MW01025981

A MORBID TASTE FOR BONES

THE RAVEN IN THE FOREGATE

THE ROSE RENT

The Complete Brother Cadfael Series

A Morbid Taste for Bones

One Corpse Too Many

Monk's Hood

Saint Peter's Fair

The Leper of Saint Giles

The Virgin in the Ice

The Sanctuary Sparrow

The Devil's Novice

Dead Man's Ransom

The Pilgrim of Hate

An Excellent Mystery

The Raven in the Foregate

The Rose Rent

The Hermit of Eyton Forest

The Confession of Brother Haluin

A Rare Benedictine

The Heretic's Apprentice

The Potter's Field

The Summer of the Danes

The Holy Thief

Brother Cadfael's Penance

A MORBID TASTE FOR BONES

THE RAVEN IN THE FOREGATE

THE ROSE RENT

ELLIS PETERS

Quality Paperback Book Club
New York

A Morbid Taste for Bones
Copyright © 1977 by Ellis Peters

The Raven in the Foregate
Copyright © 1986 by Ellis Peters

The Rose Rent
Copyright © 1986 by Ellis Peters

This edition was especially created in 1999 for Quality Paperback Book Club by arrangement with Warner Books, Inc. This edition copyright © 1999 by Book-of-the-Month Club, Inc. All rights reserved.

Printed in the United States of America

A MORBID TASTE FOR BONES

CHAPTER ONE

On the fine, bright morning in early May when the whole sensational affair of the Gwytherin relics may properly be considered to have begun, Brother Cadfael had been up long before Prime, pricking out cabbage seedlings before the day was aired, and his thoughts were all on birth, growth and fertility, not at all on graves and reliquaries and violent deaths, whether of saints, sinners or ordinary decent, fallible men like himself. Nothing troubled his peace but the necessity to take himself indoors for Mass, and the succeeding half-hour of chapter, which was always liable to stray over by an extra ten minutes. He grudged the time from his more congenial labours out here among the vegetables, but there was no evading his duty. He had, after all, chosen this cloistered life with his eyes open, he could not complain even of those parts of it he found unattractive, when the whole suited him very well, and gave him the kind of satisfaction he felt now, as he straightened his back and looked about him.

He doubted if there was a finer Benedictine garden in the whole kingdom, or one better supplied with herbs both good for spicing meats, and also invaluable as medicine. The main orchards and lands of the Shrewsbury abbey of Saint Peter and Saint Paul lay on the northern side of the road, outside the monastic enclave, but here, in the enclosed garden within the walls, close to the abbot's fish-ponds and the brook that worked the abbey mill, Brother Cadfael ruled unchallenged. The herbarium in particular was his kingdom, for he had built it up gradually through fifteen years of labour, and added to it many exotic plants of his own careful raising, collected in a roving youth that had taken him as far afield as Venice, and Cyprus and the Holy Land. For Brother Cadfael had come late to the monastic life, like a battered ship settling at last for a quiet harbour. He was well aware that in the first years of his vows the novices and lay servants had been wont to point him out to one another with awed whisperings.

'See that brother working in the garden there? The thickset fellow who rolls from one leg to the other like a sailor? You wouldn't think to look at him, would you, that he went on crusade when he was young? He was with Godfrey de Bouillon at Antioch, when the Saracens surrendered it. And he took to the seas as a captain when the king of Jerusalem ruled all the coast of the Holy Land, and served against the corsairs ten years! Hard to believe it now, eh?'

Brother Cadfael himself found nothing strange in his wide-ranging career, and had forgotten nothing and regretted nothing. He saw no contradiction in the delight he had taken in battle and adventure, and the keen pleasure he now found in quietude. Spiced, to be truthful, with more than a little mischief when he could get it, as he liked his victuals well-flavoured, but quietude all the same, a ship becalmed and enjoying it. And probably the youngsters who eyed him with such curiosity also whispered that in a life such as he had led there must have been some encounters with women, and not all purely chivalrous, and what sort of grounding was that for the conventual life?

They were right about the women. Quite apart from Richildis, who had not unnaturally tired of waiting for his return after ten years, and married a solid yeoman with good prospects in the shire, and no intention of flying off to the wars, he remembered other ladies, in more lands than one, with whom he had enjoyed encounters pleasurable to both parties, and no harm to either. Bianca, drawing water at the stone well-head in Venice—the Greek boat-girl Arianna—Mariam, the Saracen widow who sold spices and fruit in Antioch, and who found him man enough to replace for a while the man she had lost. The light encounters and the grave, not one of them had left any hard feelings behind. He counted that as achievement enough, and having known them was part of the harmonious balance that made him content now with this harboured, contemplative life, and gave him patience and insight to bear with these cloistered, simple souls who had put on the Benedictine habit as a life's profession, while for him it was a timely retirement. When you have done everything else, perfecting a conventual herb-garden is a fine and satisfying thing to do. He could not conceive of coming to this stasis having done nothing else whatever.

Five minutes more, and he must go and wash his hands and repair to the church for Mass. He used the respite to walk the length of his pale-flowered, fragrant inner kingdom, where Brother John and Brother Columbanus, two youngsters barely a year tonsured, were busy weeding and edge-trimming. Glossy and dim, oiled and furry, the leaves tendered every possible variation on green. The flowers were mostly shy, small, almost furtive, in soft, sidelong colours, lilacs and shadowy blues and diminutive yellows, for they were the unimportant and unwanted part, but for ensuring seed to follow. Rue, sage, rosemary, gilvers, gromwell, ginger, mint, thyme, columbine, herb of grace, savoury, mustard, every manner of herb grew here, fennel, tansy, basil and dill, parsley, chervil and marjoram. He had taught the uses even of the unfamiliar to all his assistants, and made plain their dangers, too, for the benefit of herbs is in their right proportion, and over-dosage can be worse than the disease. Small of habit, modest of tint, close-growing and shy, his herbs called attention to themselves only by their disseminated sweetness as the sun rose on them. But behind their shrinking ranks rose others taller and more clamorous, banks of peonies grown for their spiced seeds, and lofty, pale-leaved, budding poppies, as yet barely showing the white or purple-black petals through their close armour. They stood as tall as a short man, and their home was the eastern part of the middle sea, and from that far place Cadfael had brought their ancestors in the seed long ago, and raised and cross-bred them in his own garden, before ever he brought the perfected progeny here with him to make medicines against pain, the chief enemy of man. Pain, and the absence of sleep, which is the most beneficent remedy for pain.

The two young men, with habits kilted to the knee, were just straightening their backs and dusting the soil from their hands, as well aware as he of the hour. Brother Columbanus would not for the world have let slip one grain of his duties, or countenanced such a backsliding in any of his fellows. A very comely, well-made, upstanding young fellow he was, with a round, formidable, Norman head, as he came from a formidable, aristocratic Norman family, a younger son despatched to make his way in the monastic ranks as next-best to inheriting land. He had stiff, upstanding yellow hair and full blue eyes, and his modest demeanour and withdrawn pallor tended to obscure the muscular force of his build. Not a very comfortable colleague, Brother Columbanus, for in spite of his admirable bodily equipment he had some while since proved that he had a mental structure of alarming sensitivity, and was liable to fits of emotional stress, crises of conscience, and apocalyptic visions far removed from the implications of his solid skull. But he was young and idealistic, he had time to get over his self-torments. Brother Cadfael had worked with him for some months, and had every hope for him. He was willing, energetic, and almost too eager to please. Possibly he felt his debt to his aristocratic house too nearly, and feared a failure that would reflect on his kin. You cannot be of high Norman blood, and not excel! Brother Cadfael felt for any such victims as found themselves in this trap, coming, as he did, of antique Welsh stock without superhuman pretensions. So he tolerated Brother Columbanus with equanimity, and doctored his occasional excesses philosophically. The juice of the paynim poppies had quieted Columbanus more than once when his religious fervour prostrated him.

Well, at any rate there was no nonsense of that kind with the other one! Brother John was as plain and practical as his name, a square young man with a snub nose and an untamable ring of wiry russet curls round his tonsure. He was always hungry, and his chief interest in all things that grew in gardens was whether they were eatable, and of agreeable flavour. Come autumn he would certainly find a way of working his passage into the orchards. Just now he was content to help Brother Cadfael prick out early lettuces, and wait for the soft fruits to come into season. He was a handsome, lusty, good-natured soul, who seemed to have blundered into this enclosed life by some incomprehensible error, and not yet to have realised that he had come to the wrong place. Brother Cadfael detected a lively sense of mischief the fellow to his own, but never yet given its head in a wider world, and confidently expected that some day this particular red-crested bird would certainly fly. Meantime, he got his entertainment wherever it offered, and found it sometimes in unexpected places.

'I must be in good time,' he said, unkilting his gown and dusting his hands cheerfully on his seat. 'I'm reader this week.' So he was, Cadfael recalled, and however dull the passages they chose for him in the refectory, and innocuous the saints and martyrs he would have to celebrate at chapter, John would contrive to imbue them with drama and gusto from his own sources. Give him the beheading of Saint John the Baptist, and he would shake the foundations.

'You read for the glory of God and the saints, brother,' Columbanus reminded him, with loving reproof and somewhat offensive humility, 'not for your own!' Which showed either how little he knew about it, or how false he could be, one or the other.

'The blessed thought is ever in my mind,' said Brother John with irrepressible zest, and winked at Cadfael behind his colleague's back, and set off enthusiastically along the aisles of shrubs towards the abbot's gate and the great court. They followed him more demurely, the slender, fair, agile youth and the squat, barrel-chested, bandy-legged veteran of fifty-seven. Was I ever, wondered Cadfael, rolling with his powerful seaman's gait beside the other's long, supple strides, as young and earnest as this? It cost him an effort to recall that Columbanus was actually fully twenty-five, and the sprig of a sophisticated and ambitious house. Whose fortunes, surely, were not founded wholly on piety?

This third Mass of the day was non-parochial and brief, and after it the Benedictine brothers of the abbey of Shrewsbury filed in procession from the choir into the chapter-house, and made their way to their stalls in due order, Abbot Heribert leading.

The abbot was old, of mild nature and pliant, a gentle grey ascetic very wishful of peace and harmony around him. His figure was unimpressive, though his face was beguiling in its anxious sweetness. Novices and pupils were easy in his presence, when they could reach it, which was by no means always easy, for the extremely impressive figure of Prior Robert was liable to loom between.

Prior Robert Pennant, of mixed Welsh and English blood, was more than six feet tall, attenuated and graceful, silver-grey of hair at fifty, blanched and beautiful of visage, with long, aristocratic features and lofty marble brow. There was no man in the midland shires would look more splendid in a mitre, superhuman in height and authority, and there was no man in England better aware of it, or more determined to prove it at the earliest opportunity. His very motions, sweeping across the chapter-house to his stall, understudied the pontificate.

After him came Brother Richard the sub-prior, his antithesis, large, ungainly, amiable and benevolent, of a good mind, but mentally lazy. Doubtful if he would ever become prior when Robert achieved his end, with so many ambitious and industrious younger men eyeing the prospect of advancement, and willing to go to a great deal of trouble to secure it.

After Richard came all the other brothers in their hierarchies. Brother Benedict the sacristan, Brother Anselm the precentor, Brother Matthew the cellarer, Brother Dennis the hospitaller, Brother Edmund the infirmarer, Brother Oswald the almoner, Brother Jerome, the prior's clerk, and Brother Paul, master of the novices, followed by the commonalty of the convent, and a very flourishing number they made. Among the last of them Brother Cadfael rolled to his own chosen corner, well to the rear and poorly lit, half-concealed behind one of the stone pillars. Since he held no troublesome parchment office, he was unlikely to be called upon to speak in chapter upon the various businesses of the house, and when the matter in hand was dull into the bargain it was his habit to employ the time to good account by sleeping, which from long usage he could do bolt upright and undetected in his shadowy corner. He had a sixth sense which alerted him at need, and brought him awake instantly and plausibly. He had even been known to answer a question pat, when it was certain he had been asleep when it was put to him.

On this particular May morning he remained awake long enough to enjoy Brother John's extraction of the last improbable ounce of drama from the life of some obscure saint whose day fell on the morrow, but when the cellarer began to expound a complicated matter of a legacy partly to the altar of Our Lady, partly to the infirmary, he composed himself to slumber. After all, he knew that most of the remaining time, once a couple of minor malefactors had been dealt with, would be given to Prior Robert's campaign to secure the relics and patronage of a powerful saint for the monastery. For the past few months very little else had been discussed. The prior had had it on his mind, in fact, ever since the Cluniac house of Wenlock had rediscovered, with great pride and jubilation, the tomb of their original foundress, Saint Milburga, and installed her bones triumphantly on their altar. An alien priory, only a few miles distant, with its own miracle-working saint, and the great Benedictine house of Shrewsbury as empty of relics as a plundered almsbox! It was more than Prior Robert could stomach. He had been scouring the borderlands for a spare saint now for a year or more, looking hopefully towards Wales, where it was well known that holy men and women had been common as mushrooms in autumn in the past, and as little regarded. Brother Cadfael had no wish to hear the latest of his complaints and urgings. He slept.

The heat of the sun rebounded from honed facets of pale, baked rock, scorching his face, as the floating arid dust burned his throat. From where he crouched with his fellows in cover he could see the long crest of the wall, and the steel-capped heads of the guards on the turrets glittering in the fierce light. A landscape carved out of reddish stone and fire, all deep gullies and sheer cliffs, with never a cool green leaf to temper it, and before him the object of all his journeyings, the holy city of Jerusalem, crowned with towers and domes within its white walls. The dust of battle hung in the air, dimming the clarity of battlement and gate, and the hoarse shouting and clashing of armour filled his ears. He was waiting for the trumpet to sound the final assault, and keeping well in cover while he waited, for he had learned to respect the range of the short, curly Saracen bow. He saw the banners surge forward out of hiding, streaming on the burning wind. He saw the flash of the raised trumpet, and braced himself for the blare.

The sound that brought him leaping wide-awake out of his dream was loud enough and stirring enough, but not the brazen blast of a trumpet, nor was he launched from his stillness towards the triumphant storming of Jerusalem. He was back in his stall in the dark corner of the chapter-house, and starting to his feet as alertly as the rest, and with the same consternation and alarm. And the shriek that had awakened him was just subsiding into a series of rending moans and broken cries that might have been of extreme pain or extreme ecstasy. In the open space in the centre of the chapter-house Brother Columbanus lay on his face, threshing and jerking like a landed fish, beating his forehead and his palms against the flagstones, kicking and flailing with long, pale legs bared to the knee by his contortions, and barking out of him those extraordinary sounds of shattering physical excitement, while the nearest of the brothers hovered in helpless shock, and Prior Robert with lifted hands exhorted and exclaimed.

Brother Cadfael and Brother Edmund, the infirmarer, reached the victim together, kneeled over him one on either side, and restrained him from battering his brains out against the stones of the floor, or dislocating his joints in his flailings. 'Falling sickness!' said Brother Edmund tersely, and wedged the thick cord of Columbanus' girdle between his teeth, and a fold of his habit with it, to prevent him from biting his tongue.

Brother Cadfael was less certain of the diagnosis, for these were not the grunting, helpless noises of an epileptic in an attack, but such as might be expected from a hysterical woman in a frenzy. But at least the treatment stopped half the noise, and even appeared to diminish the vigour of the convulsions, though they resumed again as soon as the restraining grip on him was loosed.

'Poor young man!' fluttered Abbot Heribert, hovering in the background. 'So sudden, so cruel an affliction! Handle him gently! Carry him to the infirmary. We must pray for his restoration.'

Chapter broke up in some disorder. With the help of Brother John, and certain others of a practical turn of mind, they got Brother Columbanus securely but comfortably swathed in a sheet, confining arms and legs so that he could do himself no injury, wedged his teeth apart with a wooden spit instead of the cloth, on which he might have gagged and choked, and carried him on a shutter to the infirmary, where they got him into bed, and secured him there with bandages round breast and thighs. He moaned and gurgled and heaved still, but with weakening force, and when they had managed to get a draught of Brother Cadfael's poppy-juice into him his moans subsided into pitiful mutterings, and the violence of his struggles against his confinement grew feebler.

'Take good care of him,' said Prior Robert, frowning anxiously over the young man's bed. 'I think someone should be constantly by to watch over him, in case the fit comes again. You have your other sick men to attend to, you cannot sit by his side day and night. Brother Jerome, I put this sufferer in your charge, and excuse you from all other duties while he needs you.'

'Willingly,' said Brother Jerome, 'and prayerfully!' He was Prior Robert's closest associate and most devoted hanger-on, and an inevitable choice whenever Robert required strict obedience and meticulous reporting, as might well be the case where a brother of the house succumbed to what might elsewhere be whispered abroad as a fit of madness.

'Stay with him in particular during the night,' said the prior, 'for in the night a man's resistance falters, and his bodily evils may rise against him. If he sleeps peacefully, you may rest also, but remain close, in case he needs you.'

'He'll sleep within the hour,' said Cadfael confidently, 'and may pass into natural sleep well before night. God willing, he may put this off before morning.'

For his part, he thought Brother Columbanus lacked sufficient work for both mind and body, and took his revenge for his deprivation in these excesses, half-wilful, half-involuntary, and both to be pitied and censured. But he retained enough caution to reserve a doubt with every conviction. He was not sure he knew any of his adopted brothers well enough to judge with certainty. Well, Brother John—yes, perhaps! But inside the conventual life or outside, cheerful, blunt, extrovert Brother Johns are few and far between.

Brother Jerome appeared at chapter next morning with an exalted countenance, and the air of one bursting with momentous news. At Abbot Heribert's mild reproof for leaving his patient without permission, he folded his hands meekly and bowed his head, but lost none of his rapt assurance.

'Father, I am sent here by another duty, that seemed to me even more urgent. I have left Brother Columbanus sleeping, though not peacefully, for even his sleep is tormented. But two lay-brothers are watching by him. If I have done wrong, I will abide it humbly.'

'Our brother is no better?' asked the abbot anxiously.

'He is still deeply troubled, and when he wakes he raves. But, Father, this is my errand! There is a sure hope for him! In the night I have been miraculously visited. I have come to tell you what divine mercy has instructed me. Father, in the small hours I fell into a doze beside Brother Columbanus' bed, and had a marvellously sweet dream.'

By this time he had everyone's attention, even Brother Cadfael was wide awake. 'What, another of them?' whispered Brother John wickedly into his ear. 'The plague's spreading!'

'Father, it seemed to me that the wall of the room opened, and a great light shone in, and through the light and radiating the light there came in a most beautiful young virgin, and stood beside our brother's bed, and spoke to me. She told me that her name was Winifred, and that in Wales there is a holy spring, that rose to the light where she suffered martyrdom. And she said that if Brother Columbanus bathed in the water of that well, he would surely be healed, and restored at once to his senses. Then she uttered a blessing upon our house, and vanished in a great light, and I awoke.'

Through the murmur of excitement that went round the chapter-house, Prior Robert's voice rose in reverent triumph: 'Father Abbot, we are being guided! Our quest for a saint has drawn to us this sign of favour, in token that we should persevere.'

'Winifred!' said the abbot doubtfully. 'I do not recall clearly the story of this saint and martyr. There are so many of them in Wales. Certainly we ought to send Brother Columbanus to her holy spring, it would be ingratitude to neglect so clear an omen. But exactly where is it to be found?'

Prior Robert looked round for the few Welshmen among the brothers, passed somewhat hurriedly over Brother Cadfael, who had never been one of his favourites, perhaps by reason of a certain spark in his eye, as well as his notoriously worldly past, and lit gladly upon old Brother Rhys, who was virtually senile but doctrinally safe, and had the capacious if capricious memory of the very old. 'Brother, can you tell us the history of this saint, and where her well is to be found?'

The old man was slow to realise that he had become the centre of attention. He was shrunken like a bird, and toothless, and used to a tolerant oblivion. He began hesitantly, but warmed to the work as he found all eyes upon him.

'Saint Winifred, you say, Father? Everybody knows of Saint Winifred. You'll find her spring by the name they gave the place, Holywell, it's no great way in from Chester. But she's not there. You won't find her grave at Holywell.'

'Tell us about her,' coaxed Prior Robert, almost fawning in his eagerness. 'Tell us all her story.'

'Saint Winifred,' declaimed the old man, beginning to enjoy his hour of glory, 'was the only child of a knight named Tevyth, who lived in those parts when the princes were yet heathens. But this knight and all his household were converted by Saint Beuno, and made him a church there, and gave him house-room. The girl was devoted even above her parents, and pledged herself to a virgin life, hearing Mass every day. But one Sunday it happened that she was sick, and stayed at home when all the rest of the household went to church. And there came to the door the prince of those parts, Cradoc, son of the king, who had fallen in love with her at a distance. For this girl was very beautiful. *Very* beautiful!' gloated Brother Rhys, and licked his lips loudly. Prior Robert visibly recoiled, but refrained from stopping the flow by reproof. 'He pleaded that he was hot and parched from hunting,' said Brother Rhys darkly, 'and asked for a drink of water, and the girl let him in and gave him to drink. Then,' he shrilled, hunching himself in his voluminous habit and springing erect with a vigour nobody present would have credited, 'he pressed his suit upon her, and grappled her in his arms. *Thus!*' The effort was almost too much for him, and moreover, the prior was eyeing him in alarm; he subsided with dignity. 'The faithful virgin put him off with soft words, and escaping into another room, climbed from a window and fled towards the church. But finding that she had eluded him, Prince Cradoc took horse and rode after, and overtaking her just within sight of the church, and dreading that she would reveal his infamy, struck off her head with his sword.'

He paused for the murmur of horror, pity and indignation, and got it, with a flurry of prayerfully-folded hands, and a tribute of round eyes.

'Then thus piteously she came by her death and beatitude?' intoned Brother Jerome enthusiastically.

'Not a bit of it!' snapped Brother Rhys. He had never liked Brother Jerome. 'Saint Beuno and the congregation were coming out of the church, and saw what had passed. The saint drew a terrible curse upon the murderer, who at once sank to the ground, and began to melt like wax in a fire, until all his body had sunk away into the grass. Then Saint Beuno fitted the head of the virgin onto her neck, and the flesh grew together, and she stood up alive, and the holy fountain sprang up on the spot where she arose.'

They waited, spellbound, and he let them wait. He had lost interest after the death.

'And afterwards?' insinuated Prior Robert. 'What did the saint do with her restored life?'

'She went on a pilgrimage to Rome,' said Brother Rhys indifferently, 'and she attended at a great synod of saints, and was appointed to be prioress over a community of virgin sisters at Gwytherin, by Llanrwst. And there she lived many years, and did many miracles in her lifetime. If it should be called her lifetime? She was once dead already. When she died a second time, that was where it befell.' He felt nothing concerning this residue of life, he offered it with a shrug. The girl had had her chance with Prince Cradoc, and let it slip, obviously her natural bent was to be prioress of a nest of virgins, and there was nothing more to be told about her.

'And she is buried there at Gwytherin?' persisted the prior. 'And her miracles continued after death?'

'So I have heard. But it's a long time,' said the old man, 'since I've heard her name mentioned. And longer since I was in those parts.'

Prior Robert stood in the circle of sunlight that filtered between the pillars of the chapter-house, drawn to his full imposing height, and turned a radiant face and commanding eyes upon Abbot Heribert.

'Father, does it not seem to you that our reverent search for a patron of great power and sanctity is being divinely guided? This gentle saint has visited us in person, in Brother Jerome's dream, and beckoned us to bring our afflicted brother to her for healing. Shall we not hope, also, that she will again show us the next step? If she does indeed receive our prayers and restore Brother Columbanus to health of body and mind, may we not be encouraged to hope that she will come in person and dwell among us? That we may humbly beg the church's sanction to take up her blessed relics and house them fittingly here in Shrewsbury? To the great glory and lustre of our house!'

'And of Prior Robert!' whispered Brother John in Cadfael's ear.

'It certainly seems that she has shown us singular favour,' admitted Abbot Heribert.

'Then, Father, have I your leave to send Brother Columbanus with a safe escort to Holywell? This very day?'

'Do so,' said the abbot, 'with the prayers of us all, and may he return as Saint Winifred's own messenger, hale and grateful.'

The deranged man, still wandering in mind and communing with himself in incoherent ravings, was led away out of the gatehouse on the first stage of his journey immediately after the midday meal, mounted on a mule, with a high, cradling saddle to give him some security from falling, in case the violent fit took him again, and with Brother Jerome and a brawny lay-brother one on either side, to support him at need. Columbanus looked about him with wide, pathetic, childlike eyes, and seemed to know nobody, though he went submissively and trustfully where he was led.

'I could have done with a nice little trip into Wales,' said Brother John wistfully, looking after them as they rounded the corner and vanished towards the bridge over the Severn. 'But I probably shouldn't have seen the right visions. Jerome will do the job better.'

'Boy,' said Brother Cadfael tolerantly, 'you become more of an unbeliever every day.'

'Not a bit of it! I'm as willing to believe in the girl's sanctity and miracles as any man. We know the saints have power to help and bless, and I'll believe they have the goodwill, too. But when it's Prior Robert's faithful hound who has the dream, you're asking me to believe in *his* sanctity, not hers! And in any case, isn't her favour glory enough? I don't see why they should want to dig up the poor lady's dust. It seems like charnel-house business to me, not church business. And you think exactly the same,' he said firmly, and stared out his elder, eye to eye.

'When I want to hear my echo,' said Brother Cadfael, 'I will at least speak first. Come on, now, and get that bottom strip of ground dug, there are kale plants waiting to go in.'

The delegation to Holywell was gone five days, and came home towards evening in a fine shower of rain and a grand glow of grace, chanting prayers as the three entered the courtyard. In the midst rode Brother Columbanus, erect and graceful and jubilant, if that word could be used for one so humble in his gladness. His face was bright and clear, his eyes full of wonder and intelligence. No man ever looked less mad, or less likely to be subject to the falling sickness. He went straight to the church and gave thanks and praise to God and Saint Winifred on his knees, and from the altar all three went dutifully to report to the abbot, prior and sub-prior, in the abbot's lodging.

'Father,' said Brother Columbanus, eager and joyous, 'I have no skill to tell what has befallen me, for I know less than these who have cared for me in my delirium. All I know is that I was taken on this journey like a man in an ill dream, and went where I was taken, not knowing how to fend for myself, or what I ought to do. And suddenly I was like a man awakened out of that nightmare to a bright morning and a world of spring, and I was standing naked in the grass beside a well, and these good brothers were pouring water over me that healed as it touched. I knew myself and them, and only marvelled where I might be, and how I came there. Which they willingly told me. And then we went, all, and many people of that place with us, to sing Mass in a little church that stands close by the well. Now I know that I owe my recovery to the intervention of Saint Winifred, and I praise and worship her from my heart, as I do God who caused her to take pity on me. The rest these brothers will tell.'

The lay-brother was large, taciturn, weary—having done all the work throughout—and by this time somewhat bored with the whole business. He made the appropriate exclamations where needed, but left the narrative in the able hands of Brother Jerome, who told all with zest. How they had brought their patient to the village of Holywell, and asked the inhabitants for directions and aid, and been shown where the saint had risen living after her martyrdom, in the silver fountain that still sprang in the same spot, furnished now with a stone basin to hold its sacred flow. There they had led the rambling Columbanus, stripped him of habit, shirt and drawers, and poured the sacred water over him, and instantly he had stood erect and lifted his hands in prayer, and given thanks for a mind restored. Afterwards he had asked them in wonder how he came there, and what had happened to him, and had been greatly chastened and exalted at his humbling and his deliverance, and most grateful to his patroness, by whose guidance he had been made whole.

'And, Father, the people there told us that the saint is indeed buried at Gwytherin, where she died after her ministry, and that the place where her body is laid has done many miracles. But they say that her tomb, after so long, is neglected and little thought of, and it may well be that she longs for a better recognition, and to be installed in some place where pilgrims may come, where she may be revered as is her due, and have room to enlarge her grace and blessing to reach more people in need.'

'You are inspired, having been present at this miracle,' said Prior Robert, tall and splendid with faith rewarded, 'and you speak out what I have felt in listening to you. Surely Saint Winifred is calling us to her rescue as she came to the rescue of Brother Columbanus. Many have need of her goodness as he had, and know nothing of her. In our hands she would be exalted as she deserves, and those who need her grace would know where to come and seek it. I pray that we may mount that expedition of faith to which she summons us. Father Abbot, give me your leave to petition the church, and bring this blessed lady home to rest here among us, and be our proudest boast. For I believe it is her will and her command.'

'In the name of God,' said Abbot Heribert devoutly, 'I approve that project, and pray the blessing of heaven upon it!'

'He had it all planned beforehand,' said Brother John over the bed of mint, between envy and scorn. 'That was all a show, all that wonder and amazement, and asking who Saint Winifred was, and where to find her. He knew it all along. He'd already picked her out from those he's discovered neglected in Wales, and decided she was the one most likely to be available, as well as the one to shed most lustre on him. But it had to come out into the open by miraculous means. There'll be another prodigy whenever he needs his way smoothed for him, until he gets the girl here safely installed in the church, to his glory. It's a great enterprise, he means to climb high on the strength of it. So he starts out with a vision, and a prodigious healing, and divine grace leading his footsteps. It's as plain as the nose on your face.'

'And are you saying,' asked Brother Cadfael mildly, 'that Brother Columbanus is in the plot as well as Brother Jerome, and that falling fit of his was a fake, too? I should have to be very sure of my reward in heaven before I volunteered to break the paving with my forehead, even to provide Prior Robert with a miracle.'

Brother John considered seriously, frowning. 'No, that I don't say. We all know our meek white lamb is liable to the horrors over a penance scamped, and ecstasies over a vigil or a fast, and pouring ice-cold water over him at Holywell would be the very treatment to jolt him back into his right wits. We could just as well have tossed him in the fish-pond here! But of course *he'd* believe what they told him, and credit it all to the saint. Catch him missing such a chance! No, I wouldn't say he was a party to it—not knowingly. But he gave them the opportunity for a splendid demonstration of grace. You notice it was Jerome who was set to take care of him overnight! It takes only one man to be favoured with a vision, but it has to be the right man.' He rolled a sprig of the young green leaves sadly between his palms, and the fragrance distilled richly on the early morning air. 'And it will be the right men who'll accompany Prior Robert into Wales,' he said with sour certainty. 'You'll see!'

No doubt about it, this young man was hankering after a glimpse of the world again, and a breath of air from outside the walls. Brother Cadfael pondered, not only with sympathy for his young assistant, but also with some pleasurable stirrings of his own. So momentous an event in the otherwise even course of monastic life ought not to be missed. Besides the undoubted possibilities of mischief!

'True!' he said thoughtfully. 'Perhaps we ought to take some steps to leaven the lump. Wales should not be left with the notion that Jerome is the best Shrewsbury can muster, that's very true.'

'You have about as much chance of being invited as I,' said

Brother John with his customary bluntness. 'Jerome is sure of his place, Prior Robert must have his right hand with him. And Columbanus, fool innocent, was the instrument of grace, and could be made to serve the same turn again. Brother Sub-Prior they have to take along, for form's sake. Surely we could think up some way of getting a foot in the door? They can't move for a few days yet, the carpenters and carvers are working hard on this splendid reliquary coffin they're going to take with them for the lady, but it will take them a while to finish it. Get your wits to work, brother! There isn't anything you couldn't do, if you've a mind! Prior or no prior!'

'Well, well, did I say you had no faith?' wondered Brother Cadfael, charmed and disarmed. 'I might worm my own way in, there could be ways, but how am I to recommend a graceless rogue like you? What are you good at, to be taken along on such an errand?'

'I'm a good hand with mules,' said Brother John hopefully, 'and you don't think Prior Robert intends to go on foot, I suppose? Or to do the grooming and feeding and watering himself? Or the mucking-out? They'll need *somebody* to do the hard work and wait on them. Why not me?'

It was, indeed, something nobody as yet seemed to have thought of. And why take a lay-brother, if there was a cloister-brother, with a sweet voice in the Mass, willing to do the sweating into the bargain? And the boy deserved his outing, since he was willing to earn it the hard way. Besides, he might be useful before the end. If not to Prior Robert, to Brother Cadfael.

'We'll see,' he said, and with that drove his mutinous protégé back to the work in hand. But after dinner, in the somnolent half-hour of sleep for the elders and play for the novices, he sought out Abbot Heribert in his study.

'Father Abbot, it is on my mind that we are undertaking this pilgrimage to Gwytherin without full consideration. First we must send to the bishop of Bangor, in whose see Gwytherin lies, for without his approval the matter cannot proceed. Now it is not essential to have a speaker fluent in Welsh there, since the bishop is obviously conversant with Latin. But not every parish priest in Wales has that tongue, and it is vital to be able to speak freely with the priest at Gwytherin, should the bishop sanction our quest. But most of all, the see of Bangor is wholly within the sovereignty of the king of Gwynedd, and surely his goodwill and permission are essential as those of the church. The princes of Gwynedd speak only Welsh, though they have learned clerks. Father Prior, certainly, has a smattering of Welsh, but. . . .'

'That is very true,' said Abbot Heribert, easily dismayed. 'It is but a smattering. And the king's agreement is all-important. Brother Cadfael, Welsh is your first, best language, and has no mysteries for you. Could *you*. . .? The garden, I am aware. . . . But with your aid there would be no problem.

'In the garden,' said Brother Cadfael, 'everything is well forward, and can manage without me ten days or more, and take no hurt. I should be glad indeed to be the interpreter, and lend my skills also in Gwytherin.'

'Then so be it!' sighed the abbot in heartfelt relief. 'Go with Prior Robert, and be our voice to the Welsh people. I shall sanction your errand myself, and you will have my authority.'

He was old and human and gentle, full of experience, short on ambition, self-righteousness and resolution. There could have been two ways of approaching him concerning Brother John. Cadfael took the more honest and simple way.

'Father, there is a young brother concerning whose vocation I have doubts, but concerning whose goodness I have none. He is close to me, and I would that he might find his true way, for if he finds it he will not forsake it. But it may not be with us. I beg that I may take him with me, as our hewer of wood and drawer of water in this enterprise, to allow him time to consider.'

Abbot Heribert looked faintly dismayed and apprehensive, but not unsympathetic. Perhaps he remembered long-ago days when his own vocation had suffered periods of storm.

'I should be sorry,' he said, 'to refuse a choice to any man who may be better fitted to serve God elsewhere. Which of us can say he has never looked over his shoulder? You have not,' he questioned delicately, approaching the aspect that really daunted him, though with a cautiously dauntless face, 'broached this matter to Prior Robert?'

'No, Father,' said Brother Cadfael virtuously. 'I thought it wrong to charge him with so small a responsibility, when he already carries one so great.'

'Very proper!' agreed the abbot heartily. 'It would be ill-done to distract his mind from his great purpose at this stage. I should say no word to him of the reason for adding this young man to the party. Prior Robert in his own unshaken certainty is apt to take an austere view of any man who looks back, once having set his hand to the plough.'

'Yet, Father, we were not all cut out to be ploughmen. Some could be more useful labouring in other ways.'

'True!' said the abbot, and warily smiled, pondering the recurring but often forgotten riddle of Brother Cadfael himself. 'I have often wondered, I confess. . . . But never mind! Very well, tell me this young brother's name, and you shall have him.'

CHAPTER TWO

Prior Robert's fine, frosty face momentarily registered displeasure and suspicion when he heard how his delegation was to be augmented. Brother Cadfael's gnarled, guileless-eyed self-sufficiency caused him discomfort without a word amiss or a glance out of place, as though his dignity were somehow under siege. Of Brother John he knew no particular evil, but the redness of his hair, the exuberance of his health and high spirits, the very way he put live blood back into old martyrdoms with his extravagant gusto in the reading, were all offensive in themselves, and jarred on the prior's aesthetic sensibilities. However, since Abbot Heribert had innocently decreed that they should join the party, and since there was no denying that a fluent Welsh speaker might become an urgent necessity at some stage, Prior Robert accepted the fiat without demur, and made the best of it.

They set out as soon as the fine reliquary for the saint's bones was ready, polished oak ornamented with silver, to serve as a proof what honours awaited Winifred in her new shrine. In the third week of May they came to Bangor, and told their story to Bishop David, who was sympathetic, and readily gave his consent to the proposed translation, subject only to the agreement of Prince Owain, who was regent of Gwynedd owing to the illness of the old king, his father. They ran the prince to earth at Aber, and found him equally obliging, for he not only gave the desired approval, but sent his one English-speaking clerk and chaplain to show them the best and quickest way to Gwytherin, and commend them and their errand to the parish priest there. Thus episcopally and royally blessed, Prior Robert led his party on the last stage of their journey, a little too easily convinced that his progress was being divinely smoothed, and would be so to its triumphant end.

They turned aside from the Conway valley at Llanrwst, climbing away from the river into forested hill country. Beyond the watershed they crossed the Elwy where it is young and small, and moved steadily south-eastwards through thick woods, over another ridge of high land, to descend once again into the upland valley of a little river, that provided some marshy water-meadows along its banks, and a narrow band of tilled fields, sloping and sturdy but protected by the forests, above these lush pastures. The wooded ridge on either hand ran in oblique folds, richly green, hiding the scattered house-steads. The fields were already planted, and here and there orchards flowered. Below them, where the woods drew back to leave an amphitheatre of green, there was a small stone church, whitewashed and shimmering, and a little wooden house beside it.

'You see the goal of your pilgrimage,' said the chaplain Urien. He was a compact, neat, well-shaven personage, handsomely dressed and mounted, more of an ambassador than a clerk.

'That is Gwytherin?' asked Prior Robert.

'It is the church and priest's house of Gwytherin. The parish stretches for several miles along the river valley, and a mile or more from the Cledwen on either bank. We do not congregate in villages as you English do. Land good for hunting is plentiful, but good for tillage meagre. Every man lives where best suits him for working his fields and conserving his game.'

'It is a very fair place,' said the sub-prior, and meant it, for the fold on fold of well-treed hills beyond the river made a pattern of spring beauty in a hundred different greens, and the water-meadows were strung like a necklace of emeralds along the fringes of a necklace of silver and lapis-lazuli.

'Good to look at, hard to work,' said Urien practically. 'See, there's an ox-team on the far side trying to break a new strip, now all the rest are planted. Watch the beasts strain at it, and you'll know how the higher ground weighs.'

Across the river, some way below them and a great way off, the snaky curve of the furrows already won patterned the slope between cultivated fields and leaning trees, a dark brown writing upon the hillside, and on the higher furrow, as yet uncompleted, the oxen leaned into their yokes and heaved, and the ploughman behind them clung and dragged at the heavy share. Before the leading pair a man walked backwards, arms gently waving and beckoning, his goad only a wand, flourished for magic, not for its sting, his high, pure calls carried aloft on the air, cajoling and praising. Towards him the beasts leaned willingly, following his cries with all their might. The new-turned soil, greyish-brown and sluggish, heaved moist and fresh to light after the share.

'A harsh country,' said Urien, as one assessing, not complaining, and set his horse moving downhill towards the church. 'Come, I'll hand you over to Father Huw, and see you well-received.'

They followed him by a green path that wound out of the hills, and soon lost its view of the valley between scattered, flowering trees. A wooden house or two showed among the woods, surrounded by small garden plots, and again vanished.

'Did you see?' said Brother John in Cadfael's ear, pacing beside the sumpter mule. 'Did you see how the beasts laboured towards that fellow not to escape the goad, only to go where he willed, only to please him? And such labour! That I should like to learn!'

'It's labour for man as well as beast,' said Brother Cadfael.

'But for free goodwill! They wanted to go with him, to do what he wanted them to do. Brother, could devoted disciples do more? Do you tell me he takes no delight in what he does?'

'No man nor God who sees his faithful delight to serve him,' said Brother Cadfael patiently and carefully, 'but he knows delight. Hush, now, we're barely here, there'll be time to look round us.'

They were down in the little arena of grass and vegetable plots, clear of the trees. The stone church with its tiny turret and tinier bell visible within shone blindingly white, bluish-white against all the lush green. And out of the cabbage-patch, freshly planted, in the lee of the wooden cabin, rose a small, square man in a brown sackcloth gown hoisted to the knees, thick brown legs sturdy under him, and a thicket of curly brown hair and beard half-concealing a brown, broad, wondering face round two large, dark-blue eyes. He came out hastily, scrubbing his hands on his skirts. At close quarters his eyes were larger, bluer and more astonished than ever, and as timid as the mild eyes of a doe.

'Good-day to you, Father Huw,' said Urien, reining in before him, 'I've brought you distinguished guests from England, upon important church business, and with the blessing of prince and bishop.'

When they had ridden into the clearing the priest had certainly been the only man in sight, but by the time Urien had ended his greeting a score of silent, sudden figures had appeared from nowhere, and made a wary and curious half-circle about their pastor. By the distracted look in Father Huw's eyes he was busy reckoning up in some alarm how many of these strangers his modest hut could fittingly house, and where to bestow the rest of them, and how much food there was in his larder to make a meal for so many, and where he could best commandeer whatever extra was needed. But no question of not extending a welcome. Guests were sacrosanct, and must not even be questioned on the proposed length of their stay, however ruinous.

'My poor household is at the reverend fathers' disposal,' he said, 'and whatever powers I have to serve them, also. You come fresh from Aber?'

'From Aber,' said Urien, 'from Prince Owain, and I must rejoin him there tonight. I am only the herald for these Benedictine brothers, who come on a holy errand, and when I have explained their case to you, then I leave them in your hands.' He presented them by name, Prior Robert first. 'And have no fear when I have left, for Brother Cadfael here is a man of Gwynedd himself, and speaks Welsh as well as you do.'

Huw's look of harassed apprehension was immediately eased, but in case he should be in any doubt, Cadfael favoured him with a rapid brotherly greeting in the promised language, which gratifyingly produced the identical look of slight distrust and insecurity in Prior Robert's normally assured grey eyes.

'You are welcome to this poor house you honour,' said Huw, and ran a quick eye over the horses and mules and their loads, and without hesitation called a couple of names over his shoulder. A shaggy-headed elder and a sunburned boy of about ten came forward readily in answer. 'Ianto, help the good brother water the beasts, and put them in the little paddock to graze, until we see how best to stable them. Edwin, run and tell Marared we have guests, and help her bring water and wine.'

They ran to do his bidding, and several of the others who had gathered, brown, bare-legged men, slender dark women and half-naked children, drew nearer, conferred softly among themselves, and the women slipped away to their own cooking-fires and bake-ovens to bring whatever they could to contribute to Gwytherin's hospitality.

'While it's so fine and mild,' said Huw, standing aside to wave them into the little enclosure of his garden, 'it may please you best to sit in the orchard. I have benches and table there. Through the summer I live out of doors. Time enough to go within and light fires when the days draw in and the nights grow cold.'

His holding was tiny and his living poor enough, but he took good care of his fruit-trees and was a diligent gardener, Brother Cadfael noted with approval. And for one who seemed, unlike many of the parish priests of the Celtic persuasion, to be celibate, and happily so, he had the bare little house and grounds in very neat order, and could produce from his own store, or his parishioners' shared stock, clean wooden trenchers and good bread to put on them, and plain but presentable drinking-horns for his raw red wine. He performed all the ceremonies due from a host with humble dignity. The boy Edwin returned with a lively old woman, Huw's neighbour, bringing food and drink. And all the while that the visitors sat there in the sun, various of the people of Gwytherin, scattered though the parish might be, found occasion to walk past the wattle fence of the orchard and examine the party carefully, though without seeming to do so. It was not every day, or every year, indeed, that they had so momentous a visitation. Every soul in the parish would know before evening not only that monks from Shrewsbury were guests at Huw's house, but also how many they were, what they looked like, what fine horses and handsome mules they had, and most probably what they had come for, into the bargain. But the eyeing and the listening were done with perfect courtesy and discretion.

'And now, since Master Urien has to return to Aber,' said Huw, when they had eaten and were sitting at ease, 'it might be well if he would tell me in what particular I can serve the brothers of Shrewsbury, so that he may be assured we understand each other before he leaves us. And whatever is in my competence I will surely do.'

Urien told the story as he had heard it, and Prior Robert elaborated at such length that Brother John, growing bored and restless, let his eyes stray to take stock of the occasional figures that passed along the fence, with alert ears and shy but sharp eyes. His interest and curiosity were somewhat less discreet than theirs. And there were some very handsome girls among them! The one passing now, for instance, her step graceful and slow—she knew she was watched!—and her hair a great, heavy braid over her shoulder, the colour of polished oak, a light, silken brown, even with silvery dashes in it like the grain of oak. . . .

'And the bishop has given his consent to your proposal?' asked Huw, after a long minute of silence, and in a voice that suggested wonder and doubt.

'Both bishop and prince have sanctioned it.' Prior Robert was uneasy at the very hint of a hitch at this stage. 'The omens have surely not misled us? Saint Winifred is here? She lived out her restored life here, and is buried in this place?'

Huw owned that it was so, with so curious an intonation of caution and reluctance that Cadfael decided he was trying to recall exactly where the lady was to be found, and wondering in what state her grave would be discovered, after all this time since last he had so much as thought of it.

'She is here, in this cemetery?' The little whitewashed church gleamed provocatively in the sunshine.

'No, not here.' Some relief this time, he did not have to reveal her whereabouts immediately. 'This church is new since her time. Her grave is in the old burial-ground of the wooden church on the hill, a mile or more from here. It is long disused. Yes, certainly the omens favour your plans, and beyond question the saint is here in Gwytherin. But. . . .'

'But?' said Prior Robert with displeasure. 'Both prince and bishop have given us their blessing, and commended our cause to you. Moreover, we have heard, and they have agreed, that the saint in her stay here among you has been much neglected, and may well wish to be received where greater honour will be paid to her.'

'In my church,' said Huw humbly, 'I have never heard that the saints desired honour for themselves, but rather to honour God rightly. So I do not presume to know what Saint Winifred's will may be in this matter. That you and your house should desire to honour *her* rightly, that is another matter, and very proper. But. . . . This blessed virgin lived out her miraculously restored life in this place, and no other. Here she died for the second time, and here is buried, and even if my people have neglected her, being human and faulty, yet they always knew that she was here among them, and at a pinch they could rely on her, and for a Welsh saint I think that counts for much. Prince and bishop—both of whom I reverence as I ought—may not altogether understand how my flock will feel, if their holiest girl is to be dug up out of her grave and taken away into England. It may matter little to the crown and the crozier, a saint is a saint wherever her relics rest. But I tell you plainly, the people of Gwytherin are not going to like it at all!'

Brother Cadfael, stirred to an atavistic fervour of Welshness by this homely eloquence, snatched the initiative from Urien at this point, and translated with the large declamation of the bards.

In full spate, he turned his eyes away from the distracting faces, to light upon one even more distracting. The girl with the light-oak sheen on her hair was again passing the fence, and had been so charmed by what she heard, and the vehemence of its delivery, that for a moment she forgot to keep moving, and stood there at gaze, apple-blossom face radiant and rose-leaf lips laughing. And with the same fascination with which she gazed at Cadfael, Brother John gazed at her. Cadfael observed both, and was dazzled. But the next moment she caught herself up in hasty alarm, and blushed beautifully, and swept away out of sight. Brother John was still gaping long after she had vanished.

'It is hardly important, surely?' said Prior Robert with ominous mildness. 'Your bishop and your prince have made their views plain. The parishioners need not be consulted.'

That, too, Cadfael interpreted, Urien choosing to remain neutral and mute.

'Impossible!' said Huw firmly, knowing himself on secure ground. 'In such a grave matter affecting the whole parish, nothing can be done without calling together the assembly of the free men, and putting the case to them fully and publicly. Doubtless the will of prince and bishop will prevail, but even so, these must be put to the people before they can say yes or no to them. I shall call such an assembly tomorrow. Your case can only be vindicated absolutely by public acceptance.'

'He says truly,' said Urien, holding the prior's austere and half affronted eyes. 'You will do well to get the goodwill of Gwytherin, however many blessings you already have. They respect their bishop, and are very content with their king and his sons, I doubt if you need grudge the delay.'

Prior Robert accepted both the warning and the reassurance, and felt the need of a period of quietude in which to review his strategy and prepare his persuasions. When Urien rose to take his leave, his errand punctiliously completed, the prior also rose, half a head taller than the tallest there, and folded his long white hands in submissive resignation.

'We have yet two hours or more to Vespers,' he said, eyeing the angle of the sun. 'I should like to withdraw into your church and spend some while in meditation, and prayer for right guidance. Brother Cadfael, you had better remain with Father Huw, and help him in any arrangements he needs to make, and you, Brother John, bestow the horses as he directs, and see them cared for. The rest will join me in intercession, that we may conduct this enterprise rightly.'

He swept away, elongated and silvery and majestic, and had to stoop his head to enter under the low round arch of the church door. Brother Richard, Brother Jerome, Brother Columbanus vanished within on his heels. Not all the time they were together there would be spent in prayer. They would be considering what arguments would be most likely to carry the day with Father Huw's free assembly, or what oblique ecclesiastical threats daunt them into submission.

Brother John looked after the lofty silver head until it stooped with accurate dignity just low enough to pass under the stone, and let out something between a sigh and an arrested gurgle of laughter, as though he had been praying for a miscalculation. What with the journey, and the exercise, and the outdoor living, he looked ruddier and healthier and more athletic than ever.

'I've been hoping all this while for a chance to get my leg over that dapple-grey,' he said. 'Richard rides him like a badly-balanced woolsack. I hope Father Huw's stabling is a mile or more away.'

Father Huw's plans for them, it seemed, involved two of the nearer and more prosperous members of his flock, but even so, in the scattered Welsh way, their houses were dispersed in valley and forest.

'I shall give up my own house to the prior and sub-prior, of course,' he said, 'and sleep in the loft above my cow. For the beasts, my grazing here is too small, and I have no stable, but Bened the smith has a good paddock above the water-meadows, and stabling with a loft, if this young brother will not mind being lodged the better part of a mile from his fellows. And for you and your two companions, Brother Cadfael, there is open house half a mile from here through the woods, with Cadwallon, who has one of the biggest holdings in these parts.'

Brother Cadfael considered the prospect of being housed with Jerome and Columbanus, and found it unattractive. 'Since I am the only one among us who has fluent Welsh,' he said diplomatically, 'I should remain close to Prior Robert's side. With your goodwill, Huw, I'll share your loft above the cow-byre, and be very comfortable there.'

'If that's your wish,' said Huw simply, 'I shall be glad of your company. And now I must set this young man on his way to the smithy.'

'And I,' said Cadfael, 'if you don't need me along with you—and yonder boy will make himself understood in whatever language, or none!—will go a piece of the way back with Urien. If I can pick up an acquaintance or so among your flock, so much the better, for I like the look of them and their valley.'

Brother John came out from the tiny paddock leading the two tall horses, the mules following on leading reins. Huw's eyes glowed almost as bright as John's, caressing the smooth lines of neck and shoulder.

'How long it is,' he said wistfully, 'since I was on a good horse!'

'Come on, then, Father,' urged Brother John, understanding the look if not the words, 'up with you! Here's a hand, if you fancy the roan. Lead the way in style!' And he cupped a palm for the priest's lifted foot, and hoisted him, dazed and enchanted, into the saddle. Up himself on the grey, he fell in alongside, ready if the older man should need a steadying hand, but the brown knees gripped happily. He had not forgotten how. 'Bravely!' said John, hugely laughing. 'We shall get on famously together, and end up in a race!'

Urien, checking his girth, watched them ride away out of the gentle bowl of the clearing. 'There go two happy men,' he said thoughtfully.

'More and more I wonder,' said Cadfael, 'how that youngster ever came to commit himself to the monastic life.'

'Or you, for instance?' said Urien, with his toe in the stirrup. 'Come, if you want to view the ground, we'll take the valley way a piece, before I leave you for the hills.'

They parted at the crest of the ridge, among the trees but where a fold of the ground showed them the ox-team still doggedly labouring at a second strip, continuing the line of the first, above the richer valley land. Two such strips in one day was prodigious work.

'Your prior will be wise,' said Urien, taking his leave, 'to take a lesson from yonder young fellow. Leading and coaxing pays better than driving in these parts. But I need not tell you—a man as Welsh as myself.'

Cadfael watched him ride away gently along the cleared track until he vanished among the trees. Then he turned back towards Gwytherin, but went steeply downhill towards the river, and at the edge of the forest stood in green shadow under an oak tree, gazing across the sunlit meadows and the silver thread of river to where the team heaved and strained along the last furrow. Here there was no great distance between them, and he could see clearly the gloss of sweat on the pelts of the oxen, and the heavy curl of the soil as it heeled back from the share. The ploughman was dark, squat and powerful, with a salting of grey in his shaggy locks, but the ox-caller was tall and slender, and the curling hair that tossed on his neck and clung to his moist brow was as fair as flax. He managed his backward walking without a glance behind, feeling his way light-footed and gracefully, as if he had eyes in the back of his heels. His voice was hoarse and tired with long use now, but still clear and merry, more effective than any goad, as he cajoled his weary beasts along the final furrow, calling and luring and praising, telling them they had done marvels, and should get their rest and their meed for it, that in moments now they would be going home, that he was proud of them and loved them, as if he had been talking to Christian souls. And the beasts heaved and leaned, throwing their weight into the yokes and keeping their eyes upon him, and plainly would do anything in their power to please him. When the plough curved to the end and halted, and the steaming oxen stood with lowered heads, the young man came and flung an arm over the neck of the near leader, and scrubbed with brisk knuckles in the curly hair on the other's brow, and Cadfael said aloud: 'Bravely! But, my friend, how did *you* stray into Wales?'

Something small, round and hard dropped rustling through the leaves above him, and hit him neatly in the middle of his weather-beaten tonsure. He clapped a hand to his crown, and said something unbecoming his habit. But it was only one of last year's oak-balls, dried out by a winter's weathering to the hardness of a pebble. He looked up into the foliage above his head, already thick and turning rich green from its early gold, and it seemed to him that the tremor of leaves where there was no wind required more explanation than the accidental fall of one small remnant of a dead year. It stilled very quickly, and even its stillness, by contrast, seemed too careful and aware. Cadfael removed himself a few yards, as if about to walk on, and doubled round again behind the next barrier of bushes to see if the bait had been taken.

A small bare foot, slightly stained with moss and bark, reached down out of the branches to a toe-hold on the trunk. Its fellow, stretched at the end of a long, slim leg, swung clear, as the boy prepared to drop. Brother Cadfael, fascinated, suddenly averted his eyes in haste, and turned his back, but he was smiling, and he did not, after all, withdraw, but circled his screen of bushes and reappeared innocently in view of the bird that had just flown down out of its nest. No boy, as he had first supposed, but a girl, and a most personable girl, too, now standing decorously in the grass with her skirts nobly disposed round her, and even the small bare feet concealed.

They stood looking at each other with candid curiosity, neither at all abashed. She might have been eighteen or nineteen years old, possibly younger, for there was a certain erect assurance about her that gave her the dignity of maturity even when newly dropped out of an oak tree. And for all her bare feet and mane of unbraided dark hair, she was no villein girl. Everything about her said clearly that she knew her worth. Her gown was of fine homespun wool, dyed a soft blue, and had embroidery at neck and sleeves. No question but she was a beauty. Her face was oval and firm of feature, the hair that fell in wild waves about her shoulders was almost black, but black with a tint of dark and brilliant red in it where the light caught, and the large, black-lashed eyes that considered Brother Cadfael with such frank interest were of almost the same colour, dark as damsons, bright as the sparkles of mica in the river pebbles.

'You are one of the monks from Shrewsbury,' she said with certainty. And to his astonishment she said it in fluent and easy English.

'I am,' said Cadfael. 'But how did you come to know all about us so soon? I think you were not among those who made it their business to walk along Huw's garden fence while we were talking. There was one very fine girl, I remember, but not a black lass like you.'

She smiled. She had an enchanting smile, sudden and radiant. 'Oh, that would be Annest. But everybody in Gwytherin knows by now all about you, and what you've come for. Father Huw is right, you know,' she warned seriously, 'we shan't like it at all. Why do you want to take Saint Winifred away? When she's been here so long, and nobody ever paid any attention to her before? It doesn't seem neighbourly or honest to me.'

It was an excellent choice of words, he thought, and marvelled how a Welsh girl came by it, for she was using English as if she had been born to it, or come to it for love.

'I question the propriety of it myself, to be truthful,' he agreed ruefully. 'When Father Huw spoke up for his parish, I confess I found myself inclining to his side of the argument.'

That made her look at him more sharply and carefully than before, frowning over some sudden doubt or suspicion in her own mind. Whoever had informed her had certainly witnessed all that went on in Father Huw's garden. She hesitated a moment, pondering, and then launched at him unexpectedly in Welsh: 'You must be the one who speaks our language, the one who translated what Father Huw said.' It seemed to trouble her more than was reasonable. 'You do know Welsh! You understand me now.'

'Why, I'm as Welsh as you, child,' he admitted mildly, 'and only a Benedictine in my middle years, and I haven't forgotten my mother-tongue yet, I hope. But I marvel how you've come to speak English as well as I do myself, here in the heart of Rhos.'

'Oh, no,' she said defensively, 'I've only learned a very little. I tried to use it for you, because I thought you *were* English. How was I to know you'd be just *that* one?' Now why should his being bilingual cause her uneasiness? he wondered. And why was she casting so many rapid, furtive glances aside towards the river, brightly glimpsed through the trees? Where, as he saw in a glance just as swift as hers, the tall, fair youngster who was no

Welshman, and was certainly the finest ox-caller in Gwynedd, had broken away from his placidly-drinking team, and was wading the river thigh-deep towards this particular tall oak, in a flurry of sparkling spray. The girl had been ensconced in this very tree, whence, no doubt, she had a very good view of the ploughing. And came down as soon as it was finished! 'I'm shy of my English,' she said, pleading and vulnerable. 'Don't tell anyone!'

She was wishing him away from here, and demanding his discretion at the same time. His presence, he gathered, was inconvenient.

'I've known the same trouble myself,' he said comfortably, 'when first I tried getting my tongue round English. I'll never call your efforts into question. And now I'd better be on my way back to our lodgings, or I shall be late for Vespers.'

'God go with you, then, Father,' she said, radiant and relieved.

'And with you, my child.'

He withdrew by a carefully chosen route that evaded any risk of bumping into the fair young man. And she watched him go for a long moment, before she turned eagerly to meet the ox-caller as he came splashing through the shallows and climbed the bank. Cadfael thought that she was perfectly aware how much he had observed and understood, and was pleased by his reticence. Pleased and reassured. A Welsh girl of status, with embroidery along the hems of her gown, had good need to go softly if she was meeting an outlander, a man landless and rootless here in a clan society, where to be without place in a kinship was to be without the means of living. And yet a very pleasing, comely young man, good at his work and feeling for his beasts. Cadfael looked back, when he was sure the bushes covered him, and saw the two of them draw together, still and glad, not touching, almost shy of each other. He did not look back again.

Now what I really need here, he thought as he walked back towards the church of Gwytherin, is a good, congenial acquaintance, someone who knows every man, woman and child in the parish, without having to carry the burden of their souls. A sound drinking companion with good sense is what I need.

CHAPTER THREE

He found not one of what he wanted, but three at one stroke, after Compline that evening, when he walked back with Brother John in the twilight to the smithy and croft at the edge of the valley fields. Prior Robert and Brother Richard had already withdrawn for the night into Huw's house, Jerome and Columbanus were on their way through the woods to Cadwallon's holding, and who was to question whether Brother Cadfael had also gone to his pallet in the priest's loft, or was footloose among the gossips of Gwytherin? The lodging arrangements were working out admirably. He had never felt less inclined for sleep at this soft evening hour, nor was anyone going to rouse them at midnight here for Matins. Brother John was delighted to introduce him into the smith's household, and Father Huw favoured the acquaintance for his own reasons. It was well that others besides himself should speak for the people of the parish, and Bened the smith was a highly respected man, like all of his craft, and his words would carry weight.

There were three men sitting on the bench outside Bened's door when they arrived, and the mead was going round as fast as the talk. All heads went up alertly at the sound of their steps approaching, and a momentary silence marked the solidarity of the local inhabitants. But Brother John seemed already to have made himself welcome, and Cadfael cast them a greeting in Welsh, like a fisherman casting a line, and was accepted with something warmer than the strict courtesy the English would have found. Annest with the light-brown, sunflecked hair had spread word of his Welshness far and wide. Another bench was pulled up, and the drinking-horns continued their circling in a wider ring. Over the river the light was fading gradually, the dimness green with the colours of meadow and forest, and threaded through with the string of silver water.

Bened was a thickset, muscular man of middle years, bearded and brown. Of his two companions the younger was recognisable as the ploughman who had followed the ox-team that day, and no wonder he was dry after such labour. And the third was a grey-headed elder with a long, smoothly-trimmed beard and fine, sinewy hands, in an ample homespun gown that had seen better days, perhaps on another wearer. He bore himself as one entitled to respect, and got it.

'Padrig, here, is a good poet and a fine harpist,' said Bened, 'and Gwytherin is lucky to have him staying a while among us, in Rhisiart's hall. That's away beyond Cadwallon's place, in a forest clearing, but Rhisiart has land over this way, too, both sides the river. He's the biggest landowner in these parts. There are not many here entitled to keep a harp, or maybe we'd be honoured with more visits from travelling bards like Padrig. I have a little harp myself—I have that privilege—but Rhisiart's is a fine one, and kept in use, too. I've heard his girl play on it sometimes.'

'Women cannot be bards,' said Padrig with tolerant scorn. 'But she knows how to keep it tuned, and well looked after, that I will say. And her father's a patron of the arts, and a generous, open-handed one. No bard goes away disappointed from his hall, and none ever leaves without being pressed to stay. A good household!'

'And this is Cai, Rhisiart's ploughman. No doubt you saw the team cutting new land, when you came over the ridge today.'

'I did, and admired the work,' said Cadfael heartily. 'I never saw better. A good team you had there, and a good caller, too.'

'The best,' said Cai without hesitation. 'I've worked with a good many in my time, but never known one with the way Engelard has with the beasts. They'd die for him. And as good a hand with all cattle, calving or sick or what you will. Rhisiart would be a sorry man if ever he lost him. Ay, we did a good day's work today.'

'You'll have heard from Father Huw,' said Cadfael, 'that all the free men are called to the church tomorrow after Mass, to hear what our prior is proposing. No doubt we shall see Rhisiart there.'

'See and hear him,' said Cai, and grinned. 'He speaks his mind. An open-hearted, open-natured man, with a temper soon up and soon down, and never a grudge in him, but try and move him when his mind's made up, and you're leaning on Snowdon.'

'Well, a man can but hold fast to what he believes right, and even the opponent he baulks should value him for that. And have his sons no interest in the harp, that they leave it to their sister?'

'He has no sons,' said Bened. 'His wife is dead, and he never would take another, and there's only this one girl to follow him.'

'And no male heir anywhere in his kinship? It's rare for a daughter to inherit.'

'Not a man on his side the family at all,' said Cai, 'and a pity it is. The only near kin is her mother's brother, and he has no claim, and is old into the bargain. The greatest match anywhere in this valley, is Sioned, and young men after her like bees. But God willing, she'll be a contented wife with a son on her knee long before Rhisiart goes to his fathers.'

'A grandson by a good man, and what could any lord want more,' said Padrig, and emptied the jug of mead and passed the horn along. 'Understand me, I'm not a Gwytherin man myself, and have no right to give a voice one way or the other. But if I may say a word my friends won't say for themselves—you having your duty to your prior as Cai has to his lord, or I to my art and my patrons—don't look for any easy passage, and don't take offence if your way is blocked. Nothing personal to you! But where the free men of Wales see no fair dealing, they won't call it by fair names, and they won't stand aside.'

'I should be sorry if they did,' said Cadfael. 'For my part, the ending I want is the fair ending, leaving no man with a just grievance. And what of the other lords we can expect to see there? Of Cadwallon we've heard, two of our brothers are enjoying his hospitality. And his lands are neighbour to Rhisiart's?'

'It's a fair piece beyond to Rhisiart's hall, on through the forest. But they're neighbours, boundary to boundary, yes, and friends from youth. A peaceable man, Cadwallon, he likes his comfort and his hunting. His way would be to say yes to whatever bishop and prince commend, but then, his way normally is also to say yes to Rhisiart. For that matter,' owned Bened, tilting the last drop from the horn, 'I know no more than you what either of them will have to say in this matter. For all I know they'll accept your omens and bless your errand. If the free voice goes with your prior, then Saint Winifred goes home with you, and that's the end of it.'

It was the end of the mead, too, for that night.

'Bide the night here,' said Bened to Padrig, when the guests rose to walk home, 'and we'll have a little music before you leave tomorrow. My small harp needs to be played, I've kept it in fettle for you.'

'Why, so I will, since you're so kind,' said Padrig, and weaved his way gently into the house with his host. And Cai and Brother Cadfael, taking their leave, set off companionably shoulder to shoulder, to make their way back to Father Huw's house, and thence in courtesy a measure of the way through the woods towards Rhisiart's hall before they parted.

'I would not say more nor plainer,' said Cai confidingly, 'while Bened was present, nor in front of Padrig, for that matter, though he's a good fellow—so are they both!—but a traveller, not a native. This Sioned, Rhisiart's girl. . . . The truth is, Bened would like to be a suitor for her himself, and a good, solid man he is, and a girl might well do worse. But a widower, poor soul, and years older than the lass, and a poor chance he has. But you haven't seen the girl!'

Brother Cadfael was beginning to suspect that he had indeed seen the girl, and seen more than any here had ever been allowed to see. But he said nothing.

'A girl like a squirrel! As swift, as sudden, as black and as red! If she had nothing, they'd still be coming from miles around, and she will have lands any man might covet even if she squinted! And there's poor Bened, keeping his own counsel and feeding on his own silence, and still hoping. After all, a smith is respected in any company. And give him his due, it isn't her heritage he covets. It's the girl herself. If you'd seen her, you'd know. In any case,' said Cai, sighing gustily for his friend, 'her father has a favourite for son-in-law already, and has had all along. Cadwallon's lad has been in and out of Rhisiart's hall, and made free with Rhisiart's servants and hawks and horses, ever since he could run, and grown up with the girl. And he's sole heir to the neighbouring holding, and what could suit either father better? They've had it made up between them for years. And the children seem ideally matched, they know each other through and through, like brother and sister.'

'I doubt if I'd say that made for an ideal match,' said Brother Cadfael honestly.

'So Sioned seems to think, too,' said Cai drily. 'So far she's resisted all pressures to accept this lad Peredur. And mind you, he's a very gay, lively, well-looking young fellow, spoiled as you please, being the only one, but show me a girl round here who wouldn't run if he lifted his finger—all but this girl! Oh, she likes him well enough, but that's all. She won't hear of marriage yet, she's still playing the heartfree child.'

'And Rhisiart bears with her?' asked Cadfael delicately.

'You don't know him, either. He dotes on her, and well he may, and she reveres him, and well *she* may, and where does that get any of us? He won't force her choice. He never misses a chance to urge how suitable Peredur is, and she never denies it. He hopes, if he bides his time, she'll come round.'

'And will she?' asked Brother Cadfael, responding to something in the ploughman's voice. His own was milder than milk.

'No accounting,' said Cai slowly, 'for what goes on in a girl's head. She may have other plans of her own. A bold, brave one she is, clever and patient at getting her own way. But what that may be, do I know? Do you? Does any man?'

'There may be one man who does,' said Brother Cadfael with guileful disinterest.

If Cai had not risen to that bait, Cadfael would have let well alone then, for it was no business of his to give away the girl's secrets, when he had stumbled upon them himself only by chance. But he was no way surprised when the ploughman drew meaningfully close against his arm, and jabbed a significant elbow into his ribs. A man who had worked closely with the young ox-caller as he had must surely have noted a few obvious things by now. This afternoon's purposeful bee-line across the meadows and through the water to a certain well-grown oak would be enough in itself for a sharp man. And as for keeping his mouth shut about it, it was pretty plain that his sympathies were with his work-mate.

'Brother Cadfael, you wouldn't be a talking man, not out of turn, and you're not tied to one side or the other in any of our little disputes here. No reason *you* shouldn't know. Between you and me, she *has* got a man in her eye, and one that wants her worse than Bened does, and has even less chance of ever getting her. You remember we were talking of my fellow on the team, Engelard? A good man with cattle, worth plenty to his lord, and Rhisiart knows it and values him fairly on it. But the lad's an *alltud*—an outlander!'

'Saxon?' asked Cadfael.

'The fair hair. Yes, you saw him today. The length and slenderness of him too. Yes, he's a Cheshire man from the borders of Maelor, on the run from the bailiffs of Earl Ranulf of Chester. Oh, not for murder or banditry or any such! But the lad was simply the most outrageous deer-poacher in the earldom. He's a master with the short bow, and always stalked them afoot and alone. And the bailiff was after his blood. Nothing for him to do, when he was cornered on the borders, but run for it into Gwynedd. And he daren't go back, not yet, and you know what it means for a foreigner to want to make a living in Wales.'

Cadfael knew indeed. In a country where every native-born man had and knew his assured place in a clan kinship, and the basis of all relationships was establishment on the land, whether as free lord or villein partner in a village community, the man from outside, owning no land here, fitting into no place, was deprived of the very basis of living. His only means of establishing himself was by getting some overlord to make compact with him, give him house-room and a stake in the land, and employ him for whatever skills he could offer. For three generations this bargain between them was revocable at any time, and the outlander might leave at the fair price of dividing his chattels equally with the lord who had given him the means of acquiring them.

'I do know. So Rhisiart took this young man into his service and set him up in a croft?'

'He did. Two years ago now, a little more. And neither of them has had any call to regret it. Rhisiart's a fair-minded master, and gives credit where it's due. But however much he respects and values him, can you see a Welsh lord ever letting his only daughter go to an *alltud?*'

'Never!' agreed Cadfael positively. 'No chance of it! It would be against all his laws and customs and conscience. His own kinship would never forgive it.'

'True as I'm breathing!' sighed Cai ruefully. 'But you try telling that to a proud, stubborn young fellow like Engelard, who has his own laws and rights from another place, where his father's lord of a good manor, and carries every bit as much weight in his feudal fashion as Rhisiart does here.'

'Do you tell me he's actually spoken for her to her father?' demanded Cadfael, astonished and admiring.

'He has, and got the answer you might expect. No malice at all, but no hope, either. Yes, and stood his ground and argued his case just the same. And comes back to the subject every chance that offers, to remind Rhisiart he hasn't given up, and never will. I tell you what, those two are two of a kind, both hot-tempered, both obstinate, but both as open and honest as you'll find anywhere, and they've a great respect for each other that somehow keeps them from bearing malice or letting this thing break them apart. But every time this comes up, the sparks fly. Rhisiart clouted Engelard once, when he pushed him too hard, and the lad came within an ace of clouting back. What would the answer to that have been? I never knew it happen with an *alltud*, but if a slave strikes a free man he stands to lose the hand that did it. But he stopped himself in time, though I don't think it was fear that stopped him—he knew he was in the wrong. And what did Rhisiart do, not half an hour later, but fling back and ask his pardon! Said he was an insolent, unreasonable, unWelsh rascal, but he should not have struck him. There's a battle going on all the time between those two, and neither of them can get any peace, but let any man say a word against Rhisiart in Engelard's hearing, and he'll get it back down his throat with a fist behind it. And if one of the servants ever called down Engelard, thinking to curry favour with Rhisiart, he'd soon get told that the *alltud*'s an honest man and a good worker, worth ten of the likes of his backbiters. So it goes! And I can see no good end to it.'

'And the girl?' said Cadfael. 'What does she say to all this?'

'Very little, and very softly. Maybe at first she did argue and plead, but if so it was privately with her father alone. Now she's biding her time, and keeping them from each other's throat as best she can.'

And meeting her lover at the oak tree, thought Cadfael, or any one of a dozen other private places, wherever his work takes him. So that's how she learned her English, all through those two years while the Saxon boy was busy learning Welsh from her, and that's why, though she was willing to pass the time of day in his own language with a visiting monk, she was concerned about having betrayed her accomplishment to a Welsh-speaking stranger, who might innocently blurt it abroad locally. She'd hardly want to let slip how often she's been meeting Engelard in secret, if she's biding her time, and keeping father and lover from each other's throat till she can get her own way with them. And who's to say which of the three will give way first, where all look immovable?

'It seems you've your own troubles here in Gwytherin, let alone what we've brought with us,' he said, when he parted from Cai.

'God resolves all given time,' said Cai philosophically and trudged away into the darkness. And Cadfael returned along the path with the uncomfortable feeling that God, nevertheless, required a little help from men, and what he mostly got was hindrance.

All the free men of Gwytherin came to the meeting next day, and their womenfolk and all the villein community came to the

Mass beforehand. Father Huw named the chief among them softly to Brother Cadfael as they made their appearance. He had seldom had such a congregation.

'Here is Rhisiart, with his daughter and his steward, and the girl's waiting-woman.'

Rhisiart was a big, bluff, hearty-looking man of about fifty, high-coloured and dark-haired, with a short, grizzled beard, and bold features that could be merry or choleric, fierce or jovial, but were far too expressive ever to be secretive or mean. His stride was long and impetuous, and his smile quick in response when he was greeted. His dress hardly distinguished him from any of the other free landholders who came thronging into the church, being plain as any, but of good homespun cloth. To judge from his bright face, he came without prejudice, willing to listen, and for all his thwarted family plans, he looked an expansively happy man, proud and fond of his daughter.

As for the girl, she followed at his heels modestly, with poised head and serene eyes. She had shoes on for this occasion, and her hair was brushed and braided into a burnished dark coil on her neck, and covered with a linen coif, but there was no mistaking her. This was the urchin of the oak tree, and the greatest heiress and most desirable prize in marriage in all this countryside.

The steward was an older man, grey-headed and balding, with a soft, good-humoured face. 'He is Rhisiart's kinsman by marriage,' whispered Huw, 'his wife's elder brother.'

'And the other girl is Sioned's tirewoman?' No need to name her, he already knew her name. Dimpled and smiling, Annest followed her friend with demure little steps into the church, and the sun stroked all the bright, silvery grain in the sheaf of her pale hair. 'She is the smith's niece,' said Father Huw helpfully. 'A good girl, she visits him often since he buried his wife, and bakes for him.'

'Bened's niece?' Brother John pricked his ears, and looked after the shapely waist and glowing hair with fascinated eyes, no doubt hoping there would be a baking day before they had to leave Gwytherin. The lodging arrangements had certainly been inspired, though whether by an angel or an imp remained to be seen.

'Lower your eyes, brother,' said Jerome chidingly. 'It is not seemly to look so straightly upon women.'

'And how did he know there were women passing,' whispered Brother John rebelliously, 'if his own eyes were so dutifully lowered?'

Brother Columbanus, at least, was standing as prescribed in the presence of females, with pale hands prayerfully folded, and lofty eyelids lowered, his gaze upon the grass.

'And here comes Cadwallon now,' said Father Huw. 'These good brothers already know him, of course. And his lady. And his son Peredur.'

So this young man, loping after his parents with the long, springy gait of a yearling roebuck, was the chosen husband for Sioned, the lad she liked well enough, and had known familiarly all her life, but was in no way inclined to marry. It occurred to Cadfael that he had never asked how the groom felt about the situation, but it needed only a glimpse of Peredur's face when he caught sight of Sioned to settle the matter. Here was a tangle. The girl might have worn out in mere liking all her inclination to love, but the boy certainly had not. At sight of her his face paled, and his eyes took fire.

The parents were ordinary enough, comfortable people grown plump from placid living, and expecting things to go smoothly still as they always had. Cadwallon had a round, fleshy, smiling face, and his wife was fat, fair and querulous. The boy cast back to some more perilous ancestor. The spring of his step was a joy to watch. He was not above middle height, but so well-proportioned that he looked tall. His dark hair was cut short, and curled crisply all over his head. His chin was shaven clean, and all the bones of his face were as bold and elegant as his colouring was vivid, with russet brushings of sun on high cheek-bones, and a red, audacious, self-willed mouth. Such a young person might well find it hard to bear that another, and an alien at that, should be preferred to him. He proclaimed in his every movement and glance that everything and everyone in his life had responded subserviently to his charm, until now.

At the right moment, when the church was full, Prior Robert, tall and imposing and carefully groomed, swept in through the tiny sacristy and took his place, and all the Shrewsbury brothers fell into line and followed on his heels. The Mass began.

In the deliberations of the free assembly of the parish, of course, the women had no part. Neither had the villeins, though they had their indirect influence through those of their friends who were free. So while the free men lingered after the Mass, the rest dispersed, moving away with slow dignity, and not too far, just far enough to be discreetly out of sight and earshot, but handy to detect what was passing by instinct, and confirm it as soon as the meeting broke up.

The free men gathered in the open before the church. The sun was already high, for it was little more than an hour to noon. Father Huw stood up before the assembly, and gave them the gist of the matter, as it had been presented to him. He was the father of this flock, and he owed his people truth, but he also owed his church fealty. He told them what bishop and prince had answered to the request from Shrewsbury, reverently presented, and with many proofs. Which proofs he left to Robert to deliver.

The prior had never looked holier or more surely headed for sainthood himself. He had always a sense of occasion, and beyond a doubt it had been his idea to hold the meeting here in the open, where the sun could gild and illuminate his otherworldly beauty. It was Cadfael's detached opinion that he did himself more than justice, by being less overbearing than might have been expected. Usually he overdid things, this time he got it right, or as right as something only equivocally right in itself can be got.

'They're not happy!' whispered Brother John in Cadfael's ear, himself sounding far from sad about it. There were times when even Brother John could be humanly smug. And indeed, those Welsh faces ranged round them were singularly lacking in enthusiasm for all these English miracles performed by a Welsh saint. Robert at his best was not exactly carrying his audience.

They swayed and murmured, and eyed one another, and again turned as one man to eye him.

'If Owain ap Griffith wills it, and the bishop gives his blessing, too,' began Cadwallon hesitantly, 'as loyal sons of the church, and true men of Gwynedd, we can hardly. . . .'

'Both prince and bishop have blessed our errand,' said the prior loftily.

'But the girl is here, in Gwytherin,' said Rhisiart abruptly. He had the voice that might have been expected from him, large, melodious and deep, a voice that sang what it felt, and waited for thought afterwards, to find that the thought had been there already in the feeling. 'Ours, not Bishop David's! Not Owain ap Griffith's! She lived out her life here, and never said word about wanting to leave us. Am I to believe easily that she wants to leave us now, after so long? Why has she never told us? Why?'

'She has made it clear to us,' said the prior, 'by many manifestations, as I have told you.'

'But never a word to *us*,' cried Rhisiart, roused. 'Do you call that courtesy? Are we to believe that, of a virgin who chose to make her home here among us?'

They were with him, his assurance had fired their smouldering reluctance. They cried out from a dozen directions at once that Saint Winifred belonged to Gwytherin, and to no other place.

'Do you dare tell me,' said Prior Robert, high and clear, 'that you have visited her? That you have committed your prayers to her? That you have invoked the aid of this blessed virgin, and given her the honour that is her due? Do you know of any reason why she should desire to remain here among you? Have you not neglected even her grave?'

'And if we have,' said Rhisiart with blithe conviction, 'do you suppose the girl wonders at it? You have not lived here among us. She did. You are English, she was Welsh, she knew us, and was never so moved against us that she withdrew or complained. We know she is there, no need to exclaim or make any great outcry. If we have needs, she knows it, and never asks that we should come with prayers and tears, knocking our knees on the ground before her. If she grudged a few brambles and weeds, she would have found a means to tell us. Us, not some distant Benedictine house in England!'

Throats were opening joyfully, shouting where they had muttered. The man was a poet and a preacher, match for any Englishman. Brother Cadfael let loose his bardic blood, and rejoiced silently. Not even because it was Prior Robert recoiling into marble rage under Welsh siege. Only because it was a Welsh voice that cried battle.

'And do you deny,' thundered Robert, stretching his ascetic length to its loftiest, 'the truth of those omens and miracles I have declared to you, the beckoning that led us here?'

'No!' said Rhisiart roundly. 'I never doubted you believed and had experienced these portents. But portents can arise, miracles can be delivered, either from angels or devils. If these are from heaven, why have we not been instructed? The little saint is here, not in England. She owes us the courtesy of kinsmen. Dare you say she is turned traitor? Is there not a church in Wales, a Celtic church such as she served? What did she know of yours? I do not believe she would speak to you and not to us. You have been deceived by devils! Winifred never said word!'

A dozen voices took up the challenge, hallooing applause for their most articulate spokesman, who had put his finger on the very pulse of their resentment. Even the very system of bishoprics galled the devout adherents of the old, saintly Celtic church, that had no worldly trappings, courted no thrones, but rather withdrew from the world into the blessed solitude of thought and prayer. The murmur became a subdued rumbling, a thunder, a roar. Prior Robert, none too wisely, raised his commanding voice to shout them down.

'She said no word to you, for you had left her forgotten and unhonoured. She has turned to us for recognition, when she could get none from you.'

'That is not true,' said Rhisiart, 'though you in your ignorance may believe it. The saint is a good Welshwoman, and knows her countrymen. We are not quick in respect to rank or riches, we do not doff and bow and scrape when any man flaunts himself before us. We are blunt and familiar even in praise. What we value we value in the heart, and this Welsh girl knows it. She would never leave her own unfurnished, even if we have neglected to trim her grave. It is the spirit that leans to us, and is felt by us as guardian and kin. But these bones you come hunting are also hers. Not ours, not yours! Until she tells us she wills to have them moved, here they stay. We should be damned else!'

It was the bitterest blow of Prior Robert's life to know that he had met his match and overmatch in eloquence and argument, here in a half-barbaric Welsh landholder, no great lord, but a mere squireling elevated among his inferiors to a status he barely rated, at least in Norman eyes. It was the difference between them that Robert thought in hierarchies, and Rhisiart thought in blood-ties, high and low of one mind and in one kinship, and not a man among them aware of inferiority, only of his due place in a united family.

The thunder was one voice now, demanding and assured, but it was one man who had called it into being. Prior Robert, well aware that a single adversary confronted him, subdued his angry tones, and opted for the wisdom of the dove, and the subtlety of single combat. He raised his long, elegant arms, from which the wide sleeves of his habit fell free, and smiled on the assembly, turning the smile at its most compelling and fatherly upon Rhisiart.

'Come, Brother Cadfael, say this for me to the lord Rhisiart, that it is all too easy for us, who have the same devotion at heart, to disagree about the means. It is better to speak quietly, man to man, and avoid the deformation of anger. Lord Rhisiart, I beg you to come apart with me, and let us debate this matter in quietude, and then you shall have liberty to speak out what you will. And having had my say fairly with you, I will say no word further to challenge what you have to impart to your people.'

'That is fair and generous,' said Rhisiart promptly to this offer, and stood forward with ingenuous pleasure from the crowd, which parted to let him through.

'We will not take even the shadow of dissension into the church,' said Prior Robert. 'Will you come with us into Father

Huw's house?' All those bright, sullen, roused eyes followed them in through the low doorway, and clung there to wait for them to come forth again. Not a man of the Welsh moved from his place. They trusted the voice that had spoken for them hitherto to speak for them still.

In the small, wood-scented room, dark after the brightness of the day outside, Prior Robert faced his opponent with a calm and reasonable face.

'You have spoken well,' he said, 'and I commend your faith, and the high value you set on the saint, for so do we value her highly. And at her own wish, for so we believe, we have come here, solely to serve her. Both church and state are with us, and you know better than I the duty a nobleman of Wales owes to both. But I would not willingly leave Gwytherin with a sense of grievance, for I do know that by Saint Winifred's departure Gwytherin's loss is great. That we own, and I would wish to make due reparation.'

'Reparation to Gwytherin?' repeated Rhisiart, when this was translated to him. 'I do not understand how....'

'And to you,' said Robert softly and matter-of-factly, 'if you will withdraw your opposition, for then I feel sure all your fellows will do the same, and sensibly accept what bishop and prince decree.'

It occurred to Cadfael as he interpreted this, even before the prior began the slow, significant motion of one long hand into the breast of his habit, that Robert was about to make the most disastrous miscalculation of his life. But Rhisiart's face remained dubious and aloof, quite without understanding, as the prior drew from his bosom a soft leather bag drawn up with a cord at the neck, and laid it on the table, pushing it gently across until it rested against Rhisiart's right hand. Its progress over the rough boards gave out a small chinking sound. Rhisiart eyed it suspiciously, and lifted uncomprehending eyes to stare at the prior. 'I don't understand you. What is this?'

'It is yours,' said Robert, 'if you will persuade the parish to agree to give up the saint.'

Too late he felt the unbelieving coldness in the air, and sensed the terrible error he had made. Hastily he did his best to recover some of the ground lost. 'To be used as you think best for Gwytherin—a great sum. . . .' It was useless. Cadfael let it lie in silence.

'Money!' said Rhisiart in the most extraordinary of tones, at once curious, derisory and revolted. He knew about money, of course, and even understood its use, but as an aberration in human relations. In the rural parts of Wales, which indeed were almost all of Wales, it was hardly used at all, and hardly needed. Provision was made in the code for all necessary exchange of goods and services, nobody was so poor as to be without the means of living, and beggars were unknown. The kinship took care of its helpless members, and every house was open as of right. The minted coins that had seeped in through the marches were a pointless eccentricity. Only after a moment of scornful wonder did it occur to Rhisiart that in this case they were also a mortal insult. He snatched away his hand from the affronting touch, and the blood surged into his face darkly red, suffusing even the whites of his eyes.

'Money? You dare offer to *buy* our saint? To buy *me*? I was in two minds about you, and about what I ought to do, but now, by God, I know what to think! You had your omens. Now I have mine!'

'You mistake me!' cried the prior, stumbling after his blunder and seeing it outdistance him at every breath. 'One cannot buy what is holy, I am only offering a gift to Gwytherin, in gratitude and compensation for their sacrifice—'

'Mine, you said it was,' Rhisiart reminded him, glowing copper bright with dignified rage. 'Mine, if I *persuaded* . . . ! Not a gift! A bribe! This foolish stuff you hoard about you more dearly far than your reputations, don't think you can use it to buy *my* conscience. I know now that I was right to doubt you. You have said your say, now I will say mine to those people without, as you promised me I should, without hindrance.'

'No, wait!' The prior was in such agitation that he actually reached out a hand and caught his opponent by the sleeve. 'Do nothing in haste! You have mistaken my meaning indeed, and if I was wrong even to offer an alms to Gwytherin, I am sorry for it. But do not call it—'

Rhisiart withdrew himself angrily from the detaining clasp, and cut off the protest curtly, wheeling on Cadfael. 'Tell him he need not be afraid. I should be ashamed to tell my people that a prior of Shrewsbury tried to corrupt me with a bribe. I don't deal in that kind of warfare. But where I stand—that they shall know, and you, too.' And he strode out from them, and Father Huw put out a warning hand to prevent any of them from attempting to impede or follow him.

'Not now! He is hot now. Tomorrow something may be done to approach him, but not now. You must let him say what he will.'

'Then at least let's put in an appearance,' said the prior, magnificently picking up what pieces he could of the ruin he had created; and he swept out into the sunlight and took his stand close to the door of the church, with all his fellow-monks dutifully following on his heels, and stood with erect head and calmly folded hands, in full view, while Rhisiart thundered his declaration to the assembled people of Gwytherin.

'I have listened to what these men from Shrewsbury have had to say to me, and I have made my judgment accordingly, and now I deliver it to you. I say that so far from changing my views, I am confirmed a thousand times that I was right to oppose the sacrilege they desire. I say that Saint Winifred's place is here among us, where she has always belonged, and that it would be mortal sin to let her be taken away to a strange place, where not even the prayers would be in a tongue she knows, where foreigners not worthy to draw near her would be her only company. I pledge my opposition to the death, against any attempt to move her bones, and I urge upon you the same duty. And now this conference is ended.'

So he said, and so it was. There could be no possible way of prolonging it. The prior was forced to stand with marble face and quiet hands while Rhisiart strode away towards the forest path, and all the assembly, in awed and purposeful silence, melted away mysteriously in all directions after his departure, so that within minutes all that green, trodden arena was empty.

CHAPTER FOUR

'You should have told me what you intended,' said Father Huw, timidly reproachful. 'I could have told you it was folly, the worst possible. What attraction do you think money has for a man like Rhisiart? Even if he was for sale, and he is not, you would have had to find other means to purchase him. I thought you had taken his measure, and were proposing to plead to him the sorry plight of English pilgrims, who have no powerful saints of their own, and are sadly in need of such a protectress. He would have listened to something that entreated of his generosity.'

'I am come with the blessing of church and sovereign,' said the prior fiercely, though the repetition was beginning to pall even on him. 'I cannot be repudiated at the will of a local squire. Has my order no rights here in Wales?'

'Very few,' said Cadfael bluntly. 'My people have a natural reverence, but it leans towards the hermitage, not the cloister.'

The heated conference went on until Vespers, and poisoned even Vespers with its bitterness, for there Prior Robert preached a fearful sermon detailing all the omens that Winifred desired above all things to remove to the sanctity of Shrewsbury, and issuing her prophetic denunciation against all who stood in the way of her translation. Terrible would be her wrath visited on those who dared resist her will. Thus Prior Robert approached the necessary reconciliation with Rhisiart. And though Cadfael in translating toned down the threat as much as he dared, there were some among the congregation who understood enough English to get the full drift of it. He knew by their closed, mute faces. Now they would go away to spread the word to those who had not been present, until everyone in Gwytherin knew that the prior had bidden them remember what befell Prince Cradoc, whose very flesh watered away into the ground like rain, so that he vanished utterly, as to the body expunged out of the world, as to the soul, the fearful imagination dared not guess. So also it might happen to those who dared offend against Winifred now.

Father Huw, harried and anxious, cast about him as honestly as he could for a way of pleasing everybody. It took him most of the evening to get the prior to listen, but from sheer exhaustion a calm had to set in at last.

'Rhisiart is not an impious man—'

'Not impious!' fluted Brother Jerome, appealing to heaven with uplifted eyes. 'Men have been excommunicated for less!'

'Then men have been excommunicated for no evil at all,' said Huw sturdily, 'and truly I think they sometimes have. No, I say he is a decent, devout man, open-handed and fair, and had a right to resent it when he was misunderstood and affronted. If he is ever to withdraw his opposition, it must be you, Father Prior, who make the first approach to him, and upon a different footing. Not in person first, I would not ask or advise it. But if I were to go to him, perhaps with Brother Cadfael here, who is known to be a good Welshman himself, and ask him to forget all that has been said and done, and come with an open mind to begin the discussion over again, I think he would not refuse. Moreover, the very act of seeking him out would disarm him, for he has a generous heart. I don't say he would necessarily change his mind—it would depend on how he is handled this time—but I do say he would listen.'

'Far be it from me,' said Prior Robert loftily, 'to pass over any means of saving a soul from perdition. I wish the man no ill, if he tempers his offences. It is not a humiliation to stoop to deliver a sinner.'

'O wondrous clemency!' intoned Brother Jerome. 'Saintly generosity towards the ill-doer!'

Brother John flashed a narrow, glittering glance, and shifted one foot uneasily, as if restraining an impulse to kick. Father Huw, desperate to preserve his stock of goodwill with prince, bishop, prior and people alike, cast him a warning look, and resumed hurriedly: 'I will go to Rhisiart tonight, and ask him to dine here at my house tomorrow. Then if we can come to terms between us, another assembly can be called, so that all may know there is peace.'

'Very well!' said the prior, after consideration. In that way he need never actually admit any guilt on his part, or apologise for any act of his, nor need he enquire too closely what Huw might have to say on his behalf. 'Very well, do so, and I hope you may succeed.'

'It would be a mark of your status, and the importance of this gesture,' suggested Cadfael with an earnest face, 'if your messengers went mounted. It's not yet dark, and the horses would be the better for exercise.'

'True,' said the prior, mildly gratified. 'It would be in keeping with our dignity and lend weight to our errand. Very well, let Brother John bring the horses.'

'Now that's what I call a friend!' said Brother John heartily, when they were all three in the saddle, and safely away into the early dusk under the trees, Father Huw and John on the two tall horses, Brother Cadfael on the best of the mules. 'Ten more minutes, and I should have earned myself a penance that would have lasted a month or more, and now here we are in the best company around, on a decent errand, and enjoying the quiet of the evening.'

'Did I ever say word of your coming with us?' said Cadfael slyly. 'I said the horses would add lustre to the embassage, I never went so far as to say *you* would add any.'

'I go with the horses. Did you ever hear of an ambassador riding without a groom? I'll keep well out of the way while you confer, and play the dutiful servant. And by the by, Bened will be doing his drinking up there at the hall tonight. They go the rounds, and it's Cai's turn.'

'And how did you learn so much,' wondered Cadfael, 'without a word of Welsh?'

'Oh, they knock their meaning into me somehow, and I into them. Besides, I have several words of Welsh already, and if we're held up here for a while I shall soon learn a great many more, if I can get my tongue round them. I could learn the smith's art, too. I lent him a hand at the forge this morning.'

'You're honoured. In Wales not everyone can be a smith.'

Huw indicated the fence that had begun to run alongside them on the right. 'Cadwallon's holding. We have a mile of forest to go yet to Rhisiart's hall.'

It was still no more than dusk when they emerged into a large clearing, with ploughed and planted strips surrounding a long stockade fence. The smell of wood-smoke drifted on the air, and glimmer of torches lit the open doorway of the hall. Stables and barns and folds clung to the inner side of the fence, and men and women moved briskly about the evening business of a considerable household.

'Well, well!' said the voice of Cai the ploughman, from a bench under the eaves of one of the byres. 'So you've found your way by nose to where the mead is tonight, Brother Cadfael.' And he moved up obligingly to make room, shoulder to shoulder with Bened. 'Padrig's making music within, and from all I hear it may well be war music, but he'll be with us presently. Sit yourself down, and welcome. Nobody looks on you as the enemy.'

There was a third with them already, a long man seated in deeper shadow, his legs stretched well out before him at ease, and his hair showing as a primrose pallor even in the dimness. The young outlander, Engelard, willingly gathered up his long limbs and also moved to share the bench. He had a quick, open smile vivid with white teeth.

'We've come expressly to halt the war,' said Brother Cadfael as they dismounted, and a groom of the household came running to take their bridles. 'Father Huw has the peace in hand, I'm only an assessor to see fair play. And, sadly, we'll be expected back with an answer as soon as we've spoken with your lord. But if you'll take charge of Brother John while we deal, he'll be grateful. He can speak English with Engelard, a man should practise his own tongue when he can.'

But Brother John, it appeared, had at that moment completely lost the use of his tongue in any language, for he stood at gaze, and let the reins be taken from his hands like a man in a dream. Nor was he looking at Engelard, but towards the open doorway of the hall, from which a girl's figure had issued, and was crossing gaily towards the drinkers under the eaves, a large jug carried in both hands. The lively brown eyes flickered over the visitors, took in Cadfael and the priest with easy friendliness, and opened wide upon Brother John, standing like a very lifelike statue, all thorny russet hair, weather-burned cheeks and wild, admiring eyes. Cadfael looked where Annest's eyes were looking, and approved a very upstanding, ruggedly-built, ingenuous, comely young fellow, maybe two or three years older than the girl. The Benedictine habit, kilted to the knee for riding and forgotten now, looked as much like a working Welsh tunic as made no matter, and the tonsure, however well a man (or a girl!) knew it was there, was invisible behind the burning bush of curls.

'Thirsty people you are, then!' said Annest, still with one eye upon Brother John, and set down her pitcher on the bench beside Cai, and with a flick of her skirts and a wave of her light-brown mane, sat down beside it, and accepted the horn Bened offered her. Brother John stood mute and enchanted.

'Come on, then, lad,' said Bened, and made a place for him between himself and Cai, only one remove from where the girl sat delicately sipping. And Brother John, like a man walking in his sleep, though perhaps with rather more zestful purpose, strode forward towards the seat reserved for him.

'Well, well!' said Cadfael silently to himself, and left the insoluble to the solver of all problems, and with Father Huw moved on into the hall.

'I will come,' said Rhisiart, shut into a small chamber apart with his visitors. 'Of course I will come. No man should refuse another his say. No man can be sure he will not belie himself and do himself less than justice, and God forbid I should refuse anyone his second chance. I've often spoken in haste myself, and been sorry after, and said so, as your prior has said so now.' He had not, of course, nor had Huw claimed, in so many words, that he had. Rather he had expressed his own shame and regret, but if Rhisiart attributed these to Prior Robert, Huw was desperate enough to let him continue in the delusion. 'But I tell you this, I expect little from this meeting. The gap between us is too wide. To you I can say what I have not said to any who were not there, because I am ashamed. The man offered me money. He says now he offered it to Gwytherin, but how is that possible? Am I Gwytherin? I am a man like other men, I fill my place as best I can, but remain one only. No, he offered the purse to me, to take back my voice against him. To persuade my own people to go along with his wishes. I accept his desire to talk to me again, to bring me to see this matter as he sees it. But I cannot forget that he saw it as something he could buy with money. If he wishes to change me, that must change, and be shown to be changed. As for his threats, for threats they are, and I approve you for reporting them faithfully, they move me not at all. My reverence for our little saint is the equal of his or any man's. Do you think she does not know it?'

'I am sure she does,' said Father Huw.

'And if all they want is to honour and adore her rightly, why can they not do so here, where she lies? Even dress her grave, if that is what disturbs them, that we've let it run wild?'

'A good question,' said Brother Cadfael. 'I have asked it myself. The sleep of saints should be more sacred and immune even than the sleep of ordinary men.'

Rhisiart looked him over with those fine, challenging eyes, a shade or two lighter than his daughter's, and smiled. 'Howbeit, I will come, and my thanks for all your trouble. At the hour of noon, or a little after, I will come to your dinner, and I will listen faithfully to whatever may be said to me.'

There was a good laughter echoing from end to end of the bench under the eaves, and it was tempting to join the drinkers, at least for one quick cup, as Cai demanded. Bened had got up to replenish his horn from the pitcher, and Brother John, silent and flushed but glowingly happy, sat with no barrier between him and the girl, their sleeves all but touching when she leaned curiously closer, her hair dropping a stray lock against his shoulder.

'Well, how have you sped?' asked Cai, pouring mead for them. 'Will he come and talk terms with your prior?'

'He'll come,' said Cadfael. 'Whether he'll talk terms I doubt. He was greatly affronted. But he'll come to dine, and that's something.'

'The whole parish will know it before ever you get back to the parsonage,' said Cai. 'News runs faster than the wind in these parts, and after this morning they're all building on Rhisiart. I tell you, if he changed his tune and said amen, so would they. Not for want of their own doubts and waverings, but because they trust him. He took a stand, and they know he won't leave it but for good reason. Sweeten him, and you'll get your way.'

'Not my way,' said Cadfael. 'I never could see why a man can't reverence his favourite saint without wanting to fondle her bones, but there's great rivalry for such relics among the abbeys these days. A good mead, this, Cai.'

'Our Annest here brewed it,' said Bened, with tolerant pride in his niece, and clapped a hand fondly on her shoulder. 'And only one of her skills! She'll be a treasure for some man when she weds, but a sad loss to me.'

'I might bring you a good smith to work with you,' said the girl, dimpling. 'Where's the loss then?'

It was deep dusk, and with all the longing they felt to linger, they had to be away. Huw was fidgety, thinking of Prior Robert's rising impatience, his tall figure pacing the garden and looking out for the first glimpse of his messengers returning. 'We should be off. We shall be looked for. Come, brother, make your farewells.'

Brother John rose reluctantly but dutifully. The groom was leading the horses forward, an arm under each arching neck. With composed face but glowing eyes Brother John said his general goodnight and blessing. In careful but resounding Welsh!

The echo swept the riders away towards the gate on a wave of laughter and goodwill, in which the girl's light voice soared gaily, and Engelard's hearty English 'God go with you!'

balanced the tongues.

'And who taught you that between evening and dark?' asked Brother Cadfael with interest, as they entered the deep green twilight under the trees. 'Bened or Cai?'

'Neither,' said Brother John, contentedly pondering a deep private satisfaction.

Small use asking how she had managed it, she having no English and he no Welsh, to determine what the phrase was she was drumming into him. There was a kind of language at work here that made short shrift of interpreters.

'Well, you can fairly claim the day hasn't been wasted,' owned Cadfael generously, 'if something's been learned. And have you made any other discoveries to add to that?'

'Yes,' said Brother John, placidly glowing. 'The day after tomorrow is baking-day at Bened's.'

'You may rest and sleep, Father Prior,' said Huw, fronting the tall, pale forehead gallantly with his low, brown one. 'Rhisiart has said he will come, and he will listen. He was gracious and reasonable. Tomorrow at noon or soon after he will be here.'

Prior Robert certainly loosed a cautious, suppressed sigh of relief. But he required more before they could all go away and sleep. Richard loomed at his shoulder, large, benign and anxious.

'And is he sensible of the wrong-mindedness of his resistance? Will he withdraw his opposition?'

In the dimness where the candle-light barely reached, Brothers Jerome and Columbanus trembled and hoped, for while doubt remained they had not been permitted to remove to their rest at Cadwallon's house. Anxious eyes appealed, reflecting the light.

Father Huw hedged, wanting his own sleep. 'He offers friendly interest and faithful consideration. I asked no more.'

Brother Cadfael said bluntly: 'You will need to be persuasive, and sincere. *He* is sincere. I am no way convinced that he can be lightly persuaded.' He was tired of nursing wounded vanities, he spoke out what was in his mind. 'Father Prior, you made your mistake with him this morning. You will need a change of heart, *his or yours*, to undo that damage.

*

Prior Robert made his dispositions as soon as Mass was over next morning, and with some care.

'Only Brother Sub-Prior and I, with Father Huw, and Brother Cadfael as interpreter, will sit at table together. You, Brother John, will make yourself useful to the cooks, and do whatever is needed, and you may also see to Father Huw's cattle and chickens. And you two, Brother Jerome, Brother Columbanus, I have a special mission for you. Since we are about Saint Winifred's business, I would have you go and spend the hours while we deliberate in vigil and prayer, imploring her aid to bring the obdurate to reason, and our errand to a successful conclusion. Not in the church here, but in her own chapel in the old graveyard where she is buried. Take your food and your measure of wine with you, and go there now. The boy Edwin will show you the way. If we prevail upon Rhisiart, as with her aid I trust we may, I will send to release you. But continue your intercessions until I do send word.'

They scattered dutifully, John, cheerfully enough, to tend the fire for Marared, and fetch and carry as she directed. The old woman, long widowed and her own sons grown, preened herself at having a strapping young fellow to keep her company, and Cadfael reflected that John might well be favoured with the best bits before the meal ever came to table. As for Jerome and Columbanus, he saw them set out with the boy, bread and meat wrapped in napkins in the breasts of their habits, and Columbanus carrying the flask with their ration of wine, and a small bottle of spring water for himself.

'It is very little to offer,' he said meekly, 'but I will touch nothing but water until our couse has prevailed.'

'More fool he,' said Brother John blithely, 'for he may well be swearing off wine for life!'

It was a fine spring morning, but capricious as May can be. Prior Robert and his attendants sat in the orchard until they were driven indoors by a sharp and sparkling shower that lasted almost half an hour. It was then approaching noon, the time when Rhisiart should join them. He would have a wet walk by the short path through the forest. Or perhaps he had waited for the sun's return at Cadwallon's house, which was on his way. Making allowances for that, they thought little of it when another half-hour passed, and he did not put in an appearance. But when he was an hour late for the meeting, and still no sign of him, Prior Robert's face grew both grim and cautiously triumphant.

'He has heard the warning I issued against his sin, and he fears to come and face me,' he said.

'He had heard the warning, indeed,' said Father Huw heavily, 'but I saw no signs of fear in him. He spoke very firmly and calmly. And he is a man of his word. I don't understand this, it is not like him.'

'We will eat, but frugally,' said the prior, 'and give him every chance of keeping his promise, if something has happened to delay him. So it may, to any man. We will wait until it is time to prepare for Vespers.'

'I'll walk as far as Cadwallon's house,' offered Brother Richard, 'for the way is all one to that point, and see if I can meet with him, or get word if he's on his way.'

He was gone more than an hour and a half, and came back alone. 'I went beyond, some way along the ride, but saw no sign of him. On my way back I asked at Cadwallon's gate, but no one had seen him pass. I feared he might have walked by the short path while I was taking the other road.'

'We'll wait for him until Vespers, and no longer,' said the prior, and by then his voice was growing grimly confident, for now he did not expect the guest to come, and the enemy would have put himself in the wrong, to Prior Robert's great gain. Until Vespers, therefore, they waited, five hours after the appointed time. The people of Gwytherin could hardly say Rhisiart had been written off too hastily.

'So it ends,' said the prior, rising and shaking out his skirts like one shaking off a doubt or an incubus. 'He has turned tail, and his opposition will carry no weight now with any man. Let us go!'

The sunlight was still bright but slanting over the green bowl where the church stood, and a number of people were gathering for the service. And out of the deeper green shadow where the forest path began, came, not Rhisiart, but his daughter, sailing gallantly out into the sunlight in a green gown, with her wild hair tamed and braided, and a linen coif over it, Sioned in her church-going person, with Peredur on her heels, his hand possessively cupping her elbow, though she paid little heed to that attention. She saw them issuing in a silent procession from Huw's gate, and her eyes went from person to person, lingering on Cadfael who came last, and again looking back with a small frown, as though one face was missing from the expected company.

'Where is my father?' she asked, her wide eyes surprised but not yet troubled. 'Is he not still here with you? Have I missed him? I rode as far as Cadwallon's house, and he was on foot, so if he has left more than an hour ago he may well be home by now. I came to bear him company to church and go back with him afterwards.'

Prior Robert looked down at her in some wonder, the first flickering uneasiness twitching his nostrils. 'What is she saying? Do you tell me that the lord Rhisiart set out to come to our meeting?'

'Of course!' said Sioned, amazed. 'He had said he would.'

'But he did not come,' said Robert. 'We've waited for him since noon, and we've seen no sign of him. Brother Sub-Prior went a part of the way to see if he could meet with him, but in vain. He has not been here.'

She caught the meaning of that without Cadfael's services. Her eyes flashed from face to face, distrustful and ready for anger. 'Are you telling me truth? Or have you hidden him away under lock and key until you can get Winifred out of her grave and away to Shrewsbury? He was all that stood in your way. And you have threatened him!'

Peredur closed his fingers anxiously on her arm, and drew her against his side. 'Hush, you must not say such things. These brothers would not lie to you.'

'At what hour,' asked Cadfael, 'did your father set out this morning?'

She looked at him, and was a little reassured. The ring of silent onlookers drew nearer, listening attentively, ready to take her part if she needed an army.

'A good hour before noon. He was going first to the fields in the clearing, so he would be coming here by the shortest way, cutting through a quarter of a mile of forest to the usual path. He had plenty of time to be here before noon. As far as the clearing Engelard would be with him, he was going beyond, to the byres over the hill. There are two cows there ready to drop their calves.'

'We are telling you truly, child,' said Father Huw, his voice as grave and anxious as her own, 'we waited for him, and he never came.'

'What can have happened to him? Where can he be?'

'He will have crossed with us and gone home,' urged Peredur, hovering unhappily at her shoulder. 'We'll ride back, we shall surely find him there before us.'

'No! Why should he turn back, and never come to the dinner? And if he did, why so late? He would have been home long before I dressed my hair and set out to meet him, if he had changed his mind. And besides, he never would.'

'I think,' said Father Huw, 'that my whole parish has some interest in this matter, and we had better put off everything else, even the services of the church, until we have found Rhisiart and assured ourselves that all's well with him. Truly this may be no more than a tangle of mistiming and misunderstanding, but let's resolve it first, and wonder about it afterwards. There are enough of us here. Let's send out in parties along all the roads he may have taken, and Sioned shall show us where she thinks his short cut from the upland fields would bring him to the path. He could not well meet with any dangerous beasts in these woods, but he may have had a fall, an injury that has halted or slowed him. Father Prior, will you join with us?'

'With all my heart,' said Prior Robert, 'and so will we all.'

The less active among them were sent along the open ride,

with orders to scatter on either side and comb the surroundings as they went, while the more athletic took the narrow footpath beyond Cadwallon's stockade. The woods here were not yet close-set, there was thick, springy grass under the trees, and no dense undergrowth. They spread out into a half-circle, moving along within a few paces of one another, Sioned pressing purposefully forward up the path with set lips and fixed eyes, Peredur with every evidence of desperate affection following close and murmuring agitated urgings into her unheeding ears. Whether he believed in his own reassurances or not, out of all question he was a young man fathoms deep in love, and ready to do anything to serve and protect Sioned, while she saw in him nothing but the boy from the next holding, and tiresome at that.

They were perhaps half a mile beyond Cadwallon's enclosure when Father Huw suddenly plucked at Brother Cadfael's sleeve.

'We have forgotten Brother Jerome and Brother Columbanus! The hill of the chapel is off to the right here, no great way. Ask Prior Robert, should we not send and call them to join us?'

'I had indeed forgotten,' admitted the prior. 'Yes, by all means send someone. Best one of your parishioners, they'll all know the way.'

One of the young men swerved aside obediently between the trees, and ran. The slow-moving scythe swept on into deeper forest.

'About here,' said Sioned, halting, 'he would have come down from the clearing. If we go obliquely to the right here, and spread out as before, we shall be covering his likely way.'

The ground rose, the trees grew closer, the undergrowth thicker. They began to thread the encroaching bushes, having to part company by a few yards, losing sight momentarily of their neighbours. They had gone thus only a short way when Bened the smith, crashing through bushes at Brother Cadfael's left hand, uttered a great shout of discovery and dismay, and everyone in the wavering line halted and shook to the sound.

Cadfael turned towards the cry, thrusting through thorn-branches, and came out in a narrow oval of grass surrounded every way with thick bushes, through which a used track no wider than a man's shoulders clove, the long way of the oval. Just where he must have brushed through into the clear space, Rhisiart lay on his back, his right hip hollowing the grass under him, shoulders flattened to the ground and arms spread wide. His legs were drawn up under him with bent knees, the left leg crossed over the right. His short, defiant beard pointed at the sky. So, and at the very same slanting angle, did the feathered flight of the arrow that jutted out from under the cage of his ribs.

CHAPTER FIVE

From both sides they gathered, drawn to the smith's call, breaking through bushes like the running of a startled herd of deer, and halting appalled round the oval where the body lay. Cadfael went on his knees, and looked for any sign of breath within the drawn-back lips, any pulse in the stretched throat or rise and fall of the pierced breast, but there was none. And for that first moment he was the only one who moved within the open space of grass, and what he did was done in strange, too-intense silence, as though everyone round him held his breath.

Then everything broke out at once in noise and motion. Sioned clawed through the screening circle and saw her father's body, and uttered a great shriek that was more of fury even than of grief, and flung herself forward. Peredur caught her by the wrist and pulled her round into his arms, one hand cupped behind her head to press her face into his shoulder, but she shrieked again, and struck out at him with all her strength, and breaking loose, hurled herself to her knees facing Cadfael, and reached out to embrace her father's body. Cadfael leaned across to ward her off, his hand braced into the grass under Rhisiart's right armpit.

'No! Touch nothing! Not yet! Let him alone, he has things to tell us!'

By some intuitive quickness of mind that had not deserted her even at this moment, she obeyed the tone first, and awakened to the words immediately after. Her eyes questioned him, widening, and slowly she sat back in the grass, and drew her hands together in her lap. Her lips shaped the words after him silently: '—things to tell us!' She looked from his face into the face of the dead man. She knew he was dead. She also knew that the dead speak, often in thunder. And she came of proud Welsh stock to which the blood-feud is sacred, a duty transcending even grief.

When those following gathered closer, and one reached to touch, it was she who spread her arm protectively over the body, and said with authority: 'No! Let him be!'

Cadfael had drawn back his arm, and for a moment wondered what troubled him about the palm he had lifted from the grass beside Rhisiart's breast. Then he knew. Where he knelt the grass was perceptibly damp from the morning's sharp shower, he could feel the cling of the habit when he shifted his knee. Yet under the outflung right arm the grass was dry, his hand rose from it with no hint of moisture, no scent of rain. He touched again, ran his fingers up and down alongside Rhisiart's right flank. He was down to the knee before he felt the dampness and stirred the green fragrance. He felt outwards, the width of the body, to find the same signs. Strange! Very strange! His mind recorded and forbore to wonder then, because there were other things to be observed, and all manner of dangers were falling in upon all manner of people.

The tall shape looming at his back, motionless and chill, could be none other than Prior Robert, and Prior Robert in a curious state of exalted shock, nearer to Brother Columbanus' ecstatic fit than he had ever been before or would ever be again. The high, strained voice asked, over the shuddering quietness of Sioned's tearless sobs: 'He is dead?'

'Dead,' said Cadfael flatly, and looked into Sioned's wide, dry eyes and held them, promising something as yet undefined. Whatever it was, she understood it and was appeased, for he was Welsh, too, he knew about the blood-feud. And she was the only heir, the only close kin, of a murdered man. She had a task far above sorrow.

The prior's voice soared suddenly, awed and exalted. 'Behold the saint's vengeance! Did I not say her wrath would be wreaked upon all those who stood in the way of her desire? Tell them what I am saying! Tell them to look well at the fulfilment of my prophecy, and let all other obdurate hearts take warning. Saint Winifred has shown her power and her displeasure.'

There was hardly any need for translation, they had the sense of it already. A dozen of those standing close shrank warily away, a dozen voices muttered hurried submission. Not for worlds would they stand in the saint's way.

'The impious man reaps what he sows,' declaimed Robert. 'Rhisiart had his warning, and did not heed it.'

The most timorous were on their knees by then, cowed and horrified. It was not as if Saint Winifred had meant very much to them, until someone else wanted her, and Rhisiart stated a prior claim on behalf of the parish. And Rhisiart was dead by violence, struck down improbably in his own forests.

Sioned's eyes held Cadfael's, above her father's pierced heart. She was a gallant girl, she said never a word, though she had words building up in her ripe for saying, spitting, rather, into Prior Robert's pallid, aristocratic, alabaster face. It was not she who suddenly spoke out. It was Peredur.

'I don't believe it!' He had a fine, clear, vehement voice that rang under the branches. 'What, a gentle virgin saint, to take such vengeance on a good man? Yes, a good man, however mistaken! If she had been so pitiless as to want to slay—and I do not believe it of her!—what need would she have of arrows and bows? Fire from heaven would have done her will just as well, and shown her power better. You are looking at a murdered man, Father Prior. A man's hand fitted that arrow, a man's hand drew the bow, and for a man's reason. There must have been others who had a grudge against Rhisiart, others whose plans he was obstructing, besides Saint Winifred. Why blame this killing on her?'

This forthright Welsh sense Cadfael translated into English for Robert's benefit, who had caught the dissenting tone of it, but not the content. 'And the young man's right. This arrow never was shot from heaven. Look at the angle of it, up from under his ribs into the heart. Out of the earth, rather! A man with a short bow, on his knee among the bushes? True, the ground slopes, he may even have been lower than Rhisiart, but even so. . . .'

'Avenging saints may make use of earthly instruments,' said Robert overbearingly.

'The instrument would still be a murderer,' said Cadfael.

'There is law in Wales, too. We shall need to send word to the prince's bailiff.'

Bened had stood all this time darkly gazing, at the body, at the very slight ooze of blood round the wound, at the jutting shaft with its trimmed feathers. Slowly he said: 'I know this arrow. I know its owner, or at least the man whose mark it bears. Where young men are living close together in a household, they mark their own with a distinctive sign, so that there can be no argument. See the tip of the feathering on one side, dyed blue.' It was as he said, and at the mention of it several there drew breath hard, knowing the mark as well as he knew it.

'It's Engelard's,' said Bened outright, and three or four hushed voices bore him out.

Sioned raised her stricken face, shocked into a false, frozen calm that suddenly melted and crumbled into dread and anger. Rhisiart was dead, there was nothing she could do now for him but mourn and wait, but Engelard was alive and vulnerable, and an outlander, with no kinship to speak for him. She rose abruptly, slender and straight, turning her fierce eyes from face to face all round the circle.

'Engelard is the most trustworthy of all my father's men, and would cut off his own drawing hand rather than loose against my father's life. Who dares say this is his work?'

'I don't say so,' said Bened reasonably. 'I do say this is marked as his arrow. He is the best shot with the short bow in all this countryside.'

'And everybody in Gwytherin knows,' spoke up a voice from among the Welshmen, not accusing, only pointing out facts, 'that he has quarrelled often and fiercely with Rhisiart, over a certain matter at issue between them.'

'Over me,' said Sioned harshly. 'Say what you mean! I, of all people, know the truth best. Better than you all! Yes, they have had high words many times, on this one matter, and only this, and would have had more, but for all that, these two have understood each other, and neither one of them would ever have done the other harm. Do you think the prize fought over does not get to know the risks to herself and both the combatants? Fight they did, but they thought more highly of each other than either did of any of you, and with good reason.'

'Yet who can say,' said Peredur in a low voice, 'how far a man may step aside even from his own nature, for love?'

She turned and looked at him with measuring scorn. 'I thought you were his friend!'

'So I am his friend,' said Peredur, paling but steadfast. 'I said what I believe of myself, no less than of him.'

'What is this matter of one Engelard?' demanded Prior Robert, left behind in this exchange. 'Tell me what they are saying.' And when Cadfael had done so, as tersely as possible: 'It would seem that at least this young man must be asked to account for his movements this day,' decreed Robert, appropriating an authority to which he had no direct right here. 'It may be that others have been with him, and can vouch for him. But if not....'

'He set out this morning with your father,' said Huw, distressfully eyeing the girl's fixed and defiant face. 'You told us so. They went together as far as the cleared fields. Then your father turned to make his way down to us, and Engelard was to go a mile beyond, to the byres where the cows were in calf. We must send out and ask if any man has seen your father since he parted from Engelard. Is there any who can speak to that?'

There was a silence. The numbers gathered about them were growing steadily. Some of the slower searchers from the open ride had made their way up here without news of their own, to find the matter thus terribly resolved. Others, hearing rumours of the missing man, had followed from the village. Father Huw's messenger came up behind with Brother Columbanus and Brother Jerome from the chapel. But no one spoke up to say he had seen Rhisiart that day. Nor did any volunteer word of having encountered Engelard.

'He must be questioned,' said Prior Robert, 'and if his answers are not satisfactory, he must be held and handed over to the bailiff. For it's clear from what has been said that this man certainly had a motive for wishing to remove Rhisiart from his path.'

'Motive?' blazed Sioned, burning up abruptly as a dark and

quiet fire suddenly spurts flame. Instinctively she recoiled into Welsh, though she had already revealed how well she could follow what was said around her in English, and the chief reason for her reticence concerning her knowledge had been cruelly removed. 'Not so strong a motive as *you* had, Father Prior! Every soul in this parish knows what store you set upon getting Saint Winifred away from us, what glory it will be to your abbey, and above all, to you. And who stood in your way but my father? *Yours*, not the saint's! Show me a better reason for wanting him dead! Did any ever wish to lift hand against him, all these years! Until *you* came here with your quest for Winifred's relics? Engelard's disagreement with my father was constant and understood, yours was new and urgent. Our need could wait, we're young. Yours could not wait. And who knew better than you at what hour my father would be coming through the forest to Gwytherin? Or that he would not change his mind?'

Father Huw spread a horrified hand to hush her long before this, but she would not be hushed. 'Child, child, you must not make such dreadful accusations against the reverend prior, it is mortal sin.'

'I state facts, and let them speak,' snapped Sioned. 'Where's the offence in that? Prior Robert may point out the facts that suit him, I show you the others, those that do not suit him. My father was the sole obstacle in his path, and my father has been removed.'

'Child, I tell you every soul in this valley knew that your father was coming to my house, and the hour of his coming, and many would know all the possible ways, far better than any of these good brethren from Shrewsbury. The occasion might well suit another grudge. And you must know that Prior Robert has been with me, and with Brother Richard and Brother Cadfael here, ever since morning Mass.' And Father Huw turned in agitated supplication to Robert, wringing his hands. 'Father Prior, I beg you, do not hold it against the girl that she speaks so wildly. She is in great grief—a father lost. . . . You cannot wonder if she turns on us all.'

'I say no word of blame,' said the prior, though coldly. 'I gather she is casting doubts upon myself and my companions, but doubtless you have answered her. Tell the young woman, in my name, that both you and others here can witness for my own person, for all this day I have been within your sight.'

Grateful for at least one certainty, Huw turned to repeat as much to Sioned yet again, but she blazed back with biting promptness and force, forgetting all restraints in the need to confront Robert face to face, without the tedious intervention of interpreters. 'So you may have been, Father Prior,' she flashed in plain English. 'In any case I don't see *you* as likely to make a good bowman. But a man who would try to buy my father's compliance would be willing and able to buy some more pliable person to do even this work for him. You still had your purse! Rhisiart spurned it!'

'Take care!' thundered Robert, galled beyond the limits of his arduous patience. 'You put your soul in peril! I have borne with you thus far, making allowances for your grief, but go no further along this road!'

They were staring upon each other like adversaries in the lists before the baton falls, he very tall and rigid and chill as ice, she slight and ferocious and very handsome, her coif long ago lost among the bushes, and her sheaves of black hair loose on her shoulders. And at that moment, before she could spit further fire, or he threaten more imminent damnation, they all heard voices approaching from higher up among the woods, a man's voice and a girl's in quick, concerned exchanges, and coming rapidly nearer with a light threshing of branches, as though they had caught the raised tones and threatening sounds of many people gathered here improbably deep in the forest, and were hurrying to discover what was happening.

The two antagonists heard them, and their concentration on each other was shaken and disrupted. Sioned knew them, and a fleeting shadow of fear and desperation passed over her face. She glanced round wildly, but there was no help. A girl's arm parted the bushes above the oval where they stood, and Annest stepped through, and stood in astonishment, gazing round at the inexplicable gathering before her.

It was the narrowness of the track—no more than the shadow of a deer-path in the grass—and the abruptness with which she had halted that gave Sioned her one chance. She took it valiantly. 'Go back home, Annest,' she said loudly. 'I am coming with company. Go and prepare for guests, quickly, you'll have little time.' Her voice was high and urgent. Annest had not yet lowered her eyes to the ground, and grass and shadows veiled Rhisiart's body.

The effort was wasted. Another hand, large and gentle, was laid on Annest's shoulder while she hesitated, and moved her aside. 'The company sounds somewhat loud and angry,' said a man's voice, high and clear, 'so, with your leave, Sioned, we'll all go together.'

Engelard put the girl aside between his hands, as familiarly and serenely as a brother might have done, and stepped past her into the clearing.

He had eyes for no one but Sioned, he walked towards her with the straight gait of a proprietor, and as he came he took in her stiff erectness, and fixed face of fire and ice and despair, and his own face mirrored everything he saw in her. His brows drew together, his smile, taut and formidable to begin with, vanished utterly, his eyes burned bluer than cornflowers. He passed by Prior Robert as though he had not even been there, or not alive, a stock, a dead tree by the path. He put out his hands, and Sioned laid her hands in them, and for an instant closed her eyes. There was no frowning him away now, he was here in the midst, quite without defences. The circle, not all inimical but all hampering, was closing round him.

He had her by the hands when he saw Rhisiart's body.

The shock went into him as abruptly as the arrow must have gone into Rhisiart, stopping him instantly. Cadfael had him well in view, and saw his lips part and whisper soundlessly: 'Christ aid!' What followed was most eloquent. The Saxon youth moved with loving slowness, shutting both Sioned's hands into one of his, and with his freed right hand stroked softly over her hair, down temple and cheek and chin and throat, all with such mastered passion that she was soothed, as he meant, while he had barely stopped shaking from the shock.

He folded an arm about her, holding her close against his side, and slowly looked all round the circle of watching faces, and slowly down at the body of his lord. His face was bleakly angry.

'Who did this?'

He looked round, seeking the one who by rights should be spokesman, hesitating between Prior Robert, who arrogated to himself authority wherever he came, and Father Huw, who was known and trusted here. He repeated his demand in English, but neither of them answered him, and for a long moment neither did anyone else. Then Sioned said, with clear, deliberate warning: 'There are some here are saying that *you* did.'

'I?' he cried, astonished and scornful rather than alarmed, and turned sharply to search her face, which was intent and urgent.

Her lips shaped silently: 'Run! They're blaming you!'

It was all she could do, and he understood, for they had such a link between them that meanings could be exchanged in silence, in a look. He measured with a quick glance the number of his possible enemies, and the spaces between them, but he did not move. 'Who accuses me?' he said. 'And on what ground? It seems to me I might rather question all of you, whom I find standing here about my lord's dead body, while I have been all day out with the cows, beyond Bryn. When I got home Annest was anxious because Sioned had not returned, and the sheep boy told her there was no service at Vespers at the church. We came out to look for you, and found you by the noise you were making among you. And I ask again, and I will know before ever I give up: *Who did this?*'

'We are all asking that,' said Father Huw. 'Son, there's no man here has accused you. But there are things that give us the right to question you, and a man with nothing on his conscience won't be ashamed or afraid to answer. Have you yet looked carefully at the arrow that struck Rhisiart down? Then look at it now!'

Frowning, Engelard drew a step nearer, and looked indeed, earnestly and bitterly at the dead man, only afterwards at the arrow. He saw the flutter of deep blue, and gasped.

'This is one of mine!' He looked up with wild suspicion at them all. 'Either that, or someone has copied my mark. But no, this is mine, I know the trim, I fletched it new only a week or so ago.'

'He owns it his?' demanded Robert, following as best he could. 'He admits it?'

'Admit?' flashed Engelard in English. 'What is there to admit? I *say* it! How it was brought here, who loosed it, I know no more than you do, but I know the shaft for mine. God's teeth!' he cried furiously, 'do you think if I had any hand in this villainy should leave my mark flaunting in the wound? Am I fool as well as outlander? And do you think I would do anything to harm Rhisiart? The man who stood my friend and gave me the means of living here when I'd poached myself out of Cheshire?'

'He refused to consider you as a suitor for his daughter,' Bened said almost reluctantly, 'whatever good he did for you otherwise.'

'So he did, and according to his lights, rightly so. And I know it, knowing as much as I've learned of Wales, and even if I did smart under it, I knew he had reason and custom on his side. Never has he done anything I could complain of as unfair to me. He stood much arrogance and impatience from me, come to that. There isn't a man in Gwynedd I like and respect more. I'd as soon have cut my own throat as injured Rhisiart.'

'He knew and knows it,' said Sioned, 'and so do I.'

'Yet the arrow is yours,' said Huw unhappily. 'And as for reclaiming or disguising it, it may well have been that speedy flight after such an act would be more important.'

'If I had planned such an act,' said Engelard, 'though God forbid I should ever have to imagine a thing so vile, I could as easily have done what some devil has done now to me, and used another man's shaft.'

'But, son, it would be more in keeping with your nature,' the priest pursued sadly, 'to commit such a deed without planning, having with you only your own bow and arrows. Another approach, another quarrel, a sudden wild rage! No one supposes this was plotted beforehand.'

'I had no bow with me all this day. I was busy with the cattle, what should I want with a bow?'

'It will be for the royal bailiff to enquire into all possible matters concerning this case,' said Prior Robert, resolutely reclaiming the dominance among them. 'What should be asked at once of this young man is where he has been all this day, what doing, and in whose company.'

'In no man's company. The byres behind Bryn are in a lonely place, good pasture but apart from the used roads. Two cows dropped their calves today, one around noon, the second not before late afternoon, and that was a hard birth, and gave me trouble. But the young things are there alive and on their legs now, to testify to what I've been doing.'

'You left Rhisiart at his fields along the way?'

'I did, and went straight on to my own work. And have not seen him again until now.'

'And did you speak with any man, there at the byres? Can anyone testify as to where you were, at any time during the day?' No one was likely to try and wrest the initiative from Robert now. Engelard looked round him quickly, measuring chances. Annest came forward silently, and took her stand beside Sioned. Brother John's roused, anxious eyes followed her progress, and approved the loyalty which had no other way of expressing itself.

'Engelard did not come home until half an hour ago,' she said stoutly.

'Child,' said Father Huw wretchedly, 'where he was not does not in any way confirm where he says he was. Two calves may be delivered far more quickly than he claims, how can we know, who were not there? He had time to slip back here and do this thing, and be back with his cattle and never noticed. Unless we can find someone who testifies to having seen him elsewhere, at whatever time this deed may have been done, then I fear we should hold Engelard in safe-keeping until the prince's bailiff can take over the charge for us.'

The men of Gwytherin hovered, murmuring, some convinced, many angry, for Rhisiart had been very well liked, some hesitant, but granting that the outlander ought to be held until his innocence was established or his guilt proved. They shifted and closed, and their murmur became one of consent.

'It is fair,' said Bened, and the growl of assent answered him.

'One lone Englishman with his back to the wall,' whispered Brother John indignantly in Cadfael's ear, 'and what chance will he have, with nobody to bear out what he says? And plain truth, for certain! Does he act or speak like a murderer?'

Peredur had stood like a stock all this while, hardly taking his eyes from Engelard's face but to gaze earnestly and unhappily at Sioned. As Prior Robert levelled an imperious arm at Engelard, and the whole assembly closed in slowly in obedience, braced to lay hands on him, Peredur drew a little further back at the edge of the trees, and Cadfael saw him catch Sioned's eye, flash her a wild, wide-eyed look, and jerk his head as though beckoning. Out of her exhaustion and misery she roused a brief, answering blaze, and leaned to whisper rapidly in Engelard's ear.

'Do your duty, all of you,' commanded Robert, 'to your laws and your prince and your church, and lay hold of this man!'

There was one instant of stillness, and then they closed in all together, the only gap in their ranks where Peredur still hung back. Engelard made a long leap from Sioned's side, as though he would break for the thickest screen of bushes, and then, instead, caught up a dead, fallen bough that lay in the grass, and whirled it about him in a flailing circle, laying two unwary elders flat, and sending others reeling back out of range. Before they could reassemble, he had changed direction, leaped over one of the fallen, and was clean through the midst of them, arming off the only one who almost got a grip on him, and made straight for the gap Peredur had left in their ranks. Father Huw's voice, uplifted in vexed agitation, called on Peredur to halt him, and Peredur sprang to intercept his flight. How it happened was never quite clear, though Brother Cadfael had a rough idea, but at the very moment when his outstretched hand almost brushed Engelard's sleeve, Peredur stepped upon a rotten branch in the turf, that snapped under his foot and rolled, tossing him flat on his face, half-blinded among the bushes. And winded, possibly, for certainly he made no move to pick himself up until Engelard was past him and away.

Even then it was not quite over, for the nearest pursuers on either side, seeing how the hunt had turned, had also begun to run like hares, on courses converging with the fugitive's at the very edge of the clearing. From the left came a long-legged villein of Cadwallon's, with a stride like a greyhound, and from the right Brother John, his habit flying, his sandalled feet pounding the earth mightily. It was perhaps the first time Brother John had ever enjoyed Prior Robert's whole-hearted approval. It was certainly the last.

There was no one left in the race but these three, and fleet though Engelard was, it seemed that the long-legged fellow would collide with him before he could finally vanish. All three were hurtling together for a shattering collision, or so it seemed. The villein stretched out arms as formidably long as his legs. So, on the other side, did Brother John. A great hand closed on a thin fold of Engelard's tunic from one side. Brother John bounded exuberantly in from the other. The prior sighed relief, expecting the prisoner to be enfolded in a double embrace. And Brother John, diving, caught Cadwallon's villein round the knees and brought him crashing to the ground, and Engelard, plucking his tunic out of the enemy's grasp, leaped into the bushes and vanished in a receding susurration of branches, until silence and stillness closed over the path of his withdrawal.

Half the hunt, out of excitement rather than any real enmity, streamed away into the forest after the quarry, but half-heartedly now. They had little chance of capturing him. Probably they had no great desire to do anything of the kind, though once put to it, hounds must follow a scent. The real drama remained behind in the clearing. There, at least, justice had one clear culprit to enjoy.

Brother John unwound his arms from his victim's knees, sat up in the grass, fended off placidly a feeble blow the villein aimed at him, and said in robust but incomprehensible English: 'Ah, let well alone, lad! What did he ever do to you? But faith, I'm sorry I had to fetch you down so heavily. If you think you're hard-done-to, take comfort! I'm likely to pay dearer than you.'

He looked round him complacently enough as he clambered to his feet and dusted off the debris of leaves and twigs that clung to his habit. There stood Prior Robert, not yet unfrozen from the shock of incredulous disillusionment, tall and stiff and grey, a Norman lordling debating terrible penalties for treason. But there, also, stood Sioned, tired, distraught, worn out with passion, but with a small, reviving glow in her eyes, and there was Annest at her elbow, an arm protectively round her waist, but her flower-face turned towards John. Not much use Robert thundering and lightning, while she so smiled and blossomed, beaming her gratitude and admiration.

Brother Richard and Brother Jerome loomed like messengers of doom, one at either elbow. 'Brother John, you are summoned. You are in gross offence.'

He went with them resignedly. For all the threatening thunder-bolts he had never felt freer in his life. And having now nothing to lose but his own self-respect, he was sturdily determined not to sacrifice that.

'Unfaithful and unworthy brother,' hissed Prior Robert, towering in terrible indignation, 'what have you done? Do not deny what we have all witnessed. You have not merely connived at the escape of a felon, you have frustrated the attempt of a loyal servant to arrest him. You felled that good man deliberately, to let Engelard go free. Traitor against church and law, you have put yourself beyond the pale. If there is anything you can say in your defence, say it now.'

'I thought the lad was being harried beyond reason, on very suspect suspicion,' said Brother John boldly. 'I've talked with Engelard, I've got my own view of him, a decent, open soul who'd never do violence to any man by stealth, let alone Rhisiart, whom he liked and valued high. I don't believe he has any part in this death, and what's more, I think he'll not go far until he knows who had, and God help the murderer then! So I gave him his chance, and good luck to him!'

The two girls, their heads close together in women's solidarity, interpreted the tone for themselves, if they lacked the words, and glowed in silent applause. Prior Robert was helpless, though he did not know it. Brother Cadfael knew it very well.

'Shameless!' thundered Robert, bristling until even his suave purity showed knife-edged with affront. 'You are condemned out of your own mouth, and a disgrace to our order. I have no jurisdiction here as regards Welsh law. The prince's bailiff must resolve this crime that cries for vengeance here. But where my own subordinates are concerned, and where they have infringed the law of this land where we are guests, there two disciplines threaten you, Brother John. As to the sovereignty of Gwynedd, I cannot speak. As to my own discipline, I can and do. You are set far beyond mere ecclesiastical penance. I consign you to close imprisonment until I can confer with the secular authority here, and I refuse to you, meanwhile, all the comforts and consolations of the church.' He looked about him and took thought, brooding. Father Huw hovered miserably, lost in this ocean of complaints and accusations. 'Brother Cadfael, ask Father Huw where there is a safe prison, where he can be held.'

This was more than Brother John had bargained for, and though he repented of nothing, like a practical man he did begin to look round to weigh up the chances of evading the consequences. He eyed the gaps in the ring as Engelard had done, braced his sturdy feet well apart, and flexed his shoulders experimentally, as though he had thoughts of elbowing Brother Richard smartly in the belly, kicking the legs from under Jerome, and making a dash for freedom. He stopped himself just in time when he heard Cadfael report sedately: 'Father Huw suggests there is only one place secure enough. If Sioned is willing to allow her holding to be used, a prisoner could be safe enough there.'

At this point Brother John unaccountably lost interest in immediate escape.

'My house is at Prior Robert's disposal,' said Sioned in Welsh, with appropriate coldness, but very promptly. She had herself well in hand, she made no more lapses into English. 'There are storehouses and stables, if you wish to use them. I promise I shall not go near the prisoner, or hold the key to his prison myself. Father Prior may choose his guard from among my people as he sees fit. My household shall provide him his living, but even that charge I shall give to someone else. If I undertook it myself I fear my impartiality might be doubted, after what has happened.'

A good girl, Cadfael thought, translating this for Robert's benefit rather less than for John's. Clever enough to step resolutely round any actual lies even when she was thus wrung by one disaster after another, and generous enough to think for the wants and wishes of others. The someone else who would be charged with seeing Brother John decently housed and fed was standing cheek to cheek with her mistress as she spoke, fair head against dark head. A formidable pair! But they might not have found this unexpected and promising path open to them but for the innocence of celibate parish priests.

'That may be the best plan,' said Prior Robert, chilly but courteous, 'and I thank you for your dutiful offer, daughter. Keep him straitly, see he has what he needs for life, but no more. He is in great peril of his soul, his body may somewhat atone. If you permit, we will go before and bestow him securely, and let your uncle know what has happened, so that he may send down to you and bring you home. I will not intrude longer on a house of mourning.'

'I will show you the way,' said Annest, stepping demurely from Sioned's side.

'Hold him fast!' warned the prior, as they massed to follow her uphill through the woods. Though he might have seen for himself, had he looked closely, that the culprit's resignation had mellowed into something very like complacency, and he stepped out as briskly as his guards, a good deal more intent on keeping Annest's slender waist and lithe shoulders in sight than on any opportunity for escape.

Well, thought Cadfael, letting them go without him, and

turning to meet Sioned's steady gaze. God sort all! As doubtless he is doing, now as ever!

The men of Gwytherin cut young branches and made a green litter to carry Rhisiart's body home. Under the corpse, when they lifted it, there was much more blood than about the frontal wound, though the point of the arrow barely broke through skin and clothing. Cadfael would have liked to examine tunic and wound more closely, but forbore because Sioned was there beside him, stiffly erect in her stony grief, and nothing, no word or act that was not hieratic and ceremonial, was permissible then in her presence. Moreover, soon all the servants of Rhisiart's household came down in force to bring their lord home, while the steward waited at the gate with bards and mourning women to welcome him back for the last time, and this was no longer an enquiry into guilt, but the first celebration of a great funeral rite, in which probing would have been indecent. No hope of enquiring further tonight. Even Prior Robert had acknowledged that he must remove himself and his fellows reverently from a mourning community in which they had no rights.

When it was time to raise the litter and its burden, now stretched out decently with his twisted legs drawn out straight and his hands laid quietly at his sides, Sioned looked round for one more to whom she meant to confide a share in this honourable load. She did not find him.

'Where is Peredur? What became of him?'

No one had seen him go, but he was gone. No one had had attention to spare for him after Brother John had completed what Peredur had begun. He had slipped away without a word, as though he had done something to be ashamed of, something for which he might expect blame rather than thanks. Sioned was a little hurt, even in her greater hurt, at his desertion.

'I thought he would have wanted to help me bring my father home. He was a favourite with him, and fond of him. From a little boy he was in and out of our house like his own.'

'He maybe doubted his welcome,' said Cadfael, 'after saying a word that displeased you concerning Engelard.'

'And doing a thing afterwards that more than wiped that out?' she said, but for his ears only. No need to say outright before everyone what she knew very well, that Peredur had contrived a way out for her lover. 'No, I don't understand why he should slink away without a word, like this.' But she said no more then, only begged him with a look to walk with her as she fell in behind the litter. They went some distance in silence. Then she asked, without looking aside at him: 'Did my father yet tell you those things he had to tell?'

'Some,' said Cadfael. 'Not all.'

'Is there anything I should do, or not do? I need to know. We must make him seemly tonight.' By the morrow he would be stiff, and she knew it. 'If you need anything from me, tell me now.'

'Keep me the clothes he's wearing, when you take them off him, and take note for me where they're damp from this morning's rain, and where they're dry. If you notice anything strange, remember it. Tomorrow, as soon as I can, I'll come to you.'

'I must know the truth,' she said. 'You know why.'

'Yes, I know. But tonight sing him and drink to him, and never doubt but he'll hear the singing.'

'Yes,' she said, and loosed a great, renewing sigh. 'You are a good man. I'm glad you're here. You do not believe it was Engelard.'

'I'm as good as certain it was not. First and best, it isn't in him. Lads like Engelard hit out in a passion, but with their fists, not with weapons. Second, if it had been in his scope, he'd have made a better job of it. You saw the angle of the arrow. Engelard, I judge, is the breadth of three fingers taller than your father. How could he shoot an arrow under a man's rib-cage who is shorter than he, even from lower ground? Even if he kneeled or crouched in the undergrowth in ambush, I doubt if it could be done. And why should it ever be tried? No, this is folly. And to say that the best shot in all these parts could not put his shaft clean through his man, at any distance there where he could see him? Not more than fifty yards clear in any direction. Worse folly still, why should a good bowman choose such a blind tangled place? They have not looked at the ground, or they could not put forward such foolishness. But first and last and best, that young man of yours is too open and honest to kill by stealth, even a man he hated. And he did not hate Rhisiart. You need not tell me, I know it.'

Much of what he had said might well have been hurtful to her, but none of it was. She went with him every step of that way, and flushed and warmed into her proper, vulnerable girlhood at hearing her lover thus accepted.

'You've said no word in wonder,' she said, 'that I have not been more troubled over what has become of Engelard, and where he is gone to earth now.'

'No,' said Cadfael, and smiled. 'You know where he is, and how to get in touch with him whenever you need. I think you two have two or three places better for secrecy than your oak tree, and in one of them Engelard is resting now, or soon will be. You seem to think he'll be safe enough. Tell me nothing, unless you need a messenger, or help.'

'You can be my messenger, if you will, to another,' she said. They were emerging from the forest at the edge of Rhisiart's home fields, and Prior Robert stood tall and grim and non-committal aside from their path, his companions discreetly disposed behind him, his hands, features, and the angle of his gently bowed head all disposed to convey respect for death and compassion for the bereaved without actually owning to forgiveness of the dead. His prisoner was safely lodged, he was waiting only to collect the last stray from his flock, and make an appropriately impressive exit. 'Tell Peredur I missed him from among those my father would have liked to carry him home. Tell him what he did was generous, and I am grateful. I am sorry he should ever have doubted it.'

They were approaching the gate, and Uncle Meurice, the steward, came out to meet them with his kindly, soft-lined face quaking and shapeless with shock and distress.

'And come tomorrow,' said Sioned on an almost soundless breath, and walked away from him alone, and entered the gateway after her father's body.

CHAPTER SIX

Sioned's message might not have been delivered so soon, for it would not have been any easy matter to turn aside at Cadwallon's house, without a word of request or excuse to Prior Robert; but in the dimness of the woods, a little above the holding, Cadfael caught a glimpse of a figure withdrawing from them, with evident intent, some fifty yards into cover, and knew it for Peredur. He had not expected to be followed, for he went only far enough to be secure from actual encounter on the path, and there sat down moodily on a fallen trunk, his back against a young tree that leaned with him, and kicked one foot in the litter of last year's leaves. Cadfael asked no permission, but went after him.

Peredur looked up at the sound of other feet rustling the beech-mast, and rose as if he would have removed further to avoid speech, but then gave up the thought, and stood mute and unwelcoming, but resigned.

'I have a word to you,' said Brother Cadfael mildly, 'from Sioned. She bade me tell you that she missed you when she would gladly have asked you to lend a shoulder for her father's bier. She sends you word that what you did was generous, and she is grateful.'

Peredur stirred his feet uneasily, and drew a little back into deeper shadow.

'There were plenty of her own people there,' he said, after a pause that seemed awkward rather than sullen. 'She had no need of me.'

'Oh, there were hands enough, and shoulders enough,' agreed Cadfael, 'nevertheless, she missed you. It seems to me that she looks upon you as one having a forward place among her own people. You have been like a brother to her from children, and she could well do with a brother now.'

The stiffness of Peredur's young body was palpable even in the green dusk, a constraint that crippled even his tongue. He got out, with a bitter spurt of laughter: 'It was not her brother I wanted to be.'

'No, that I understand. Yet you behaved like one, towards her and towards Engelard, when it came to the testing.'

What was meant to comfort and compliment appeared, instead, to hurt. Peredur shrank still deeper into his morose stillness. 'So she feels she has a debt to me, and wants to pay it but not for my sake. She does not want *me*.'

'Well,' said Cadfael equably, 'I have delivered her message, and if you'll go to her she'll convince you, as I cannot. There was another would have wanted you there, if he could have spoken.'

'Oh, hush!' said Peredur, and jerked his head aside with a motion of sudden pain. 'Don't say more. . . .'

'No, pardon me, I know this is a grief to you, as well as to her. She said so. "He was a favourite with him," she said, "and fond of him—" '

The boy gave a sharp gasp, and turning with blundering haste, walked away rapidly through the trees, deeper into the wood, and left Brother Cadfael to return very thoughtfully to his companions, with the feel of that unbearably tender spot still wincing under his probing finger.

'You and I,' said Bened, when Cadfael walked down to the smithy after Compline, 'must do our drinking alone tonight, my friend. Huw has not yet come down from Rhisiart's hall, and Padrig will be busy singing the dead man till the small hours. Well that he was there at this time. A man's all the better for being sung to his grave by a fine poet and harpist, and it's a great thing for his children to remember. And Cai—Cai we shan't be seeing down here much for a while, not until the bailiff comes to take his prisoner off his hands.'

'You mean Brother John has *Cai* for his gaoler?' asked Cadfael, enlightened.

'He volunteered for the job. I fancy that girl of mine ran and prompted him, but he wouldn't need much prodding. Between them, Brother John will be lying snug enough for a day or two. You need not worry about him.'

'Nothing was further from my mind,' said Cadfael. 'And it's Cai who keeps the key on him?'

'You may be sure. And what with Prince Owain being away in the south, as I hear he is, I doubt if sheriff or bailiff will have much time to spare for a small matter of insubordination in Gwytherin.' Bened sighed heavily over his horn, filled this time with coarse red wine. 'It grieves me now that ever I spoke up and called attention to the blue on the feathers, at least in front of the lass. But someone would have said it. And it's truth that now, with only her Uncle Meurice as guardian, she could have got her own way. She twists him round her finger, he wouldn't have stood in her road. But now I misdoubt me, no man would be such a fool as to leave his private mark on a dead man for all to see. Not unless he was disturbed and had to take to his heels. All it needed was the corner clipping, how long does that take if you've a knife on you? No, it's hard to understand. And yet it could be so!'

By his deep gloom there was more on Bened's mind than that. Somewhere within, he was in abysmal doubt whether he had not spoken up in the hope of having a better chance with Sioned himself if his most favoured rival was removed. He shook his head sadly. 'I was glad when he broke clear as he did, but I'll be satisfied if he makes his way back to Cheshire after this alarm. And yet it's hard to think of him as a murderer.'

'We might give our minds to that, if you're willing,' said Cadfael, 'for you know the people of these parts better than I do. Let's own it, the girl's suspicion, that she spoke out to Prior Robert's face, will be what many a one here is thinking, whether he says it or not. Here are we come into the place and starting a great contention, chiefly with this one lord—no need to argue who's in the right—and there he stands as the one obstacle to what we've come for, and suddenly he's dead, murdered. What's more natural than to point the finger at us, all of us?'

'It's blasphemy even to consider such a charge against such reverend brothers,' said Bened, shocked.

'Kings and abbots are also men, and can fall to temptation. So how do we all stand in regard to this day's doings? All six of us were together or close within sight of one another until after Mass. Then Prior Robert, Brother Richard and I were with Father Huw, first in the orchard, and when it rained, half an hour before noon, in the house. None of the four of us could have gone into the forest. Brother John, too, was about the house and holding, Marared can vouch for him as well as we. The only one who left, before we all came forth for Vespers and set off to search for Rhisiart, was Brother Richard, who offered to go and see if he could meet with him or get word of him, and was gone perhaps an hour and a half, and came back empty-handed. From an hour after noon he was gone, and into the forest, too, for what it's worth, and makes no claim to have spoken with anyone until he enquired at Cadwallon's gate on his way back, which would be nearing half past two. I must speak with the gate-keeper, and see if he bears that out. Two of us are left, but not unaccounted for. Brother Jerome and Brother Columbanus were sent off to keep a vigil together at Saint Winifred's chapel, to pray for a peaceful agreement. We all saw them set off together, and they'd be in the chapel and on their knees long before ever Rhisiart came down towards the path. And there they stayed until Father Huw's messenger went to fetch them to join us. Each of them is warranty for the other.'

'I said so,' said Bened, reassured. 'Holy men do not do murder.'

'Man,' said Cadfael earnestly, 'there are as holy persons outside orders as ever there are in, and not to trifle with truth, as good men out of the Christian church as most I've met within it. In the Holy Land I've known Saracens I'd trust before the common run of the crusaders, men honourable, generous and courteous, who would have scorned to haggle and jostle for place and trade as some of our allies did. Meet every man as you find him, for we're all made the same under habit or robe or rags. Some better made than others, and some better cared for, but on the same pattern all. But there it is. As far as I can see, only one of us, Brother Richard, had any chance at all to be in the neighbourhood when Rhisiart was killed, and of all of us he makes the least likely murderer. So we're forced to look if the ground is not wide open for others, and Saint Winifred only an opportunity and an excuse. Had Rhisiart any enemies around Gwytherin? Some who might never have moved against him if we had not blown up this storm and put the temptation in their way?'

Bened considered gravely, nursing his wine. 'I wouldn't say there's a man anywhere who has not someone to wish him ill, but it's a far cry from that to murder. Time was when Father Huw himself came up against Rhisiart over a patch of land both claimed, and tempers ran high, but they settled it the proper way, by witness from the neighbours, and there's been no malice after. And there have been lawsuits—did you ever hear of a Welsh landholder without one or two lawsuits in hand? One with Rhys ap Cynan over a disputed boundary, one over some beasts that strayed. Nothing to make lasting bad blood. We thrive on suits at law. One thing's true, with the interest you've roused here, every soul for miles around knew that Rhisiart was due at Father Huw's parsonage at noon. No limit at all, there, on who might have decided to waylay him on the road.'

That was as far as they could get. The field was wide, wide enough still to include Engelard, however persuaded Cadfael might be that he was incapable of such an act. Wide enough to enfold even neighbours like Cadwallon, villeins from the village, servants of the household.

But not, surely, thought Brother Cadfael, making his way back to Huw's loft in the green and fragrant dark, not that strange young man who had been a favourite of Rhisiart, and fond of him, and in and out of his house like a son from childhood? The young man who had said of Engelard, and of himself, that a man might step far aside even from his own nature, for love, and then, presumably for love, had opened a way for Engelard to escape, as Cadfael had seen for himself. And who was now avoiding Sioned's gratitude and affection, either because it was not love, and love was the only thing he wanted from her, or for some darker reason. When he flung away in silence into the forest he had had the look of one pursued by a demon. But surely not *that* demon? So far from furthering his chances, Rhisiart's death robbed him of his most staunch ally, who had waited patiently and urged constantly, to bring his daughter to the desired match in the end. No, whichever way a man looked at him, Peredur remained mysterious and disturbing.

Father Huw did not come back from Rhisiart's house that night. Brother Cadfael lay alone in the loft, and mindful that Brother John was locked up somewhere in Sioned's barns, and there was no one to prepare food, got up in good time and went to do it himself, and then set off to Bened's paddock to see to the horses, who were also left without a groom. It suited him better to be out and working in the fresh morning than cooped up with Prior Robert, but he was obliged to return in time for chapter, which the prior had decreed should be held daily as at home, however brief the business they had to transact here.

They met in the orchard, the five of them, Prior Robert presiding in as solemn dignity as ever. Brother Richard read out the saints to be celebrated that day and the following day. Brother Jerome composed his wiry person into his usual shape of sycophantic reverence, and made all the appropriate responses. But it seemed to Cadfael that Brother Columbanus looked unusually withdrawn and troubled, his full blue eyes veiled. The contrast between his athletic build and fine, autocratic head, and his meek and anxious devoutness of feature and bearing, was always confusing to the observer, but that morning his extreme preoccupation with some inward crisis of real or imagined sin made it painful to look at him. Brother Cadfael sighed, expecting another falling fit like the one that had launched them all on this quest. Who knew what this badly-balanced half-saint, half-idiot would do next?

'Here we have but one business in hand,' said Prior Robert firmly, 'and we shall pursue it as in duty bound. I mean to press more resolutely than ever for our right to take up the relics of the saint, and remove them to Shrewsbury. But we must admit, at this moment, that we have not so far been successful in carrying the people with us. I had great hopes yesterday that all would be resolved. We made every reverent preparation to deserve success. . . .'

At this point he was interrupted by an audible sob from Brother Columbanus, that drew all eyes to that young man. Trembling and meek, he rose from his place and stood with lowered eyes and folded hands before Robert.

'Father Prior, alas, *mea culpa*! I am to blame! I have been unfaithful, and I desire to make confession. I came to chapter determined to cleanse my bosom and ask penance, for my backsliding is the cause of our continued distresses. May I speak?'

I knew there was something brewing, thought Brother Cadfael, resigned and disgusted. But at least without rolling on the ground and biting the grass, this time!

'Speak out,' said the prior, not unkindly. 'You have never sought to make light of your failings, I do not think you need fear our too harsh condemnation. You have been commonly your own sternest judge.' So he had, but that, well handled, can be one way of evading and forestalling the judgments of others.'

Brother Columbanus sank to his knees in the orchard turf. And very comely and aristocratic he looked, Cadfael admitted, again admiring with surprise the compact grace and strength of his body, and the supple flow of his movements.

'Father, you sent me with Brother Jerome, yesterday, to keep vigil in the chapel, and pray earnestly for a good outcome, in amity and peace. Father, we came there in good time, before eleven, as I judge, and having eaten our meal, we went in and took our places, for there are prayer-desks within, and the altar is kept clean and well-tended. Oh, Father, my will to keep vigil was good, but the flesh was weak. I had not been half an hour kneeling in prayer, when I fell asleep on my arms on the desk, to my endless shame. It is no excuse that I have slept badly and thought much since we came here. Prayer should fix and purify the mind. I slept, and our cause was weakened. I must have slept all the afternoon, for the next thing I remember is

Brother Jerome shaking me by the shoulder and telling me there was a messenger calling us to go with him.'

He caught his breath, and a frantic tear rolled down his cheek, circling the bold, rounded Norman bone. 'Oh, do not look askance at Brother Jerome, for he surely never knew I had been sleeping, and there is no blame at all to him for not observing and reporting my sin. I awoke as he touched me, and arose and went with him. He thought me as earnest in prayer as he, and knew no wrong.'

Nobody, probably, had thought of looking askance at Brother Jerome until then, but Cadfael was probably the quickest and most alert, and the only one who caught the curious expression of apprehension, fading rapidly into complacency, that passed over Brother Jerome's normally controlled countenance. Jerome had not been pursuing the same studies as Cadfael, or he would have been far from complacent. For Brother Columbanus in his self-absorbed innocence had just removed all certainty that Jerome had spent the previous noon and afternoon motionless in Saint Winifred's chapel, praying for a happy solution. His only guarantor had been fast asleep throughout. He could have sauntered out and gone anywhere he chose.

'Son,' said Prior Robert, in an indulgent voice he would certainly never have used to Brother John, 'your fault is human, and frailty is in our nature. And you redeem your own error, in defending your brother. Why did you not tell us of this yesterday?'

'Father, how could I? There was no opportunity, before we learned of Rhisiart's death. Thus burdened, how could I burden you further at that time? I kept it for this chapter, the right place for erring brothers to receive their penance, and make their abasement. As I do abase myself, as all unworthy the vocation I chose. Speak out sentence on me, for I desire penance.'

The prior was opening his lips to give judgment, patiently enough, for such devout submission and awareness of guilt disarmed him, when they were distracted by the clap of the wooden bar of the garden gate, and there was Father Huw himself advancing across the grass towards them, hair and beard even more disordered than usual, and his eyes heavy and tired with sleeplessness, but his face resolved and calm.

'Father Prior,' he said, halting before them, 'I have just come from holding council with Cadwallon, and Rhys, and Meurice, and all the men of substance in my parish. It was the best opportunity, though I'm sad indeed about the cause. They all came to the mourning for Rhisiart. Every man there knew how he had been struck down, and how such a fate was prophesied. . . .'

'God forbid,' said Prior Robert hastily, 'that I should threaten any man's death. I said that Saint Winifred would be revenged in her own time on the man who stood in the way and did her offence, I never said word of killing.'

'But when he was dead you did claim that this was the saint's vengeance. Every man there heard it, and most believed. I took this chance of conferring with them again in the matter. They do not wish to do anything that is against the will of heaven, nor to give offence to the Benedictine order and the abbey of Shrewsbury. They do not think it right or wise, after what has happened, even to put any man, woman or child of Gwytherin in peril. I am commissioned, Father Prior, to tell you that they withdraw all opposition to your plans. The relics of Saint Winifred are yours to take away with you.'

Prior Robert drew a great breath of triumph and joy, and whatever will he might have had to deal even the lightest punishment left him in an instant. It was everything he had hoped for. Brother Columbanus, still kneeling, cast up his eyes radiantly towards heaven and clasped his hands in gratitude, and somehow contrived to look as though he had brought about this desired consummation himself, the deprivation caused by his unfaithfulness compensated in full by this reward of his penitence. Brother Jerome, just as determined to impress prior and priest with his devotion, threw up his hands and uttered a reverent Latin invocation of praise to God and the saints.

'I am certain,' said Prior Robert magnanimously, 'that the people of Gwytherin never wished to offend, and that they have done wisely and rightly now. I am glad, for them as for my abbey, that we may complete our work here and take our leave in amity with you all. And for your part in bringing about this good ending, Father Huw, we are all grateful. You have done well for your parish and your people.'

'I am bound to tell you,' said Huw honestly, 'that they are not at all happy at losing the saint. But none of them will hinder what you wish. If you so will, we will take you to the burial place today.'

'We will go in procession after the next Mass,' said the prior, unwonted animation lighting up his severe countenance now that he had his own way, 'and not touch food until we have knelt at Saint Winifred's altar and given thanks.' His eyes lit upon Brother Columbanus, patiently kneeling and gazing upon him with doglike eyes, still insistent upon having his sin recognised. Robert looked faintly surprised for a moment, as if he had forgotten the young man's existence. 'Rise, brother, and take heart, for you see that there is forgiveness in the air. You shall not be deprived of your share in the delight of visiting the virgin saint and paying honour to her.'

'And my penance?' insisted the incorrigible penitent. There was a good deal of iron in Brother Columbanus' meekness.

'For penance you shall undertake the menial duties that fell to Brother John, and serve your fellows and their beasts until we return home. But your part in the glory of this day you shall have, and help to bear the reliquary in which the saint's bones are to rest. We'll carry it with us, and set it up before the altar. Every move we make I would have the virgin approve plainly, in all men's sight.'

'And will you break the ground today?' asked Father Huw wearily. No doubt he would be glad to have the whole episode over and forgotten, and be rid of them all, so that Gwytherin could settle again to its age-old business, though short of one good man.

'No,' said Prior Robert after due thought. 'I wish to show forth at every stage our willingness to be guided, and the truth of what we have claimed, that our mission was inspired by Saint Winifred herself. I decree that there shall be three nights of vigil and prayer before the chapel altar, before ever we break the sod, to confirm to all that what we are doing is indeed right and blessed. We are six here, if you will join us, Father Huw. Two by two we will watch nightlong in the chapel, and pray to be guided rightly.'

They took up the silver-inlaid coffin made in implicit faith in Shrewsbury, and carried it in procession up through the woods, past Cadwallon's house, taking the right-hand path that led them obliquely away from the scene of Rhisiart's death, until they came to a small clearing on a hillside, ringed round on three sides by tall, thick clumps of hawthorn, then in snowy bloom. The chapel was of wood, dark with age, small and shadowy within, a tiny bell-turret without a bell leaning over the doorway. Round it the old graveyard lay spread like billowing green skirts, thick with herbs and brambles and tall grasses. By the time they reached this place they had a silent and ever-growing company of local inhabitants following them, curious, submissive, wary. There was no way of telling whether they still felt resentment. Their eyes were steady, observant and opaque, determined to miss nothing and give nothing away.

At the sagging wooden gate that still hung where the path entered, Prior Robert halted, and made the sign of the cross with large, grave gestures. 'Wait here!' he said, when Huw would have led him forward. 'Let us see if prayer can guide my feet, for I have prayed. You shall not show me the saint's grave. I will show it to you, if she will be my aid.'

Obediently they stood and watched his tall figure advance with measured steps, as if he felt his way, the skirts of his habit sweeping through the tangles of grass and flowers. Without hesitation and without haste he made his way to a little, overgrown mound aligned with the east end of the chapel, and sank to his knees at its head.

'Saint Winifred lies here,' he said.

Cadfael thought about it every step of the way, as he went up through the woods that afternoon to Rhisiart's hall. A man could count on Prior Robert to be impressive, but that little miracle had been a master-stroke. The breathless hush, the rippling outbreak of comment and wonder and awe among the men of Gwytherin were with him still. No question but the remotest villein hut and the poorest free holding in the parish would be buzzing with the news by now. The monks of Shrewsbury were vindicated. The saint had taken their prior by the hand and led him to her grave. No, the man had never before been to that place, nor had the grave been marked in any way, by a belated attempt to cut the brambles from it, for instance. It was as it had always been, and yet he had known it from all the rest.

No use at all pointing out, to a crowd swayed by emotion, that if Prior Robert had not previously been to the chapel, Brothers Jerome and Columbanus, his most faithful adherents, had, only the previous day, and with the boy Edwin to guide them, and what more probable than that one of them should have asked the child the whereabouts of the lady they had come all this way to find?

And now, with this triumph already establishing his claim, Robert had given himself three whole days and nights of delay, in which other, similar prodigies might well confirm his ascendancy. A very bold step, but then, Robert was a bold and resourceful man, quite capable of gambling his chances of providing further miracles against any risk of contrary chance refuting him. He meant to leave Gwytherin with what he had come for, but to leave it, if not fully reconciled, then permanently cowed. No scuttling away in haste with his prize of bones, as though still in terror of being thwarted.

But he could not have killed Rhisiart, thought Cadfael with certainty. That I know. Could he have gone so far as to procure . . . ? He considered the possibility honestly, and discarded it. Robert he endured, disliked, and in a fashion admired. At Brother John's age he would have detested him, but Cadfael was old, experienced and grown tolerant.

He came to the gatehouse of Rhisiart's holding, a wattle hut shored into a corner of the palisade fence. The man knew him again from yesterday, and let him in freely. Cai came across the enclosed court to meet him, grinning. All grins here were somewhat soured and chastened now, but a spark of inward mischief survived.

'Have you come to rescue your mate?' asked Cai. 'I doubt he wouldn't thank you, he's lying snug, and feeding like a fighting cock, and no threats of the bailiff yet. *She's* said never a word, you may be sure, and Father Huw would be in no hurry. I reckon we've a couple of days yet, unless your prior makes it his business, where it's none. And if he does, we have boys out will give us plenty of notice before any horseman reaches the gate. Brother John's in good hands.'

It was Engelard's fellow-worker speaking, the man who knew him as well as any in this place. Clearly Brother John had established himself with his gaoler, and Cai's mission was rather to keep the threatening world from him, than to keep him from sallying forth into the world. When the key was needed for the right purpose, it would be provided.

'Take care for your own head,' said Cadfael, though without much anxiety. They knew what they were doing. 'Your prince may have a lawyer's mind, and want to keep in with the Benedictines along the border.'

'Ah, never fret! An escaped felon can be nobody's fault. And everybody's quarry and nobody's prize! Have you never hunted zealously in all the wrong places for something you desired not to find?'

'Say no more,' said Cadfael, 'or I shall have to stop my ears. And tell the lad I never even asked after him, for I know there's no need.'

'Would you be wishing to have a gossip with him?' offered Cai generously. 'He's lodged over yonder in a nice little stable that's clean and empty, and he gets his meals princely, I tell you!'

'Tell me nothing, for I might be asked,' said Cadfael. 'A blind eye and a deaf ear can be useful sometimes. I'll be glad to spend a while with you presently, but now I'm bound to *her*. We have business together.'

Sioned was not in the hall, but in the small chamber curtained off at its end, Rhisiart's private room. And Rhisiart was private there with his daughter, stretched out straight and still on draped furs, on a trestle table, with a white linen sheet covering him. The girl sat beside him, waiting, very formally attired, very grave, her hair austerely braided about her head. She looked older, and taller, now that she was the lady-lord of this holding. But she rose to meet Brother Cadfael with the bright, sad, eager smile of a child sure now of counsel and guidance.

'I looked for you earlier. No matter, I'm glad you're here. I have his clothes for you. I did not fold them; if I had, the damp would have spread evenly through, and now, though they may have dried off, I think you'll still feel a difference.' She brought them, chausses, tunic and shirt, and he took them from her one by one and felt at the cloth testingly. 'I see,' she said, 'that you already know where to feel.'

Rhisiart's hose, though partly covered by the tunic he had worn, were still damp at the back of the thighs and legs, but in front dry, though the damp had spread round through the threads to narrow the dry part to a few inches. His tunic was moist all down the back to the hem, the full width of his shoulders still shaped in a dark patch like spread wings, but all the breast of it, round the dark-rimmed slit the arrow had made, was quite dry. The shirt, though less definitely, showed the same pattern. The fronts of the sleeves were dry, the backs damp. Where the exit wound pierced his back, shirt and tunic were soaked in blood now drying and encrusted.

'You remember,' said Cadfael, 'just how he lay when we found him?'

'I shall remember it my life long,' said Sioned. 'From the hips up flat on his back, but his right hip turned into the grass, and his legs twisted, the left over the right, like. . . .' She hesitated, frowning, feeling for her own half-glimpsed meaning, and found it. 'Like a man who has been lying on his face, and heaves himself over in his sleep on to his back, and sleeps again at once.'

'Or,' said Cadfael, 'like a man who has been taken by the left shoulder, as he lay on his face, and heaved over on to his back. After he was well asleep!'

She gazed at him steadily, with eyes hollow and dark like

wounds. 'Tell me all your thoughts. I need to know. I must know.'

'First, then,' said Brother Cadfael, 'I call attention to the place where this thing happened. A close-set, thicketed place, with plenty of bushes for cover, but not more than fifty paces clear view in any direction. Is that an archer's ground? I think not. Even if he wished the body to be left in woodlands where it might lie undiscovered for hours, he could have found a hundred places more favourable to him. An expert bowman does not need to get close to his quarry, he needs room to draw on a target he can hold in view long enough for a steady aim.'

'Yes,' said Sioned. 'Even if it could be believed of him that he would kill, that rules out Engelard.'

'Not only Engelard, any good bowman, and if someone so incompetent as to need so close a shot tried it, I doubt if he could succeed. I do not like this arrow, it has no place here, and yet here it is. It has one clear purpose, to cast the guilt on Engelard. But I cannot get it out of my head that it has some other purpose, too.'

'To kill!' said Sioned, burning darkly.

'Even that I question, mad though it may seem. See the angle at which it enters and leaves. And then see how the blood is all at the back, and not where the shaft entered. And remember all we have said and noted about his clothes, how they were wet behind, though he lay on his back. And how you yourself said it was the attitude of a man who had heaved himself over from lying on his face. And one more thing I found out yesterday, as I kneeled beside him. Under him the thick grass was wet. But all down by his right side, shoulder to hip and body-wide, it was bone-dry. There was a brisk shower yesterday morning, half an hour of rain. When that rain began, your father was lying on his face, already dead. How else could that patch of grass have remained dry, but sheltered by his body?'

'And then,' said Sioned low but clearly, 'as you say, he was taken by his left shoulder and heaved over on to his back. When he was well asleep. Deep asleep!'

'So it looks to me!'

'But the arrow entered his breast,' she said. 'How, then, could he fall on his face?'

'That we have to find out. Also why he bled behind, and not in front. But lie on his face he did, and that from before the rain began until after it ceased, or the grass beneath him could not have been dry. From half an hour before noon, when the first drops fell, until some minutes past noon, when the sun came out again. Sioned, may I, with all reverence, look closely again now at his body?'

'I know no greater reverence anyone can pay to a murdered man,' she said fiercely, 'than to seek out by all possible means and avenge him on his murder. Yes, handle him if you must. I'll help you. No one else! At least,' she said with a pale and bitter smile, 'you and I are not afraid to touch him, in case he bleeds in accusation against us.'

Cadfael was sharply arrested in the act of drawing down the sheet that covered Rhisiart's body, as though what she had said had put a new and promising idea into his head. 'True! There are not many who do not believe in that trial. Would you say everyone here holds by it?'

'Don't your people believe it? Don't you?' She was astonished. Her eyes rounded like a child's

'My cloister-brothers. . . . Yes, I dare say all or most believe in it. I? Child, I've seen too many slaughtered men handled over and over after a battle by those who finish them off, and never known one of them gush fresh blood, once the life was out of him. But what I believe or don't believe is not to the point. What the murderer believes well may be. No, you have endured enough. Leave him now to me.'

Nevertheless, she did not turn her eyes away, as Cadfael drew off the covering sheet. She must have anticipated the need to examine the body further, for as yet she had left him naked, unshrouded. Washed clean of blood, Rhisiart lay composed and at rest, a thick, powerful trunk brown to the waist, whiter below. The wound under his ribs, an erect slit, now showed ugly and torn, with frayed, bluish lips, though they had done their best to smooth the lacerated flesh together.

'I must turn him,' said Cadfael. 'I need to see the other wound.'

She did not hesitate, but with the tenderness of a mother rather than a daughter she slipped an arm under her father's shoulders, and with her free hand flattened under him from the other side, raised the stiffened corpse until he lay on his right side, his face cradled in the hollow of her arm. Cadfael steadied the stretched-out legs, and leaned to peer closely at the wound high on the left side of the back.

'You would have trouble pulling out the shaft. You had to withdraw it frontally.'

'Yes.' She shook for a moment, for that had been the worst of the ordeal. 'The tip barely broke the skin behind, we had no chance to cut it off. Shame to mangle him so, but what could we do? And yet all that blood!'

The steel point had indeed done little more than puncture the skin, leaving a small, blackened spot, dried blood with a bluish bruise round it. But there was a further mark there, thin and clear and faint. From the black spot the brown line of another upright slit extended, a little longer above the arrow-mark than below, its length in all about as great as the width of Cadfael's thumb-joint, and a faint stain of bruising extending it slightly at either end, beyond where the skin was broken. All that blood—though in fact it was not so very much, though it took Rhisiart's life away with it—had drained out of this thin slit, and not from the wound in his breast, though that now glared, and this lay closed and secret.

'I have done,' said Cadfael gently, and helped her to lay her father at peace again. When they had smoothed even the thick mane of his hair, they covered him again reverently. Then Cadfael told her exactly what he had seen. She watched him with great eyes, and thought for some moments in silence. Then she said: 'I did see this mark you speak of. I could not account for it. If you can, tell me.'

'It was there his life-blood came out,' said Cadfael. 'And not by the puncture the arrow certainly made, but by a prior wound. A wound made, as I judge, by a long dagger, and a very thin and sharp one, no common working knife. Once it was withdrawn, the wound was nearly closed. Yet the blade passed clean through him. For it was possible, afterwards, to trace and turn that same thrust backwards upon itself, and very accurately, too. What we took for the exit wound is no exit wound at all, but an entry wound. The arrow was driven in from the front after he was dead, to hide the fact that he was stabbed in the back. That was why the ambush took place in thick undergrowth, in a tangled place. That was why he fell on his face, and why, afterwards, he was turned on his back. And why the upward course of the arrow is so improbable. It never was shot from any bow. To *thrust* in an arrow is hard work, it was made to get its power from flight. I think the way was opened first with a dagger.'

'The same that struck him down from behind,' she said, white and translucent as flame.

'It would seem so. Then the arrow was inserted after. Even so he could not make it penetrate further. I mistrusted that shot from the first. Engelard could have put a shaft through a couple of oak boards and clean away at that distance. So could any archer worth his pay. But to thrust it in with your hands—no, it was a strong, lusty arm that made even this crude job of it. And at least he got the line right. A good eye, a sensitive hand.'

'A devil's heart,' said Sioned, 'and Engelard's arrow! Someone who knew where to find them, and knew Engelard would not be there to prevent.' But for all her intolerable burdens, she was still thinking clearly. 'I have a question yet. Why did this murderer leave it so long between killing and disguising his kill? My father was dead before ever the rain came. You have shown it clearly. But he was not turned on his back to receive Engelard's arrow until after the rain had stopped. More than half an hour. Why? Was his murderer startled away by someone passing close? Did he wait in the bushes to be sure Rhisiart was dead before he dared touch him? Or did he only think of this devilish trick later, and have to go and fetch the shaft for his purpose? Why so long?'

'That,' said Cadfael honestly, 'I do not know.'

'What do we know? That whoever it was wished to pin this thing upon Engelard. Was that the whole cause? Was my father just a disposable thing, to get rid of Engelard? Bait to trap another man? Or did someone want my father disposed of, and only afterwards realise how easy, how convenient, to dispose of Engelard, too?'

'I know no more than you,' said Cadfael, himself shaken. And he thought, and wished he had not, of that young man fretting his feet tormentedly among the leaves, and flinching from Sioned's trust as from a death-wound. 'Perhaps whoever it was did the deed, and slipped away, and then paused to think, and saw how easy it might be to point the act away from himself, and went back to do it. All we are sure of is this, and, child, thank God for it. Engelard has been set up as a sacrificial victim, and is clear of all taint. Keep that at heart, and wait.'

'And whether we discover the real murderer or not, if ever it should be needful you will speak out for Engelard?'

'That I will, with all my heart. But for now, say nothing of this to anyone, for *we* are still here, the troublers of Gwytherin's peace, and never think that I have set us apart as immaculate. Until we know the guilty, we do not know the innocent.'

'I take back nothing,' said Sioned firmly, 'of what I said concerning your prior.'

'Nevertheless, he could not have done it. He was not out of my sight.'

'No, that I accept. But he buys men, and he is utterly set upon getting his saint, and now, as I understand, he has his will. It is a cause. And never forget, Welshman, as well as Englishmen, may be for sale. I pray not many. But a few.'

'I don't forget,' said Cadfael.

'Who is he? *Who?* He knows my father's movements. He knows where to lay hands on Engelard's arrows. He wants God knows what from my father's death, but certainly he wants to pin murder on Engelard. Brother Cadfael, who can this man be?'

'That, God willing,' he said, 'you and I between us will find out. But as at this moment, I cannot judge nor guess, I am utterly astray. What was done I see, but why, or by whom, I know no more than you. But you have reminded me how the dead are known to rebel against the touch of those who struck them down, and as Rhisiart has told us much, so he may yet tell us all.

He told her, then, of the three nights of prayer and vigil Prior Robert had decreed, and how all the monks and Father Huw, by turns, would share the duty. But he did not tell her how Columbanus, in his single-minded innocence and his concern for his own conscience, had added one more to those who had had the opportunity to lie in wait for her father in the forest. Nor did he admit to her, and hardly to himself, that what they had discovered here lent a sinister meaning to Columbanus' revelation. Jerome out hunting his man with bow and arrow was a most unlikely conception, but Jerome creeping up behind a man's back in thick cover, with a sharp dagger in hand. . . .

Cadfael put the thought behind him, but it did not go far. There was a certain credibility about it that he did not like at all.

'Tonight and for two nights following, two of us will be keeping watch in the chapel from after Compline in the evening until Prime in the morning. All six of us can be drawn into the same trial, and not one can feel himself singled out. After that, we'll see. Now this,' said Brother Cadfael, 'is what you must do. . . .'

CHAPTER SEVEN

After Compline, in the soft evening light, with the slanting sunset filtering through young viridian leaves, they went up, all six together, to the wooden chapel and the solitary graveyard, to bring their first pair of pilgrims to the vigil. And there, advancing to meet them in the clearing before the gate, came another procession, eight of Rhisiart's household officers and servants, winding down out of the woods with their lord's bier upon their shoulders, and their lord's daughter, now herself their lord, walking erect and dignified before them, dressed in a dark gown and draped with a grey veil, under which her long hair lay loose in mourning. Her face was calm and fixed, her eyes looked far. She could have daunted any man, even an abbot. Prior Robert baulked at sight of her. Cadfael was proud of her.

So far from checking at sight of Robert, she gave a slight spring of hope and purpose to her step, and came on without pause. Face to face with him at three paces distance, she halted and stood so still and quiet that he might have mistaken this for submission, if he had been fool enough. But he was not a fool, and he gazed and measured silently, seeing a woman, a mere girl, who had come to match him, though not yet recognising her as his match.

'Brother Cadfael,' she said, without taking her eyes from Robert's face, 'stand by me now and make my words plain to the reverend prior, for I have a prayer to him for my father's sake.'

Rhisiart was there at her back, not coffined, only swathed and shrouded in white linen, every line of body and face standing clear under the tight wrappings, in a cradle of leafy branches, carried on a wooden bier. All those dark, secret Welsh eyes of the men who bore him glowed like little lamps about a catafalque, betraying nothing, seeing everything. And the girl was so young, and so solitary. Prior Robert, even in his assured situation, was uneasy. He may even have been moved.

'Make your prayer, daughter,' he said.

'I have heard that you intend to watch three nights in reverence to Saint Winifred, before you take her hence with you. I ask that for the ease of my father's soul, if he has offended against her, which was never his intent, he may be allowed to lie those three nights before her altar, in the care of those who keep watch. I ask that they will spare one prayer for forgiveness and rest to his soul, one only, in a long night of prayer. Is that too much to ask?'

'It is a fair asking,' said Robert, 'from a loyal daughter.' And after all, he came of a noble family, and knew how to value the ties of blood and birth, and he was not all falsity.

'I hope for a sign of grace,' said Sioned, 'all the more if you approve me.'

There was no way that such a request could do anything but add lustre and glory to his reputation. His opponent's heiress and only child came asking his countenance and patronage. He was more than gratified, he was charmed. He gave his consent graciously, aware of more pairs of Gwytherin eyes watching him than belonged to Rhisiart's bearers. Scattered though the households were, apart from the villein community that farmed as one family, the woods were full of eyes now wherever the strangers went. A pity they had not kept as close a watch on Rhisiart when he was man alive!

They installed his green bier on the trestles before the altar, beside the reliquary that awaited Saint Winifred's bones. The altar was small and plain, the bier almost dwarfed it, and the light that came in through the narrow east window barely illuminated the scene even by morning sunlight. Prior Robert had brought altar-cloths in the chest, and with these the trestles were draped. There the party from Rhisiart's hall left their lord lying in state, and quietly withdrew on the way home.

'In the morning,' said Sioned, before she went with them, 'I shall come to say my thanks to those who have asked grace for my father during the night. And so I shall do each morning, before we bury him.'

She made the reverence due to Prior Robert, and went away without another word, without so much as a glance at Brother Cadfael, drawing the veil close round her face.

So far, so good! Robert's vanity and self-interest, if not his compunction, had assured her of her chance, it remained to be seen what would come of it. The order of their watches had been decreed by Robert himself, in consultation with no one but Father Huw, who wished to be the first to spend the night opening his heart to the saint's influence, if she pleased to make her presence known. His partner was Brother Jerome, of whose obsequious attendance the prior occasionally grew weary, and Cadfael was thankful for the accidental choice that suited him best. That first morning, at least, no one would know what to expect. After that the rest would have due warning, but surely no way of evading the issue.

In the morning, when they went to the chapel, it was to find a fair number of the inhabitants of Gwytherin already gathered there, though unobtrusively, lurking in the edges of the woods and under the fragrant shadow of the hawthorn hedges. Only when the prior and his companions entered the chapel did the villagers emerge silently from cover and gather close, and the first of them to draw near was Sioned, with Annest at her elbow. Way was opened for the two girls, and the people of Gwytherin closed in after them, filling the doorway of the chapel and blocking off the early light, so that only the candles on the altar cast a pale glow over the bier where the dead man lay.

Father Huw got up from his knees somewhat creakily, leaning on the solid wood of the desk till he could get his old legs straightened and working again. From the other desk beside him Jerome rose briskly and supply. Cadfael thought suspiciously of devout watchkeepers who fell asleep as comfortably as possible on their folded arms, but at the moment that was of no importance. He would hardly have expected heaven to open and rain down roses of forgiveness at Jerome's request, in any case.

'A quiet watch,' said Huw, 'and all most calm. I was not

visited by any great experience, but such hardly fall to humble parish priests. We have prayed, child, and I trust we have been heard.'

'I am grateful,' said Sioned. 'And before you go, will you do one more kindness for me and mine? As you have all been sufferers in this trouble and dissension, will you show your own will to mercy? You have prayed for him, now I ask you to lay your hand, each of you, upon my father's heart, in token of reassurance and forgiveness.'

The people of Gwytherin, still as trees in the doorway, but live as trees, too, and all eyes as a tree is all leaves, made never a sound, and missed never a move.

'Gladly!' said Father Huw, and stepped to the bier and laid his rough hand gently on the stilled heart, and by the wagging of his beard his lips were again moving in silent intercession. All eyes turned upon Brother Jerome, for Brother Jerome was hesitating.

He did not look greatly disturbed, but he did look evasive. The face he turned upon Sioned was benevolent and sweet, and having bestowed on her the obligatory glance of compassion, he modestly lowered his eyes before her as was prescribed, and turned to look trustfully at Prior Robert.

'Father Huw holds the cure of this parish, and is subject to one discipline, but I to another. The lord Rhisiart surely carried out his religious duties faithfully, and I feel with him. But he died by violence, unconfessed and unshriven, and such a death leaves the health of his soul in doubt. I am not fit to pronounce in this case. I have prayed, but blessing is not for me to dispense without authority. If Prior Robert feels it is justified, and gives me leave, I will gladly do as I am asked.'

Along this devious path Cadfael followed him with some amazement and considerable doubt. If the prior had himself authorised the death, and sent his creature out to accomplish it, Jerome could not have turned the threat back on his superior more neatly. On the other hand, knowing Jerome, this could as well be his way of flattering and courting, at this opportunity as at every other. And if Robert graciously gave his leave, did he suppose that would protect him, as having plainly handed on the guilt and the threat where they truly belonged, and leave him free to touch his victim with impunity? It would have mattered less if Cadfael had firmly believed that the murdered bleed when the murderer touches, but what he believed was very different, simply that the belief was general among most people, and could drive the guilty, when cornered, to terror and confession. That very terror and stress might even produce some small effusion of blood, though he doubted it. He was beginning to think that Jerome doubted it, too.

The watching eyes had changed their quarry, and hung heavily upon the prior. He frowned, and considered gravely for some moments, before he gave judgment. 'You may do what she wishes, with a good conscience. She is asking only for forgiveness, which is every man's to give, not for absolution.'

And Brother Jerome, gratefully acknowledging the instruction, stepped readily to the bier, and laid his hand upon the swathed heart without a tremor. No spurt of red showed through the shroud to accuse him. Complacently he followed Prior Robert out of the chapel, the others falling in behind, and the silent, staring people fell back from the doorway and let them pass.

And where, thought Cadfael, following, does that leave us? Is he quite hardy about the ordeal, not believing in it at all, or does he feel he has passed the guilt to the guilty, whatever his own part in it, and is therefore out of danger? Or had he no part in it at all, and was all this to no purpose? He is quite narrow enough to refuse the girl a kindness, unless he could turn it to his own credit and advantage.

Well, we shall see tomorrow, reasoned Cadfael, what Robert will do when he's asked for his own forgiveness, instead of being generous with another man's.

However, things did not turn out quite as he had expected. Prior Robert had certainly elected to take that night's watch himself, along with Brother Richard. But as the two were on their way to the chapel, and passing by Cadwallon's holding, the prior was hailed by the gateman, and Cadwallon himself came hastening out to intercept him, with a burly, handsomely-dressed Welshman in a short riding tunic at his heels.

The first Cadfael knew of it was when the prior came striding back into Huw's garden with the stranger beside him, just at the hour when he should have been sinking to his knees in the sombre chapel with its tiny lights, to keep nightlong company with his dead man, in a confrontation which might yet produce fruitful evidence. But here he was, just in time to prevent Cadfael from slipping away to Bened's smithy to exchange the news of the day, and share a cup of wine. And plainly not seriously displeased at having his night's vigil disrupted, either.

'Brother Cadfael, we have a visitor, and I shall require your services. This is Griffith ap Rhys, Prince Owain's bailiff in Rhos. Cadwallon sent to him concerning the death of the lord Rhisiart, and I must make my own statement to him, and discuss what is to be done. He will be enquiring of all those who may have witness to deliver, but now he requires that I shall render my account first. I have had to send Brother Richard on to the chapel without me.'

Jerome and Columbanus had been about to set out for their own beds in Cadwallon's house, but they lingered dutifully at hearing this. 'I will go in your place, Father Prior,' offered Jerome devotedly, certain he would be refused.

'No, you have had one sleepless night.' (Had he? In that dim interior there was no being sure, even if Father Huw had been a suspicious man. And Jerome was not the kind to wear himself out needlessly.) 'You must get your rest.'

'I would gladly take your place, Father Prior,' offered Columbanus just as ardently.

'You have your turn tomorrow. Beware, brother, of taking too much to yourself, of arrogance in the guise of humility. No, Brother Richard will keep the vigil alone tonight. You may wait, both, until you have given your witness as to what you did and saw the day before yesterday, and then leave us, and get your proper sleep.'

That was a long and tedious session, and greatly fretted Brother Cadfael, who was obliged to fall back on his own conception of truth, not, indeed, by translating falsely, but by adding his own view of those things that had happened in the forest by Rhisiart's body. He did not suppress anything Robert said, but he severed plain fact from supposition, the thing observed from the conclusion leaped to, on his own authority. Who was there with Welsh enough to challenge him, except Griffith ap Rhys himself? And that experienced and sceptical officer soon proved himself not only a quick and agile listener, but a very shrewd dissector of feelings and motives, too. He was, after all, Welsh to the bone, and Welsh bones were at the heart of this tangle. By the time he had dealt with Columbanus and Jerome, those two faithful watchers of whom one had turned out to be a treasonous sleeper-on-duty (though neither they nor Prior Robert saw fit to mention that lapse!), Cadfael was beginning to feel he could rely on the good sense of the prince's bailiff, and need not have gone to so much trouble to suppress most of what he himself knew and was about. Better so, though, he decided finally, for what he most needed now was time, and a day or two saved by sending Griffith all round the parish after evidence might see the satisfactory conclusion of his own enquiries. Official justice does not dig deep, but regards what comes readily to the surface, and draws conclusions accordingly. A nagging doubt now and then is the price it pays for speedy order and a quiet land. But Cadfael was not prepared to let the nagging doubt occur in the person of either Engelard or Brother John. No, better go his own way to the end, and have a finished case to present to bailiff and prince.

So there was nothing at all for Sioned to do, when she came the next morning, but to ask Brother Richard, that large, lazy, kindly man who willed peace and harmony all round him, for his personal pity towards her father, and his benediction in the laying on of hands. Which he gave willingly and guilelessly, and departed still in ignorance of what he had done, and what he had been absolved from doing.

'I missed you,' said Bened, briefly visited between Mass and dinner. 'Padrig came down for a while, we were talking over the old days, when Rhisiart was younger. Padrig's been coming here a good many years now. He knows us all. He asked after you.'

'Tell him we'll share a cup one of these days, here or there. And say I'm about Rhisiart's business, if that's any comfort.'

'We're getting used to you,' said Bened, stooping to his fire, where a sinewy boy was bending into the bellows. 'You should stay, there'd be a place for you.'

'I've got my place,' said Cadfael. 'Never fret about me. I chose the cowl with both eyes open. I knew what I did.'

'There are some I can't reconcile with you,' said Bened, with the iron in hand for the shoe that waited.

'Ah, priors and brothers come and go, as mixed as the rest of men, but the cloister remains. Now, there are some who did lose their way, I grant you,' said Cadfael, 'mostly young things who mistook a girl's "no" for the end of the world. Some of them might make very useful craftsmen, if ever they broke free. Always supposing they were free men, and could get entry to, say, the smith's mystery....'

'He has a good arm and wrist on him, that one,' said Bened reflectively, 'and knows how to jump and do as he's bid when the man bidding knows his business. That's half the craft. If he hasn't let Rhisiart's killer loose on the world, then there isn't an outlander would be more welcome here. But that I don't yet know, though the poor girl up yonder may think she does. How if she's wrong? Do *you* know?'

'Not yet,' owned Cadfael. 'But give us time, and we shall know.'

On this third day of Brother John's nominal captivity he found himself more closely confined. The word had gone round that the bailiff was in the parish and asking questions everywhere concerning the circumstances of Rhisiart's death, and it was known that he had had a lengthy session with the prior at Father Huw's parsonage, and must certainly have been urged and admonished as to his duty to take action also in the matter of Brother John's crime. Not that John had any complaints as to his lodging, his food or his company; he had seldom been so completely content. But for two days, with brief intervals when caution had seemed advisable, he had been out from dawn to dusk about the holding, lending a hand with the cattle, replenishing the wood-pile, fetching and carrying, planting out in the vegetable garden, and had had neither time nor inclination to worry about his situation. Now that he was hustled out of sight, and sat idle in the stable, the realities fretted even John, and the want of Welsh, or of Brother Cadfael to supply the want, was a frustration no longer so easy to bear. He did not know what Cadfael and Sioned were up to, he did not know what was happening to Saint Winifred, or to Prior Robert and his fellows, and above all he did not know where Engelard was, or how he was to be extricated from the tangle of suspicion roused against him. Since his instinctive gesture of solidarity, John took a proprietorial interest in Engelard, and wanted him safe, vindicated, and happy with his Sioned.

But Sioned, true to her word, did not come near him, and there was no one else in the holding who could talk to him freely. Simple things could be conveyed, but there was no way of communicating to him everything he wanted and needed to know. There was he, willing but useless, wondering and fretting how his friends were faring, and quite unable to do anything to aid them.

Annest brought his dinner, and sat by him while he ate, and the same want of words troubled her. It was all very well teaching him simple words and phrases in Welsh by touching the thing she meant, but how to set about pouring out to him, as she would have liked, all that was happening at the chapel, and what the village was saying and thinking? The helplessness of talking at all made their meetings almost silent, but sometimes they did speak aloud, he in English, she in Welsh, saying things because they could not be contained, things that would be understood by the other only in some future day, though the tone might convey at least the sense of friendship, like a kind of restrained caress. Thus they conducted two little monologues which yet were an exchange and a comfort.

Sometimes, though they did not know it, they were even answering each other's questions.

'I wonder who she was,' said Annest, soft and hesitant, 'that one who drove you to take the cowl? Sioned and I, we can't help wondering how a lad like you ever came to do it.' Now if he had known Welsh, she could never have said that to him.

'How did I ever come to think that Margery such a beauty!' marvelled John. 'And take it so hard when she turned me down? But I'd never really seen beauty then—I'd never seen *you*!'

'She did us all a bad turn,' said Annest, sighing, 'whoever she was, driving you into that habit for life!'

'Dear God,' said John, 'to think I might have married her! At least she did me that much of a favour, with her "no". There's only the matter of a cowl between you and me, not a wife.' And that was the first moment when he had entertained the dazzling idea that escape from his vows might be possible at all. The thought caused him to turn his head and look with even closer and more ardent attention at the fair face so close to his. She had smooth, rounded, apple-blossom cheeks, and delicate, sun-glossed bones, and eyes like brook-water in the sun over bright pebbles, glittering, polished, crystal-clear.

'Do you still fret after her?' wondered Annest in a whisper. 'A conceited ninny who hadn't the wit to know a good man when she saw one?' For he was indeed a very well-grown, handy, handsome, good-humoured young fellow, with his long, sturdy legs and his big, deft hands, and his bush of russet curls, and the girl who thought herself too good for him must have been the world's fool. 'I hate her!' said Annest, leaning unwarily towards him.

The lips that tantalised him with soft utterances he could not understand were only a little way from his own. He resorted in desperation to a kind of sign-language that needed no interpreter. He hadn't kissed a girl since Margery, the draper's daughter, threw him over when her father became bailiff of Shrewsbury, but it seemed he hadn't forgotten how. And Annest melted into his arms, where she fitted a great deal better than his too-hasty vows had ever fitted him.

'Oh, Annest!' gasped Brother John, who had never in his life felt less like a brother, 'I think I love you!'

Brother Cadfael and Brother Columbanus walked up through the woodland together, to keep the third night of prayer. The evening was mild and still but overcast, and under the trees the light grew dusky green. Until the last moment it had remained a possibility that Prior Robert, having missed his chosen night of duty, might elect to be present on this last occasion, but he had said no word, and to tell the truth, Cadfael was beginning to wonder if that long session with the bailiff had really been necessary at all, or whether the prior had welcomed it as an alternative to keeping the night-watch and facing Sioned with her request in the morning. Not necessarily a proof of any guilt on his part, beyond the guilt of still wishing to refuse grace to Rhisiart, without actually having to do so face to face with his daughter. For whatever virtues might be found in Prior Robert, humility was not one, nor magnanimity. He was invariably sure of his own rightness, and where it was challenged he was not a forgiving man.

'In this quest and this vigil, brother,' said Columbanus, his long young steps keeping easy pace with Cadfael's seaman's roll, 'we are greatly privileged. The history of our abbey will record our names, and brothers in the generations to come will envy us.'

'I have already heard,' said Cadfael drily, 'that Prior Robert is proposing to write a life of Saint Winifred, and complete it with the story of this translation to Shrewsbury. You think he'll record the names of *all* his companions?' Yours, however, he thought, he well might mention, as the afflicted brother who first fell sick and was sent to Holywell to be cured. And Jerome's, who had the dream that took you there. But mine, I feel sure, will remain a silence, and so much the better!

'I have a fault to atone for,' recalled Columbanus devoutly, 'having betrayed my trust once in this same chapel, I, who most of all should have been faithful.' They were at the decrepit gate, the tangle of the graveyard before them, threaded by a narrow path just discernible through the long grass. 'I feel a holy air reaching out to me,' said the young man, quivering, his face uplifted and pale. 'I am drawn into a light. I believe we are approaching a wonder, a miracle of grace. Such mercy to me, who fell asleep in betrayal of her service!' And he led the way to the open door, his stride lengthening in eagerness, his hands extended as if to clasp a mistress rather than make obeisance before a saint. Cadfael followed morosely but resignedly, used to these uncomfortable ardours, but not looking forward to being confined in so small a chapel with them overnight. He had thinking as well as praying to do, and Columbanus was not conducive to either activity.

Inside the chapel the air was heavy with the scent of old wood, and the spices and incense of the draperies on which the reliquary lay, and the faint, aromatic aura of years of dust and partial disuse. A small oil-lamp burned with a dark yellow flame on the altar, and Cadfael went forward and lit the two altar candles from it, and set them one on either side. Through the narrow east window the fragrance of the falling may-blossom breathed freshness on a very light breeze, causing the flames to flicker for a few minutes. Their faint, dancing radiance glanced from every near surface, but did not reach the corners of the roof, or fix the walls in place. They were in a narrow cavern of brown, wood-scented darkness, with a dim focus of light before them, that shone on an empty coffin and an uncoffined body, and just showed them the rough outlines of the two prayer-desks drawn up side by side at a little distance from the catafalque. Rhisiart lay nearer to them, the black and silver bulk of the reliquary like a low wall shading him from the altar lights.

Brother Columbanus bowed humbly low to the altar, and took his place at the desk on the right. Brother Cadfael settled solidly at the one on the left, and with practised movements sought and found the best place for his knees. Stillness came down on them gently. He composed himself for a long watch, and said his prayer for Rhisiart, not the first he had said for him. Great darkness and constant, feeble light, the slow flowing of time from far beyond his conception to far beyond his power to follow, the solitude about him and the troubled and peopled world within, all these settled into their perpetual pattern, a steady rhythm as perfect as sleep. He thought no more of Columbanus, he forgot that Columbanus existed. He prayed as he breathed, forming no words and making no specific requests, only holding in his heart, like broken birds in cupped hands, all those people who were in stress or in grief because of this little saint, for if he suffered like this for their sake, how much more must she feel for them?

The candles would last the night, and by instinct he traced time by the rate at which they dwindled, and knew when it was near to midnight.

He was thinking of Sioned, to whom he had nothing but himself to offer in the morning, this pietistic innocent being essentially nothing, and Cadfael himself by no means enough, when he heard the faintest and strangest of sounds issuing from the prie-dieu on his right, where Columbanus leaned in total absorption. Not now with face hidden on his linked hands, but uplifted and strained upwards into what light could reach him, and faint though it was, it conjured his sharp profile into primrose pallor. His eyes were wide open and staring beyond the chapel wall, and his lips open and curved in ecstasy, and singing, a mere thread of Latin chant in praise of virginity. It was barely audible, yet clear as in a dream. And before Cadfael was fully aware of what he heard, he saw the young man thrust himself upwards, holding by the desk, and stand upright before the altar. The chant ceased. Suddenly he reared himself erect to his tallest, drawing back his head as though he would see through the roof into a spring night full of stars, and spreading out his arms on either side like a man stretched on a cross. He gave a great, wordless cry, seemingly both of pain and triumph, and fell forward full-length on the earthen floor, crashing to the ground stiffly, arms still outspread, body stretched to the very toes, and lay still, his forehead against the trailing fringe of the altar-cloth that spilled from beneath Rhisiart's body.

Cadfael got up in a hurry and went to him, torn between anxiety and alarm on one hand, and disgusted resignation on the other. Exactly what was to be expected of the idiot, he thought with exasperation, even as he was on his knees feeling at the prone brow, and adjusting a fold of the altar drapery under it to ease the position of nose and mouth, turning the young man's head to one side so that he could breathe freely. I should have recognised the signs! Never an opportunity but he can produce a devotional fit or a mystic ecstasy to order. One of these days he'll be drawn into that light of his, and never come back. Yet I've noticed he can fall flat on his face without hurting himself, and go into pious convulsions over his visions or his sins without ever hurling himself against anything sharp or hard, or even biting his tongue. The same sort of providence that takes care of drunken men looks out for Columbanus in his throes. And he reflected at the back of his mind, and tartly, that there ought somewhere to be a moral in that, lumping all excesses together.

No convulsions this time, at any rate. He had simply seen whatever he had seen, or thought he had seen, and fallen down before it in this destroying rapture. Cadfael shook him by the shoulder gently, and then more sharply, but he was rigid and unresponsive. His forehead was cool and smooth, his features, very dimly seen, yet looked serene, composed, if anything, in a gentle and joyful peace. But for the rigidity of body and limbs, and that unnatural attitude as though he lay stretched on a cross, he might have been asleep. All Cadfael had been able to do by way of easing him was to turn his head so that he lay on his right cheek, pillowed on the draperies. When he tried to bend the right arm and turn the young man more comfortably on his side, the joints resisted him, so he let well alone.

And now, he thought, what am I supposed to do? Abandon my watch and go down and fetch the prior with help for him? What could they do for him that I cannot do here? If I can't rouse him, then neither could they. He'll come out of it when the right time comes, and not before. He's done himself no injury, his breathing is steady and deep. His heart beats strongly and regularly, he has no fever. Why interfere with a man's peculiar pleasures, if they're doing him no harm? It isn't cold here, and he can have one of these altar-cloths for blanket, a fancy that ought to please him. No, we came to watch out the night together, and so we will, I here on my knees as is due, and he wherever he may be at this moment in his dreams.

He covered Columbanus, adjusted the cloths to cushion his head, and went back to his own prie-dieu. But whatever this visitation had done for Columbanus, it had shattered all possibility of thought or concentration for Cadfael. The more he tried to focus his mind, whether upon his duty of prayer and meditation, or the urgent need to consider where Sioned stood now, and what more could be done, the more was he drawn to look again at the prone body, and listen again to make sure it still breathed as evenly as ever. What should have been a profitable night hung heavy upon him, wasted as worship, useless as thought, as long and dreary and tedious a night as he had ever passed.

The first dove-grey softening of the darkness came as a blessing, bringing release at least within sight. The narrow space of sky seen through the altar window changed from grey to pale, clear green, from green to saffron, from saffron to gold, a cloudless morning, the first sunray piercing through the slit and falling on the altar, the reliquary, the shrouded body, and then striking like a golden sword across the chapel, leaving Columbanus in darkness. Still he lay rigid, yet breathing deeply and softly, and no touch or word could reach him.

He was in the same condition when Prior Robert came with his fellows, and Sioned with Annest in attendance, and all the people from the village and the nearby holdings, silent and watchful as before, to see the end of this three-night vigil.

Sioned was the first to enter, and the dimness within, after the brightness without, made her blind for a moment, so that she halted in the doorway until her eyes should grow accustomed to the change. Prior Robert was close behind her when she saw the soles of Brother Columbanus' sandals upturned before her, just touched by the sunray from the window, while the rest of him lay still in shadow. Her eyes widened in wonder and horror, and before Cadfael could rise and turn to reassure her she had uttered a sharp cry: 'What is it? Is he dead?'

The prior put her aside quickly, and strode past her, and was brought up short with his foot on the hem of Columbanus' habit.

'What happened here? Columbanus! Brother!' He stooped and laid his hand upon a rigid shoulder. Columbanus slept and dreamed on, unmoved and unmoving. 'Brother Cadfael, what does this mean? What has befallen him?'

'He is not dead,' said Cadfael, putting first things first, 'nor do I think he is in any danger. He breathes like a man peacefully sleeping. His colour is good, he is cool to the touch, and has no injury. Simply, at midnight he suddenly stood up before the altar, and spread out his arms and fell forward thus in trance. He has lain all night like this, but without distress or agitation.'

'You should have called us to his aid,' said the prior, shaken and dismayed.

'I had also a duty,' said Cadfael shortly, 'to remain here and keep the vigil I was sent to keep. And what could have been done for him more than I have done, in giving him a pillow for his head and a cover against the chill of the night? Nor, I think, would he have been grateful if we had carried him away before the appointed time. Now he has kept his own watch faithfully, and if we cannot rouse him we may bear him away to his bed, without doing violence to his sense of duty.'

'There is something in that,' said Brother Richard earnestly, 'for you know that Brother Columbanus has several times been visited and favoured by visions, and it might have been a great wrong to take him away from the very place where such blessings befell him. An offence, perhaps, against the saint herself, if she was pleased to reveal herself to him. And if that is so, then he will awake when the time is right that he should, and it might do him great harm to try and hasten the hour.'

'It is true,' said the prior, a little reassured, 'that he seems at peace, and has a good colour, and no sign of trouble or pain. This is most strange. Is it possible that this young brother will be the occasion of another such prodigy as when his affliction first drew us to Saint Winifred?'

'He was the instrument of grace once,' said Richard, 'and may be so again. We had better carry him down to his bed at Cadwallon's house, and keep him quiet and warm, and wait. Or had we not better take him to Father Huw's parsonage, so that he may be close to the church? It may be that his first need will be to give thanks.'

With a heavy altar-cloth and their girdles they made a sling in which to carry Columbanus, lifting him from the floor, stiff as a branch, even his extended arms still rigid. They laid him on his back in their improvised litter, and he suffered whatever they did to him, and made no sound or sign. A few of the watching natives, moved and awed by the spectacle, came forward to lend a hand in carrying him down through the forest to Huw's house. Cadfael let them go. He turned to look at Sioned, as she was looking at him, with dubious and speculative eyes.

'Well, I, at least,' he said, 'am in my right senses, and can and will do what you have not asked of me.' And he stepped to Rhisiart's side, and laid his hand upon the dead man's heart, and signed his forehead with a cross.

She walked beside him as they followed the slow procession down towards the village.

'What more can we do? If you know of anything, only tell me. We have not been favoured so far. And today is to be his burial.'

'I know it,' said Cadfael, and brooded. 'As for this affair in the night, I'm torn two ways. I should think it possible it was all planned, to reinforce our cause with another miracle, but for two things. To me Prior Robert's amazement and concern, however I look at them, seem to be true and not false. And Columbanus has shown these strange properties before, and the way they overtake him is violent and perilous, and it's hard to believe he is feigning. A tumbler at a fair, making his living by playing the devil with his own body, could not outdo Columbanus when the fit comes on him. I am not able to judge. I think there are some who live on a knife-edge in the soul, and at times are driven to hurl themselves into the air, at the mercy of heaven or hell which way to fall.'

'All I know,' said Sioned, burning darkly red like a slow torch, 'is that my father whom I loved is murdered, and I want justice on the murderer, and I do not want a blood price. There is no price I will accept for Rhisiart's blood.'

'I know, I know!' said Cadfael. 'I am as Welsh as you. But keep a door open to pity, as who knows when you or I may need it! And have you spoken with Engelard? And is all well with him?'

She quivered and flushed and softened beside him, like a frost-blighted flower miraculously revived by a southern wind. But she did not answer. There was no need.

'Ah, you'll live!' said Brother Cadfael, satisfied. 'As he'd want you to. Even if he did set his face against, like a proper Welsh lord. You'd have got your way in the end, you were right about that. And listen, I have thought of two things you should yet do. We must try whatever we can. Don't go home now. Let Annest take you to Bened's smithy to rest, and the both of you come to Mass. Who knows what we may learn once our half-fledged saint regains his senses? And then, also, when you bury your father, make certain Peredur comes with *his* father. He might try to avoid else, if he's eluded you this far, but if you ask him, he cannot refuse. I am still in more minds than one, and none of them very clear, concerning Master Peredur.'

CHAPTER EIGHT

It was the little brazen bell ringing for Mass that penetrated Brother Columbanus' enchanted sleep at last. It could not be said that it awoke him, rather it caused him to open his closed eyes, quiver through all his frozen members, flex his stiff arms, and press his re-quickened hands together over his breast. Otherwise his face did not change, nor did he seem to be aware of those who were gathered anxiously about the bed on which he lay. They might not have been there at all. All Brother Columbanus responded to was the bell, the first call to worship. He stirred and sat up. He rose from the bed, and stood firmly on his feet. He looked radiant, but still private and apart.

'He is preparing to take his usual place with us,' said the prior, moved and awed. 'Let us go, and make no attempt yet to rouse him. When he has given thanks he'll come back to us, and speak out what he has experienced.'

And he led the way to the church, and as he had supposed, Columbanus fell into his usual place as the youngest in the attendant brotherhood now that John was disgraced, and followed modestly, and modestly took part in the service, still like a man in a dream.

The church was full as it would hold, and there were more people clustered outside the doorway. The word had gone round already that something strange and wonderful had happened at Saint Winifred's chapel, and revelations might very well follow at Mass.

Not until the end did any further change occur in the condition of Brother Columbanus. But when the prior, slowly and expectantly, as one turning a key and almost confident of entry, took the first step towards the doorway, suddenly Columbanus gave a great start, and uttered a soft cry, staring wonderingly about him at all these known faces. His own visage came to life, smiling. He put out a hand as if to arrest the prior's departure, and said in a high voice: 'Oh, Father, I have been so blessed, I have known such bliss! How did I come here, when I know I was elsewhere, and translated out of night's darkness into so glorious a light? And surely this is again the world I left! A fair world enough, but I have been in a fairer, far beyond any deserts of mine. Oh, if I could but tell you!'

Every eye was upon him, and every ear stretched to catch his least word. Not a soul left the church, rather those without crowded in closer.

'Son,' said Prior Robert, with unwontedly respectful kindness, 'you are here among your brothers, engaged in the worship of God, and there is nothing to fear and nothing to regret, for the visitation granted you was surely meant to inspire and arm you to go fearless through an imperfect world, in the hope of a perfect world hereafter. You were keeping night watch with Brother Cadfael at Saint Winifred's chapel—do you remember that? In the night something befell you that drew your spirit for a time away from us, out of the body, but left that body unharmed and at rest like a child asleep. We brought you back here still absent from us in the spirit, but now you are here with us again, and all is well. You have been greatly privileged.'

'Oh, greatly, far more than you know,' sang Columbanus, glowing like a pale lantern. 'I am the messenger of such goodness, I am the instrument of reconciliation and peace. Oh, Father. . . . Father Huw . . . brothers . . . let me speak out here before all, for what I am bidden to tell concerns all.'

Nothing, thought Cadfael, could have stopped him, so plainly did his heavenly embassage override any objection mere prior or priest might muster. And Robert was proving surprisingly compliant in accepting this transfer of authority. Either he already knew that the voice from heaven was about to say something entirely favourable to his plans and conducive to his glory, or else he was truly impressed, and inclining heart and ear to listen as devoutly as any man there present.

'Speak freely, brother,' he said, 'let us share your joy.'

'Father, at the hour of midnight as I knelt before the altar I heard a sweet voice crying my name, and I arose and went forward to obey the call. What happened to my body then I do not know, you tell me it was lying as if asleep when you came. But it seemed to me that as I stepped towards the altar there was suddenly a soft, golden light all about it, and there rose up, floating in the midst of the light, a most beautiful virgin, who moved in a miraculous shower of white petals, and distilled most sweet odours from her robe and from her long hair. And this gracious being spoke to me, and told me that her name was Winifred, and that she was come to approve our enterprise, and also to forgive all those who out of mistaken loyalty and reverence had opposed it hitherto. And then, oh, marvellous goodness! —she laid her hand on Rhisiart's breast, as his daughter has begged us to do in token of our mere personal forgiveness, but she in divine absolution, and with such perfection of grace, I cannot describe it.'

'Oh, son,' said Prior Robert in rapture, riding over the quivering murmurs that crossed the church like ripples on a pool, 'you tell a greater wonder than we dared hope. Even the lost saved!'

'It is so! And, Father, there is more! When she laid her hand on him, she bade me speak out to all men in this place, both native and stranger, and make known her merciful will. And it is this: "Where my bones shall be taken out of the earth," she said, "there will be an open grave provided. What I relinquish, I may bestow. In this grave," said Winifred, "let Rhisiart be buried, that his rest may be assured, and my power made manifest." '

'What could I do,' said Sioned, 'but thank him for his good offices, when he brought divine reassurance for my father's weal? And yet it outrages me, I would rather have stood up and said that I am not and never have been in the least doubt that my father is in blessedness this moment, for he was a good man who never did a mean wrong to anyone. And certainly it's kind of Saint Winifred to offer him the lodging she's leaving, and graciously forgive him, but—forgiveness for what? Absolution for what? She might rather have praised him while she was about it, and said outright that he was justified, not forgiven.'

'Yet a very ambassadorial message,' admitted Cadfael appreciatively, 'calculated to get us what we came for, assuage the people of Gwytherin, make peace all round—'

'And to placate me, and cause me to give up the pursuit of my father's murderer,' said Sioned, 'burying the deed along with the victim. Except that I will not rest until I know.'

'—and shed reflected glory upon Prior Robert, I was going to say. And I wish I knew which mind conceived the idea!'

They had met for a few hurried minutes at Bened's smithy, where Cadfael had gone to borrow mattock and spade for the holy work now to be undertaken. Even a few of the men of Gwytherin had come forward and asked to have a share in breaking the sacred earth, for though they were still reluctant to lose their saint, if it was her will to leave them they had no wish to cross her. Prodigious things were happening, and they intended to be in receipt of her approval and blessing rather than run the risk of encountering her arrows.

'It seems to me most of the glory is falling, rather, on Brother Columbanus of late,' said Sioned shrewdly. 'And the prior took it meekly, and never made any attempt to filch it back from him. That's the one thing that makes me believe he may be honest.'

She had said something that caused Cadfael to pause and look attentively at her, scrubbing dubiously at his nose. 'You may well be right. And certainly this story is bound to go back to Shrewsbury with us, and spread through all our sister houses, when we come home with our triumph. Yes, Columbanus will certainly have made himself a great name for holiness and divine favour in the order.'

'They say an ambitious man can make a grand career in the cloister,' she said. 'Maybe he's busy laying the foundations, a great step up towards being prior himself when Robert becomes abbot. Or even abbot, when Robert supposes *he's* about to become abbot! For it's not *his* name they'll be buzzing round the shires as the visionary the saints use to make their wants known.'

'That,' agreed Cadfael, 'may not even have dawned on Robert yet, but when the awe of the occasion passes it will. And he's the one who's pledged to write a life of the saint, and complete it with the account of this pilgrimage. Columbanus may very well end up as an anonymous brother who happened to be charged with a message to the prior from his patroness. Chroniclers can edit names out as easily as visionaries can noise them abroad. But I grant you, this lad comes of a thrusting Norman family that doesn't put even its younger sons into the Benedictine habit to spend their lives doing menial work like gardening.'

'And we're no further forward,' said Sioned bitterly.

'No. But we have not finished yet.'

'But as I see it, this is devised to be an ending, to close this whole episode in general amity, as if everything was resolved. But everything is *not* resolved! Somewhere in this land there is a man who stabbed my father in the back, and we're all being asked to draw a veil over that and lose sight of it in the great treaty of peace. But I want that man found, and Engelard vindicated, and my father avenged, and I won't rest, or let anyone else rest, until I get what I want. And now tell me what I am to do.'

'What I've already told you,' said Cadfael. 'Have all your household party and friends gathered at the chapel to watch the grave opened, and make sure that Peredur attends.'

'I've already sent Annest to beg him to come,' said Sioned. 'And then? What have I to say or do to Peredur?'

'That silver cross you wear round your neck,' said Cadfael. 'Are you willing to part with it in exchange for one step ahead towards what you want to know?'

'That and all the rest of the valuables I own. You know it.'

'Then this,' said Cadfael, 'is what you will do....'

With prayers and psalms they carried their tools up to the tangled graveyard by the chapel, trimmed back the brambles and wild flowers and long grass from the little mound of Winifred's grave, and reverently broke the sod. By turns they laboured, all taking a share in the work for the merit to be acquired. And most of Gwytherin gathered round the place in the course of the day, all work left at a standstill in the fields and crofts, to watch the end of this contention. For Sioned had spoken truly. She and all her household servants were there among the rest, in mourning and massed to bring out Rhisiart's body for burial when the time came, but this funeral party had become, for the time being, no more than a side-issue, an incident in the story of Saint Winifred, and a closed incident at that.

Cadwallon was there, Uncle Meurice was there, and Bened, and all the other neighbours. And there at his father's elbow, withdrawn and brooding, stood young Peredur, by the look of him wishing himself a hundred leagues away. His thick dark brows were drawn together as though his head ached, and wherever his brown eyes wandered, it was never towards Sioned. He had crept here reluctantly at her express asking, but he could not or would not face her. The bold red mouth was chilled and pale from the tension with which it was tightened against his teeth. He watched the dark pit deepen in the grass, and breathed hard and deep, like a man containing pain. A far cry from the spoiled boy with the long, light step and the audacious smile, who so plainly had taken it for granted that the world was his for the wooing. Peredur's demons were at him within.

The ground was moist but light, not hard to work, but the grave was deep. Gradually the diggers sank to the shoulders in the pit, and by mid-afternoon Brother Cadfael, shortest of the party, had almost disappeared from view when he took his final turn in the depths. No one dared to doubt openly if they were in the right place, but some must have been wondering. Cadfael, for no good reason that he could see, had no doubts at all. The girl was here. She had lived many years as an abbess after her brief martyrdom and miraculous restoration, yet he thought of her as that devout, green girl, in romantic love with celibacy and holiness, who had fled from Prince Cradoc's advances as from the devil himself. By some perverse severance of the heart in two he could feel both for her and for the desperate lover, so roughly molten out of the flesh and presumably exterminated in the spirit. Did anyone ever pray for him? He was in greater need than Winifred. In the end, perhaps the only prayers he ever benefited by were Winifred's prayers. She was Welsh, and capable of detachment and subtlety. She might well have put in a word for him, to reassemble his liquefied person and congeal it again into the shape of a man. A chastened man, doubtless, but still the same shape as before. Even a saint may take pleasure, in retrospect, in having been once desired.

The spade grated on something in the dark, friable soil, something neither loam nor stone. Cadfael checked his stroke instantly at its suggestion of age, frailty and crumbling dryness. He let the blade lie, and stooped to scoop away with his hands the cool, odorous, gentle earth that hid the obstruction from him. Dark soil peeled away under his fingers from a slender, pale, delicate thing, the gentle dove-grey of pre-dawn, but freckled with pitted points of black. He drew out an arm-bone, scarcely more than child size, and stroked away the clinging earth. Islands of the same soft colouring showed below, grouped loosely together. He did not want to break any of them. He hoisted the spade and tossed it out of the pit.

'She is here. We have found her. Softly, now, leave her to me.'

Faces peered in upon him. Prior Robert gleamed in silvery agitation, thirsting to plunge in and dredge up the prize in person, but deterred by the clinging darkness of the soil and the whiteness of his hands. Brother Columbanus at the brink towered and glittered, his exalted visage turned, not towards the depths where this fragile virgin substance lay at rest, but rather to the heavens from which her diffused spiritual essence had addressed him. He displayed, no doubt of it, an aura of distinct proprietorship that dwarfed both prior and sub-prior, and shone with its full radiance upon all those who watched from the distance. Brother Columbanus meant to be, was, and knew that he was, memorable in this memorable hour.

Brother Cadfael kneeled. It may even have been a significant omen that at this moment he alone was kneeling. He judged that he was at the feet of the skeleton. She had been there some centuries, but the earth had dealt kindly, she might well be whole, or virtually whole. He had not wanted her disturbed at all, but now he wanted her disturbed as little as might be, and delved carefully with scooping palms and probing, stroking finger-tips to uncover the whole slender length of her without damage. She must have been a little above medium height, but willowy as a seventeen-year-old girl. Tenderly he stroked the earth away from round her. He found the skull, and leaned on stretched arms, fingering the eye-sockets clear, marvelling at the narrow elegance of the cheek-bones, and the generosity of the dome. She had beauty and fineness in her death. He leaned over her like a shield, and grieved.

'Let me down a linen sheet,' he said, 'and some bands to raise it smoothly. She shall not come out of here bone by bone, but whole woman as she went in.'

They handed a cloth down to him, and he spread it beside the slight skeleton, and with infinite care eased her free of the loose soil, and edged her by inches into the shroud of linen, laying the disturbed arm-bone in its proper place. With bands of cloth slung under her she was drawn up into the light of day, and laid tenderly in the grass at the side of her grave.

'We must wash away the soil-marks from her bones,' said Prior Robert, gazing in reverent awe upon the prize he had gone to such trouble to gain, 'and wrap them afresh.'

'They are dry and frail and brittle,' warned Cadfael impatiently. 'If she is robbed of this Welsh earth she may very well crumble to Welsh earth herself in your hands. And if you keep her here in the air and the sun too long, she may fall to dust in any case. If you are wise, Father Prior, you'll wrap her well as she lies, and get her into the reliquary and seal her from the air as tight as you can, as quickly as you can.'

That was good sense, and the prior acted on it, even if he did not much relish being told what to do so brusquely. With hasty but exultant prayers they brought the resplendent coffin out to the lady, to avoid moving her more than they must, and with repeated swathings of linen bound her little bones carefully together, and laid her in the coffin. The brothers who made it had realised the need for perfect sealing to preserve the treasure, and taken great pains to make the lid fit down close as a skin, and line the interior with lead. Before Saint Winifred was carried back into the chapel for the thanksgiving Mass the lid was closed upon her, the catches secured, and at the end of the service the prior's seals were added to make all fast. They had her imprisoned, to be carried away into the alien land that desired her patronage. All the Welsh who could crowd into the chapel or cling close enough to the doorway to catch glimpses of the proceedings kept a silence uncannily perfect, their eyes following every move, secret eyes that expressed no resentment, but by their very attention, fixed and unwavering, implied an unreconciled opposition they were afraid to speak aloud.

'Now that this sacred duty is done,' said Father Huw, at once relieved and saddened, 'it is time to attend to the other duty which the saint herself has laid upon us, and bury Rhisiart honourably, with full absolution, in the grave she has bequeathed to him. And I call to mind, in the hearing of all, how great a blessing is thus bestowed, and how notable an honour.' It was as near as he would go to speaking out his own view of Rhisiart, and in this, at least, he had the sympathy of every Welshman there present.

That burial service was brief, and after it six of Rhisiart's oldest and most trusted servants took up the bier of branches, a little wilted now but still green, and carried it out to the graveside. The same slings which had lifted Saint Winifred waited to lower Rhisiart into the same bed.

Sioned stood beside her uncle, and looked all round her at the circle of her friends and neighbours, and unclasped the silver cross from her neck. She had so placed herself that Cadwallon and Peredur were close at her right hand, and it was simple and natural to turn towards them. Peredur had hung back throughout, never looking at her but when he was sure she was looking away, and when she swung round upon him suddenly he had no way of avoiding.

'One last gift I want to give to my father. And I would like you, Peredur, to be the one to give it. You have been like a son to him. Will you lay this cross on his breast, where the murderer's arrow pierced him? I want it to be buried with him. It is my farewell to him here, let it be yours, too.'

Peredur stood dumbstruck and aghast, staring from her still

and challenging face to the little thing she held out to him, in front of so many witnesses, all of whom knew him, all of whom were known to him. She had spoken clearly, to be heard by all. Every eye was on him, and all recorded, though without understanding, the slow draining of blood from his face, and his horror-stricken stare. He could not refuse what she asked. He could not do it without touching the dead man, touching the very place where death had struck him.

His hand came out with aching reluctance, and took the cross from her. To leave her thus extending it in vain was more than he could stand. He did not look at it, but only desperately at her, and in her face the testing calm had blanched into incredulous dismay, for now she believed she knew everything, and it was worse than anything she had imagined. But as he could not escape from the trap she had laid for him, neither could she release him. It was sprung, and now he had to fight his way out of it as best he could. They were already wondering why he made no move, and whispering together in concern at his hanging back.

He made a great effort, drawing himself together with a frantic briskness that lasted only a moment. He took a few irresolute steps towards the bier and the grave, and then baulked like a frightened horse, and halted again, and that was worse, for now he stood alone in the middle of the circle of witnesses, and could go neither forward nor back. Cadfael saw sweat break in great beads on his forehead and lip.

'Come, son,' said Father Huw kindly, the last to suspect evil, 'don't keep the dead waiting, and don't grieve too much for them, for that would be sin. I know, as Sioned has said, he was like another father to you, and you share her loss. So do we all.'

Peredur stood quivering at Sioned's name, and at the word 'father', and tried to go forward, and could not move. His feet would not take him one step nearer to the swathed form that lay by the open grave. The light of the sun on him, the weight of all eyes, bore him down. He fell on his knees suddenly, the cross still clutched in one hand, the other spread to hide his face.

'He cannot!' he cried hoarsely from behind the shielding palm.

'He cannot accuse me! I am not guilty of murder! What I did was done when Rhisiart was already dead!'

A great, gasping sigh passed like a sudden wind round the clearing and over the tangled grave, and subsided into a vast silence. It was a long minute before Father Huw broke it, for this was his sheep, not Prior Robert's, a child of his flock, and hitherto a child of grace, now stricken into wild self-accusation of some terrible sin not yet explained, but to do with violent death.

'Son Peredur,' said Father Huw firmly, 'you have not been charged with any ill-doing by any other but yourself. We are waiting only for you to do what Sioned has asked of you, for her asking was a grace. Therefore do her bidding, or speak out why you will not, and speak plainly.'

Peredur heard, and ceased to tremble. A little while he kneeled and gathered his shattered composure about him doggedly, like a cloak. Then he uncovered his face, which was pale, despairing but eased, no longer in combat with truth but consenting to it. He was a young man of courage. He got to his feet and faced them squarely.

'Father, I come to confession by constraint, and not gladly, and I am as ashamed of that as of what I have to confess. But it is not murder. I did not kill Rhisiart. I found him dead.'

'At what hour?' asked Brother Cadfael, wholly without right, but nobody questioned the interruption.

'I went out after the rain stopped. You remember it rained.' They remembered. They had good reason. 'It would be a little after noon. I was going up to the pasture our side of Bryn, and I found him lying on his face in that place where afterwards we all saw him. He was dead then, I swear it! And I was grieved, but also I was tempted, for there was nothing in this world I could do for Rhisiart, but I saw a way. . . .' Peredur swallowed and sighed, bracing his forehead against his fate, and went on. 'I saw a means of ridding myself of a rival. Of the favoured rival. Rhisiart had refused his daughter to Engelard, but Sioned had not refused him, and well I knew there was no hope for me, however her father urged her, while Engelard was there between us. Men might easily believe that Engelard should kill Rhisiart, if—if there was some proof....'

'But *you* did not believe it,' said Cadfael, so softly that hardly anyone noticed the interruption, it was accepted and answered without thought.

'No!' said Peredur almost scornfully. 'I knew him, he never would!'

'Yet you were willing he should be taken and accused. It was all one to you if it was death that removed him out of your way, so he was removed.'

'No!' said Peredur again, smouldering but aware that he was justly lashed. 'No, not that! I thought he would run, take himself away again into England, and leave us alone, Sioned and me. I never wished him worse than that. I thought, with him gone, in the end Sioned would do what her father had wished, and marry me. I could wait! I would have waited years....'

He did not say, but there were two there, at least, who knew, and remembered in his favour, that he had opened the way for Engelard to break out of the ring that penned him in, and deliberately let him pass, just as Brother John, with a better conscience, had frustrated the pursuit.

Brother Cadfael said sternly: 'But you went so far as to steal one of this unfortunate young man's arrows, to make sure all eyes turned on him.'

'I did not steal it, though no less discredit to me that I used it as I did. I was out with Engelard after game, not a week earlier, with Rhisiart's permission. When we retrieved our arrows, I took one of his by error among mine. I had it with me then.'

Peredur's shoulders had straightened, his head was up, his hands, the right still holding Sioned's cross, hung gently and resignedly at his sides. His face was pale but calm. He had got the worst of it off his back, after what he had borne alone these last days confession and penance were balm.

'Let me tell the whole of it, all the thing I did, that has made me a monster in my own eyes ever since. I will not make it less than it was, and it was hideous. Rhisiart was stabbed in the back, and the dagger withdrawn and gone. I turned him over on his back, and I turned that wound back to front, and I tell you, my hands burn now, but I did it. He was dead, he suffered nothing. I pierced my own flesh, not his. I could tell the line of the wound, for the dagger had gone right through him, though the breast wound was small. I took my own dagger, and opened the way for Engelard's arrow to follow, and I thrust it through and left it standing in him for witness. And I have not had one quiet moment, night or day,' said Peredur, not asking pity, rather grateful that now his silence was broken and his infamy known, and nothing more to hide, 'since I did this small, vile thing, and now I am glad it's out, whatever becomes of me. And at least grant me this, I did not make my trap in such a way as to accuse Engelard of shooting a man in the back! I knew him! I lived almost side by side with him since he came here a fugitive, we were of an age, we could match each other. I have liked him, hunted with him, fought with him, been jealous of him, even hated him because he was loved where I was not. Love makes men do terrible things,' said Peredur, not pleading, marvelling, 'even to their friends.'

He had created, all unconsciously, a tremendous hush all about him, of awe at his blasphemy, of startled pity for his desolation, of chastened wonder at their own misconceivings. The truth fell like thunder, subduing them all. Rhisiart had not been shot down with an arrow, but felled from behind at close quarters, out of thick cover, a coward's killing. Not saints, but men, deal in that kind of treachery.

Father Huw broke the silence. In his own province, where no alien dignitaries dared intrude, he grew taller and more secure in his gentle, neighbourly authority. And great violence had been done to what he knew to be right, and great requital was due from the sinner, and great compassion due to him.

'Son Peredur,' he said, 'you stand in dire sin, and cannot be excused. Such violation of the image of God, such misuse of a clean affection—for such I know you had with Rhisiart—and such malice towards an innocent man—for such you proclaimed Engelard—cannot go unpunished.'

'God forbid,' said Peredur humbly, 'that I should escape any part of what is due. I want it! I cannot live with myself if I have only this present self to live with!'

'Child, if you mean that, then give yourself into my hands, to be delivered up both to secular and religious justice. As to the law, I shall speak with the prince's bailiff. As to the penance due before God, that is for me as your confessor, and I require that you shall wait my considered judgment.'

'So I will, Father,' said Peredur. 'I want no unearned pardon. I take penance willingly.'

'Then you need not despair of grace. Go home now, and remain withindoors until I send for you.'

'I will be obedient to you in all things. But I have one prayer before I go.' He turned slowly and faced Sioned. She was standing quite still where the awful dread had fallen upon her, her hands clutched to her cheeks, her eyes fixed in fascination and pain upon the boy who had grown up as her playfellow. But the rigidity had ebbed out of her, for though he called himself a monster, he was not, after all, the monster she had briefly thought him. 'May I now do what you asked of me? I am not afraid now. He was a fair man always. He won't accuse me of more than my due.'

He was both asking her pardon and saying his farewell to any hope he had still cherished of winning her, for now that was irrevocably over. And the strange thing was that now he could approach her, even after so great an offence, without constraint, almost without jealousy. Nor did her face express any great heat or bitterness against him. It was thoughtful and intent.

'Yes,' she said, 'I still wish it.' If he had spoken the whole truth, and she was persuaded that he had, it was well that he should take his appeal to Rhisiart, in a form every man there would acknowledge. In otherworldly justice the body would clear him of the evil he had not committed, now that confession was made of what he had.

Peredur went forward steadily enough now, sank to his knees beside Rhisiart's body, and laid first his hand, and then Sioned's cross, upon the heart he had pierced, and no gush of blood sprang at his touch. And if there was one thing certain, it was that here was a man who did believe. He hesitated a moment, still kneeling, and then, feeling a need rather to give thanks for this acceptance than to make any late and unfitting display of affection, stooped and kissed the right hand that lay quiet over the left on Rhisiart's breast, their clasped shape showing through the close shroud. That done, he rose and went firmly away by the downhill path towards his father's house. The people parted to let him through in a great silence, and Cadwallon, starting out of a trance of unbelieving misery, lurched forward in haste and went trotting after his son.

CHAPTER NINE

The evening was drawing in by the time they had buried Rhisiart, and it was too late for Prior Robert and his companions to take their prize and leave at once for home, even if it had been a seemly thing to do, after all that had happened. Some ceremony was due to the community the saint was leaving, and the houses that had offered hospitality freely even to those who came to rob them.

'We will stay this night over, and sing Vespers and Compline in the church with you, and give due thanks,' said the prior. 'And after Compline one of us will again watch the night through with Saint Winifred, as is only proper. And should the prince's bailiff require that we stay longer, we will do as he asks. For there is still the matter of Brother John, who stands in contempt of the law, to our disgrace.'

'At present,' said Father Huw deprecatingly, 'the bailiff is giving his attention to the case of Rhisiart's murder. For though we have suffered many revelations in that matter, you see that we are no nearer knowing who is guilty. What we have seen today is one man who certainly is innocent of the crime, whatever his other sins may be.'

'I fear,' said Prior Robert with unwonted humility, 'that without ill intent we have caused you great grief and trouble here, and for that I am sorry. And greatly sorry for the parents of that sinful young man, who are suffering, I think, far worse than he, and without blame.'

'I am going to them now,' said Huw. 'Will you go on ahead, Father Prior, and sing Vespers for me? For I may be delayed some time. I must do what I can for this troubled household.'

The people of Gwytherin had begun to drift away silently by many paths, vanishing into the woods to spread the news of the day's happening to the far corners of the parish. In the long grass of the graveyard, trampled now by many feet, the dark, raw shape of Rhisiart's grave made a great scar, and two of his men were filling in the earth over him. It was finished. Sioned turned towards the gate, and all the rest of her people followed.

Cadfael fell in beside her as the subdued, straggling procession made its way home towards the village.

'Well,' he said resignedly, 'it was worth trying. And we can't say it got us nothing. At least we know now who committed the lesser crime, if we're very little nearer knowing who committed the greater. And we know why there were two, for they made no sense, being one and the same. And at any rate, we have shaken the devil off that boy's back. Are you quite revolted at what he did? As *he* is?'

'Strangely,' said Sioned, 'I don't believe I am. I was too sick with horror, that short time while I thought him the murderer. After that, it was simple relief that he was not. He has never gone short of anything he wanted, you see, until he wanted me.'

'It was a real wanting,' said Brother Cadfael, remembering long-past hungers of his own. 'I doubt if he'll ever quite get over it, though I'm pretty sure he'll make a sound marriage, and get handsome children like himself, and be very fairly content. He grew up today, she won't be disappointed, whoever she may be. But she'll never be Sioned.'

Her tired, woeful, discouraged face had softened and warmed, and suddenly she was smiling beside him, faintly but reassuringly. 'You are a good man. You have a way of reconciling people. But no need! Do you think I did not see how he dragged himself painfully to this afternoon's business, and has gone striding away with his head up to embrace his punishment? I might really have loved him a little, if there had been no Engelard. But only a little! He may do better than that.'

'You are a fine girl,' said Brother Cadfael heartily. 'If I had met you when I was thirty years younger, I should have made Engelard sweat for his prize. Peredur should be thankful even for such a sister. But we're no nearer knowing what we want and need to know.'

'And have we any more shafts left to loose?' she asked ruefully. 'Any more snares to set? At least we've freed the poor soul we caught in the last one.'

He was silent, glumly thinking.

'And tomorrow,' she said sadly, 'Prior Robert will take his saint and all his brothers, and you with them, and set out for home, and I shall be left with nobody to turn to here. Father Huw is as near a saint himself, in his small, confused way, as ever Winifred was, but no use to me. And Uncle Meurice is a gentle creature who knows about running a manor, but nothing about anything else, and wants no trouble and no exertion. And Engelard must go on hiding, as well you know. Peredur's plot against him is quite empty now, we all know it. But does that prove he did not kill my father, after a raging quarrel?'

'In the back?' said Cadfael, unguardedly indignant.

She smiled. 'All that proves is that you know him! Not everyone does. Some will be saying at this moment, perhaps, after all . . . that Peredur may have been right without even knowing it.'

He thought about it and was dismayed, for no question but she was right. What, indeed, did it prove if another man had wished to burden him with the guilt? Certainly not that the guilt was *not* his. Brother Cadfael confronted his own voluntarily assumed responsibility, and braced himself to cope with it.

'There is also Brother John to be considered,' said Sioned. It may well be that Annest, walking behind, had prodded her.

'I have not forgotten Brother John,' agreed Cadfael.

'But I think the bailiff well may have done. He would shut his eyes or look the other way, if Brother John left for Shrewsbury with the rest of you. He has troubles enough here, what does he want with alien trouble?'

'And if Brother John should seem to him to have left for Shrewsbury, he would be satisfied? And ask no questions about one more outlander taken up by a patron here?'

'I always knew you were quick,' said Sioned, brown and bright and animated, almost herself again. 'But would Prior Robert pursue him still, when he hears he's gone from custody? I don't see him as a forgiving man.'

'No, nor he is, but how would he set about it? The Benedictine order has no real hold in Wales. No, I think he'd let it ride, now he has what he came for. I'm more concerned for Engelard. Give me this one more night, child, and do this for me! Send your people home, and stay the night over with Annest at Bened's croft, and if God aids me with some new thought—for never forget God is far more deeply offended even than you or I by this great wrong!—I'll come to you there.'

'We'll do that,' said Sioned. 'And you'll surely come.'

They had slowed to let the cortège move well ahead of them, so that they could talk freely. They were approaching the gatehouse of Cadwallon's holding, and Prior Robert and his companions were far in front and had passed by the gate, bent upon singing Vespers in good time. Father Huw, issuing forth in haste and agitation in search of help, seemed relieved rather than dismayed to find only Cadfael within call. The presence of Sioned checked him to a decent walk and a measured tone, but did nothing to subdue the effect of his erected hair and frantic mien.

'Brother Cadfael, will you spare some minutes for this afflicted household? You have some skills with medicines, you may be able to advise....'

'His mother!' whispered Sioned in immediate reassurance. 'She weeps herself into a frenzy at everything that crosses her. I knew this would set her off. Poor Peredur, he has his penance already! Shall I come?'

'Better not,' he said as softly, and moved to meet Father Huw. Sioned was, after all, the innocent cause of Peredur's fall from grace, she would probably be the last person calculated to calm his mother's anguish. And Sioned understood him so, and went on, and left the matter to him, so calmly that it was clear she expected no tragic results from the present uproar. She had known Cadwallon's wife all her life, no doubt she had learned to treat her ups and downs as philosophically as Cadfael did Brother Columbanus' ecstasies and excesses. He never really hurt himself in his throes, either!

'Dame Branwen is in such a taking,' fluttered Father Huw distractedly, steering Cadfael in haste towards the open door of the hall. 'I fear for her wits. I've seen her upset before, and hard enough to pacify, but now, her only child, and such a shock. . . . Really, she may do herself an injury if we cannot quiet her.'

Dame Branwen was indeed audible before they even entered the small room where husband and son were trying to soothe her, against a tide of vociferous weeping and lamentation that all but deafened them. The lady, fat and fair and outwardly fashioned only for comfortable, shallow placidity, half-sat, half-lay on a couch, throwing her substantial person about in extravagant distress, now covering her silly, fond face, now throwing her arms abroad in sweeping gestures of desolation and despair, but never for one moment ceasing to bellow her sorrow and shame. The tears that flowed freely down her round cheeks and the shattering sobs that racked her hardly seemed to impede the flow of words that poured out of her like heavy rain.

Cadwallon on one side and Peredur on the other stroked and patted and comforted in vain. As often as the father tried to assert himself she turned on him with wild reproaches, crying that he had no faith in his own son, or he could never have believed such a terrible thing of him, that the boy was bewitched, under some spell that forced false confession out of him, that he ought to have stood up for him before everybody and prevented the tale from being accepted so lightly, for somewhere there was witchcraft in it. As often as Peredur tried to convince her he had told truth, that he was willing to make amends, and she must accept his word, she rounded on him with fresh outbursts of tears, screaming that her own son had brought dreadful disgrace upon himself and her, that she wondered he dare come near her, that she would never be able to lift up her head again, that he was a monster. . . .

As for poor Father Huw, when he tried to assert his spiritual authority and order her to submit to the force of truth and accept her son's act with humility, as Peredur himself had done in making full confession and offering full submission, she cried out that she had been a God-fearing and law-abiding woman all her life, and done everything to bring up her child in the same way, and she could not now accept his guilt as reflecting upon her.

'Mother,' said Peredur, haggard and sweating worse than when he faced Rhisiart's body, 'nobody blames you, and nobody will. What I did I did, and it's I who must abide the consequence, not you. There isn't a woman in Gwytherin won't feel for you.'

At that she let out a great wail of grief, and flung her arms about him, and swore that he should not suffer any grim penalties, that he was her own boy, and she would protect him. And when he extricated himself with fading patience, she screamed that he meant to kill her, the unfeeling wretch, and went off into peals of ear-piercing, sobbing laughter.

Brother Cadfael took Peredur firmly by the sleeve, and hauled him awav to the back of the room. 'Show a little sense, lad, and take yourself out of her sight, you're fuel to her fire. If nobody marked her at all she'd have stopped long ago, but now she's got herself into this state she's past doing that of her own accord. Did our two brothers stop in here, do you know, or go on with the prior?'

Peredur was shaking and tired out, but responded hopefully to this matter-of-fact treatment. 'They've not been here, or I should have seen them. They must have gone on to the church.'

Naturally, neither Columbanus nor Jerome would dream of absenting himself from Vespers on such a momentous day.

'Never mind, you can show me where they lodge. Columbanus brought some of my poppy syrup with him, in case of need, the phial should be there with his scrip, he'd hardly have it on him. And as far as I know, he's had no occasion to use it, his cantrips here in Wales have been of a quieter kind. We can find a use for it now.'

'What does it do?' asked Peredur, wide-eyed.

'It soothes the passions and kills pain—either of the body or the spirit.'

'I could use some of that myself,' said Peredur with a wry smile, and led the way out to one of the small huts that lined the stockade. The guests from Shrewsbury had been given the best lodging the house afforded, with two low brychans, and a small chest, with a rush lamp for light. Their few necessaries occupied almost no space, but each had a leather scrip to hold them, and both of these dangled from a nail in the timber wall. Brother Cadfael opened first one, and then the other, and in the second found what he was seeking.

He drew it out and held it up to the light, a small phial of greenish glass. Even before he saw the line of the liquid in it, its light weight had caused him to check and wonder. Instead of being full to the stopper with the thick, sweet syrup, the bottle was three-quarters empty.

Brother Cadfael stood stock-still for a moment with the phial in his hand, staring at it in silence. Certainly Columbanus might at some time have felt the need to forestall some threatening spiritual disturbance but Cadfael could recall no occasion when he had said any word to that effect, or shown any sign of the rosy, reassuring calm the poppies could bring. There was enough gone from the bottle to restore serenity three times over, enough to put a man to sleep for hours. And now that he came to think back, there had been at least one occasion when a man had slept away hours of the day, instead of keeping the watch he was set to keep. The day of Rhisiart's death Columbanus had failed of his duty, and confessed as much with heartfelt penitence. Columbanus, who had the syrup in his possession, and knew its use. . . .

'What must we do?' asked Peredur, uneasy in the silence. 'If it tastes unpleasant you'll have trouble getting her to drink it.'

'It tastes sweet.' But there was not very much of it left, a little reinforcement with something else soothing and pleasant might be necessary. 'Go and get a cup of strong wine, and we'll see how that goes down.'

They had taken with them a measure of wine that day, he remembered, the ration for the two of them, when they set off for the chapel. Columbanus had drawn and carried it. And a bottle of water for himself, since he had made an act of piety of renouncing wine until their mission was accomplished. Jerome had done well, getting a double ration.

Brother Cadfael stirred himself out of his furious thoughts

to deal with the immediate need. Peredur hurried to do his bidding, but brought mead instead of wine.

'She's more likely to drink it down before she thinks to be obstinate, for she likes it better. And it's stronger.'

'Good!' said Cadfael. 'It will hide the syrup better. And now, go somewhere quiet, and harden your heart and stop your ears and stay out of her sight, for it's the best thing you can do for her, and God knows the best for yourself, after such a day. And leave agonising too much over your sins, black as they are, there isn't a confessor in the land who hasn't heard worse and never turned a hair. It's a kind of arrogance to be so certain you're past redemption.'

The sweet, cloying drink swirled in the cup, the syrup unwinding into it in a long spiral that slowly melted and vanished. Peredur with shadowy eyes watched and was silent.

After a moment he said, very low: 'It's strange! I never could have done so shabbily by anyone I hated.'

'Not strange at all,' said Cadfael bluntly, stirring his potion. 'When harried, we go as far as we dare, and with those we're sure of we dare go very far, knowing where forgiveness is certain.'

Peredur bit his lip until it was biddable. '*Is* it certain?'

'As tomorrow's daylight, child! And now be off out of my way, and stop asking fool questions. Father Huw will have no time for you today, there's more important business waiting.'

Peredur went like a docile child, startled and comforted, and wherever he hid himself, he did it effectively, for Cadfael saw no more of him that evening. He was a good lad at heart, and this wild lunge of his into envy and meanness had brought him up short against an image of himself that he did not like at all. Whatever prayers Huw set him by way of penance were likely to hit heaven with the irresistible fervour of thunderbolts, and whatever hard labour he was given, the result was likely to stand solid as oak and last for ever.

Cadfael took his draught, and went back to where Dame Branwen was still heaving and quivering with uncontrollable sobs, by this time in genuine distress, exhausted by her efforts but unable to end them. He took advantage of her sheer weariness to present the cup to her as soon as he reached her side, and with abrupt authority that acted on her before she could muster the fibre of stubbornness.

'Drink this!' And automatically she drank it, half of it going down out of pure surprise, the second half because the first had taught her how dry and sore her throat was from all its exertions, and how smooth was the texture and how sweet the taste of this brew. The very act of swallowing it broke the frightening rhythm of the huge sighs that had convulsed her almost worse than the sobbing. Father Huw had time to mop his brow with a fold of his sleeve before she was able to resume her complaints. Even then, by comparison with what had gone before, they sounded half-hearted.

'We women, we mothers, we sacrifice our lives to bringing up children, and when they're grown they reward us by bringing disgrace upon us. What did I ever do to deserve this?'

'He'll do you credit yet,' said Cadfael cheerfully. 'Stand by him in his penance, but never try to excuse his sin, and he'll think the better of you for it.'

That went by her like the wind sighing at the time, though she may have remembered it later. Her voice declined gradually from its injured self-justification, dwindled into a half-dreamy monologue of grief, and took on at length a tone of warm and drowsy complacency, before it lapsed into silence. Cadwallon breathed deep and cautiously, and eyed his advisers.

'I should call her women and get her to bed,' said Cadfael. 'She'll sleep the night through, and it'll do her nothing but good.' And you more good still, he thought but did not say. 'Let your son rest, too, and never say another word about his trouble but by the way, like any other daily business, unless he speaks up first. Father Huw will take care of him faithfully.'

'I will,' said Huw. 'He's worth our efforts.'

Dame Branwen went amiably where she was led, and the house was wonderfully quiet. Cadfael and Huw went out together, pursued as far as the gate by Cadwallon's distracted gratitude. When they were well away from the holding, at the end of the stockade, the quietness of the dusk came down on them softly, a cloud descending delicately upon a cloud.

'In time for supper, if not for Vespers,' said Huw wearily. 'What should we have done without you, Brother Cadfael? I have no skill at all with women, they confuse me utterly. I marvel how you have learned to deal with them so ably, you, a cloistered brother.'

Cadfael thought of Bianca, and Arianna, and Mariam, and all the others, some known so briefly, all so well.

'Both men and women partake of the same human nature, Huw. We both bleed when we're wounded. That's a poor, silly woman, true, but we can show plenty of poor, silly men. There are women as strong as any of us, and as able.' He was thinking of Mariam—or was it of Sioned? 'You go to supper, Huw, and hold me excused, and if I can be with you before Compline, I will. I have some business first at Bened's smithy.'

The empty phial swung heavily in the pocket in his right sleeve, reminding him. His mind was still busy with the implications. Before ever he reached Bened's croft he had it clear in his mind what must be done, but was no nearer knowing how to set about it.

Cai was with Bened on the bench under the eaves, with a jug of rough wine between them. They were not talking, only waiting for him to appear, and there could be no reason for that, but that Sioned had told them positively that he would.

'A fine tangle it turns out,' said Bened, shaking his grizzled head. 'And now you'll be off and leave us holding it. No blame to you, you have to go where your duty is. But what are we to do about Rhisiart when you're gone? There's more than half this parish thinks your Benedictines have killed him, and the lesser half thinks some enemy here has taken the chance to blame you, and get clean away into cover. We were a peaceful community until you came, nobody looked for murder among us.'

'God knows we never meant to bring it,' said Cadfael. 'But there's still tonight before we go, and I haven't shot my last bolt yet. I must speak with Sioned. We've things to do, and not much time for doing them.'

'Drink one cup with us before you go in to her,' insisted Cai. 'That takes no time at all, and is a powerful aid to thought.'

They were seated all together, three simple, honest men, and the wine notably lower in the jug, when someone turned in at the gate, light feet came runing in great haste along the path, and suddenly there was Annest confronting them, skirts flying and settling about her like wings folding, her breath short and laboured, and excitement and consternation in her face. And ready to be indignant at the very sight of them sitting peacefully drinking wine.

'You'd better stir yourselves,' she said, panting and sparkling. 'I've been along to Father Huw's house to see what's going on there—Marared and Edwin between them have been keeping an eye open for us. Do you know who's there taking supper with the Benedictines? Griffith ap Rhys, the bailiff! And do you know where he's bound, afterwards? Up to our house, to take Brother John to prison!'

They were on their feet fast enough at this news, though Bened dared to question it. 'He can't be there! The last I heard of him he was at the mill.'

'And that was this morning, and I tell you now he's eating and drinking with Prior Robert and the rest. I've seen him with my own eyes, so don't tell me he can't be there. And here I find you sitting on your hams drinking, as though we had all the time in the world!'

'But *why* in such a hurry tonight?' persisted Bened. 'Did the prior send for him, because he's wanting to be away tomorrow?'

'The devil was in it! He came to Vespers just by way of compliment to Father Huw, and who should he find celebrating instead but Prior Robert, and the prior seized on it as just the chance he wanted, and has hung on to him and persuaded him Brother John must be taken in charge tonight, for he can't leave without knowing he's safely in the hands of the law. He says the bailiff should deal with him for the secular offence of hindering the arrest of a criminal, and when he's served his penalty he's to be sent back to Shrewsbury to answer for his defiance of discipline, or else the prior will send an escort to fetch him. And what could the bailiff do but fall in with it, when it was put to him like that? And here you sit—!'

'All right, girl, all right,' said Cai placatingly. 'I'm off this minute, and Brother John will be out of there and away to a safe place before ever the bailiff gets near us. I'll take one of your ponies, Bened....'

'Saddle another for me,' said Annest with determination. 'I'm coming with you.'

Cai went off at a jogtrot to the paddock, and Annest, drawing breath more easily now that the worst was told, drank off the wine he had left in his cup, and heaved a huge, resolute sigh.

'We'd better be out of here fast, for that young brother who looks after the horses now will be coming down after supper to get them. The prior means to be there to see John safe bound. "There's time yet before Compline," he said. He was complaining of wanting you, too, to interpret for him, they were managing lamely with only Latin between them. Dear God, what a day it's been!'

And what a night, thought Cadfael, it's still likely to be. 'What else was going on there?' he asked. 'Did you hear anything that might give me a light? For heaven knows I need one!'

'They were debating which one of them should watch the night through at the chapel. And that same young fair one, the one who has visions, up and prayed it might be him. He said he'd been unfaithful to his watch once, and longed still to make amends. And the prior said he might. That much I understood myself. All the prior's thinking about seems to be making all the trouble he can for John,' said Annest resentfully, 'or I should think he might have sent somebody else instead. That young brother—what is it you call him?'

'Columbanus,' said Brother Cadfael.

'That's him, Columbanus! He begins to put on airs as if he *owned* Saint Winifred. I don't want her to go away at all, but at least it was the prior who first thought of it, and now if there's a halo for anybody it's shifted to this other fellow's head.'

She did not know it, but she had indeed given Cadfael a light, and with every word she said it burned more steadily. 'So he's to be the one who watches the night through before the altar—and alone, is he?'

'So I heard.' Cai was coming with the ponies, at a gay trot out of the meadow. Annest rose eagerly and kilted her gown, knotting her girdle tightly about the broad pleat she drew up over her hips. 'Brother Cadfael, you don't think it wrong of me to love John? Or of him to love me? I don't care about the rest of them, but I should be sorry if *you* thought we were doing something wicked.'

Cai had not bothered with a saddle for himself, but had provided one for her. Quite simply and naturally Brother Cadfael cupped his hands for her foot, to give her a lift on to the pony's broad back, and the fresh scent of her linen and the smooth coolness of her ankle against his wrists as she mounted made one of the best moments of that interminably long and chaotic day. 'As long as I may live, girl,' he said, 'I doubt if I shall ever know two creatures with less wickedness between them. He made a mistake, and there should be provision for everybody to make one fresh start. I don't think he's making any mistake this time.'

He watched her ride away, setting an uphill pace to which Cai adapted himself goodhumouredly. They had a fair start, it would be ten minutes or more yet before Columbanus came to fetch the horses, and even then he had to take them back to the parsonage. It might be well to put in an appearance and go with Robert dutifully to interpret his fulminations, too, in which case there was need of haste, for he had now a great deal to say to Sioned, and this night's moves must be planned thoroughly. He withdrew into the croft as soon as Annest and Cai were out of sight, and Sioned came out of the shadows eagerly to meet him.

'I expected Annest to be here before you. She went to find out what's happening at Father Huw's. I thought best to stay out of sight. If people think I'm away home, so much the better. You haven't seen Annest?'

'I have, and heard all her news,' said Cadfael, and told her what was in the wind, and where Annest was gone. 'Never fear for John, they'll be there well ahead of any pursuit. We have other business, and no time to waste, for I shall be expected to ride with the prior, and it's as well I should be there to see fair play. If we manage our business as well as I fancy Cai and Annest will manage theirs, before morning we may know what we want to know.'

'You've found out something,' she said with certainty. 'You are changed. You are sure!'

He told her briefly all that had happened at Cadwallon's house, how he had brooded upon it without enlightenment as to how it was to be used, and how Annest in innocence had shown him. Then he told her what he required of her.

'I know you can speak English, you must use it tonight. This may be a more dangerous trap than any we've laid before, but I shall be close by. And you may call in Engelard, too, if he'll promise to stay close in cover. But, child, if you have any doubts or fears, if you'd rather let be, and have me try some other way, say so now, and so be it.'

'No,' she said, 'no doubts and no fears. I can do anything. I dare do anything.'

'Then sit down with me, and learn your part well, for we haven't long. And while we plan, can I ask you to bring me some bread and a morsel of cheese? For I've missed my supper.'

Prior Robert and Brother Richard rode into Rhisiart's yard with the prince's bailiff between them, his two henchmen and Brother Cadfael close behind, at about half past seven, in a mild twilight, with all the unhurried ceremony of the law, rather as if Griffith ap Rhys held his commission from Saint Benedict, and not from Owain Gwynedd. The bailiff was, in fact, more than a little vexed at this unfortunate encounter, which had left him no alternative but to comply with Robert's demands. An offence against Welsh law was alleged, and had been reported to him, and he was obliged to investigate it, where, considering the circumstances, he would much have preferred to pack all the Benedictine delegation back to Shrewsbury, and let them sort out their own grudges there, without bothering a busy man who had plenty of more important things on his mind. Unhappily

Cadwallon's villein, the long-legged fellow who had been brought down by Brother John, had given vociferous evidence in support of the accusation, or it would have been easier to ignore it.

There was no one on duty at the gate, which was strange, and as they rode in, a number of people seemed to be running hither and thither in a distracted way, as if something unforeseen had happened, and confused and conflicting orders were being given from several authorities at once. No groom ran to attend to them, either. Prior Robert was displeased. Griffith ap Rhys was mildly and alertly interested. When someone did take notice of them, it was a very handsome young person in a green gown, who came running with her skirts gathered in her hands, and her light-brown hair slipping out of its glossy coil to her shoulders.

'Oh, sirs, you must excuse us this neglect, we've been so disturbed! The gate-keeper was called away to help, and all the grooms are hunting. . . . But I'm ashamed to let our troubles cast a shadow over our hospitality. My lady's resting, and can't be disturbed, but I'm at your service. Will it please you light down? Shall I have lodgings made ready?'

'We don't propose to stay,' said Griffith ap Rhys, already suspecting this artless goodwill, and approving the way she radiated it. 'We came to relieve you of a certain young malefactor you've had in hold here. But it seems you've suffered some further calamity, and we should be sorry to add to your troubles, or disturb your lady, after the grievous day she's endured.'

'Madam,' said Prior Robert, civilly but officiously, 'you are addressing the prince's bailiff of Rhos, and I am the prior of Shrewsbury abbey. You have a brother of that abbey in confinement here, the royal bailiff is come to relieve you of his care.'

All of which Cadfael duly and solemnly translated for Annest's benefit, his face as guileless as hers.

'Oh, sir!' She opened her eyes wide and curtseyed deeply to Griffith and cursorily to the prior, separating her own from the alien. 'It's true we had such a brother here a prisoner. . . .'

'Had?' said Robert sharply, for once detecting the change of tense.

'Had?' said Griffith thoughtfully.

'He's gone, sir! You see what confusion he's left behind. This evening, when his keeper took him his supper, this brother struck him down with a board torn loose from the manger in his prison, and dropped the bolt on him and slipped away. It was some time before we knew. He must have climbed the wall, you see it is not so high. We have men out now looking for him in the woods, and searching everywhere here within. But I fear he's clean gone!'

Cai made his entrance at the perfect time, issuing from one of the barns with shaky steps, his head wreathed in a white cloth lightly dabbled with red.

'The poor man, the villain broke his head for him! It was some time before he could drag himself to the door and hammer on it, and make himself heard. There's no knowing how far the fellow may have got by now. But the whole household is out hunting for him.'

The bailiff, as in duty bound, questioned Cai, but gently and briefly, questioned all the other servants, who ran to make themselves useful and succeeded only in being magnificently confusing. And Prior Robert, burning with vengeful zeal, would have pressed them more strenuously but for the bailiff's presence and obvious prior right, and the brevity of the time at his disposal if he was to get back for Compline. In any case, it was quite clear that Brother John was indeed over the wall and clean gone. Most willingly they showed the place where he had been confined, and the manger from which he had ripped the board, and the board itself, artistically spattered at one end with spots of Cai's gore, though it may, of course, have been pigment borrowed from the butcher.

'It seems your young man has given us all the slip,' said Griffith, with admirable serenity for a man of law who has lost a malefactor. 'There's nothing more to be done here. They could hardly expect such violence from a Benedictine brother, it's no blame to them.'

With considerable pleasure Cadfael translated that neat little stab. It kindled a spark in the speaking eyes of the young person in green, and Griffith did not miss it. But to challenge it would have been folly. The clear brown eyes would have opened wide enough and deep enough to drown a man in their innocence. 'We'd best leave them in peace to mend their broken mangers and broken heads,' said Griffith, 'and look elsewhere for our fugitive.'

'The wretch compounds his offences,' said Robert, furious. 'But I cannot allow his villainy to disrupt my mission. I must set out for home tomorrow, and leave his capture to you.'

'You may trust me to deal properly with him,' said Griffith drily, 'when he is found.' If he laid the slightest of emphasis on the 'when', no one appeared to remark it but Cadfael and Annest. By this time Annest was quite satisfied that she liked this princely official, and could trust him to behave like a reasonable man who is not looking for trouble, or trying to make it for others as harmless as himself.

'And you will restore him to our house when he has purged his offences under Welsh law?'

'When he has done so,' said Griffith, decidedly with some stress this time on the 'when', 'you shall certainly have him back.'

With that Prior Robert had to be content, though his Norman spirit burned at being deprived of its rightful victim. And on the ride back he was by no means placated by Griffith's tales of the large numbers of fugitive outlaws who had found no difficulty in living wild in these forests, and even made friends among the country people, and been accepted into families, and even into respectability at last. It galled his orderly mind to think of insubordination mellowing with time and being tolerated and condoned. He was in no very Christian mood when he swept into Father Huw's church, only just in time for Compline.

They were all there but Brother John, the remaining five brethren from Shrewsbury and a good number of the people of Gwytherin, to witness the last flowering of Brother Columbanus' devotional gift of ecstasy, now dedicated entirely to Saint Winifred, his personal patroness who had healed him of madness, favoured him with her true presence in a dream, and made known her will through him in the matter of Rhisiart's burial.

For at the end of Compline, rising to go to his self-chosen vigil, Columbanus turned to the altar, raised his arms in a sweeping gesture, and prayed aloud in a high, clear voice that the virgin martyr would deign to visit him once more in his holy solitude, in the silence of the night, and reveal to him again the inexpressible bliss from which he had returned so reluctantly to this imperfect world. And more, that this time, if she found him worthy of translation out of the body, she would take him up living into that world of light. Humbly he submitted his will to endure here below, and do his duty in the estate assigned him, but rapturously he sent his desire soaring to the timber roof, to be uplifted out of the flesh, transported through death without dying, if he was counted ready for the assumption.

Everyone present heard, and trembled at such virtue. Everyone but Brother Cadfael, who was past trembling at the arrogance of man, and whose mind, in any case, was busy and anxious with other, though related, matters.

CHAPTER TEN

Brother Columbanus entered the small, dark, wood-scented chapel, heavy with the odours of centuries, and closed the door gently behind him, without latching it. There were no candles lighted, tonight, only the small oil-lamp upon the altar, that burned with a tall, unwavering flame from its floating wick. That slender, single turret of light cast still shadows all around, and being almost on a level with the bier of Saint Winifred, braced on trestles before it, made of it a black coffin shape, only touched here and there with sparkles of reflected silver.

Beyond the capsule of soft golden light all was darkness, perfumed with age and dust. There was a second entrance, from the minute sacristy that was no more than a porch beside the altar, but no draught from that or any source caused the lamp-flame to waver even for an instant. There might have been no storms of air or spirit, no winds, no breath of living creature, to disturb the stillness.

Brother Columbanus made his obeisance to the altar, briefly and almost curtly. There was no one to see, he had come alone, and neither seen nor heard any sign of another living soul in the graveyard or the woods around. He moved the second prayer-desk aside, and set the chosen one squarely in the centre of the chapel, facing the bier. His behaviour was markedly more practical and moderate than when there were people by to see him, but did not otherwise greatly differ. He had come to watch out the night on his knees, and he was prepared to do so, but there was no need to labour his effects until morning, when his fellows would come to take Saint Winifred in reverent procession on the first stage of her journey. Columbanus padded the prie-dieu for his knees with the bunched skirts of his habit, and made himself as comfortable as possible with his gowned arms broadly folded as a pillow for his head. The umber darkness was scented and heavy with the warmth of wood, and the night outside was not cold. Once he had shut out the tiny, erect tower of light and the few bright surfaces from which it was reflected, the drowsiness he was inviting came stealing over him in long, lulling waves until it washed over his head, and he slept.

It seemed, after the fashion of sleep, no time at all before he was startled awake, but in fact it was more than three hours, and midnight was approaching, when his slumbers began to be strangely troubled with a persistent dream that someone, a woman, was calling him by name low and clearly, and over and over and over again: 'Columbanus. . . . Columbanus . . .' with inexhaustible and relentless patience. And he was visited, even in sleep, by a sensation that this woman had all the time in the world, and was willing to go on calling for ever, while for him there was no time left at all, but he must awake and be rid of her.

He started up suddenly, stiff to the ends of fingers and toes, ears stretched and eyes staring wildly, but there was the enclosing capsule of mild darkness all about him as before, and the reliquary dark, too, darker than before, or so it seemed, as if the flame of the lamp, though steady, had subsided, and was now more than half hidden behind the coffin. He had forgotten to check the oil. Yet he knew it had been fully supplied when last he left it, after Rhisiart's burial, and that was only a matter of hours ago.

It seemed that of all his senses, hearing had been the last to return to him, for now he was aware, with a cold crawling of fear along his skin, that the voice of his dream was still with him, and had been with him all along, emerging from dream into reality without a break. Very soft, very low, very deliberate, not a whisper, but the clear thread of a voice, at once distant and near, insisting unmistakably: 'Columbanus . . . Columbanus . . . Columbanus, what have you done?'

Out of the reliquary the voice came, out of the light that was dwindling even as he stared in terror and unbelief.

'Columbanus, Columbanus, my false servant, who blasphemes

against my will and murders my champions, what will you say in your defence to Winifred? Do you think you can deceive me as you deceive your prior and your brothers?'

Without haste, without heat, the voice issued forth from the darkening apse of the altar, so small, so terrible, echoing eerily out of its sacred cave.

'You who claim to be my worshipper, you have played me false like the vile Cradoc, do you think you will escape his end? I never wished to leave my resting-place here in Gwytherin. Who told you otherwise but your own devil of ambition? I laid my hand upon a good man, and sent him out to be my champion, and this day he has been buried here, a martyr for my sake. The sin is recorded in heaven, there is no hiding-place for you. Why,' demanded the voice, cold, peremptory and menacing in its stillness, 'have you killed my servant Rhisiart?'

He tried to rise from his knees, and it was as if they were nailed to the wood of the prie-dieu. He tried to find a voice, and only a dry croaking came out of his stiff throat. She could not be there, there was no one there! But the saints go where they please, and reveal themselves to whom they please, and sometimes terribly. His cold fingers clutched at the desk, and felt nothing. His tongue, like an unplaned splinter of wood, tore the roof of his mouth when he fought to make it speak.

'There is no hope for you but in confession, Columbanus, murderer! Speak! Confess!'

'No!' croaked Columbanus, forcing out words in frantic haste. 'I never touched Rhisiart! I was here in your chapel, holy virgin, all that afternoon, how could I have harmed him? I sinned against you, I was faithless, I slept. . . . I own it! Don't lay a greater guilt on me. . . .'

'It was not you who slept,' breathed the voice, a tone higher, a shade more fiercely, 'liar that you are! Who carried the wine? Who poisoned the wine, causing even the innocent to sin? Brother Jerome slept, not you! *You* went out into the forest and waited for Rhisiart, and struck him down.'

'No . . . no, I swear it!' Shaking and sweating, he clawed at the desk before him, and could get no leverage with his palsied hands to prise himself to his feet and fly from her. How can you fly from beings who are everywhere and see everything? For nothing mortal could possibly know what this being knew. 'No, it's all wrong, I am misjudged! I was asleep here when Father Huw's messenger came for us. Jerome shook me awake. . . . The messenger is witness. . . .'

'The messenger never passed the doorway. Brother Jerome was already stirring out of his poisoned sleep, and went to meet him. As for you, you feigned and lied, as you feign and lie now. Who was it brought the poppy syrup? Who was it knew its use? You were pretending sleep, you lied even in confessing to sleep, and Jerome, as weak as you are wicked, was glad enough to think you could not accuse him, not even seeing that you were indeed accusing him of worse, of *your* act, of *your* slaying! He did not know you lied, and could not charge you with it. But *I* know, and I do charge you! And my vengeance loosed upon Cradoc may also be loosed upon you, if you lie to me but once more!'

'No!' he shrieked, and covered his face as though she dazzled him with lightnings, though only a thin, small, terrible sound threatened him. 'No, spare! I am not lying! Blessed virgin, I have been your true servant . . . I have tried to do your will . . . I know nothing of this! I never harmed Rhisiart! I never gave poisoned wine to Jerome!'

'Fool!' said the voice in a sudden loud cry. 'Do you think you can deceive *me? Then what is this?*'

There was a sudden silvery flash in the air before him, and something fell and smashed with a shivering of glass on the floor just in front of the desk, spattering his knees with sharp fragments and infinitesimal, sticky drops, and at the same instant the flame of the lamp died utterly, and black darkness fell.

Shivering and sick with fear, Columbanus groped forward along the earth floor, and slivers of glass crushed and stabbed under his palms, drawing blood. He lifted one hand to his face, whimpering, and smelled the sweet, cloying scent of the poppy syrup, and knew that he was kneeling among the fragments of the phial he had left safe in his scrip at Cadwallon's house.

It was no more than a minute before the total darkness eased, and there beyond the bier and the altar the small, oblong shape of the window formed in comparative light, a deep, clear sky, moonless but starlit. Shapes within the chapel again loomed very dimly, giving space to his sickening terror. There was a figure standing motionless between him and the bier.

It took a little while for his eyes to accustom themselves to the dimness, and assemble out of it this shadowy, erect pallor, a woman lost in obscurity from the waist down, but head and shoulders feebly illuminated by the starlight from the altar window. He had not seen her come, he had heard nothing. She had appeared while he was dragging his torn palm over the shards of glass, and moaning as if at the derisory pain. A slender, still form swathed from head to foot closely in white, Winifred in her grave clothes, long since dust, a thin veil covering her face and head, and her arm outstretched and pointing at him.

He shrank back before her, scuffling abjectly backwards along the floor, making feeble gestures with his hands to fend off the very sight of her. Frantic tears burst out of his eyes, and frantic words from his lips.

'It was for you! It was for you and for my abbey! I did it for the glory of our house! I believed I had warranty—from you and from heaven! He stood in the way of God's will! He would not let you go. I meant only rightly when I did what I did!'

'Speak plainly,' said the voice, sharp with command, 'and say out what you did.'

'I gave the syrup to Jerome—in his wine—and when he was asleep I stole out to the forest path, and waited for Rhisiart. I followed him. I struck him down. . . . Oh, sweet Saint Winifred, don't let me be damned for striking down the enemy who stood in the way of blessedness. . . .'

'Struck in the back!' said the pale figure, and a sudden cold gust of air swept over her and shuddered in her draperies, and surging across the chapel, blew upon Columbanus and chilled him to the bone. As if she had touched him! And she was surely a pace nearer, though he had not seen her move. 'Struck in the back, as mean cowards and traitors do! Own it! Say it all!'

'In the back!' babbled Columbanus, scrambling back from her like a broken animal, until his shoulders came up against the wall, and he could retreat no farther. 'I own it. I confess it all! Oh, merciful saint, you know all, and I cannot hide from you! Have pity on me! Don't destroy me! It was all for you, I did it for you!'

'You did it for yourself,' charged the voice, colder than ice and burning like ice. 'You who would be master of whatever order you enter, you with your ambitions and stratagems, you setting out wilfully to draw to yourself all the glory of possessing me, to work your way into the centre of all achievements, to show as the favourite of heaven, the paragon of piety, to elbow Brother Richard out of his succession to your prior, and if you could, the prior out of his succession to your abbot. You with your thirst to become the youngest head under a mitre in this or any land! I know you, and I know your kind. There is no way too ruthless for you, provided it leads to power.'

'No, no!' he panted, bracing himself back against the wall, for certainly she was advancing upon him, and now in bitter, quiet fury, jetting menace from her outstretched finger-tips. 'It was all for you, only for you! I believed I was doing your will!'

'My will to evil?' the voice rose into a piercing cry, sharp as a dagger. 'My will to murder?'

She had taken one step too many. Columbanus broke in frenzied fear, clawed himself upright by the wall, and struck out with both hands, beating at her blindly to fend her off from touching, and uttering thin, babbling cries as he flailed about him. His left hand caught in her draperies and dragged the veil from her face and head. Dark hair fell round her shoulders. His fingers made contact with the curve of a smooth, cool cheek, cool, but not cold, smooth with the graceful curves of firm young flesh, where in his sick horror he had expected to plunge his hand into the bony hollows of a skull.

He uttered a scream that began in frantic terror and ended in soaring triumph. The hand that had shrunk from contact turned suddenly to grasp hold, knotting strong fingers in the dark tangle of hair. He was very quick, Columbanus. It took him no more than the intake of a breath to know he had a flesh-and-blood woman at the end of his arm, and scarcely longer to know who she must be, and what she had done to him, with this intolerable trap in which she had caught him. And barely another breath to consider that she was here alone, and to all appearances had set her trap alone, and if she survived he was lost, and if she did not survive, if she vanished—there was plenty left of the night!—he was safe, and still in command of all this expedition, and inheritor of all its glory.

It was his misfortune that Sioned was almost as quick in the uptake as he. In a darkness in which vision hardly helped or hindered, she heard the great, indrawn breath that released him from the fear of hell and heaven together, and felt the wave of animal anger that came out from him like a foul scent, almost as sickening as the odour of his fear. She sprang back from it by instinct, and repeated the lunge of intent, dragging herself out of his grasp at the price of a few strands of hair. But his clawing hand, cheated, loosed the fragments and caught again at the linen sheet that draped her, and that would not tear so easily. She swung round to her left, to put as much distance as she could between her body and his right hand, but she saw him lunge into the breast of his habit, and saw the brief, sullen flash of the steel as he whipped it out and followed her swing, hacking into dimness. The same dagger, she thought, swooping beneath its first blind stab, that killed my father.

Somewhere a door had opened fully on the night, for the wind blew through the chapel suddenly, and sandalled feet thudded in with the night air, a thickset, powerful body driving the draught before it. A loud voice thundered warning. Brother Cadfael erupted into the chapel from the sacristy like a bolt from a crossbow, and drove at full speed into the struggle.

Columbanus was in the act of striking a second time, and with his left hand firmly clutching the linen sheet wound about Sioned's body. But she was whirling round away from him to unloose those same folds that held her, and the blow that was meant for her heart only grazed painfully down her left forearm. Then his grip released her, and she fell back against the wall, and Columbanus was gone, hurtling out at the door in full flight, and Brother Cadfael was embracing her with strong, sustaining arms, and upbraiding her with a furious, bracing voice, while he held her in a bear's hug, and felt at her as tenderly and fervently as a mother.

'For God's sake, fool daughter, why did you get within his reach? I *told* you, keep the bier between you and him . . . !'

'Get after him,' shouted Sioned wrathfully, 'do you want him clean away? I'm sound enough, go get *him*! He killed my father!'

They headed for the door together, but Cadfael was out of it first. The girl was strong, vigorous and vengeful, a Welshwoman to the heart, barely grazed, he knew the kind. The wind of action blew her, she felt no pain and was aware of no effusion of blood, blood she wanted, and with justification. She was close on his heels as he rolled like a thunderbolt down the narrow path through the graveyard towards the gate. The night was huge, velvet, sewn with stars, their veiled and delicate light barely casting shadows. All that quiet space received and smothered the sound of their passage, and smoothed the stillness of the night over it.

Out of the bushes beyond the graveyard wall a man's figure started, tall, slender and swift, leaping to block the gateway. Columbanus saw him, and baulked for a moment, but Cadfael was running hard behind him, and the next instant the fugitive made up his mind and rushed on, straight at the shadow that moved to intercept him. Hard on Cadfael's heels, Sioned suddenly shrieked: 'Take care, Engelard! He has a dagger!'

Engelard heard her, and swerved to the right at the very moment of collision, so that the stroke meant for his heart only ripped a fluttering ribbon of cloth from his sleeve. Columbanus would have bored his way past at speed, and run for the cover of the woods, but Engelard's long left arm swept round hard into the back of his neck, sending him off-balance for a moment, though he kept his feet, and Engelard's right fist got a tight grip on the flying cowl, and twisted. Half-strangled, Columbanus whirled again and struck out with the knife, and this time

Engelard was ready for the flash, and took the thrusting wrist neatly in his left hand. They swayed and wrestled together, feet braced in the grass, and they were very fairly matched if both had been armed. That unbalance was soon amended. Engelard twisted at the wrist he held, ignoring the clawing of Columbanus' free hand at his throat, and the numbed fingers opened at last and let the dagger fall. Both lunged for it, but Engelard scooped it up and flung it contemptuously aside into the bushes, and grappled his opponent with his bare hands. The fight was all but over. Columbanus hung panting and gasping, both arms pinned, looking wildly round for a means of escape and finding none.

'Is this the man?' demanded Engelard.

Sioned said: 'Yes. He has owned to it.'

Engelard looked beyond his prisoner then for the first time, and saw her standing in the soft starlight that was becoming to their accustomed eyes almost as clear as day. He saw her dishevelled and bruised and gazing with great, shocked eyes, her left arm gashed and bleeding freely, though the cut was shallow. He saw smears of her blood dabbling the white sheet in which she was swathed. By starlight there is little or no colour to be seen, but everything that Engelard saw at that moment was blood-red. This was the man who had murdered in coward's fashion Engelard's well-liked lord and good friend—whatever their differences!—and now he had tried to kill the daughter as he had killed the father.

'You dared, you dared touch her!' blazed Engelard in towering rage. 'You worthless cloister rat!' And he took Columbanus by the throat and hoisted him bodily from the ground, shook him like the rat he had called him, cracked him in the air like a poisonous snake, and when he had done with him, flung him down at his feet in the grass.

'Get up!' he growled, standing over the wreckage. 'Get up now, and I'll give you time to rest and breathe, and then you can fight a man to the death, without a dagger in your hand, instead of writhing through the undergrowth and stabbing him in the back, or carving up a defenceless girl. Take your time, I can wait to kill you till you've got your breath.'

Sioned flew to him, breast to breast, and held him fast in her arms, pressing him back. 'No! Don't touch him again! I don't want the law to have any hold on *you*, even the slenderest.'

'He tried to kill you—you're hurt. . . .'

'No! It's nothing . . . only a cut. It bleeds, but it's nothing!'

His rage subsided slowly, shaking him. He folded his arms round her and held her to him, and with a disdainful but restrained jab of a toe urged his prostrate enemy again: 'Get up! I won't touch you. The law can have you, and welcome!'

Columbanus did not move, not by so much as the flicker of an eyelid or the twitching of a finger. All three of them stood peering down at him in sudden silence, aware how utterly still he was, and how rare such stillness is among living things.

'He's foxing,' said Engelard scornfully, 'for fear of worse, and by way of getting himself pitied. I've heard he's a master at that.'

Those who feign sleep and hear themselves talked of, usually betray themselves by some exaggeration of innocence. Columbanus lay in a stillness that was perfectly detached and indifferent.

Brother Cadfael knelt down beside him, shook him by the shoulder gently, and sat back with a sharp sigh at the broken movement of the head. He put a hand inside the breast of the habit, and stooped to the parted lips and wide nostrils. Then he took the head between his hands, and gently turned and tilted it. It rolled back, as he released it, into a position so improbable that they knew the worst even before Cadfael said, quite practically: 'You'd have waited a long time for him to get his breath back, my friend. You don't know your own strength! His neck is broken. He's dead.'

Sobered and shocked, they stood dumbly staring down at what they had hardly yet recognised for disaster. They saw a regrettable accident which neither of them had ever intended, but which was, after all, a kind of justice. But Cadfael saw a scandal that could yet wreck their young lives, and others, too, for without Columbanus alive, and forced by two respected witnesses to repeat his confession, how strong was all their proof against him? Cadfael sat back on his heels, and thought. It was startling to realise, now that the unmoved silence of the night came down on them again, how all this violence and passion had passed with very little noise, and no other witnesses. He listened, and no stirring of foot or wing troubled the quiet. They were far enough away from any dwelling, not a soul had been disturbed. That, at least, was time gained.

'He can't be dead,' said Engelard doubtfully. 'I barely handled him at all. Nobody dies as easily as that!'

'This one did. And now what's to be done? I hadn't bargained for this.' He said it not complainingly, but as one pointing out that further urgent planning would now be necessary, and they had better keep their minds flexible.

'Why, what can be done?' To Engelard it was simple, though troublesome. 'We shall have to call up Father Huw and your prior, and tell them exactly what's happened. What else can we do? I'm sorry to have killed the fellow, I never meant to, but I can't say I feel any *guilt* about it.' Nor did he expect any blame. The truth was always the best way. Cadfael felt a reluctant affection for such innocence. The world was going to damage it sooner or later, but one undeserved accusation had so far failed even to bruise it, he still trusted men to be reasonable. Cadfael doubted if Sioned was so sure. Her silence was anxious and foreboding. And her grazed arm was still oozing blood. First things first, and they might as well be sensibly occupied while he thought.

'Here, make yourself useful! Help me get this carrion back into the chapel, out of sight. And, Sioned, find his dagger, we can't leave that lying about to bear witness. Then let's get that arm of yours washed and bound up. There's a stream at the back of the hawthorn hedge, and of linen we've plenty.'

They had absolute faith in him, and did his bidding without question, though Engelard, once he had assured himself that Sioned was not gravely hurt, and had himself carefully and deftly bandaged her scratch, returned to his dogged opinion that their best course was to tell the whole story, which could hardly cast infamy upon anyone but Columbanus. Cadfael busied himself with flint and tinder until he had candles lighted, and the lamp refilled, from which he himself had drained a judicious quantity of oil before Sioned took her place under the draperies of the saint's catafalque.

'You think,' he said at length, 'that because you've done nothing wrong, and we've all of us banded together to expose a wrong, that the whole world will be of the same opinion, and honestly come out and say so. Child, I know better! The only proof we have of Columbanus' guilt is his confession, which both of us here heard. Or rather, the only proof we had, for we no longer have even that. Alive, we two could have forced the truth out of him a second time. Dead, he's never going to give us that satisfaction. And without that, our position is vulnerable enough. Make no mistake, if we accuse him, if this fearful scandal breaks, to smirch the abbey of Shrewsbury, and all the force of the Benedictine order, backed here by the bishop and the prince, take my word for it, all the forces of authority will band together to avert the disaster, and nobody, much less a friendless outlander, will be allowed to stand in the way. They simply can't afford to have their acquisition of Saint Winifred called in question and brought to disrepute. Rather than that, they'll call this an outlaw killing by a desperate man, a fugitive already, wanted for another crime, and trying to escape both together. A pity,' he said, 'I ever suggested that Sioned should call you in to wait in reserve, in case we had trouble. But none of this is your fault, and I won't have you branded with it. I made the plot, and I must unravel it. But give up all idea of going straight to Father Huw, or the bailiff, or anyone else, with the true story. Far better use the rest of this night to rearrange matters to better advantage. Justice can be arrived at by more routes than one.'

'They wouldn't dare doubt Sioned's word,' said Engelard stoutly.

'Fool boy, they'd say that Sioned, for love's sake, might go as far aside from her proper nature as Peredur did. And as for me, my influence is small enough, and I am not interested in protecting only myself, but as many of those in this coil as I can reach. Even my prior, who is arrogant and rigid, and to tell the truth, sometimes rather stupid, but not a murderer and not a liar. And my order, which has not deserved Columbanus. Hush, now, and let me think! And while I do, you can be clearing away the remains of the syrup bottle. This chapel must be as neat and quiet tomorrow as before we ever brought our troubles into it.'

Obediently they went about removing the traces of the night's alarms, and let him alone until he should have found them a way through the tangle.

'And I wonder, now,' he said at length, 'what made you improve on all the speeches I made for you, and put such fiery words into Saint Winifred's mouth? What put it into your head to say that you'd never wanted to leave Gwytherin, and did not want it now? That Rhisiart was not merely a decent, honest man, but your chosen champion?'

She turned and looked at him in astonishment and wonder. 'Did I say that?'

'You did, and very well you delivered it, too. And very proper and apt it sounded, but I think we never rehearsed it so. Where did you get the words?'

'I don't know,' said Sioned, puzzled. 'I don't remember what I did say. The words seemed to come freely of themselves, I only let them flow.'

'It may be,' said Engelard, 'that the saint was taking her chance when it offered. All these strangers having visions and ecstasies, and interpreting them to suit themselves, yet nobody ever really asked Saint Winifred what *she* wanted. They all claimed they knew better than she did.'

'Out of the mouths of innocents!' said Cadfael to himself, and pondered the road that was gradually opening before his mind's eye. Of all the people who ought to be left happy with the outcome, Saint Winifred should surely come first. Aim, he thought, at making everybody happy, and if that's within reach, why stir up any kind of unpleasantness? Take Columbanus, for instance! Only a few hours ago at Compline he prayed aloud before us all that if the virgin deemed him worthy, he might be taken up out of this world this very night, translated instantly out of the body. Well, that was one who got his wish! Maybe he'd have withdrawn his request if he'd known it was going to be taken up so literally, for its purpose was rather to reflect incomparable holiness upon him while he was still alive to enjoy it. But saints have a right to suppose that their devotees mean what they say, and bestow gifts accordingly. And if the saint has really spoken through Sioned, he thought—and who am I to question it?—if she really wants to stay here in her own village, which is a reasonable enough wish, well, the plot where she used to sleep has been newly turned today, no one will notice anything if it's turned again tonight.

'I believe,' said Sioned, watching him with the first faint smile, wan but trusting, 'you're beginning to see your way.'

'I believe,' said Cadfael, 'I'm beginning to see *our* way, which is more to the point. Sioned, I have something for you to do, and you need not hurry, we have work to do here while you're away. Take that sheet of yours, and go and spread it under the may trees in the hedge, where they're beginning to shed, but not yet brown. Shake the bushes and bring us a whole cloud of petals. The last time she visited him, it was with wondrous sweet odours and a shower of white flowers. Bring the one, and we shall have the other.'

Confidently, understanding nothing as yet, she took the linen sheet from which she had unwound herself as from a shroud, and went to do his bidding.

'Give me the dagger,' said Cadfael briskly when she was gone. He wiped the blade on the veil Columbanus had torn from Sioned's head, and moved the candles so that they shone upon the great red seals that closed Winifred's reliquary. 'Thank God he didn't bleed,' he said. 'His habit and clothes are unmarked. Strip him!'

And he fingered the first seal, nodded satisfaction at its fatness and the thinness and sharpness of the dagger, and thrust the tip of the blade into the flame of the lamp.

Long before daylight they were ready. They walked down all three together from the chapel towards the village, and separated at the edge of the wood, where the shortest path turned off uphill towards Rhisiart's holding.

Sioned carried with her the blood-stained sheet and veil, and the fragments of glass they had buried in the forest. A good thing the servants who had filled in Rhisiart's grave had left their spades on the scene, meaning to tidy the mound next day. That had saved a journey to borrow without leave, and a good hour of time.

'There'll be no scandal,' said Cadfael, when they halted at the place where the paths divided. 'No scandal, and no accusations. I think you may take him home with you, but keep him out of sight until we're gone. There'll be peace when we're gone. And you needn't fear that the prince or his bailiff will ever proceed further against Engelard, any more than against John. I'll speak a word in Peredur's ear, Peredur will speak it into the bailiff's ear, the bailiff will speak it into Owain Gwynedd's ear—Father Huw we'll leave out of it, no need to burden his conscience, the good, simple man. And if the monks of Shrewsbury are happy, and the people of Gwytherin are happy—for they'll hear the whisper fast enough—why should anyone want to upset such a satisfactory state of affairs, by speaking the word aloud? A wise prince—and Owain Gwynedd seems to me very wise—will let well alone.'

'All Gwytherin,' said Sioned, and shivered a little at the thought, 'will be there in the morning to watch you take the reliquary away.'

'So much the better, we want all the witnesses we can have, all the emotion, all the wonder. I am a great sinner,' said Cadfael philosophically, 'but I feel no weight. Does the end justify the means, I wonder?'

'One thing I know,' she said. 'My father can rest now, and that he owes to you. And I owe you that and more. When I first came down to you out of the tree—you remember?—I thought you would be like other monks, and not want to look at me.'

'Child, I should have to be out of my wits, not to want to look at you. I've looked so attentively, I shall remember you all my life. But your love, my children, and how you manage it—with that I can't help you.'

'No need,' said Engelard. 'I am an outlander, with a proper agreement. That agreement can be dissolved by consent, and I can be a free man by dividing all my goods equally with my lord, and now Sioned *is* my lord.'

'And then there can no man prevent,' said Sioned, 'if I choose to endow him with half *my* goods, as is only fair. Uncle Meurice won't stand in our way. And it won't even be hard for him to justify. To marry an heiress to an outlander servant is one thing, to marry her to a free man and heir to a manor, even if it's in England and can't be claimed for a while, is quite another.'

'Especially,' said Cadfael, 'when you already know he's the best hand with cattle in the four cantrefs.'

It seemed that those two, at any rate, were satisfied. And Rhisiart in his honoured grave would not grudge them their happiness. He had not been a grudging man.

Engelard, no talker, said his thanks plainly and briefly when they parted. Sioned turned back impulsively, flung her arms round Cadfael's neck, and kissed him. It was their farewell, for he had thought it best to advise them not to show themselves at the chapel again. It was a wry touch that she smelled so heady and sweet with flowering may, and left so saintly a fragrance in his arms when she was gone.

On his way down to the parsonage Cadfael made a detour to the mill-pond, and dropped Columbanus' dagger into the deepest of the dark water. What a good thing, he thought, making for the bed he would occupy for no more than an hour or so before Prime, that the brothers who made the reliquary were such meticulous craftsmen, and insisted on lining it with lead!

CHAPTER ELEVEN

Prior Robert arose and went to the first service of the day in so great content with his success that he had almost forgotten about the escape of Brother John, and even when he remembered that one unsatisfactory particular, he merely put it away in the back of his mind, as something that must and would be dealt with faithfully in good time, but need not cloud the splendour of this occasion. And it was indeed a clear, radiant morning, very bright and still, when they came from the church and turned towards the old graveyard and the chapel, and all the congregation fell in at their heels and followed, and along the way others appeared silently from every path, and joined the procession, until it was like some memorable pilgrimage. They came to Cadwallon's gatehouse, and Cadwallon came out to join them, and Peredur, who had hung back in strict obedience to his orders to remain at home until his penance was appointed, was kindly bidden forth by Father Huw, and even smiled upon, though as saint to sinner, by Prior Robert. Dame Branwen, if not still asleep, was no doubt recuperating after her vapours. Her menfolk were not likely to be very pressing in their invitations to her to go with them, and perhaps she was still punishing them by withdrawing herself. Either way, they were relieved of her presence.

The order of procession having only a loose form, brothers and villagers could mingle, and greet, and change partners as they willed. It was a communal celebration. And that was strange, considering the contention that had threatened it for some days. Gwytherin was playing it very cautiously now, intent on seeing everything and giving nothing away.

Peredur made his way to Cadfael's side, and remained there thankfully, though silently. Cadfael asked after his mother, and the young man coloured and frowned, and then smiled guiltily like a child, and said that she was very well, a little dreamy still, but placid and amiable.

'You can do Gwytherin and me a good service, if you will,' said Brother Cadfael, and confided to his ear the word he had in mind to pass on to Griffith ap Rhys.

'So that's the way it is!' said Peredur, forgetting altogether about his own unforgivable sins. His eyes opened wide. He whistled softly. 'And that's the way you want it left?'

'That's the way it is, and that's the way I want it left. Who loses? And everyone gains. We, you, Rhisiart, Saint Winifred —Saint Winifred most of all. And Sioned and Engelard, of course,' said Cadfael firmly, probing the penitent to the heart.

'Yes . . . I'm glad for them!' said Peredur, a shade too vehemently. His head was bent, and his eyelids lowered. He was not yet as glad as all that, but he was trying. The will was there. 'Given a year or two longer, nobody's going to remember about the deer Engelard took. In the end he'll be able to go back and forth to Cheshire if he pleases, and he'll have lands when his father dies. And once he's no longer reckoned outlaw and felon he'll have no more troubles. I'll get your word to Griffith ap Rhys this very day. He's over the river at his cousin David's but Father Huw will give me indulgence if it's to go voluntarily to the law.' He smiled wryly. 'Very apt that I should be your man! I can unload my own sins at the same time, while I'm confiding to him what everyone must know but no one must say aloud.'

'Good!' said Brother Cadfael, contented. 'The bailiff will do the rest. A word to the prince, and that's the whole business settled.'

They had come to the place where the most direct path from Rhisiart's holding joined with their road. And there came half the household from above, Padrig the bard nursing his little portable harp, perhaps bound for some other house after this leave-taking, Cai the ploughman still with an impressive bandage round his quite intact head, an artistic lurch to his gait, and a shameless gleam in his one exposed eye. No Sioned, no Engelard, no Annest, no John. Brother Cadfael, though he himself had given the orders, felt a sudden grievous deprivation.

Now they were approaching the little clearing, the woodlands fell back from them on either side, the narrow field of wild grass opened, and then the stone-built wall, green from head to foot, of the old graveyard. Small, shrunken, black, a huddled shape too tall for its base, the chapel of Saint Winifred loomed, and at its eastern end the raw, dark oblong of Rhisiart's grave scarred the lush spring green of the grass.

Prior Robert halted at the gate, and turned to face the following multitude with a benign and almost affectionate countenance, and through Cadfael addressed them thus:

'Father Huw, and good people of Gwytherin, we came here with every good intent, led, as we believed and still believe, by divine guidance, desiring to honour Saint Winifred as she had instructed us, not at all to deprive you of a treasure, rather to allow its beams to shine upon many more people as well as you. That our mission should have brought grief to any is great grief to us. That we are now of one mind, and you are willing to let us take the saint's relics away with us to a wider glory, is relief and joy. Now you are assured that we meant no evil, but only good, and that what we are doing is done reverently.'

A murmur began at one end of the crescent of watchers, and rolled gently round to the other extreme, a murmur of acquiescence, almost of complacency.

'And you do not grudge us the possession of this precious thing we are taking with us? You do believe that we are doing justly, that we take only what has been committed to us?'

He could not have chosen his words better, thought Brother Cadfael, astonished and gratified, if he had known everything—or if I had written this address for him. Now if there comes an equally well-worded answer, I'll believe in a miracle of my own.

The crowd heaved, and gave forth the sturdy form of Bened, as solid and respectable and fit to be spokesman for his parish as any man in Gwytherin, barring, perhaps, Father Huw, who here stood in the equivocal position of having a foot in both camps, and therefore wisely kept silence.

'Father Prior,' said Bened gruffly, 'there's not a man among us now grudges you the relics within there on the altar. We do believe they are yours to take, and you take them with our consent home to Shrewsbury, where by all the omens they rightly belong.'

It was altogether too good. It might bring a blush of pleasure, even mingled with a trace of shame, to Prior Robert's cheek, but it caused Cadfael to run a long, considering glance round all those serene, secretive, smiling faces, all those wide, honest, opaque eyes. Nobody fidgeted, nobody muttered, nobody, even at the back, sniggered. Cai gazed with simple admiration from his one visible eye. Padrig beamed benevolent bardic satisfaction upon this total reconciliation.

They knew already! Whether through some discreet whisper started on its rounds by Sioned, or by some earth-rooted intuition of their own, the people of Gwytherin knew, in essence if not in detail, everything there was to be known. And not a word aloud, not a word out of place, until the strangers were gone.

'Come, then,' said Prior Robert, deeply gratified, 'let us release Brother Columbanus from his vigil, and take Saint Winifred on the first stage of her journey home.' And he turned, very tall, very regal, very silvery-fine, and paced majestically to the door of the chapel, with most of Gwytherin crowding into the graveyard after him. With a long, white, aristocratic hand he thrust the door wide and stood in the doorway.

'Brother Columbanus, we are here. Your watch is over.'

He took just two paces into the interior, his eyes finding it dim after the brilliance outside, in spite of the clear light pouring in through the small east window. Then the dark-brown, wood-scented walls came clear to him, and every detail of the scene within emerged from dimness into comparative light, and then into a light so acute and blinding that he halted where he stood, awed and marvelling.

There was a heavy, haunting sweetness that filled all the air within, and the opening of the door had let in a small morning wind that stirred it in great waves of fragrance. Both candles burned steadily upon the altar, the small oil-lamp between them. The prie-dieu stood centrally before the bier, but there was no one kneeling there. Over altar and reliquary a snowdrift of white petals lay, as though a miraculous wind had carried them in its arms across two fields from the hawthorn hedge, without spilling one flower on the way, and breathed them in here through the altar window. The snowy sweetness carried as far as the prie-dieu, and sprinkled both it and the crumpled, empty garments that lay discarded there.

'Columbanus . . . ! What is this? He is not here!'

Brother Richard came to the prior's left shoulder, Brother Jerome to the right, Bened and Cadwallon and Cai and others crowded in after them and flowed round on either side to line the dark walls and stare at the marvel, nostrils widening to the drowning sweetness. No one ventured to advance beyond where the prior stood, until he himself went slowly forward, and leaned to look more closely at all that was left of Brother Columbanus.

The black Benedictine habit lay where he had been kneeling, skirts spread behind, body fallen together in folds, sleeves spread like wings on either side, bent at the elbow as though the arms that had left them had still ended in hands pressed together in prayer. Within the cowl an edge of white showed.

'Look!' whispered Brother Richard in awe. 'His shirt is still within the habit, and look!—his sandals!' They were under the hem of the habit, neatly together, soles upturned, as the feet had left them. And on the book-rest of the prie-dieu, laid where his prayerful hands had rested, was a single knot of flowering may.

'Father Prior, all his clothes are here, shirt and drawers and all, one within another as he would wear them. As though—as though he had been lifted out of them and left them lying, as a snake discards its old skin and emerges bright in a new. . . .'

'This is most marvellous,' said Prior Robert. 'How shall we understand it, and not sin?'

'Father, may we take up these garments? If there is trace or mark on them. . . .'

There was none, Brother Cadfael was certain of that. Columbanus had not bled, his habit was not torn, nor even soiled. He had fallen only in thick spring grass, bursting irresistibly through the dead grass of last autumn.

'Father, it is as I said, as though he has been lifted out of these garments quite softly, and let them fall, not needing them any more. Oh, Father, we are in the presence of a great wonder! I am afraid!' said Brother Richard, meaning the wonderful, blissful fear of what is holy. He had seldom spoken with such eloquence, or been so moved.

'I do recall now,' said the prior, shaken and chastened (and that was no harm!), 'the prayer he made last night at Compline. How he cried out to be taken up living out of this world, for pure ecstasy, if the virgin saint found him fit for such favour and bliss. Is it possible that he was in such a state of grace as to be found worthy?'

'Father, shall we search? Here, and without? Into the woods?'

'To what end?' said the prior simply. 'Would he be running naked in the night? A sane man? And even if he ran mad, and shed the clothes he wore, would they be thus discarded, fold within fold as he kneeled, here in such pure order? It is not possible to put off garments thus. No, he is gone far beyond these forests, far out of this world. He has been marvellously favoured, and his most demanding prayers heard. Let us say a Mass here for Brother Columbanus, before we take up the blessed lady who has made him her herald, and go to make known this miracle of faith.'

There was no knowing, Prior Robert being the man he was, at what stage his awareness of the use to be made of this marvel thrust his genuine faith and wonder and emotion into the back of his mind, and set him manipulating events to get the utmost glory out of them. There was no inconsistency in such behaviour. He was quite certain that Brother Columbanus had been taken up living out of this world, just as he had wished. But that being so, it was not only his opportunity, but his duty, to make the utmost use of the exemplary favour to glorify the abbey of Saint Peter and Saint Paul of Shrewsbury, and not only his duty, but his pleasure, to make use of the same to shed a halo round the head of Prior Rcbert, who had originated this quest. And so he did. He said Mass with absolute conviction, in the cloud of white flowers, the huddle of discarded garments at his feet.

Almost certainly he would also inform Griffith ap Rhys, through Father Huw, of all that had befallen, and ask him to keep an alert eye open in case any relevant information surfaced after the brothers from Shrewsbury were gone. Brother Prior was the product of his faith and his birth, his training for sanctity and for arbitrary rule, and could shake off neither.

The people of Gwytherin, silent and observant, crowded in to fill the space available, made no sound, expressed no opinion. Their presence and silence passed for endorsement. What they really thought they kept to themselves.

'Now,' said Prior Robert, moved almost to tears, 'let us take up this blessed burden, and praise God for the weight we carry.'

And he moved forward to offer his own delicate hands and frail shoulder, first of the devout.

That was Brother Cadfael's worst moment, for it was the one thing he had overlooked. But Bened, unwontedly quick at the right moment, called aloud: 'Shall Gwytherin be backward, now peace is made?' and rolled forward with less stateliness and greater speed, and had a solid shoulder under the head end of the reliquary before the prior was able to reach it, and half a dozen of the smith's own powerful but stocky build took up the challenge with enthusiasm. Apart from Cadfael, the only monk of Shrewshbury who got a corner hoisted into his neck was Jerome, being of much the same height, and his was the sole voice that cried out in astonishment at the weight, and sagged under it until Bened shifted nearer and hefted most of the load from him.

'Your pardon, Father Prior! But who would have thought those slender little bones could weigh so heavily?'

Cadfael spoke up in hasty interpretation: 'We are surrounded here by miracles, both small and great. Truly did Father Prior say that we thank God for the weight we carry. Is not this evidence of singular grace, that heaven has caused the weight of her worthiness to be so signally demonstrated?'

In his present state, at once humbled and exalted, Prior Robert apparently did not find the logic of this nearly as peculiar as did Brother Cadfael himself. He would have accepted and embraced anything that added to his own triumph. So it was on sturdy Gwytherin shoulders that the reliquary and its contents were hoisted out of the chapel and borne in procession down to the parsonage, with such brisk enthusiasm that it almost seemed the parish could hardly wait to get rid of them. It was Gwytherin men who fetched the horses and mules, and rigged a little cart, spread with cloths, on which the precious casket could be drawn home. Once installed on this vehicle, which, after all, cost little in materials or labour, given the smith's benevolent interest, the casket need not be unloaded until it reached Shrewsbury. Nobody wanted anything untoward to happen to it on the way, such as Brother Jerome crumpling under his end, and starting the joints by dropping it.

'But you we'll miss,' said Cai regretfully, busy with the harness. 'Padrig has a song in praise of Rhisiart you'd have liked to hear, and one more companionable drinking night would have been pleasant. But the lad sends you his thanks and his godspeed. He's only in hiding until the pack of you have gone. And Sioned told me to tell you from him, look out for your pear trees, for the winter moth's playing the devil with some of ours here.'

'He's a good helper in a garden,' Cadfael confirmed judicially. 'A shade heavy-handed, but he shifts the rough digging faster than any novice I ever had under me. I shall miss him, too. God knows what I shall get in his place.'

'A light hand's no good with iron,' said Bened, standing back to admire the banded wheels he had contributed to the cart. 'Deft, yes! Not light. I tell you what, Cadfael! I'll see you in Shrewsbury yet. For years I've had a fancy to make a great pilgrimage across England some day and get to Walsingham. I reckon Shrewsbury would be just about on my way.'

At the last, when all was ready and Prior Robert mounted, Cai said in Cadfael's ear: 'When you're up the hill, where you saw us ploughing that day, cast a look the other way. There's a place where the woods fall away, and an open hillock just before they close again. We'll be there, a fair gathering of us. And that's for you.'

Brother Cadfael, without shame, for he had been up and busy

all night and was very tired, annexed the gentler and cleverer of the two mules, a steady pad that would follow where the horses led, and step delicately on any ground. It had a high, supporting saddle, and he had not lost the trick of riding through his knees, even when asleep. The larger and heavier beast was harnessed to draw the cart, but the carriage was narrow yet stable, rode well even on a forest floor, and Jerome, no great weight, could still ride, either on the mule's back or the shafts and yoke. In any case, why trouble too much about the comfort of Jerome, who had concocted that vision of Saint Winifred in the first place, almost certainly knowing that the prior's searches in Wales had cast up this particular virgin as one most desirable, and most available? Jerome would have been courting Columbanus just as assiduously, if he had survived to oust Robert.

The cortège set forth ceremoniously, half of Gwytherin there to watch it go, and sigh immense relief when it was gone. Father Huw blessed the departing guests. Peredur, almost certainly, was away across the river, planting the good seed in the bailiff's mind. He deserved that his errand should be counted to his own credit. Genuine sinners are plentiful, but genuine penitents are rare. Peredur had done a detestable thing, but remained a very likeable young man. Cadfael had no serious fears for his future, once he was over Sioned. There were other girls, after all. Not many her match, but some not so very far behind.

Brother Cadfael settled himself well down in the saddle, and shook his bridle to let the mule know it might conduct him where it would. Very gently he dozed. It could not yet be called sleep. He was aware of the shifting light and shadow under the trees, and the fresh cool air, and movement under him, and a sense of something completed. Or almost completed, for this was only the first stage of the way home.

He roused when they came to the high ridge above the river valley. There was no team ploughing down there now, all the ploughing, even the breaking of new ground, was done. He turned his head towards the wooded uplands on his right, and waited for the opening vista between the trees. It was brief and narrow, a sweep of grass soaring to a gentle crest beyond which the trees loomed close and dark. There were a number of people clustered there on the rounded hillock, most of Sioned's household, far enough removed to be nameless to anyone who knew them less well than he. A cloud of dark hair beside a cap of flaxen, Cai's flaunting bandage shoved back like a hat unseated in a hot noon, a light brown head clasped close against a red thorn-hedge that looked very like Brother John's abandoned tonsure. Padrig, too, not yet off on his wanderings. They were all waving and smiling, and Cadfael returned the salute with enthusiasm. Then the ambulant procession crossed the narrow opening, and the woods took away all.

Brother Cadfael, well content, subsided into his saddle comfortably, and fell asleep.

Overnight they halted at Penmachmo, in the shelter of the church, where there was hospitality for travellers. Brother Cadfael, without apology to any, withdrew himself as soon as he had seen to his mule, and continued his overdue sleep in the loft above the stables. He was roused after midnight by Brother Jerome in delirious excitement.

'Brother, a great wonder!' bleated Jerome, ecstatic. 'There came a traveller here in great pain from a malignant illness, and made such outcry that all of us in the hostel were robbed of sleep. And Prior Robert took a few of the petals we saved from the chapel, and floated them in holy water, and gave them to this poor soul to drink, and afterwards we carried him out into the yard and let him kiss the foot of the reliquary. And instantly he was eased of his pain, and before we laid him in his bed again he was asleep. He feels nothing, he slumbers like a child! Oh, brother, we are the means of astonishing grace!'

'Ought it to astonish you so much?' demanded Brother Cadfael censoriously, malicious half out of vexation at being awakened, and half in self-defence, for he was considerably more taken aback than he would admit. 'If you had any faith in what we have brought from Gwytherin, you should not be amazed that it accomplishes wonders along the way.'

But by the same token, he thought honestly, after Jerome had left him to seek out a more appreciative audience, *I* should! I do believe I begin to grasp the nature of miracles! For would it be a miracle, if there was any reason for it? Miracles have nothing to do with reason. Miracles contradict reason, overturn reason, make game of reason, they strike clean across mere human deserts, and deliver and save where they will. If they made sense, they would not be miracles. And he was comforted and entertained, and fell asleep again readily, feeling that all was well with a world he had always known to be peculiar and perverse.

Minor prodigies, most of them trivial, some derisory, trailed after them all the way to Shrewsbury, though how many of the crutches discarded had been necessary, and how many, even of those that were, had to be resumed shortly afterwards, how many of the speech impediments had been in the will rather than in the tongue, how many feeble tendons in the mind rather than in the legs, it was difficult to judge, not even counting all the sensation-seekers who were bound to bandage an eye or come over suddenly paralytic in order to be in with the latest cult. It all made for a great reputation that not only kept pace with them, but rushed ahead, and was already bringing in awestruck patronage in gifts and legacies to the abbey of Saint Peter and Saint Paul, in the hope of having dubious sins prayed away by a grateful saint.

When they reached the outskirts of Shrewsbury, crowds of people came out to meet them, and accompany the procession as far as the boundary church of Saint Giles, where the reliquary was to await the great day of the saint's translation to the abbey church. This could hardly take place without the blessing of the bishop, and due notice to all churches and religious houses, to add to the glory accruing. It was no surprise to Brother Cadfael that when the day came it should come with grey skies and squally rain, to leave room for another little miracle. For though it rained heavily on all the surrounding fields and countryside, not a drop fell on the procession, as they carried Saint Winifred's casket at last to its final resting-place on the altar of the abbey church, where the miracle-seekers immediately betook themselves in great numbers, and mostly came away satisfied.

In full chapter Prior Robert gave his account of his mission to Abbot Heribert. 'Father, to my grief I must own it, we have come back only four, who went out from Shrewsbury six brethren together. And we return without both the glory and the blemish of our house, but bringing with us the treasure we set out to gain.'

On almost all of which counts he was in error, but since no one was ever likely to tell him so, there was no harm done. Brother Cadfael dozed gently behind his pillar through the awed encomiums on Brother Columbanus, out of whom they would certainly have wished to make a new saint, but for the sad fact that they supposed all his relics but his discarded clothes to be for ever withdrawn from reach. Letting the devout voices slip out of his consciousness, Cadfael congratulated himself on having made as many people as possible happy, and drifted into a dream of a hot knife-blade slicing deftly through the thick wax of a seal without ever disturbing the device. It was a long time since he had exercised some of his more questionable skills, he was glad to be confirmed in believing that he had forgotten none of them, and that every one had a meritorious use in the end.

CHAPTER TWELVE

It was more than two years later, and the middle of a bright June afternoon, when Brother Cadfael, crossing the great court from the fish-ponds, saw among the travellers arriving at the gate a certain thickset, foursquare, powerful figure that he knew. Bened, the smith of Gwytherin, a little rounder in the belly and a little greyer in the hair, had found the time ripe for realising an old ambition, and was on his way in a pilgrim's gown to the shrine of Our Lady of Walsingham.

'If I'd put it off much longer,' he confided, when they were private together with a bottle of wine in a corner of the herb-garden, 'I should have grown too old to relish the journey. And what was there to keep me now, with a good lad ready and able to take over the smithy while I'm gone? He took to it like a duck to water. Oh, yes, they've been man and wife eighteen months now, and as happy as larks. Annest always knew her own mind, and this time I will say she's made no mistake.'

'And have they a child yet?' asked Brother Cadfael, imagining a bold, sturdy boy-baby with a bush of red hair, rubbed away by his pillow in an infant tonsure.

'Not yet, but there's one on the way. By the time I get back he'll be with us.'

'And Annest is well?'

'Blossoming like a rose.'

'And Sioned and Engelard? They had no troubles after we were gone?'

'None, bless you! Griffith ap Rhys let it be known that all was well, and should be let well alone. They're married, and snug, and I'm to bring you their warmest greetings, and to tell you they have a fine son—three months old, I reckon he'd be now—dark and Welsh like his mother. And they've named him Cadfael.'

'Well, well!' said Brother Cadfael, absurdly gratified. 'The best way to get the sweet out of children and escape the bitter is to have them by proxy. But I hope they'll never find anything but sweet in their youngster. There'll be a Bened yet, in one household or the other.'

Bened the pilgrim shook his head, but without any deep regret, and reached for the bottle. 'There was a time when I'd hoped. . . . But it would never have done. I was an old fool ever to think of it, and it's better this way. And Cai's well, and sends you remembrances, and says drink down one cup for him.'

They drank many more than one before it was time for Vespers. 'And you'll see me again at chapter tomorrow,' said Bened, as they walked back to the great court, 'for I'm charged with greetings from Father Huw to Prior Robert and Abbot Heribert, and I'll need you to be my interpreter.'

'Father Huw must be the one person in Gwytherin, I suppose, who doesn't know the truth by this time,' said Cadfael, with some compunction. 'But it wouldn't have been fair to lay such a load on his conscience. Better to let him keep his innocence.'

'His innocence is safe enough,' said Bened, 'for he's never said word to bring it in question, but for all that I wouldn't be too sure that he doesn't know. There's a lot of merit in silence.'

The next morning at chapter he delivered his messages of goodwill and commendation to the monastery in general, and the members of Prior Robert's mission in particular, from the parish of Saint Winifred's ministry to the altar of her glorification. Abbot Heribert questioned him amiably about the chapel and the graveyard which he himself had never seen, and to which, as he said, the abbey owed its most distinguished patroness and most precious relics.

'And we trust,' he said gently, 'that in our great gain you have not suffered equally great deprivation, for that was never our intent.'

'No, Father Abbot,' Bened reassured him heartily, 'you need have no regrets upon that score. For I must tell you that at the place of Saint Winifred's grave wonderful things are happening.

More people come there for help than ever before. There have been marvellous cures.'

Prior Robert stiffened in his place, and his austere face turned bluish-white and pinched with incredulous resentment.

'Even now, when the saint is here on our altar, and all the devout come to pray to her here? Ah, but small things—the residue of grace. . . .'

'No, Father Prior, great things! Women in mortal labour with cross-births have been brought there and laid on the grave from which she was taken, where we buried Rhisiart, and their children have been soothed into the world whole and perfect, with no harm to the mothers. A man blind for years came and bathed his eyes in a distillation of her may-blossoms, and threw away his stick and went home seeing. A young man whose leg-bone had been broken and knitted awry came in pain, and set his teeth and danced before her, and as he danced the pain left him, and his bones straightened. I cannot tell you half the wonders we have seen in Gwytherin these last two years.'

Prior Robert's livid countenance was taking on a shade of green, and under his careful eyelids his eyes sparkled emerald jealousy. How dare that obscure village, bereft of its saint, outdo the small prodigies of rain that held off from falling, and superficial wounds that healed with commendable but hardly miraculous speed, and even the slightly suspicious numbers of lame who brought their crutches and left them before the altar, and walked away unsupported?

'There was a child of three who went into a fit,' pursued Bened with gusto, 'stiff as a board in his mother's arms, and stopped breathing, and she ran with him all the way from the far fields, fording the river, and carried him to Winifred's grave, and laid him down in the grass there dead. And when he touched the chill of the earth, he breathed and cried out, and she picked him up living, and took him home joyfully, and he is live and well to this day.'

'What, even the dead raised?' croaked Prior Robert, almost speechless with envy.

'Father Prior,' said Brother Cadfael soothingly, 'surely this is but another proof, the strongest possible, of the surpassing merit and potency of Saint Winifred. Even the soil that once held her bones works wonders, and every wonder must redound to the credit and glory of that place which houses the very body that blessed the earth that still blesses others.'

And Abbot Heribert, oblivious of the chagrin that was consuming his prior, benignly agreed that it was so, and that universal grace, whether it manifested itself in Wales, or England, or the Holy Land, or wheresoever, was to be hailed with universal gratitude.

'Was that innocence or mischief?' demanded Cadfael, when he saw Bened off from the gatehouse afterwards.

'Work it out for yourself! The great thing is, Cadfael, it was truth! These things happened, and are happening yet.'

Brother Cadfael stood looking after him as he took the road towards Lilleshall, until the stocky figure with its long, easy strides dwindled to child-size, and vanished at the curve of the wall. Then he turned back towards his garden, where a new young novice, barely sixteen and homesick, was waiting earnestly for his orders, having finished planting out lettuces to follow in succession. A silent lad as yet. Maybe once he had taken Brother Cadfael's measure his tongue would begin to wag, and then there'd be no stopping it. He knew nothing, but was quick to learn, and though he was still near enough to childhood to attract any available moist soil to his own person, things grew for him. On the whole, Cadfael was well content.

I don't see, he thought, reviewing the whole business again from this peaceful distance, how I could have done much better. The little Welsh saint's back where she always wanted to be, bless her, and showing her pleasure by taking good care of her own, it seems. And we've got what belonged to us in the first place, all we have a right to, and probably all we deserve, too, and by and large it seems to be thought satisfactory. Evidently the body of a calculating murderer does almost as well as the real thing, given faith enough. Almost, but never quite! Knowing what they all know by now, those good people up there in

Gwytherin may well look forward to great things. And if a little of their thanks and gratitude rubs off on Rhisiart, well, why not? He earned it, and it's a sign she's made him welcome. She may even be glad of his company. He's no threat to her virginity now, and if he is trespassing, that's no fault of his. His bed-fellow won't grudge him a leaf or two from her garland!

THE RAVEN IN THE FOREGATE

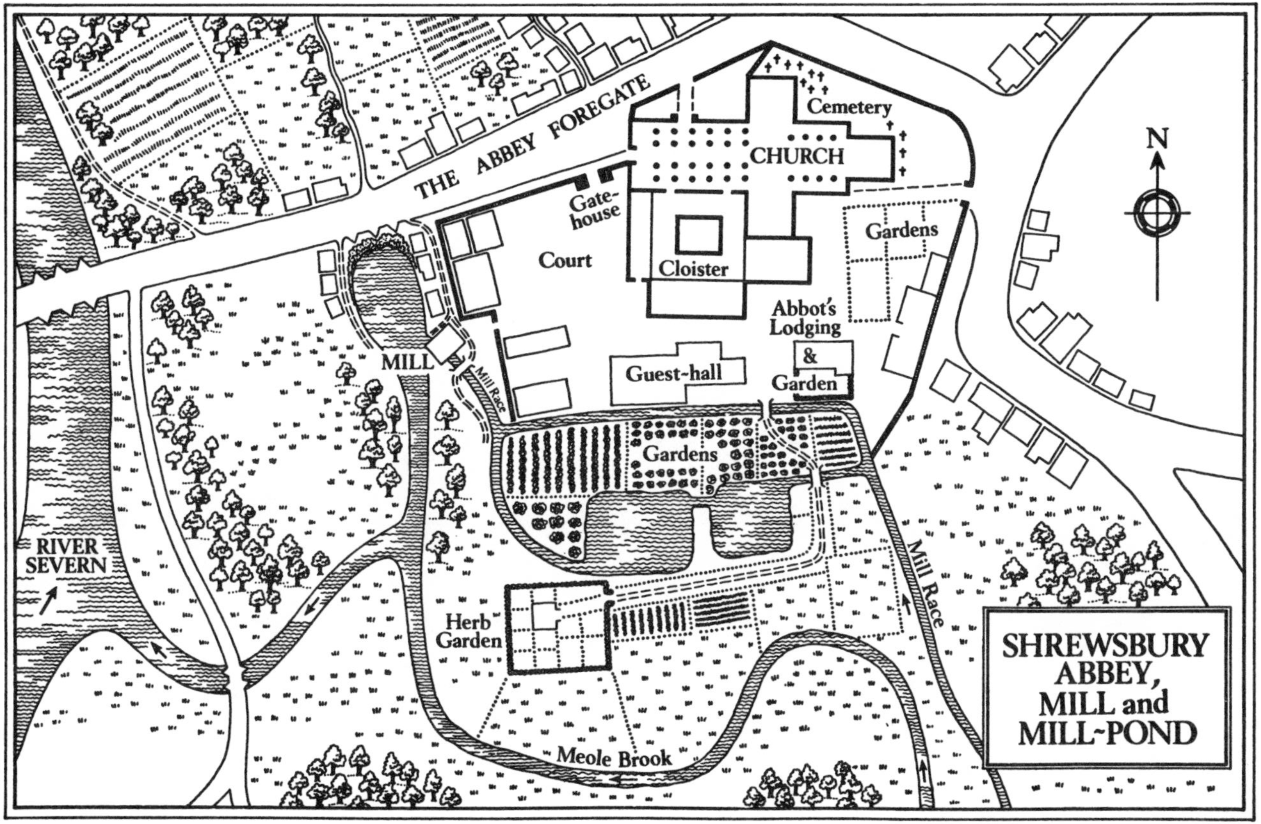
SHREWSBURY ABBEY, MILL and MILL-POND
N
THE ABBEY FOREGATE
Cemetery
CHURCH
Gate-house
Court
Cloister
Gardens
Abbot's Lodging
& Garden
Guest-hall
MILL
Mill Race
Gardens
Herb Garden
Mill Race
Meole Brook
RIVER SEVERN

Chapter One

Abbot Radulfus came to chapter, on this first day of December, with a preoccupied and frowning face, and made short work of the various trivialities brought up by his obedientiaries. Though a man of few words himself, he was disposed, as a rule, to allow plenty of scope to those who were rambling and loquacious about their requests and suggestions, but on this day, plainly, he had more urgent matters on his mind.

'I must tell you,' he said, when he had swept the last trifle satisfactorily into its place, 'that I shall be leaving you for some days to the care of Father Prior, to whom, I expect and require, you shall be as obedient and helpful as you are to me. I am summoned to a council to be held at Westminster on the seventh day of this month, by the Holy Father's legate, Henry of Blois, bishop of Winchester. I shall return as soon as I can, but in my absence I desire you will make your prayers for a spirit of wisdom and reconciliation in this meeting of prelates, for the sake of the peace of this land.'

His voice was dry and calm to the point of resignation. For the past four years there had been precious little inclination to reconciliation in England between the warring rivals for the crown, and no very considerable wisdom shown on either side. But it was the business of the Church to continue to strive, and if possible to hope, even when the affairs of the land seemed to have reverted to the very same point where the civil war had begun, to repeat the whole unprofitable cycle all over again.

'I am well aware there are matters outstanding here,' said

the abbot, 'which equally require our attention, but they must wait for my return. In particular there is the question of a successor to Father Adam, lately vicar of this parish of Holy Cross, whose loss we are still lamenting. The advowson rests with this house. Father Adam has been for many years a much valued associate with us here in the worship of God and the cure of souls, and his replacement is a matter for both thought and prayer. Until my return, Father Prior will direct the parish services as he thinks fit, and all of you will be at his bidding.'

He swept one long, dark glance round the chapter house, accepted the general silence as understanding and consent, and rose.

'This chapter is concluded.'

'Well, at least if he leaves tomorrow he has good weather for the ride,' said Hugh Beringar, looking out from the open door of Brother Cadfael's workshop in the herb garden over grass still green, and a few surviving roses, grown tall and spindly by now but still budding bravely. December of this year of Our Lord 1141 had come in with soft-stepping care, gentle winds and lightly veiled skies, treading on tiptoe. 'Like all those shifting souls who turned to the Empress when she was in her glory,' said Hugh, grinning, 'and are now put to it to keep well out of sight while they turn again. There must be a good many holding their breath and making themselves small just now.'

'Bad luck for his reverence the papal legate,' said Cadfael, 'who cannot make himself small or go unregarded, whatever he does. His turning has to be done in broad daylight, with every eye on him. And twice in one year is too much to ask of any man.'

'Ah, but in the name of the Church, Cadfael, in the name of the Church! It's not the man who turns, it's the representative of Pope and Church, who must preserve the infallibility of both at all costs.'

Twice in one year, indeed, had Henry of Blois summoned

his bishops and abbots to a legatine council, once in Winchester on the seventh of April to justify his endorsement of the Empress Maud as ruler, when she was in the ascendant and had her rival King Stephen securely in prison in Bristol, and now at Westminster on the seventh of December to justify his swing back to Stephen, now that the King was free again, and the city of London had put a decisive end to Maud's bid to establish herself in the capital, and get her hands at last on the crown.

'If his head is not going round by now, it should be,' said Cadfael, shaking his own grizzled brown tonsure in mingled admiration and deprecation. 'How many spins does this make? First he swore allegiance to the lady, when her father died without a male heir, then he accepted his brother Stephen's seizure of power in her absence, thirdly, when Stephen's star is darkened he makes his peace – a peace of sorts, at any rate! – with the lady, and justifies it by saying that Stephen has flouted and aggrieved Holy Church. . . . Now must he turn the same argument about, and accuse the Empress, or has he something new in his scrip?'

'What is there new to be said?' asked Hugh, shrugging. 'No, he'll wring the last drop from his stewardship of Holy Church, and make the best of it that every soul there will have heard it all before, no longer ago than last April. And it will convince Stephen no more than it did Maud, but he'll let it pass with only a mild snarl or two, since he can no more afford to reject the backing of Henry of Blois than could Maud in her day. And the bishop will grit his teeth and stare his clerics in the eyes, and swallow his gall with a brazen face.'

'It may well be the last time he has to turn about-face,' said Cadfael, feeding his brazier with a few judiciously placed turves, to keep it burning with a slow and tempered heat. 'She has thrown away what's likely to be her only chance.'

A strange woman she had proved, King Henry's royal daughter. Married in childhood to the Holy Roman Emperor Henry V, she had so firmly ingratiated herself with her husband's people in Germany that when she was recalled to England, after his death, the populace had risen in consternation and grief to plead with her to stay. Yet here at home, when fate threw her enemy into her hands and held the crown suspended over her head, she had behaved with such vengeful arrogance, and exacted such penalties for past affronts, that the men of her capital city had risen just as indignantly, not to appeal to her to remain, but to drive her out and put a violent end to her hopes of ever becoming their ruler. And it was common knowledge that though she could turn even upon her own best allies with venom, yet she could also retain the love and loyalty of the best of the baronage. There was not a man of the first rank on Stephen's side to match the quality of her half-brother, Earl Robert of Gloucester, or her champion and reputed lover, Brian FitzCount, her easternmost paladin in his fortress at Wallingford. But it would take more than a couple of heroes to redeem her cause now. She had been forced to surrender her royal prisoner in exchange for her half-brother, without whom she could not hope to achieve anything. And here was England back to the beginning, with all to do again. For if she could not win, neither could she give up.

'From here where I stand now,' said Cadfael, pondering, 'these things seem strangely distant and unreal. If I had not been forty years in the world and among the armies myself, I doubt if I could believe in the times we live in but as a disturbed dream.'

'They are not so to Abbot Radulfus,' said Hugh with unwonted gravity. He turned his back upon the mild, moist prospect of the garden, sinking gently into its winter sleep, and sat down on the wooden bench against the timber wall. The small glow of the brazier, damped under the turf, burned on the bold, slender bones of his cheeks and jaw and brows, conjuring them out of deep shadows, and sparkling briefly in his black eyes before the lids and dark lashes quenched the sparks. 'That man would make a better adviser to kings than most that cluster round Stephen now he's free again. But he would not tell them what they want to hear, and they'd all stop their ears.'

'What's the news of King Stephen now? How has he borne this year of captivity? Is he likely to come out of it fighting, or has it dimmed his ardour? What is he likely to do next?'

'That I may be better able to answer after Christmas,' said Hugh. 'They say he's in good health. But she put him in chains, and that even he is not likely to forgive too readily. He's come out leaner and hungrier than he went in, and a gnaw in the belly may well serve to concentrate the mind. He was ever a man to begin a campaign or siege all fire the first day, weary of it if he got no gain by the third, and go off after another prey by the fifth. Maybe now he's learned to keep an unwavering eye fixed on one target until he fetches it down. Sometimes I wonder why we follow him, and never look round, then I see him roaring into personal battle as he did at Lincoln, and I know the reason well enough. Even when he has the woman as good as in his hands, as when she first landed at Arundel, and gives her an escort to her brother's fortress instead of having the good sense to seize her, I curse him for a fool, but I love him while I'm cursing him. What monumental folly of mistaken chivalry he'll commit next, only God knows. But I'll welcome the chance to see him again, and try to guess at his mind. For I'm bidden forth, Cadfael, like the abbot. King Stephen means to keep Christmas at Canterbury this year, and put on his crown again, for all to see which of two heads is the anointed monarch here. And he's called all his sheriffs to attend him and render account of their shires. Me among the rest, seeing we have here no properly appointed sheriff to render account.'

He looked up with a dark, sidelong smile into Cadfael's attentive and thoughtful face. 'A very sound move. He needs to know what measure of loyalty he has to rely on, after a year in prison, or close on a year. But there's no denying it may bring me a fall.'

For Cadfael it was a new and jolting thought. Hugh had

stepped into the office of sheriff perforce, when his superior, Gilbert Prestcote, had died of his battle wounds and the act of a desperate man, at a time when the King was already a prisoner in Bristol castle, with no power to appoint or to demote any officer in any shire. And Hugh had served him and maintained his peace here without authority, and deserved well of him. But now that he was free to make and break again, would Stephen confirm so young and so minor a nobleman in office, or use the appointment to flatter and bind to himself some baron of the march?

'Folly!' said Cadfael firmly. 'The man is a fool only towards himself. He made you deputy to his man out of nowhere, when he saw your mettle. What does Aline say of it?'

Hugh could not hear his wife's name spoken without a wild, warm softening of his sharp, subtle face, nor could Cadfael speak it without relaxing every solemnity into a smile. He had witnessed their courtship and their marriage, and was godfather to their son, two years old this coming Christmastide. Aline's girlish, flaxen gentleness had grown into a golden, matronly calm to which they both turned in every need.

'Aline says that she has no great confidence in the gratitude of princes, but that Stephen has the right to choose his own officers, wisely or foolishly.'

'And you?' said Cadfael.

'Why, if he gives me his countenance and writ I'll go on keeping all his borders for him, and if not, then I'll go back to Maesbury and keep the north, at least, against Chester, if the earl tries again to enlarge his palatinate. And Stephen's man must take charge of west, east and south. And you, old friend, must pay a visit or two over Christmas, while I'm away, and keep Aline company.'

'Of all of us,' said Cadfael piously, 'that makes me the best blessed at this coming feast. I'll pray good joy to my abbot in his mission, and to you in yours. My joy is assured.'

* * *

They had buried old Father Adam, seventeen years vicar of the parish of Holy Cross in the Foregate of Shrewsbury, only one week before Abbot Radulfus was summoned to the legatine council at Westminster. The advowson of the living was vested in the abbey, and the great church of Saint Peter and Saint Paul was equally the parish church of Holy Cross, the nave open to the people living here outside the town gates, in this growing suburb which almost considered itself a borough like the borough within the walls. The reeve of the Foregate, Erwald the wheelwright, publicly if unofficially used the title of provost, and abbey, church and town humoured his harmless flourish, for the Monks' Foregate was a relatively law-abiding, respectable district, and gave barely any trouble to the properly constituted authorities of the town itself. An occasional squabble between seculars and abbey, a brief tangle between the high-spirited young of Foregate and town, what was there in that to worry anyone beyond the day?

Father Adam had been there so long that all the young had grown up under his easy-going shadow, and all the old had known him as one of themselves, hardly set apart by his office. He had lived alone in his little house up a narrow alley opposite the church, looking after himself, with only an elderly freeman to take care of his glebe and his strip fields in the country part of the parish, for Holy Cross spread wide outside the main street of the Foregate. A big parish, a population made up equally of the craftsmen and merchants of the suburb and the cottars and villagers in the countryside. It was a matter of importance to them all what manner of priest they got in succession to Father Adam. The old man himself, from whatever gentle purgatory now contained him, would be keeping an anxious eye on his own.

Abbot Radulfus had presided at Adam's funeral, and Prior Robert at his most dignified and elegiac, tall and silvery and consciously patrician, had pronounced his eulogy, perhaps with a slight touch of condescension, for Adam had been barely literate, and a man of humble origins and no pretentions. But it was Cynric, the verger of Holy Cross, who had been with the priest through most of his years of office, who had best spoken his epitaph, and that privately, over the trimming of the candles on the parish altar, to Brother Cadfael, who had halted in passing through to say a word of personal sympathy to the man who would surely miss the dead most deeply.

'A sad, kind man,' said Cynric, his deep-sunk eyes narrowed on the wick he was trimming, and his low voice as grainy and grudging as ever, 'a tired man, with a soft spot for sinners.'

It was rare enough for Cynric to utter thirteen words together, except by way of the responses learned by heart in the holy office. Thirteen words of his own had the force of prophecy. A sad man, because he had been listening to and bearing with the perpetual failures of humankind for seventeen years, a tired man because endless consoling and chiding and forgiving takes it out of any man by the time he's sixty, especially one with neither malice nor anger in his own make-up. A kind man, because he had somehow managed to preserve compassion and hope even against the tide of human fallibility. Yes, Cynric had known him better than anyone. He had absorbed, in the years of his service, something of the same qualities without the authority.

'You'll feel the want of him,' said Cadfael. 'So shall we all.'

'He'll not be far,' said Cynric, and snipped the dead wick with thumb and finger.

The verger was a man past fifty, but there was no knowing by how many years, for he himself did not know the exact year of his birth, though he knew the day and month. He was dark of hair and eyes, and sallow-skinned, and went in a rusty black gown somewhat frayed at the hems from long years of wear, and he lived in the tiny upper room over the north porch where Father Adam robed and kept his church furnishings. A taciturn, grave, durable man, built upon long, strong bones, but very meagre in flesh, as much by reason of the hermit's forgetfulness as any want of means. He came of a country family of free folk, and had a brother somewhere north of the town with a grown family, and very occasionally at feast or holiday he visited there, but that happened very rarely now, his whole life being centred here in the great church and the small upper room. So spare, silent and dark a form and face might have aroused awe and avoidance, but did not, since what the darkness and the silence covered was known to all, even the mischievous boys of the Foregate, and inspired no fear or revulsion at all. A good man, with his own preferences and peculiarities, and certainly no talker, but if you needed him, he was there, and like his master, would not send you away empty.

Those who could not be easy with his mute company at least respected him, and those who could included the most innocent and guileless. Children and dogs would sit companionably on the steps of the north porch with him in summer weather, and do all the talking necessary to such a friendship, after their own fashion, while he listened. Many a mother in the Foregate, content to see her young consorting so familiarly with a respectable churchman, had wondered why Cynric had never married and had children of his own, since plainly he had an affinity for them. It could not be because of his office of verger, for there were still plenty of married priests scattered through the parishes of the shire, and no one thought any wrong of them. The new order of clerics without women was only just beginning to make headway here, no one, not even bishops, had yet begun to look sidewise at those of the old school who did not conform. Monks were monks, and had made their choice, but surely the secular clergy could still be secular without reproach.

'He had no living kin?' asked Cadfael. For of all men remaining behind, Cynric would know.

'None.'

'He was newly priest here,' said Cadfael, 'when I came first from Woodstock with Abbot Heribert – Prior Heribert he was then, for Abbot Godefrid was still alive. You came, as I remember, a year or two later. You're a younger man than I. You and I between us could put together a history of cowl and cassock here in the Foregate all this long while. It would make a very handsome memorial to Father Adam. No falling out, no falling off. He had his everlasting penitents, but that was his glory, that they always came back. They could not do without him. And he kept his thread that drew them back, whether they would or no.'

'So he did,' said Cynric, and clipped the last blackened wick with a snap of his finger-nails, and straightened the candlesticks on the parish altar, standing back a pace with narrowed lids to check that they stood correct as soldiers on guard.

His throat creaked, forcing unwilling chords to flex, when he used more words. The strings protested now. 'Is there a man in mind?'

'No,' said Cadfael, 'or Father Abbot would have told you. He goes south by forced rides tomorrow to the legate's council in Westminster, and this presentation must wait his return, but he's promised haste. He knows the need. You may well get Brother Jerome now and again until the abbot returns, but never doubt that Radulfus has the parish very much at heart.'

To that Cynric nodded silent assent, for the relations between cloister and parish here had been harmonious under three abbots in succession, all the years of Father Adam's incumbency, whereas in some churches thus shared, as everyone knew, there was constant friction, the monastics grudging the commonalty room in their enclave and entry to their privileged buildings, and the secular priest putting up a fight for his rights to avoid being elbowed out. Not so here. Perhaps it was the modest goodness of Father Adam that had done the lion's share in keeping the peace, and making the relationship easy.

'He liked a sup now and again,' said Cadfael meditatively. 'I still have some of a wine he liked – distilled with herbs, good for the blood and heart. Come and take a cup with me in the garden, some afternoon, Cynric, and we'll drink to him.'

'I will so,' said Cynric, and relaxed for one moment into his rare, indulgent smile, the same by which children and dogs found him out and approached him with confidence.

They crossed the chill tiles of the nave together, and Cynric went out by the north porch, and up to his little dark room above. Cadfael looked after him until the door had closed between. All these years they had been within arm's reach of each other, and on the best of terms, yet never familiar. Who had ever been familiar with Cynric? Since the ties with his mother loosened, and he turned his back on home, whatever and wherever that home had been, perhaps only Father Adam had truly drawn near to him. Two solitaries together make a very special matched pair, two in one. Yes, of all the mourners for Father Adam, and they must be many, Cynric must now be the most painfully bereaved.

They had lighted the fire in the warming room for the first time when December came in, and in the relaxed half-hour between Collations and Compline, when tongues were allowed considerable licence, there was far more talk and speculation about the parish cure than about the legate's council in Westminster, to which Abbot Radulfus had just set out. Prior Robert had withdrawn into the abbot's lodging, as representing that dignitary in his absence, which gave further freedom to the talkative, but his chaplain and shadow, Brother Jerome, in his turn took upon himself the duty and privilege of representing the prior, and Brother Richard, the sub-prior, was too easy-going, not to say indolent, to assert himself with any vigour.

A meagre man in the flesh was Brother Jerome, but he made up for it in zeal, though there were those who found that zeal too narrowly channelled, and somewhat dehydrated of the milk of human tolerance. Which rendered it understandable that he should consider Father Adam to have been rather over-supplied with that commodity.

'Certainly a man of virtue himself,' said Jerome, 'I would not for a moment take that from him, we all know he served devotedly. But somewhat loose upon others who did offend. His discipline was too slack, and his penances too light and too indulgently given. Who spares the sinner condones the sin.'

'There's been good order and neighbourliness in his parish the length of his life here,' said Brother Ambrose the almoner, whose office brought him into contact with the poorest of the poor throughout the Foregate. 'I know how they speak of him. He left a cure ready and fit for another to step into, with the general goodwill open to whoever comes, because the general goodwill was there to speed the one departed.'

'Children will always be glad of a weak master who never uses the rod,' said Jerome sagely, 'and rascals of a judge who lets them off lightly. But the payment that falls due later will be fearful. Better they should be brought up harshly against the wages of sin now, and lay up safety for their souls hereafter.'

Brother Paul, master of the novices and the boys, who very rarely laid a hand upon his pupils, and certainly only when they had well deserved it, smiled and held his peace.

'In too much mercy is too little kindness,' pronounced Jerome, conscious of his own eloquence, and mindful of his reputation as a preacher. 'The Rule itself decrees that where the child offends he must be beaten, and these folk of the Foregate, what are they but children?'

They were called by the bell to Compline at that moment, but in any case it was unlikely that any of them would have troubled to argue with Jerome, whose much noise and small effect hardly challenged notice. No doubt he would preach stern sermons at the parish Mass, on the two days allotted to him, but there would be very few of the regular attenders there to listen to him, and even those who did attend would let his homily in at one ear and out at the other, knowing his office here could last but a few days.

For all that, Cadfael went to his bed that night very thoughtful, and though he heard a few whispered exchanges in the dortoir, himself kept silence, mindful of the rule that the words of Compline, the completion, the perfecting of the day's worship, should be the last words uttered before sleep, that the mind should not be distracted from the '*Opus Dei*'. Nor was it. For the words lingered with him between sleep and waking, the same words over and over, faintly returning. By chance the psalm was the sixth. He took it with him into slumber.

'*Domine, ne in furore* – O Lord, rebuke me not in thine anger, neither chasten me in thy displeasure. . . . Have mercy upon me, O Lord, for I am weak. . . .'

Chapter Two

On the tenth day of December, Abbot Radulfus returned, riding in at the gatehouse just as the daylight was fading, and the brethren were within at Vespers. Thus the porter was the only witness of his arrival, and of the embellished entourage he brought back with him, and not until the next day at chapter did the brothers hear all that he had to tell, or as much of it as concerned the abbey itself. But Brother Porter, the soul of discretion when required, could also be the best-informed gossip in the enclave to his special friends, and Cadfael learned something of what was toward that same night, in one of the carrels in the cloister, immediately after Vespers.

'He's brought back with him a priest, a fine tall fellow – not above thirty-five years or so I'd guess him to be. He's bedded now in the guest hall, they rode hard today to get home before dark. Not a word has Father Abbot said to me, beyond giving me my orders to let Brother Denis know he has a guest for the night, and to take care of the other two. For there's a woman come with the priest, a decent soul going grey and very modestly conducted, that I take to be some sort of aunt or housekeeper to the priest, for I was bidden get one of the lay grooms to show her the way to Father Adam's cottage, and that I did. And not the woman alone, there's another young servant lad with her, that waits on the pair of them and does their errands. A widow and her son they could be, in the priest's service. Off he goes with only Brother Vitalis, as always, and comes back with three more, and two extra horses. The young lad brought the woman pillion behind him. And what do you make of all that?'

'Why, there's but one way of it,' said Cadfael, after giving the matter serious thought. 'The lord abbot has brought back a priest for Holy Cross from the southlands, and his household with him. The man himself is made comfortable in the guest hall overnight, while his domestics go to open up the empty house and get a good fire going for him, and food in store, and the place warmed and ready. And tomorrow at chapter, no doubt, we shall hear how the abbot came by him, and which of all the bishops gathered there recommended him to the benefice.'

'It's what I myself was thinking,' agreed the porter, 'though it would have been more to the general mind, I fancy, if a local man had been advanced to the vacancy. Still, it's what a man is that counts, not his name nor where he came from. No doubt the lord abbot knows his business best.' And he went off briskly, probably to whisper the news into one or two other discreet ears before Compline. Certainly several of the brothers came to the next morning's chapter already forewarned and expectant, alertly waiting for the new man to be first heralded, and then produced for inspection. For though it was very unlikely that anyone would raise objections to a man chosen by Abbot Radulfus, yet the whole chapter had rights in the presentation to the living, and Radulfus was not the man to infringe its privileges.

'I have made all possible haste to return to you,' the abbot began, when the normal routine matters had been quickly dealt with. 'In brief, I must report to you of the legatine council held at Westminster, that the discussions and decisions there have brought the Church back into full allegiance to King Stephen. The King himself was present to confirm the establishment of this relationship, and the legate to declare him blessed by the countenance of the Apostolic See, and the followers of the Empress, if they remain recalcitrant, as enemies of King and Church. There is no need,' said the abbot, somewhat drily, 'to go into further detail here.'

None, thought Cadfael, attentive in his chosen stall, conveniently sheltered behind a pillar in case he nodded off when material matters became tiresome. No need for us to hear the spiral manipulations by which the legate extricated himself from all his difficulties. But beyond doubt, Hugh would get a full account of all.

'What does more nearly concern this house,' said Radulfus, 'is certain conference I had with Bishop Henry of Winchester in private. Knowing of the cure left vacant here at Holy Cross, he recommended to me a priest of his own following, at present waiting for a benefice. I have talked with the man in question, and found him in every way able, scholarly and fitted for advancement. His personal life is austere and simple, his scholarship I have myself tested.'

It was a point powerful enough, by contrast with Father Adam's want of learning, though it would count for more with the brothers here than with the folk of the Foregate.

'Father Ailnoth is thirty-six years of age,' said the abbot, 'and comes rather late to a parish by reason of having served as a clerk to Bishop Henry, loyally and efficiently, for four years, and the bishop desires to reward his diligence now by seeing him settled in a cure. For my part, I am satisfied that he is both suitable and deserving. But if you will bear with me so far, brothers, I will have him called in to give account of himself, and answer whatever you may wish to ask him.'

A stir of interest, consent and curiosity went round the chapter house, and Prior Robert, surveying the heads nodding in anticipation and obeying the abbot's glance, went out to summon the candidate.

Ailnoth, thought Cadfael, a Saxon name, and reported as a fine, tall fellow. Well, better than some Norman hanger-on from the fringes of the court. And he formed a mental picture of a big young man with fresh, ruddy skin and fair hair, but dismissed it in a breath when Father Ailnoth came in on Prior Robert's heels, and took his stand with composed grace in the middle of the chapter house, where he could be seen by all.

He was indeed a fine, tall fellow, wide-shouldered, muscular, fluent and rapid in gait, erect and very still when he had taken his stand. And a very comely man, too, in his own fashion, but so far from Saxon pallor that he was blacker of hair and eye than Hugh Beringar himself. He had a long, patrician countenance, olive-skinned and with no warmer flush of red in his well-shaven cheeks. The black hair that ringed his tonsure was straight as wire, and thick, and clipped with such precision that it looked almost as if it had been applied with black paint. He made an austere obeisance to the abbot, folded his hands, which were large and powerful, at the waist of his black gown, and waited to be catechised.

'I present to this assembly Father Ailnoth,' said Radulfus, 'whom I propose we should prefer to the cure of Holy Cross. Examine him of his own wishes in this matter, his attainments and his past service, and he will answer freely.'

And freely indeed he did answer, launched by a first gracious word of welcome from Prior Robert, who clearly found his appearance pleasing. He answered questions briefly and fluently, like one who never has had and never expects to have any lack of confidence or any time to waste, and his voice, pitched a shade higher than Cadfael had expected from so big a man and so broad a chest, rang with an assured authority. He accounted for himself forcefully, declared his intent to pursue his duty with energy and integrity, and awaited the verdict upon himself with steely confidence. He had excellent Latin, some Greek, and was versed in accountancy, which promised well for his church management. His acceptance was assured.

'If I may make one request, Father Abbot,' he said finally, 'I should be greatly thankful if you could find some work here among your lay servants for the young man who has travelled here with me. He is the nephew and only kin of my housekeeper, the widow Hammet, and she entreated me to let him come here with her and find some employment locally. He is landless and without fortune. My lord abbot, you have seen that he is healthy and sturdy and not afraid of hard work, and he has been willing and serviceable to us all on the journey. He has, I believe, some inclination to the cloistered life, though as yet he is undecided. If you could give him work for a while it might settle his mind.'

'Ah, yes, the young man Benet,' said the abbot. 'He seems a well-conditioned youth, I agree. Certainly he may come, upon probation, no doubt work can be found for him. There must be a deal of things to be done about the grange court, or in the gardens. . . .'

'Indeed there is, Father,' Cadfael spoke up heartily. 'I could make good use of a younger pair of hands, there's much of the rough digging for the winter still to be done, some of the ground in the kitchen garden has only now been cleared. And the pruning in the orchard – heavy work. With the winter coming on, short days, and Brother Oswin gone to Saint Giles, to the hospice, I shall be needing a helper. I should shortly have been asking for another brother to come and work with me, as is usual, though through the summer I've managed well enough.'

'True! And some of the ploughing in the Gaye remains to be done, and around Christmas, or soon after, the lambing will begin in the hill granges, if the young man is no longer needed here. Yes, by all means send Benet to us. Should he later find other employment more to his advantage, he may take it with our goodwill. In the meantime hard labour here for us will do him no harm.'

'I will tell him so,' said Ailnoth, 'and he will be as thankful to you as I am. His aunt would have been sad at leaving him behind, seeing he is the only younger kinsman she has, to be helpful to her. Shall I send him here today?'

'Do so, and tell him he may ask at the gatehouse for Brother Cadfael. Leave us now to confer, Father,' said the abbot, 'but wait in the cloister, and Father Prior will bring you word of our decision.'

Ailnoth bowed his head with measured reverence, withdrew a respectful pace or two backwards from the abbot's presence, and strode out of the chapter house, his black, handsome head erect and confident. His gown swung like half-spread wings to the vigour of his stride. He was already sure, as was everyone present, that the cure of Holy Cross was his.

'It went much as you have probably supposed,' said Abbot Radulfus, somewhat later in the day, in the parlour of his own lodging, with a modest fire burning on the chimney stone, and Hugh Beringar seated opposite him across the glow. The abbot's face was still a little drawn and grey with tiredness, his deep-set eyes a little hollow. The two knew each other very well by this time, and had grown accustomed to sharing with complete confidence, for the sake of order and England, whatever they gathered of events and tendencies, without ever questioning whether they shared the same opinions. Their disciplines were separate and very different, but their acceptance of service was one, and mutually recognised.

'The bishop had little choice,' said Hugh simply. 'Virtually none, now the King is again free, and the Empress again driven into the west, with little foothold in the rest of England. I would not have wished myself in his shoes, nor do I know how I would have handled his difficulties. Let him who is certain of his own valour cast blame, I cannot.'

'Nor I. But for all that can be said, the spectacle is not edifying. There are, after all, some who have never wavered, whether fortune favoured or flayed them. But it is truth that the legate had received the Pope's letter, which he read out to us in conference, reproving him for not enforcing the release of the King, and urging him to insist upon it above all else. And who dare wonder if he made the most of it? And besides, the King came there himself. He entered the hall and made formal complaint against all those who had sworn fealty to him, and then suffered him to lie in prison, and come near to slaying him.'

'But then sat back and let his brother use his eloquence to

worm his way out of the reproach,' said Hugh, and smiled. 'He has the advantage of his cousin and rival, he knows when to mellow and forget. She neither forgets nor forgives.'

'Well, true. But it was not a happy thing to hear. Bishop Henry made his defence, frankly owning he had had no choice open to him but to accept the fortune as it fell, and receive the Empress. He said he had done what seemed the best and only thing, but that she had broken all her pledges, outraged all her subjects, and made war against his own life. And to conclude, he pledged the Church again to King Stephen, and urged all men of consequence and goodwill to serve him. He took some credit,' said Abbot Radulfus with sad deliberation, 'for the liberation of the King to himself. And outlawed from the Church all those who continued to oppose him.'

'And mentioned the Empress, or so I've heard,' said Hugh equally drily, 'as the countess of Anjou.' It was a title the Empress detested, as belittling both her birth and her rank by her first marriage, a king's daughter and the widow of an emperor, now reduced to a title borrowed from her none-too-loved and none-too-loving second husband, Geoffrey of Anjou, her inferior in every particular but talent, common sense and efficiency. All he had ever done for Maud was give her a son. Of the love she bore to the boy Henry there was no doubt at all.

'No one raised a voice against what was said,' the abbot mentioned almost absently. 'Except an envoy from the lady, who fared no better than the one who spoke, last time, for King Stephen's queen. Though this one, at least, was not set upon by assassins in the street.'*

Inevitably those two legatine councils, one in April, one in December, had been exact and chilling mirror-images, fortune turning her face now to one faction, now to the other, and taking back with the left hand what she had given with the right. There might yet be as many further reversals

* *The Pilgrim of Hate.*

before ever there was an end in sight.

'We are back where we began,' said the abbot, 'and nothing to show for months of misery. And what will the King do now?'

'That I shall hope to find out during the Christmas feast,' said Hugh, rising to take his leave. 'For I'm summoned to my lord, Father, like you. King Stephen wants all his sheriffs about him at his court at Canterbury, where he keeps the feast, to render account of our stewardships. Me among them, as his sheriff here for want of a better. What he'll do with his freedom remains to be seen. They say he's in good health and resolute spirits, if that means anything. As for what he means to do with me – well, that, no doubt, I shall discover, in due time.'

'My son, I trust he'll have the good sense to leave well alone. For here,' said Radulfus, 'we have at least preserved what good we can, and by the present measure in this unhappy realm, it *is* well with this shire. But I doubt whatever he does else can only mean more fighting and more wretchedness for England. And you and I can do nothing to prevent or better it.'

'Well, if we cannot give England peace,' said Hugh, smiling somewhat wryly, 'at least let's see what you and I can do between us for Shrewsbury.'

After dinner in the refectory Brother Cadfael made his way across the great court, rounded the thick, dark mass of the box hedge – grown straggly now, he noted, and ripe for a final clipping before growth ceased in the cold – and entered the moist flower gardens, where leggy roses balanced at a man's height on their thin, leafless stems, and still glowed with invincible light and life. Beyond lay his herb garden, walled and silent, all its small, square beds already falling asleep, naked spears of mint left standing stiff as wire, cushions of thyme flattened to the ground, crouching to protect their remaining leaves, yet over all a faint surviving fragrance of the summer's spices. Partly a memory, perhaps, partly drifting out from the open door of his workshop, where bunches of dried herbs swung from the eaves and the beams within, but surely, also, still emanating from these drowsy minor manifestations of God, grown old and tired now only to grow young and vigorous again with the spring. Green phoenixes every one, visible proof, if any were needed, of perpetual life.

Within the wall it was mild and still, a sanctuary within a sanctuary. Cadfael sat down on the bench in his workshop, facing the open door, and composed himself at ease to employ his half-hour of permitted repose in meditation rather than sleep. The morning had provided plenty of food for thought, and he did his best thinking alone here in his own small kingdom.

So that, he thought, is the new priest of Holy Cross. Now why did Bishop Henry take the trouble to bestow on us one of his own household clerks, and one he valued, at that? One who either was born with or has acquired by reverent imitation what I take to be his overlord's notable qualities? Is it possible that two masterful, confident, proud men had become one too many for comfort, and Henry was glad to part with him? Or is the legate, after the humiliation of publicly eating his own words twice in one year, and the damage that may well have done to his prestige – after all that, has he been taking this opportunity of courting all his bishops and abbots by taking a fatherly interest in all their wants and needs? Flattering them by his attentions to prop up what might be stumbling allegiance? That is also possible, and he might be willing to sacrifice even a valued clerk to feel certain of a man like Radulfus. But one thing is sure, Cadfael concluded firmly, our abbot would not have been a party to such an appointment if he had not been convinced he was getting a man fit for the work.

He had closed his eyes, to think the better, and braced his back comfortably against the timber wall, sandalled feet crossed before him, hands folded in the sleeves of his habit, so still that to the young man approaching along the gravel path he seemed asleep. Others, unused to such complete stillness in a waking man, had sometimes made that mistake with Brother Cadfael. Cadfael heard the footsteps, wary and soft as they were. Not a brother, and the lay servants were few in number, and seldom had occasion to come here. Nor would they approach so cautiously if they had some errand here. Not sandals, these, but old, well-worn shoes, and their wearer imagined they trod silently, and indeed they came close to it, if Cadfael had not had the hearing of a wild creature. Outside the open door the steps halted, and for a long moment the silence became complete. He studies me, thought Cadfael. Well, I know what he sees, if I don't know what he makes of it: a man past sixty, in robust health, bar the occasional stiffness in the joints proper to his age, squarely made, blunt-featured, with wiry brown hair laced with grey, and in need of a trim, come to think of it! – round a shaven crown that's been out in all weathers for many a year. He weighs me, he measures me, and takes his time about it.

He opened his eyes. 'I may look like a mastiff,' he said amiably, 'but it's years now since I bit anyone. Step in, and never hesitate.'

So brisk and unexpected a greeting, so far from drawing the visitor within, caused him to take a startled pace backwards, so that he stood full in the soft noon light of the day, to be seen clearly. A young fellow surely not above twenty, of the middle height but very well put together, dressed in wrinkled cloth hose of an indeterminate drab colour, scuffed leather shoes very down at heel, a dark brown cotte rubbed slightly paler where the sleeves chafed the flanks, and belted with a frayed rope girdle, and a short, caped capuchon thrown back on his shoulders. The coarse linen of his shirt showed at the neck, unlaced, and the sleeves of the cotte were short on him, showing a length of paler wrist above good brown hands. A compact, stout pillar of young manhood stood sturdily to be appraised, and once the immediate check had passed, even a long and silent appraisal seemed to reassure him rather than to make him uneasy, for a distinct spark lit in his eye, and an irrepressible grin hovered about his mouth as he said very respectfully:

'They told me at the gatehouse to come here. I'm looking for a brother named Cadfael.'

He had a pleasant voice, pitched agreeably low but with a fine, blithe ring to it, and just now practising a meekness which did not seem altogether at home on his tongue. Cadfael continued to study him with quickening interest. A mop of shaggy light-brown curls capped a shapely head poised on an elegant neck, and the face that took such pains to play the rustic innocent abashed before his betters was youthfully rounded of cheek and chin, but very adequately supplied with bone, too, and shaven clean as the schoolboy it aimed at presenting. A guileless face, but for the suppressed smoulder of mischief in the wide hazel eyes, changeable and fluid like peat water flowing over sunlit pebbles of delectable, autumnal greens and browns. There was nothing he could do about that merry sparkle. Asleep, the angelic simpleton might achieve conviction, but not with those eyes open.

'Then you have found him,' said Cadfael. 'That name belongs to me. And you, I take it, must be the young fellow who came here with the priest, and wants work with us for a while.' He rose, gathering himself without haste. Their eyes came virtually on a level. Dancing, brook-water eyes the boy had, scintillating with winter sunlight. 'What was the name they gave you, son?'

'N . . . name?' The stammer was a surprise, and the sudden nervous flickering of long brown lashes that briefly veiled the lively eyes was the first sign of unease Cadfael had detected in him. 'Benet – my name's Benet. My Aunt Diota is widow to a decent man, John Hammet, who was a groom in the lord bishop's service, so when he died Bishop Henry found a place for her with Father Ailnoth. That's how we came here. They're used to each other now for three years and more. And I begged to come here along with them to see could I find work near to her. I'm not skilled, but what I don't know I can learn.'

Very voluble now, all at once, and no more stammering, either, and he had stepped within, into shadow from the midday light, quenching somewhat of his perilous brightness. 'He said you could make use of me here,' said the vibrant voice, meekly muted. 'Tell me what to do, and I'll do it.'

'And a very proper attitude to work,' allowed Cadfael. 'You'll be sharing the life here within the enclave, so I'm told. Where have they lodged you? Among the lay servants?'

'Nowhere yet,' said the boy, his voice cautiously recovering its spring and resonance. 'But I'm promised a bed here within. I'd just as soon be out of the priest's house. There's a parish fellow looks after his glebe, they tell me, so there's no need for me there.'

'Well, there's need enough here,' said Cadfael heartily, 'for what with one thing and another I'm behind with the rough digging that ought to be done before the frosts come, and I've half a dozen fruit trees here in the small orchard that need pruning about Christmas time. Brother Bernard will be wanting to borrow you to help with the ploughing in the Gaye, where our main gardens are – you'll scarcely be familiar with the lie of the land yet, but you'll soon get used to it. I'll see you're not snatched away until I've had the worth of you here. Come, then, and see what we have for you within the walls.'

Benet had come a few paces more into the hut, and was looking about him with curiosity and mild awe at the array of bottles, jars and flagons that furnished Brother Cadfael's shelves, the rustling bunches of herbs that sighed overhead in the faint stirrings of air from the open door, the small brass scales, the three mortars, the single gently bubbling wine-jar, the little wooden bowls of medicinal roots, and a batch of small white lozenges drying on a marble slab. His round-eyed, open-mouthed stare spoke for him. Cadfael half-expected him to cross himself defensively against such ominous mysteries, but Benet stopped short of that. Just as well, thought Cadfael, alerted and amused, for I should not quite have believed in it.

'This, too, you can learn, if you put your mind to it diligently enough,' he said drily, 'but it will take you some years. Mere medicines – God made every ingredient that goes into them, there's no other magic. But let's begin with what's needed most. There's a good acre of vegetable garden beds to rough-dig, and a small mountain of well-weathered stable muck to cart and spread on the main butts and the rose beds. And the sooner we get down to it, the sooner it will be done. Come and see!'

The boy followed him willingly enough, his light, lively eyes scanning everything with interest. Beyond the fish ponds, in the two pease fields that ran down the slope to the Meole Brook, the western boundary of the enclave, the haulms had long since been cut close and dried for stable bedding, and the roots ploughed back into the soil, but there would be a heavy and dirty job there spreading much of the ripened and tempered manure from the stable yard and the byres. There were the few fruit trees in the small orchard to be pruned, but such growth as remained in the grass, in this mild opening of the month, was cropped neatly by two yearling lambs. The flower beds wore their usual somewhat ragged autumn look, but would do with one last weeding, if time served, before all growth ceased in the cold. The kitchen garden, cleared of its crops, lay weedy and trampled, waiting for the spade, a dauntingly large expanse. But it seemed that nothing could daunt Benet.

'A goodish stretch,' he said cheerfully, eyeing the long main butt with no sign of discouragement. 'Where will I find the tools?'

Cadfael showed him the low shed where they were to be found, and was interested to note that the young man looked round him among the assembly with a slightly doubtful face, though he soon selected the iron-shod wooden spade appropriate to the job in hand, and even viewed the length of the ground ahead and started his first row with judgement and energy, if not with very much skill.

'Wait!' said Cadfael, noting the thin, worn shoes the boy wore. 'If you thrust like that in such wear you'll have a swollen foot before long. I have wooden pattens in my hut that you can strap under your feet and shove as hard as you please. But no need to rush at it, or you'll be in a muck sweat before you've done a dozen rows. What you must do is set an even pace, get a rhythm into it, and you can go on all day, the spade will keep time for you. Sing to it if you have breath enough, or hum with it and save your breath. You'll be surprised how the rows will multiply.' He caught himself up there, somewhat belatedly aware that he was giving away too much of what he had already observed. 'Your work's been mainly with horses, as I heard,' he said blandly. 'There's an art in every labour.' And he went to fetch the wooden pattens he had himself carved out to shoe his own feet against either harsh digging or deep mire, before Benet could bridle in self-defence.

Thus shod and advised, Benet began very circumspectly, and Cadfael stayed only to see him launched into a good, steady action before he took himself off into his workshop, to be about his ordinary business of pounding up green herbs for an ointment of his own concoction, good against the chapped hands that would surely make their usual January appearance among the copyists and illuminators in the scriptorium. There would be coughs and colds, too, no doubt, later on, and now was the right time to prepare such of his medicines as would keep through the winter.

When it was almost time to clear away his impedimenta and prepare for Vespers he went out to see how his acolyte was faring. No one likes to be watched at his work, especially if he comes raw to the practice, and maybe a thought sensitive about his lack of skill and experience. Cadfael was impressed by the great surge the young man had made down the formidable butt of ground. His rows were straight, clearly he had a good eye. His cut appeared to be deep, by the rich black of the upturned tilth. True, he had somewhat sprayed soil over the border paths, but he had also ferreted out a twig broom from the shed, and was busy brushing back the spilled earth to where it belonged. He looked up a little defensively at Cadfael, flicking a glance towards the spade he had left lying.

'I've blunted the iron edge against a stone,' he said, and dropped his broom to up-end the spade and run his fingers gingerly along the metal rim that bound the wood. 'I'll hammer it out fine before I leave it. There's a hammer in the shed there, and your water trough has a good wide rim to the stone. Though I was aiming at two rows more before the light goes.'

'Son,' said Cadfael heartily, 'you've already done more than ever I expected of you. As for the spade, that edge has been replaced three times at least since the tool was made, and I know well enough it's due for a fourth sheathing very soon. If you think it will do yet a while, at least to finish this task, then beat if out again by all means, but then put it away, and wash, and come to Vespers.'

Benet looked up from the dented edge, suddenly aware of cautious praise, and broke into the broadest and most unguarded grin Cadfael could ever recall seeing, and the speckled, limpid light blazed up in his trout-stream eyes.

'I'll do, then?' he said, between simple pleasure and subtle impudence, flushed and exhilarated with his own energy; and added with unwary honesty: 'I've hardly had a spade in my hands before.'

'Now that,' said Cadfael, straight faced, and eyeing with interest the form and trim of the hands that jutted a little too far from the outgrown sleeves, 'that I never would have suspected.'

'I've worked mostly with –' Benet began in slight haste.

'. . . with horses. Yes, I know! Well, you match today's effort tomorrow, and tomorrow's the next day, and yes, you'll do.'

Cadfael went to Vespers with his mind's eye full of the jaunty figure of his new labourer, striding away to beat out the dented iron edge of the spade into even sharpness, and his ears were still stretched to catch the whistled tune, certainly not liturgical in character, to which Benet's large young feet in their scuffed shoes and borrowed pattens kept time.

'Father Ailnoth was installed in his cure this morning,' said Cadfael, coming fresh from the induction on the second day. 'You didn't want to attend?'

'I?' Benet straightened up over his spade in ingenuous surprise. 'No, why should I? I've got my work here, he can take care of his without any help from me. I hardly knew the man until we set off to come here. Why, did all go well?'

'Yes – oh, yes, all went well. His sermon was perhaps a little harsh on poor sinners,' said Cadfael, doubtfully pondering. 'No doubt he wanted to begin by showing his zeal at the outset. The rein can always be slackened later, when priest and people come to know each other better, and know where they stand. It's never easy for a younger man and a stranger to follow one old and accustomed. The old shoe comforts, the new pinches. But given time enough, the new comes to be the old, and fits as gently.'

It seemed that Benet had very quickly developed the ability to read between lines where his new master was concerned. He stood gazing earnestly at Cadfael with a slight frown, his curly head on one side, his smooth brown forehead creased in unaccustomed gravity, as if he had been brought up without warning against some unforeseen question, and was suddenly aware that he ought to have been giving thought to it long ago, if he had not been totally preoccupied with some other enterprise of his own.

'Aunt Diota has been with him over three years,' he said consideringly, 'and she's never made any complaint of him, as far as I know. I only rubbed shoulders with him on the way here, and I was thankful to him for bringing me. Not a man a servant like me could be easy with, but I minded my tongue and did what he bade me, and he was fair enough in his dealings with me.' Benet's buoyancy returned like a gust of the western wind, blowing doubts away. 'Ah, here is he as raw in his new work as I am in mine, but he sets out to cudgel his way through, and I have the good sense to worm my way in gently. Let him alone, and he'll get his feet to the ground.'

He was right, of course, a new man comes unmeasured and uneasy into a place not yet mellowed to him, and must be given time to breathe, and listen to the breathing of others. But Cadfael went to his own work with fretting memories of a homily half frenetic dream, half judgement day, eloquently phrased, beginning with the pure air of a scarcely accessible heaven, and ending with the anatomy of a far-too-visual hell.

'. . . that hell which is an island, for ever circled by four seas, the guardian dragons of the condemned. The sea of bitterness, whose every wave burns more white-hot than the mainland fires of hell itself; the sea of rebellion, which at every stroke of swimmer or rower casts the fugitive back into the fire; the sea of despair, in which every barque founders, and every swimmer sinks like a stone. And last, the sea of penitence, composed of all the tears of all the damned, by which alone, for the very few, escape is possible, since a single tear of Our Lord over sinners once fell into the fiery flood, and permeated, cooled and calmed the entire ocean for such as reach the perfection of remorse . . .'

A narrow and terrifying mercy, thought Cadfael, stirring a balsam for the chests of the old, imperfect men in the infirmary, human and fallible like himself, and not long for this world. Hardly mercy at all!

Chapter Three

The first small cloud that showed in the serene sky of the Foregate came when Aelgar, who had always worked the field strips of the priest's glebe, and cared for the parish bull and the parish boar, came with a grievance to Erwald the wheelwright, who was provost of the Foregate, rather in anxiety than in any spirit of rebellion, complaining that his new master had raised doubts about whether his servant was free or villein. For there was one strip in the more distant fields which was in mild dispute at the time of Father Adam's death, and the tenure had not been agreed between priest and man when Adam died. Had he lived there would have been an amicable arrangement, since Adam certainly had no greed in his make-up, and there was a fair claim on Aelgar's part through his mother. But Father Ailnoth, unswervingly exact, had insisted rather that the case should come to court, and further, had said outright that in the King's court Aelgar would have no standing, since he was not free, but villein.

'And everyone knows,' said Aelgar, fretting, 'that I'm a free man and always have been, but he says I have villein kin, for my uncle and my cousin have a yardland in the manor of Worthin, and hold it by customary services, and that's the proof. And true enough, for my father's younger brother, being landless, took the yardland gladly when it fell vacant, and agreed to do service for it, but for all that he was born free, like all my kin. It's not that I grudge him or the church that strip, if it's justly his, but how if he bring case to prove me a villein and no free man?'

'He'll not do that,' said Erwald comfortably, 'for it would never stand if he did. And why should he want to do you wrong? He's a stickler for the letter of the law, you'll find, but nothing more than that. Why, every soul in the parish would testify. I'll tell him so, and he'll hear reason.'

But the tale had gone round before nightfall.

The second small blot in the clear sky was an urchin with a broken head, who admitted, between sniffs and sobs, that he and a few more of his age had been playing a somewhat rumbustious ball game against the wall of the priest's house, a clear, windowless wall well suited for the purpose, and that they had naturally made a certain amount of noise in the process. But so they had many times before, and Father Adam had never done worse than shake a tolerant fist at them, and grin, and finally shoo them away like chickens. This time a tall black figure had surged out of the house crying anathema at them and brandishing a great long staff, and even their startled speed had not been enough to bring them off without damage. Two or three had bad bruises to show for it, and this unfortunate had taken a blow on the head that all but stunned him, and left him with a broken wound that bled alarmingly for a while, as head wounds do.

'I know they can be imps of Satan,' said Erwald to Brother Cadfael, when the child had been soothed and bandaged and lugged away by an indignant mother, 'and many a time I expect you and I have clouted a backside or boxed an ear, but not with a great walking-staff like that one he carries.'

'That could well have been an unlucky stroke that was never meant to land,' said Cadfael. 'But I wouldn't say he'll ever be as easy on the scamps as Father Adam was. They'd best learn to stay out of his way, or mind their manners within reach of him.'

It was soon plain that the boys thought so, too, for there were no more noisy games outside the small house at the end of the alley, and when the tall, black-clad figure was seen stalking down the Foregate, cloak flying like a crow's wings in time to his impetuous stride, the children melted away to safe distances, even when they were about blameless business.

It certainly could not be said that Father Ailnoth neglected his duties. He was meticulous in observing the hours, and let nothing interrupt his saying of the office, he preached somewhat stern sermons, conducted his services reverently, visited the sick, exhorted the backsliding. His comfort to the ailing was austere, even chilling, and his penances heavier than those to which his flock was accustomed, but he did all that his cure required of him. He also took jealous care of all the perquisites of his office, tithe and tilth, to the extent that one of his neighbours in the fields was complaining of having half his headland ploughed up, and Aelgar was protesting that he had been ordered to plough more closely, for the waste of ground was blameworthy.

The few boys who had been learning a smattering of letters from Father Adam, and had continued their lessons under his successor, grew less and less willing to attend, and muttered to their parents that they were beaten now for the least error, let alone a real offence.

'It was a mistake,' said Brother Jerome loftily, 'ever to let them run wild, as Father Adam did. They feel a proper curb now as affliction, instead of fair usage. What says the Rule on this head? That boys or youths who cannot yet understand how great a punishment excommunication is, must be punished for their offences either by fasting, or by sharp stripes, for their own good. The priest does very properly by them.'

'I cannot regard a simple mistake in letters,' retorted Brother Paul, up in arms for lads no older than his own charges, 'as an offence. Offence argues a will to offend, and these children answer as best they know, having no will but to do well.'

'The offence,' said Jerome pompously, 'is in the neglect and inattention which caused them to be imperfect in answering. Those who attend diligently will be able to answer without fault.'

'Not when they are already afraid,' snapped Brother Paul, and fled the argument for fear of his own temper. Jerome had a way of presenting his pious face as a target, and Paul, who like most big, powerful men could be astonishingly gentle and tender with the helpless, like his youngest pupils, was only too well aware of what his fists could do to an opponent of his own size, let alone a puny creature like Jerome.

It was more than a week before the matter came to the notice of Abbot Radulfus, and even then it was a relatively minor complaint that set the affair in motion. For Father Ailnoth had publicly accused Jordan Achard, the Foregate baker, of delivering short-weight loaves, and Jordan, rightly pricked in his professional pride, meant to rebut the charge at all costs.

'And a lucky man he is,' said Erwald the provost heartily, 'that he's charged with the one thing every soul in the Foregate will swear is false, for he gives just measure and always has, if he does nothing else justly in his life. If he'd been charged with fathering one or two of the recent bastards in these parts, he'd have had good cause to sing very low. But he bakes good bread, and never cheats on the weight. And how the priest came by this error is a mystery, but Jordan wants blood for it, and he has a fluent mouth on him that might well speak up usefully for others less bold.'

So it was that the provost of the Foregate, backed by Jordan the baker and one or two more of the notables of the parish, came to ask audience of Abbot Radulfus in chapter on the eighteenth day of December.

'I have asked you here into private with me,' said the abbot, when they had withdrawn at his request into the parlour in his lodging, 'so that the daily duties of the brothers may not be disrupted. For I see that you have much to discuss, and I would like you to speak freely. Now we have time enough. Master Provost, you have my attention. I desire the prosperity and happiness of the Foregate, as you do.'

His very use of the courtesy title, to which Erwald had no official right, was meant as an invitation, and as such accepted.

'Father Abbot,' began Erwald earnestly, 'we are come to you thus because we are not altogether easy at the rule of our new priest. Father Ailnoth has his duties in the church, and performs them faithfully, and there we have no complaint of him. But where he moves among us in the parish we are not happy with his dealings. He has called into question whether Aelgar, who works for him, is villein or free, and has not asked of us, who know very well he is a free man. He has also caused Aelgar to plough up a part of the headland of his neighbour Eadwin, without Eadwin's knowledge or leave. He has accused Master Jordan, here, of giving short weight, while all of us here know that is false. Jordan is known for good bread and good measure.'

'That is truth,' said Jordan emphatically. 'I rent my bakery ovens from the abbey, it is on your land I work, you have known me for years, that I take pride in my bread.'

'You have that right,' agreed Radulfus, 'it is good bread. Go on, Master Provost, there is more to tell.'

'My lord, there is,' said Erwald, very gravely now. 'You may have heard with what strict dealing Father Ailnoth keeps his school. The same severity he uses towards the boys of the parish, wherever he sees them gathered, if they put a foot aside – and you know that the young are liable to folly. He is too free with his blows, he has done violence where it was not called for, not by our measure. The children are afraid of him. That is not good, though not everyone has patience with children. But the women are frightened, too. He preaches such dire things, they are afraid of hell.'

'There is no need to fear,' said the abbot, 'unless by reason of a consciousness of sin. I do not think we have here in the parish such great sinners.'

'No, my lord, but women are tender and easily frightened. They look within for sins they may have committed, unknowing. They are no longer sure what is sin and what is not, so they dare not breathe without wondering if they do wrong. But there is more still.'

'I am listening,' said the abbot.

'My lord, there's a decent poor man of this parish, Centwin, whose wife Elen bore a very weakly child, a boy, four days ago. It was about Sext when the baby was born, and it was so small and feeble, they were sure it must die, and Centwin ran quickly to the priest's house, and begged him to come and baptise the boy before he died, that his soul might be saved. And Father Ailnoth sent out word that he was at his devotions, and could not come until he had completed the office. Centwin begged him, but he would not interrupt his prayers. And when he did go, Father, the baby was dead.'

The small, chill silence seemed to bring down a looming darkness on the panelled room.

'Father, he would not give the child Christian burial, because it was not baptised. He said it could not come within the hallowed ground, though he would say what prayers he could at its burial – which was in a grave outside the pale. The place I can show.'

Abbot Radulfus said with infinite heaviness: 'He was within his rights.'

'His rights! What of the child's rights? It might have been christen soul if he had come when he was called for.'

'He was within his rights,' said Radulfus again, inexorably but with deep detestation. 'The office is sacrosanct.'

'So is the newborn soul,' said Erwald, remorselessly eloquent.

'You say well. And God hears us both. There can and shall be dispensation. If you have more to tell, go on, tell me all.'

'My lord, there was a girl of this parish – Eluned – very beautiful. Not like other girls, wild as a hare. Everyone knew her. God knows she never harmed a soul but herself, the creature! My lord, she could not say no to men. Time and again she went with this one or that, but always she came back, as wild returning as going, in tears, and made her confession, and swore amendment. And meant it! But she never could keep it, a lad would look at her and sigh. . . . Father Adam always took her back, confessed her, gave her penance, and afterwards absolution. He knew she could not help it. And she as kind a creature to man or child or beast as ever breathed – too kind!'

The abbot sat still and silent, foreseeing what was to come.

'Last month she bore a child. When she was delivered and recovered she came, as she always came, mad with shame, to make her confession. He refused her countenance. He told her she had broken every promise of amendment, and so she had, but still . . . He would not give her penance, because he would not take her word, and so he refused her absolution. And when she came humbly to enter the church and hear Mass, he turned her away, and shut the door against her. Publicly and loudly he did it, in front of all.'

There was a long and deep silence before the abbot asked, perforce: 'What became of her?' For clearly she was already in the past, an outcast shade.

'They took her out of the mill-pond, my lord. By good fortune she had drifted down to the brook, and those who drew her out were from the town, and did not know her, so they took her with them back to their own parish, and the priest of Saint Chad's has buried her. It was not clear how she came to drown, it was taken for accident.'

Though of course everyone knew it was none. That was clear in look and voice. Despair is deadly sin. Then what of the record of those who deal out despair?

'Leave all this in my hands,' said Abbot Radulfus. 'I will speak to Father Ailnoth.'

There was no trace of guilt, trepidation or want of assurance in the long, austere, handsome face that confronted Abbot Radulfus across the desk in his parlour, after Mass. The man stood quite erect and still, with hands folded at ease and face invincibly calm.

'Father Abbot, if I may speak freely, the souls of my cure had been long neglected, to their own ruin. The garden is full of weeds, they starve and strangle the good grain. I am pledged to do whatever is needed to bring a clean crop, and so I must and will endeavour. I can do no other. The child spared will be the man spoiled. As for the matter of Eadwin's headland, it has been shown me that I have removed his boundary stone. That was in error, and the error has been made good. I have replaced the stone and drawn my own bounds short of it. I would not possess myself of one hand's breadth of land that belonged to another man.'

And that was surely truth. Not a hand's breadth of land nor a penny in money. Nor let go of one or the other that belonged to him. The bare razor of justice was his measure.

'I am less concerned for a yard of headland,' said the abbot drily, 'than for matters that touch a man's being even more nearly. Your man Aelgar was born free, is free man now, and so are his uncle and cousin, and if they take steps to assert it there will be no man query it hereafter. They assumed such customary duties as they do by way of payment for a piece of land, there is no disfranchisement, no more than when a man pays in money.'

'So I have found by enquiry,' said Ailnoth imperturbably, 'and have said as much to him.'

'Then that was properly done. But it would have been better to enquire first and accuse afterwards.'

'My lord, no just man should resent the appeal to justice. I am new among these people, I heard of the kinsmen's land, that it was held by villein service. It was my duty to find out the truth, and it was honest to speak first to the man himself.'

Which was true enough, if not kindly, and it seemed he had acknowledged the truth against himself, once established, with the same steely integrity. But what is to be done with such a man, among the common, fallible run of humanity? Radulfus went on to graver matters.

'The child that was born to the man Centwin and his wife, and lived barely an hour. . . . The man came to you, urging haste, since the baby was very feeble and likely to die. You did not go with him to give it Christian baptism, and since your ministration came too late, as I hear, you denied the infant burial in consecrated ground. Why did you not go at once when you were called, and with all haste?'

'Because I had but just begun the office. My lord, I never have broken off my devotions according to my vows, and never will, for any cause, though it were my own death. Until I had completed the act of worship I could not go. As soon as it was ended, I did go. I could not know the child would die so soon. But if I had known, still I could not have cut short the worship I owe.'

'There are other obligations you owe no less,' said Radulfus with some asperity. 'There are times when it is needful to make a choice between duties, and yours, I think, is first to the souls of those within your care. You chose rather the perfection of your own personal worship, and consigned the child to a grave outside the pale. Was that well done?'

'My lord,' said Ailnoth, unflinching, and with the high and smouldering gleam of self-justification in his black eyes, 'as I hold, it was. I will not go aside from the least iota of my service where the sacred office is concerned. My own soul and all others must bow to that.'

'Even the soul of the most innocent, new come into the world, the most defenceless of God's creatures?'

'My lord, you know well that the letter of divine law does not permit the burial of unchristened creatures within the pale. I keep the rules by which I am bound. I can do no other. God will know where to find Centwin's babe, if his mercy extends to him, in holy ground or base.'

After its merciless fashion it was a good answer. The abbot pondered, eyeing the stony, assured face.

'The letter of the rule is much, I grant you, but the spirit is more. And you might well have jeopardised your own soul to ensure that of a newborn child. An office interrupted can be completed without sin, if the cause be urgent enough. And there is also the matter of the girl Eluned, who went to her death after – I say after, mark, I do not say because! – you turned her away from the church. It is a grave thing to refuse confession and penance even to the greatest sinner.'

'Father Abbot,' said Ailnoth, with the first hot spurt of

passion, immovable in righteousness, 'where there is no penitence there can be neither penance nor absolution. The woman had pleaded penitence and vowed amendment time after time, and never kept her word. I have heard from others all her reputation, and it is past amendment. I could not in conscience confess her, for I could not take her word. If there is no truth in the act of contrition, there is no merit in confession, and to absolve her would have been deadly sin. A whore past recovery! I do not repent me, whether she died or no. I would do again what I did. There is no compromise with the pledges by which I am bound.'

'There will be no compromise with the answer you must make for two deaths,' said Radulfus solemnly, 'if God should take a view different from yours. I bid you recall, Father Ailnoth, that you are summoned to call not the righteous, but sinners to repentance, the weak, the fallible, those who go in fear and ignorance, and have not your pure advantage. Temper your demands to their abilities, and be less severe on those who cannot match your perfection.' He paused there, for it was meant as irony, to bite, but the proud, impervious face never winced, accepting the accolade. 'And be slow to lay your hand upon the children,' he said, 'unless they offend of malicious intent. To error we are all liable, even you.'

'I study to do right,' said Ailnoth, 'as I have always, and always shall.' And he went away with the same confident step, vehement and firm, the skirts of his gown billowing like wings in the wind of his going.

'A man abstemious, rigidly upright, inflexibly honest, ferociously chaste,' said Radulfus in private to Prior Robert. 'A man with every virtue, except humility and human kindess. That is what I have brought upon the Foregate, Robert. And now what are we to do about him?'

Dame Diota Hammet came on the twenty-second day of December to the gatehouse of the abbey with a covered basket, and asked meekly for her nephew Benet, for whom she had brought a cake for his Christmas, and a few honey buns from her festival baking. The porter, knowing her for the parish priest's housekeeper, directed her through to the garden, where Benet was busy clipping the last straggly growth from the box hedges.

Hearing their voices, Cadfael looked out from his workshop, and divining who this matronly woman must be, was about to return to his mortar when he was caught by some delicate shade in their greeting. A matter-of-fact affection, easy-going and undemonstrative, was natural between aunt and nephew, and what he beheld here hardly went beyond that, but for all that there was a gloss of tenderness and almost deference in the woman's bearing towards her young kinsman, and an unexpected, childish grace in the warmth with which he embraced her. True, he was already known for a young man who did nothing by halves, but here were certainly aunt and nephew who did not take each other for granted.

Cadfael withdrew to his work again and left them their privacy. A comely, well-kept woman was Mistress Hammet, with decent black clothing befitting a priest's housekeeper, and a dark shawl over her neat, greying hair. Her oval face, mildly sad in repose, brightened vividly in greeting the boy, and then she looked no more than forty years old, and perhaps, indeed, she was no more. Benet's mother's sister, wondered Cadfael? If so, he took after his father, for there was very little resemblance here. Well, it was none of his business!

Benet came bounding into the workshop to empty the basket of its good things, spreading them out on the wooden bench. 'We're in luck, Brother Cadfael, for she's as good a cook as you'd find in the King's own kitchen. You and I can eat like princes.'

And he was off again as blithely to restore the empty basket. Cadfael looked out after him through the open door, and saw him hand over, besides the basket, some small thing he drew from the breast of his cotte. She took it, nodding earnestly, unsmiling, and the boy stooped and kissed her cheek. She smiled then. He had a way with him, no question. She turned and went away, and left him looking after her for a long moment, before he also turned, and came back to the workshop. The engaging grin came back readily to his face.

'"On no account,"' quoted Cadfael, straight-faced, '"may a monk accept small presents of any kind, from his parents or anyone else, without the abbot's permission." That, sweet son, is in the Rule.'

'Lucky you, then, and lucky I,' said the boy gaily, 'that I've taken no vows. She makes the best honey cakes ever I tasted.' And he sank even white teeth into one of them, and reached to offer another to Cadfael.

'". . . nor may the brethren exchange them, one with another,"' said Cadfael, and accepted the offering. 'Lucky, indeed! Though I transgress in accepting, you go sinless in offering. Have you quite abandoned your inclination to the cloistered life, then?'

'Me?' said the youth, startled out of his busy munching, and open-mouthed. 'When did I ever profess any?'

'Not you, lad, but your sponsor on your account, when he asked work for you here.'

'Did he say that of me?'

'He did. Not positively promising it, mark you, but holding out the hope that you might settle to it one day. I grant you I've never seen much sign of it.'

Benet thought that over for a moment, while he finished his cake and licked the sticky crumbs from his fingers. 'No doubt he was anxious to get rid of me, and thought it might make me more welcome here. My face was never in any great favour with him – too much given to smiling, maybe. No, not even you will pen me in here for very long, Cadfael. When the time comes I'll be on my way. But while I'm here,' he said, breaking into the bountiful smile that might well strike an ascetic as far too frivolous, 'I'll do my fair share of the work.'

And he was off back to his box hedge, swinging the shears in one large, easy hand, and leaving Cadfael gazing after him with a very thoughtful face.

Chapter Four

Dame Diota Hammet presented herself later that afternoon at a house near Saint Chad's church, and asked timidly for the lord Ralph Giffard. The servant who opened the door to her looked her up and down and hesitated, never having seen her before.

'What's your business with him, mistress? Who sends you?'

'I'm to bring him this letter,' said Diota submissively, and held out a small rolled leaf fastened with a seal. 'And to wait for an answer, if my lord will be so good.'

He was in two minds about taking it from her hand. It was a small and irregularly shaped slip of parchment, with good reason, since it was one of the discarded edges from a leaf Brother Anselm had trimmed to shape and size for a piece of music, two days since. But the seal argued matter of possible importance, even on so insignificant a missive. The servant was still hesitating when a girl came out into the porch at his back, and seeing a woman unknown but clearly respectable, stayed to enquire curiously what was to do. She accepted the scroll readily enough, and knew the seal. She looked up with startled, intent blue eyes into Diota's face, and abruptly handed the scroll back to her.

'Come in, and deliver this yourself. I'll bring you to my step-father.'

The master of the house was sitting by a comfortable fire in a small solar, with wine at his elbow and a deerhound coiled about his feet. A big, ruddy, sinewy man of fifty, balding and bearded, very spruce in his dress and only just beginning to put on a little extra flesh after an active life, he looked what he was, the lord of two or three country manors and this town house, where he preferred to spend his Christmas in comfort. He looked up at Diota, when the girl presented her, with complete incomprehension, but he comprehended all too well when he looked at the seal that fastened the parchment. He asked no questions, but sent the girl for his clerk, and listened intently as the content was read to him, in so low a voice that it was plain the clerk understood how dangerous its import could be. He was a small, withered man, grown old in Giffard's service, and utterly trustworthy. He made an end, and watched his master's face anxiously.

'My lord, send nothing in writing! Word of mouth is safer, if you want to reply. Words said can be denied, to write them would be folly.'

Ralph sat pondering for a while in silence, and eyeing the unlikely messenger, who stood patiently and uneasily waiting.

'Tell him,' he said at last, 'that I have received and understood his message.'

She hesitated, and ventured at last to ask: 'Is that all, my lord?'

'It's enough! The less said the better, for him and for me.'

The girl, who had remained unobtrusive but attentive in a corner of the room, followed Diota out to the shadow of the porch, with doors closed behind them.

'Mistress,' she said softly in Diota's ear, 'where is he to be found – this man who sent you?'

By the brief, blank silence and the doubtful face of the older woman she understood her fears, and made impatient haste to allay them, her voice low and vehement. 'I mean him no harm, God knows! My father was of the same party – did you not see how well I knew the seal? You can trust me, I won't say word to any, nor to him, either, but I want to know how I may know him, where I may find him, in case of need.'

'At the abbey,' said Diota as softly and hurriedly, making up her mind. 'He's working in the garden, by the name of Benet, under the herbalist brother.'

'Oh, Brother Cadfael – I know him!' said the girl, breathing satisfaction. 'He treated me once for a bad fever, when I was ten years old, and he came to help my mother, three Christmases ago, when she fell into her last illness. Good, I know where his herbarium is. Go now, quickly!'

She watched Diota scurry hastily out of the small courtyard, and then closed the door and went back to the solar, where Giffard was sitting sunk in anxious consideration, heavy-browed and sombre.

'Shall you go to this meeting?'

He had the letter still in his hand. Once already he had made an impulsive motion towards the fire, to thrust the parchment into it and be rid of it, but then had drawn back again, rolled it carefully and hid it in the breast of his cotte. She took that for a sign favourable to the sender, and was pleased. It was no surprise that he did not give her a direct answer. This was a serious business and needed thought, and in any case he never paid any great heed to his step-daughter, either to confide in her or to regulate her actions. He was indulgent rather out of tolerant indifference than out of affection.

'Say no word of this to anyone,' he said. 'What have I to gain by keeping such an appointment? And everything to lose! Have not your family and mine lost enough already by loyalty to that cause? How if he should be followed to the mill?'

'Why should he be? No one has any suspicion of him. He's accepted at the abbey as a labourer in the gardens, calling himself Benet. He's vouched for. Christmas Eve, and by night, there'll be no one abroad but those already in the church. Where's the risk? It was a good time to choose. And he needs help.'

'Well. . . .' said Ralph, and drummed his fingers irresolutely on the small cylinder in the breast of his cotte. 'We have two days yet, we'll watch and wait until the time comes.'

Benet was sweeping up the brushings from the hedge, and whistling merrily over the work, when he heard brisk, light steps stirring the moist gravel on the path behind him, and turned to behold a young woman in a dark cloak and hood advancing upon him from the great court. A small, slender girl of erect and confident bearing, the outline of her swathed form softened and blurred by the faint mist of a still day, and the hovering approach of dusk. Not until she was quite near to him and he had stepped deferentially aside to give her passage could he see clearly the rosy, youthful face within the shadow of the hood, a rounded face with apple-blossom skin, a resolute chin, and a mouth full and firm in its generosity of line, and coloured like half-open roses. Then what light remained gathered into the harebell blue of her wide-set eyes, at once soft and brilliant, and he lost sight of everything else. And though he had made way for her to pass him by, and ducked his head to her in a properly servantlike reverence, she did not pass by, but lingered, studying him closely and candidly, with the fearless, innocent stare of a cat. Indeed there was something of the kitten about the whole face, wider at the brow and eyes than its length from brow to chin, tapered and tilted imperiously, as a kitten confronts the world, never having experienced fear. She looked him up and down gravely, and took her time about it, in a solemn inspection that might have been insolent if it had not implied a very serious purpose. Though what interest some noble young woman of the county or well-to-do merchant daughter of the town could have in him was more than Benet could imagine.

Only when she was satisfied of whatever had been in question in her mind did she ask, in a clear, firm voice: 'Are you Brother Cadfael's new helper here?'

'Yes, my lady,' said the dutiful labourer bashfully, shuffling his feet and somehow even contriving a blush that sat rather oddly on so positive and cheerful a countenance.

She looked at the trimmed hedge and the newly weeded and manured flower beds, and again at him, and for a dazzling instant he thought she smiled, but in the flicker of an eyelash she was solemn again.

'I came to ask Brother Cadfael for some herbs for my kitchen forcemeats. Do you know were I shall find him?'

'He's in his workshop within,' said Benet. 'Please to walk through into the walled garden there.'

'I remember the way,' she said, and inclined her head to him graciously, as noble to simple, and swept away from him through the open gate into the walled enclosure of the herbarium.

It was almost time for Vespers, and Benet could well have quit his labours and gone to make himself ready, but he prolonged his sweeping quite unnecessarily, gathering the brushings into a pile of supererogatory neatness, scattering them a little and massing them again, in order to get another close glimpse of her when she came blithely back with a bunch of dried herbs loosely wrapped in a cloth and carried carefully in her hands. She passed him this time without a glance, or seemed to do so, but still he had the feeling that those wide and wide-set eyes with their startling blueness took him in methodically in passing. The hood had slipped back a little from her head, and showed him a coiled braid of hair of an indefinable spring colour, like the young fronds of bracken when they are just unfolding, a soft light brown with tones of green in the shadows. Or hazel withies, perhaps! Hazel eyes are no great rarity, but how many women can boast of hazel hair?

She was gone, the hem of her cloak whisking round the box hedge and out of his sight. Benet forsook his broom in haste, left his pile of brushings lying, and went to pick Brother Cadfael's brains.

'Who was that lady?' he asked, point-blank.

'Is that a proper question for a postulant like you to be asking?' said Cadfael placidly, and went on cleaning and putting away his pestle and mortar.

Benet made a derisive noise, and interposed his sturdy person to confront Cadfael eye to eye, with no pretence whatsoever to notions of celibacy. 'Come, you know her, or at least she knows you. Who is she?'

'She spoke to you?' Cadfael wondered, interested.

'Only to ask me where she would find you. Yes, she spoke to me!' he said, elated. 'Yes, she stopped and looked me up and down, the creature, as though she found herself in need of a page, and thought I might do, given a little polishing. Would I do for a lady's page, Cadfael?'

'What's certain,' said Cadfael tolerantly, 'is that you'll never do for a monk. But no, I wouldn't say a lady's service is your right place, either.' He did not add: 'Unless on level terms!' but that was what was in his mind. At this moment the boy had shed all pretence of being a poor widow's penniless kinsman, untutored and awkward. That was no great surprise. There had been little effort spent on the imposture here in the garden for a week past, though the boy could reassume it at a moment's notice with others, and was still the rustic simpleton in Prior Robert's patronising presence.

'Cadfael . . .' Benet took him cajolingly by the shoulders and held him, tilting his curly head coaxingly, with a wilfully engaging intimacy. Given the occasion, he was well aware he could charm the birds from the trees. Nor did he have any difficulty in weighing up elder sympathisers who must once have shared much the same propensities. 'Cadfael, I may never speak to her again, I may never see her again – but I can *try*! Who is she?'

'Her name,' said Cadfael, capitulating rather from policy than from compulsion, 'is Sanan Bernières. Her father held a manor in the north-east of the shire, which was confiscated when he fought for his overlord FitzAlan and the Empress at the siege here, and died for it. Her mother married another vassal of FitzAlan, who had suffered his losses, too – the faction holds together, though they're all singing very small and lying very low here now. Giffard spends his winters mainly in his house in Shrewsbury, and since her mother died he brings his step-daughter to preside at his table-head. That's the lady you've seen pass by.'

'And had better let pass by?' said Benet, ruefully smiling in acknowledgement of a plain warning. 'Not for me?' He burst into the glowing grin to which Cadfael was becoming accustomed, and which sometimes gave him such qualms on behalf of his protégé, who was far too rash in the indulgence of his flashing moods. Benet laughed, and flung his arms about his mentor in a bear's hug. 'What will you wager?'

Cadfael freed an arm, without much ado, and held off his boisterous aggressor by a fistful of his thick curls.

'Where you're concerned, you madcap, I would not risk a hair that's left me. But watch your gait, you move out of your part. There are others here have keen eyes.'

'I do know,' said Benet, brought up short and sharp, his smile sobered into gravity. 'I do take care.'

How had they come by this secret and barely expressed understanding? Cadfael wondered as he went to Vespers. A kind of tacit agreement had been achieved, with never a word said of doubt, suspicion or plain, reckless trust. But the changed relationship existed, and was a factor to be reckoned with.

Hugh was gone, riding south for Canterbury in uncustomary state, well escorted and in his finery. He laughed at himself, but would not abate one degree of the dignity that was his due. 'If I come back deposed,' he said, 'at least I'll make a grand departure, and if I come back sheriff still, I'll do honour to the office.'

After his going Christmas seemed already on the doorstep, and there were great preparations to be made for the long night vigil and the proper celebration of the Nativity, and it was past Vespers on Christmas Eve before Cadfael had time to make a brief visit to the town, to spend at least an hour with Aline, and take a gift to his two-year-old godson, a little wooden horse that Martin Bellecote the master-carpenter had made for him, with gaily coloured harness and trappings fit for a knight, made out of scraps of felt and cloth and leather by Cadfael himself.

A soft, sleety rain had fallen earlier, but by that hour in the evening it was growing very cold, and there was frost in the air. The low, moist sky had cleared and grown infinitely tall, there were stars snapping out in it almost audibly, tiny but brilliant. By the morning the roads would be treacherous, and the frozen ruts a peril to wrenched ankles and unwary steps. There were still people abroad in the Foregate, most of them hurrying home by now, either to stoke up the fire and toast their feet, or to make ready for the long night in church. And as Cadfael crossed the bridge towards the town gate, the river in full, silent dark motion below, there was just enough light left to put names to those he met, coming from their shopping laden and in haste to get their purchases home. They exchanged greetings with him as they passed, for he was well known by his shape and his rolling gait even in so dim a light. The voices had the ring of frost about them, echoing like the chime of glass.

And here, striding across the bridge towards the Foregate, just within the compass of the torches burning under the town gate, came Ralph Giffard, on foot. Without the sidelong fall of the torchlight he would not have been recognised, but thus illuminated he was unmistakable. And where could Giffard be going at this time of the evening, and out of the town? Unless he meant to celebrate Christmas at the church of Holy Cross instead of in his own parish of Saint Chad. That was possible, though if so he was over-early. A good number of the wealthier townsfolk would also be making for the abbey this night.

Cadfael went on up the long curve of the Wyle, between the sparkling celestial darkness and the red, warm, earthy torchlight, to Hugh's house close by Saint Mary's church, and in through the courtyard to the hall door. No sooner had he set foot within than the excited imp Giles bore down upon him, yelling, and embraced him cripplingly round the thighs, which was as high as he could reach. To detach him was easy enough. As soon as the small, cloth-wrapped parcel was lowered into his sight he held up his arms for it gleefully, and plumped down in the rushes of the hall floor to unwrap it with cries of delight. But he did not forget, once the first transports were over, to make a rush for his godfather again, and clamber into his lap by the fireside to present him with a moist but fervent kiss in thanks. He had Hugh's self-reliant nature, but something also of his mother's instinctive sweetness.

'I can stay no more than an hour,' said Cadfael, as the boy scrambled down again to play with his new toy. 'I must be back for Compline, and very soon after that begins Matins, and we shall be up all the night until Prime and the dawn Mass.'

'Then at least rest an hour, and take food with me, and stay until Constance fetches my demon there away to his bed. Will you believe,' said Aline, smiling indulgently upon her offspring, 'what he says of this house without Hugh? Though it was Hugh told him what to say. He says he is the man of the house now, and asks how long his father will be away. He's too proud of himself to miss Hugh. It pleases his lordship to be taking his father's place.'

'You'd find his face fall if you told him longer than three or four days,' said Cadfael shrewdly. 'Tell him he's gone for a week, and there'll be tears. But three days? I daresay his pride will last out that long.'

At that moment the boy had no attention to spare for his dignity as lord of the household or his responsibilities as its protector in his father's absence, he was wholly taken up with galloping his new steed through the open plain of rushes, on some heroic adventure with an imaginary rider. Cadfael was left at liberty to sit with Aline, take meat and wine with her, and think and talk about Hugh, his possible reception at Canterbury, and his future, now hanging in the balance.

'He has deserved well of Stephen,' said Cadfael firmly, 'and Stephen is not quite a fool, he's seen too many change their coats, and change them back again when the wind turned. He'll know how to value one who never changed.'

When he noted the sand in the glass and rose to take his leave, he went out from the hall into the bright glitter of frost, and a vault of stars now three times larger than when first they appeared, and crackling with brilliance. The first real frost of the winter. As he made his way cautiously down the Wyle and out at the town gate he was thinking of the hard winter two years earlier, when the boy had been born, and hoping that this winter there would be no such mountainous snows and ferocious winds to drive it.* This night, the eve of the Nativity, hung about the town utterly still and silent, not a breath to temper the bite of the frost. Even the movements of such men as were abroad seemed hushed and almost stealthy, afraid to shake the wonder.

The bridge had a sheen of silver upon it after the earlier fine rain. The river ran dark and still, with too strong a flow for frost to have any hold. A few voices gave him good night as he passed. In the rutted road of the Foregate he began to hurry, fearing he had lingered a little too long. The trees that sheltered the long riverside level of the Gaye loomed like the dark fur of the earth's winter pelt on his left hand, the flat, pale sheen of the mill-pond opened out on his right, beyond the six little abbey houses of grace, three on either side the near end of the water, a narrow path slipping away from the road to serve each modest row. Silver and dark fell behind, he saw the torchlight glow from the gatehouse golden before him.

Still some twenty paces short of the gate he glimpsed a tall black figure sweeping towards him with long, rapid, fierce strides. The sidelong torchlight snatched it into momentary brightness as it strode past, the darkness took it again as it swept by Cadfael without pause or glance, long staff ringing

**The Virgin in the Ice.*

against the frosty ruts, wide black garments flying, head and shoulders thrusting forward hungrily, long pale oval of face fixed and grim, and for one instant a vagrant light from the opened door of the nearest house by the pool plucked two crimson sparks of fire from the dark pits of the eyes.

Cadfael called a greeting that was neither heeded nor heard. Father Ailnoth swept by, engendering round him the only turbulence in the night's stillness, and was lost in the dark. Like an avenging fury, Cadfael thought later, like a scavenging raven swooping through the Foregate to hunt out little venial sins, and consign the sinners to damnation.

In the church of Saint Chad, Ralph Giffard bent the knee with a satisfactory feeling of a duty done and fences securely mended. He had lost one manor through loyalty to the cause of his overlord FitzAlan and his sovereign, the Empress Maud, and it had taken him a good deal of cautious treading and quiet submission to achieve the successful retention of what remained. He had but one cause that mattered to him now, and that was to preserve his own situation and leave his remaining estate intact to his son. His life had never been threatened, he had not been so deeply involved as to invite death. But possessions are possessions, and he was an ageing man, by no means minded to abandon his lands and flee either abroad, to Normandy or Anjou, where he had no status, or to Gloucester, to take up arms for the liege lady who had already cost him dear. No, better far to sit still, shun every tempter, and forget old allegiance. Only so could he ensure that young Ralph, busy this Christmas happily playing lord of the manor at home, should survive this long conflict for the crown without loss, no matter which of the two claimants finally triumphed.

Ralph welcomed midnight with deep and genuine gratitude for the mercies shown forth upon men, and not least upon Ralph Giffard.

Benet slipped into the abbey church by the parish door, and made his way softly forward towards a spot where he could look through into the choir, and see the monks in their stalls, faintly lit by the yellow sheen of candles and the red glow of the altar lamps. The chanting of psalms came out into the nave muted and mild. Here the lighting was dim, and the cloaked assembly of the Foregate laity shifted and stirred, kneeled and rose again, every man nameless. There was a little while yet to wait before Matins began at the midnight hour, the celebration of God made flesh, virgin-born and wonderful. Why should not the Holy Spirit engender, as fire kindles fire and light light, the necessary instrument of flesh no more than the fuel that renders its substance to provide warmth and enlightenment? He who questions has already denied himself any answer. Benet did not question. He was breathing hard with haste and excitement, and even elation, for risk was meat to him. But once within here, in the obscurity that was at once peopled and isolated, he lost himself in awe, like the child he would never quite outgrow. He found himself a pillar, rather to brace himself by than to hide behind, and laid a hand to the cold stone, and waited, listening. The matched voices, soft as they were, expanded to fill the vault. The stone above, warmed by the music, reflected its arching radiance to the stone below.

He could see Brother Cadfael in his stall, and moved a little to have him more clearly in view. Perhaps he had chosen this spot purely to have in his sights the person most near to him in this place, a man already compromised, already tolerant, and all without any intent, on either part, to invade another's peace of mind. Only a little while, thought Benet, and you shall be free of me. Will you regret it, now and then, if you never again hear of me? And he wondered if he ought to say something clearly, something to be remembered, while there was still time.

A soft voice, just avoiding the sibilance of a whisper, breathed in his ear: 'He did not come?'

Benet turned his head very slowly, entranced and afraid, for surely it could not be the same voice, heard only once before, and briefly, but still causing the strings of his being to vibrate. And she was there, close at his right shoulder, the veritable, the unforgettable she. A dim, reflected light conjured her features out of the dark hood, broad brow, wide-set eyes, deeply blue. 'No,' she said. 'He didn't come!' And having answered herself, she heaved a great sigh. 'I never thought he would. Don't move – don't look round at me.'

He turned his face obediently towards the parish altar again. The soft breath fanned his cheek as she leaned close. 'You don't know who I am, but I know you.'

'I do know you,' said Benet as softly. Nothing more, and even that was uttered like a man in a dream.

Silence for a moment; then she said: 'Brother Cadfael told you?'

'I asked. . . .'

Silence again, with some soft implication of a smile in it, as though he had said something to please her, even distract her for a moment from whatever purpose had brought her here to his side.

'I know you, too. If Giffard is afraid, I am not. If he won't help you, I will. When can we two talk?'

'Now!' he said, suddenly wide awake and grasping with both hands at an opportunity for which he had never dared to hope. 'After Matins some people will be leaving, so may we. All the brothers will be here until dawn. As good a time as any!'

He felt her warm at his back, and knew when she shook softly with silent, excited laughter. 'Where?'

'Brother Cadfael's workshop.' It was the place he knew best as a possible solitude, while its proprietor kept the Christmas vigil here in the church. The brazier in the hut was turfed down to burn slowly through the night, he could easily blow it into life again to keep her warm. Clearly he could not take advantage of this delicate young being's partisan loyalty so far as to put her in peril, but at least this once he could speak with her alone, feast his eyes on her grave, ardent face, share with her the confidences of allies. Something to remember lifelong, if he never saw her again.

'By the south door, through the cloisters,' he said. 'No one will be there to see us tonight.'

The soft, warm breath in his ear said: 'Need we wait? I could slip into the porch now. Matins will be so long tonight. Will you follow?'

And she was away, not waiting for an answer, stealing silently and reverently across the tiles of the nave, and taking station for a few moments where she could be seen to be gazing devoutly in towards the high altar, beyond the chanting in the choir, in case anyone should be taking note of her movements. By that time he would have followed her wherever she chose to lead him. It hurt even to wait patiently the many minutes she delayed, before she chose her moment to withdraw into the darkness of the south porch. When he followed her, by cautious stages, reaching the darkness of the closed doorway with a great heaved breath of relief, he found her waiting with the heavy latch in her hand, motionless against the door. There they waited, close and quivering, for the first jubilant antiphon of Matins, and the triumphant answering cry:

'Christ is born unto us!'

'Oh, come, let us worship!'

Benet set his hand over hers on the massive latch, and lifted it softly as the hymn began. Outside, the night's darkness matched the darkness within. Who was to pay any attention now to two young creatures slipping through the chink of the door into the cold of the night, and cautiously letting the latch slide back into place? There was no one in the cloister, no one in the great court as they crossed it. Whether it was Benet who reached for her hand, or she for his, they rounded the corner of the thick box hedge in the garden hand in hand, and slowed to a walk there, panting and smiling, palms tightly clasped together, their breath a faint silver mist. The vast inverted bowl of sky, dark blue almost to blackness but polished bright and scintillating with stars, poured down upon them a still coldness they did not feel.

Brother Cadfael's timbered hut, solid and squat in the

sheltered enclosure, never quite lost its warmth. Benet closed the door gently behind them, and groped along the little shelf he knew now almost as well as did Cadfael himself, where the tinder box and lamp lay ready to hand. It took him two or three attempts before the charred linen caught at the spark, and let him blow it carefully into a glow. The wick of the lamp put up a tiny, wavering flame that grew into a steady flare, and stood up tall and erect. The leather bellows lay by the brazier, he had only to shift a turf or two and spend a minute industriously pumping, and the charcoal glowed brightly, and accepted a feeding of split wood to burn into a warm hearth.

'He'll know someone has been here,' said the girl, but very tranquilly.

'He'll know I was here,' said Benet, getting up lithely from his knees, his bold, boy's face conjured into summer bronze by the glow from the brazier. 'I doubt if he'll say so. But he may wonder why. And with whom!'

'You've brought other women here?' She tilted her head at him in challenge, abruptly displeased.

'Never any, till now. Never any, hereafter. Unless you so pleasure me a second time,' he said, and stared her down with fiery solemnity.

Some resinous knot in the new wood caught and hissed, sending up a clear, white flame for a moment between them. Across its pale, pure gold the two young faces sprang into mysterious brightness, lit from below, lips parted, eyes rounded in astonished gravity. Each of them stared into a mirror, matched and mated, and could not look away from the unexpected image of love.

Chapter Five

Prime was said at an early hour, after a very short interlude for sleep, and the dawn Mass followed with first light. Almost all the people of the Foregate had long since gone home, and the brothers, dazed with long standing and strung taut with the tensions of music and wonder, filed a little unsteadily up the night stairs to rest briefly before preparing for the day.

Brother Cadfael, stiff with being still for so long a time, felt himself in need rather of movement than of rest. Solitary in the lavatorium, he made unusually leisurely ablutions, shaved with care, and went out into the great court, just in time to see Dame Diota Hammet come hurrying in through the wicket in the gate, stumbling and slipping on the glazed cobbles, clutching her dark cloak about her, and gazing round in evident agitation. A furry fringe of hoar frost had formed on the collar of her cloak from her breath. Every outline of wall or bush or branch was silvered with the same glittering whiteness.

The porter had come out to greet her and ask her business, but she had observed Prior Robert emerging from the cloisters, and made for him like a homing bird, making him so low and unwary a reverence that she almost fell on her knees.

'Father Prior, my master – Father Ailnoth – has he been all night in the church with you?'

'I have not seen him,' said Robert, startled, and put out a hand in haste to help her keep her feet, for the rounded stones were wickedly treacherous. He held on to the arm he had grasped, and peered concernedly into her face. 'What is amiss? Surely he has his own Mass to take care of soon. By this time he should be robing. I should not interrupt him now, unless for some very grave reason. What is your need?'

'He is not there,' she said abruptly. 'I have been up to see. Cynric is there waiting, ready, but my master has not come.'

Prior Robert had begun to frown, certain that this silly woman was troubling him for no good reason, and yet made uneasy by her agitation. 'When did you see him last? You must know when he left his house.'

'Last evening, before Compline,' she said bleakly.

'What? And has not been back since then?'

'No, Father. He never came home all night. I thought he might have come to take part in your night offices, but no one has seen him even here. And as you say, by now he should be robing for his own Mass. But he is not there!'

Halted at the foot of the day stairs, Cadfael could not choose but overhear, and having overheard, inevitably recalled the ominous black-winged bird swooping along the Foregate towards the bridge at very much the same hour, according to Diota, when Ailnoth had left his own house. On what punitive errand, Cadfael wondered? And where could those raven wings have carried him, to cause him to fail of his duty on such a festal day?

'Father,' he said, coming forward with unwary haste, slithering on the frosty cobbles, 'I met the priest last night as I was coming back from the town to be in time for Compline. Not fifty paces from the gatehouse here, going towards the bridge, and in a hurry.'

Prior Robert looked round, frowning, at this unsolicited witness, and gnawed a lip in doubt how to proceed. 'He did not speak to you? You don't know where he was bound in such haste?'

'No. I spoke to him,' said Cadfael drily, 'but he was too intent to mark me. No, I have no notion where he was bound. But it was he. I saw him pass the light of the torches under the gate. No mistaking him.'

The woman was staring at him now with bruised, hollow eyes and still face, and the hood had slipped back from her forehead unnoticed, and showed a great leaden bruise on her left temple, broken at the centre by a wavering line of dried blood.

'You're hurt!' said Cadfael, asking no leave, and put back the folds of cloth from her head and turned her face to the dawning light. 'This is a bad blow you've suffered, it needs tending. How did you come by it?'

She shrank a little from his touch, and then submitted with a resigned sigh. 'I came out in the night, anxious about him, to see if there was anyone stirring, or any sign of him. The doorstone was frozen, I fell and struck my head. I've washed it well, it's nothing.'

Cadfael took her hand and turned up to view a palm rasped raw in three or four grazes, took up its fellow and found it marked almost as brutally. 'Well, perhaps you saved yourself worse by putting out these hands. But you must let me dress them for you, and your brow, too.'

Prior Robert stood gazing beyond them, pondering what it was best to do. 'Truly I wonder . . . If Father Ailnoth went out at that hour, and in such haste, may not he also have fallen, somewhere, and so injured himself that he's lying helpless? The frost was already setting in. . . .'

'It was,' said Cadfael, remembering the glassy sheen on the steep slope of the Wyle, and the icy ring of his own steps on the bridge. 'And sharply! And I would not say he was minding his steps when I saw him.'

'Some charitable errand. . .' murmured Robert anxiously. 'He would not spare himself. . . .'

No, neither himself nor any other soul! But true enough, those hasty steps might well have lunged into slippery places.

'If he has lain all night helpless in the cold,' said Robert, 'he may have caught his death. Brother Cadfael, do you tend to this lady, do whatever is needful, and I will go and speak to

Father Abbot. For I think we had best call all the brothers and lay brothers together, and set in hand a hunt for Father Ailnoth, wherever he may be.'

In the dim, quiet shelter of the workshop in the garden Cadfael sat his charge down on the bench against the wall, and turned to his brazier, to uncover it for the day. All the winter he kept it thus turfed overnight, to be ready at short notice if needed, the rest of the year he let it out, since it could easily be rekindled. None of his brews within here required positive warmth, but there were many among them that would not take kindly to frost.

The thick turves now damping it down were almost fresh, though neatly placed, and the fire beneath them live and comforting. Someone had been here during the night, and someone who knew how to lay his hand on the lamp and the tinder without disturbing anything else, and how to tend the fire to leave it much as he had found it. Young Benet had left few traces, but enough to set his signature to the nocturnal invasion. Even by night, it seemed, he practised very little dissembling where Cadfael was concerned, he was intent rather on leaving everything in order than on concealing his intrusion.

Cadfael warmed water in a pan, and diluted a lotion of betony, comfrey and daisy to cleanse the broken bruise on her forehead and the scored grazes in both palms, scratches that ran obliquely from the wrist to the root of the forefinger and thumb, torn by the frozen and rutted ground. She submitted to his ministrations with resigned dignity, her eyes veiled.

'That's a heavy fall you had,' said Cadfael, wiping away the dried line of blood from her temple.

'I was not minding myself,' she said, so simply that he knew it for plain truth. 'I am not of any importance.'

Her face, seen thus below him as he fingered her forehead, was a long oval, with fine, elongated features. Large, arched eyelids hid her eyes, her mouth was well shaped and generous but drooping with weariness. She braided her greying hair severely and coiled it behind her head. Now that she had told what she had come to tell, and laid it in other hands, she was calm and still under his handling.

'You'll need to get some rest now,' said Cadfael, 'if you've been up fretting all night, and after this blow. Whatever needs to be done Father Abbot will do. There! I'll not cover it, better to have it open to the air, but as soon as you're dismissed go home and keep from the frost. Frost can fester.' He made a leisurely business of putting away such things as he had used, to give her time to think and breathe. 'Your nephew works here with me. But of course you know that. I remember you visited him here in the garden a few days ago. A good lad, your Benet.'

After a brief, deep silence she said: 'So I have always found him.' And for the first time, though pallidly and briefly, she smiled.

'Hard-working and willing! I shall miss him if he goes, but he's worth a more testing employment.'

She said nothing to that. Her silence was marked, as though words hovered behind it ready for spilling, and were strongly held back. She said no more, barring a sedate word of thanks, when he led her back to the great court, where a buzzing murmur of voices like a disturbed hive met them before ever they rounded the hedge. Abbot Radulfus was there, and had the brothers already mustering about him, bright and quivering with curiosity, their sleepiness almost forgotten.

'We have cause to fear,' said Radulfus, wasting no words, 'that some accident has befallen Father Ailnoth. He went out from his house towards the town last night, before Compline, and no one has any word of him since. He has not been home, nor did he attend with us in church overnight. He may have suffered a fall on the ice, and lain either senseless, or unable to walk, through the night. It is my order that those of you who did not serve throughout the night in the choir should take some food quickly, and go out to search for him. The last we know of him is that he had passed our gate before Compline, hurrying towards the town. From that point we must consider and attempt every path he may have taken, for who knows upon what parish errand he was called forth? Those of you who have been wakeful all night long, take food and then sleep, and you are excused attendance from the office, so that you may be fit to take up the search when your fellows return. Robert, see to it! Brother Cadfael will show where Father Ailnoth was last seen. The searchers had best go forth in pairs or more, for two at least may be needed if he is found injured. But I pray he may be found in reasonable case, and quickly.'

Brother Cadfael intercepted a startled and solemn Benet at the edge of the dispersing crowd. The boy had a distracted look about him, between mild guilt and deep bewilderment. He jutted a dubious underlip at Cadfael, and shook his head vehemently, as if to shake off some clinging illusion that made no sense, and yet would not be ignored.

'You won't need me today. I'd best go with them.'

'No,' said Cadfael decidedly. 'You stay here and look after Mistress Hammet. Take her home if she'll go, or find her a warm corner in the gatehouse and stay with her. I know where I met with the priest, and I'll see the hunt started. If anyone wants me, you can answer for me that I'll be back as soon as may be.'

'But you've been up the better part of the night,' protested Benet, hesitating.

'And you?' said Cadfael, and made off towards the gatehouse before Benet could reply.

Ailnoth had passed by in the evening like a black arrow from a war-bow, so blind, so deaf that he had neither seen Brother Cadfael nor heard his greeting, called clearly into a brazen frost that rang like bells. At that point in the Foregate he could have been making for the bridge, in which case his urgent business was with someone in the town itself, or for any of the paths which diverged from the Foregate beyond this point. Of these there were four, one to the right, down into the riverside level of the Gaye, where the abbey's main gardens spread for almost half a mile in plots, fields and orchards, and gave place at last to woodland, and a few scattered homesteads; three to the left, a first path turning in on the near side of the mill-pond, to serve the mill and the three small houses fringing the water there, the second performing the same function for the three on the opposite side. Each of these paths was prolonged alongside the water, but to end blindly at the obstacle of the Meole Brook. The third was the narrow but well-used road that turned left just short of the Severn bridge, crossed the Meole Brook by a wooden foot-bridge where it emptied into the river, and continued south-west into woodland country leading towards the Welsh border.

And why should Father Ailnoth be hurtling like the wrath of God towards any one of these paths? The town had seemed a likelier aim, but others were taking care of enquiries there, whether the watch at the gate had seen him, whether he had stopped to enquire for anyone, whether a black, menacing shadow had passed by under the gatehouse torches. Cadfael turned his attention to the more devious ways, and halted to consider, on the very spot, so far as he could judge, where Ailnoth had passed him by.

The Foregate parish of Holy Cross embraced both sides of the road, on the right stretching well into the scattered hamlets beyond the suburb, on the left as far as the brook. Had Ailnoth been bent upon visiting someone in a country croft, he would have started directly eastward from his house in the alley opposite the abbey gatehouse, and never entered the Foregate highway at all, unless his goal was one of the few dwellings beyond the Gaye. Small ground to cover there. Cadfael deployed two parties in that direction, and turned his attention towards the west. Three paths here, one that became a regular road and would take time, two that were near, short and could surely be cleared up with little delay. And in any case, what would Ailnoth be doing at that late hour, setting out on a longer journey? No, he was on his way to some place or person close by, for what purpose only he knew.

The path on the near side of the mill-pond left the road as a decent cart track, since it had to carry the local corn to the mill, and bring the flour homeward again. It passed by the three small houses that crowded close to the highway, between their doors and the boundary wall of the abbey, reached the small plateau by the mill, where a wooden bridge crossed the head-race, and thence wandered on as a mere footpath in rough meadow grass by the edge of the water, where several pollarded willows leaned crookedly from the high bank. The first and second cottages were occupied by elderly people who had purchased bed and board for life by the grant of their own property to the abbey. The third belonged to the miller, who had been in the church throughout the night offices, to Cadfael's knowledge, and was here among the searchers now in mid morning. A devout man, as well as sedulous in preserving the favour he enjoyed with the Benedictines, and the security of his employment.

'Not a soul did I see along the waterside,' said the miller, shaking his head, 'when I came out last night to go to church, and that must have been much the same time as Brother Cadfael met with Father Ailnoth on the road. But I went straight through the wicket into the great court, not along the track, so he could have been bound this way only a matter of minutes later, for all I know. The old dame in the house next mine is house-bound once the frosts begin, she'd be home.'

'And deaf as a stone,' said Brother Ambrose flatly. 'Any man who called for help outside her door, no matter how loudly, would call in vain.'

'I meant, rather,' said the miller, 'that Father Ailnoth may have set out to visit her, knowing she dared not stir out even as far as the church. It's his duty to visit the aged and infirm, for their comfort. . . .'

The face Cadfael had glimpsed in the frosty night, flaring and fading as it surged past the torches, had not looked to him as if its errand was one of comfort, but he did not say so. Even the miller, charitably advancing the possibility, had sounded dubious.

'But even if he did not,' he said, rallying stoutly, 'the maidservant who looks after the old dame has sharp enough ears, and may have heard or seen him if he did pass this way.'

They separated into two parties, to comb the paths on either side the water, Brother Ambrose taking the far side, where it was but a narrow, beaten footpath serving the three little houses and continuing along the waterside under their sloping gardens, Cadfael the cart track that led to the mill, and there dwindled into a footpath in its turn. On both the white sheen of frost was dimpled and darkened by a few footprints, but those belonged all to the morning. The rime had silvered and concealed any that might have been made by night.

The elderly couple living retired in the first house had not been out of their door since the previous day, and had heard nothing of the priest being missing. Such sensational news had them gaping in an excitement partly pleasurable, and set their tongues wagging in exclamation and lamentation, but elicited no information at all. They had shuttered their window and barred their door early, made up a steady fire, and slept undisturbed. The man, once a forester in the abbey's portion of the forest of Eyton, went in haste to pull on his boots and wrap himself in a sacking cape, and join the hunt.

At the second house the door was opened to them by a pretty slattern of about eighteen, with a mane of dark hair and bold, inquisitive eyes. The tenant was merely a high, querulous voice from the inner room, demanding why the door stood open to let in the cold. The girl whisked away for a moment to reassure her, speaking in a loud screech and perhaps with much gesture, for the complaint sank to a satisfied mumble. The girl came back to them, swathing a shawl about her and closing the door behind her to forestall further complaint.

'No,' she said, shaking her dark mane vigorously, 'not a soul that I know of came along here in the night, why should they? Never a sound did I hear after dark, and she was in her bed as soon as the daylight went, and she'd sleep through the trump of doom. But I was awake until later, and there was nothing to hear or see.'

They left her standing on the doorstone, curious and eager, gazing after them along the track as they passed the third house and came to the tall bulk of the mill. Here, with no houses in between, the still surface of the mill-pond opened on their right hand, dull silver, widening and shallowing into a round pool towards the road from which they had come, tapering gradually before them into the stream that carried the water back to the Meole Brook and the river. Rimy grass overhung the high bank, undercut here by the strength of the tail-race. And still no sign of any black form anywhere in the wintry pallor. The frost had done no more than form a thin frill of ice in the shallows, where the reed beds thickened and helped to hold it. The track reached the mill and became a narrow path, winding between the steep-roofed building and the precinct wall, and crossing the head-race by a little wooden bridge with a single hand-rail. The wheel was still, the sluice above it closed, and the overflow discharging its steady stream aside into the tail-race deep below, and so out into the pool, a silent force perceptible only as a shudder along the surface, which otherwise lay so still.

'Even if he came here,' said the miller, shaking his head, 'he would not go further. There's nothing beyond.'

No, nothing beyond but the path ambling along the grassy plain of the narrow meadow, to dwindle into nothing above the junction of brook and outflow. Fishermen came there sometimes, in season, children played there in the summer, lovers walked there in the twilight, perhaps, but who would walk that way on a frosty night? None the less, Cadfael walked on a little way. Here a few willows grew, leaning out over the water at a drunken angle by reason of the current which was gnawing under the bank. The younger ones had never yet been trimmed, but there were also two or three pollarded trunks, and one cut right down to a stump and bristling with a circle of new wands fine and springy as hairs on a giant, tonsured head. Cadfael passed by the first trees, and stood in the tufted wintry grass on the very edge of the high bank.

The motion of the tail-race, flowing out into the centre of the pool, continued its rippling path through the leaden stillness. Its influence, diminished but present, caused the faintest tremor under the bank on either side for a matter of perhaps ten paces, dying into the metallic lustre just beneath where Cadfael stood. It was that last barely perceptible shimmer that first drew his eyes down, but it was the dull fold of underlying darkness, barely stirring, that held his gaze. An edge of dark cloth, sluggishly swaying beneath the jutting grass of the bank. He went on his knees in the lingering rime, parting the grass to lean over and peer into the water. Black cloth, massed against the naked soil and the eroded willow roots, where the thrust of the tail-race had pushed it aside and tidied it out of the way, and almost out of sight. Twin pallors swayed gently, articulated like strange fish Cadfael had once seen drawn in a traveller's book. Open and empty, Father Ailnoth's hands appealed to a clearing sky, while a fold of his cloak half-covered his face.

Cadfael rose to his feet, and turned a sombre face upon his companions, who were standing by the plank bridge, gazing across the open water to where the other party was just appearing below the gardens of the townward cottages.

'He is here,' said Cadfael. 'We have found him.'

It was no small labour to get him out, even when Brother Ambrose and his fellows, hailed from their own fruitless hunt by the miller's bull's bellow and excited waving, came hurrying round from the road to lend a hand in the work.

The high, undercut bank, with deep water beneath it, made it impossible to reach down and get a hold on his clothing, even when the lankiest of them lay flat on his face and stretched long arms down, to grope still short of the surface. The miller brought a boat hook from among his store of tools, and with care they guided the obdurate body along to the edge of the tail-race, where they could descend to water level and grasp the folds of his garments.

The black, ominous bird had become an improbable fish. He lay in the grass, when they had carried him up to level ground, streaming pond-water from wiry black hair and sodden black garments, his uncovered face turned up to the chill winter light marbled blue and grey, with lips parted and eyes half-open, the muscles of cheeks and jaw and neck drawn tight with a painful suggestion of struggle and terror. A cold, cold, lonely death in the dark, and mysteriously his corpse bore the marks of it even when the combat was over. They looked down at him in awe, and no one had anything to say. What they did they did practically, without fuss, in blank silence.

They took a door from its hinges in the mill, and laid him on it, and carried him away through the wicket in the wall into the great court, and thence to the mortuary chapel. They dispersed then about their various businesses, as soon as Abbot Radulfus and Prior Robert had been apprised of their return, and what they brought with them. They were glad to go, to be off to the living, and to the festival the living were still keeping, glad to have the sanction of the season to feel happiness and have a great thing to celebrate.

The word went round the Foregate almost furtively, whispered from ear to ear, without exclaim, without many words, taking its time to reach the outer fringes of the parish, but by nightfall it was known to all. The thanksgiving made no noise, no one acknowledged it or mentioned it, no one visibly exulted. Nevertheless, the parishioners of the Foregate kept Christmas with the heartfelt fervour of a people from whom an oppressive shadow had been lifted overnight.

In the mortuary chapel, where even at this end of the year no warmth could be employed, those gathered about the bier shivered and blew into their bunched fingers wringing the rough, fingerless mittens to set the chill blood flowing and work off the numbness. Father Ailnoth, colder than them all, nevertheless lay indifferent to the gathering frost even in his nakedness, and on his bed of stone.

'We must, then, conclude,' said Abbot Radulfus heavily, 'that he fell into the pool and drowned. But why was he there at such an hour, and on the eve of the Nativity?'

There was no one prepared to answer that. To reach the place where he had been found he must have passed by every near habitation without word or sign, to end in a barren, unpeopled solitude.

'He drowned, certainly,' said Cadfael.

'Is it known,' wondered Prior Robert, 'whether he could swim?'

Cadfael shook his head. 'I've no knowledge of that, I doubt if anyone here knows. But it might not be of much importance whether he could or no. Certainly he drowned. It is less certain, I fear, that he simply fell into the water. See here – the back of his head . . .'

He raised the dead man's head with one hand, and propped head and shoulders with the right arm, and Brother Edmund, who had already viewed this corpse with him before ever Abbot Radulfus and Prior Robert were summoned, held a candle to show the nape and the thick circlet of wiry black hair. A broken wound, with edges of skin grazed loose round it and a bleached, moist middle now only faintly discoloured with blood after its soaking in the pool, began just at the rim of the tonsure, and scraped down raggedly through the circle of hair, to end where the inward curve of the nape began.

'He suffered a blow on the head here, before ever he entered the water,' said Cadfael.

'Struck from behind him,' said the abbot, with fastidious disdain, and peered closer. 'You are sure he drowned? This blow could not have killed him? For what you are saying is that this was no accident, but a deliberate assault. Or could he have come by this innocently? Is it possible? The track there is rutted, and it was icy. Could he have fallen and injured himself thus?'

'I doubt it. If a man's feet go from under him he may sit down heavily, even sprawl back on his shoulders, but he seldom goes full-length so violently as to hit his head forcibly on the ground and break his crown. That could not happen on such rough ground, only on smooth sheet ice. And mark, this is not on the round of his head, which would have taken such a shock, but lower, even moving into the curve of his neck, and lacerated, as if he was struck with something rough and jagged. And you saw the shoes he was wearing, felted beneath the sole. I think he went safer from a fall, last night, than most men.'

'Certainly, then, a blow,' said Radulfus. 'Could it have killed?'

'No, impossible! His skull is not broken. Not enough to kill, nor even to do him much lasting harm. But he might well have been stunned for a while, or so dazed that he was helpless when he fell into the water. Fell,' said Cadfael with deliberation, but ruefully, 'or was pushed in.'

'And of those two,' said the abbot with cold composure, 'which is the more likely?'

'In darkness,' said Cadfael, 'any man may step too near a sloping edge and misjudge his footing where a bank overhangs water. But whatever his reason for going along that path, why should he persist beyond the last dwelling? But this broken head I do not believe he got by any natural fall, and he got it before he went into the water. Some other hand, some other person, was there with him, and party to this death.'

'There is nothing in the wound, no fragment to show what manner of weapon it was that struck him?' ventured Brother Edmund, who had worked with Brother Cadfael in similar cases, and found good reason to require his judgement even in the minutest details. But he did not sound hopeful.

'How could there be?' said Cadfael simply. 'He has lain in the water all through the night, everything about him is bleached and sodden. If there had ever been soil or grass in his grazes, it would have soaked away long ago. But I do not think there was. He cannot alone have staggered far after that blow was struck, and he was just past the tail-race, or it would have drifted him the opposing way. Nor would anyone have carried or dragged him far if he was stunned, he being a big, heavy man, and the blow being only briefly disabling, not killing. Not ten paces from where we found him, I judge, he went into the pool. And close by that same stretch he got this blow. On top of all, there he was on grass unrutted by wheels, being past the mill – only rough and tufted, as winter turf is. If he had slipped and fallen, the ground there might have half-stunned him, but it would not have broken his head and fetched blood. I have told you all I can tell from this poor body,' he said wearily. 'Make what you can of it.'

'Murder!' said Prior Robert, rigid with indignation and horror. 'Murder is what I make of it. Father Abbot, what is now to be done?'

Radulfus brooded for some minutes over the indifferent corpse which had been Father Ailnoth, and never before so still and quiet, so tolerant of the views of others. Then he said, with measured regret: 'I am afraid, Robert, we have no choice but to inform the lord sheriff's deputy, since Hugh Beringar himself is elsewhere about his own duties.' And with his eyes still upon the livid face on the stone slab he said, with bleak wonder: 'I knew he had not made himself loved. I had not realised that in so short a time he could make himself so hated.'

Chapter Six

Young Alan Herbard, who was Hugh's deputy in his absence, came down hot-foot from the castle with the most experienced of his sergeants, William Warden, and two other officers in his train. Even if Herbard had not been well acquainted with the Foregate and its people, Will Warden certainly was, and went in no misapprehension concerning the degree of love the congregation of Holy Cross had for its new priest.

'There'll be very little mourning for him hereabouts,' he said bluntly, viewing the dead man without emotion. 'He made a thorough job of turning every soul in the parish against him. A poor end, though, for any man. A poor, cold end!'

They examined the head wound, noted the account rendered by every man who had taken part in the search, and listened to the careful opinions put forward by Brother Edmund and Brother Cadfael, and to everything Dame Diota had to say of her master's evening departure, and the anxious night she had spent worrying about his failure to return.

She had refused to depart, and waited all this time to repeat her story, which she did with a drained but steady composure, now that the matter and the mystery were out of her hands. Benet was beside her, attentive and solicitous, a very sombre Benet, with creased brows and hazel eyes clouded by something between anxiety on her account and sheer puzzlement on his own.

'If you'll give me leave,' said the boy, as soon as the

officers had withdrawn from the precinct to go in search of the provost of the Foregate, who knew his people as well as any man could, 'I'll take my aunt back to the house now, and see her settled with a good fire. She needs to rest.' And he added, appealing to Cadfael: 'I won't stay long. I may be wanted here.'

'Stay as long as is needful,' said Cadfael readily. 'I'll answer for you if there should be any questions. But what could you have to tell? I know you were in the church well before Matins began.' And knew, moreover, where the boy had been later on, and probably not alone, but he said nothing about that. 'Has anything been said about making provision for Mistress Hammet's future? This leaves her very solitary, but for you, and still almost a stranger here. But I'm sure Abbot Radulfus will see to it she's not left friendless.'

'He came himself to speak to her,' said Benet, a faint flush and gleam of his usual brightness appearing for a moment, in appreciation of such considerate usage. 'He says she need not be troubled at all, for she came here in good faith to serve the church in her proper station, and the church will see to it that she is provided for. Dwell in the house and care for it, he said, until a new priest is preferred to the benefice, and then we'll see. But in no case shall she be cast away.'

'Good! Then you and she can rest with easy minds. Terrible this may be, but it's no fault of yours or hers, and you should not brood on it.' They were both looking at him then with still, shocked faces that expressed nothing of grief or reassurance, but only stunned acceptance. 'Stay and sleep there, if you see fit,' he said to Benet. 'She may be glad of having you close by, tonight.'

Benet said neither yes nor no to that, nor did the woman. They went out silently from the ante-room of the gatehouse, where they had sat out the long uncertainty of the morning together, and crossing the wide highway of the Foregate, vanished into the narrow mouth of the alley opposite, still silvered with hoar-frost between its enclosing walls.

Cadfael felt no great surprise when Benet was back within

the hour, instead of taking advantage of the permission to absent himself overnight. He came looking for Cadfael in the garden, and found him, for once, virtually idle in his workshop, sitting by the glowing brazier. The boy sat down silently beside him, and heaved a glum sigh.

'Agreed!' said Cadfael, stirring out of his thoughts at the sound. 'We're none of us quite ourselves today, small wonder. But no need for you to rack your conscience, surely. Have you left your aunt all alone?'

'No,' said Benet. 'There's a neighbour with her, though I doubt if she's all that glad of the kind attention. There'll be more of them, I daresay, before long, bursting with curiosity and worming the whole story out of her. Not for grief, either, to judge by the one I left with her. They'll be chattering like starlings all over the parish, and never stop until night falls.'

'They'll stop fast enough, you'll find,' said Cadfael drily, 'as soon as Alan Herbard or one of his sergeants puts a word in. Let one officer show his face, and silence will fall. There's not a soul in the Foregate will own to knowing anything about anything once the questions begin.'

Benet shifted uneasily on the wooden bench, as though his bones rather than his conscience felt uncomfortable. 'I never understood that he was quite so blackly disliked. Do you truly think they'll hang together so close, and never betray even if they know who brought him to his death?'

'Yes, I do think it. For there's hardly a soul but will feel it might as easily have been his own act, but for God's grace. But it need not fret you, one way or the other. Unless it was you who broke his head?' said Cadfael mildly. 'Was it?'

'No,' said Benet as simply, staring down into his linked hands; and the next moment looked up with sharp curiosity: 'But what makes *you* so sure of it?'

'Well, firstly, I saw you in church well before it was time for Matins, and though there's no certainty just when Ailnoth went into the pool, I should judge it was probably after that time. Secondly, I know of no reason why you should bear him any grudge, and you said yourself it comes as a surprise to you he was so hated. But thirdly and best, from what I know of you, lad, if you took such dire offence as to up and hit a man, it would not be from behind, but face to face.'

'Well, thank you for that!' said Benet, briefly recovering his blazing smile. 'But, Cadfael, what *do* you think happened? It was you saw him last, alive, at least as far as is known. Was there any other soul about there? Did you see anyone else? Anyone, as it might be, following him?'

'Never a creature beyond the gatehouse here. There were folk from the Foregate just coming in for the service, but none going on towards the town. Any others who may have seen Ailnoth can only have seen him before ever I did, and with nothing to show where he was bound. Unless someone had speech with him. But by the way he went scurrying past me, I doubt if he halted for any other.'

Benet considered that in silence for a long moment, and then said, rather to himself than to Cadfael: 'And from his house it's so short a way. He'd come into the Foregate just opposite the gatehouse. Small chance of being seen or stopped in that distance.'

'Leave it to the King's officers to scratch their heads over the how and why,' Cadfael advised. 'They'll find no lack of folk who'll pretend no sorrow at seeing the last of Ailnoth, but I doubt if they'll get much information out of anyone, man, woman or child. No blinking it, the man generated grudges wherever he stepped. He may well have made the most perfect of clerks, where he had to deal only with documents, charters and accounts, but he had no notion how to coax and counsel and comfort common human sinners. And what else is a parish priest for?'

The frost continued that night, harder than ever, freezing over the reedy shallows in the mill-pond, and fringing the townward shore with a white shelf of ice, but not yet sealing over the deeper water or the tremulous path of the tail-race, so that the little boys who went hopefully to examine the ice in the early morning returned disappointed. No point as yet in trying to break the iron ground for Father Ailnoth's grave, even if Herbard would have permitted an early burial, but at least the clear cold made delay acceptable.

In the Foregate a kind of breathless hush brooded. People talked much but in low voices and only among trusted friends, and yet everywhere there was a feeling of suppressed and superstitious gladness, as if a great cloud had been lifted from the parish. Even those who did not confide in one another in words did so in silent glances. The relief was everywhere, and palpable.

But so was the fear. For someone, it seemed, had rid the Foregate of its blight, and all those who had wished it away felt a morsel of the guilt sticking to their fingers. They could not but speculate on the identity of their deliverer, even while they shut their mouths and their eyes, and put away all knowledge of their own suspicions, for fear of betraying them to the law.

All through the routine of the day Cadfael pursued his own thoughts, and they centred, inevitably, on Ailnoth's death. No one would tell Alan Herbard about Eadwin's headland or Aelgar's grievance, or the unconsecrated grave of Centwin's son, or any of the dozen or more other wounds that had made Ailnoth a hated man, but there would be no need. Will Warden would know them all already, and maybe other, lesser offences of which even the abbot had not been told. Every one of those thus aggrieved would be examined as to his movements on the eve of the Nativity, and Will would know where to look for confirmation. And much as the Foregate might sympathise with whoever had killed Ailnoth, and loyally as they would close round him and cover him, it was nevertheless vital that the truth should be known, for there would be no real peace of mind for anyone until it was discovered. That was the first reason why Cadfael, almost against his will, wished for a solution. The second was for the sake of Abbot Radulfus, who carried, in his own mind, a double guilt, for bringing to the fold so ill-fitted a shepherd, and for suffering him to be done to death by some enraged ram among the flock. Bitter though it may be to many, Cadfael concluded, there is no substitute for truth, in this or any case.

Meantime, in occasional reversions to the day's labours, he was thankful that Benet had completed the winter digging just in time, before the hard frost came, and attacked the final thin crop of weeds in all the flower beds so vigorously that now the earth could sleep snugly under the rime, and the whole enclosed garden looked neat and clean, and content as a hedge-pig curled up an arm's length down under leaves and grass and dry herbage until the spring.

A good worker, the boy Benet, cheerful and ungrudging, and good company. Somewhat clouded by the death of this man who had brought him here, and at least never done him any harm, but his natural buoyancy would keep breaking through. Not much was left, now, of the candidate for the cloister. Had that been the one sign of human frailty in Father Ailnoth, that he had deliberately represented his groom on the journey north as desirous of the monastic life, though still a little hesitant to take the final step? A lie to get the boy off his hands? Benet was firm that he had never given voice to any such wish, and Benet, in Cadfael's considered opinion, would make a very poor liar. Come to think of it, not very much left, either, of the wide-eyed, innocent, unlettered bumpkin Benet had first affected, at least not here in the solitude of the garden. He could still slip it on like a glove if for any reason the prior accosted him. Either he thinks me blind, said Cadfael to himself, or he does not care at all to pretend with me. And I am very sure he does not think me blind!

Well, a day or two more, and surely Hugh would be back. As soon as he was released from attendance on the King he would be making his way home by forced marches. Aline and Giles between them would take care of that. God send he would come home with the right answer!

And it seemed that Hugh had indeed made all haste to get home to his wife and son, for he rode into Shrewsbury late in the evening of the twenty-seventh, to hear from a relieved Alan Herbard of the turmoil that awaited solution, the death that came rather as blessing than disaster to the people of the Foregate, but must none the less be taken very seriously by the King's officers. He came down immediately after Prime next morning, to get the most authoritative account from the abbot, and confer with him over the whole troublesome matter of the priest's relationship with his flock. He had also another grave matter of his own to confide.

Cadfael knew nothing of Hugh's return until mid morning, when his friend sought him out in the workshop. The broken-glass grating of boots on the frozen gravel made Cadfael turn from his mortar, knowing the step but hardly believing in it.

'Well, well!' he said, delighted. 'I hadn't thought to clap eyes on you for a day or two yet. Glad I am to see you, and I hope I read the signs aright?' He broke free from Hugh's embrace to hold him off at arm's length and study his face anxiously. 'Yes, you have the look of success about you. Do I see you confirmed in office?'

'You do, old friend, you do! And kicked out promptly to my shire to be about my master's business. Trust me, Cadfael, he's come back to us lean and hungry and with the iron-marks on him, and he wants action, and vengeance, and blood. If he could but keep up this fury of energy, he could finish this contention within the year. But it won't last,' said Hugh philosophically, 'it never does. God, but I'm still stiff with all the riding I've done. Have you got a cup of wine about you, and half an hour to sit and waste with me?'

He flung himself down gratefully on the wooden bench and stretched out his feet to the warmth of the brazier, and Cadfael brought cups and a flagon, and sat down beside him, taking pleasure in viewing the slight figure and thin, eloquent face that brought in with them the whole savour of the outside world, fresh from the court, ratified in office, a man whose energy did not flag as Stephen's did, who did not abandon one enterprise to go off after another, as Stephen did. Or were those days now over? Perhaps the King's privations and grievances in prison in Bristol had put an end to all half-hearted proceedings in the future. But plainly Hugh did not think him capable of sustaining so great a change.

'He wore his crown again at the Christmas feast, and a sumptuous affair it was. Give him his due, there's no man living could look more of a king than Stephen. He questioned me closely in private as to how things shape in these parts, and I gave him a full account of how we stand with the earl of Chester, and the solid ally Owain Gwynedd has been to us there in the north of the shire. He seemed content enough with me – at least he clouted me hard on the back – a fist like a shovel, Cadfael! – and gave me his authority to get on with the work as sheriff confirmed. He even recalled how I ever came to get his countenance as Prestcote's deputy. I fancy that's a rare touch in kings, part of the reason why we cling to Stephen even when he maddens us. So I got not only his sanction, but a great shove to get back on the road and back to my duty. I think he means to make a visit north when the worst of the winter's over, to buckle a few more of the waverers to him again. Lucky I'd thought to get a change of horses four times on the way south,' said Hugh thankfully, 'thinking I might be in haste coming back. I'd left my grey in Oxford, going down. And here I am, glad to be home.'

'And Alan Herbard will be glad to see you home,' said Cadfael, 'for he's been dropped into deep water while you've been away. Not that he shrinks from it, though he can hardly have welcomed it. He'll have told you what's happened here? On the very Nativity! A bad business!'

'He's told me. I've just come from the abbot, to get his

view of it. I saw but little of the man, but I've heard enough from others. A man well hated, and in so short a time. Is their view of him justified? I could hardly ask Abbot Radulfus to cry his candidate down, but I would not say he had any great regard for him.'

'A man without charity or humility,' said Cadfael simply. 'Salted with those, he might have been a decent fellow, but both were left out of him. He came down over the parish like a cloud of blight, suddenly.'

'And you're sure it was murder? I've seen his body, I know of the head wound. Hard to see, I grant you, how he could have come by that by accident, or alone.'

'You'll have to pursue it,' said Cadfael, 'whatever poor angry soul struck the blow. But you'll get no help from the Foregate folk. Their hearts will be with whoever rid them of the shadow.'

'So Alan says, too,' said Hugh, briefly smiling. 'He knows these people pretty shrewdly, young as he is. And he'd rather I should harry them than he. And inasmuch as I must, I will. I'm warned off charity and humility myself,' said Hugh ruefully, 'on the King's affairs. He wants his enemies hunted down without remorse, and is giving orders right and left to that effect. And I have a charge to be the hunter here in my shire, for one of them.'

'Once before, as I recall,' said Cadfael, refilling his friend's cup, 'he gave you a task to do that you did in your own way, which certainly was not his when he gave the order. He never questioned your way, after. He may as well repent of this, later, and be glad if you shuffle your feet somewhat in the hunt. Not that I need to tell you as much, since you know it all before.'

'I can make a goodly show,' agreed Hugh, grinning, 'and still bear in mind that he might not be grateful for overmuch zeal, once he gets over his grudges. I never knew him bear malice for long. He did his worst here in Shrewsbury, and dislikes to be reminded of it now. The thing is this, Cadfael. Back in the summer, when it seemed the Empress had crown and sceptre and all in her hands, FitzAlan in Normandy is known to have sent over a couple of scouts of his following, to sound out the extent of her support, and see if the time was ripe to bring a fresh force over to add to her strength. How they were discovered I haven't heard, but when her fortunes were reversed, and the Queen brought her army up into London and beyond, these two venturers were cut off from return, and have been one leap ahead of capture ever since. One of them is thought to have got off successfully from Dunwich, but the other is still loose somewhere, and since he's been hunted without result in the south, the cry is now that he's made his way north to get out of range, and try to make contact with sympathisers of Anjou for help. So all the King's sheriffs are ordered to keep a strict watch for him. After his rough treatment, Stephen's in no mind to forgive and forget. I'm obliged to make a show of zeal, and that means making the matter public by proclamation, and so I shall. For my part, I'm glad to know that one of them has slipped overseas again safely, back to his wife. Nor would I be sorry if I heard that the second had followed him. Two bold boys venturing over here alone, putting their skins at risk for a cause – why should I have anything against them? Nor will Stephen, when he comes to himself.'

'You use very exact terms,' said Cadfael curiously. 'How do you know they are mere boys? And how do you know that the one who's fled back to Normandy has a wife?'

'Because, my Cadfael, it's known who they are, the pair of them, youngsters very close to FitzAlan. The hart we're still hunting is one Ninian Bachiler. And the lad who's escaped us, happily, is a certain young fellow named Torold Blund, whom both you and I have good cause to remember.' He laughed, seeing how Cadfael's face brightened in astonished pleasure. 'Yes, the same long lad you hid in the old mill along the Gaye, some years back. And now reported as son-in-law to FitzAlan's closest friend and ally, Fulke Adeney. Yes, Godith got her way!'

Good cause to remember, indeed! Cadfael sat warmed

through by the recollection of Godith Adeney, for a short time his garden boy Godric to the outer world, and the young man she had helped him to succour and send away safely into Wales. Man and wife now, it seemed. Yes, Godith had got her way!

'To think,' said Hugh, 'that I might have married her! If my father had lived longer, if I'd never come to Shrewsbury to put my newly inherited manors at Stephen's disposal, and never set eyes on Aline, I might well have married Godith. No regrets, I fancy, on either side. She got a good lad, and I got Aline.'

'And you're sure he's slipped away safely out of England, back to her?'

'So it's reported. And so may his fellow slip away, with my goodwill,' said Hugh heartily, 'if he's Torold's match, and can oblige me by keeping well out of my way. Should you happen on him, Cadfael – you have a way of happening on the unexpected – keep him out of sight. I'm in no mind to clap a good lad into prison for being loyal to a cause which isn't mine.'

'You have a good excuse for setting his case aside,' Cadfael suggested thoughtfully, 'seeing you're come home to find a slain man on the doorstep, and a priest at that.'

'True, I could argue that as the prior case,' agreed Hugh, setting his empty cup aside and rising to take his leave. 'All the more as this affair is indeed laid right at my door, and for all I know young Bachiler may be a hundred miles away or more. A small show of zeal, however, won't come amiss, or do any harm.'

Cadfael went out into the garden with him. Benet was just coming up over the far rim of the rose garden, where the ground sloped away to the pease fields and the brook. He was whistling jauntily as he came, and swinging an axe lightly in one hand, for a little earlier he had been breaking the ice on the fish ponds, to let air through to the denizens below.

'What did you say, Hugh, was the christened name of this

young man Bachiler you're supposed to be hunting?'

'Ninian, or so he's reported.'

'Ah, yes!' said Cadfael. 'That was it – Ninian.'

Benet came back into the garden after his dinner with the lay servants, and looked about him somewhat doubtfully, kicking at the hard-frozen ground he had recently dug, and viewing the clipped hedges now silvered with rime that lasted day-long and increased by a fresh frilling of white every night. Every branch that stirred tinkled like glass. Every clod was solid as stone.

'What is there for me to do?' he demanded, tramping into Cadfael's workshop. 'This frost halts everything. No man could plough or dig, a day like this. Let alone copy letters,' he added, round eyed at the thought of the numb fingers in the scriptorium trying to line in a capital with precious gold-leaf, or even write an unshaken line. 'They're still at it, poor wretches. At least there's some warmth in handling a spade or an axe. Can I split you some wood for the brazier? Lucky for us you need the fire for your brews, or we should be as blue and stiff as the scribes.'

'They'll have lighted the fire in the warming room early, a day like this,' said Cadfael placidly, 'and when they can no longer hold pen or brush steady they have leave to stop work. You've done all the digging within the walls here, and the pruning's finished, no need to feel guilty if you sit idle for once. Or you can take a turn at these mysteries of mine if you care to. Nothing learned is ever quite wasted.'

Benet was ready enough to try his hand at anything. He came close, to peer curiously at what Cadfael was stirring in a stone pot on a grid on the side of the brazier. Here in their shared solitude he was quite easy, and had lost the passing disquiet and dismay that had dimmed his brightness on Christmas Day. Men die, and thinking men see a morsel of their own death in every one that draws close to them, but the young soon recover. And what was Father Ailnoth to Benet, after all? If he had done him a kindness in letting him come here with his aunt, the priest had none the less had the benefit of the boy's willing service on the journey, a fair exchange.

'Did you visit Mistress Hammet last evening?' asked Cadfael, recalling another possible source of concern. 'How is she now?'

'Still bruised and shaken,' said Benet, 'but she has a stout spirit, she'll do well enough.'

'She hasn't been greatly worried by the sergeants? Hugh Beringar is home now, and he'll want to hear everything from her own lips, but she need not trouble for that. Hugh has been told how it was, she need only repeat it to him.'

'They've been civility itself with her,' said Benet. 'What is this you're making?'

It was a large pot, and a goodly quantity of aromatic brown syrup bubbling gently in it. 'A mixture for coughs and colds,' said Cadfael. 'We shall be needing it any day now, and plenty of it, too.'

'What goes into it?'

'A great many things. Bay and mint, coltsfoot, horehound, mullein, mustard, poppy – good for the throat and the chest – and a small draught of the strong liquor I distil does no harm in such cases, either. But if you want work, here, lift out that big mortar . . . yes, there! Those frost-gnawed hands you were pitying, we'll make something for those.'

The chilblains of winter were always a seasonal enemy, and an extra batch of ointment for treating them could not come amiss. He began to issue orders briskly, pointing out the herbs he wanted, making Benet climb for some, and move hastily up and down the hanging bunches for others. The boy took pleasure in this novel entertainment, and jumped to obey every crisp command.

'The small scale, there, at the back of the shelf – fetch that out, and while you're in the corner there, the little weights are in the box beside. Oh, and, Ninian . . .' said Cadfael, sweet and calm and guileless as ever.

The boy, interested and off his guard, halted and swung about in response to his name, waiting with a willing smile to hear what next he should bring. And on the instant he froze where he stood, the serene brightness still visible on a face turned to marble, the smile fixed and empty. For a long moment they contemplated each other eye to eye, Cadfael also smiling, then warm blood flushed into Benet's face and he stirred out of his stillness, and the smile, wary as it was, became live and young again. The silence endured longer, but it was the boy who broke it at last.

'Now what should happen? Am I supposed to overturn the brazier, set the hut on fire, rush out and bar the door on you, and run for my life?'

'Hardly,' said Cadfael, 'unless that's what you want. It would scarcely suit me. It would become you better to put that scale down on the level slab there, and pay attention to what you and I are about. And while you're at it, that jar by the shutter is hog's fat, bring that out, too.'

Benet did so, with admirable calm now, and turned a wryly smiling face. 'How did you know? How did you know even my name?' He was making no further pretence at secrecy, he had even relaxed into a measure of perverse enjoyment.

'Son, the story of your invasion of this realm, along with another mad-head as reckless as yourself, seems to be common currency by this time, and the whole land knows you are supposed to have fled northwards from regions where you were far too hotly hunted for comfort. Hugh Beringar got his orders to keep an eye open for you, at the feast in Canterbury. King Stephen's blood is up, and until it cools your liberty is not worth a penny if his officers catch up with you. For I take it,' he said mildly, 'that you *are* Ninian Bachiler?'

'I am. But how did you know?'

'Why, once I heard that there was a certain Ninian lost somewhere in these midland counties, it was not so hard. Once you all but told me yourself. "What's your name?" I asked you, and you began to say "Ninian", and then caught yourself up and changed it to a clownish echo of the question, before you got out "Benet". And oh, my child, how soon you gave over pretending with me that you were a simple country groom. Never had a spade in your hand before! No, I swear you never had, though I grant you you learn very quickly. And your speech, and your hands — No, never blush or look mortified, it was not so obvious, it simply added together grain by grain. And besides, you stopped counting me as someone to be deceived. You may as well admit it.'

'It seemed unworthy,' said the boy, and scowled briefly at the beaten earth floor. 'Or useless, perhaps! I don't know! What are you going to do with me now? If you try to give me up, I warn you I'll do all I can to break away. But I won't do it by laying hand on you. We've been friendly together.'

'As well for both you and me,' said Cadfael, smiling, 'for you might find you'd met your match. And who said I had any notion of giving you up? I am neither King Stephen's partisan nor the Empress Maud's, and whoever serves either of them honestly and at risk to himself may go about his business freely for me. But you may as well tell me what that business is. Without implicating any other, of course. I take it, for instance, that Mistress Hammet is not your aunt?'

'No,' said Ninian slowly, his eyes intent and earnest on Cadfael's face. 'You will respect her part in this? She was in my mother's service before she married the bishop's groom. She was my nurse when I was a child. When I was in flight I went to her for help. It was thoughtless, and I wish it could be undone, but believe it, whatever she has done has been done in pure affection for me, and what I've been about is nothing to do with her. She got me these clothes I wear – mine had been living rough in the woods and in and out of rivers, but they still marked me for what I am. And it was of her own will that she asked leave to bring me here with her as her nephew, when Father Ailnoth got this preferment. To get me away from the hunters. She had asked and been given his leave before ever I knew of it, I could not avoid. And it did come as a blessing to me, I own it.'

'What was your intent when you came over from Normandy?' asked Cadfael.

'Why, to make contact with any friends of the Empress who might be lying very low in the south and east, where she's least loved, and urge them to be ready to rise if FitzAlan should think the time ripe for a return. It looked well for her chances then. But when the wind changed, someone – God knows which of those we'd spoken with – took fright and covered himself by betraying us. You know we were two?'

'I know it,' said Cadfael. 'Indeed I know the second. He was of FitzAlan's household here in Shrewsbury before the town fell to the King. He got off safely from an eastern port, as I heard. You were not so lucky.'

'Is Torold clean away? Oh, you do me good!' cried Ninian, flushed with joy. 'We were separated when they almost cornered us near Bury. I feared for him! Oh, if he's safe home . . .' He caught himself up there, wincing at the thought of calling Normandy home. 'For myself, I can deal! Even if I do end in the King's prison – but I won't! Fending for one is not so hard as fretting for two. And Torold's a married man!'

'And the word is, he's gone, back to his wife. And what,' wondered Cadfael, 'is your intention now? Plainly the one you came with is a lost cause. What now?'

'Now,' said the boy with emphatic gravity, 'I mean to get across the border into Wales, and make my way down to join the Empress's army at Gloucester. I can't bring her FitzAlan's army, but I can bring her one able-bodied man to fight for her – and not a bad hand with sword or lance, though I do say it myself.'

By the lift of his voice and the sparkle in his eyes he meant it ardently, and it was a course much more congenial to him than acting as agent to reluctant allies. And why should he not succeed? The Welsh border was not so far, though the journey to Gloucester through the ill-disciplined wilds of

Powys might be long and perilous. Cadfael considered his companion thoughtfully, and beheld a young man somewhat lightly clad for winter travelling afoot, without weapons, without a horse, without wealth to grease his journeying. None of which considerations appeared to discourage Ninian.

'An honest enough purpose,' said Cadfael, 'and I see nothing against it. We have a few adherents of your faction even in these parts, though they keep very quiet these days. Could not one of them be of use to you now?'

The bait was not taken. The boy closed his lips firmly, and stared Cadfael out with impregnable composure. If he had indeed attempted to contact one of the Empress's partisans here, he was never going to admit it. With his own confidences he might favour his too perceptive mentor, but he was not going to implicate any other man.

'Well,' said Cadfael comfortably, 'it seems that you are not being hunted here with any great zeal, and your position with us is well established, no reason why Benet should not continue to do his work here quietly and modestly, and never be noticed. And if this iron frost goes on as it's begun, your work will be here among the medicines, so we may as well go on with your lesson. Look lively, now, and pay attention to what I show you.'

The boy burst into a soft, half-smothered peal of laughter in sheer relief and pleasure, like a child, and bounded to Cadfael's elbow at the mortar like a hound puppy excited by a fresh scent.

'Good, then tell me what to do, and I'll do it. I'll be half an apothecary before I leave you. Nothing learned,' said Ninian, with an impudently accurate imitation of Cadfael's more didactic style, 'is ever quite wasted.'

'True, true!' agreed Cadfael sententiously. 'Nothing observed, either. You never know where it may fit into a larger vision.'

Exactly as certain details were beginning to fit together and elaborate for him the picture he had of this venturesome, light-hearted, likeable young man. A destitute young man, urgently in need of the means to make his way undetected to Gloucester, one who had come to England, no doubt, with a memorised list of names that should prove sympathetic to the Empress's cause, a few of them even here in Shropshire. A devoted woman all anxiety for her nurseling, bringing honey cakes and carrying away a small token thing that slipped easily into the breast of her gown, from the breast of Benet's cotte. And shortly thereafter, the lady Sanan Bernières, daughter of a father dispossessed for his adherence to Maud, and step-daughter to another lord of the same party, paying a brief visit from Giffard's house near Saint Chad's to buy herbs for her Christmas kitchen, and pausing in the garden to speak to the labouring boy, and look him up and down, as though, as the boy himself had reported, she were in need of a page, 'and thought I might do, given a little polishing'.

Well, well! So far everything in harmony. But why, then, was the boy still here at all, if aid had been asked and given?

Upon this incomplete picture the sudden death of Father Ailnoth intruded like a black blot in a half-written page, complicating everything, relating, apparently, to nothing, a bird of as ill omen dead as alive.

Chapter Seven

The hunt for Ninian Bachiler, as a proscribed agent of the Empress Maud at large in Stephen's territory, was duly proclaimed in Shrewsbury, and the word went round in voluble gossip, all the more exuberantly as a relief from the former sensation of Ailnoth's death, concerning which no one in the Foregate had been voluble, unless in privacy. It was good to have a topic of conversation which departed at so marked a tangent from what really preoccupied the parishioners of Holy Cross. Since none of the gossips cared a pin how many dissident agents were at large in the county, none of the talk was any threat to the fugitive, much less to Mistress Hammet's dutiful nephew Benet, who came and went freely between abbey and parsonage.

In the afternoon of the twenty-ninth of December, Cadfael was called out to the first sufferers from coughs and colds in the Foregate, and extended his visits to one elderly merchant in the town itself, a regular chest patient of his in the winter. He had left Ninian sawing and splitting wood from the pruning of the trees, and keeping cautious watch on a pot of herbs in oil of almonds, which had to warm on the edge of the brazier without simmering, to make a lotion for the frost-nipped hands too tender to endure the hog's fat base of the ointment. The boy could be trusted to abide by his instructions, and whatever he did he did with his might.

Cadfael's errands had taken him rather less time than he had expected, and the weather was not such as to encourage him to linger. He re-entered at the gatehouse with more than an hour still in hand before Vespers, and made his way across the great court and out into the garden, rounding the box hedge into the alley that led to his herbarium. In the frost he had wrapped woollen cloths about his boots to give him a grip on the icy roads, and the same sensible precaution made his steps silent on the path. So it happened that he heard the voices before he himself was heard, rapid and soft and vehement from within his workshop. And one of the voices was Ninian's, a tone above its usual pitch by reason of some fierce but subdued excitement. And the other was a girl's, insistent and agitated. Curious that she, too, should convey this same foolhardy sense of enjoyment in the experience of danger and dread. A good match! And what other girl had had to do with this place and this youth, but Sanan Bernières?

'Oh, but he would!' she was saying emphatically. 'He's there by now, he'll tell them everything, where to find you, how you sent to him – all! You must come now, quickly, before they come to take you.'

'Impossible by the gatehouse,' said Ninian, 'we should run into their arms. But I can't believe – why should he betray me? Surely he knows I'd never mention his name?'

'He's been in dread,' said the girl impatiently, 'ever since your message came, but now you're cried publicly as a wanted man, he'll do anything to shake off his own danger. He's not evil – he does as other men do, protects his own life and lands, and his son's, too – he lost enough before. . . .'

'So he did,' said Ninian, penitent. 'I never should have drawn him in. Wait, I must lift this aside, I can't leave it to boil. Cadfael. . . .'

The shameless listener, who at least had heard one motion of consideration towards him and his art, in that last utterance, suddenly came to his senses, and to the awareness that in a matter of seconds these two would be issuing forth from the hut and taking to flight, by whatever road this resourceful girl had devised. Just as soon as Ninian had lifted the soothing oil from the heat and laid it carefully in a secure spot. Bless the boy, he deserved to reach Gloucester in safety! Cadfael made haste to dart round behind the barrier of the box hedge, and freeze into stillness there. He had not time to withdraw completely, but it is not certain, in any case, that he would have done so.

They burst out of the workshop hand in hand, she leading, for she knew by what route she had entered here unobserved. Through the garden she drew him, over the rim of the slope, and down towards the Meole Brook. A dark little figure swathed in a cloak, she vanished first, dwindling rapidly out of sight down the field; Ninian followed. They were gone, along the edge of the newly ploughed and manured pease fields and out of sight. So the brook was frozen over, and so must the mill-pond be. That way she had come, straight to where she knew he would be. Yet she might, just as easily, have found Cadfael there as well. Which meant, surely, that she had had converse with Ninian since he had confided in Cadfael, and saw no reason to fear the encounter, when the need was great.

Well, they were gone. No sound came up from the hollow of the brook, and there were trees quite close on the further side for cover, and all they had to do after that was wait for the right moment, cross the brook again by the bridge that carried the westward road, and make their way discreetly to whatever hiding place she had devised for her hostage, whether in the town or out of it. If out of it, surely to the west, since that was the way he desired, at last, to go. But would Ninian consent to depart until he knew that Dame Diota was safe and suspect of nothing in connection with his own expedition? If his cover was stripped from him, then she was also exposed to question. He would not leave her so. Cadfael had begun to know this young man well enough to be certain of that.

It had grown profoundly quiet, as if the very air waited for the next and inevitable alarm. Cadfael spared a moment to peer into his workshop, saw his pot of oil placed carefully on the stone cooling slab close to the brazier, and withdrew again in some haste to the great court, and across it into the cloister, but hovering anxiously where he could watch for any invasion at the gatehouse, without himself being immediately observed.

They were longer in coming than he had expected, and for that he was grateful. Moreover, a sudden flurry of fine snow had begun to fall, and that would soon cover up the footsteps crossing the brook, and in the rising wind of evening even disguise any tracks left in the garden. Until this moment he had not had time to consider the implications of what he had overheard. Clearly Ninian's appeal had gone to Ralph Giffard, who had turned a deaf ear, all too conscious of his own danger if he responded. But the girl, born into another family no less devoted to the Empress's cause, had taken up the charge and made it her own. And now, affrighted by the public crying of an enemy spy, Giffard had thought it best to ensure his own position by carrying the whole story to Hugh Beringar. Who would not be grateful for the attention, but would be forced to act upon it, or at least to put up a fair show of doing so.

All of which left one curious point at issue: Where had Ralph Giffard been going in such purposeful haste on Christmas Eve, striding across the bridge towards the Foregate almost as impetuously as Father Ailnoth had been hastening in the opposite direction an hour or so later? The two intent figures began to look like mirror images of the same man. Giffard, perhaps, the more afraid, Ailnoth the more malevolent. There was a link somewhere there, though the join was missing.

And here they came, in at the gatehouse arch, all of them on foot, Hugh with Ralph Giffard hard and erect at his elbow, Will Warden and a couple of young officers in arms following. No need here for mounted men, they were in search of a youngster horseless and penniless, labouring in the abbey gardens, and the prison that waited for him was only walking distance away.

Cadfael took his time about appearing. Others were there first, and so much the better. Brother Jerome did not love the cold, but kept a watchful eye on the outer world whenever he hopped into the warming room on such frosty days, ready to appear at any moment, dutiful and devout. Moreover, he always knew where to find Prior Robert at need. By the time Cadfael emerged innocently from the cloister they were both there, confronting the visitors from the secular world, and a few other brethren had noted the gathering, and halted within earshot in pure human curiosity, forgetting their chilled hands and feet.

'The boy Benet?' Prior Robert was saying in tones of astonishment and disdain as Cadfael approached. 'Father Ailnoth's groom? The good father himself asked employment for this young man. What absurdity is this? The boy is scarcely better than a simpleton, a mere country lad! I have often spoken with him, I know him for an innocent. My lord sheriff, I fear this gentleman wastes your time in a mistake. This cannot be true.'

'Father Prior, by your leave,' Ralph Giffard spoke up firmly, 'it is only too true, the fellow is not what he seems. I received a message, written in a fair hand, from this same simpleton, sealed with the seal of the traitor and outlaw FitzAlan, the Empress's man who is now in France, and asking me for help in FitzAlan's name – an appeal I rightly left unanswered. I have kept the leaf, the lord sheriff has seen it for himself. He was here, he said, come with the new priest, and he needed help, news and a horse, and laid claim to my aid to get what he wanted. He begged me to meet him at the mill an hour short of midnight on Christmas Eve, when all good folk would be making ready for church. I did not go, I would not touch such treason against our lord the King. But the proof I've given to the sheriff here, and there is not nor cannot be any mistake. Your labourer Benet is FitzAlan's agent Ninian Bachiler, for so he signed himself with his own hand.'

'I fear it's true enough, Father Prior,' said Hugh briskly. 'There are questions to be asked later, but now I must ask your leave at once to seek out this Benet, and he must answer for himself. There need be no disturbance for the brothers, I am asking access only to the garden.'

It was at this point that Cadfael ambled forward out of the cloister, secure across the glazed cobbles, since his feet were still swathed in wool. He came with ears benignly pricked and countenance open as the air. The snow was still falling, in an idle, neglectful fashion, but every flake froze where it fell.

'Benet?' said Cadfael guilelessly. 'You're looking for my labouring boy? I left him not a quarter of an hour since in my workshop. What do you want with him?'

He went with them, all concern and astonishment, as they proceeded into the garden, and threw open the workshop door upon the soft glow of the brazier, the pot of herbal oil drawn close on its stone slab, and the aromatic emptiness, and from that went on to quarter the whole of the garden and the fields down to the brook, where the helpful snow had obliterated every footprint. He was as mystified as the best of them. And if Hugh avoided giving him a single sidelong look, that did not mean he had not observed every facet of this vain pursuit, rather that he had, and was in little doubt as to the purveyor of mystification. There was usually a reason for Brother Cadfael's willing non-cooperation. Moreover, there were other points to be pursued before the search was taken further.

'You tell me,' said Hugh, turning to Giffard, 'that you received this appeal for your help a day or so before Christmas Eve, when a meeting at the mill was requested, somewhat before midnight. Why did you not pass it on at once to my deputy? Something might have been done about it then. Plainly he had wind of us now, since he's fled.'

If Giffard was uneasy at this dereliction of a loyal subject's duty, he gave no sign of it, but stared Hugh fully and firmly in the face. 'Because he was merely your deputy, my lord. Had you been here. . . . You got your office first after the siege of Shrewsbury, you know how we who had taken the oath to the Empress fared then, you know of my losses.

Since then I have submitted to King Stephen, and held by my submission faithfully. But a young man like Herbard, new here, left in charge and liable to stand on his dignity and status – one ignorant of the past, and what it cost me . . . I was afraid of being held still as one attainted, even if I told honestly all that I knew. And recollect, we had then heard nothing about this Bachiler being hunted in the south, the name meant nothing to me. I thought him probably of no importance, and with no prospect of any success in whipping up support for a lost cause. So I held my peace, in spite of FitzAlan's seal. There were several of his knights held such seals in his name. Do me justice, as soon as you made public the hue and cry, and I understood what was afoot, I came to you and told you the truth.'

'I grant you did,' said Hugh, 'and I understand your doubts, though it's no part of my office to hound any man for what's past and done.'

'But now, my lord . . .' Giffard had more to say, and had plainly taken great encouragement from his own eloquence and Hugh's acquiescence, for he had burned into sudden hopeful fervour. 'Now I see more in this than either you or I have thought. For I have not quite told you all, there has hardly been time to think of everything. For see, it was this young man who came here under the protection of Father Ailnoth, vilely deceiving the priest in the pretence that he was a harmless youth seeking work, and kin to the woman who kept the priest's household. And is not Father Ailnoth, who brought him here in all innocence, now done to death and waiting for burial? Who is more likely to stand guilty of his murder than the man who took wicked advantage of his goodness, and made him an unwitting accomplice in treason?'

He knew very well what manner of bolt he was hurling into the circle of listeners, he had even drawn back a pace or two to observe the shock and to distance himself from it. There was no length to which he would not go, now, to prove his own loyal integrity, to keep what he still had, if he must eternally grudge and lament what he had lost by his former allegiance. Perhaps he was secretly relieved that the boy he traduced was well away, and need never answer, but what most troubled him was his own inviolability.

'You're accusing him of the priest's murder?' said Hugh, eyeing him narrowly. 'That's going far. On what grounds do you make such a charge?'

'The very fact that he is fled points to him.'

'That might be valid enough, but not – mark me! – not unless the priest had got wind of the deception practised on him. To the best we know there was no quarrel between them, nothing had arisen to set them at odds. Unless the priest had found out how he had been abused, there could be no ground for any hostility between them.'

'He did know,' said Giffard.

'Go on,' said Hugh after a brief, profound silence. 'You cannot stop there. How do you know the priest had found him out?'

'For the best reason. I told him! I said there was still more that I had not yet told you. On the eve of the Nativity I came down here to his house, and told him how he was cheated and abused by one he had helped. I had given it anxious thought, and though I did not go to your deputy, I felt it only right to warn Father Ailnoth how he had harboured an enemy unawares. Those of the Empress's party are threatened with excommunication now, as you, my lord sheriff, are witness. The priest had been shamefully imposed upon, and so I told him.'

So that was the way of it! That was where he had been bound in such determined haste before Compline. And that was why Father Ailnoth had rushed away vengefully to keep the nocturnal tryst and confront in person the youth who had imposed upon him. Give him his due, he was no coward, he would not run first to the sergeants and get a bodyguard, he would storm forth by the mill-pool to challenge his opponent face to face, denounce, possibly even attempt to overpower him with his own hands, certainly cry him outlaw to the abbot and to the castle if he could not himself hale him to judgement. But things had gone very differently, for Ninian had come unharmed to church, and Ailnoth had ended in the pool with a broken head. And who could avoid making the simple connection now? Who that had not spent so many days in Ninian's blithe company as had Cadfael, and got to know him so well?

'And after you had left him,' said Hugh, eyeing Giffard steadily, 'he knew the time and place appointed for you to meet with Bachiler, and the invitation you had rejected you think he went to accept? But without an acceptance from you, would Bachiler keep the appointment?'

'I made no answer. I had not rejected it outright. He was asking for help, for news, for a horse. He would come! He could not afford not to come.'

And he would meet with a very formidable and very angry enemy, bent on betraying him to the law, a man who verily held himself to be the instrument of the wrath of God. Yes, death could well come of such a meeting.

'Will,' said Hugh, turning abruptly to his sergeant, 'get back to the castle and bring down more men. We'll get the lord abbot's permission to search the gardens here, and the stables and the barns, grange court, storehouses, all. Begin with the mill, and have a watch on the bridge and the highway. If this youngster was in the hut here not half an hour ago, as Cadfael says, he cannot be far. And whether he has killed or no is still open, but the first need is to lay hands on him and have him safe in hold.'

'You will not forget,' said Cadfael, alone with Hugh in the workshop later, 'that there are others, many others, who had as good reason as Ninian, and better, to wish Ailnoth dead?'

'I don't forget it. Far too many others,' agreed Hugh ruefully. 'And all you tell me of this boy – not that I'm dull enough, mind, to suppose you've told me all you could! – shows him as one who might very well hit out boldly in his own defence, but scarcely from behind. Yet he might, in the heat of conflict. Who knows what any of us might do, in extremes? And by what I hear of the priest, he would lash out with all his might and whatever weapon came to hand. It's the lad's vanishing now that suggests the worst.'

'He had good reason to vanish,' pointed out Cadfael, 'if he heard that Giffard was on his way to the castle to betray him. You'd have had to clap him into prison, guilty or innocent of the priest's death. Your hand's forced. Of course he'd run.'

'*If* someone warned him,' agreed Hugh with a wry smile. 'You, for instance?'

'No, not I,' said Cadfael virtuously. 'I knew nothing about Giffard's errand, or I might have dropped a word in the boy's ear. But no, certainly not I. I do know that Benet – Ninian we must call him now, I suppose! – was in the church some time before midnight on Christmas Eve. If he went to the mill at all, he went early for the meeting, and left early, also.'

'So you told me, and I believe it. But so, by your own account, did Ailnoth go early to the meeting place, perhaps to hide himself and spring out on Bachiler by surprise. There was still time for them to clash and one to die.'

'The boy had not the marks of any agitation or dismay upon him in the church. A little excitement, perhaps, but pleasurable, I would say. And how much have you managed to worm out of the parish folk about this business? There are a number who had justifiable grudges against Ailnoth, what have they to say for themselves?'

'In general, as you'd expect, as little as possible. One or two make no secret of their gratitude that the man's gone, none at all. Eadwin, the one whose boundary stone he moved, he's neither forgotten nor forgiven, even if the stone was replaced afterwards. His wife and children swear he never left the house that night – but so do they all, and so, of course, they would. Jordan Achard, the baker, now there's a man who might kill in a rage. He has a real grievance. His bread is his pride, and there was never any amends made for that insult. It hurt far more than if the priest had denounced him for a notorious lecher, which would at least have had the merit of being true. There are some give him the credit for being the father of that poor girl's baby, the lass who drowned herself, but from all I hear it could as well have been half the other men in the parish, for she couldn't say no to any of them. Our Jordan says he was home and sober every moment of Christmas Eve, and his wife bears him out, but she's a poor, subdued creature who wouldn't dare cross him. But from all accounts it's few nights he does spend in his own bed, and to judge by his wife's sidelong looks and wary answers he may well have been sleeping abroad that night. But we shall never get her to say so. She's both afraid of him and loyal to him.'

'The rest of his women may be less so,' said Cadfael. 'But I hardly see Jordan as a man of violence.'

'Perhaps not. But I do see Father Ailnoth as a man of violence, whether bodily or spiritual. And consider, Cadfael, how he might behave if he happened on one of his flock sneaking into the wrong bed. If not a violent man, Jordan is a big and strong one, and by no means meek enough to suffer assault tamely. He might end the fight another man began, without ever meaning to. But Jordan is one among many, and not the most likely.'

'Your men have been diligent,' said Cadfael with a sigh.

'They have. Alan was on his mettle, and determined to deserve his place. There's a decent poor soul called Centwin, who lives along the Foregate towards the horse-fair ground. You'll have heard his story. It was new to me until I heard it from Alan. The babe that died unchristened because Ailnoth could not interrupt his prayers. That sticks in the craw of every man in the parish, worse than all.'

'You cannot have found out anything black against Centwin?' protested Cadfael. 'As quiet a creature as breathes, never a trouble to any.'

'Never with occasion until now. But this goes deep. And Centwin, quiet as he may be, is also deep. He keeps his own counsel, and broods over his own grievances. I've spoken with him. We questioned the watch on the town gate,

Christmas Eve,' said Hugh. 'They saw you go out, and you best know the time that was, and where you met the priest. They also saw Centwin go out not many minutes after you, on his way home, he said, from visiting a friend in the town to whom he owed a small debt. True enough, for the tanner he paid has confirmed it. He wanted, he said, to have all his affairs clear and all dues paid before he went to Matins, as indeed he did go, and left before Lauds for home. But you see how the time fits. One coming a few minutes behind you may also have met with Ailnoth, may have seen him turn from the Foregate along the path to the mill. There in darkness and loneliness, think, might not even a mild, submissive man with that wound burning in his belly have seen suddenly an opportunity to pay off yet another and a more bitter debt? And there was the time between then and Matins for two men to clash in the darkness, and one to die.'

'No,' said Cadfael, 'I do not believe it!'

'Because it would be one cruelty piled upon another? But such things happen. No, take heart, Cadfael, neither do I quite believe it, but it is *possible.* There are too many by far who are not vouched for, or whose guarantors cannot be trusted, too many who hated him. And there is still Ninian Bachiler. Whatever the truth of him, you do understand that I must do my best to find him?'

He looked down at his friend with a dark, private smile that was more eloquent than the words. It was not the first time they had agreed, with considerate courtesy and no need of many words, to pursue each what he held to be his own duty, and bear no malice if the two crossed like swords.

'Oh, yes!' said Cadfael. 'Yes, that I fully understand.'

Chapter Eight

Cadfael had returned to the church after Prime to replenish the perfumed oil in the lamp on Saint Winifred's altar. The inquisitive skills which might have been frowned upon if they had been employed to make scents for women's vanity became permissible and even praiseworthy when used as an act of worship, and he took pleasure in trying out all manner of fragrant herbs and flowers in many different combinations, plying the sweets of rose and lily, violet and clover against the searching aromatic riches of rue and sage and wormwood. It pleased him to think that the lady must take delight in being so served, for virgin saint though she might be, she was a woman, and in her youth had been a beautiful and desirable one.

Cynric the verger came in from the north porch with the twig broom in his hand, from brushing away the night's sprinkling of fine snow from porch and steps, and went to open the great service-book on the reading desk, and trim the candles on the parish altar ready for the communal Mass, and set two new ones on the prickets of the wall brackets on either side. Cadfael gave him good day as he came back into the nave, and got the usual tranquil but brief acknowledgement.

'Freezing as hard as ever,' said Cadfael. 'There'll be no breaking the ground for Ailnoth today.' For it would be Cynric who had to dig the grave, in the green enclosure east of the church, where priests and abbots and brothers were laid to rest.

Cynric sniffed the air and considered, his deep eyes veiled.

'A change by tomorrow, maybe. I smell a thaw coming.'

It could be true. He lived on close, if neutral, terms with the elements, tolerating them as they seemed to refrain from harming him, for it must be deathly cold in that small, stony room over the porch.

'The ground's chosen for him?' asked Cadfael, catching the taciturn habit.

'Close under the wall.'

'Not next to Father Adam, then? I thought Prior Robert would have wanted to put him there.'

'He did,' said Cynric shortly. 'I said the earth there was not yet settled, and must have time to bed down.'

'A pity the hard frost came now. A dead man still lying among us unburied makes the young ones uneasy.'

'Ay,' said Cynric. 'The sooner he's in the ground the better for all. Now that he's gone.' He straightened the second thick candle on its spike, stepped back to make sure it stood erect and would not gutter, and brushed the clinging feel of tallow from his hands, for the first time turning his eyes in their hollow caverns upon Cadfael, and lighting up his lantern countenance with the smile of singular if rueful sweetness that brought the children to him with such serene confidence. 'Do you go into the Foregate this morning? I heard there's a few folk having trouble with the cold.'

'No wonder they should!' said Cadfael. 'I'm away to have a look at one or two of the children, but there's no great harm yet. Why, do you know of someone who needs me? I have leave, I can as well make one more visit. Who is sick?'

'It's the little wooden hovel on the left, along the back lane from the horse-fair, the widow Nest. She's caring for her grandchild, the poor worm, Eluned's baby, and she's fretted for it.' Cynric, perforce, was unusually loquacious in explaining. 'Won't take its milk, and cries with the wind in its belly.'

'It was born a healthy child?' asked Cadfael. For it could not be many weeks old, and motherless, deprived of its best food. He had not forgotten the shock and anger that had swept through the Foregate, when they lost their favourite whore. If indeed Eluned had ever been a whore. She never asked payment. If men gave her things, it was of their own will. She, it seemed, had done nothing but give, however unwisely.

'A bonny girl, big and lusty, so Nest said.'

'Then she'll have it in her, infant though she may be, to fight her way into life,' said Cadfael comfortably. 'I must go get the right cordial for an infant's inside. I'll make it fresh. Who sings Mass for you today?'

'Brother Anselm.'

'Well for you!' said Brother Cadfael, making for the south porch and his quickest way to the garden and his workshop. 'It might as easily have been Brother Jerome.'

The house was low and narrow, but sturdy, and the dark passage in which it stood braced against a taller dwelling looked crisp and clean in the hard frost, though in moist, mild weather it might have been an odorous hole. Cadfael rapped at the door, and for immediate reassurance called out loudly: 'Brother Cadfael from the abbey, mistress. Cynric said you need me for the child.'

Whether it was his own name or Cynric's that made him welcome there was no knowing, but instantly there was a stir of movement within, a baby howled fretfully, probably at being laid down in haste, and then the door was opened wide, and from half-darkness a woman beckoned him within, and made haste to close the door after him against the cold.

This one small room was all the house, and its only inlet for light or outlet for smoke was a vent in the roof. In clement weather the door would always be open from dawn to dusk, but frost had closed it, and the dwelling was lit only by a small oil lamp and the dim but steady glow of a fire penned in an iron cage on a flat stone under the vent. But blessedly someone had supplied charcoal for the widow's needs, and there was a mild fume in the nostrils here but little smoke. Furnishings were few, a low bench-bed in a corner, a few pots on the firestone, a rough, small table. Cadfael took a little time to accustom his eyes to the dim light, and the shapes of things emerged gradually. The woman stood by him, waiting, and like all else here, grew steadily out of the gloom, a perceptible human being. The cradle, the central concern of this house, was placed in the most sheltered corner, where the warmth of the fire could come, but not the draught from door or vent. And the child within was wailing indignantly within its wrappings, half-asleep but unable by reason of discomfort to fall deeper into peace.

'I brought an end of candle with me,' said Cadfael, taking in everything about him without haste. 'I thought we might need more light. With your leave!' He took it out from his scrip, tilted the wick into the small flame of the lamp in its clay saucer, and stood the stump upon the corner of the table, where it shed light closely upon the cradle. It was a broad-based end discarded from one of the prickets in the wall brackets of the church, he found them useful for carrying on his errands because they would stand solidly on any flat surface, and run no risk of being overturned. Among flimsy wooden cottages there was need of such care. This dwelling, poor as it was, had been more solidly built than many.

'They keep you in charcoal?' asked Cadfael, turning to the woman, who stood quite still, gazing at him with fixed and illusionless eyes.

'My man who's dead was a forester in Eyton. The abbey's man there remembers me. He brings me wood, as well, the dead twigs and small chippings for kindling.'

'That's well,' said Cadfael. 'So young a babe needs to be kept warm. Now you tell me, what's her trouble?'

She was telling him herself, in small, fretful wails from her cradle, but she was well wrapped and clean, and had a healthy, well-nourished voice with which to complain.

'Three days now she's sickened on her milk, and cries with the wind inside. But I've kept her warm, and she's taken no chill. If my poor girl had lived this chit would have been at her breast, not sipping from a spoon or my fingers, but she's gone, and left this one to me, all I have now, and I'll do anything to keep her safe.'

'She's been feeding well enough, by the look of her,' said Cadfael, stooping over the whimpering child. 'How old is she now? Six weeks is it, or seven? She's big and bonny for that age.'

The small, contorted face, all wailing mouth and tight-shut eyes screwed up with annoyance, was round and clear-skinned, though red now with exertion and anger. She had abundant, fine hair of a bright autumn brown, and inclined to curl.

'Feed well, yes, indeed she did, until this upset. A greedy-gut, even. I was proud of her.'

And kept plying her too long, thought Cadfael, and she without the sense yet to know when she had enough. No great mystery here.

'That's a part of her trouble, you'll find. Give her only a little at a time, and often, and put in the milk a few drops of the cordial I'll leave with you. Three or four drops will be enough. Get me a small spoon, and she shall have a proper dose of it now to soothe her.'

The widow brought him a little horn spoon, and he unstoppered the glass bottle he had brought, moistened the tip of a finger at its lip, and touched it to the lower lip of the baby's angry mouth. In an instant the howling broke off short, and the contorted countenance resumed a human shape, and even a human expression of wonder and surprise. The mouth closed, small moist lips folding on an unexpected sweetness; and miraculously this became a mouth too shapely and delicate for a baby of seven weeks, with a distant promise of beauty. The angry red faded slowly to leave the round cheeks flushed with rose, and Eluned's daughter opened great eyes of a blue almost as dark as the night sky, and smiled an aware, responsive smile, too old for her few weeks of life. True, she wrinkled her face and uttered a warning wail the next moment, but the far-off vision of loveliness remained.

'The creature!' said her grandmother, ruefully fond. 'She likes it!'

Cadfael half-filled the little spoon, touched it gently to the baby's lower lip, and instantly her mouth opened, willing to suck in the offering. It went down fairly tidily, leaving only a gloss upon the relaxed lips. She gazed upward in silence for a moment, from those eyes that devoured half her face under the rounded brow and fluff of auburn hair. Then she turned her cheek a little into the flat pillow under her, belched resoundingly, and lay quiescent with lids half-closed, her infinitesimal fingers curled into small, easy fists under her chin.

'Nothing amiss with her that need cause you any worry,' said Cadfael, re-stoppering the bottle. 'If she wakes and cries in the night, and is again in pain, you can give her a little of this in the spoon, as I did. But I think she'll sleep. Give her somewhat less food at a time than you've been giving, and put three or four drops of this in the milk, and we'll see how she fares in a few days more.'

'What is in it?' asked the widow, looking curiously at the bottle in her hand.

'There's dill, fennel, mint, just a morsel of poppy-juice . . . and honey to make it agreeable to the taste. Put it somewhere safe and use it as I've said. If she's again troubled this way, give her the dose you saw me give. If she does well enough without it, then spare it but for the drop or two in her food. Medicines are of more effect if used only when there's need.'

He blew out the end of candle he had brought, leaving it to cool and congeal, for it had still an hour or so of burning left in it, and could serve again in the same office. On the instant he was sorry he had diminished the light in the room so soon, for only now had he leisure to look at the woman. This was the widowed mother of the girl who had been shut out of the church as an irredeemable sinner, whose very penitence and confession were not to be trusted, and therefore could justifiably be rejected. Out of this small, dark dwelling that disordered beauty had blossomed, borne fruit, and died.

The mother must herself have been comely, some years ago, she had still fine features, though worn and lined now in shapes of discouragement, and her greying hair, drawn back austerely from her face, was still abundant, and bore the shadowy richness of its former red-brown colouring. There was no saying whether the dark, hollow eyes that studied her grandchild with such a bitter burden of love were dark blue, but they well might have been. She was probably barely forty. Cadfael had seen her about the Foregate now and then, but never before paid close attention to her.

'A fine babe you have there,' said Cadfael. 'She may well grow into a beautiful child.'

'Better she should be plain as any drab,' said the widow with abrupt passion, 'than take after her mother's beauty, and go the same way. You do know whose child she is? Everyone knows it!'

'No fault of this little one she left behind,' said Cadfael. 'I hope the world will treat her better than it treated her mother.'

'It was not the world that cast her off,' said Nest, 'but the church. She could have lived under the world's malice, but not when the priest shut her out of the church.'

'Did her worship truly mean so much to her,' asked Cadfael gravely, 'that she could not live excommunicate?'

'Truly it did. You never knew her! As wild and rash as she was beautiful, but such a bright, kind, warm creature to have about the house, and for all her wildness she was easily hurt. She who never could bear to wound any other creature was open to wounds herself. But for the thing she could not help, no one could have been a better and sweeter daughter to me. You can't know how it was! She could not refuse to anyone whatever he asked of her, if it was in her power to give it. And the men found it out, and having no shame – for sin was something she spoke of without understanding – she could not say no to men, either. She would go with a man because he was melancholy, or because he begged her, or because he had been blamed or beaten unjustly and was aggrieved at the world. And then it would come over her that this might indeed be sin, as Father Adam had told her, though she could not see why. And then she went flying to confession, in tears, and promised amendment, and meant it, too. Father Adam was gentle with her, seeing she was not like other young women. He always spoke her kindly and fair, and gave her light penance, and never refused her absolution. Always she promised to amend, but then she forgot for some boy's light tongue or dark eyes, and sinned again, and again confessed and was shriven. She couldn't keep from men, but neither could she live without the blessing and comfort of the church. When the door was shut in her face she went solitary away, and solitary she died. And for all she was a torment to me, living, she was a joy, too, and now I have only torment, and no joy – but for this fearful joy here in the cradle. Look, she's asleep!'

'Do you know,' asked Cadfael, brooding, 'who fathered the child?'

Nest shook her head, and a faint, dry smile plucked at her lips. 'No. As soon as she understood it might bring blame on him, whoever he was, she kept him a secret even from me. If, indeed, she knew herself which one of them had quickened her! Yet I think she did know. She was neither mad nor dull of understanding. She was brighter than most, but for the part of caution that was left out of her. She might have confronted the man to his face, but she would never betray him to the black priest. Oh, he asked her! He threatened her, he raged at her, but she said that for her sins she would answer and do penance, but another man's sins were his own, and so must his confession be.'

A good answer! Cadfael acknowledged it with a nod and a sigh.

The candle was cold and set. He restored it to his scrip, and turned to take his leave. 'Well, if she's fretful again and you need me, let me know of it by Cynric, or leave word at the gatehouse, and I'll come. But I think you'll find the cordial will serve your turn.' He looked back for a second with his hand on the latch of the door. 'What have you named her? Eluned, for her mother?'

'No,' said the widow. 'It was Eluned chose her name. Praise God, it was Father Adam who christened her, before he fell ill and died. She's called Winifred.'

Cadfael walked back along the Foregate with that last echo still ringing in his mind. The daughter of the outcast and excommunicate, it seemed, was named for the town's own saint, witness enough to the truth of Eluned's undisciplined devotion. And doubtless Saint Winifred would know where to find and watch over both the living child and the dead mother, whom the parish of Saint Chad, more prodigally merciful than Father Ailnoth, had buried decently, observing a benevolent Christian doubt concerning the circumstances of her unwitnessed death. A strong strain, these Welsh women married into Shropshire families. He knew nothing of the English forester who had been husband to the widow Nest, but surely it must be she who had handed on to her self-doomed child the fierce beauty that had been her downfall, and the same face, in prophetic vision, waited for the infant Winifred in her cradle. Perhaps the choice of her venerated name had been a brave gesture to protect a creature otherwise orphaned and unprotected, a waif in an alien world where too prodigal a union of beauty and generosity brought only grief.

Now there, in the cottage he had left behind, was one being who had the best of all reasons to hate Ailnoth, and might have killed him if a thought could have done it, but was hardly likely to follow him through the winter night and strike him down from behind, much less roll him, stunned, into the pool. She had too powerful a lodestone to keep her watchful and protective at home. But the vengeful fire in her might drive a man to do it for her sake, if she had so close and resolute a friend. Among all those men who had taken comfort from the world's spite in Eluned's arms, might there not be more than one ready and willing? And in particular, if he knew what seed he had sown, the father of the infant Winifred.

At this rate, thought Cadfael, mildly irritated with his own preoccupation, I shall be looking sidewise at every comely man I see, to try if I can find in his face any resemblance to a murderer. I'd best concern myself with my own duties, and leave official retribution to Hugh – not that he'll be grateful for it!

He was approaching the gatehouse, and had just come to the entrance to the twisting alley that led to the priest's house. He halted there, suddenly aware that the heavy covering cloud had lifted, and a faint gleam of sun showed through. Not brilliantly and icily out of a pale, cold sky, but timidly and grudgingly through untidy, wallowing shreds of cloud. The glitter coruscating from icicles and swags of frozen snow along the eaves had acquired a softer, moist brightness. There was even a drip here and there from a gable end where the timorous sun fell. Cynric might be right in his prediction, and a thaw on the way by nightfall. Then they could at least put Ailnoth out of the chapel and under the ground, though his baleful shadow would still be with them.

There was no haste to return to the abbey and his workshop, half an hour more would not do any harm. Cadfael turned into the alley and walked along to the priest's house. He was none too sure of his own motives in paying this visit. Certainly it was his legitimate business to make sure that Mistress Hammet's injuries had healed properly, and she had taken no lingering harm from the blow to her head, but pure curiosity had a part in what prompted him, too. Here was another woman whose attitude to Father Ailnoth might be exceedingly ambivalent, torn between gratitude for a patronage which had given her status and security, and desperation at his raging resentment of the deception practised on him, if she knew how he had found it out, and his all too probable intent to see her nurseling unmasked and thrown into prison. Cadfael's judgement of Diota was that she went in considerable awe and fear of her master, but also that she would dare much for the boy she had nursed. But any suspicion of her was quickly tempered by his recollection of her state on Christmas morning. Almost certainly, whatever her fears after a night of waiting in vain, she had not known that Ailnoth was dead until the searchers returned with his body. As often as Cadfael told himself he could be deceived in believing that, his own memory rejected the doubt.

Just beyond the priest's house the narrow alley opened out into a small grassy space, now a circle of trampled rime, but with the green of grass peeping through by small, indomitable tufts here and there. To this confined playground the house presented its fine, unbroken wall, the one that attracted the players of ball games and the like, to their peril. There were half a dozen urchins of the Foregate playing there now, rolling snowballs and hurling them from an ambitiously remote mark at a target set up on an abandoned fence-post at the corner of the green. A round black cap, with a fluttering end of torn braid quivering in the light wind. A skull cap, such as a priest would wear, or a monk, to cover his tonsure from cold when the cowl was inconvenient.

One small possession of Ailnoth's which had not been recovered with him, nor missed. Cadfael stood and gazed, remembering sharply the clear image of the priest's set and formidable face as he passed the gatehouse torches, unshadowed by any cowl, and capped, yes, certainly capped in black, this meagre circle that cast no shadows, but left his apocalyptic rage plain to view.

One of the marksmen, luckier or more adroit, had knocked the target flying into the grass. The victor, without great interest now, having prevailed, went to pick it up, and stood dangling it in one hand, while the rest of the band, capricious as children can be, burst into a spirited argument as to what they should do next, and like a wisp of snipe rising, suddenly took off across the grass towards the open field beyond.

The marksman made to follow them, but with no haste, knowing they would settle as abruptly as they had taken flight, and he could be up with them whenever he willed. Cadfael went a few paces to intercept his passage, and the boy halted readily enough, knowing him. A bright boy, ten years old, the reeve's sister's son. He had a charming, inscrutable smile.

'What's that you have there, Eddi?' asked Cadfael, nodding at the dangling cap. 'May I see it?'

It was handed over willingly, indifferently. No doubt they had played various games with it for several days now, and were weary of it. Some other brief foundling toy would take its place, and it would never be missed. Cadfael turned it in his hands, and marked how the braid that bound its rim was ripped clear on one side, and dangled the loose end. When he drew it into place there was still a strand missing, perhaps the length of his little finger, and the stitching of two of the segments that made up the circle had been frayed apart with the lost shred. Good black cloth, carefully made, the braid hand-plaited wool.

'Where did you find this, Eddi?'

'In the mill-pond,' said the boy readily. 'Someone threw it away because it was torn. We went down early in the morning to see if the pond was frozen, but it wasn't. But we found this.'

'Which morning was that?' asked Cadfael.

'Christmas Day. It was only just getting light.' The boy was grave, demure of countenance, impenetrable as clever children can be.

'Where in the mill-pond? On the mill side?'

'No, we went along the other path, where it's shallow. That's where it freezes first. The tail-race keeps it open the other side.'

So it did, the movement enough to preserve an open channel until all froze over, and the same stream of moving water would carry a light thing, like this cap, over to lodge in the shallows.

'This was caught among the reeds there?'

The boy said yes, serenely.

'You know whose this is, do you, Eddi?'

'No, sir,' said Eddi, and smiled a brief, guileless smile. He was, Cadfael recalled, one of those unfortunate children who had been learning their letters with Father Adam, and had fallen into less tolerant hands after his death. And wronged and injured children are not themselves merciful to their tyrants.

'No matter, son. Are you done with it? Will you leave it with me? I'll bring you a few apples to your father's, a fair exchange. And you may forget it.'

'Yes, sir,' said the boy, and turned and skipped away without another glance, rid of his prize and his burden.

Cadfael stood looking down at the small, drab thing in his hands, damp now and darkening from the comparative warmth of being handled, but fringed with rime and still stiff. How unlike Father Ailnoth to be seen wearing a cap with a tattered braid and a seam beginning to lose its stitches! If, indeed, it had been in this condition when he put it on? It had been tossed around at random since Christmas Day, and might have come by its dilapidations at any time since it was plucked out of the frosty reeds, where the drift of the tail-race had carried it, while the heavier body from which it had been flung was gradually edged aside under the leaning bank.

And was there not something else that had been forgotten, as this cap had been forgotten? Something else they should have looked for, and had never thought of? Something nagging at the back of Cadfael's mind but refusing to show itself?

He thrust the cap into his scrip, and turned back to rap at the door of the priest's house. It was opened to him by Diota, prim and composed in her customary black. She stepped back readily, unsmiling but hospitable, and beckoned him at once into a small, warm room dimly lit by a brownish light from two small windows, into the shutters of which thin sheets of horn had been set. A bright wood fire burned on the clay hearth in the centre of the room, and on the cushioned bench beside it a young woman was sitting, alert and silent, and to one entering from broad daylight not immediately recognisable.

'I came only to ask how you are,' said Cadfael as the door was closed behind him, 'and to see if you need anything more for your grazes.'

Diota came round to face him and let herself be seen, the palest of smiles visiting a face habitually grave and anxious. 'That was kind of you, Brother Cadfael. I am well, I thank you, quite well. You see the wound is healed.'

She turned her injured temple docilely to the best of the light at the urging of his hand, and let him study what had faded now to a yellow bruise and a small dry scar.

'Yes, that's well, there'll be no mark left to show for it. But I should go on using the ointment for a few days yet, in this frost the skin dries and abrades easily. And you've had no headaches?'

'No, none.'

'Good! Then I'll be off back to my work, and not take up your time, for I see you have a visitor.'

'Oh, no,' said the visitor, rising briskly from the bench, 'I was about to take my leave.' She stepped forward, raising to the light a rounded young face, broad at the brow and tapering gently to a resolute chin. Challenging harebell-blue eyes, set very wide apart, confronted Cadfael with a direct and searching stare. 'If you must really go so soon,' said Sanan Bernières, with the serene confidence of a masterful child, 'I'll walk with you. I've been waiting to find a right time to talk to you.'

There was no gainsaying such a girl. Diota did not venture to try and detain her, and Brother Cadfael, even if he had wished, would have hesitated before denying her. Law itself, he thought with amused admiration, might come off the loser if it collided with the will of Sanan Bernières. In view of all that had happened, that was a distinct if as yet distant possibility, but she would not let the prospect deter her.

'That will be great pleasure for me,' said Cadfael. 'The walk is very short – but perhaps you'll be needing some more herbs for your kitchen? I have ample supplies, you may come in and take what you wish.'

She did give him a very sharp glance for that, and as suddenly dimpled, and to hide laughter turned to embrace Diota, kissing her thin cheek like a daughter. Then she drew her cloak about her and led the way out into the alley, and together they walked the greater part of the way out into the Foregate in silence.

'Do you know,' she said then, 'why I went to see Mistress Hammet?'

'Out of womanly sympathy, surely,' said Cadfael, 'with her loss. Loss and loneliness – still a virtual stranger here . . .'

'Oh, come!' said Sanan bluntly. 'She worked for the priest, I suppose it was a secure life for a widow woman, but loss . . .? Lonely she may well be.'

'I was not speaking of Father Ailnoth,' said Cadfael.

She gave him another straight glance of her startling blue eyes, and heaved a thoughtful sigh. 'Yes, you've worked with him, you know him. He told you, didn't he, that she was his nurse, no blood kin? She never had children in her own marriage, he's as dear as a son to her. I . . . have talked with him, too – by chance. You know he sent a message to my step-father. Everyone knows that now. I was curious to see this young man, that's all.'

They had reached the abbey gatehouse. She stood hesitant, frowning at the ground.

'Now everyone is saying that he – this Ninian Bachiler – killed Father Ailnoth, because the priest was going to betray him to the sheriff. I knew she must have heard it. I knew she would be alone, afraid for him, now he's fled, and hunted for his life – for it *is* his life, now!'

'So you came to bear her company,' said Cadfael, 'and reassure her. Come through into the garden, and if you have all the pot-herbs you want, I daresay we can find another good reason. You won't be any the worse for having something by you to cure the cough that may be coming along in a week or two.'

She looked up with a flashing smile. 'The same remedy you gave me when I was ten? I've changed so much you can hardly have known me again. Such excellent health I have, I need you only once every seven or eight years.'

'If you need me now,' said Cadfael simply, leading the way across the great court towards the gardens, 'that's enough.'

She followed demurely, lowering her eyes modestly in this male seclusion, and in the safe solitude of the workshop she allowed herself to be installed comfortably with her small feet towards the brazier before she drew breath again and went on talking, now more freely, having left all other ears outside the door.

'I came to see Mistress Hammet because I was afraid that, now that he is so threatened, she might do something foolish. She is devoted to Ninian, in desperation she might do anything – *anything*! – to ensure that he goes free. She might even come forward with some mad story about being to blame herself. She would, I am sure, for him! If she thought it would clear him of all guilt, she would confess to murder.'

'So you came,' said Cadfael, moving about his private world quietly to leave her the illusion that she was not closely observed, 'to urge her to hold her peace and wait calmly, for he's still at liberty and in no immediate danger. Is that it?'

'Yes. And if you go to see her again, or she comes to you, please urge the same upon her. Don't let her do anything to harm herself.'

'Did he send you, to see her and tell her this?' asked Cadfael directly.

She was not yet quite ready to be drawn into the open, though fleetingly she smiled. 'It's simply that I know, I understand, how anxious he must be now about her. He would be glad if he knew I had talked to her.'

As he will know, before many hours are out, thought Cadfael. Now I wonder where she has hidden him? There could well be old retainers of her own father here in Shrewsbury, or close by, men who would do a great deal for Bernières's daughter.

'I know,' said Sanan with slow solemnity, following Cadfael's movements with intent eyes, 'that you discovered Ninian before ever my step-father betrayed him. I know he told you freely who he is and what he's about, and you said you had nothing against any honest man of either party, and would do nothing to harm him. And you've kept his secret until now, when it's no longer a secret. He trusts you, and I am resolved to trust you.'

'No,' said Cadfael hastily, 'tell me nothing! If I don't know where the boy is now, no one can get it out of me, and I can declare my ignorance with a good conscience. I like a gallant lad, even if he is too rash for his own good. He tells me his whole aim now is to reach the Empress, at whatever cost, and offer her his services. He has a right to dispose of his own efforts as he pleases, and I wish him a safe arrival and long life. Such a madcap deserves to have luck on his side.'

'I know,' she said, flushing and smiling, 'he is not very discreet. . . .'

'Discreet? I doubt if he knows the meaning of the word! To write and send such a letter, open as the day, signed with his own name and telling where and under what pretence he's to be found! No, never tell me where he is now, but wherever you've hidden him, keep a weather eye on him, for there's no knowing what breathless foolishness he'll be up to next.' He had been busy filling a small flask, to provide her with a respectable reason for emerging from his herbarium. He sealed it with a wooden stopper and tied it down at the neck under a wisp of thin parchment before wrapping it in a piece of linen and putting it into her hands. 'There, madam, is your permit to be here. And my advice is, get him away as soon as you can.'

'But he won't go,' she said, sighing, but with pride rather than exasperation, 'not while this matter is unresolved. He won't budge until he knows Diota is safe. And there are preparations to make – means to provide. . . .' She shook herself bracingly, tossed her brown head, and made briskly for the door.

'His first need,' said Cadfael thoughtfully after her, 'will be a good horse.'

She turned about abruptly in the doorway, and gave him a blazing smile, throwing aside all reservations.

'Two horses!' she said in a soft, triumphant whisper. 'I am of the Empress's party, too. I am going with him!'

Chapter Nine

Cadfael was uneasy in his mind all that day, plagued on the one hand by misgivings about Sanan's revelation, and on the other by the elusive gnat that sang in the back of his consciousness, telling him persistently that he had failed to notice the loss of one item that should have been sought with Ailnoth, and might very well have missed another. There was certainly something he should have thought of, something that might shed light, if only he could discover what it was, and go, belatedly, to look for it.

In the meantime, he pursued the round of his duties through Vespers and supper in the refectory, and tried in vain to concentrate upon the psalms for this thirtieth day of December, the sixth day in the octave of Christmas.

Cynric had been right about the thaw. It came furtively and grudgingly, but it was certainly on its way by mid afternoon. The trees were shedding their tinkling filigree of frozen rime and standing starkly black against a low sky. Drips perforated the whiteness under the eaves with small dark pockmarks, and the black of the road and the green of grass were beginning to show through the covering of snow. By morning it might even be possible to break the ground, in that chosen spot sheltered under the precinct wall, and dig Father Ailnoth's grave.

Cadfael had examined the skull-cap closely, and could make no great sense of it. Yet it fretted him simply because he had failed to think of it when the body was found. As for the damage to it, that suggested a connection with the blow to the head, and yet at the same time contradicted that connection, since in that event the cap would surely have fallen on land, when the blow was struck. True, the assailant might very well have thrown it into the water after the priest, but in the dark would he have noticed or thought of it, and if he had, would he necessarily have been able to find it? A small black thing in tufted grass not yet white with rime – not easy to see, and unlikely to be remembered as too dangerous to leave, when murder had been committed. Who was going to grope around in the dark in rough grass, when he had just killed a man? His one thought would be to get well away from the scene as quickly as possible.

Well, if Cadfael had missed this one thing, he might have missed – his demon was nagging at him that he *had* missed! – another as important. And if he had, it was still there by the mill, either along the bank or in the water, or even within the mill itself. No use looking for it elsewhere.

There was half an hour left before Compline, and most of the brothers, very sensibly, were in the warming room, getting the chill out of their bones. It was folly to think of going near the mill at this hour, in the dark, but for all that Cadfael could not keep away, his mind so dwelt upon the place, as though the very ambience of the pool, the mill and the solitary night might reproduce the events of Christmas Eve, and prod his memory into recapturing the lost factor. He crossed the great court to the retired corner by the infirmary, where the wicket in the precinct wall led through directly to the mill.

Outside, with no moon and only ragged glimpses of stars, he stood until his eyes grew accustomed to the night, and the shapes of things grew out of obscurity. The rough grass of the field, the dark bulk of the mill to his right, with the little wooden bridge at the corner of the building immediately before him, crossing the head-race to the overhanging bank of the pool. He crossed, his feet making a small, clear, hollow sound on the planks, and walked across the narrow strip of grass to the bank. The expanse of the water opened beneath him, pale, leaden-still, dappled with patches of open water, rimmed round with half-thawed ice.

Nothing moved here but himself, there was nothing to be heard, not even a breath of wind stirring in the lissome naked shoots of the pollarded willows at his left hand along the bank. A few yards along there, just past the nearest stump, cut down to hip-height and bristling with wands like hair on the giant head of a terrified man, they had drawn Ailnoth's body laboriously along under the eroded bank, and brought him to shore where the meadow sloped down more gently to the outflow of the tail-race.

In his recollection of the morning every detail stood sharply defined, but shed no light at all on what had happened in the night. He turned from the high bank and walked back across the bridge, and for no good reason that he could see continued round the mill, and down the sloping bank to the big doors where the grain was carried in. Only an outer bar fastened the door, and that, he saw dimly by the faint reflection from bleached timber, was drawn back from its socket. There was a small door on the higher level, giving quick access to the wicket in the precinct wall. That could be fastened within. But why should this heavy bar be drawn back unless someone had made entry from without?

Cadfael set his hand to the closed but unbarred door, eased it open by a hand's breadth, and stiffened to listen with an ear to the chink. Nothing but silence from within. He opened it a little wider, slid quietly through, and eased the door back again behind him. The warm scents of flour and grain tickled his nostrils. He had a nose sharp as fox or hound, and trusted to it in the dark, and there was another scent here, very faint, utterly familiar. In his own workshop he was unaware of it from long and constant acquaintance, but in any other place it pricked his consciousness with a particular insistence, as of a stolen possession of his own, and a valued one, that had no business to stray. A man cannot be in and out of a workshop saturated with years of harvesting herbs, and not carry the scent of them about in his garments. Cadfael froze with his back against the closed door, and waited.

The faintest stir reached his ears, as of a foot carefully placed in dust and husk that could not choose but rustle, however cautiously trodden. Somewhere above him, on the upper floor. So the hatch was open, and someone was leaning there, carefully shifting his stance to drop through. Cadfael moved obligingly in that direction, to give him encouragement. Next moment a body dropped neatly behind him, and an arm clamped about his neck, bracing him back against his assailant, while its fellow embraced him about chest and arms, pinning him close. He stood slack within the double grip, and continued to breathe easily, and with wind to spare.

'Not badly done,' he said with mild approval. 'But you have no nose, son. What are four senses, without the fifth?'

'Have I not?' breathed Ninian's voice in his ear, shaken by a quaver of suppressed laughter. 'You came in at the door so like a waft of wind through your eaves, I was back there with that oil I had to abandon. I hope it took no harm.' Hard and vehement young arms hugged Cadfael close, let him loose gently, and turned him about at arm's length, as though to view him, where there was no light to see more than a shape, a shadow. 'I owed you a fright. You had the wits scared out of me when you eased the door ajar,' said Ninian reproachfully.

'I was none too easy in my own mind,' said Cadfael, 'when I found the bar out of its socket. Lad, you take far too many chances. For God's sake and Sanan's, what are you doing here?'

'I could as well ask you that,' said Ninian. 'And might get the same answer, too. I ventured here to see if there was anything more to be found, though after so many days, heaven knows why there should be. But how can any of us be easy until we know? *I* know I never laid hands on the man, but what comfort is that when everyone else lays it at my door? I should be loth to leave here until it's shown I'm no murderer, even if there were nothing more in it than that, but there is. There's Diota! Wanting the chance to get at me, how long before they begin to turn on her, if not for murder, then for treason in helping me to escape the hunt in the south, and cover my guilt here?'

'If you think Hugh Beringar has any ill intent against Mistress Hammet, or will suffer anyone else to make her a victim,' said Cadfael firmly, 'you may put that out of your mind at once. Well, now, since we're both here, and the time and place as good as any, we may as well sit down somewhere in the warmest corner we can find, and put together whatever we have to share. Two heads may make more of it than my one has been able to do. There should be plenty of sacks here somewhere – better than nothing. . . .'

Evidently Ninian had been here long enough to know his way about, for he took Cadfael by the arm, and drew him confidently into a corner where a pile of clean, coarse bags was folded and stacked against the timber wall. They settled themselves close there, flank by flank for warmth, and Ninian drew round them both a thick cloak which had certainly never been in Benet's possession.

'Now,' said Cadfael briskly, 'I should first tell you that this very morning I've spoken with Sanan, and I know what you and she are planning. Probably she's told you as much. I'm half in and half out of your confidence and hers, and if I'm to be of any help to you in putting an end to this vexatious business that holds you here, you had better let me in fully. I do *not* believe you guilty of the priest's death, and I have no reason in the world to stand in your way. But I do believe that you know more of what happened here that night than you have told. Tell the rest, and let me know where we really stand. You did come here to the mill, did you not?'

Ninian blew out a gusty, rueful breath that warmed Cadfael's leaning cheek for a moment. 'I did. I had to. I got no more answer from Giffard than that he'd received and understood the message I sent. I'd no means of knowing whether he meant to come or not. But I came very early, to view the place and find a corner to hide in until I saw what came of it. I stayed there in the doorway in the abbey wall, with the wicket ajar, so that I could watch for whoever came. I had to make haste round the corner of the infirmary, I can tell you, when the miller came bustling through on his way to church, but I had the place to myself after that, to keep watch on the path.'

'And it was Ailnoth who came?' said Cadfael.

'Storming along the path like a bolt from God. Dark as it was, there was no mistaking him, he had a gait all his own. There was no possible reason he should be there at such an hour, unless he'd got wind of what I was up to, and meant all manner of mischief. He was striding up and down and round the mill and along the bank, thumping the ground like a cat lashing its tail. And I'd perhaps got another man into the mud with me, and must make some shift to get him, at least, out of it, even if I was still stuck in the mire.'

'So what did you do?'

'It was still early. I couldn't leave Giffard to come to the meeting all unsuspecting, could I? I didn't know if he meant to come at all, but still he might, I couldn't take the risk. I hared away back through the court and out at the gatehouse, and went to earth among the bushes close by the end of the bridge. If he came at all, he had to come that way from the town. And I didn't even know what the man looked like, though I knew his name and his allegiance from others. But I thought there'd be very few men coming out from the town at that hour, and I could risk accosting any who looked of his age and quality.'

'Ralph Giffard had already come over the bridge,' said Cadfael, 'a good hour earlier, to visit the priest and send him hot-foot to confront you at the mill, but you could hardly know that. I fancy he was already back in his own house while you were watching for him in the bushes. Did you see any others pass by you there?'

'Only one, and he was too young, and too poor and simple in his person and gear to be Giffard. He went straight along the Foregate, and turned in at the church.'

Centwin, perhaps, thought Cadfael, coming from paying

his debt, to have his mind free and at peace, owing no man, as he went to celebrate the birth of Christ. Well for him if it proved that Ninian could speak for him, and show clearly that his own bitter debt had gone unreclaimed.

'And you?'

'I waited until I was sure he was not coming – it was past the time. So I made haste back to be in time for Matins.'

'Where you met with Sanan.' Cadfael's smile was invisible in the dark, but perceptible in his voice. 'She was not so foolish as to go to the mill, for like you, she could not be quite sure her step-father would not keep the tryst. But she knew where to find you, and she was determined to respond to the appeal Giffard had preferred to reject. Indeed, as I recall, she had already taken steps to get a good look at you, as you yourself told me. Maybe you'll do for a lady's page, after all. With a little polishing!'

Within the muffling folds of the cloak he heard Ninian laughing softly. 'I never believed, that first day, that anything would really come of it. And now see – everything I owe to her. She would not be put off. . . . You've seen her, you've talked to her, you know how splendid she is. . . . Cadfael, I must tell you – she's coming with me to Gloucester, she's promised herself to me in marriage.' His voice was low and solemn now, as though he had already come to the altar. It was the first time Cadfael had known him in awe of anything or anyone.

'She is a very valiant lady,' said Cadfael slowly, 'and knows her own mind very well, and I, for my part, wouldn't say a word against her choice. But, lad, is it right to let her do this for you? Is she not abandoning property, family, everything? Have you considered that?'

'I have, and urged her to consider it, too. How much do you know, Cadfael, of her situation? She has no land to abandon. Her father's manor was taken from him after the siege here, because he supported FitzAlan and the Empress. Her mother is dead. Her step-father – she has no complaint of him, he has always cared for her in duty bound, but not gladly. He has a son by his first marriage to inherit from him, he will be only too pleased to have an estate undivided, and to escape providing her a dowry. But from her mother she has a good provision in jewels, undeniably her own. She says she loses nothing by coming with me, and gains what she most wants in the world. I do love her!' said Ninian with abrupt and moving gravity. 'I will make a fit place for her. I can! I will!'

Yes, thought Cadfael on reflection, on balance she may be getting none so bad a bargain. Giffard himself lost certain lands for his adherence to the Empress, no wonder he wants all he has left to go to his son. It may even be more for his son's sake than his own that he has so ruthlessly severed himself now from any lingering devotion to his former overlord, and even sought to buy his own security with this boy's freedom. Men do things far out of their nature when deformed by circumstances. And the girl knew a good lad when she saw one, she'll be his fair match.

'Well, I wish you a fortunate journey through Wales, with all my heart,' he said. 'You'll need horses for the journey, is that already arranged?'

'We have them, she procured them. They're stabled where I'm in hiding,' said Ninian, candid and thoughtless, 'out by—'

Cadfael clapped a hand hastily over the boy's mouth, fumbling in the dark but effectively silencing him out of sheer surprise. 'No, hush, tell me nothing! Better I know nothing of where you are, or where you got your horses. What I don't know I can't even be expected to tell.'

'But I can't go,' said Ninian firmly, 'while there's a shadow hanging over me. I won't be remembered, here or anywhere, as a fugitive murderer. Still less can I go while there's such a shadow hanging over Diota. I owe her more already than I know how to repay, I must see her secure and protected before I go.'

'The more credit to you, and we must try by any means we have for a resolution. As it seems we've both been doing tonight, though with very sorry success. But now, had you not best be getting back to your hiding place? How if Sanan should send to you, and you not there?'

'And you?' retorted Ninian. 'How if Prior Robert should make a round of the dortoir, and you not there?'

They rose together, and unwound the cloak from about them, drawing in breath sharply at the invading cold.

'You haven't told me,' said Ninian, opening the heavy door on the comparative light outside, 'just what thought brought you here tonight – though I'm glad it did. I was not happy at leaving you without a word. But you can hardly have been hunting for me! What were you hoping to find?'

'I wish I knew. This morning I found a gaggle of goslings playing in the snow with a black skull-cap that surely belonged to Ailnoth, for the boys had found it here in the shallows of the pool, among the reeds. And I had seen him wearing it that evening, and clean forgotten so small a thing. And it's been nagging at me all day long since then that there was something else I had noted about him, and likewise never missed and never looked for afterwards. I don't know that I came here with any great expectation of finding anything. Perhaps I simply hoped that being here might bring the thing back to mind. Did ever you get up to do something, and then clean forget what it was?' wondered Cadfael. 'And have to go back to where you first thought of it, to bring it back to mind? No, surely not, you're too young, for you to think of doing a thing is to do it. But ask the elders like me, they'll all admit to it.'

'And it still hasn't come back to you?' asked Ninian, delicately sympathetic towards the old and forgetful.

'It has not. Not even here. Have you fared any better?'

'It was a thin hope to find what I came for,' said Ninian ruefully, 'though I did risk coming before the light was quite gone. But at least I know what I came looking for. I was there with Diota when you brought him back on Christmas Day, and I never thought what was missing until later. After all, it's a thing that could well go astray, not like the clothes he was wearing. But I knew he had it with him when he came stamping along the path and stabbing at the ground. Coming all this way through England in his company, I got to know it very well. That great staff he was always so lungeous with – ebony, tall as his elbow, with a stag's-horn handle – that's what I came to look for. And somewhere here it must still be.'

They had emerged on to the low shore, dappled now with moist dark patches of grass breaking through the tattered snow. The dull, pale level of the water stretched away to the dark slope of the further bank. Cadfael had stopped abruptly, staring over the shield of pallor in startled enlightenment.

'So it must!' he said devoutly. 'So it must! Child, that's the will-o'-the-wisp I've been chasing all this day. You get back to your refuge and keep snug within, and leave this search to me now. You've read my riddle for me.'

By morning half the snow had melted and vanished, and the Foregate was like a coil of tattered and threadbare lace. The cobbles of the great court shone moist and dark, and in the graveyard east of the church Cynric had broken the turf for Father Ailnoth's grave.

Cadfael came from the last chapter of the year with a strong feeling that more things than the year were ending. No word had yet been said of who was to succeed to the living of Holy Cross, no word would be said until Ailnoth was safely under the ground, with every proper rite and as much mourning as brotherhood and parish could muster between them. The next day, the birth of another year, would see the burial of a brief tyranny that would soon be gratefully forgotten. God send us, thought Cadfael, a humble soul who thinks himself as fallible as his flock, and labours modestly to keep both from falling. If two hold fast together they stand steadily, but if one holds aloof the other may find his feet betraying him in slippery places. Better a limping prop than a solid rock for ever out of reach of the stretched hand.

Cadfael made for the wicket in the wall, and went through to the shores of the mill-pond. He stood on the edge of the overhanging bank between the pollarded willows, at the spot where he had found Ailnoth's body, the pool widening and shallowing on his right hand into the reed beds below the highway, and on his left gradually narrowing to the deeper stream that carried the water back to the brook, and shortly thereafter to the Severn. The body had entered the water probably a few yards to the right, and been nudged aside here under the bank by the tail-race. The skull-cap had been found in the reeds, somewhere accessible from the path on the opposite side. A small, light thing, it would go with the current until reeds or branch or debris in the water arrested it. But where would a heavy ebony staff be carried, whether it flew from his hand as he was struck down, or whether it was thrown in after him, from this spot? It would either be drifted aside in the same direction as the body, in which case it might be sunk deep somewhere in the narrowing channel, or else, if it fell on the other side of the main force of the tail-race, edged away like the skull-cap into the far shore. At least there was no harm in circling the shallow bowl and looking for it.

He re-crossed the little bridge over the head-race, circled the mill and went down to the edge of the water. There was no real path here, the gardens of the three small houses came almost to the lip of the bank, where a narrow strip of open grass just allowed of passage. For some way the path was still raised above water level, and somewhat hollowed out beneath, then it dropped gradually into the first growth of reeds, and he walked in tufted grass, with moisture welling round every step he took. Under the miller's house and garden, under the house where the deaf old woman lived with her pretty slattern of a maidservant, and then he was bearing somewhat away from the final house, round the rim of the broad shallows. Silver of water gleamed through the blanched, pallid green of winter reeds, but though an accumulation of leaves, dead twigs and branches had drifted and lodged here, he saw no sign of an ebony walking-staff. Other cast-offs, however, showed themselves, broken crockery, discarded shards and a holed pot, too far gone to be worth mending.

He went on, round the broad end of the pool, to the trickle of water that came down from the conduit under the highway, stepped over that, and on beneath the gardens of the second trio of abbey houses. Somewhere here the boys had found the cap, but he could not believe he would find the staff here. Either he had missed it, or, if it had been flung well out over the drift of the tail-race, he must look for it on the far side of the channel opposite where the body had been found. The water was still fairly wide there, but what fell beyond its centre might well fetch up on this far side.

He halted to consider, glad he had put on boots to wade about this thawing quagmire. His friend and fellow Welshman, Madog of the Dead Boat, who knew everything there was to be known about water and its properties, given an idea of the thing sought, could have told him exactly where to seek it. But Madog was not here, and time was precious, and he must manage on his own. Ebony was heavy and solid, but still it was wood, and would float. Nor would it float evenly, having a stag's-horn handle, a tip should break the surface, wherever it lodged, and he did not believe it would be carried so far as the brook and the river. Doggedly he went on, and on this side the water there was a trodden path, which gradually lifted out of the boggy ground, and carried him dry-shod a little above the surface of the pool.

He drew level with the mill opposite, and was past the sloping strips of garden on this side the water. The stunted willow stump, defiantly sprouting its head of startled hair, matched his progress and held his eye. Just beyond that the body had lain, nuzzling the undercut bank.

Three paces more, and he found what he was seeking. Barely visible through the fringe of rotting ice and the protruding ends of grass, only its tip emerging, Ailnoth's staff lay at his feet. He took it gingerly by its tapered end, and plucked it out of the water. No mistaking it, once found, there could hardly be two exactly alike. Black and long, with a metal-shod tip and a grooved horn handle, banded to the shaft by a worn silver band embossed in some pattern worn very smooth with age. Whether flying out of the victim's hand or thrown in afterwards, it must have fallen into the water on this side of the current's main flow, and so been cast up here into the encroaching border of grass.

Melting snow dripped from the handle and ran down the shaft. Carrying it by the middle of the shaft, Cadfael turned back on his tracks, and circled the reedy shallows back to the mill. He was not yet ready to share his prize with anyone, not even Hugh, until he had had a close look at it, and extracted from it whatever it had to tell him. His hopes were not high, but he could not afford to let any hint slip through his fingers. He hurried through the wicket in the precinct wall, and across the great court, and went to earth in his own workshop. He left the door open for the sake of light, but also lit a wooden spill at the brazier and kindled his little lamp to make a close examination of the trophy.

The hand-long piece of horn, pale brown furrowed with wavy ruts of darker brown, was heavy and polished from years of use, and its slight curve fitted well into the hand. The band of silver was a thumb-joint wide, and the half-eroded vine leaves with which it was engraved reflected the yellow light of the lamp from worn highlights as Cadfael carefully dabbed off the moisture and held it close to the flame. The silver had worn thin as gauze, and grown so pliant to every touch that both rims had frayed up into rough edges here and there, sharp as knife blades. Cadfael had scratched a finger in drying the metal before he realised the danger.

This was the formidable weapon with which Father Ailnoth had lashed out at the vexatious urchins who played games against the wall of his house, and no doubt prodded the ribs or thumped the shoulders of the unlucky pupils who were less than perfect in their lessons. Cadfael turned it slowly in his hands in the close light of the lamp, and shook his head over the sins of the virtuous. It was while he was so turning it that his eye was caught by the brief, passing gleam of a drop of moisture, spinning past an inch or more from the rim of silver. Hastily he checked, and turned the staff counterwise, and the bead of brightness reappeared. A single minute drop, clinging not to the metal, but to a fine thread held by the metal, something that appeared and vanished in a silvery curve. He uncoiled on his finger-end a long, greying hair, drawing it forth until it resisted, caught in a sharp edge of silver. Not one hair only, for now a second was partly drawn forth with it, and a third made a small, tight ring, stuck fast in the same tiny nick.

It took him some little time to detach them all from the notch in the lower rim of the band, five of them in all, as well as a few tangled ends. The five were all of fine hair, some brown, some greying to silver, and long, too long for any tonsure, too long for a man, unless he wore his hair neglected and untrimmed. If there had ever been any further mark, of blood, or grazed skin, or thread from a cloth, the water had soaked it away, but these hairs, caught fast in the worn metal, had held their place, to give up their testimony at last.

Cadfael ran a careful hand up the shaft of the staff, and felt the needle-stabs of three or four rough points in the silver. In the deepest of these five precious hairs had been dragged by violence from a head. A woman's head!

Diota opened the door to him, and on recognising her visitor seemed to hesitate whether to open it wider and step aside to let him in, or hold her ground and discourage any lengthy conversation by keeping him on the doorstep. Her face was guarded and still, and her greeting resigned rather than welcoming. But the hesitation was only momentary. Submissively she stepped back into the room, and Cadfael followed her within and closed the door upon the world. It was early afternoon, the light as good as it would be this day, and the fire in the clay hearth bright and clear, almost without smoke.

'Mistress Hammet,' said Cadfael, with no more than a yard of dim, warm air between their faces, 'I must talk with you, and what I have to say concerns also the welfare of Ninian Bachiler, whom I know you value. I am in his confidence, if that helps me to yours. Now sit, and listen to me, and believe in my goodwill, as you have nothing on your conscience but the heart's affection. Which God saw clearly, before ever I held a key to it.'

She turned from him abruptly, but with a suggestion rather of balance and resolution than shock and dread, and sat down on the bench where Sanan had been sitting on his former visit. She sat erect, drawn up with elbows tight at her sides and feet firmly planted.

'Do you know where he is?' she asked in a low voice.

'I do not, though he made to tell me. Rest easy, I talked with him only last night, I know he is well. What I have to say has to do with you, and with what happened on the eve of the Nativity, when Father Ailnoth died, and you . . . had a fall on the ice.'

She was already certain that he had knowledge she had hoped to keep from the light, but she did not know what it was. She kept silence, her eyes lifted steadily to his face, and left it to him to continue.

'A fall – yes! You won't have forgotten. You fell on the icy road and struck your head on the doorstone. I dressed the wound then, I saw it again yesterday, and it has healed over, but it still shows the bruise, and the scar where the skin was broken. Now hear what I have found this morning, in the mill-pond. Father Ailnoth's staff, drifted across to the far shore, and caught in the worn silver band, where the thin edges have turned, and are rough and sharp, five long hairs, the like of yours. Yours I saw closely, when I bathed your wound, I know there were broken ends there. I have the means to match them now.'

She had sunk her head into her hands, the long, work-worn fingers clutched cheek and temple hard.

'Why should you hide your face?' he said temperately.

'That was not your sin.'

In a little while she raised a tearless face, blanched and wary, and peered at him steadily between her supporting hands. 'I was here,' she said slowly, 'when the nobleman came. I knew him again, I knew why he was here. Why else should he come?'

'Why, indeed! And when he was gone, the priest turned upon you. Reviled you, perhaps cursed you, for an accomplice in treason, for a liar and deceiver. . . . We have learned to know him well enough to know that he would not be merciful, nor listen to excuse or pleading. Did he threaten you? Tell you how he would crush your nurseling first, and discard you with ignominy afterwards?'

Her back stiffened. She said with dignity: 'I nursed my lamb at this breast after my own child was born dead. He had a sickly mother, poor sweet lady. When he came to me, it was as if a son of my own had come home in need. Do you think I cared what he – my master – might do against me?'

'No, I believe you,' said Cadfael. 'Your thought was all of Ninian when you went out after Father Ailnoth that night, to try to turn him from his purpose of challenge and betrayal. For you did follow him, did you not? You must have followed him. How else have I teased your hairs out of the worn band of his staff? You followed and pleaded with him, and he struck you. Clubbed his staff and struck out at your head.'

'I clung to him,' she said, with stony calm now, 'fell on my knees in the frosty grass there by the mill, and clung to the skirts of his gown to hold him, and would not let go. I prayed him, I pleaded, I begged him for mercy, but he had none. Yes, he struck me. He could not endure to be so held and crossed, it enraged him, he might well have killed me. Or so I dreaded then. I tried to fend off his blows, but I knew he would strike again if he could not rid himself of me. So I loosed hold and got to my feet, God knows how, and ran from him. And that was the last I ever saw of him living.'

'And you neither saw nor heard any other creature there?

You left him whole, and alone?'

'I tell you truth,' she said, shaking her head, 'I neither heard nor saw any other soul, not even when I reached the Foregate. But neither my eyes nor my ears were clear, my head so rang, and I was in such sick despair. The first I was truly aware of was blood running down my forehead, and then I was in this house, crouched on the floor by the hearth, and shivering with the cold of fear, with no notion how I got here. I ran like an animal to its den, and that was all I knew. Only I am sure I met no one on the way, because if I had I should have had to master myself, walk like a woman in her senses, even give a greeting. And when you have to, you can. No, I know nothing more after I fled from him. All night I waited in fear of his return, knowing he would not spare me, and dreading he had already done his worst against Ninian. I was sure then that we were both lost – that everything was lost.'

'But he did not come,' said Cadfael.

'No, he did not come. I bathed my head, and stanched the blood, and waited without hope, but he never came. It was no help to me. Fear of him turned about into fear for him, for what could he be doing, out in the frost all night long? Even if he had gone up to the castle and called out the guard there, still it could not have kept him so long. But he didn't come. Think for yourself what manner of night I spent, sleepless in his house, waiting.'

'There was also, perhaps worst of all,' said Cadfael gently, 'your fear that he had indeed met with Ninian at the mill after you fled, and come to grief at Ninian's hands.'

She said, 'Yes,' in a dry whisper, and shivered. 'It could have been so. A boy of such spirit, challenged, accused, perhaps attacked. . . . It could have been so. Thanks be to God, it was not so!'

'And in the morning? You could not leave it longer or leave it to others to raise an alarm. So you came to the church.'

'And told half a story,' she said with a brief, twisted smile, like a contortion of pain. 'What else could I do?'

'And while we went searching for the priest, Ninian stayed with you, and told you, doubtless, how he had spent the night, knowing nothing at all of what had happened after he left the mill. As doubtless you told him the rest of your story. But neither of you could shed light on the man's death.'

'That is true,' said Diota, 'I swear it. Neither then nor now. And now what do you intend for me?'

'Why, simply that you should do what Abbot Radulfus charged you, continue here and keep this house in readiness for another priest, and trust his word that you shall not be abandoned, since the church brought you here. I must be free to make use of what I know, but it shall be done with as little harm to you as possible, and only when I have understood more than now I understand. I wish you could have helped me one more step on the road, but never mind, truth is there to be found, and there must be a way to it. There were three people, besides Ailnoth, went to the mill that night,' said Cadfael, pausing at the door. 'Ninian was the first, you were the second. I wonder – I wonder! – who was the third?'

Chapter Ten

Cadfael had been back in his workshop no more than half an hour, and the light was only just beginning to dim towards the Vesper office, when Hugh came seeking him, as he usually did if shire affairs brought him to confer with the abbot. He brought in with him a gust of moist, chill air and the quiver of a rising breeze that might bring more snow, now that the hard frost had eased, or might blow away the heavy cloud and clear the sky for the morrow.

'I've been with Father Abbot,' said Hugh, and sat down on the familiar bench by the wall and spread his feet appreciatively towards the brazier. 'Tomorrow, I hear, you're burying the priest. Cynric has the grave dug for him so deep you'd think he feared the man might break out of it without six feet of earth on top of him to hold him down. Well, he's going to his funeral unavenged, for we're no nearer knowing who killed him. You said from the first that the entire Foregate would turn blind, deaf and dumb. A man would think the whole parish had been depeopled on Christmas Eve, no one will admit to having been out of his own house but to hurry to church, and not a man of them set eyes on any other living being in the streets that night. It took a stranger to let fall even one little word of furtive comings and goings at an ungodly hour, and I place no great credence in that. And how have you been faring?'

Cadfael had been wondering the same thing in his own mind ever since leaving Diota, and could see no possibility of keeping back from Hugh what he had learned. He had not promised secrecy, only discretion, and he owed help to Hugh as surely as to the woman caught in the trap of her own devotion.

'Better, perhaps, than I deserve,' he said sombrely, and put aside the tray of tablets he had just set out to dry, and went to sit beside his friend. 'If you had not come to me, Hugh, I should have had to come to you. Last night it was brought back to me what I had seen in Ailnoth's possession that night, and had not found nor thought to look for again the next day, when we brought him back here dead. Two things, indeed, though the first I did not find myself, but got it from the little boys who went down hopefully to the pool on Christmas morning, thinking it might be frozen over. Wait a moment, I'll bring both, and you shall hear.'

He brought them, and carried the lamp closer, to show the detail that might mean so much or so little.

'This cap the children found among the reeds of the shallows. You see how the stitches are started in the one seam, and the binding ripped loose. And this staff – this I found only this morning, almost opposite the place where we found Ailnoth.' He told that story simply and truthfully, but for omitting any mention of Ninian, though that, too, might have to come. 'You see how the silver band is worn into a mere wafer from age, and crumpled at the edges, being so thin. This notch here. . .' He set a finger-tip to the razor-sharp points. 'From this I wormed out *these!*'

He had dabbed a tiny spot of grease into one of his clay saucers for selecting seed, and anchored the rescued hairs to the congealed fat, so that no chance draught should blow them away. In the close yellow light of the lamp they showed clearly. Cadfael drew out one of them to its full length.

'A metal edge fissured like this might pick up a stray hair almost anywhere,' said Hugh, but not with any great conviction.

'So it might, but here are five, captured at the same mis-stroke. Which makes this a different matter. Well?'

Hugh likewise laid a finger to the glistening threads and said deliberately: 'A woman's. Not young.'

'Whether you yet know it or no,' said Cadfael, 'there are but two women in all this coil, and one of them is young, and will not be grey, please God, for many years yet.'

'I think,' said Hugh, eyeing him with a faint, wise smile, 'you had better tell me. You were here from the beginning, I came late, and brought with me another matter warranted to confuse the first. I am not interested in preventing young Bachiler from making clean away to Gloucester to fight for his Empress, if he has nothing on his conscience that chances to be more particularly my business. But I *am* interested in burying the ugly fact of murder along with Ailnoth tomorrow, if by any means I can. I want the town and the Foregate going about their day's work with a quiet mind, and the way cleared for another priest, and let's hope one easier to live with. Now, what I make of these hairs is that they came from the head of Dame Diota Hammet. I have not even seen the woman in a good light, to know if this colouring is hers, but even there indoors the bruise on her brow was plain to be seen. She had a fall on the icy step – so I had been told, and so she told me. I think you are saying she came by that injury in a very different manner.'

'She came by it,' said Cadfael, 'by the mill that night, when she followed the priest in desperation, to plead with him to let well alone and turn a blind eye to the boy's deception, instead of confronting him like an avenging demon and fetching your sergeants down on him to throw him into prison. She was Ninian's nurse, she would dare almost anything for his sake. She clung about Ailnoth's skirts and begged him to let be, and because he could not shake her off, he clubbed this staff of his and struck her on the head, and would have struck again if she had not loosed him and scrambled away half-stunned, and run for her life back to the house.'

He told the whole of it as he had had it from Diota herself, and Hugh listened with a grave face but the hint of the smile lingering thoughtfully in his eyes. 'You believe this,' he said at the end of it; not a question, but a fact, and relevant to his own thinking.

'I do believe it. Entirely.'

'And she can add nothing more, to point us to any other person. Or would she, even if she could?' wondered Hugh. 'She may very well feel with the Foregate, and prefer to keep her own counsel.'

'So she might, I won't deny, but for all that, I think she knows no more. She ran from him dazed and in terror. I think there's no more to be got from her.'

'Nor from your boy Benet?' said Hugh slyly, and laughed at seeing Cadfael turn a sharp glance on him and bridle for a moment. 'Oh, come now, I do accept that it was not you who warned the boy to make himself scarce when Giffard brought the law down on him. But only because someone else had already spared you the trouble. You were very well aware that he was gone, when you so helpfully led us all round the garden here hunting for him. I'll even believe that you *had* seen him here not half an hour before. You have a way of telling simple truths which is anything but simple. And when did you ever have a young fellow in trouble under your eye, and not wind your way into his confidence? Of course he'll have opened his mind to you. I daresay you know where he is this very moment. Though I'm not asking!' he added hastily.

'No,' said Cadfael, well satisfied with the way that was phrased, 'no, that I don't know, so you may ask, for I can't tell you.'

'Having gone to some trouble not to find out or be told,' agreed Hugh, grinning. 'Well, I did tell you to keep him out of sight if you should happen on him. I might even turn a blind eye myself, once this other matter is cleared up.'

'As to that,' said Cadfael candidly, 'he's of the same mind as you, for until he knows that all's made plain, and Dame Hammet safe and respected, he won't budge. Much as he wants to get to honest service in Gloucester, here he stays while she's in trouble. Which is only fair, seeing the risks she has taken for him. But once this is over, he'll be away, out of your territory. And not alone!' said Cadfael, meeting Hugh's quizzical glance with a complacent countenance. 'Is it possible I still know something you do not know?'

Hugh furrowed his brow and considered this riddle at leisure. 'Not Giffard, that's certain! He could not get himself out of the trap fast enough. Two women in the affair, you said, one of them young. . . . Do you tell me this young venturer has found himself a wife in these parts? Already? These imps of Anjou work briskly, I grant them that! Let's see, then. . . .' He pondered, drumming his fingers thoughtfully on the rim of the clay saucer. 'He had got himself into a monastery, where women do not abound, and I think you will have got your due of work out of him, he had small opportunity to go wooing among the townswomen. And as far as I know, he made no approach to any other of the local lordlings. I'm left with Giffard's household, where the boy's embassage may have been a none too well-kept secret, and where there's a very pleasing young woman, of the Empress's faction by blood, and bold and determined enough to choose differently from her step-father. Why, pure curiosity would have brought her to have a close look at such a paladin of romance, come in peril of his liberty and life from over the sea. Sanan Bernières? Is he truly wanting to take her with him?'

'Sanan it is. But I think it was she who made the decision. They have horses hidden away ready for departure, and she has her own small estate in jewels from her mother, easily carried. No doubt she's provided him sword and dagger, too. She'll not let him come before the Empress or Robert of Gloucester shabby, or without arms and horse.'

'They mean this earnestly?' wondered Hugh, frowning over a private doubt as to what his own course ought to be in such a case.

'They mean it. Both of them. I doubt if Giffard will mind much, though he's done his duty by her fairly enough. It saves him a dowry. And the man's had his losses, and is ambitious for his son.'

'And what,' demanded Hugh, 'does she get out of it?'

'She gets her own way. She gets what she wants, and the man she's chosen for herself. She gets Ninian. I think it may not be a bad bargain.'

Hugh sat silent for a brooding while, weighing the rights and wrongs of allowing such a flight, and recalling, perhaps, his own determined pursuit of Aline, not so long past. After a while his brow smoothed, and the private gleam of mischief quickened in his black eyes and twitched at the corner of his mouth. An eloquent eyebrow tilted above a covert glance at Cadfael.

'Well, I can as easily put a stop to that as cross the court here, yes, and bring the lad flying out of hiding into my arms, if I choose. You've taught me the way to flush him out of cover. All I need do is arrest Mistress Hammet, or even put it abroad that I'm about to, and he'll come running to defend her. If I accused her of murder, as like as not he'd go so far as to confess to an act he never committed, to see her free and vindicated.'

'You could do it,' Cadfael admitted, without any great concern, 'but you won't. You are as convinced as I am that neither he nor Dame Diota ever laid hand on Ailnoth, and you certainly won't pretend otherwise.'

'I might, however,' said Hugh, grinning, 'try the same trick with another victim, and see if the man who did drown Ailnoth will be as honest and chivalrous as your lad would be. For I came here today with a small item of news you will not yet have heard, concerning one of Ailnoth's flock who'll be none the worse for a salutary shock. Who knows, there are plenty of rough and ready fellows who would kill lightly enough, but not stand by and let another man be hanged for it. It would be worth the trial, to hook a murderer, and even if it failed, the bait would come to no lasting harm.'

'I would not do it to a dog!' said Cadfael.

'Neither would I, dogs are honest, worthy creatures that fight fair and bear no grudges. When they set out to kill, they do it openly in broad daylight, and never care how many witnesses there may be. I have less scruples about some men.

This one – ah, he's none so bad, but a fright won't hurt him, and may do a very sound turn for his poor drab of a wife.'

'You have lost me,' said Cadfael.

'Let me find you again! This morning Alan Herbard brought me a man he'd happened on by chance, a country kinsman of Erwald's who came to spend Christmas with the provost and his family here in the Foregate. The man's a shepherd by calling, and Erwald had a couple of ewes too early in lamb, penned in his shed out beyond the Gaye, and one of them threatened to cast her lamb too soon. So his cousin the shepherd went to the shed after Matins and Lauds on Christmas morning, to take a look at them, and brought off the threatened lamb safely, too, and was on his way back, just coming up from the Gaye and along to the Foregate at first light. And who do you suppose he saw sneaking very furtively up from the path to the mill and heading for home, but Jordan Achard, rumpled and bleared from sleep and hardly expecting to be seen at that hour. By chance one of the few people our man would have known by sight and name here, being the baker from whose oven he'd fetched his cousin's bread the day before. It came out in purest gossip, in all innocence. The countryman knew Jordan's reputation, and thought it a harmless joke to have seen him making for home from some strange bed.'

'Along that path?' said Cadfael, staring.

'Along that path. It was well trodden that night, it seems.'

'Ninian was the first,' said Cadfael slowly. 'I never told you that, but he went there early, not being sure of Giffard. He took himself off smartly when he saw Ailnoth come raging to the meeting, and nothing more did he know of it until morning, when Diota came crying the priest was lost. She was there, as I've told you. I said there must be a third. But Jordan? And blundering homeward at first light? It's hard to believe he had so much durable malice in him as to carry his grudge so long. A big, spoiled babe, I should have said, but for being an excellent baker.'

'So should I. But he was there, no question. Who's abroad

at first light on Christmas morning, after a long night's worship? Barring, of course, a shepherd anxious about an ailing ewe! That was very ill luck for Jordan. But it goes further, Cadfael. I went myself to talk to Jordan's wife, while he was busy at his ovens. I told her what news we had of his moves, and made her understand it was proven beyond doubt where he'd been. I think she was ready to break like a branch over-fruited. Do you know how many children she's borne, poor soul? Eleven, and only two of them living. And how he managed to engender so many, considering how seldom he lies at home, only the recording angel can tell. Not a bad-looking woman, if she were not so worn and harried. And still fond of him!'

'And this time,' said Cadfael, awed, 'she really told you truth?'

'Of course she did, she was rightly afraid for him. Yes, she told truth. Yes, he was out all that night, it was nothing new. But not murdering anyone! No, on that she was insistent, he would not hurt a fly. He's done his worst by a poor wretch of a wife, however! All he'd been about, she said, was bedding his latest fancy girl, and that was the bold little bitch who's maidservant to the old woman who lives next to the miller, by the pool.'

'Ah, now that's a far more likely thing,' said Cadfael, enlightened. 'That rings true! We talked to her,' he recalled, fascinated, 'next morning, when we were looking for Ailnoth.' A pretty slut of about eighteen, with a mane of dark hair and bold, inquisitive eyes, saying: 'Not a soul that I know of came along here in the night, why should they?' No, she had not been lying. She had never thought of her covert lover as counting among the furtive visitors to the mill in the darkness. His errand was known, and if not innocent, entirely natural and harmless. She spoke according to her understanding.

'And she never said word of Jordan! No, why should she? She knew what he'd been up to, it was not about him you were asking. Oh, no, I've nothing against the girl. But I would stake much that she knows nothing of time, and has no notion exactly when he came or when he left, except by the beginning of light. He could have killed a man before ever he whispered at the deaf woman's door, for ears that were forewarned and sharp enough.'

'I doubt if he did,' said Cadfael.

'So do I. But see how beautiful a case I can make against him! His wife has admitted that he went there. The shepherd saw him leaving. We know that Father Ailnoth went along that same path. After Mistress Hammet had fled from him, still he waited for his prey. And how if he saw a parishioner of his, already in dispute with him, and whose reputation he may well have heard before then, whispering his way furtively into a strange house, and being let in by a young woman? How then? His nose was expert at detecting sinners, he might well be distracted from his first purpose to flush out an evil-doer on the spot. The old woman is stone deaf. The girl, if she witnessed such a collision, and saw its end, would hold her tongue and tell a good story. In such a case, Cadfael, old friend, the priest might well have started too hot a hare, and got the worst of it, ending in the pool.'

'The blow to Ailnoth's head,' said Cadfael, jolted, 'was deep to the back. Men in conflict go face to face.'

'True, but one may easily be spun aside and involuntarily turn his back for an instant. But you know how the wound lay, and I know. But do the commons know?'

'And you will really do this?' marvelled Cadfael.

'Most publicly, my friend, I will do it. Tomorrow morning, at Ailnoth's funeral – even those who most hated him will be there to make sure he's safely underground, what better occasion could there be? If it bears fruit, then we have our answer, and the town can be at peace, once the turmoil's over. If not, Jordan will be none the worse for a short-lived fright, and a few nights, perhaps,' pondered Hugh, gleaming mischief, 'on a harder bed than usual with him, and lying alone. He may even learn that his own bed is the safest from this on.'

'And how if no man speaks up to deliver him,' said Cadfael with mild malice, 'and the thing happened just as you have pictured it to me a minute ago, and Jordan really is your man? What then? If he keep his head and deny all, and the girl bears witness for him, you'll have trailed your bait in vain.'

'Ah, you know the man better than that,' said Hugh, undisturbed. 'Big-boned and hearty, but no great stiffening in his back. If he did it, deny it as loudly as he may when he's first accused, a couple of nights on stone and he'll be blabbing out everything, how he did no more than defend himself, how it was mere accident, and he could not haul the priest out of the water, and took fright, and dared not speak, knowing that the bad blood between them was common knowledge. A couple of nights in a cell won't hurt him. And if he holds out stoutly any longer than that,' said Hugh, rising, 'then he deserves to get away with it. The parish will think so.'

'You are a devious creature,' said Cadfael, in a tone uncertain between reproach and admiration. 'I wonder why I bear with you?'

Hugh turned in the doorway to give him a flashing glance over his shoulder. 'Like calling to like, I daresay!' he suggested, and went striding away along the gravel path, to disappear into the gathering dusk.

At Vespers the psalms had a penitential solemnity, and at Collations in the chapter house after supper the readings were also of a funereal colouring. The shadow of Father Ailnoth hung over the death of the year, and it seemed that the year of Our Lord 1142 would be born, not at midnight, but only after the burial service was over, and the grave filled in. The morrow might, according to the Church's calendar, be the octave of the Nativity and the celebration of the Circumcision of Our Lord, but to the people of the Foregate it was rather the propitiatory office that would lift their incubus from them. A wretched departure for any man, let alone a priest.

'On the morrow,' said Prior Robert, before dismissing them to the warming room for the blessed last half-hour of ease before Compline, 'the funeral office for Father Ailnoth will follow immediately after the parish Mass, and I myself shall preside. But the homily will be delivered by Father Abbot, at his desire.' The prior's incisive and well-modulated voice made this statement with a somewhat ambiguous emphasis, as if in doubt whether to welcome the abbot's decision as a devout compliment to the dead, or to regret and perhaps even resent it as depriving him of an opportunity to exercise his own undoubted eloquence. 'Matins and Lauds will be said according to the Office of the Dead.'

That meant that they would be long, and prudent brothers would be wise to make straight for their beds after Compline. Cadfael had already turfed down his brazier to burn slowly through the night, and keep lotions and medicines from freezing and bottles from bursting, should a hard frost set in again in the small hours. But the air was certainly not cold enough yet for frost, and he thought by the slight wind and lightly overcast sky that they would get through the night safely. He went thankfully to the warming room with his brothers, and settled down to half an hour of pleasant idleness.

This was the hour when even the taciturn relaxed into speech, and not even the prior frowned upon a degree of loquacity. And inevitably the subject of their exchanges tonight was the brief rule of Father Ailnoth, his grim death, and the coming ceremonial of his burial.

'So Father Abbot means to pronounce the eulogy himself, does he?' said Brother Anselm in Cadfael's ear. 'That will make interesting listening.' Anselm's business was the music of the Divine Office, and he had not quite the same regard for the spoken word, but he appreciated its power and influence. 'I had thought he'd be only too glad to leave it to Robert. *Nil nisi bonum. . . .* Or do you suppose he looks upon it as a fitting penance for bringing the man here in the first place?'

'There may be something in that,' admitted Cadfael. 'But

more, I think, in a resolve that only truth shall be told. Robert would be carried away into paeans of praise. Radulfus intends clarity and honesty.'

'No easy task,' said Anselm. 'Well for me no one expects words from me. There's been no hint yet of who's to follow in the parish. They'll be praying for a man they know, whether he has any Latin or not. Even a man they did not much like would be welcomed, if he belongs here, and knows them. You can deal with the devil you know.'

'No harm in hoping for better than that,' said Cadfael, sighing. 'A very ordinary man, more than a little lower than the angels, and well aware of his own shortcomings, would do very nicely for the Foregate. A pity these few weeks were wasted, wanting him.'

In the big stone hearth the fire of logs burned steadily, sinking down now into a hot core of ash, nicely timed to last the evening out, and die down with little waste when the bell rang for Compline. Faces pinched with cold and outdoor labour during the day flushed into rosy content, and chapped hands smoothed gratefully at the ointment doled out from Cadfael's store. Friends foregathered in their own chosen groups, voices decorously low blended into a contented murmur like a hive of bees. Some of the healthy young, who had been out in the air most of the day, had much ado to keep their eyelids open in the warmth. Compline would be wisely brief tonight, as Matins would be long and sombre.

'Another year tomorrow,' said Brother Edmund the infirmarer, 'and a new beginning.'

Some said: 'Amen!' whether from habit or conviction, but Cadfael stuck fast at the word. 'Amen' belongs rather to an ending, a resolution, an acceptance into peace, and as yet they were within reach of none of these things.

A mile to the west of Cadfael's bed in his narrow cell in the dortoir, Ninian lay in the plenteous hay of a well-stocked loft, rolled in the cloak Sanan had brought for him, and with the heartening warmth of her still in his arms, though she had been gone two hours and more, in time to have her pony back in the town stable before her step-father returned from the night office at Saint Chad's church. Ninian had been urgent with her that she should not venture alone by night, but as yet he had no authority over her, and she would do what she would do, having been born into the world apparently without fear. This byre and loft on the edge of the forest belonged to the Giffards, who had grazing along the open meadow that rimmed the trees, but the elderly hind who kept the cattle was from Sanan's own household, and her willing and devoted slave. The two good horses she had bought and stabled here were his joy, and his privity to Sanan's marriage plans would keep him proud and glad to the day of his death.

She had come, and she had lain with Ninian in the loft, the two rolled in one cloak and anchored with embracing arms, not yet for the body's delight but rather for its survival and comfort. Snug like dormice in their winter sleep, alive and awake enough to be aware of profound pleasure, they had talked together almost an hour, and now that she had left him he hugged the remembrance of her and got warmth from it to keep him glowing through the night. Some day, some night, please God soon, she would not have to rise and leave him, he would not have to open reluctant arms and let her go, and the night would be perfect, a lovely, starry dark shot through with flame. But now he lay alone, and ached a little, and fretted about her, about the morrow, about his own debts, which seemed to him so inadequately paid.

With her hair adrift against his cheek, and her breath warm in the hollow of his throat, she had told him everything that had happened during these last days of the old year, how Brother Cadfael had found the ebony staff, how he had visited Diota and got her story out of her, how Father Ailnoth's funeral was to take place next day after the parish Mass. And when he started up in anxiety for Diota, she had drawn him down to her again with her arms wreathed about his neck, and told him he need have no uneasiness, for she had promised to go with Diota to the priest's funeral Mass, and take as great care of her as he himself could have done, and deal with any threat that might arise against her as valiantly as even he would have dealt with it. And she had forbidden him to stir from where he lay hidden until she should come to him again. But just as she was a lady not lightly to be disobeyed, so he was a man not lightly to be forbidden.

All the same, she had got a promise out of him that he would wait, as she insisted, unless something unforeseen should arise to make action imperative. And with that she had had to be content, and they had kissed on it, and put away present anxieties to whisper about the future. How many miles to the Welsh border? Ten? Certainly not much more. And Powys might be a wild land, but it had no quarrel with a soldier of the Empress more than with an officer of King Stephen, and would by instinct take the part of the hunted rather than the forces of English law. Moreover, Sanan had claims to a distant kinship there, through a Welsh grandmother, who had bequeathed her her un-English name. And should they encounter masterless men in the forests, Ninian was a good man of his hands, and there was a good sword and a long dagger hidden away in the hay, arms once carried by John Bernières at the siege of Shrewsbury, where he had met his death. They would do well enough on the journey, they would reach Gloucester and marry there, openly and honourably.

Except that they could not go, not yet, not until he was satisfied that all danger to Diota was past, and her living secure under the abbot's protection. And now that he lay alone, Ninian could see no present end to that difficulty. The morrow would lay Ailnoth's body to rest, but not the ugly shadow of his death. Even if the day passed without threat to Diota, that would not solve anything for the days yet to come.

Ninian lay wakeful until past midnight, fretting at the threads that would not untangle for him. Over the watershed between the old year and the new he drifted at last into an uneasy sleep, and dreamed of fighting his way through interminable forest tracks overgrown with bramble and thorn towards a Sanan forever withdrawn from him, and leaving behind for him only a sweet, aromatic scent of herbs.

Under the vast inverted keel of the choir, dimly lit for Matins, the solemn words of the Office of the Dead echoed and re-echoed as sounds never seemed to do by day, and the fine, sonorous voice of Brother Benedict the sacristan was magnified to fill the whole vault as he read the lessons in between the spoken psalms, and at every ending came the insistent versicle and response:

'Requiem aeternam dona eis, Domine. . . .'

'Et lux perpetua luceat eis. . . .'

And Brother Benedict, deep and splendid: ' "My soul is weary of my life. . . . I will speak in the bitterness of my soul, I will say unto God, Do not condemn me, show me wherefore thou contendest with me. . . ." '

Not much comfort in the book of Job, thought Cadfael, listening intently in his stall, but a great deal of fine poetry – could not that in itself be a kind of comfort, after all? Making even discomfort, degradation and death, everything Job complained of, a magnificent defiance?

'"O that thou wouldst hide me in the grave, that thou wouldst keep me secret until thy wrath be past. . . .

'"My breath is corrupt, my days are extinct, the grave is ready for me. . . . I have made my bed in the darkness, I have said to corruption, Thou art my father, to the worm, Thou art my mother. And where is now my hope?

'"Cease, then, and let me alone, that I may take comfort a little, before I go whence I shall not return, even to the land of darkness and the shadow of death . . . land without order, where even the light is as darkness. . . ."'

Yet in the end the entreaty that was itself a reassurance rose again, one step advanced beyond hope towards certainty:

'Rest eternal grant unto them, O Lord. . . .'

'And let light perpetual shine upon them. . . .'

Stumbling up the night stairs back to bed after Lauds, half asleep, Cadfael still had that persistent appeal echoing in his mind, and by the time he slept again it had become almost a triumphant claim reaching up to take what it pleaded for. Rest eternal and light perpetual . . . even for Ailnoth.

Not only for Ailnoth, but for most of us, thought Cadfael, subsiding into sleep, it will be a long journey through purgatory, but no doubt even the most winding way gets there in the end.

Chapter Eleven

The first day of the New Year, 1142, dawned grey and moist, but with a veiled light that suggested the sun might come through slowly, and abide for an hour or so in the middle of the day, before mist again closed in towards nightfall. Cadfael, who was often up well before Prime, awakened this morning only when the bell sounded, and made his way down the night stairs with the others still drowsy from so short a rest. After Prime he went to make sure that all was well in the workshop, and brought away with him fresh oil for the altar lamps. Cynric had already trimmed the candles, and gone out through the cloister to the graveyard, to see all neat and ready where the open grave waited under the precinct wall, covered decorously with planks. The body in its wooden coffin rested on a bier before the parish altar, decently draped. After the Mass it would be carried in procession from the north door, along the Foregate, and in at the great double gate just round the corner from the horse-fair ground, where the laity had access, instead of through the monastic court. A certain separateness must be preserved, for the sake of the quietude necessary to the Rule.

There was a subdued bustle about the great court well before the hour for Mass, brothers hurrying to get their work ready for the rest of the day, or finish small things left undone the previous day. And the people of the Foregate began to gather outside the great west door of the church, or hover about the gatehouse waiting for friends before entering. They came with faces closed and shuttered, dutifully grave and ceremonious, but with quick and careful eyes watching from ambush, uncertain still whether they were really out of the shadow of that resented presence. Perhaps after today they would draw breath and come out of hiding, no longer wary of speaking openly to their neighbours. Perhaps! But what if Hugh should spring his trap in vain?

Cadfael was uneasy about the entire enterprise, but even more dismayed at the thought of this uncertainty continuing for ever, until distrust and fear died at last only from attrition and forgetfulness. Better to have it out into the light, deal with it, and be done. Then at least all but one could be at peace. No – he, too! He most of all!

The notabilities of the Foregate had begun to appear, Erwald the reeve, sombre-faced and aware of his dignity, as befitted and almost justified his use of the title of provost. The smith from his forge, Rhys ab Owain the Welsh farrier – several of the craftsmen of the Foregate were Welsh – Erwald's shepherd kinsman, and Jordan Achard the baker, big and burly and well fleshed, wooden-faced like the rest but nevertheless with a sort of glossy content about him, having survived to bury his detractor. And the little people, too. Aelgar who had worked for the priest and been affronted by the doubt whether he was villein or free, Eadwin whose boundary stone had been shifted by Ailnoth's too close ploughing, Centwin whose child had been buried in unblessed ground and abandoned as lost, the fathers of boys who had learned the hard way to stay out of range of the ebony staff, and shivered in their shoes at having to attend Ailnoth's lessons. The boys themselves gathered at a little distance from their elders, whispering, shuffling, shifting to get a view within but never entering, and sometimes their wary faces showed a sudden fleeting grin here and there, and sometimes their whispering turned briefly to sniggering, half from bravado and half from involuntary awe. The Foregate dogs, sensing the general excitement and unease, ran about between the crowding watchers, snapped edgily at the hooves of passing horses, and loosed volleys of high-pitched barking at every sudden noise.

The women, for the most part, had been left at home. No doubt Jordan's wife was looking after his bakery, raking out the ashes from the early morning firing, and making ready for the second batch, the loaves already shaped and waiting. Just as well for her to be at a safe distance from what was to come, though surely Hugh would not involve the poor soul, when she had only admitted her husband's sleeping abroad in order to save him from this worse accusation. Well, that must be left to Hugh, and Hugh was usually adroit about his manipulations of people and events. But some of the women were here, the elders, the matrons, the widows of solid craftsmen, those who upheld the church even when others became backsliders. The stalwarts at all the least timely services, attending doggedly even at the monastic Vespers as well as the parish Mass, were mostly these sturdy she-elders in their decent black, like lay members of the community itself. They would not miss the ceremonies of this day.

Cadfael was watching the arrivals with a half-attentive gaze and his mind elsewhere, when he saw Diota Hammet come in at the gate, with Sanan's hand solicitous at her elbow. It came both as an anxious reminder and a pleasant refreshment to his eyes, two comely women thus linked in a carefully groomed and perhaps brittle dignity, very calm and stiff with resolution. Autumn and spring came gallantly supporting each other. Ninian in his banishment and solitude would require a full account, and never have an easy moment until he got it. Two hours more and the thing would be done, one way or the other.

They had come in through the gate to the court, and were looking about them, clearly seeking someone. It was Sanan who saw him first, and brightened as she turned to speak quickly into Diota's ear. The widow turned to look, and at once started towards him. He went to meet them, since it seemed he must be the one they were seeking.

'I'm glad to have found you thus before the service,' said

the widow. 'The ointment you gave me – there's the half of it left, and you see I don't need it any more. It would be a shame to waste it, you must have a deal of call for it in this wintry weather.' She had it put away safely in the little bag slung from her girdle, and had to fumble under her cloak to get it out. A small, rough pottery jar, with a wooden lid stoppered tightly into the neck to seal it. She held it out to him on her open palm, and offered him with it a pale but steady smile. 'All my grazes are gone, this can still serve someone else. Take it, with my thanks.'

The last of her grazes, faded now almost to invisibility, hair-fine threads of white, showed elusively round the jar in her palm. The mark on her temple was merely a hyacinth oval, the bruise all but gone.

'You could have kept it against future need, with all my goodwill,' said Cadfael, accepting the offering.

'Well, should I ever have need again, I hope I shall still be here, and able to send to you,' said Diota.

She made him a small, dignified reverence, and turned back towards the church. Over her shoulder Cadfael caught Sanan's confiding blue gaze, harebell-soft and sky-bright, almost as intimate as a signal between conspirators. Then she, too, turned, taking the older woman's arm, and the two of them walked away from him, across the court to the gate, and in at the west door of the church.

Ninian awoke when it was full daylight, thick-headed and slow to collect his wits from having lain half the night wakeful, and then fallen into too profound a slumber. He rose, and swung himself down from the loft without using the ladder, and went out into the fresh, chill, moist morning to shake off the lingering cobwebs. The stalls below were empty. Sanan's man Sweyn had been here already from his own cottage nearer the town, and turned out the two horses into the fenced paddock. They needed a little space for exercise, after the harder frosts when they had been kept indoors, and they were making good use of their freedom, glad of the air and the light. Young and high-spirited and short of work, they would not easily let themselves be caught and bridled, but it was unlikely they would be needed this day.

The cattle byre was still peopled, they would not be let out to the grazing along the riverside until Sweyn was near to keep an eye on them. The byre and stable stood in a large clearing between slopes of woodland, with an open side only to the river, pleasantly private, and under the western stand of trees a little stream ran down to the Severn. Ninian made for it sleepily, stripped off coat and shirt, shivering a little, and plunged head and arms into the water, flinching and drawing in hissing breath at the instant coldness, but taking pleasure in feeling his wits start into warm wakefulness. Shaking off drops from his face and wringing his hands through his thick thatch of curls, he ran a couple of circuits of the open grass at full gallop, caught up his discarded clothes and ran back with them into the shelter of the stable, to scrub himself vigorously with a clean sack until he glowed, and dress himself to face the day. Which might be long and lonely and full of anxieties, but at this moment felt bracing and hopeful.

He had combed his hair into such order as his fingers could command, and was sitting on a bale of straw eating a hunk of bread and an apple from the store Sanan had provided, when he heard the herdsman come along the rough path towards the door. Or was this some other man, and not Sweyn at all? Ninian stiffened to listen, with his cheek bulging with apple, and his jaws motionless. No whistling, and Sweyn always whistled, and these feet came in unusual haste, clearly audible in the rough grass and small stones. Ninian was up in still greater haste, and swung himself up into the loft and hung silent over the hatch, ready for whoever should come.

'Young master . . .' called a voice in the open doorway, without any suggestion of caution. Sweyn, after all, but a Sweyn who had been hurrying, was a little out of breath, and had no thought to spare for whistling this morning. 'Lad, where are you? Come down!'

Ninian let out his breath in a great gust, and slid back through the hatch to hang at arm's length and drop beside the herdsman. 'God's love, Sweyn, you had me reaching for a knife then! I never thought it was you. I thought I had you by heart, by this time, but you came like a stranger. What is it?' He flung an arm about his friend and ally boisterously in his relief, and as quickly held him off to look him up and down from head to foot. 'Lord, lord, in your best, too! In whose honour?'

Sweyn was a thickset, grizzled man of middle age, with a ragged brown beard and a twinkling glance. Whatever warm clothing he put on against the winter he must have put on underneath, for he had but the one stout pair of cloth hose, and Ninian had never yet seen him in any coat but the much-mended drab brown, but evidently he possessed another, for this morning he had on a green coat, unpatched, and a dark brown capuchon protecting head and shoulders.

'I've been into Shrewsbury,' he said shortly, 'fetching a pair of shoes my wife left to be clouted at Provost Corviser's. I was here at first light and let out the horses, they've been penned long enough, and then I went back to fettle myself for the town, and I've had no time to put on my working gear again. There's word going round the town, master, that the sheriff means to attend the Foregate priest's funeral, and fetch a murderer away with him. I thought I'd best bring you word as fast as I could. For it may be true.'

Ninian stood gaping at him aghast for a moment in stricken silence. 'No! He's going to take her? Is that the word? Oh, God, not Diota! And she there to be seized, all unsuspecting. And I not there!' He clutched earnestly at Sweyn's arm. 'Is this certain?'

'It's the common talk about the town. Folks are all agog, there'll be a stream of them making haste over the bridge to see it done. They don't say who – leastways, they guess at it, two or three ways, but they all agree it's coming, be the poor wretch who he may.'

Ninian flung away the apple he had still been holding, and beat his fists together in frantic thought. 'I must go! The parish Mass won't be until ten, there's still time. . . .'

'You can't go. The young mistress said—'

'I know what she said, but this is my business now. I must and will get Diota out of it. Who else can it be the sheriff means to accuse? But he shan't have her! I won't suffer it!'

'You'll be known! It may not be your woman he has in mind, how then? He may have the rights of it, and know well what he's doing. And you'll have thrown yourself away for nothing,' urged the herdsman reasonably.

'No, I needn't be known. One in a crowd – and only the people of the abbey and a few in the Foregate know me well by sight. In any case,' said Ninian grimly, 'let anyone lay a hand on her and I *will* be known, and with a vengeance, too. But I can be lost among a crowd, why not? Lend me that coat and capuchon, Sweyn, who's to know me under a hood? And they've never seen me but in this gear, yours is far too fine for the Benet they've seen about the place. . . .'

'Take the horse,' said Sweyn, stripping off his capuchon without protest, and hoisting the loose cotte over his head.

Ninian did cast one glance out into the field where the two horses kicked up their heels, happy to be at large. 'No, no time! I can do it as fast afoot. And I'd be more noticeable, mounted. How many horsemen will there be about Ailnoth's funeral?' He thrust his way into the over-ample garment already warmed for him, and emerged ruffled and flushed. 'I daren't show a sword. But the dagger I can hide about me.' He was up into the loft to fetch it, and fasten it safely out of sight under his coat, secure in the belt of his hose.

At the doorway, poised to run, he was stricken with another qualm, and turned to clutch again at the herdsman's arm. 'Sweyn, if I'm taken – Sanan will see you shan't be the loser. Your good clothes – I've no right . . .'

'Ah, go on with you!' said Sweyn, half-affronted, and gave him a shove out into the field and towards the trees. 'I can go in sacking if needs must. You bring yourself back safe, or the young mistress will have my head for it. And put up your hood, fool boy, before you come near the road!'

Ninian ran, across the meadow and into the slope of trees, heading for the track that would bring him, within a mile or so, to the Meole Brook, and across it into the Foregate, close by the bridge into the town.

Word of the fat rumour that was running round Shrewsbury reached Ralph Giffard some time later, none of his household having been abroad in the town before nine o'clock, when a maidservant went out to fetch a pitcher of milk, and was a long time about it by reason of the juicy gossip she learned on her errand. Even when she returned to the house the news took some time to be carried from the kitchen to the clerk, who had come to see what all the chatter was about, and thence to Giffard himself, who was at that moment reflecting whether it was not time to leave the town house to the caretaker and make for his chief manor in the north-east. It was pleasant to prolong the comfortable stay here, and he had taken pleasure in falling in with his young son's wish to practise the skills of managing a manor for himself, unsupervised. The boy was sixteen, two years younger than his step-sister, and somewhat jealous of her show of maturity and responsibility in running the distaff side of the household. He was already affianced, a good match with a neighbour's daughter, and naturally he was eager to try his wings. And no doubt he would be doing well enough, and proud of his prowess, but still a father would be only prudent to keep an eye on affairs. There was no bad blood between boy and girl, but for all that, young Ralph would not be sorry to have Sanan safely married and out of the house. If only her marriage did not threaten to cost so much!

'My lord,' said the old clerk, coming in upon his ponderings towards mid morning, 'I think you are rid of your incubus this day, or soon will be. It seems it's all round the town, being bandied across every counter and every doorstep, that Beringar has his murderer known and proved, and means to take him at the priest's burial. And who can it be but that youngster of FitzAlan's? He may have made his escape once, but it seems they've run him to earth this time.'

He brought it as good news, and as such Giffard received it. Once the troublesome fellow was safely in hold, and his own part in the matter as clearly decorous and loyal, he could be at ease. While the rogue ran loose, there might still be unpleasant echoes for any man who had had to do with him.

'So I did well to uncover him,' he said, breathing deeply. 'I might still have been suspect else, when they lay hands on him. Well, well! So the thing's as good as over, and no harm done.'

The thought was very satisfying, even though he would have been just as pleased if it could have been achieved without the act of betrayal with which a lingering scruple in his own mind still reproached him. But now, if it was to be proven that the young fellow really had murdered the priest, then there was no longer need to feel any qualms on his behalf, for he had his deserts.

It was some last superstition that something might yet go wrong, added to a contradictory desire to see the successful consummation in person, that made him think again, and make up his mind, somewhat belatedly, to be in at the death. To make sure, and to wring the fullest savour out of his own preservation.

'After the parish Mass, this was to be? They'll be well into the abbot's sermon by now. I think I'll ride down and see the end of it.' And he was out of his chair and shouting across the yard for the groom to saddle his horse.

Abbot Radulfus had been speaking for some time, slowly, with the high, withdrawn voice of intense thought, every word measured. In the choir it was always dim, a parable of the life of man, a small, lighted space arched over by a vast shadowy darkness, for even in darkness there are degrees of shadow. The crowded nave was lighter, and with so many people in attendance not even notably cold. When choir monks and secular congregation met for worship together, the separation between them seemed accentuated rather than softened. We here, you out there, thought Brother Cadfael, and yet we are all like flesh, and our souls subject to the same final judgement.

'The company of the saints,' said Abbot Radulfus, his head raised so that he looked rather into the vault than at those he addressed, 'is not to be determined by any measure within our understanding. It cannot be made up of those without sin, for who that ever wore flesh, except one, can make so high a claim? Surely there is room within it for those who have set before themselves lofty aims, and done their best to reach them, and so, we believe, did our brother and shepherd here dead. Yes, even though they fail of attaining their aims, more, even though those aims may have been too narrow, the mind that conceived them being blinded by prejudice and pride, and channelled too greedily towards a personal excellence. For even the pursuit of perfection may be sin, if it infringes the rights and needs of another soul. Better to fail a little, by turning aside to lift up another, than to pass by him in haste to reach our own reward, and leave him to solitude and despair. Better to labour in lameness, in fallibility, but holding up others who falter, than to stride forward alone.

'Again, it is not enough to abstain from evil, there must also be an outgoing goodness. The company of the blessed may extend justifiably to embrace even men who have been great sinners, yet also great lovers of their fellow men, such as have never turned away their eyes from other men's needs, but have done them such good as they might, and as little harm as they must. For in that they saw a neighbour's need, they saw God's need, as he himself has shown us, and inasmuch as they saw a neighbour's face more clearly than their own, so also they saw God's face.

'Further, I show you certainly that all such as are born into this world and die untainted by personal sin partake of the martyred purity of the Holy Innocents, and die for Our Lord, who also will embrace them and quicken them living, where they shall no more partake of death. And if they died without name here, yet their name is written in his book, and no other need know it, until the day come.

'But we, all we who share the burden of sin, it behoves us not to question or fret concerning the measure dealt out to us, or try to calculate our own merit and deserving, for we have not the tools by which to measure values concerning the soul. That is God's business. Rather it behoves us to live every day as though it were our last, to the full of such truth and kindness as is within us, and to lie down every night as though the next day were to be our first, and a new and pure beginning. The day will come when all will be made plain. Then shall we know, as now we trust. And in that trust we commit our pastor here to the care of the shepherd of shepherds, in the sure hope of the resurrection.'

He uttered the blessing with his face lowered at last to those who listened. Probably he wondered how many had understood, and how many, indeed, had need of understanding.

It was over here, people stirred stealthily in the nave, sliding towards the north door to be first out and secure a good place ahead of the procession. In the choir the three ministering priests, abbot, prior and sub-prior, descended to the bier, and the brothers formed silent file, two by two, after them. The party of bearers took up the burden, and made towards the open north doorway into the Foregate. How is it, thought Cadfael, watching, and glad of a distraction, however sinful at such a moment, how is it that there is always one out of step, or just a little too short in height and stride to match the others? Is it so that we should not fall into the error of taking even death too seriously?

It was no great surprise to find the Foregate crowded when the procession issued from the north porch and turned to the right along the precinct wall, but at first glance it did come as a surprise to find half the townspeople among the starers, as well as the men of the parish. Then Cadfael understood the reason. Hugh had had discreet whispers of his plans leaked within the town walls, too late for them to be carried out here to the folk most concerned, and give warning, but in time to bring the worthies of Shrewsbury – or perhaps even more surely the unworthies, who had time to waste on curiosity – hurrying here to be witnesses of the ending.

Cadfael was still wondering what that ending was to be. Hugh's device might provoke some man's conscience and make him speak out, to deliver a neighbour mistakenly accused, but equally it might come as an immense relief to the guilty, and be accepted as a gift – certainly not from heaven, rather from the other place! At every step along the Foregate he fretted at the tangle of details churning in his mind, and found no coherence among them. Not until the little jar of ointment he had thrust into the breast of his habit nodded against his middle as his foot slid in a muddy rut. The touch was like an impatient nudge at his mind. He saw it again, resting in the palm of a shapely but work-worn hand, as Diota held it out to him. A hand seamed with the lines proper to the human palm, graven deep with lifelong use, but also bearing thread-like white lines that crossed these, fanning from wrist to fingers, barely visible now, soon to vanish altogether.

An icy night, certainly, he had trodden cautiously through it himself, he knew. And a woman slipping as she turned to step back on to the frozen doorstone of a house, and falling forward, naturally puts out her hands to save herself, and her hands take the rough force of the fall, even though they may not quite save her head. Except that Diota had not fallen. Her head injury was sustained in quite a different way. She had fallen on her knees that night, yes, but of desperate intent, with hands clutching not at frozen ground, but at the skirts of Ailnoth's cassock and cloak. So how did she get those scored grazes in both palms?

In innocence she had told him but half a story, believing she told him all. And here was he helpless now, he must hold his place in this funeral procession, and she must hold hers, and he could not get to her, to probe the corners of memory which had eluded her then. Not until this solemn rite was over and done would he be able to speak again with Diota. No, but there were other witnesses, mute by their nature but possibly eloquent in what they might be able to demonstrate. He walked on perforce, keeping pace with Brother Henry along the Foregate and round the corner by the horse-fair ground, unable to break the decorum of burial. Not yet! But perhaps within? For there would be no procession through the street afterwards, not for the brethren. They would be already within their chosen enclave, to disperse severally to their ablutions and their dinner in the refectory. Once within, why should he be missed if he slipped quietly away?

The broad double doors in the precinct wall stood wide open to let the mourning column into the wide prospect of the cemetery garth, giving place on the left to kitchen gardens, and beyond, the long roof of the abbot's lodging, and the small enclosed flower garden round it. The brothers were buried close under the east end of the church, the vicars of the parish a little removed from them, but in the same area. The number of graves as yet was not large, the foundation being no more than fifty-eight years old, and though the parish was older, it had then been served by the small wooden church Earl Roger had replaced in stone and given to the newly founded abbey. There were trees here, and grass, and meadow flowers in the summer, a pleasant enough place. Only the dark, raw hole close to the wall marred the green enclosure. Cynric had placed trestles to receive the coffin before it was lowered into the grave, and he was stooped over the planks he had just removed, stacking them tidily against the wall.

Half the Foregate and a good number of the inhabitants of the town came thronging through the open doors after the brothers, crowding close to see all there was to be seen. Cadfael drew back from his place in the ranks, and contrived to be swallowed up by their inquisitive numbers. No doubt Brother Henry would eventually miss him from his side, but in the circumstances he would say no word. By the time Prior Robert had got out the first sonorous phrases of the committal, Cadfael was round the corner of the chapter house and scurrying across the great court towards the wicket by the infirmary, that led through to the mill.

Hugh had brought down with him from the castle two sergeants and two of the young men of the garrison, all mounted, though they had left their horses tethered at the abbey gatehouse, and allowed the funeral procession to make its way along the Foregate to the cemetery before they showed themselves. While all eyes were on the prior and the coffin Hugh posted two men outside the open doors, to make a show of preventing any departures, while he and the sergeants went within, and made their way unobtrusively forward through the press. The very discretion with which they advanced, and the respectful silence they preserved when they had drawn close to the bier, which should have kept them inconspicuous, perversely drew every eye, so that by the time they were where Hugh had designed they should be, himself almost facing the prior across the coffin, the sergeants a pace or two behind Jordan Achard, one on either side, many a furtive glance had turned on them, and there was a wary shifting and staring and stealthy shuffling of feet on all sides. But Hugh held his hand until all was over.

Cynric and his helpers hoisted the coffin, and fitted the slings to lower it into the grave. Earth fell dully. The last prayer was said. There was the inevitable stillness and hush, before everyone would sigh and stir, and very slowly begin to move away. The sigh came like a sudden gust of wind, it fell from so many throats. The stir followed like the rustle of leaves in the gust. And Hugh said loudly and clearly, in a voice calculated to arrest any movement on the instant:

'My lord abbot, Father Prior . . . I must ask your pardon for having placed a guard at your gate – outside your walls, but even so I beg your indulgence. No one must leave here until I've made known my purpose. Hold me excused that I must come at such a time, but there's no help for it. I am here in the name of the King's law, and in pursuit of a murderer. I am here to take into charge a felon suspected of the slaying of Father Ailnoth.'

Chapter Twelve

There was not very much to be found, but there was enough. Cadfael stood on the rim of the high bank where Ailnoth's body had bobbed and nestled, held fast there by the slight side impulse from the tail-race of the mill. The stump of the felled willow, no more than hip-high, bristled with its whips of blanched green hair. Some broken shoots among them, at the rim of the barren, dead surface, dried and cracked with time and jagged from the axe. And a finger length of black thread fluttering, one end securely held in the frayed ridge of dead wood. A finger length of unravelled woollen braid, just enough to complete the binding of a black skull-cap. Frost and thaw had come and gone, whitened and moistened and changed and obliterated whatever else had once been there to be found, a smear of blood, perhaps, some minute fragments of torn skin. Nothing left but a fluttering black roving, clawed loose when the cap flew wide and went with the current into the reeds.

Cadfael went back in haste with the infinitesimal scrap of wool in his hand. Halfway across the great court he heard the clamour of voices howling protest, excitement and confusion, and slackened his pace, for clearly there was no more need for haste. The trap was sprung, and must hold whatever it caught. Too late to prevent, at least he could undo whatever harm came of it, and if none came, so much the better. What he had to say and to show would keep.

Ninian reached the open track and the bridge over the Meole Brook in a glow from running most of the way, and remembered to slow to a walk before he reached the highway, close to the end of the bridge into Shrewsbury, and to haul up the hood of Sweyn's capuchon to shadow his face. At the turning into the Foregate he first checked in mild alarm, and then realised his luck and took heart, for so many people were still hurrying out of the town towards the abbey that it was very simple to mingle with them and be lost. He went with the stream, ears pricked for every word uttered around him, and heard his own name bandied back and forth with anticipatory relish. So that was the arrest some of these were expecting, though it could hardly be what Hugh Beringar had in mind, since he had lost the scent some days ago, and had no reason to suppose that he would recover it today. But others spoke of the woman, the priest's servant, not even knowing a name by which to call her. Others again were speculating wildly between two or three names unknown to Ninian, but who had evidently suffered under Ailnoth's unbending severities.

It seemed he had come only in time to join the stragglers in the traffic from the town, those who had been late in hearing the gossip, for the Foregate from the gatehouse of the abbey on was already crowded. Just as Ninian reached the gatehouse the clergy were emerging from the north door, and after them the coffin, and all the brothers in solemn procession. This was the one danger he must avoid, at least until he knew whether he had to face the worst, and deliver himself up of his own will. These were the men, any one of whom might know him on sight if he caught a clear glimpse of his face, indeed might be able to place him even by his build and gait. He withdrew hastily, weaving between the curious watchers to the far side of the street, and slipped into the mouth of the narrow alley until the monks had all passed by. After them came those of the parish worthies whose dignity had forbidden them to scurry first out of the church and secure a favourable place in the cemetery garth. And after them streamed the watchers in the Foregate, intent and avid as children and dogs after a travelling tumbler, though not so candidly loud in their anticipation of wonders.

To be the last and alone would be as bad as thrusting himself to the fore. Ninian slid out of concealment in time to join the rear guard, and hung just within the fringes as the cortège made its way along the Foregate to the corner by the horse-fair, and rounded it to the cemetery doors, which stood wide open.

There were a few besides himself, it seemed, who wanted to see everything there was to be seen, without making themselves conspicuous, and likewise preferred to hang upon the fringes of the crowd outside the gates, peering within. And that might be because two men of the castle garrison stood one on either side the entrance, very casually, not interfering with those who went in, but nevertheless to be eyed with caution.

Ninian halted in the wide opening, neither in nor out, and peered forward, craning to see between the massed heads, and reach the group gathered about the grave. Both abbot and prior were more than commonly tall, he could see them clearly above the rest, and hear the prayers of the committal ring aloud in Prior Robert's consciously mellifluous tones, to reach every ear. The prior had a genuinely splendid voice, and loved to exercise it in all the highly dramatic possibilities of the liturgy.

Edging a step or two to one side, Ninian caught a glimpse of Diota's face, a pale oval under her black hood. She stood close beside the bier, her due as the only member of the priest's household. The curve of a shoulder pressed close to hers, the arm linked in her arm, could only belong to Sanan, though no matter how he craned to one side and the other, he could not get a view of the beloved face, taller heads moved always between.

There was a ripple of movement as the priests advanced to the grave-side, the crowd swinging that way with them. The coffin was being lowered, the last dismissal spoken. Under the high precinct wall the first clods of earth fell on Father Ailnoth's coffin. It was almost over, and nothing had broken the decorum of the occasion. The first shuffle and rustle and stir passed through the assembly, acknowledging an ending. Ninian's heart settled in him, cautiously hoping, and as suddenly seemed to heave over in his breast as another voice, raised to carry clearly, spoke up from the grave-side:

'My lord abbot, Father Prior . . . I must ask your pardon for having placed a guard at your gate. . . .'

For the beating of the blood in his ears Ninian missed what came next, but he knew the voice must belong to the sheriff, for who else bore such authority even here, within the enclave? And the end he heard all too clearly: 'I am here to take into charge a felon suspected of the slaying of Father Ailnoth.'

So the worst had fallen on them, after all, just as rumour had foretold. There was a sudden stunned silence, and then a great buzz of confusion and excitement that shook the crowd like a gale of wind. The next words were lost, though Ninian held his breath and strained to hear. Some of those standing with him outside the gate had pressed forward, to miss nothing of this sensation, and no one had any ears for the clatter of hooves coming briskly round the corner by the horse-fair, and heading towards them at a trot. Within the walls there came a sudden wild outcry, a babel of voices exclaiming and protesting, bombarding those before them with questions, passing back probably inaccurate answers to those behind. Ninian braced himself to plunge in and shoulder his way through to where his womenfolk stood embattled and defenceless. For it was over, his liberty was forfeit, if not his life. He drew breath deep, and laid his hand on the shoulder of the nearest body that barred his way, for the curious had abandoned caution and filled up the open gateway.

The bellow of dismay and indignation that suddenly rose from under the precinct wall stopped him in his tracks and hurled him back almost physically from the doorway. A man's voice, howling protests, calling heaven to witness his innocence. Not Diota! Not Diota, but a man!

'My lord, I swear to you I know nothing of it. . . . I never saw hide or hair of him that day or that night. I was fast at home, my wife will tell you so! I never harmed any man, much less a priest. . . . Someone has lied about me, lied! My lord abbot, as God sees me . . .'

The name was borne back to Ninian's ears rank by rank through the crowd. 'Jordan Achard . . . it was Jordan Achard. . . . They're seizing Jordan Achard. . . .'

Ninian stood trembling, weak with reaction, and so neglectful of his own situation that he had let the hood of Sweyn's capuchon slip back from his head and lie in folds on his shoulders. Behind him the hooves had halted, shifting lightly in the thin mud of the thaw.

'Hey, you, fellow!'

The butt of a whip jabbed him sharply in the back, and he swung about, startled, to look up directly into the face of a rider who leaned down to him from the saddle of a fine roan horse. A big, ruddy, sinewy man in his fifties, perhaps, very spruce in his own gear and the accoutrements of his mount, and with the nobleman's authority in his voice and face. A handsome face, bearded and strong-featured, now just beginning to run to flesh and lose its taut, clear lines, but still memorable. The brief moment they spent staring closely at each other was terminated by a second impatient but good-natured prod of the whip's butt against Ninian's shoulder, and the brisk order:

'Yes, you, lad! Hold my horse while I'm within, and you shan't be the loser. What's afoot in there, do you know? Someone's making a fine noise about it.'

In the exuberance of relief from his terror for Diota, Ninian rebounded into impudent glee, knuckled his forehead obsequiously, and reached willingly for the bridle, once again the penniless peasant groom Benet to the life. 'I don't rightly know, master,' he said, 'but there's some in there saying a man's been taken up for killing the priest. . . .' He smoothed a hand over the horse's silken forehead and between the pricked ears, and the roan tossed his head, turned a soft, inquisitive muzzle to breathe warmth at him, and accepted the caress graciously. 'A lovely beast, my lord! I'll mind him well.'

'So the murderer's taken, is he? Rumour told truth for once.' The rider was down in a moment, and off through the quivering crowd like a sickle cutting grass, a brusque, hard shoulder forward and a masterful tongue ready to demand passage. Ninian was left with his cheek against a glossy shoulder, and a tangle of feelings boiling within him, laughter and gratitude, and the joyful anticipation of a journey now free from all regrets and reservations, but also a small, bitter jet of sadness that one man was dead untimely, and another now accused of his murder. It took him some little time to remember to pull the hood over his head again, and well forward to shadow his face, but luckily all attention was fixed avidly upon the hubbub within the cemetery garth, and no one was paying any heed to a hind holding his master's horse in the street. The horse was excellent cover, but it did prevent him from advancing again into the wide-open doorway, and even by straining his ears he could make little sense out of the babel from within. The clamour of terrified protest went on for some time, that was plain enough, and the shrill commentary from the bystanders made a criss-cross of conflicting sounds around it. If there were saner voices speaking, Hugh Beringar's or the abbot's, they were drowned in the general chaos.

Ninian leaned his forehead against the warm hide that quivered gently under his touch, and offered devout thanks for so timely a deliverance.

In the heart of the tumult Abbot Radulfus raised a voice that seldom found it necessary to thunder, and thundered to instant effect.

'Silence! You bring shame on yourselves and desecrate this holy place. Silence, I say!'

And there was silence, sudden and profound, though it might as easily break out in fresh chaos if the rein was not tightened.

'So, and keep silence, all you who have nothing here to plead or deny. Let those speak and be heard who have. Now, my lord sheriff, you accuse this man Jordan Achard of murder. On what evidence?'

'On the evidence,' said Hugh, 'of a witness who has said and will say again that he lies in saying he spent that night at home. Why, if he has nothing to hide, should he find it necessary to lie? On the evidence also of a witness who saw him creeping out from the mill path and making for his home at earliest light on Christmas morning. It is enough to hold him upon suspicion,' said Hugh crisply, and motioned to the two sergeants, who grasped the terrified Jordan almost tenderly by the arms. 'That he had a grievance against Father Ailnoth is known to everyone.'

'My lord abbot,' babbled Jordan, quaking, 'on my soul I swear I never touched the priest. I never saw him, I was not there . . . it's false . . . they lie about me. . . .'

'It seems there are those,' said Radulfus, 'who will equally swear that you were there.'

'It was I who told that I'd seen him,' spoke up the reeve's shepherd cousin, worried and shaken by the result he had achieved. 'I could say no other, for I did see him, and it was barely light, and all I've told is truth. But I never intended mischief, and I never thought any harm but that he was at his games, for I knew what's said of him. . . .'

'And what is said of you, Jordan?' asked Hugh mildly.

Jordan swallowed and writhed, agonised between shame at owning where he had spent his night, and terror of holding out and risking worse. Sweating and wriggling, he blurted: 'No evil, I'm a man well respected. . . . If I was there, it was for no wrong purpose. I . . . I had business there early, charitable business there early – with the old Widow Warren who lives along there. . . . .'

'Or late, with her slut of a maidservant,' called a voice from the safe anonymity of the crowd, and a great ripple of laughter went round, hastily suppressed under the abbot's flashing glare.

'Was that the truth of it? And by chance under Father Ailnoth's eye?' demanded Hugh. 'He would look very gravely upon such depravity, from all accounts. Did he catch you sneaking into the house, Jordan? I hear he was apt to reprove sin on the spot, and harshly. Is that how you came to kill him and leave him in the pool?'

'I never did!' howled Jordan. 'I swear I never had ado with him. If I did fall into sin with the girl, that was all I did. I never went past the house. Ask her, she'll tell you! I was there all night long. . . .'

And all this time Cynric had gone on patiently and steadily filling in the grave, without haste, without apparently paying any great attention to all the tumult at his back. During this last exchange he had straightened up creakily, and stretched until his joints cracked. Now he turned to thrust his way into the centre of the circle, the iron-shod spade still dangling in his hand.

So strange an intrusion from so solitary and withdrawn a man silenced all voices and drew all eyes.

'Let him be, my lord,' said Cynric. 'Jordan had nought to do with the man's death.' He turned his greying head and long, sombre, deep-eyed face from Hugh to the abbot, and back again. 'There's none but I,' he said simply, 'knows how Ailnoth came by his end.'

Then there was utter silence, beyond what the abbot's authority had been able to invoke, a silence deep enough to drown in, as Ailnoth had drowned. The verger stood tall and dignified in his rusty black, waiting to be questioned further, without fear or regret, seeing nothing strange in what he had said, and no reason why he should have said more or said it earlier, but willing to bear with those who demanded explanations.

'You know?' said the abbot, after long and astonished contemplation of the man before him. 'And you have not spoken before?'

'I saw no need. There was no other soul put in peril, not till now. The thing was done, best leave well alone.'

'Are you saying,' demanded Radulfus doubtfully, 'that you were there, that you witnessed it? . . . Was it *you* . . .?'

'No,' said Cynric with a slow shake of his long, grizzled head. 'I did not touch him.' His voice was patient and gentle, as it would have been to questioning children. 'I was there, I witnessed it. But I did not touch him.'

'Then tell us now,' said Hugh quietly. 'Who killed him?'

'No one killed him,' said Cynric. 'Those who do violence die by the same. It's only just.'

'Tell us,' said Hugh again as softly. 'Tell us how this befell. Let us all know, and be at peace again. You are saying his death was an accident?'

'No accident,' said Cynric, and his eyes burned in their deep sockets. 'A judgement.'

He moistened his lips, and lifted his head to stare into the wall of the Lady Chapel, above their heads, as if he, who was illiterate, could read there the words he had to say, he who was a man of few words by nature.

'I went out that night to the pool. I have often walked there by night, when there has been no moon, and none awake to see. Between the willow trees there, beyond the mill, where she went into the water . . . Eluned, Nest's girl . . . because Ailnoth refused her confession and the uses of the church, denounced her before all the parish and shut the door in her face. He could as well have stabbed her to the heart, it would have been kinder. All that brightness and beauty taken from us. . . . I knew her well, she came so often for comfort while Father Adam lived, and he never failed her. And when she was not fretting over her sins she was like a bird, like a flower, a joy to see. There are not so many things of beauty in the world that a man should destroy one of them, and make no amends. And when she fell into remorse she was like a child . . . she *was* a child, it was a child he cast out. . . .'

He fell silent for a moment, as though the words had become hard to read by reason of the blindness of grief, and furrowed his high forehead to decipher them the better, but no one ventured to speak.

'There I was standing, where Eluned went into the pool, when he came along the path. I did not know who it was, he did not come as far as where I stood – but someone, a man stamping and muttering, there by the mill. A man in a rage, or so it sounded. Then a woman came stumbling after him, I heard her cry out to him, she went on her knees to him, weeping, and he was trying to shake her off, and she would not let go of him. He struck her – I heard the blow. She made no more than a moan, but then I did go towards them, thinking there could be murder done, and therefore I saw – dimly, but I had my night eyes, and I did see – how he swung his stick at her again, and she clung with both hands to the head of it to save herself, and how he tugged at it with all his strength and tore it out of her hands. . . . The woman ran from him, I heard her stumbling away along the path, but I doubt she ever heard what I heard, or knows what I know. I heard him reel backwards and crash into the stump of the willow. I heard the withies lash and break. I heard the splash – it was not a great sound – as he went into the water.'

There was another silence, long and deep, while he thought, and laboured to remember with precision, since that was required of him. Brother Cadfael, coming up quietly behind the ranks of the awestruck brothers, had heard only the latter part of Cynric's story, but he had the poor, draggled proof of it in his hand as he listened. Hugh's trap had caught nothing, rather it had set everyone free. He looked across the mute circle to where Diota stood, with Sanan's arm about her. Both women had drawn their hoods close round their faces. One of the hands torn by the sharp edges of the silver band held the folds of Diota's cloak together.

'I went towards the place,' said Cynric, 'and looked into the water. It was only then I knew him certainly for Ailnoth. He drifted at my feet, stunned or dazed. . . . I knew his face. His eyes were open. . . . And I turned my back and walked away from him, as he turned his back on her and walked away from her, shutting the door on her tears as he struck at this other woman's tears. . . . If God had willed him to live, he would have lived. Why else should it happen there, in that very place? And who am I, to usurp the privilege of God?'

All this he delivered in the same reasonable voice with which he would have rendered account of the number of candles bought for the parish altar, though the words came slowly and with effort and thought, studying to make all plain now that plainness was needed. But to Abbot Radulfus it had some distant echo of the voice of prophecy. Even if the man had wished to save, could he have saved? Might not the priest have been already past saving? And there in the dark, alone, with no time to summon help, since everyone was preparing for the night office, and with that undercut bank to contend with, and the dead weight of a big man to handle – could any man, singly, have saved? Better to suppose that the thing had been impossible, and accept what to Cynric was the will of God!

'And now, with your leave, my lord abbot,' said Cynric, having waited courteously but vainly for some comment or question, 'if you've no more need of me I'll be getting on with filling in the grave, for I'll need the most of the daylight to make a good job of it.'

'Do so,' said the abbot, and looked at him for a moment, eye to eye, with no shadow of blame, and saw no shadow of doubt. 'Do so, and come to me for your fee when it is done.'

Cynric went as he had come, back to his work, and those who watched him in awe-stricken silence saw no change in his long-legged walk, or in the quiet, steady rhythm with which he plied his spade.

Radulfus looked at Hugh, and then to Jordan Achard, mute and wilting with relief from terror between his guards. For a brief instant the abbot's austere face was shaken by the merest fleeting shadow of a smile. 'My lord sheriff, I think your charge against this man is already answered. What other offences he may have on his conscience,' said the abbot, fixing the demoralised Jordan with a severe eye, 'I recommend him to bring to confession. And to avoid henceforward!

He may well reflect on the dangers into which such a manner of life has led him, and take this day as a warning.'

'For my part, I'm glad to know the truth and find that none of us here has the guilt of murder on his soul,' said Hugh. 'Master Achard, take yourself home and be glad you have a loyal and dutiful wife. Lucky for you there was one here to speak for you, for there was a strong case against you had there been no such witness. Loose him!' he said to his sergeants. 'Let him be about his business. By rights he owes a gift to the parish altar, by way of thanks for a good deliverance.'

Jordan all but sagged to the ground when the two officers took their hands from him, and Will Warden was moved in good humour to lend him a supporting hand again under one arm until he got his legs to stand solid under him. And now at last it was truly over, but that every soul there was so petrified with wonder that it took another benediction by way of dismissal to start them moving.

'Go now, good people,' said the abbot, somewhat brusquely accepting the need. 'Make your prayers for the soul of Father Ailnoth, and bear in mind that our neighbour's failings should but make us mindful rather of our own. Go, and trust to us who have the grant of this parish to bestow, to consider your needs above all in whatever we determine.' And he blessed them departing, with a vigour and brevity that actually set them in motion. Silent as yet, even as they melted like snow and began to move away, but soon they would be voluble enough. Town and Foregate would ring with the many and contradictory accounts of this morning's events, to be transmuted at last into myth, a folk memory of momentous things witnessed, once, long ago.

'And you, brothers,' said Radulfus shortly, turning to his own flock, doves with fluttered feathers now and disrupted cooing, 'go now to your daily duties, and make ready for dinner.'

They broke ranks almost fearfully, and drifted apart as the

rest were doing, apparently aimlessly at first, then making slowly for the places where now they should be. Like sparks from a fire, or dust scattered on a wind, they disseminated, still half-dazed with revelation. The only one who went about his business with purpose and method was Cynric, busy with his spade under the wall.

Brother Jerome, deeply disturbed by proceedings which in no way fitted in with his conception of the rule and routine of the Benedictine order, went about rounding up some of his strayed chicks towards the lavatorium and the frater, and shooing some of the lingering parishioners out of the abbey's confines. In so doing he drew near to the wide-open doors upon the Foregate, and became aware of a young man standing in the street outside, holding the bridle of a horse, and casting an occasional brief glance over those emerging, but from within a close-drawn capuchon, so that his face was not clearly visible. But there was something about him that held Jerome's sharp eyes. Something not quite recognised, since the coat and capuchon were strange, and the face obstinately averted, and yet something reminiscent of a certain young fellow known for a while to the brethren, and later vanished in strange circumstances. If only the fellow would once turn his face fully!

Cadfael, lingering to watch Sanan and Diota depart, saw them instead draw back into the shadow of the chapel wall, and wait there until the greater part of the throng had moved towards the Foregate. The impulse came from Sanan, he saw her restraining hand laid upon the older woman's arm, and wondered why she should delay. Had she seen someone among the crowd whom she was anxious not to encounter? In search of such a person, he scanned the retreating backs, and saw one at least whose presence there would certainly not be too welcome to her. And had she not, like Diota, drawn the hood of her cloak closely round her face, during the time that Cadfael himself had been absent, as if to avoid being noticed and recognised by someone?

Now the two women began to move after the rest, but

with cautious slowness, and Sanan's eyes were intent upon the back of the tall man who had almost reached the open doorway. Thus both Sanan and Cadfael at the same moment also saw Brother Jerome, hovering hesitant for a moment, and then making purposefully for the street. And following the converging courses of these two very dissimilar backs, the one erect and confident, the other meagre and stooped, inevitably lighted upon the horse waiting in the Foregate, and the young man holding his bridle.

Brother Jerome was still not quite sure, though he was bent on making sure, even if it meant leaving the precinct without due reason or permission. It would be counted due reason enough if he succeeded in raising a righteous alarm, and handing over a fugitive enemy of the King to the King's justice. A guard outside the gates, the sheriff had said. He had but to halloo the soldiers on to their quarry, who stood within arm's reach, believing himself safe. If, of course, *if* this really was the youngster once known as Benet?

But if Jerome was not yet certain, Sanan was, and Cadfael was. Who, in these parts, had known that figure and stance and carriage as well as they? And there was Jerome bearing down upon him with plainly malevolent intent, before their eyes, and they had no way of preventing the disaster.

Sanan dropped Diota's arm and started forward. Cadfael, approaching from another angle, bellowed: '*Brother*!' peremptorily after Jerome, in a self-righteous and scandalised voice of which Jerome himself need not have been ashamed, in the hope of diverting his attention, but vainly. Jerome nose-down on the trail of a malefactor was almost as undeflectable as Father Ailnoth himself. It was left to someone else to turn the trick.

Ninian's horseman, long-legged and striding briskly away from a field which left him unthreatened and well satisfied, arrived at the doorway only a pace or two ahead of Jerome, indeed he brushed past him into the Foregate. Not the ending he had expected, but on the whole he was glad of it. As long as he was neither suspect of disloyalty nor threatened with loss of lands of status, he bore no grudge now against the rash young man who had caused him so much anxiety. Let him get away unscathed, provided he never came back here to make trouble for others.

Ninian had glanced round to see his patron approaching, and saw at the same time, very belatedly, the ferret countenance of Brother Jerome, all too clearly making for him with no kindly intent. There was no time to evade, he had no choice but to stand his ground. Blessedly the horseman reached him barely ahead of the hunter, and blessedly he was well content with whatever he had witnessed within, for he clapped his horse-boy on the shoulder as the bridle was surrendered into his hand. Ninian made haste to stoop to the stirrup, and hold it for the rider to mount.

It was enough! Jerome stopped so abruptly in the gateway that Erwald, coming behind, collided with him, and put him aside good-naturedly with one large hand as he passed. And by that time the horseman had dropped a careless word of thanks into Ninian's ear and a silver penny into his hand, and set off back along the Foregate at a leisurely trot, to vanish round the corner by the horse-fair ground, with his supposed groom loping behind him on foot.

A lucky escape, thought Ninian, dropping into a walk as soon as he was round the corner of the high wall and out of sight. And he span delightedly in his hand the silver penny a satisfied and lavish patron had tossed to him as he rode away. God bless the man, whoever he may be, he's saved my life, or at least my hide! A man of consequence, and evidently well known here. Just as well for me his grooms are not equally well known, and all over fifty and bearded, or I should have been a lost man.

A lucky escape, thought Cadfael, heaving a great sigh of relief, and turning back to where Hugh still stood in earnest talk with Abbot Radulfus, under the great east window of the Lady Chapel. Salvation comes from strange places and unexpected friends. And a very apt ending, too!

A lucky escape, thought Sanan, shaking with dismay and fear suddenly transmuted into triumphant laughter. And he has no idea what has just happened! Neither of them has! Oh, to see Ninian's face when I tell him!

A lucky escape, thought Jerome, scurrying thankfully back to his proper duties. I should have made a sorry fool of myself if I had challenged him. A mere chance resemblance in figure and bearing, after all, nothing more. What a blessing for me that his master brushed by in time to acknowledge him as his, and warn me of my error.

For of course, Ralph Giffard, of all people, could scarcely be harbouring in his own service the very man he himself had so properly denounced to the law!

Chapter Thirteen

'There is one question,' said the abbot, 'which not only has not been answered, it has not yet been asked.'

He had waited until the table was cleared, and his guest supplied with the final cup of wine. Radulfus never allowed business of any kind to be discussed during a meal. The pleasures of the table were something he used sparingly, but respected.

'What is that?' asked Hugh.

'Has he told all the truth?'

Hugh looked up sharply across the table. 'Cynric? Who can say of any man that he never lies? But general report of Cynric says that he never speaks at all unless he must, and then to the point. It is why he said nothing until Jordan was accused. Words come very hard to Cynric. I doubt if he ever in his life used as many in one day as we heard from him in a handful of moments this morning. I doubt if he would waste breath on lying, when even necessary truth costs him such labour.'

'He was eloquent enough today,' said Radulfus with a wry smile. 'But I should be glad if we had some sure sign to confirm what he told us. He may very well have done no more than turn and walk away, and leave the issue of life and death to God, or whatever force he regards as the arbiter of justice in such a strange case. Or he may have struck the blow himself. Or he may have seen the thing happen, much as he says, but helped the priest into the water while he was stunned. Granted I do not think Cynric would be very ingenious at making up plausible tales to cover the event, yet we cannot *know*. Nor do I think him at all a man of violence, even where he found much to provoke it, but again we cannot *know*. And even if we have the entire truth from him, what should be done about such a man? How proceed with him?'

'For my part,' said Hugh firmly, 'nothing can or will be done. There is no law he has broken. It may be a sin to allow a death to take place, it is not a crime. I hold fast to my own writ. Sinners are in your province, not mine.' He did not add that there was some accounting due from the man who had brought Ailnoth, a stranger scarcely known, to assume the pastoral care of a bereaved flock that had no voice in the choosing of their new shepherd. But he suspected that the thought was in the abbot's mind, and had been ever since the first complaints were brought to his ears. He was not a man to shut his eyes to his own errors, or shirk his own responsibilities.

'This I can tell you,' said Hugh. 'What he said of the woman who followed Ailnoth and was struck down by him is certainly true. Mistress Hammet claimed then that she had fallen on the icy ground. That was a lie. The priest did that to her, she has owned it since to Brother Cadfael, who treated her injuries. And since I have now brought Cadfael into this, I think you would do well, my lord, to send for him. I have had no chance to speak with him since the events of this morning, and it's in my mind that he may have something further to say in this matter. He was missing from the ranks of the brothers in the cemetery when I came, for I looked for him and couldn't find him. He came later, not from the Foregate but from within the court. He would not have absented himself but for good reason. If he has things to tell me, I cannot afford to neglect them.'

'Neither, it seems, can I,' said Radulfus, and reached for the little bell that lay on his desk. The small silver chime brought in his secretary from the ante-room. 'Brother Vitalis, will you find Brother Cadfael, and ask him to come here to us?'

When the door had closed again the abbot sat silent for a while, considering. 'I know now, of course,' he said at last, 'that Father Ailnoth was indeed grossly deceived, and that is some extenuation for him. But the woman – I gather she is no kin to the youth she sheltered, the one we knew as Benet? – she had been an exemplary servant to her master for three years, her only offence was in protecting the young man, an offence which sprang only from affection. There shall be no penalty visited upon her, never by my authority. She shall have quiet living here, since it was I who brought her here. If we get a new priest who has neither mother nor sister to mind his dwelling, then she may serve him as she did Ailnoth, and I hope there may never be reason for her to kneel to him but in the confessional, and none ever for him to strike her. And as for the boy . . .' He looked back with a resigned and tolerant eye, and shook his head a little, smiling. 'I remember we gave him to Cadfael to do the rough work before the winter freeze. I saw him once in the garden, digging the long butt. At least he gave honest value. FitzAlan's squire was not afraid to dig, nor ashamed.' He looked up, head tilted, into Hugh's face. 'You don't, by any chance, know . . .?'

'I have been rather careful not to know,' said Hugh.

'Well . . . I am glad he never fouled his hands with murder. I saw them black enough with soil, from plucking out the weeds too gross to be dug in,' said Radulfus, and smiled distantly, looking out of the window at a pearl-grey, low hanging sky. 'I expect he'll do well enough. Pity of all pities there should be one such young man in arms against another in this land, but at least let the steel be bared only in the open field, not privily in the dark.'

Cadfael laid out on the abbot's desk the remaining relics of Father Ailnoth, the ebony staff, the draggled black skull-cap with its torn binding, and the unravelled woollen remnant of braid that completed the circle.

'Cynric told simple truth, and here are the proofs of it.

Only this morning, when I saw Mistress Hammet's open hand once again, and remembered the grazes I had dressed, did I understand how she got those injuries. Not from a fall – there was no fall. The wound on her head was dealt by this staff, for I found several long hairs of her greying light-brown colour here, caught in the frayed edges of this silver band. You see it's worn wafer-thin, and the edges turned and cracking.'

Radulfus ran a long, lean finger round the crumpled, razor-sharp rim, and nodded grimly. 'Yes, I see. And from this same band she got the grazes to her hands. He swung his staff at her a second time, so Cynric said, and she caught and clung to it, to save her head. . . .'

'. . . and he tugged at it with all his strength, and tore it by main force out of her hands,' said Hugh, 'to his own undoing.'

'They could not have been many paces past the mill,' said Cadfael, 'for Cynric was some way beyond, among the willows. On the side of that first stump that overhangs the pool I found a few broken withies, and this black ravelling of wool braid snagged in the cracked, dead wood of the stump. The priest went stunned or dazed into the water, the cap flew from his head, leaving this scrap held fast in the tree, as the silver band held her torn hairs. The staff was flung from his hand. The winter turf is tufted and rough there, no wonder if he caught his heel, as he reeled backwards when she loosed her hold. He crashed into the stump. The axe that felled it, long ago, left it uneven, the jagged edge took him low at the back of the head. Father, you saw the wound. So did the sheriff.'

'I saw it,' said Radulfus. 'And the woman knew nothing from the time she ran from him?'

'She barely knows how she got home. Certainly she waited out the night in dread, expecting him to finish what he intended against the boy, and return to his house to denounce and cast her out. But he never came.'

'Could he have been saved?' wondered the abbot, grieving

as much for the roused and resentful flock as for the dead shepherd.

'In the dark,' said Cadfael, 'I doubt if any one man could have got him from under that bank, however he laboured at it. Even had there been help within reach, I think he would have drowned before ever they got him out.'

'At the risk of falling into sin,' said Radulfus, with a smile that began sourly and ended in resignation, 'I find that comforting. We have not a murderer among us, at any rate.'

'Talk of falling into sin,' said Cadfael later, when he and Hugh were sitting easy together in the workshop in the herb garden, 'forces me to examine my own conscience. I enjoy some privileges, by reason of being called on to attend sick people outside the enclave, and also by virtue of having a godson to visit. But I ought not to take advantage of that permission for my own ends. Which I have done shamelessly on three or four occasions since Christmas. Indeed, Father Abbot must be well aware that I went out from the precinct this very morning without leave, but he's said no word about it.'

'No doubt he takes it for granted you'll be making proper confession voluntarily, at chapter tomorrow,' said Hugh, straight-faced.

'That I doubt! He'd hardly welcome it. I should have to explain the reason, and I know his mind by now. There are old hawks like Radulfus and myself in here, who can stand the gales, but there are also innocents who will not benefit by too stormy a wind blowing through the dovecote. He's fretted enough about Ailnoth's influence, now he wants it put by and soon forgotten. And I prophesy, Hugh, that the Foregate will soon have a new priest, and one who is known and welcome not only to us who have the bestowing of the benefice, but to those who are likely to reap the results. No better way of burying Ailnoth.'

'In all fairness,' said Hugh thoughtfully, 'it would have been a very delicate matter to reject a priest recommended by the papal legate, even for a man of your abbot's stature. And the fellow was impressive to the eye and the ear, and had scholarship. . . . No wonder Radulfus thought he was bringing you a treasure. God send you a decent, humble, common man next time.'

'Amen! Whether he has Latin or not! And here am I the well-wisher, if not the accomplice, of an enemy of the King, criminal as well as sinner! Did I say I was being obliged to search my conscience? But not too diligently – that always leads to trouble.'

'I wonder,' said Hugh, smiling indulgently into the glow of the brazier, 'if they'll have set out yet?'

'Not until dark, I fancy. Overnight they'll be gone. I hope she has somehow left word for Ralph Giffard,' said Cadfael, considering. 'He's no bad man, only driven, as so many are now, and mainly for his son. She had no complaint of him, except that he had compounded with fortune, and given up his hopes for the Empress. Being more than thirty years short of his age, she finds that incomprehensible. But you and I, Hugh, can comprehend it all too well. Let the young ones go their own gait, and find their own way.'

He sat smiling, thinking of the pair of them, but chiefly of Ninian, lively and bold and impudent, and a stout performer with the spade, even though he had never had one in his hand before, and had to learn the craft quickly. 'I never had such a stout-hearted labourer under me here since Brother John – that must be nearly five years now! The one who stayed in Gwytherin, and married the smith's niece. He'll have made a doughty smith himself by now. Benet reminded me of him, some ways . . . all or nothing, and ready for every venture.'

'Ninian,' said Hugh, correcting him almost absently.

'True, Ninian we must call him now, but I tend to forget. But I haven't told you,' said Cadfael, kindling joyfully to the recollection, 'the very best of the ending. In the middle of so much aggravation and suspicion and death, a joke is no bad thing.'

'I wouldn't say no to that,' agreed Hugh, leaning forward

to mend the fire with a few judiciously placed pieces of charcoal, with the calculated pleasure of one for whom such things are usually done by others. 'But I saw very little sign of one today. Where did you find it?'

'Why, you were kept busy talking with Father Abbot, close by the grave, while the rest were dispersing. You had no chance to observe it. But I was loose, and so was Brother Jerome, with his nose twitching for officious mischief, as usual. Sanan saw it,' said Cadfael, with fond recollection. 'It scared the wits out of her for a moment or two, but then it was all resolved. You know, Hugh, how wide those double doors of ours are, in the wall. . . .'

'I came that way,' said Hugh patiently, a little sleepy with relief from care, the fumes of the brazier, and the early start to a day now subsiding into a dim and misty evening. 'I know!'

'There was a young fellow holding a horse, out there in the Foregate. Who was to notice him until everyone began streaming out by that way? Jerome was running like a sheep-dog about the fringes, hustling them out, he was bound to take a frequent look out there to the streets. He saw a man he thought he recognised, and went closer to view, all panting with fervour and zeal – you know him!'

'Every uncoverer of evil acquires merit,' said Hugh, taking idle pleasure in the mild satire upon Brother Jerome. 'What merit could there be for him there, in a lad holding a horse?'

'Why, one Benet, or Ninian, hunted as recreant to our lord King Stephen, and denounced to our lord sheriff – saving your presence, Hugh, but you know you were just confirmed in office, you mean more now to Brother Jerome than ever before! – by Ralph Giffard, no less. That is what Jerome saw, barring that the malefactor did seem to be wearing clothes never seen on him before.'

'Now you do surprise me,' said Hugh, turning a gleaming and amused face upon his friend. 'And this really was the said Benet or Ninian?'

'It was indeed. I knew him, and so did Sanan when she

looked ahead, where Jerome was looking, and saw him there. The lad himself, Hugh, bold as ever to plunge his head into whatever snare. Come to make sure himself where the blame was flying, and see that none of it fell upon his nurse. God knows what he would have done, if you had not carolled aloud your preference for Jordan. After all, what did he know of all that happened after he came panting into the church, that night? It could have been Jordan, for all he knew. No doubt he believed it was, once you bayed the quarry.'

'I have a fine, bell-mouthed bay,' acknowledged Hugh, grinning. 'And just as well Father Abbot kept me talking and would have me stay and dine with him, or I might have run my nose full into this madcap lad of yours, and just as Jerome plucked him by the hood. So how did all this end? I heard no foray in the Foregate.'

'There was none,' agreed Cadfael complacently. 'Ralph Giffard was there among the crowd, did you never see him? He's tall enough to top most of the Foregate folk. But there, you were held fast in the middle, no time to look about you. He was there. At the end he turned to go, not worst pleased, I fancy, that you had no hold on the lad he'd felt obliged to hand to you earlier. It was good to see, Hugh! He shouldered past Jerome, having legs so much longer, just as our most eager hound had his nose down on a hot scent. And he took the bridle from the lad's hand, and even smiled at him, eye to eye, and the lad held his stirrup for him and steadied him astride, as good a groom as ever you saw. And Jerome baulked like a hound at a loss, and came scuttling back, aghast that he'd as good as howled accusation at Giffard's own groom, waiting honestly for his master. That was when I saw Sanan shudder into such laughter as might almost have broken her apart, but that she's very sturdily made, that lady! And Giffard rode away, back along the Foregate, and the groom that was no groom of his went trotting after him afoot, out of sight and away.'

'And this verily happened?' demanded Hugh.

'Son, I saw it. I shall cherish it. Off they went, and Ralph Giffard threw a silver penny to young Ninian, and Ninian caught it and went on his way round the corner and out of sight, before he stopped for breath. And still does not know, I suppose,' said Cadfael, peering through the doorway into a late afternoon light that still lacked an hour or so to Vespers, 'still does not know to whom he owes his salvation. How I would love to be by, when Sanan tells him to whom he owes his fat pay for less than an hour of holding a horse! I wager that lad will never part with that penny, he'll have it pierced for his neck or for hers. There are not many such keepsakes,' said Cadfael smugly, 'in one lifetime.'

'Are you telling me,' said Hugh, delighted, 'that those two met so and parted so, in mutual service, and had no notion with whom they dealt?'

'No notion in the world! They had exchanged messages, they were allies, adversaries, friends, enemies, what you please, in the most intimate degree,' said Cadfael, with deep and grateful contentment, 'but neither of them had the least idea what the other one looked like. They had never once set eyes on each other.'

THE ROSE RENT

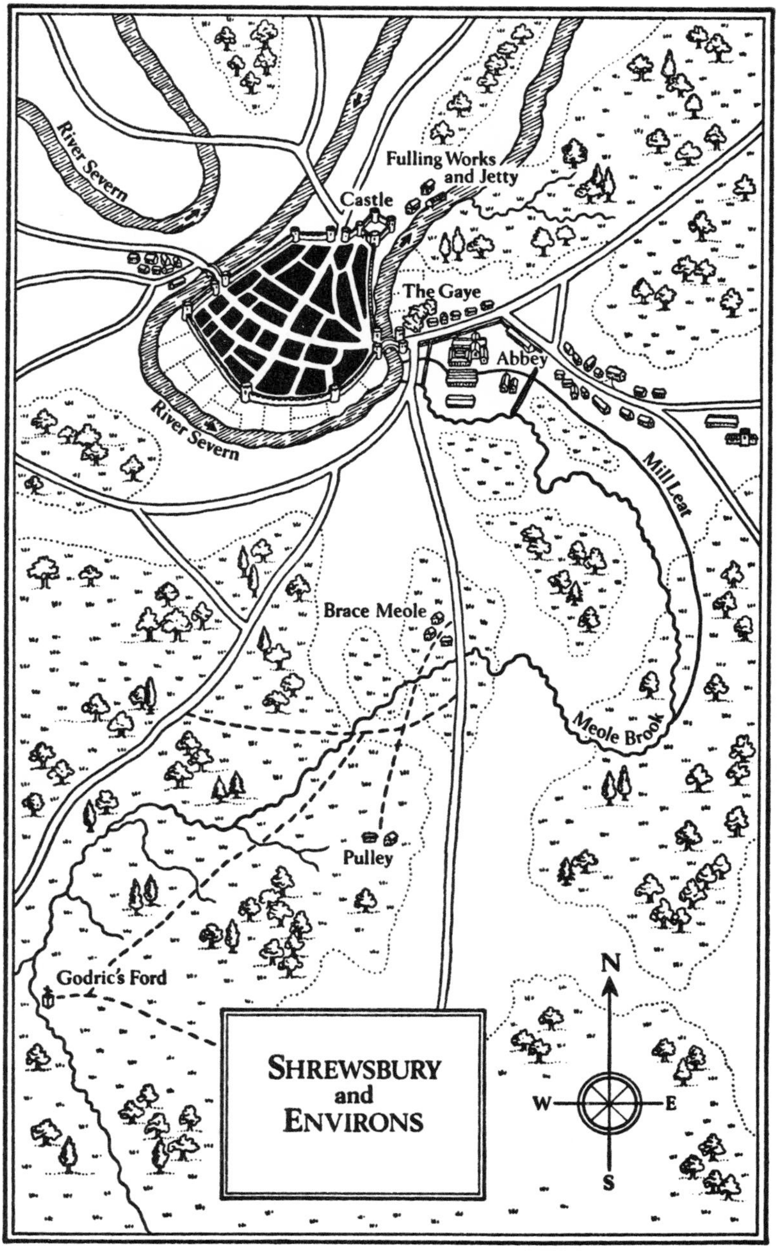
River Severn
Fulling Works
and Jetty
Castle
The Gaye
Abbey
River Severn
Mill Leat
Brace Meole
Meole Brook
Pulley
Godric's Ford
SHREWSBURY
and
ENVIRONS
N
W
E
S

Chapter One

By reason of the prolonged cold, which lingered far into April, and had scarcely mellowed when the month of May began, everything came laggard and reluctant that spring of 1142. The birds kept close about the roofs, finding warmer places to roost. The bees slept late, depleted their stores, and had to be fed, but neither was there any early burst of blossom for them to make fruitful. In the gardens there was no point in planting seed that would rot or be eaten in soil too chilly to engender life.

The affairs of men, stricken with the same petrifying chill, seemed to have subsided into hibernation. Faction held its breath. King Stephen, after the first exhilaration of liberation from his prison, and the Easter journey north to draw together the frayed strings of his influence, had fallen ill in the south, so ill that the rumour of his death had spread throughout England, and his cousin and rival, the Empress Maud, had cautiously moved her headquarters to Oxford, and settled down there to wait patiently and vainly for him to make truth of rumour, which he stubbornly declined to do. He had still business to settle with the lady, and his constitution was more than a match for even this virulent fever. By the end of May he was on his way manfully back to health. By the early days of June the long sub-frost broke. The biting wind changed to a temperate breeze, the sun came out over the earth like a warm hand stroking, the seed stirred in the ground and put forth green blades, and a foam of flowers, all the more exuberant for having been so long restrained, burst forth in gold and purple and white over garden and meadow. The belated sowing began in jubilant haste. And King Stephen, like a giant breaking loose from some crippling enchantment, surged out of his convalescence into vigorous action, and bearing down on the port of Wareham, the most easterly still available to his enemies, seized both town and castle with hardly a graze to show for it.

'And is making north again now towards Cirencester,' reported Hugh Beringar, elated by the news, 'to pick off the empress's outposts one by one, if only he can keep up this storm of energy.' It was the one fatal flaw in the king's military make-up that he could not sustain action for long if he failed to get instant results, but would abandon a siege after three days, and go off to start another elsewhere, squandering for no gain the energy devoted to both. 'We may see a tidy end to it yet!'

Brother Cadfael, preoccupied with his own narrower concerns, continued to survey the vegetable patch outside the wall of his herb-garden, digging an experimental toe into soil grown darker and kinder after a mild morning shower. 'By rights,' he said thoughtfully, 'carrots should have been in more than a month ago, and the first radishes will be fibrous and shrunken as old leather, but we might get something with more juices in it from now on. Lucky the fruit-blossom held back until the bees began to wake up, but even so it will be a thin crop this year. Everything's four weeks behind, but the seasons have a way of catching up, somehow. Wareham, you were saying? What of Wareham?'

'Why, that Stephen has taken it, town and castle and harbour and all. So Robert of Gloucester, who went out by that gate barely ten days earlier, has it slammed in his face now. Did I not tell you? The word came three days since. It seems there was a meeting back in April, in Devizes, between the empress and her brother, and they made it up between them that it was high time the lady's husband should pay a little heed to her affairs, and come over in person to help her get her hands on Stephen's crown. They sent envoys over to Normandy to meet with Geoffrey, but he sent back to say he was well disposed, no question, but the men sent out to him were unknown to him, name or reputation, and he would be uneasy in dealing with any but the Earl of Gloucester himself. If Robert will not come, says Geoffrey, no use sending me any other.'

Cadfael was momentarily distracted from his laggard crops. 'And Robert let himself be persuaded?' he said, marvelling.

'Very reluctantly. He feared to leave his sister to the loyalties of some who were all but ready to desert her after the Westminster shambles, and I doubt if he has any great hopes of getting anything out of the Count of Anjou. But yes, he let himself be persuaded. And he's sailed from Wareham, with less trouble than he'll have sailing back into the same port, now the king holds it. A good, fast move, that was. If he can but maintain it now!'

'We said a Mass in thanksgiving for his recovery,' said Cadfael absently, and plucked out a leggy sow-thistle from among his mint. 'How is it that weeds grow three times faster than the plants we nurse so tenderly? Three days ago that was not even there. If the kale shot up like that I should be pricking the plants out by tomorrow.'

'No doubt your prayers will stiffen Stephen's resolution,' Hugh said, though with less than complete conviction. 'Have they not given you a helper yet, here in the garden? It's high time, there's more than one's work here in this season.'

'So I urged at chapter this morning. What they'll offer me there's no knowing. Prior Robert has one or two among the younger ones he'd be glad to shuffle off his hands and into mine. Happily the ones he least approves tend to be those with more wit and spirit than the rest, not less. I may yet be lucky in my apprentice.'

He straightened his back, and stood looking out over the newly turned beds, and the pease-fields that sloped down to the Meole Brook, mentally casting an indulgent eye back over the most recent of his helpers here in the herbarium. Big, jaunty, comely Brother John, who had blundered into the cloister by mistake, and backed out of it, not without the connivance of friends, in Wales, to exchange the role of brother for that of husband and father; Brother Mark, entering here as an undersized and maltreated sixteen-year-old, shy and quiet, and grown into a clear, serene maturity of spirit that drew him away inevitably towards the priesthood. Cadfael still missed Brother Mark, attached now to the household chapel of the Bishop of Lichfield, and already a deacon. And after Mark, Brother Oswin, cheerful, confident and ham-fisted, gone now to do his year's service at the lazarhouse of Saint Giles at the edge of the town. What next, wondered Cadfael? Put a dozen young men into the same rusty black habits, shave their heads, fit them into a single horarium day after day and year after year, and still they will all be irremediably different, every one unique. Thank God!

'Whatever they send you,' said Hugh, keeping pace with him along the broad green path that circled the fish-ponds, 'you'll have transformed by the time he leaves you. Why should they waste a simple, sweet saint like Rhun on you? He's made already, he came into the world made. You'll get the rough, the obdurate, the unstable to lick into shape. Not that it ever comes out the shape that was expected,' he added, with a flashing grin and a slanted glance along his shoulder at his friend.

'Rhun has taken upon himself the custody of Saint Winifred's altar,' said Cadfael. 'He has a proprietorial interest in the little lady. He makes the candles for her himself, and borrows essences from me to scent them for her. No, Rhun will find his own duties, and no one will stand in his way. He and she between them will see to that.'

They crossed the little foot-bridge over the leat that fed the pools and the mill, and emerged into the rose-garden. The trimmed bushes had made little growth as yet, but the first buds were swelling at last, the green sheaths parting to show a sliver of red or white. 'They'll open fast now,' said Cadfael contentedly. 'All they needed was warmth. I'd begun to wonder whether the Widow Perle would get her rent on time this year, but if these are making up for lost time, so will her white ones be. A sad year, if there were no roses by the twenty-second day of June!'

'The Widow Perle? Oh, yes, the Vestier girl!' said Hugh. 'I remember! So it's due on the day of Saint Winifred's translation, is it? How many years is it now since she made the gift?'

'This will be the fourth time we've paid her her annual rent. One white rose from that bush in her old garden, to be delivered to her on the day of Saint Winifred's translation—'

'Supposed translation,' said Hugh, grinning. 'And you

should blush when you name it.'

'So I do, but with my complexion who notices?' And he was indeed of a rosy russet colouring, confirmed by long years of outdoor living in both east and west, so engrained now that winters merely tarnished it a little, and summers regularly renewed the gloss.

'She made modest demands,' observed Hugh thoughtfully, as they came to the second plank-bridge that spanned the channel drawn off to service the guest-hall. 'Most of our solid merchants up in the town value property a good deal higher than roses.'

'She had already lost what she most valued,' said Cadfael. 'Husband and child both, within twenty days. He died, and she miscarried. She could not bear to go on living, alone, in the house where they had been happy together. But it was because she valued it that she wanted it spent for God, not hoarded up with the rest of a property large enough to provide handsomely even without it for herself and all her kinsfolk and workfolk. It pays for the lighting and draping of Our Lady's altar the whole year round. It's what she chose. But just the one link she kept – one rose a year. He was a very comely man, Edred Perle,' said Cadfael, shaking his head mildly over the vulnerability of beauty, 'I saw him pared away to the bone in a searing fever, and had no art to cool him. A man remembers that.'

'You've seen many such,' said Hugh reasonably, 'here and on the fields of Syria, long ago.'

'So I have! So I have! Did ever you hear me say I'd forgotten any one of them? But a young, handsome man, shrivelled away before his time, before even his prime, and his girl left without even his child to keep him in mind . . . A sad enough case, you'll allow.'

'She's young,' said Hugh with indifferent practicality, his mind being on other things. 'She should marry again.'

'So think a good many of our merchant fathers in the town,' agreed Cadfael with a wry smile, 'the lady being as wealthy as she is, and sole mistress of the Vestiers' clothier business. But after what she lost, I doubt if she'll look at a grey old skinflint like Godfrey Fuller, who's buried two wives already and made a profit out of both of them, and has his eye on a third fortune with the next. Or a fancy young fellow in search of an easy living!'

'Such as?' invited Hugh, amused.

'Two or three I could name. William Hynde's youngster, for one, if my gossips tell me truth. And the lad who's foreman of her own weavers is a very well-looking young man, and fancies his chance with her. Even her neighbour the saddler is looking for a wife, I'm told, and thinks she might very well do.'

Hugh burst into affectionate laughter, and clapped him boisterously on the shoulders as they emerged into the great court, and the quiet, purposeful bustle before Mass. 'How many eyes and ears have you in every street in Shrewsbury? I wish my own intelligencers knew half as much of what goes on. A pity your influence falls short of Normandy. I might get some inkling then of what Robert and Geoffrey are up to there. Though I think,' he said, growing grave again as he turned back to his own preoccupations, 'Geoffrey is far more concerned with getting possession of Normandy than with wasting his time on England. From all accounts he's making fast inroads there, he's not likely to draw off now. Far more like to inveigle Robert into helping him than offering much help to Robert.

'He certainly shows very little interest in his wife,' agreed Cadfael drily, 'or her ambitions. Well, we shall see if Robert can sway him. Are you coming in to Mass this morning?'

'No, I'm away to Maesbury tomorrow for a week or two. They should have been shearing before this, but they put it off for a while because of the cold. They'll be hard at it now. I'll leave Aline and Giles there for the summer. But I'll be back and forth, in case of need.'

'A summer without Aline, and without my godson,' said Cadfael reprovingly, 'is no prospect to spring on me without preamble, like this. Are you not ashamed?'

'Not a whit! For I came, among other errands, to bid you to supper with us tonight, before we leave early in the morning. Abbot Radulfus has given his leave and blessing. Go, pray for fair weather and a smooth ride for us,' said Hugh heartily, and gave his friend a vigorous shove towards the corner of the cloister and the south door of the church.

* * *

It was purely by chance, or a symbol of that strange compulsion that brings the substance hard on the heels of the recollection, that the sparse company of worshippers in the parish part of the church at the monastic Mass that day should include the Widow Perle. There were always a few of the laity there on their knees beyond the parish altar, some who had missed their parish Mass for varying reasons, some who were old and solitary and filled up their lonely time with supererogatory worship, some who had special pleas to make, and sought an extra opportunity of approaching grace. Some, even, who had other business in the Foregate, and welcomed a haven meantime for thought and quietness, which was the case of the Widow Perle.

From his stall in the choir Brother Cadfael could just see the suave line of her head, shoulder and arm, beyond the bulk of the parish altar. It was strange that so quiet and unobtrusive a woman should nevertheless be so instantly recognisable even in this fragmentary glimpse. It might have been the way she carried her straight and slender shoulders, or the great mass of her brown hair weighing down the head so reverently inclined over clasped hands, hidden from his sight by the altar. She was barely twenty-five years old, and had enjoyed only three years of a happy marriage, but she went about her deprived and solitary life without fuss or complaint, cared scrupulously for a business which gave her no personal pleasure, and faced the prospect of perpetual loneliness with a calm countenance and a surprising supply of practical energy. In happiness or unhappiness, living is a duty, and must be done thoroughly.

A blessing, at any rate, thought Cadfael, that she is not utterly alone, she has her mother's sister to keep the house for her now she lives, as it were, over her shop, and her cousin for a conscientious foreman and manager, to take the weight of the business off her shoulders. And one rose every year for the rent of the house and garden in the Foregate, where her man died. The only gesture of passion and grief and loss she ever made, to give away voluntarily her most valuable property, the house where she had been happy, and yet ask for that one reminder, and nothing more.

She was not a beautiful woman, Judith Perle, born Judith Vestier, and sole heiress to the biggest clothiers' business in the town. But she had a bodily dignity that would draw the eye even in a market crowd, above the common height for a woman, slender and erect, and with a carriage and walk of notable grace. The great coils of her shining light-brown hair, the colour of seasoned oak timber, crowned a pale face that tapered from wide and lofty brow to pointed chin, by way of strong cheekbones and hollow cheeks, and an eloquent, mobile mouth too wide for beauty, but elegantly shaped. Her eyes were of a deep grey, and very clear and wide, neither confiding nor hiding anything. Cadfael had been eye to eye with her, four years ago now, across her husband's death-bed, and she had neither lowered her lids nor turned her glance aside, but stared unwaveringly as her life's happiness slipped irresistibly away through her fingers. Two weeks later she had miscarried, and lost even her child. Edred had left her nothing.

Hugh is right, thought Cadfael, forcing his mind back to the liturgy. She is young, she should marry again.

The June light, now approaching the middle hours of the day, and radiant with sunshine, fell in long golden shafts across the body of the choir and into the ranks of the brothers and obedientiaries opposite, gilding half a face here and throwing its other half into exaggerated shade, there causing dazzled eyes in a blanched face to blink away the brightness. The vault above received the diffused reflections in a soft, muted glow, plucking into relief the curved leaves of the stone bosses. Music and light seemed to mate only there in the zenith. Summer trod hesitantly into the church at last, after prolonged hibernation.

It seemed that brother Cadfael was not the only one whose mind was wandering when it should have been fixed. Brother Anselm the precentor, absorbed into his singing, lifted a rapt face into the sun, his eyes closed, since he knew every note without study or thought. But beside him Brother Eluric, custodian of Saint Mary's altar in the Lady Chapel, responded only absently, his head turned aside, towards the parish altar and the soft murmur of responses from beyond.

Brother Eluric was a child of the cloister, not long a full brother, and entrusted with his particular charge by reason of his undoubted deserving, tempered by the reserve that was felt about admitting child oblates to full office, at least until they had been mature for a number of years. An unreasonable reserve, Cadfael had always felt, seeing that the child oblates were regarded as the perfect innocents, equivalent to the angels, while the *conversi*, those who came voluntarily and in maturity to the monastic life, were the fighting saints, those who had endured and mastered their imperfections. So Saint Anselm had classified them, and ordered them never to attempt reciprocal reproaches, never to feel envy. But still the *conversi* were preferred for the responsible offices, perhaps as having experience of the deceits and complexities and temptations of the world around them. But the care of an altar, its light, its draperies, the special prayers belonging to it, this could well be the charge of an innocent.

Brother Eluric was past twenty now, the most learned and devout of his contemporaries, a tall, well-made young man, black-haired and black-eyed. He had been in the cloister since he was three years old, and knew nothing outside it. Unacquainted with sin, he was all the more haunted by it, as by some unknown monster, and assiduous in confession, he picked to pieces his own infinitesimal failings, with the mortal penitence due to deadly sins. A curious thing, that so over-conscientious a youth should be paying so little heed to the holy office. His chin was on his shoulder, his lips still, forgetting the words of the psalm. He was gazing, in fact, precisely where Cadfael had been gazing only moments earlier. But from Eluric's stall there would be more of her to see, Cadfael reflected, the averted face, the linked hands, the folds of linen over her breast.

The contemplation, it seemed, gave him no joy, but only a brittle, quivering tension, taut as a drawn bow. When he recollected himself and tore his gaze away, it was with a wrench that shook him from head to foot.

Well, well! said Cadfael to himself, enlightened. And in eight days more he has to carry the rose rent to her. That task they should have allotted to some old hardened sinner like me, who would view and enjoy, and return untroubled and untroubling, not this vulnerable boy who surely can never else have been alone in a room with a woman since his mother let him be taken out of her arms. And a pity she ever did!

And this poor girl, the very image to wring him most painfully, grave, sad, with a piteous past and yet composed and calm like the Blessed Virgin herself. And he coming to her bearing a white rose, their hands perhaps touching as he delivers it. And now I recall that Anselm says he's something of a poet. Well, what follies we commit without evil intent!

It was far too late now to devote his mind to its proper business of prayer and praise. He contented himself with hoping that by the time the brothers emerged from the choir after service the lady would be gone.

By the mercy of God, she was.

But she was gone, it seemed, no further than Cadfael's workshop in the herb-garden, where he found her waiting patiently outside the open door when he came to decant the lotion he had left cooling before Mass. Her brow was smooth and her voice mild, and everything about her practical and sensible. The fire that burned Eluric was unknown to her. At Cadfael's invitation she followed him in, under the gently swaying bunches of herbs that rustled overhead from the beams.

'You once made me an ointment, Brother Cadfael, if you remember. For a rash on the hands. There's one of my carders breaks out in little pustules, handling the new fleeces. But not every season – that's strange too. This year she has trouble with it again.'

'I remember it,' said Cadfael. 'It was three years ago. Yes, I know the receipt. I can make some fresh for you in a matter of minutes, if you've leisure to wait?'

It seemed that she had. She sat down on the wooden bench against the timber wall, and drew her dark skirts close about her feet, very erect and still in the corner of the hut, as Cadfael reached for pestle and mortar, and the little scale with its brass weights.

'And how are you faring now?' he asked, busy with hog's fat and herbal oils. 'Up there in the town?'

'Well enough,' she said composedly. 'The business gives

me plenty to do, and the wool clip has turned out better than I feared. I can't complain. Isn't it strange,' she went on, warming, 'that wool should bring up this rash for Branwen, when you use the fat from wool to doctor skin diseases for many people?'

'Such contrary cases do happen,' he said. 'There are plants some people cannot handle without coming to grief. No one knows the reason. We learn by observing. You had good results with this salve, I remember.'

'Oh, yes, her hands healed very quickly. But I think perhaps I should keep her from carding, and teach her weaving. When the wool is washed and dyed and spun, perhaps she could handle it more safely. She's a good girl, she would soon learn.'

It seemed to Cadfael, working away with his back turned to her, that she was talking to fill the silence while she thought, and thought of something far removed from what she was saying. It was no great surprise when she said suddenly, and in a very different voice, abrupt and resolute: 'Brother Cadfael, I have thoughts of taking the veil. Serious thoughts! The world is not so desirable that I should hesitate to leave it, nor my condition so hopeful that I dare look for a better time to come. The business can do very well without me; Cousin Miles runs it very profitably, and values it more than I do. Oh, I do my duty well enough, as I was always taught to do, but he could do it every bit as well without me. Why should I hesitate?'

Cadfael turned to face her, the mortar balanced on his palm. 'Have you said as much to your aunt and your cousin?'

'I have mentioned it.'

'And what do they say to it?'

'Nothing. It's left to me. Miles will neither commend nor advise, he brushes it aside. I think he doesn't take me seriously. My aunt – you know her a little? She's widowed like me, and for ever lamenting it, even after years. She talks of the peace of the cloister, and release from the cares of the world. But she always talks so, though I know she's well content with her comfortable life if the truth were told. I live, Brother Cadfael, I do my work, but I am not content. It would be something settled and stable, to take to the cloister.'

'And wrong,' said Cadfael firmly. 'Wrong, at least, for you.'

'Why would it be so wrong?' she challenged. The hood had slipped back from her head, the great braid of light-brown hair, silver-lit like veined oak, glowed faintly in the subdued light.

'No one should take to the cloistered life as a second-best, and that is what you would be doing. It must be embraced out of genuine desire, or not at all. It is not enough to wish to escape from the world without, you must be on fire for the world within.'

'Was it so with you?' she asked, and suddenly she smiled, and her austere face kindled into warmth for a moment.

He considered that in silence for a brief, cautious while. 'I came late to it, and it may be that my fire burned somewhat dully,' he said honestly at length, 'but it gave light enough to show me the road to what I wanted. I was running towards, not away.'

She looked him full in the face with her daunting, direct eyes, and said with abrupt, bleak deliberation: 'Have you never thought, Brother Cadfael, that a woman may have more cause to run away than ever you had? More perils to run from, and fewer alternatives than flight?'

'That is truth,' admitted Cadfael, stirring vigorously. 'But you, as I know, are better placed than many to hold your own, as well as having more courage than a good many of us men. You are your own mistress, your kin depend on you, and not you on them. There is no overlord to claim the right to order your future, no one can force you into another marriage – yes, I have heard there are many would be only too pleased if they could, but they have no power over you. No father living, no elder kinsman to influence you. No matter how men may pester you or affairs weary you, you know you are more than equal to them. And as for what you have lost,' he said, after a moment's hesitation as to whether he should tread so near, 'it is lost only to this world. Waiting is not easy, but no harder, believe me, among the vexations and distractions of the world than in the solitude and silence of the cloister. I have seen men make that mistake, for as reasonable cause, and suffer all the more with the double deprivation. Do not you take that risk. Never unless you are sure of what you want, and want it with all your heart and soul.'

It was as much as he dared say, as much as and perhaps more than he had any right to say. She heard him out without turning her eyes away. He felt their clear stare heavy upon him all the time he was smoothing his ointment into its jar for her, and tying down the lid of the pot for safe carriage.

'Sister Magdalen, from the Benedictine cell at Godric's Ford,' he said, 'is coming to Shrewsbury in two days' time, to fetch away Brother Edmund's niece, who wants to join the sisterhood there. As for the girl's motives, I know nothing of them, but if Sister Magdalen is accepting her as a novice it must be from conviction, and moreover, the child will be carefully watched, and get no further than her novitiate unless Magdalen is satisfied of her vocation. Will you speak with her about this? I think you already know something of her.'

'I do.' Judith's voice was soft, and yet there was a shade of quiet amusement in the tone. 'Her own motives, I think, when she entered Godric's Ford, were scarcely what you are demanding.'

That was something he could not well deny. Sister Magdalen had formerly been, for many years, the constant mistress of a certain nobleman, and on his death had looked about her with single-minded resolution for another field in which to employ her undoubted talents. No question but the choice of the cloister had been coolly and practically made. What redeemed it was the vigour and loyalty she had devoted to it since the day of her entry, and would maintain, without question, until the day of her death.

'In no way that I know of,' admitted Cadfael, 'is Sister Magdalen anything but unique. You are right, she entered the cell seeking not a vocation, but a career, and a career she is making, and a notable one, too. Mother Mariana is old and bedridden now; the weight of the cell falls all on Magdalen, and I know no shoulders better fitted to carry it. And I do not think she would say to you, as I said, that there is but one good reason for taking the veil, true longing for the life of the spirit. The more reason you could and should listen to her advice and weigh it carefully, before you take so grave a step. And bear in mind, you are young, she had said goodbye to her prime.'

'And I have buried mine,' said Judith very firmly, and as one stating truth, without self-pity.

'Well, if it comes to second-bests,' said Cadfael, 'they can be found outside the cloister as well as within. Managing the business your fathers built up, providing employment for so many people, is itself a sufficient justification for a life, for want of better.'

'It does not put me to any great test,' she said indifferently. 'Ah, well, I said only that I had been thinking of quitting the world. Nothing is done, as yet. And whether or no, I shall be glad to talk with Sister Magdalen, for I do value her wit, and know better than to discard unconsidered whatever she may say. Let me know when she comes, and I will send and bid her to my house, or go to her wherever she is lodged.'

She rose to take the jar of ointment from him. Standing, she was the breadth of two fingers taller than he, but thin and slender-boned. The coils of her hair would have seemed over-heavy if she had not carried her head so nobly.

'Your roses are budding well,' she said, as he went out with her along the gravel path from the workshop. 'However late they come, they always bloom equally in the end.'

It could have been a metaphor for the quality of a life, he thought, as they had been discussing it. But he did not say so. Better leave her to the shrewd and penetrating wisdom of Sister Magdalen. 'And yours?' he said. 'There'll be a choice of blooms when Saint Winifred's feast comes round. You should have the best and freshest for your fee.'

The most fleeting of smiles crossed her face, and left her sombre again, her eyes on the path. 'Yes,' she said, and nothing more, though it seemed there should have been more. Was it possible that she had noted and been troubled by the same trouble that haunted Eluric? Three times he had carried the rose rent to her, a matter of . . . how long . . . in her presence? Two minutes annually? Three, perhaps? But no man's shadow clouded Judith Perle's eyes, no living man's. She might, none the less, have become somehow aware, thought Cadfael, not of a young man's physical entrance into her house and presence, but of the nearness of pain.

'I'm going there now,' she said, stirring out of her preoccupation. 'I've lost the buckle of a good girdle, I should like to have a new one made, to match the rosettes that decorate the leather, and the end-tag. Enamel inlay on the bronze. It was a present Edred once made to me. Niall Bronzesmith will be able to copy the design. He's a fine craftsman. I'm glad the abbey has such a good tenant for the house.'

'A decent, quiet man,' agreed Cadfael, 'and keeps the garden well tended. You'll find your rose-bush in very good heart.'

To that she made no reply, only thanked him simply for his services as they entered the great court together, and there separated, she to continue along the Foregate to the large house beyond the abbey forge, where she had spent the few years of her married life, he to the lavatorium to wash his hands before dinner. But he turned at the corner of the cloister to look after her, and watched until she passed through the arch of the gatehouse and vanished from his sight. She had a walk that might be very becoming in an abbess, but to his mind it looked just as well on the capable heiress of the chief clothier in the town. He went on to the refectory convinced that he was right in dissuading her from the conventual life. If she looked upon it as a refuge now, the time might come when it would seem to her a prison, and none the less constricting because she would have entered it willingly.

Chapter Two

The house in the Foregate stood well along towards the grassy triangle of the horse-fair ground, where the high road turned the corner of the abbey wall. A lower wall on the opposite side of the road closed in the yard where Niall the bronzesmith had his shop and workshop, and beyond lay the substantial and well-built house with its large garden, and a small field of grazing land behind. Niall did a good trade in everything from brooches and buttons, small weights and pins, to metal cooking pots, ewers and dishes, and paid the abbey a suitable rent for his premises. He had even worked occasionally with others of his trade in the founding of bells, but that was a very rare commission, and demanded travel to the site itself, rather than having to transport the heavy bells after casting.

The smith was working in a corner of his shop, on the rim of a dish beaten out in sheet metal, pecking away with punch and mallet at an incised decoration of leaves, when Judith came in to his counter. From the unshuttered window above the work-bench the light fell softly sidewise upon her face and figure, and Niall, turning to see who had entered, stood for a moment at gaze with his tools dangling in either hand, before he laid them down and came to wait upon her.

'Your servant, mistress! What can I do for you?'

They were barely acquaintances, merely shopkeeper-craftsman and customer, and yet the very fact that he now did his work in the house which she had given to the abbey made them study each other with a special intensity. She had been in his shop perhaps five times in the few years since he had rented it; he had supplied her with pins, points for the laces of bodices, small utensils for her kitchen, the matrix for the seal of the Vestier household. He knew her history, the gift of the house had made it public. She knew little of him beyond the fact that he had come to her erstwhile property as the abbey's tenant, and that the man and his work were well regarded in town and Foregate.

Judith laid her damaged girdle upon the long counter, a strip of fine, soft leather, excellently worked and ornamented with a series of small bronze rosettes round the holes for the tongue, and a bronze sheath protecting the end of the belt. The bright enamel inlays within the raised outlines were clear and fresh, but the stitching at the other end had worn through, and the buckle was gone.

'I lost it somewhere in the town,' she said, 'one night after dark, and never noticed under my cloak that girdle and all had slipped down and were gone. When I went back to look for it I could find only the belt, not the buckle. It was muddy weather, and the kennel running with the thaw. My own fault, I knew it was fraying, I should have made it secure.'

'Delicate work,' said the smith, fingering the end-tag with interest. 'That was not bought here, surely?'

'Yes, it was, but at the abbey fair, from a Flemish merchant. I wore it much,' she said, 'in earlier days, but it's been laid by since the winter, when I lost the buckle. Can you make me a new one, to match these colours and designs? It was a long shape – thus!' She drew it on the counter with a fingertip. 'But it need not be so, you could make it oval, or whatever you think suits best.'

Their heads were close together over the counter. She looked up into his face, mildly startled by its nearness, but he was intent upon the detail of the bronzework and inlay, and unaware of her sharp scrutiny. A decent, quiet man, Cadfael had called him, and coming from Cadfael there was nothing dismissive in that description. Decent, quiet men were the backbone of any community, to be respected and valued beyond those who made the biggest commotion and the most noise in the world. Niall the bronzesmith could have provided the portrait for them all. He was of the middle height and the middle years, and even of the middle brown colouring, and his voice was pitched pleasantly low. His age, she thought, might be forty years. When he straightened up they stood virtually eye to eye, and the movements of his large, capable hands were smooth, firm and deft.

Everything about him fitted into the picture of the ordinary, worthy soul almost indistinguishable from his neighbour, and yet the sum of the parts was very simply and positively himself and no other man. He had thick brown brows in a wide-boned face, and wide-set eyes of a deep, sunny hazel. There were a few grizzled hairs in his thick brown thatch, and a solid, peaceful jut to his shaven chin.

'Are you in haste for it?' he asked. 'I should like to make a good job of it. If I may take two or three days over it.'

'There's no hurry,' she said readily. 'I've neglected it long enough, another week is no great matter.'

'Then shall I bring it up to you in the town? I know the place, I could save you the walk.' He made the offer civilly but hesitantly, as though it might be taken as presumption rather than simply meant as a courtesy.

She cast a rapid glance about his shop, and saw evidences enough that he had in hand a great deal of work, more than enough to keep him busy all through the labouring day. 'But I think your time is very well filled. If you have a boy, perhaps – but I can as well come for it.'

'I work alone,' said Niall. 'But I'd willingly bring it up to you in the evening, when the light's going. I've no other calls on my time, it's no hardship to work the clock round.'

'You live alone here?' she asked, confirmed in her assumptions about him. 'No wife? No family?'

'I lost my wife, five years ago. I'm used to being alone, it's a simple enough matter to take care of my few needs. But I have a little girl. Her mother died bearing her.' He saw the sudden tension in her face, the faint spark in her eyes as she reared her head and glanced round, half expecting to see some evidence of a child's presence. 'Oh, not here! I should have been hard put to it to care for a newborn babe, and there's my sister, out at Pulley, no great distance, married to Mortimer's steward at the demesne there, and with two boys and a girl of her own, not very much older. My little lass stays there with them, where she has other children for playmates, and a woman's care. I walk over to see her every Sunday, and sometimes in the evenings, too, but she's better with Cecily and John and the youngsters than here solitary with me, leastways while she's still so young.'

Judith drew breath long and deeply. Widower he might be, and his loss there as bitter as hers, but he had one priceless pledge left to him, while she was barren. 'You don't know,' she said abruptly, 'how I envy you. My child I lost.' She had not meant to say so much, but it came out of her naturally and bluntly, and naturally and bluntly he received it.

'I heard of your trouble, mistress. I was mortally sorry then, having known the like myself not so long before. But the little one at least was spared to me. I thank God for that. When a man suffers such a wound, he also finds out how to value such a mercy.'

'Yes,' she said, and turned away sharply. 'Well . . . I trust your daughter thrives,' she said, recovering, 'and will always be a joy to you. I'll come for the girdle in three days' time, if that's enough for you. No need to bring it.'

She was in the doorway of the shop before he could speak, and then there seemed nothing of any significance to say. But he watched her cross the yard and turn into the Foregate, and turned back to his work at the bench only when she had vanished from his sight.

It was late in the afternoon, but still an hour short of Vespers at this season of the year, when Brother Eluric, custodian of Saint Mary's altar, slipped almost furtively away from his work in the scriptorium, crossed the great court to the abbot's lodging in its small fenced garden, and asked for audience. His manner was so taut and brittle that Brother Vitalis, chaplain and secretary to Abbot Radulfus, raised questioning eyebrows, and hesitated before announcing him. But Radulfus was absolute that every son of the house in trouble or need of advice must have ready access to him. Vitalis shrugged, and went in to ask leave, which was readily given.

In the panelled parlour the bright sunlight softened into a mellow haze. Eluric halted just within the doorway, and heard the door gently closed at his back. Radulfus was sitting at his desk near the open window, quill in hand, and did not look up for a moment from his writing. Against the light his aquiline profile showed dark and calm, an outline of gold shaping lofty brow and lean cheek. Eluric went in great awe of him, and yet was drawn gratefully to that composure and certainty, so far out of his own scope.

Radulfus put a period to his well-shaped sentence, and laid down his quill in the bronze tray before him. 'Yes, my son? I am here. I am listening.' He looked up. 'If you have need of me, ask freely.'

'Father,' said Eluric, from a throat constricted and dry, and in a voice so low it was barely audible across the room, 'I have a great trouble. I hardly know how to tell it, or how far it must be seen as shame and guilt to me, though God knows I have struggled with it, and been constant in prayer to keep myself from evil. I am both petitioner and penitent, and yet I have not sinned, and by your grace and understanding may still be saved from offence.'

Radulfus eyed him more sharply, and saw the tension that stiffened the young man's body, and set him quivering like a drawn bowstring. An over-intense boy, always racked by remorse for faults as often as not imaginary, or so venial that to inflate them into sins was itself an offence, being a distortion of truth.

'Child,' said the abbot tolerantly, 'from all I know of you, you are too forward to take to your charge as great sins such small matters as a wise man would think unworthy of mention. Beware of inverted pride! Moderation in all things is not the most spectacular path to perfection, but it is the safest and the most modest. Now speak up plainly, and let's see what between us we can do to end your trouble.' And he added briskly: 'Come closer! Let me see you clearly, and hear you make good sense.'

Eluric crept closer, linked his hands before him in a nervous convulsion that whitened the knuckles perceptibly, and moistened his dry lips. 'Father, in eight days' time it will be the day of Saint Winifred's translation, and the rose rent must be paid for the property in the Foregate . . . to Mistress Perle, who gave the house by charter on those terms . . .'

'Yes,' said Radulfus, 'I know it. Well?'

'Father, I came to beg you to release me from this duty. Three times I have carried the rose to her, according to the charter, and with every year it grows harder for me. Do not send me there again! Lift this burden from me, before I founder! It is more than I can bear.' He was shaking violently, and had difficulty in continuing to speak, so that the words came in painful bursts, like gouts of blood from a wound. 'Father, the very sight and sound of her are torment to me, to be in the same room with her is the pain of death. I have prayed, I have kept vigil, I have implored God and the saints for deliverance from sin, but not all my prayers and austerities could keep me from this uninvited love.'

Radulfus sat silent for a while after the last word had been said, and his face had not changed, beyond a certain sharpening of his attention, a steady gleam in his deep-set eyes.

'Love, of itself,' he said at last with deliberation, 'is not sin, cannot be sin, though it may lead into sin. Has any word of this inordinate affection ever been said between you and the woman, any act or look that would blemish your vows or her purity?'

'No! No, Father, never! Never word of any sort but in civil greeting and farewell, and a blessing, due to such a benefactress. Nothing wrong has been done or said, only my heart is the offender. She knows nothing of my torment, she never has nor never will give one thought to me but as the messenger of this house. God forbid she should ever come to know, for she is blameless. It is for her sake, as well as mine, that I pray to be excused from ever seeing her again, for such pain as I feel might well disturb and distress her, even without understanding. The last thing I wish is for her to suffer.'

Radulfus rose abruptly from his seat, and Eluric, drained with the effort of confession and convinced of guilt, sank to his knees and bowed his head into his hands, expecting condemnation. But the abbot merely turned away to the window, and stood for a while looking out into the sunlit afternoon, where his own roses were coming into lavish bud.

No more oblates, the abbot was reflecting ruefully, and thanking God for it. No more taking these babes out of their cradles and severing them from the very sight and sound of women, half the creation stolen out of their world. How can they be expected to deal capably at last with something as strange and daunting to them as dragons? Sooner or later a woman must cross their path, terrible as an army with banners, and these wretched children without arms or armour to withstand the onslaught! We wrong women, and we wrong these boys, to send them unprepared into maturity, whole men, defenceless against the first pricking of the flesh. In defending them from perils we have deprived them of the means to defend themselves. Well, no more now! Those who enter here henceforward will be of manhood's years, enter of their own will, bear their own burdens. But this one's burden falls upon me.

He turned back into the room. Eluric knelt brokenly, his smooth young hands spread painfully to cover his face, and slow tears sliding between the fingers.

'Look up!' said Radulfus firmly, and as the young, tortured face was turned up to him fearfully: 'Now answer me truly, and don't be afraid. You have never spoken word of love to this lady?'

'No, Father!'

'Nor she ever offered such a word to you, nor such a look as could inflame or invite love?'

'No, Father, never, never! She is utterly untouched. I am nothing to her.' And he added with despairing tears: 'It is I who have in some way besmirched her, to my shame, by loving her, though she knows nothing of it.'

'Indeed? In what way has your unhappy affection befouled the lady? Tell me this, did ever you let your fancy dwell on touching her? On embracing her? On possessing her?'

'No!' cried Eluric in a great howl of pain and dismay. 'God forbid! How could I so profane her? I revere her, I think of her as of the company of the saints. When I trim the candles her goodness provides, I see her face as a brightness. I am no more than her pilgrim. But ah, it hurts . . .' he said, and bowed himself into the skirts of the abbot's gown and clung there.

'Hush!' said the abbot peremptorily, and laid his hand on the bowed head. 'You use extravagant terms for what is wholly human and natural. Excess is blameworthy, and in that field you do indeed offend. But it is plain that in the matter of this unhappy temptation you have not done ill, but in truth rather well. Nor need you fear any reproach to the lady, whose virtue you do well to extol. You have not harmed her. I know you for one unfailingly truthful, insofar as you see and understand truth. For truth is no simple matter, my son, and the mind of man is stumbling and imperfect in wisdom. I blame myself that I submitted you to this trial. I should have foreseen its severity for one as young and unpractised as you. Get up now! You have what you came to ask. You are excused from this duty henceforth.'

He took Eluric by the wrists, and hoisted him firmly to his feet, for he was so drained and trembling with weakness that it seemed doubtful if he could have risen unaided. The boy began to utter stumbling thanks, his tongue lame now even upon ordinary words. The calm of exhaustion and relief came back gradually to his face. But still he found something to fret him even in his release.

'Father . . . the charter . . . It will be void if the rose is not delivered and the rent paid.'

'The rose will be delivered,' said Radulfus forcibly. 'The rent will be paid. This task I lift here and now from your shoulders. Tend your altar, and give no further thought to how or by whom the duty is undertaken from this day.'

'Father, what more should I do for the cleansing of my soul?' ventured Eluric, quivering to the last subsiding tremors of guilt.

'Penance may well be salutary for you,' admitted the abbot somewhat wearily. 'But beware of making extravagant claims even upon punishment. You are far from a saint – so are we all – but neither are you a notable sinner; nor, my child, will you ever be.'

'God forbid!' whispered Eluric, appalled.

'God does indeed forbid,' said Radulfus drily, 'that we should make more of our virtues or our failings than is due. More than your due you shall not have of, neither praise nor blame. For your soul's ease, go and make your confession as I have ordered, with moderation, but say to your confessor that you have also been with me, and have my countenance and blessing, and are by me delivered from the duty which was too heavy for you. Then perform whatever penance he may give you, and beware of asking or expecting more.'

Brother Eluric went out from the presence on shaky legs, emptied of all feeling, and dreading that this emptiness could not last. It was not pleasure, but at least it was not pain. He had been dealt with kindly, he who had come to this interview looking upon success and release from the ordeal of the woman's nearness as the end of all his troubles, yet now this void within him was like the house swept clean in the Bible, ready for residence, aching to be filled, and as apt for devils as for angels.

He did as he had been bidden. Until the end of his novitiate his confessor had been Brother Jerome, ear and shadow of Prior Robert, and from Jerome he could have counted on all the chastisement his over-anxious soul desired. But now it was to the sub-prior, Richard, that he must turn, and Richard was known to be easy and consoling to his penitents, as much out of laziness as kindliness. Eluric did his best to obey the abbot's injunction, not to spare himself but not to accuse himself of what he had not committed, even in his secret mind. When it was done, penance allotted and absolution given, still he kneeled, with closed eyes and brows painfully drawn together.

'Is there more?' asked Richard.

'No, Father . . . No more to tell of what is done. Only I am afraid . . .' The numbness was beginning to melt, a small ache had begun in his guts, the empty house would not long be uninhabited. 'I will do all I may to put away even the memory of this illicit affection, but I am not sure . . . I am not sure! How if I fail? I go in dread of my own heart . . .'

'My son, whenever that heart fails you, you must go to the source of all strength and compassion, and pray to be aided, and grace will not fail you. You serve the altar of Our Lady, who is perfect purity. Where better could you turn for grace?'

Where, indeed! But grace is not a river into which a man can dip his pail at will, but a fountain that plays when it lists, and when it lists is dry and still. Eluric performed his penance before the altar he had newly trimmed, kneeling on the chill tiles of the floor, his whispering voice half-choked with passion, and kneeled still when he was done, with every nerve and sinew of his body imploring plenitude and peace.

Surely he should have been happy, for he was vindicated, delivered from the weight of mortal guilt, saved from ever having to see the face of Judith Perle again, or hear her voice, or breathe the faint sweetness that distilled out of her clothing as she moved. Free of that torment and temptation, he had believed his troubles were at an end. Now he knew better.

He knotted his hands into pain, and burst into a fury of passionate, silent prayers to the Virgin whose faithful servant he was, and who could and must stand by him now. But when he opened his eyes and looked up into the mellow golden cones of the candle-flames, there was the woman's face radiant before him, a dazzling, insistent brightness.

He had escaped nothing, all he had done was to cast away with the unbearable pain the transcendent bliss, and now all he had left was his barren virgin honour, this grim necessity to keep his vows at all costs. He was a man of his word, he would keep his word.

But he would never see her again.

Cadfael came back from the town in good time for Compline, well fed and well wined, and content with his evening's entertainment, though regretful that he would see no more of Aline and his godson Giles for three or four months. Doubtless Hugh would bring them back to the town house for the winter, by which time the boy would be grown out of all knowledge, and approaching his third birthday. Well, better they should spend the warm months up there in the north, at Maesbury, in the healthy caput of Hugh's modest honour, rather than in the congested streets of Shrewsbury, where disease had easier entry and exaggerated power. He ought not to grudge their going, however he was bound to miss them.

It was a warm early twilight as he crossed the bridge, matching his mood of content with its mild and pleasant melancholy. He passed the spot where trees and bushes bordered the path down to the lush riverside level of the Gaye, the abbey's main gardens, and the still silver gleam of the mill-pond on his right, and turned in at the gatehouse. The porter was sitting in the doorway of his lodge in the mild sweet air, taking the cool of the evening very pleasurably, but he also had an eye to his duties and the errand he had been given.

'So there you are!' he said comfortably, as Cadfael entered through the open wicket. 'Gallivanting again! I wish I had a godson up in the town.'

'I had leave,' said Cadfael complacently.

'I've known times when you couldn't have said that so smugly! But yes, I know you had leave tonight, and are back in good time for the office. But that's all one for tonight – Father Abbot wants you in his parlour. As soon as he returns, he said.'

'Does he so, indeed?' Cadfael echoed, brows aloft. 'What's afoot, then, at this hour? Has something wild been happening?'

'Not that I know of, there's been no stir about the place at all, everything as quiet as the night. Just the simple summons. Brother Anselm is sent for, too,' he added placidly. 'No mention of the occasion. Better go now and see.'

So Cadfael thought, too, and betook himself briskly down the length of the great court to the abbot's lodging. Brother Anselm the precentor was there before him, already ensconced on a carved bench against the panelled wall, and it appeared that nothing of too disturbing a nature was towards, for abbot and obedientiary were provided with wine-cups, and the like was offered to Cadfael as soon as he had reported himself in response to the abbot's summons. Anselm moved up on the bench to make room for his friend. The precentor, who also presided over the library, was ten years younger than Cadfael, a vague, unworldly man except where his personal enthusiasms were concerned, but alert and subtle enough in anything that concerned books, music or the instruments that make music, best of all the most perfect, the human voice. The blue eyes that peered out beneath his bushy brown eyebrows and shock of shaggy brown hair might be short-sighted, but they missed very little that went on, and had a tolerant twinkle for fallible human creatures and their failings, especially among the young.

'I have sent for you two,' said Radulfus, when the door

was firmly closed, and there was no fourth to overhear, 'because a thing has arisen that I would as lief not bring up in chapter tomorrow. It will certainly be known to one other, but through the confessional, which is secret enough. But else I want it kept within here, between us three. You have both long experience of the world and its pitfalls before you entered the cloister, you will comprehend my reasons. What is fortunate is that you were also the abbey witnesses to the charter by which we acquired the Widow Perle's house here in the Foregate. I have asked Anselm to bring with him a copy of the charter from the lieger-book.'

'I have it here,' said Brother Anselm, half-unfolding the leaf of vellum on his knee.

'Good! Presently! Now the matter is this. This afternoon Brother Eluric, who as custodian of the Lady Chapel altar, which benefits from the gift, seemed the natural person to pay the stipulated rent to the lady each year, came to me and requested to be excused from this duty. For reasons which I should have foreseen. For there is no denying that Mistress Perle is an attractive woman, and Brother Eluric is quite unpractised, young and vulnerable. He says, and I am sure truly, that no ill word or look has ever passed between them, nor has he ever entertained a single lustful thought concerning her. But he wished to be relieved of any further meeting, since he suffers and is tempted.'

It was a carefully temperate description, Cadfael thought, of what ailed Brother Eluric, but mercifully it seemed the disaster had been averted in time. The boy had got his asking, that was plain.

'And you have granted his wish,' said Anselm, rather stating than asking.

'I have. It is our work to teach the young how to deal with the temptations of the world and the flesh, but certainly not our duty to subject them to such temptations. I blame myself that I did not pay sufficient attention to what was arranged, or foresee the consequences. Eluric has behaved emotionally, but I believe him absolutely when he says he has not sinned, even in thought. I have therefore relieved him of his task. And I do not wish anything of his ordeal to be known among the other brothers. At best it will not be easy for him, let it at least be private, or confined to the few of us. He need not even know that I have confided in you.'

'He shall not,' said Cadfael firmly.

'So, then,' said Radulfus, 'having rescued one fallible child from the fire, I am all the more resolved not to subject another equally unprepared to the same danger. I cannot appoint another boy of Eluric's years to carry the rose. And if I nominate an elder, such as yourself, Cadfael, or Anselm here, it will be known all too well what the change means, and Brother Eluric's trouble will become matter for gossip and scandal. Oh, be sure I know that no rule of silence keeps news from spreading like bindweed. No, this must be seen as a change of policy for good and canonical reasons. Which is why I asked for the charter. Its purport I know, but its exact wording I cannot recall. Let us see what the possibilities are. Will you read it aloud, Anselm?'

Anselm unrolled his leaf and read, in the mellifluous voice that rejoiced in swaying hearers in the liturgy:

'"Be it known to all, present and future, that I, Judith, daughter of Richard Vestier and widow of Edred Perle, being in full health of mind, give and bestow, and by this present charter confirm to God and to the altar of Saint Mary in the church of the monks of Shrewsbury, my house in the Monks' Foregate, between the abbey forge and the messuage of Thomas the farrier, together with the garden and field pertaining to it, for an annual rent, during my lifetime, of one rose from the white rose-bush growing beside the north wall, to be delivered to me, Judith, upon the day of the translation of Saint Winifred. By these witnesses recorded: as to the abbey, Brother Anselm, precentor, Brother Cadfael; as to the town, John Ruddock, Nicholas of Meole, Henry Wyle."'

'Good!' said the abbot with a deep, satisfied breath, as Anselm lowered the leaf into the lap of his habit. 'So there is no mention of who is to deliver the rent, merely that it must be paid on the fixed day, and into the donor's own hand. So we may excuse Brother Eluric without infringing the terms, and as freely appoint another to bear the rose. There is no restriction, any man appointed may act for the abbey in this matter.'

'That's certain, agreed Anselm heartily. 'But if you purpose to exclude all the young, Father, for fear of bringing them into temptation, and all of us elders for fear of exposing Brother Eluric to suspicion of, at least, weakness, and at worst, misconduct, are we to look to a lay servant? One of the stewards, perhaps?'

'It would be perfectly permissible,' said Radulfus practically, 'but perhaps might lose something of relevance. I would not wish to diminish the gratitude we feel, and should feel, for the lady's generous gift, nor the respect with which we regard the gesture of her choice of rent. It means much to her, it should and must be dealt with by us with equal gravity. I would welcome your thoughts on the matter.'

'The rose,' said Cadfael, slowly and consideringly, 'comes from the garden and the particular bush which the widow cherished during the years of her marriage, and tended along with her husband. The house has a tenant now, a decent widower and a good craftsman, who has cared for the bush, pruned and fed it ever since he took up household there. Why should not he be asked to deliver the rose? Not roundabout, through a third and by order, but direct from bush to lady? This house is his landlord, as it is her beneficiary, and its blessing goes with the rose without further word said.'

He was not sure himself what had moved him to make the suggestion. It may have been that the evening's wine, rewarmed in him now by the abbot's wine, rekindled with it the memory of the close and happy family he had left up in the town, where the marital warmth as sacred in its way as any monastic vows gave witness to heaven of a beneficent purpose for mankind. Whatever it was that had moved him to speak, surely they were here dealing with a confrontation of special significance between man and woman, as Eluric had all too clearly shown, and the champion sent into the lists might as well be a mature man who already knew about women, and about love, marriage and loss.

'It's a good thought,' said Anselm, having considered it dispassionately. 'If it's to be a layman, who better than the tenant? He also benefits from the gift, the premises suit him very well, his former quarters were too distant from the town and too cramped.'

'And you think he would be willing?' asked the abbot.

'We can but ask. He's already done work for the lady,' said Cadfael, 'they're acquainted. And the better his contacts with the townsfolk, the better for trade. I think he'd have no objection.'

'Then tomorrow,' decided the abbot with satisfaction, 'I will send Vitalis to put the matter to him. And our problem, small though it is, will be happily solved.'

Chapter Three

Brother Vitalis had lived so long with documents and accounts and legal points that nothing surprised him, and about nothing that was not written down on vellum did he retain any curiosity. The errands that fell to his lot he discharged punctiliously but without personal interest. He delivered the abbot's message to Niall the bronzesmith word for word, expecting and receiving instant agreement, carried the satisfactory answer back, and promptly forgot the tenant's face. Not one word of one parchment that ever passed through his hands did he forget, those were immutable, even years would only slightly fade them, but the faces of laymen whom he might well never see again, and whom he could not recall ever noticing before, these vanished from his mind far more completely than words erased deliberately from a leaf of vellum to make way for a new text.

'The smith is quite willing,' he reported to Abbot Radulfus on his return, 'and promises faithful delivery.' He had not even wondered why the duty should have been transferred from a brother to a secular agent. It was in any case more seemly, since the donor was a woman.

'That's well,' said the abbot, content, and as promptly dismissed the matter from his mind as finished.

Niall, when he was left alone, stood for some minutes gazing after his departed visitor, leaving the all but completed dish with its incised border neglected on his workbench, the punch and mallet idle beside it. A small sector of the rim left to do, and then he could turn his hand to the supple leather girdle rolled up on a shelf and waiting for his attention. There would be a small mould to make, the body of the buckle to cast, and then the hammering out of the fine pattern and the mixing of the bright enamels to fill the incisions. Three times since she had brought it in he had unrolled it and run it caressingly through his fingers, dwelling on the delicate precision of the bronze rosettes. For her he would make a thing of beauty, however small and insignificant, and even if she never noticed it but as an article of apparel, a thing of use, at least she would wear it, it would encircle that body of hers that was so slender, too slender, and the buckle would rest close against the womb that had conceived but once and miscarried, leaving her so lasting and bitter a grief.

Not this night, but the night following, when the light began to fade and made fine work impossible, he would close the house and set out on the walk down through Brace Meole to the hamlet of Pulley, a minor manor of the Mortimers, where his sister's husband John Stury farmed the demesne as steward, and Cecily's boisterous children kept his own little girl company, made much of her, and ran wild with her among the chickens and the piglets. He was not utterly bereft, like Judith Perle. There was great consolation in a little daughter. He pitied those who had no children, and most of all such as had carried a child half the long, hard way into this world, only to lose it at last, and too late to conceive again. Judith's child had gone in haste after its father. The wife was left to make her way slowly, and alone.

He had no illusions about her. She knew little of him, desired no more, and thought of him not at all. Her composed courtesy was for every man, her closer regard for none. That he acknowledged without complaint or question. But fate and the lord abbot, and certain monastic scruples about encountering women, no doubt, had so decreed that on one day in the year, at least, he was to see her, to go to her house, to stand in her presence and pay her what was due, exchange a few civil words with her, see her face clearly, even be seen clearly by her, if only for a moment.

He left his work and went out by the house door into the garden. Within the high wall there were fruit trees bedded in grass, and a patch of vegetables, and to one side a narrow, tangled bed of flowers, overcrowded but spangled with bright colour. The white rose-bush grew against the north wall, tall as a man, and clutching the stonework with a dozen long, spiny arms. He had cut it back only seven weeks before, but it made rapid and lengthy growth every year. It was old; dead wood had been cut away from its stem several times, so that it had a thick, knotty bole at the base, and a sinewy stalk that was almost worthy of being called a trunk. A snow of white, half-open buds sprinkled it richly. The blooms were never very large, but of the purest white and very fragrant. There would be no lack of them at their best to choose from, when the day of Saint Winifred's translation came.

She should have the finest to be found on the tree. And even before that day he would see her again, when she came to fetch her girdle. Niall went back to his work with goodwill, shaping the new buckle in his mind while he completed the decoration of the dish for the provost's kitchen.

The burgage of the Vestier family occupied a prominent place at the head of the street called Maerdol, which led downhill to the western bridge. A right-angled house, with wide shop-front on the street, and the long stem of the hall and chambers running well back behind, with a spacious yard and stables. There was room enough in all that elongated building, besides the living rooms of the family, to house ample stores in a good dry undercroft, and provide space for all the girls who carded and combed the newly dyed wool, besides three horizontal looms set up in their own outbuilding, and plenty of room in the long hall for half a dozen spinsters at once. Others worked in their own homes, and so did five other weavers about the town. The Vestiers were the biggest and best-known clothiers in Shrewsbury.

Only the dyeing of the fleeces and fulling of the cloth were put out into the experienced hands of Godfrey Fuller, who had his dye-house and fulling-works and tenterground just down-river, under the wall of the castle.

At this time of year the first fleeces of the clip had already been purchased and sorted, and sent to be dyed, and on this same day had been duly delivered in person by Godfrey. Nor did he seem to be in any hurry to be off about his business, though he was known for a man to whom time was money, and money very dear. So was power. He enjoyed being one of the wealthiest of the town's guildsmen, and was always on the look-out for an extension to his realm and influence. He had his eye, so the common gossip said, on the almost comparable wealth of the Widow Perle, and never neglected an opportunity of urging the benefits of bringing the two together by a match.

Judith had sighed at his staying, but dutifully offered refreshment, and listened patiently to his dogged persuasions, which at least had the decency to avoid any semblance of loving courtship. He spoke solid sense, not dalliance, and all he said was true. His business and hers, put together, and run as well as they were being run now, would become a power in the shire, let alone the town. She would be the gainer, in terms of wealth at least, as well as he. Nor would he make too repulsive a husband, for if he was turned fifty he was still a presentable figure of a man, tall, vigorous, with a long stride on him, and a thick crop of steel-grey hair capping sharp features, and if he valued money, he also valued appearances and refinements, and would see to it, if only for his own prestige, that his wife went decked out as handsomely as any in the county.

'Well, well!' he said, recognising his dismissal and accepting it without resentment, 'I know how to bide my time, mistress, and I'm not one to give up short of the victory, nor one to change my mind, neither. You'll come to see the rights of what I've said, and I'm not afraid to stand my ground against any of these young fly-by-nights that have nothing to offer you but their pretty faces. Mine has seen long service, but I'll back it against theirs any day. You have too much good sense, girl, to choose a lad for his dainty seat on a horse, or his pink and yellow beauty. And think well on all we could do between us, if we had the whole of the trade brought together in our hands, from the ewe's back to the cloth on the counter and the gown on the customer's back.'

'I have thought of it,' she said simply, 'but the truth is, Master Fuller, I do not purpose to marry again.'

'Purposes can change,' said Godfrey firmly, and rose to take his leave. The hand she gave him resignedly he raised to his lips.

'Yours, too?' she said with a faint smile.

'My mind won't change. If yours does, here am I waiting.' And with that he did leave her, as briskly as he had come. Certainly there seemed to be no end to his persistence and patience, but fifty can ill afford to wait too long. Very soon she might have to do something decisive about Godfrey Fuller, and against that massive assurance it was hard to see what she could do but what she had been doing all along, fend him off and be as constant in denial as he was in demanding. She had been brought up to take good care of her business and her labourers, no less than he, she could ill afford to take her dyeing and fulling to another master.

Aunt Agatha Coliar, who had sat a little apart, sewing, bit off her thread, and said in the sweet, indulgent voice she affected sometimes towards the niece who kept her in comfort: 'You'll never rid yourself of him by being too civil. He takes it for encouragement.'

'He has a right to speak his mind,' said Judith indifferently, 'and he's in no doubt about mine. As often as he asks, I can refuse.'

'Oh, my dear soul, I trust you can. He's not the man for you. Nor none of those youngsters he spoke of, neither. You well know there's no second in the world for one who's known joy with the first. Better by far go the leave of the way alone! I still grieve for my own man, after all these years. I could never look at any other, after him.' So she had said, sighing and shaking her head and wiping away a facile tear, a thousand times since she had kept the storehouse and the linen here, and brought her son to help manage the business. 'If it had not been for my boy, who was young then to fend for himself, I would have taken the veil that same year that Will died. There'd be no fortune-hunting lads pestering a woman in the cloister. Peace of mind there'd be, there.' She was off upon her best theme, and sometimes seemed almost to forget that she was talking to anyone but herself.

She had been a pretty woman in youth, and still had a round, rosy, comfortable freshness, somewhat contradicted by the alert sharpness of her blue eyes, and the taut smile that visited her mouth very often when it should have been relaxed and easy in repose, as if shrewd thoughts within wore her soft outward seeming like a disguise. Judith could not remember her own mother, and often wondered if there had been much resemblance between the sisters. But these, mother and son, were the only kin she had, and she had taken them in without hesitation. Miles more than earned his keep, for he had shown himself an excellent manager during the long decline of Edred's health, when Judith had had no thought to spare for anything but her husband and the child to come. She had not had the heart, when she returned to the shop, to take back the reins into her own hands. Though she did her share, and kept a dutiful eye upon everything, she let him continue as master-clothier. So influential a house fared better with a man in the forefront.

'But there,' sighed Agatha, folding her sewing on her spacious lap and dropping a tear on the hem, 'I had my duty to do in the world, there was to be no such calm and quiet for me. But you have no chick nor child to cling to you, my poor dear, and nothing now to tie you to the world, if it should please you to leave it. You did speak of it once. Oh, take good thought, do nothing in haste. But should it come to that, there's nothing to hold you back.'

No, nothing! And sometimes the world did seem to Judith a waste, a tedium, hardly worth keeping. And in a day or two, perhaps tomorrow, Sister Magdalen would be coming from Godric's Ford, from the forest cell of the abbey of Polesworth, to fetch away Brother Edmund's niece as a postulant. She could as well take back with her two aspiring novices as one.

Judith was in the spinning room with the women when Sister Magdalen arrived, early the following afternoon. As heiress to the clothier's business for want of a brother, she had learned all the skills involved, from teasing and carding to the loom and the final cutting of garments, though she found herself much out of practice now at the distaff. The sheaf of carded wool before her was russet-red. Even the dye-stuffs came seasonally, and last summer's crop of woad for the blues was generally used up by April or May, to be followed by these variations on reds and browns and yellows, which Godfrey Fuller produced from the lichens and madders. He knew his craft. The lengths of cloth he would finally get back for fulling had a clear, fast colour, and fetched good prices.

It was Miles who came looking for her. 'You have a visitor,' he said, reaching over Judith's shoulder to rub a strand of wool from the distaff between finger and thumb, with cautious approval. 'There's a nun from Godric's Ford sitting in your small chamber, waiting for you. She says they told her at the abbey you'd be glad of a word with her. You're not still playing with the notion of quitting the world, are you? I thought that nonsense was over.'

'I did tell Brother Cadfael I should like to see her,' said Judith, stilling her spindle. 'No more than that. She's here to fetch a new novice away – the infirmarer's sister's girl.'

'Then don't you be fool enough to offer her a second. Though you do have your follies, as I know,' he said lightly, and clapped her affectionately on the shoulder. 'Like giving away for a rose-leaf the best property in the Foregate. Do you intend to cap that by giving away yourself?'

He was two years older than his cousin, and given to playing the elder, full of sage advice, though with a lightness that tempered the image. A young man very neatly and compactly made, strong and lissome, and as good at riding and wrestling and shooting at the butts by the riverside as he was at managing a clothier's business. He had his mother's blue, alert eyes and light-brown hair, but none of her blurred complacency. All that was, or seemed, vague and shallow in the mother became clear and decisive in the son. Judith had had good cause to be glad of him, and to rely on his solid good sense in all matters concerning commerce.

'I may do as I please with myself,' she said, rising and laying her spindle down in safety with its cone of russet yarn, 'if only I knew what *does* best please me! But truth to tell, I'm utterly in the dark. All I've done is to say I should be glad to talk to her. So I shall. I like Sister Magdalen.'

'So do I,' agreed Miles heartily. 'But I should grudge *you* to her. This house would founder without you.'

'Folly!' said Judith sharply. 'You know well enough it could fare as well without me as with me. It's you who hold up the roof, not I.'

If he disclaimed that, she did not wait to hear, but gave

him a sudden reassuring smile and a touch of her hand on his sleeve as she passed, and went to join her guest. Miles had a ruthless honesty, he knew that what she had said was no more than truth, he could have run everything here without her. The sharp reminder pricked her. She was indeed expendable, a woman without purpose here in this world, she might well consider whether there was not a better use for her out of the world. In urging her against it, he had reopened the hollow in her heart, and turned her thoughts again towards the cloister.

Sister Magdalen was sitting on a cushioned bench beside the unshuttered window in Judith's small private chamber, broad, composed and placid in her black habit. Agatha had brought her fruit and wine, and left her to herself, for she went in some awe of her. Judith sat down beside her visitor.

'Cadfael has told me,' said the nun simply, 'what ails you, and what you have confided to him. God forbid I should press you one way or the other, for in the end the decision is yours to make, and no other can make it for you. I am taking into account how grievous your losses have been.'

'I envy you,' said Judith, looking down into her linked hands. 'You are kind, and I am sure you are wise and strong. I do not believe I am now any of these things, and it is tempting to lean upon someone who is. Oh, I do live, I do work, I have not abandoned house, or kinsfolk, or duties. Yet all this could as well go on without me. My cousin has just shown me as much by denying it. It would be a most welcome refuge, to have a vocation elsewhere.'

'Which you have not,' said Sister Magdalen shrewdly, 'or you could not have said that.' Her sudden smile was like a ray of warmth, and the dimple that darted in and out of her cheek sparkled and was gone.

'No. Brother Cadfael said as much. He said the religious life should not be embraced as a second-best, but only as the best – not a hiding-place, but a passion.'

'He would be hard put to it to apply that to me,' said Sister Magdalen bluntly. 'But neither do I recommend to others what I myself do. If truth be told, I am no example to any woman. I took what I chose, I have still some years of life in which to pay for it. And if the debt is not discharged by then,

I'll pay the balance after, ungrudging. But you have incurred no such debt, and I do not think you should. The price comes high. You, I judge, will do better to wait, and spend your substance for something different.'

'I know of nothing,' said Judith bleakly, after a long moment of thought, 'that I find worth buying in this world now. But you and Brother Cadfael are right, if I took the veil I should be hiding behind a lie. All I covet in the cloister is the quiet, and the wall around me, keeping the world out.'

'Bear in mind, then,' said the nun emphatically, 'that our doors are not closed against any woman in need, and the quiet is not reserved for those who have taken vows. The time may come when you truly need a place to be apart, time for thought and rest, even time to recover lost courage, though of that I think you have enough. I said I would not advise, and I am advising. Wait, bear with things as they are. But if ever you need a place to hide, for a little while or a long while, come to Godric's Ford and bring all your frets in with you, and you shall find a refuge for as long as you need, with no vows taken, never unless you come to it with a whole heart. And I will keep the door against the world until you see fit to go forth again.'

Late after supper that night, in the small manor-house of Pulley, in the open scrubland fringes of the Long Forest, Niall opened the outer door of his brother-in-law's timber hall, and looked out into the twilight that was just deepening into night. He had a walk of three miles or so before him, back to his house in the Foregate of the town, but it was a familiar and pleasant walk in fair weather, and he was accustomed to making the trip two or three times in the week after work, and home in the early dark, to be up and at work again betimes in the morning. But on this night he saw with some surprise that there was a steady rain falling, so quietly and straightly that within the house they had been quite unaware of it.

'Bide overnight,' said his sister at his shoulder. 'No need to get wet through, and this won't last the night out.'

'I don't mind it,' said Niall simply. 'I shan't hurt.'

'With all that way to go? Get some sense,' advised Cecily

comfortably, 'and stay here in the dry, there's room enough, and you know you're welcome. You can be up and away in good time tomorrow, no fear of oversleeping, these early dawns.'

'Shut the door on it,' urged John from the table, 'and come and have another sup. Better wet inside than out. It's not often we have time for a talk among the three of us, after the children are all abed and asleep.'

With four of them about the place, and all lively as squirrels, that was true enough; the grown folk were at the beck and call of their young for all manner of services, mending toys, joining in games, telling stories, singing rhymes. Cecily's two boys and a girl ranged from ten years old down to six, and Niall's own chick was the youngest and the pet. Now all four were curled up like a litter of puppies on their hay mattresses in the little loft, fast asleep, and round the trestle table in the hall the elders could talk freely without disturbing them.

It had been a good day for Niall. He had cast and decorated and polished the new buckle for Judith's girdle, and was not displeased with his work. Tomorrow she might come to fetch it, and if he saw pleasure in her eyes when she took it, he would be well rewarded. Meantime, why not settle here cosily for the night, and get up with the dawn to a newly washed world, and a sweet green walk home?

He slept well, and was roused at first light by the usual wild, waking rapture of the birds, at once sweet and strident. Cecily was up and busy, and had small ale and bread ready for him. She was younger than he, fair and benign, happy in her husband and a born hand with children, no wonder the motherless child thrived here. Stury would take nothing for her keep. What was one more little bird, he said, in a full nest? And indeed the family was well provided here, keeping Mortimer's little manor prosperous and in good repair, the cleared fields productive, the forest well managed, the small coppice ditched against the invading deer. A good place for children. And yet it was always an effort to set out for the town, and leave her behind, and he visited often for fear she should begin to forget that she was his, and not the youngest of the Stury brood, fathered and mothered here from birth.

Niall set out through an early morning moist and sweet, the rain over, seemingly, for some hours, for though the grass sparkled, the open soil had swallowed up the fall, and was beginning to dry. The first long, low beams of the rising sun lanced through the trees and drew patterns of light and dark along the ground. The first passion of bird-song gradually softened and lost its belligerence, grew busy and sweet and at ease. Here also the nests were full of fledgelings, hard work day-long to feed them all.

The first mile was through the edges of the forest, the ground opening gradually into heath and scrub, dotted with small groves of trees. Then he came to the hamlet of Brace Meole, and from there it was a beaten road, widening as it neared the town into a cart-track, which crossed the Meole Brook by a narrow bridge, and brought him into the Foregate between the stone bridge into the town and the mill and mill-pond at the edge of the abbey enclave. He had set off early and walked briskly, and the Foregate was still barely awake; only a few cottagers and labourers were up and about their business, and gave him good day as he passed. The monks were not yet down for Prime, there was no sound in the church as Niall went by, but faintly from the dortoir the waking bell was ringing. The high road had dried after the rain, but the soil of the gardens showed richly dark, promising grateful growth.

He came to the gate in his own burgage wall, and let himself through into the yard, set the door of his shop open, and made ready for the day's work. Judith's girdle lay coiled on a shelf. He held his hand from taking it down to caress yet again, for he had no rights in her, and never would have. But this very day he might at least see her again and hear her voice, and in five days' time he surely would, and that in her own house. Their hands might touch on the stem of the rose. He would choose carefully, wary of offering her thorns, who had been pierced by too many and too sharp thorns already in her brief life.

The thought drove him out into the garden, which lay behind the yard, entered by a door from the house and a wicket in the wall from the yard. After the indoor chill left from the night, the bright sunlight embraced him in the doorway, a scarf of warmth, and gleamed moistly through the branches of the fruit trees and over the tangled flower-bed. He took one step over the threshold and halted, stricken and appalled.

Against the north wall the white rose-bush sagged sidelong, its thorny arms dragged from the stone, its thickened bole hacked in a long, downward gash that split away a third of its weight and growth dangling into the grass. Beneath it the soil of the bed was stirred and churned as if dogs had battled there, and beside the battlefield lay huddled a still heap of rusty black, half sunk in the grass. Niall took no more than three hasty steps towards the wreckage when he saw the pale gleam of a naked ankle jutting from the heap, an arm in a wide black sleeve flung out, a hand convulsively clenched into the soil, and the pallid circle of a tonsure startlingly white in all the blackness. A monk of Shrewsbury, young and slight, almost more habit than body within it, and what, in God's name, was he doing here, dead or wounded under the wounded tree?

Niall went close and kneeled beside him, in too much awe, at first, to touch. Then he saw the knife, lying close beside the outstretched hand, its blade glazed with drying blood. There was a thick dark moisture that was not rain, sodden into the soil under the body. The forearm exposed by the wide black sleeve was smooth and fair. This was no more than a boy. Niall reached a hand to touch at last, and the flesh was chill but not yet cold. Nevertheless, he knew death. With careful dread he eased a hand under the head, and turned to the morning light the soiled young face of Brother Eluric.

Chapter Four

Brother Jerome, who counted heads and censored behaviour in all the brothers, young and old, and whether within his province or no, had marked the silence within one dormitory cell when all the rest were rising dutifully for Prime, and made it his business to look within, somewhat surprised in this case, for Brother Eluric rated normally as a model of virtue. But even the virtuous may backslide now and then, and the opportunity to reprove so exemplary a brother came rarely, and was certainly not to be missed. This time Jerome's zeal was wasted, and the pious words of reproach died unspoken, for the cell was empty, the cot immaculately neat, the breviary open on the narrow desk. Brother Eluric had surely risen ahead of his kin, and was already on his knees somewhere in the church, engaged in supererogatory prayer. Jerome felt cheated, and snapped with more than his usual acidity at any who looked blear-eyed with sleep, or came yawning to the night-stairs. He was equally at odds with those who exceeded him in devotion and those who fell short. One way or another, Eluric would pay for this check.

Once they were all in their stalls in the choir, and Brother Anselm was launched into the liturgy – how could a man past fifty, who spoke in a round, human voice deeper than most, sing at will in that upper register, like the most perfect of boy cantors? And how dared he! – Jerome again began to count heads, and grew even happier in his self-vindication, for there was one missing, and that one was Brother Eluric. The fallen paragon, who had actually won his way into Prior Robert's dignified and influential favour, to Jerome's jealous concern! Let him look to his laurels now! The prior would never demean himself to count or search for defections, but he would listen when they were brought to his notice.

Prime came to its end, and the brothers began to file back to the night-stairs, to complete their toilets and make ready for breakfast. Jerome lingered to sidle confidentially to Prior Robert's elbow, and whisper into his ear, with righteous disapproval: 'Father, we have a truant this morning. Brother Eluric was not present in church. Nor is he in his cell. All is left in order there, I thought surely he was before us into the church. Now I cannot think where he may be, nor what he is about, to neglect his duties so.'

Prior Robert in his turn paused and frowned. 'Strange! He of all people! Have you looked in the Lady Chapel? If he rose very early to tend the altar and has lingered long in prayer he may have fallen asleep. The best of us may do so.'

But Brother Eluric was not in the Lady Chapel. Prior Robert hurried to detain the abbot on his way across the great court towards his lodging.

'Father Abbot, we are in some concern over Brother Eluric.'

The name produced instant and sharp attention. Abbot Radulfus turned a fixed and guarded countenance. 'Brother Eluric? Why, what of him?'

'He was not in attendance at Prime, and he is nowhere to be found. Nowhere, at least, that he should be at this hour. It is not like him to absent himself from the office,' said the prior fairly.

'It is not. He is a devoted soul.' The abbot spoke almost absently, for his mind was back in the privacy of his parlour, facing that all too brittle devotee as he poured out his illicit and bravely resisted love. This reminder came all too aptly. How if confession and absolution and the release from temptation had not been enough? Radulfus, not a hesitant man, was still hesitating how to act now, when they were interrupted by the sight of the porter coming down from the gatehouse at a scurrying run, skirts and sleeves flying.

'Father Abbot, there's one here at the gate, the bronze-smith who rents the Widow Perle's old house, says he has dire news that won't wait. He asks for you – would not give me the message—'

'I'll come,' said Radulfus instantly. And to the prior, who would have made to follow him: 'Robert, do you have someone search further, the gardens, the grange court . . . If you do not find him, come back to me.' And he was off at a long, raking stride towards the gate, and the authority of his voice and the vehemence of his going forbade pursuit. There were too many interwoven threads here – the lady of the rose, the house of the rose, the tenant who had willingly undertaken the errand Eluric dreaded, and now Eluric lost from within, and dire news entering from without. A woven pattern began to appear, and its colours were sombre.

Niall was waiting at the door of the porter's lodge, his broad, strongly boned face very still and blanched with shock under its summer brown.

'You asked for me,' said Radulfus quietly, viewing him with a steady, measuring stare. 'I am here. What is this news you bring?'

'My lord,' said Niall, 'I thought best you should know it first alone, and then dispose as you see fit. Last night I lay at my sister's house overnight because of the rain. When I came back this morning I went into the garden. My lord, Mistress Perle's rose-bush has been hacked and broken, and one of your brothers lies dead there under it.'

After a brief, profound silence Radulfus said: 'If you know him, name him.'

'I do know him. For three years he came to the garden to cut the rose for Mistress Perle. He is Brother Eluric, the custodian of Saint Mary's altar.'

This time the silence was longer and deeper. Then the abbot asked simply: 'How long since you discovered him there?'

'About the length of Prime, my lord, for it was nearly the hour when I passed the church on my way home. I came at once, but the porter would not disturb you during the office.'

'And you left all as you found it? Touched nothing?'

'I lifted his head to see his face. Nothing else. He lies just as I found him.'

'Good!' said Radulfus, and winced at using the word even for one right act, where everything else went grimly awry. 'Then wait but a moment, while I send for certain others, and we will go back with you to that garden.'

* * *

Those he took with him, saying nothing as yet to any other, even the prior, were Brother Anselm and Brother Cadfael, witnesses for the abbey to the charter drawn up with Judith Perle. They alone had been told of Brother Eluric's trouble, and shared the sorry knowledge that might be relevant here. The young man's confessor was silenced by his office, and in any case Sub-Prior Richard was not the man Radulfus would have chosen as a wise counsellor in such dark matters.

The four of them stood in silence round the body of Brother Eluric, taking in the pitiful heap of black folds, the outflung hand, the mangled tree and the bloody knife. Niall had withdrawn a few paces to leave them alone, but stood watchful in attendance, to answer whatever they might ask.

'Poor, tormented child,' said Radulfus heavily. 'I doubt I failed him fatally, his disease was worse than I knew. He begged to be relieved of his task, but surely he grudged it to any other, and has tried here to destroy the bush. And himself with it.'

Cadfael was silent, his eyes roving thoughtfully over the trampled ground. They had all refrained from treading too close, nothing had been disturbed since Niall went on his knees to turn the pallid face up to the light.

'Is that how you read it?' asked Anselm. 'Are we to condemn him as a suicide? However we may pity?'

'What else can it be? Surely this involuntary love had so eaten into him that he could not bear another should take his place with the woman. Why else should he steal out by night and come here to this garden, why else should he hack at the roots of the tree? And from that it would be but a step, in his despair, to the unholy temptation to destroy himself with the roses. What could fix his image more terribly and for ever in her memory than such a death? For you know – you two do know – the measure of his desperation. And there lies the knife beside his hand.'

It was not a dagger, but a good, long-hafted knife, sharp and thin, such as any practical man might carry on him for a dozen lawful purposes, from carving his meat at the table to scaring off footpads on a journey, or the occasional wild boar in the forest.

'Beside it,' said Cadfael shortly, 'not in it.'

They turned their eyes on him cautiously, even hopefully.

'You see how his hand is clenched into the soil,' he went on slowly, 'and there is no blood upon it, though the knife is bloodied to the hilt. Touch his hand – I think you'll find it is already stiffening as it lies, clutching the earth. He never held this knife. And if he had, would not the sheath be on his girdle? No man in his senses would carry such a knife about him unsheathed.'

'A man not in his right senses might, however,' said Radulfus ruefully. 'He needed it, did he not, for what he has done to the rose-bush.'

'What was done to the rose-bush,' said Cadfael firmly, 'was not done with that knife. Could not be! A man would have to saw away for half an hour or more, even with a sharp knife, at such a thick bole. That was done with a heavier weapon, meant for such work, a broom-hook or a hatchet. Moreover, you see the gash begins higher, where a single blow, or two at the most, should have severed the stem, but it swerves downwards into the thick of the bole, where dead wood has been cut away for years, and left this woody encrustation.'

'I fear,' said Brother Anselm wryly, 'that Brother Eluric would hardly be expert with such a tool.'

'And there was no second blow,' said Cadfael, undeterred. 'If there had been, the bush would be severed utterly. And the first blow, I think, the only blow – even that was deflected. Someone interrupted the act. Someone clutched at the arm that was swinging the hatchet, and sent the blade down into the thick of the bole. I think – I *think* – it stuck fast there, and the man who held it had not time to get both hands to the haft and pull it out. Why else should he draw his knife?'

'You are saying,' said Radulfus intently, 'that there were two men here in the night, not one? One who tried to destroy, and one who tried to prevent?'

'Yes, that is what I see here.'

'And that the one who tried to protect the tree, who caught at the attacker's arm and caused his weapon to lodge fast – and who was struck down instead with the knife . . .'

'Is Brother Eluric. Yes. How else can it have been?

Certainly he came here secretly in the night of his own will, but not to destroy, rather to take a last farewell of this wild dream of his, to look for one last time on the roses, and then never no more. But he came just in time to see another man here, one who had other thoughts, and for other motives, one who had come to destroy the rose-bush. Would Eluric endure to see that done? Surely he leaped to protect the tree, clutched at the arm wielding the hatchet, drove the blade down to stick fast in the bole. If there was a struggle, as the ground shows, I do not think it lasted long. Eluric was unarmed. The other, if he could not then make use of his hatchet, carried a knife. And used it.'

There was a long silence, while they all stared at him and thought out slowly the implications of what he was saying. And gradually something of conviction came easefully into their faces, even something of relief and gratitude. For if Eluric was not a suicide, but had gone to his end faithfully bearing his burden and seeking to prevent an evil act, then his resting-place in the cemetery was assured, and his passage through death, however his account might stand for little sins needing purging, as safe as a prodigal son re-entering his father's house.

'If it were not as I've said,' Cadfael pointed out, 'then the hatchet would still be here in the garden. It is not. And certainly it was not our brother here who carried it away. And neither did he bring it here, I pledge my word on that.'

'Yet if this is true,' said Anselm consideringly, 'the other did not stay to complete his work.'

'No, he lugged out his hatchet and made off as fast as he could, away from the place where he had made himself a murderer. A thing I daresay he never intended, done in a moment of alarm and terror, when this poor lad in his outrage lunged at him. He would run from Eluric dead in far greater horror than he ever need have done from Eluric living.'

'Nevertheless,' said Abbot Radulfus strongly, 'this is murder.'

'It is.'

'Then I must send word to the castle. It is for the secular authorities to pursue murderers. A pity,' he said, 'that Hugh

Beringar is gone north, we shall have to wait for his return, though no doubt Alan Herbard will send to him at once, and let him know what has happened. Is there more that we here must do, before we have Brother Eluric carried home?'

'We can at least observe whatever is here to be seen, Father. One thing I can tell you, indeed you yourself will see it, what happened here happened after the rain stopped. The ground was soft when they came together here, see how they've marked it. And back and shoulder of the boy's habit are dry. May we now move him? There are witnesses enough here as to how he was found.'

They stooped in all reverence and lifted the stiffening but not yet rigid body, and laid him out on the grass, stretched on his back. From throat to toes the front of his habit was dark with the moisture from the earth, and the great dark stain of his blood clotted the cloth over his left breast. His face, if it had borne the stamp of sudden anger, dread and pain, had now lost that tension, and eased into the smoothness of youth and innocence. Only his eyes, half-open, retained the frowning anxiety of a troubled soul. Radulfus stooped and closed them gently, and wiped the mud from the pale cheeks.

'You take a load from my heart, Cadfael. Surely you are right, he did not take his own life, it was rapt from him cruelly and unjustly, and there must be a price to pay for it. But as for this child here, he is safe enough. I would I had known better how to deal with him, he might still have been living.' He drew the two smooth hands together, and folded them on the bloodied breast.

'I sleep too well,' said Cadfael wryly, 'I never heard when the rain ceased. Did anyone mark the end of it?'

Niall had drawn a little nearer, waiting patiently in case anything further should be required of him.

'It was over by about midnight,' he said, 'for before we went to our beds, there at Pulley, my sister opened the door and looked out, and said that the sky had cleared and it was bidding to be a fine night. But it was too late to start out then.' He added, putting his own interpretation on the way they turned to look at him, after so long of forgetting his presence: 'My sister and her man and the children will tell you I stayed the night over, and left in the dawn. It might be said a family will hold together, however. But I can tell you the names of two or three I said good day to, coming back along the Foregate this morning. They'll bear me out.'

The abbot gave him a startled and preoccupied look, and understood. 'Such checks and counter-checks are for the sheriff's men,' he said. 'But I make no doubt you've told us simple truth. And the rain was over by midnight, you say?'

'It was, my lord. There's but three miles between, it would surely be much the same here.'

'It fits well,' said Cadfael, kneeling over the body. 'He must surely have died about six or seven hours ago. And since he came after the rain stopped, when the ground was soft and moist to tread, there should be traces they've left after them. Here they've stamped the ground raw between them, there's nothing clear, but by one way or another they walked in here in the night, and one walked out again.'

He rose from his knees and rubbed his moist palms together. 'Hold your places where you stand, and look about you. We may have trampled out something of value ourselves, but at least all of us here but one wear sandals, and so did Eluric. Master Bronzesmith, how did you enter here this morning, when you found him?'

'Through the house-door,' said Niall, nodding in that direction.

'And when Brother Eluric came each year to fetch the rose, how did he enter?'

'Through the wicket from the front yard, as we did now. And was very quiet and modest about it.'

'Then this night past, coming with no ill intent, though so secretly, surely he would come as he always came. Let us see,' said Cadfael, treading carefully along the grass to the wicket gate in the wall, 'if any but sandalled feet came that way.'

The earth path, watered into mud by the rain, and again dried into a smooth, soft surface, had taken all their entering footprints and held them clear to view, three pairs of flat soles, here and there overlaid one on another. Or were there four pairs? With these common sandals size meant nothing very helpful, but Cadfael thought he could detect, among all those prints entering and none leaving, one which had trodden deeper than the rest, having entered here while the ground was wetter than now, and by lucky chance escaped being trodden out of shape with their morning invasion. There was also a broad, sturdy shoe-sole, recent like the sandals, which Niall claimed for his, and showed as much by fitting his foot to it.

'Whoever the second was,' said Cadfael, 'I fancy he did not come by the front way, as innocent men do. Nor leave by it, either, having left a dead man behind here. Let us look elsewhere.'

On the eastward side the garden was hemmed in by the wall of the house belonging to Thomas the farrier, on the west by Niall's workshop and dwelling; there was no way out there. But to the rear, on the other side of the north wall, lay a paddock, very easily entered from the fields, and no way overlooked by any building. A few paces along the wall from the mutilated rose-bush there was a vine growing, crabbed and old and seldom fruitful. A part of its twisted trunk had been pulled away from the wall, and when Niall approached it closely he saw that where the trunk turned sidelong and afforded a foothold, a foot had indeed scored it, mounting in panic haste.

'Here! Here he climbed. The ground is higher outside in the paddock, but leaving he needed a holt on the way.'

They drew close, peering. The climber's boot had scratched the bark and left soil in the scratches. And below, in the exposed earth of the bed, the other foot, the left, had stamped a deep and perfect print as he lunged upward, for he had had to reach high. A booted foot, with a raised heel that had dug deep, but less deep on the outer edge at the back, where the wearer habitually trod his boot down. By the shape his footgear had been well made, but well worn also. There was a fine ridge of earth that crossed from below the great toe diagonally half across the sole, narrowing to vanishing point as it went, left by a crack in the leather. Opposite the downtrodden heel, the toe also had left an imprint shallowing slightly. Whoever the man was, he trod from the left of the heel clean to the right of the toe with this left foot. His spring from the ground had forced the print in deep, but his foot had left the soil cleanly, and the wet earth, gradually drying, had preserved the perfect mould.

'A little warm wax,' said Cadfael, half to himself, intently staring, 'a little warm wax and a steady hand, and we have him by the heel!'

They were so intent upon that single spot, the last remaining trace of Brother Eluric's murderer, that none of them heard the light footsteps approaching the open house-door from within, or caught in the corner of an eye the slight gleam of the sun upon movement and colour, as Judith came into the doorway. She had found the workshop empty, and waited some minutes for Niall to appear. But since the door into his living quarters was wide open as he had left it, and the shifting green and gold of sunlit branches stirring showed in reflection across the room within, and since she knew the house so well, she had ventured to pass through to find him in the garden, where she judged he must be.

'I ask pardon,' she was saying as she stepped into the doorway, 'but the doors were open. I did call—'

She broke off there, startled and bewildered to see the whole group of them swing about and stare in consternation at her. Three black Benedictine habits gathered beside the old, barren vine, and one of them the lord abbot himself. What errand could they possibly have here?

'Oh, forgive me,' she began haltingly. 'I didn't know . . .'

Niall sprang out of his shocked stillness and came running, putting himself between her and what else she might see if once she took her eyes off the abbot. He spread an arm protectively to urge her back into the house.

'Come within, mistress, here's nothing to trouble you. I have the girdle ready. You're early, I hadn't expected you. . .'

He was not good at providing a flood of reassuring words. She held her ground, and over his shoulder she swept the enclosed space of the garden with dilated eyes blanched into the chill grey of glass, and found the still body lying aloof and indifferent in the grass. She saw the pale oval of the face, the pale cross of the hands on the breast of the habit, the hacked bole of the rose-bush, and its sagging branches torn from the wall. As yet she neither recognised the dead youth, nor understood at all what could have been happening here.

But all too well she understood that whatever befell in this place, between these walls which had once been hers, somehow lay heavy upon her, as if she had set in motion some terrible procession of events which she was powerless to stop, as if a gathering guilt had begun to fold round her, and mock her with her purity of intent and the corruption of its consequences.

She made no sound at all, she did not shrink, or yield to Niall's awkward, concerned pleading: 'Come, come within and sit you down quietly, and leave all here to the lord abbot. Come!' He had an arm about her, rather persuading than supporting, for she stood quite still and erect, not a quiver in her body. She laid her hands on his shoulders, resisting his urging with resigned determination.

'No, let me be. This has to do with me. I know it.'

They were all drawing anxiously about her by then. The abbot accepted necessity. 'Madam, there is here matter that must distress you, that we cannot deny. I will not hide anything from you. This house is your gift, and truth is your due. But you must not take to yourself more than is customary from any godly gentlewoman in compassion for a young life taken untimely. No part of this stems from you, and no part of what must be done about it falls to your duty. Go within, and all that we know – all that is of consequence – you shall be told. I promise it.'

She hesitated, her eyes still on the dead youth. 'Father, I will not further embitter what is surely hard enough for you,' she said slowly. 'But let me see him. I owe him that.'

Radulfus looked her in the eyes, and stood aside. Niall took away his arm from about her almost stealthily, for fear she should suddenly become aware of his touch in the instant when it was removed. She crossed the grass with a firm and steady step, and stood looking down at Brother Eluric. In death he looked even younger and more vulnerable than in life, for all his immovable calm. Judith reached over him to the dangling, wounded bush, plucked one of the half-open buds, and slipped it carefully into his folded hands.

'For all those you brought to me,' she said. And to the rest of those present, raising her head: 'Yes, it is he. I knew it must be he.'

'Brother Eluric,' said the abbot.

'I never knew his name. Is not that strange?' She looked round them all, from face to face, with drawn brows. 'I never asked, and he never told. So few words we ever had to say to each other, and too late now for more.' She fastened last and longest, and with the first returning warmth of pain in her eyes as the numbness passed, on Cadfael, whom she knew best here. 'How could this happen?' she said.

'Come within now,' said Cadfael, 'and you shall know.'

Chapter Five

The abbot and Brother Anselm departed, back to the abbey to send men with a litter to bring Brother Eluric home, and a messenger to Hugh's young deputy at the castle, to warn him he had a murder on his hands. Very soon word would go forth through the Foregate that a brother was mysteriously dead, and many and strange rumours would be blown on the summer winds all through the town. Some carefully truncated version of Eluric's tragedy the abbot would surely make public, to silence the wildest tales. He would not lie, but he would judiciously omit what was eternally private between himself, the two brother witnesses, and the dead man. Cadfael could guess how it would read. It had been decided, on maturer reflection, that it would be more suitable for the rose rent to be paid direct by the tenant, rather than by the custodian of the altar of Saint Mary, and therefore Brother Eluric had been excused from the duty he had formerly fulfilled. That he had gone in secret to the garden was perhaps foolish, but not blameworthy. No doubt he had simply wished to verify that the bush was well cared for and in blossom, and finding a malefactor in the very act of destroying it, he had naturally tried to prevent the act, and had been struck down by the attacker. A creditable death, an honourable grave. What need to mention the conflict and suffering that lay behind it?

But in the meantime here was he, Cadfael, confronted with a woman who surely had the right to know everything. It would not, in any case, be easy to lie to this woman, or even to prevaricate. She would not be satisfied with anything less than truth.

Since the sun was now reaching the flower-bed under the north wall of the garden, and the edge of the deep print might become dry and friable before noon, and perhaps powder away, Cadfael had borrowed some ends of candle from Niall on the spot, melted them in one of the smith's small crucibles, and gone to fill in carefully the shape of the bootprint. With patient coaxing the congealed form came away intact. It would have to go into a cold place to preserve its sharpness, but for good measure he had also purloined a discarded offcut of thin leather, and made a careful outline of the print, marking where heel and toe were worn down, and the diagonal crack across the ball of the foot. Sooner or later boots come into the hands of the cobbler, they are far too precious to be discarded until they are completely worn out and can no longer be mended. Often they are handed down through three generations before finally being thrown away. So, reflected Cadfael, would this boot some day need attention from Provost Corviser or one of his trade. How soon there was no telling, but justice has to learn to wait, and not to forget.

Judith sat waiting for him now in Niall's neat, bare and austere living room, the room of a man living alone, orderly and clean, but with none of the small adornments a woman would have added. The doors still stood wide open, there were two unshuttered windows, green of foliage and gold of sun came quivering in, and filled the chamber with light. She was not afraid of light, she sat where it played over her, gilding and trembling as the breeze quickened. She was alone when Cadfael came back from the garden.

'The smith has a customer,' she said with the palest of smiles. 'I bade him go. A man must tend to his trade.'

'So must a woman,' said Cadfael, and laid his moulded waxen form carefully down on the stone floor, where the draught would play over it as the sunlight did over her.

'Yes, so I shall. You need not fear me, I have a respect for life. All the more,' she said gravely, 'now that I have seen death close to, yet again. Tell me! You said you would.'

He sat down with her on the uncushioned bench, and told her fully all that had happened that morning – the defection of Eluric, the coming of Niall with his story of finding the crumpled body and the broken bush, even the first grim suspicion of deliberate damage and self-murder, before sign after sign pointed another way. She heard him out with unwavering attention, those arresting grey eyes dauntingly wide and intelligent.

'But still,' she said, 'I do not understand. You speak as if there was nothing of note or consequence in his leaving the enclave by night as he did. But you know it is something utterly unknown, for a young brother so to dare. And he, I thought, so meek and dutiful, no breaker of rules. Why did he do so? What can have made it so important to him to visit the rose-bush? Secretly, illicitly, by night? What did it mean to him, to drive him so far out of his proper way?'

No question but she was asking honestly. She had never thought of herself as a disturber of any man's peace. And she meant to have an answer, and there was none to give her but the truth. The abbot might have hesitated at this point. Cadfael did not hesitate.

'It meant to him,' he said simply, 'the memory of you. It was no change of policy that removed him from being bearer of the rose. He had begged to be relieved of a task which had become torment to him, and his request was granted. He could no longer bear the pain of being in your presence and as far from you as the moon, of seeing you, and being within touch of you, and forbidden to love. But when he was released, it seems he could not bear absence, either. In a manner, he was saying his goodbye to you. He would have got over it,' said Cadfael with resigned regret, 'if he had lived. But it would have been a long, bleak sickness.'

Still her eyes had not wavered nor her face changed, except that the blood had drained from her cheeks and left her pale and translucent as ice. 'Oh, God!' she said in a whisper. 'And I never knew! There was never word said, never a look . . . And I so much his elder, and no beauty! It was like sending one of the singing boys from the school to me. Never a wrong thought, how could there be?'

'He was cloistered almost from his cradle,' said Cadfael gently, 'he had never had to do with a woman since he left his mother. He had no defence against a gentle face, a soft voice and a motion of grace. You cannot see yourself with his eyes, or you might find yourself dazzled.'

After a moment of silence she said: 'I did feel, somehow,

that he was not happy. No more than that. And how many in this world can boast of being happy?' And she asked, looking up again into Cadfael's face: 'How many know of this? Need it be spoken of?'

'No one but Father Abbot, Brother Richard his confessor, Brother Anselm and myself. And now you. No, it will never be spoken of to any other. And none of these can or will ever think one thought of blame for you. How could we?'

'But I can,' said Judith.

'Not if you are just. You must not take to yourself more than your due. That was Eluric's error.'

A man's voice was raised suddenly in the shop, young and agitated, and Niall's voice replying in hasty reassurance. Miles burst in through the open doorway, the sunlight behind him casting him into sharp silhouette, and shining through his ruffled fair hair, turning light brown into flaxen. He was flushed and out of breath, but he heaved a great, relieved sigh at the sight of Judith sitting composed and tearless and in calm company.

'Dear God, what has been happening here? The tales they're buzzing along the Foregate of murder and malice! Brother, is it true? My cousin . . . I knew she was coming here this morning. Thank God, girl dear, I find you safe and well befriended. No harm has come to you? I came on the run as soon as I heard what they were saying, to take you home.'

His boisterous coming had blown away, like a March wind, the heavy solemnity that had pervaded the room, and his vigour had brought back some rising colour to Judith's frozen face. She rose to meet him, and let him embrace her in an impulsive hug, and kiss her cold cheek.

'I've taken no harm, no need to fret for me. Brother Cadfael has been kind enough to keep me company. He was here before I came, and Father Abbot also, there was never any threat or danger to me.'

'But there *has* been a death?' With his arms still protectively about her he looked from her face to Cadfael's, anxiously frowning. 'Or is it all a false tale? They were saying – a brother of the abbey was carried home from this place, and his face covered . . .'

'It's all too true,' said Cadfael, rising somewhat wearily. 'Brother Eluric, the custodian of Saint Mary's altar, was found here this morning stabbed to death.'

'Here? What, within the house?' He sounded incredulous, as well he might. What would a brother of the abbey be doing invading a craftsman's house?

'In the garden. Under the rose-tree,' said Cadfael briefly, 'and that rose-tree hacked and damaged. Your cousin will tell you all. Better you should hear truth than the common rumours none of us will quite escape. But the lady should be taken home at once and allowed to rest. She has need of it.' He took up from the stone threshold the form of wax, on which the young man's eyes rested with wondering curiosity, and laid it carefully away in his linen scrip to avoid handling.

'Indeed!' agreed Miles, recalled to his duty and flushing boyishly. 'And thank you, Brother, for your kindness.'

Cadfael followed them out into the workshop. Niall was at his bench, but he rose to meet them as they took their leave, a modest man, who had had the delicacy to remove himself from any attendance on what should be private between comforter and comforted. Judith looked at him gravely, and suddenly recovered from some deep reserve of untouched innocence within her a pale but lovely smile. 'Master Niall, I grieve that I have caused you so much trouble and distress, and I do thank you for your goodness. And I have a thing to collect, and a debt to pay – have you forgotten?'

'No,' said Niall. 'But I would have brought it to you when the time was better suited.' He turned to the shelf behind him, and brought out to her the coiled girdle. She paid him what he asked, as simply as he asked it, and then she unrolled the buckle end in her hands, and looked long at her dead husband's mended gift, and for the first time her eyes moistened with a pearly sheen, though no tears fell.

'It is a time very well suited now,' she said, looking up into Niall's face, 'for a small, precious thing to provide me with a pure pleasure.'

It was the only pleasure she had that day, and even that carried with it a piercing undercurrent of pain. Agatha's flustered and voluble fussing and Miles's restrained but all too attentive concern were equally burdensome to her. The dead face of Brother Eluric remained with her every moment. How could she have failed to feel his anguish? Once, twice, three times she had received him and parted from him, with no deeper misgiving than a mild sense of his discomfort, which could well be merely shyness, and a conviction that here was a young man none too happy, which she had attributed to want of a true vocation in one cloistered from childhood. She had been so deeply sunk in her own griefs as to be insensitive to his. Even in death he did not reproach her. He had no need. She reproached herself.

She would have sought distraction at least in occupying her hands, but she could not face the awed whispers and heavy silences of the girls in the spinning room. She chose rather to sit in the shop, where, if the curious came to stare and exclaim, at least they were likely to come one at a time, and some at least might come honestly to buy cloth, not even having heard yet the news that was being blown round the alleys of Shrewsbury like thistledown, and taking root as blithely.

But even that was hard to bear. She would have been glad when evening came, and the shutters were put up, but that one late customer, coming to collect a length of cloth for his mother, elected to stay a while and commiserate with the lady in private, or at least as much privacy as he could contrive between the clucking forays of Agatha, who could not leave her niece unattended for many minutes together. Those brief intervals, however, Vivian Hynde knew how to use to the best advantage.

He was the only son of old William Hynde, who ran the biggest flocks of sheep in the central western uplands of the shire, and who for years had regularly sold the less select fleeces of his clip to the Vestiers, while the finest were reserved to be collected by the middlemen for shipping to the north of France and the wool towns of Flanders, from his warehouse and jetty downstream, beyond Godfrey Fuller's workshops. The partnership between the two families for business purposes had existed for two generations, and made close contact plausible even for this young sprig who was said to be at odds with his father, and highly unlikely to prove a third successful woolman, his talent being more highly developed in spending the money his father made. So much so that it was rumoured the old man had put his foot down heavily, and refused to pay any more debts for his son and heir, or allow him any more funds to squander on dice, and girls, and riotous living. William had bailed him out of trouble often enough already, but now, without his backing, Vivian's usual resources were far less likely to lend to him or give him extended credit. And easy friends fall off from an idol and patron who no longer has money to spend.

There was no sign of drooping as yet, however, in Vivian's bright crest when he came, with his considerable charm and grace, to console a dismayed widow. He was a very personable young man indeed, tall and athletic, with corn-yellow hair that curled becomingly, and dancing pebble-brown eyes in which a full light found surprising golden glints. He was invariably elegant in his gear and wear, and knew very well how pleasant a picture he made in most women's eyes. And if he had made no headway yet with the Widow Perle, neither had anyone else, and there was still hope.

He had the wit to approach delicately on this occasion, with a declaration of sympathy and concern that stopped short of probing too deeply. Excellent at keeping his feet on thin ice, indeed sensible enough to know himself a man for surfaces, not for depths, he also had the gall to rally and tease a little in the hope of raising a smile.

'And now if you shut yourself up here and grieve in private for someone you hardly knew, that aunt of yours will drive you ever more melancholy. She has you talked halfway to a nunnery already. And that,' said Vivian with emphatic pleading, 'you *must not do*.'

'Many another has,' she said, 'with no better cause. Why not I?'

'Because,' he said, glittering, and leaning closer to lower his voice for fear Agatha should choose that moment to enter yet again on some pretext or other, 'because you are young and beautiful, and have no real wish to bury yourself in a convent. You know it! And because I am your devoted worshipper, as well you know, and if you vanish from my life it will be the death of me.'

She took that as a well-intended if ill-judged flourish, and was even a little touched by his suddenly caught breath and stricken gaze as he realised what he had said, and how it must bite home on this of all days. He caught at her hand, voluble and honeyed in dismay. 'Oh, forgive me, forgive me! Fool that I am, I never meant ... There is no blame, none, can touch you. Let me in to your life closer, and I'll convince you. Marry me, and I'll shut out all vexations and doubts from you ...'

She did begin to wonder, afterwards, if it was all calculated, for he was a subtle and persuasive young man; but then she was disarmed and self-doubting, and could not bring herself to attribute deceit or self-interest to any other. Vivian had often enough pressed his attentions upon her and made no impression. Now what she saw in him was a boy no more than a year older than Brother Eluric, one who might, for all his flattery and exaggeration, be suffering something of what Brother Eluric had suffered. She had so lamentably failed to offer the slightest help to the one, the more reason she should deal considerately with the other. So she tolerated him, and made firm but gentle answers, longer than she would have done at any other time.

'It's foolish to talk so,' she said. 'You and I have known each other from childhood. I'm your elder, and a widow, by no means a match for you, and I do not intend to marry again with any man. You must accept that for an answer. Waste no more time here on me.'

'You are fretting now,' he said vehemently, 'over this monk who is dead, though God knows that's none of your fault. But it will not always be so, you'll see all very differently in a month or so. And for this charter that troubles you, it can be changed. You can, you should rid yourself of the bargain, and with it the reproach. You see now it was folly.'

'Yes,' she agreed resignedly, 'it was indeed folly to put a price, even a nominal price, upon a gift. I should never have done it. It has brought nothing but grief. But yes, it can be undone.'

It seemed to her that he was drawing encouragement from this lengthening colloquy, and that she certainly did not desire. So she rose, and pleaded her very real weariness to rid herself of his continuing assiduities as gently as possible. Vivian departed reluctantly but still gracefully, looking back from the doorway for a long, ingratiating moment before he swung about and went, lithe and long-legged and elegant, down the street called Maerdol towards the bridge.

But even when he was gone, the evening was full of echoes of the morning, reminders of disaster, reproaches of folly, as Agatha worried away at the past.

'You see now how foolish it was to make such a ballad-romance agreement, like any green girl. A rose, indeed! You should never have given away half your patrimony so rashly, how could you know when you and yours might have great need of it? And now see what it's come to! A death, and all at the door of that foolish charter.'

'You need not trouble any longer,' said Judith wearily. 'I do repent it. It is not too late to amend it. Let me alone now. There is nothing you could say to me that I have not already said to myself.'

She went early to her bed, and the girl Branwen, relieved of the carding that brought her out in a rash, and put to work for a time in the household, came to fetch and carry for her, fold away into the chest the gown her mistress discarded, and curtain the unshuttered window. Branwen was fond of Judith, but not sorry, on this occasion, to be dismissed early, for Vivian's serving-man, left behind to carry home the bolt of cloth for Mistress Hynde, was settled cosily in the kitchen, throwing dice with Bertred, the foreman of the weavers, and both of them were personable fellows with an eye for a pretty girl. Branwen was not at all averse to being the desirable bone between two handsome dogs. Sometimes she had felt that Bertred had ideas above his station, and was casting a greedy eye in the direction of his mistress, being vain of his sturdy, straight body and fresh, comely face, and a silver tongue to match. But nothing would ever come of that! And when he had Master Hynde's Gunnar across the table from him, plainly captivated, he might better appreciate more accessible meat.

'Go now,' said Judith, loosing the great sheaf of her hair about her shoulders. 'I shan't need you tonight. But call me very early in the morning,' she added with sudden resolution, 'for I'm going to the abbey. I'll not leave this matter lying one hour more than need be. Tomorrow I'll go to the abbot and have a new charter drawn up. No more roses! The gift I made for so foolish a fee I'll now make unconditional.'

Branwen was proud of her advancement into Judith's personal service, and fondly imagined herself closer in her mistress's confidence than in fact she was. And with two young men in the kitchen already interested in her and prepared to be impressed, what wonder if she boasted of being the first to be entrusted with Judith's plans for the morrow? It seemed a pity that Gunnar should so soon afterwards recall that he had to carry home Mistress Hynde's cloth, and might end with a flea in his ear if he delayed too long. And though that left her the attentions of Bertred, whom on the whole she preferred, his pricked sense of proprietorship in a woman of this household seemed to flag disappointingly once his rival was out of the house. It was not, after all, a satisfactory evening. Branwen went to her bed out of temper between disillusionment and dudgeon, and out of sorts with men.

Young Alan Herbard, Hugh's deputy, dutiful and determined though he was, drew the line at coping unaided with murder, and had had a courier on the road as soon as the news came to his ears. By noon of the next day, which was the eighteenth day of June, Hugh would surely be back in Shrewsbury, not in his own house, where only one elderly servant remained during the family's absence, but at the castle, where garrison, sergeant and all were at his disposal.

Meantime, Cadfael betook himself and his waxen footprint, with the abbot's blessing, into the town, and showed mould and drawing to Geoffrey Corviser, the provost, and his son Philip, the foremost shoemakers and leather workers in the town. 'For sooner or later every boot comes into the cobbler's hands,' he said simply, 'though it may be a year ahead or more. No harm, at least, in keeping a copy of such witness as you see there, and looking out for the like among any you repair.'

Philip handled the wax delicately, and nodded over the evidence it provided of its wearer's tread. 'I don't know it, but it will be easily seen if ever it does find its way in here. And I'll show it to the cobbler over the bridge, in Frankwell. Between us, who knows, we may run the fellow down in the end. But there's many a man patches his own,' said the good craftsman with professional disdain.

A thin chance enough, Cadfael admitted to himself on his way back over the bridge, but one that could not be neglected. What else had they to offer a lead? Little enough, except the inevitable and unanswerable question: Who could possibly have wanted to destroy the rose-bush? And for what conceivable reason? A question they had all voiced already, without profit, and one that would be posed all over again when Hugh arrived.

Instead of turning in at the gatehouse Cadfael passed by and walked the length of the Foregate, along the dusty highway, past the bakery, past the forge, exchanging greetings in at doorways and over hedges as he went, to turn in at the gate of Niall's yard, and cross to the wicket which led through into the garden. It was bolted fast on the inner side. Cadfael turned instead to the shop, where Niall was at work with a small ceramic crucible and a tiny clay mould for a brooch.

'I came to see if you'd had any further night visitors,' said Cadfael, 'but I see you've secured one way in, at least. A pity there's no wall ever built high enough to keep out a man determined to get in. But even stopping one hole is something. What of the bush? Will it live?'

'Come and see. One side may die off, but it's no more than two or three branches. It may leave the tree lopsided, but a year or so, and pruning and growth will balance all.'

In the green and sunlight and tangled colour of the garden the rose-bush spread its arms firmly against the north wall, the dangling trailers pegged back to the stone with strips of cloth. Niall had wound a length of stout canvas round and round the damaged bole, binding the severed wood together, and coated the covering with a thick layer of wax and grease.

'There's love been put into this,' said Cadfael approvingly, but wisely did not say whether for the bush or the woman. The leaves on the half-severed part had wilted, and a few had fallen, but the bulk of the tree stood green and glossy, and full of half-open buds. 'You've done well by it. I could use you inside the enclave, if ever you tire of bronze and the world.'

The quiet, decent man never opened his mouth to answer that. Whatever he felt for woman or rose was his business, no other man's. Cadfael respected that, and viewing the wide, wide-set, honest and yet reticent eyes, he took his leave and set off back to his proper duties feeling somewhat reproved, and curiously elated. One man at least in this sorry business kept his eyes on his own course, and would not easily be turned aside. And he, surely, looking for no gain. Somewhere in all this there was greed of gain more than enough, and little enough of love.

It was almost noon by this time, and the sun high and hot, a true June day. Saint Winifred must have been at work coaxing the heavens to do her honour for the festival of her translation. As so often happened in a late season, the summer had all but caught up with the laggard spring, flowers which had lingered shivering and reluctant to bloom suddenly sprang into fevered haste, bursting their buds overnight into a blazing prime. The crops, slower to take risks, might still be as much as a month late, but they would be lavish and clean, half their hereditary enemies chilled to death in April and May.

In the doorway of his lodge in the gatehouse Brother Porter was standing in earnest talk with an agitated young man. Cadfael, always vulnerable to curiosity, his prevalent sin, halted, wavered and turned aside, recognising Miles Coliar, that tidy, practical, trim young fellow a great deal less trim than usual, his hair blown and teased erect in disorder, his bright blue eyes dilated beneath drawn and anxious copper brows. Miles turned his head, hearing a new step approaching, and recognised, through a haze of worry, a brother he had seen only the previous day sitting amicably with his cousin. He swung about eagerly.

'Brother, I remember you – you were of some comfort and

help yesterday to Judith. You have not seen her today? She has not spoken again with you?'

'She has not,' said Cadfael, surprised. 'Why? What is new now? She went home with you yesterday. I trust she has met with no further grief?'

'No, none that I know of. I do know she went to her bed in good time, and I hoped she would sleep well. But now ...' He cast a vague, distracted glance about him: 'They tell me at home she set out to come here. But ...'

'She has not been here,' said the porter positively. 'I have not left my post, I should know if she had entered the gate. I know the lady from the time she came here making her gift to the house. I have not set eyes on her today. But Master Coliar here says she left home very early ...'

'*Very* early,' Miles confirmed vehemently. 'Before I was waking.'

'And with intent to come here on some errand to the lord abbot,' concluded the porter.

'So her maid told me,' said Miles, sweating. 'Judith told her so last night, when the girl attended her to bed. I knew nothing of it until this morning. But it seems she has not been here. She never reached here. And she has not come home again. Midday, and she has not come home! I dread something ill has befallen her.'

Chapter Six

There were five of them gathered in the abbot's parlour that afternoon, in urgent conclave: Radulfus himself, Brothers Anselm and Cadfael, witnesses to the charter which had somehow precipitated these dire events, Miles Coliar, restless and fevered with anxiety, and Hugh Beringar, who had ridden south in haste from Maesbury with Eluric's murder on his mind, to find on arrival that a second crisis had followed hard on the heels of the first. He had already deputed Alan Herbard to send men hunting through the town and the Foregate for any sign or news of the missing lady, with orders to send word if by any chance she should have returned home. There could, after all, be legitimate reasons for her absence, something unforeseen that had met and deflected her on her way. But minute by minute it began to look less likely. Branwen had told her tearful story, and there was no question but Judith had indeed set out from home to visit the abbey. None, either, that she had never reached it.

'The girl never told me what my cousin had said, until this morning,' said Miles, twisting frustrated hands. 'I knew nothing of it, or I could have borne her company. So short a walk, down here from the town! And the watchman at the town gate said good day to her and saw her start across the bridge, but after that he was busy, and had no call to watch her go. And not a sign of her from that moment.'

'And she said her errand was to remit the rose rent,' said Hugh intently, 'and make her gift to the abbey free of all conditions?'

'So her maid says. So Judith told her. She was much distressed,' said Miles, 'over the young brother's death. She surely took it to heart that it was her whim brought about that murder.'

'It has yet to be explained,' said Abbot Radulfus, 'why that should be. Truly it does appear that Brother Eluric interrupted the attack upon the rose-bush, and was killed for his pains, perhaps in mere panic, yet killed he was. What I do not understand is why anyone should wish to destroy the rose-bush in the first place. But for that inexplicable deed there would have been no interruption and no death. Who could want to hack down the bush? What possible motive could there be?'

'Ah, but, Father, there could!' Miles turned on him with feverish vehemence. 'There were some not best pleased when my cousin gave away so valuable a property, worth the half of all she has. If the bush was hacked down and all the roses dead by the day of Saint Winifred's translation, the rent could not be paid, and the terms of the charter would have been broken. The whole bargain could be repudiated.'

'Could,' Hugh pointed out briskly, 'but would not. The matter would still be in the lady's hands, she could remit the rent at will. And you see she had the will.'

'She *could* remit it,' Miles echoed with sharp intent, '*if she were here to do it.* But she is not here. Four days until the payment is due, and she has vanished. Time gained, time gained! Whoever failed to destroy the bush has now abducted my cousin. She is not here to grant or deny. What he did not accomplish by one way he now approaches by another.'

There was a brief, intent silence, and then the abbot said slowly: 'Do you indeed believe that? You speak as one believing.'

'I do, my lord. I see no other possibility. Yesterday she announced her intention of making her gift unconditional. Today that has been prevented. There was no time to be lost.'

'Yet you yourself did not know what she meant to do,' said Hugh, 'not until today. Did any other know of it?'

'Her maid owns she repeated it in the kitchen. Who knows how many heard it then, or got it from those who did? Such things come out through keyholes and the chinks of shutters. Moreover, Judith may have met with some acquaintance on the bridge or in the Foregate, and told them where she was bound. However lightly and thoughtlessly she had that provision written into the charter, the failure to observe it would render the bargain null and void. Father, you know that is true.'

'I do know it,' acknowledged Radulfus, and came at last to the unavoidable question: 'Who, then, could possibly stand to gain by breaking the agreement, by whatever means?'

'Father, my cousin is young, and a widow, and a rich prize in marriage, all the richer if her gift to you could be annulled. There are a bevy of suitors about the town pursuing her, and have been now for a year and more, and every one of them would rather marry the whole of her wealth than merely the half. Me, I manage the business for her, I'm very well content with what I have, and with the wife I'm to marry before the year's out, a good match. But even if we were not first cousins I should have no interest in Judith but as a loyal kinsman and craftsman should. But I cannot choose but know how she is pestered with wooers. Not that she encourages any of them, nor ever gives them grounds for hope, but they never cease their efforts. After three years and more of widowhood, they reason, her resolution must surely weaken, and she'll be worn down into taking a second husband at last. It may be that one of them is running out of patience.'

'To name names,' said Hugh mildly, 'may sometimes be dangerous, but to call a man a wooer is not necessarily to call him an abductor and murderer into the bargain. And I think you have gone so far, Master Coliar, that in this company you may as well go the rest of the way.'

Miles moistened his lips and brushed a sleeve across his beaded forehead. 'Business looks to business for a match, my lord. There are two guildsmen in the town, at least, who would be only too glad to get hold of Judith's trade, and both of them work in with us, and know well enough what she's worth. There's Godfrey Fuller does all the dyeing of our fleeces, and the fulling of the cloth at the end of it, and he'd dearly like to make himself the master of the spinning and weaving, too, and have all in one profitable basket. And then there's old William Hynde, he has a wife still, but by another road he could get his hands on the Vestier property, for he has a young spark of a son who comes courting her day in, day out, and has the entry because they know each other from children. The father might be willing to use him as bait for a woman, though he's drawn his purse-strings tight from paying the young fellow's debts any longer. And the son – if he could win her I fancy he'd be set up for life, but not dance to his father's tune, more likely to laugh in his face. And that's not the whole of it, for our neighbour the saddler is just of an age to feel the want of a wife, and in his plodding way has settled on her as suitable. And our best weaver chances to be a very good craftsmen and a fine-looking man, and fancies himself even prettier than he is, and he's been casting sheep's eyes at her lately, though I doubt if she even noticed. There's more than one comely journeyman has caught his mistress's eye and done very well for himself.'

'Hard to imagine our solid guildsmen resorting to murder and abduction,' objected the abbot, unwilling to accept so readily a suggestion so outrageous.

'But the murder,' Hugh pointed out alertly, 'seems to have been done in alarm and terror, and probably never was intended. Yet having so far committed himself, why should a man stop at the second crime?'

'Still it seems to me a hazardous business, for from all I know or have heard about the lady, she would not easily give way to persuasion. Captive or free, she has thus far resisted all blandishments, she will not change now. I do understand,' said Radulfus ruefully, 'what force of compulsion the common report may bring to bear in such a case, how a woman might feel it better to yield and marry than endure the scandal of suspicion and the ill will between families that must follow. But this lady, it seems to me, might well survive even that pressure. Then her captor would have gained nothing.'

Miles drew deep breath, and ran a hand through his fair curls, dragging them wildly awry. 'Father, what you say is true, Judith is a strong spirit, and will not easily be broken. But, Father, there may be worse! Marriage by rape is no new thing. Once in a man's power, hidden away with no means of escape, if coaxing and persuasion have no effect, there remains force. It has been known time and time again. My lord Beringar here will witness it happens among the nobility, and I know it happens among the commonalty. Even a town tradesman might resort to it at last. And I know my cousin, if once her virtue was lost, she might well think it best to mend her sorry state by marriage. Wretched though that remedy must be.'

'Wretched indeed!' agreed Radulfus with detestation. 'Such a thing must not be. Hugh, this house is deeply committed here, the charter and the gift draw us in, and whatever aid we can lend you to recover this unhappy lady is at your disposal, men, funds, whatever you require. No need to ask – take! And as for our prayers, they shall not be wanting. There is still some frail chance that no harm has come to her, and she may yet return home of her own volition, and wonder at this fury and alarm. But now we must reckon with the worst, and hunt as for a soul in danger.'

'Then we'd best be about it,' said Hugh, and rose to take his leave. Miles was on his feet with a nervous spring, eager and anxious, and would have been first out at the door if Cadfael had not opened his mouth for the first time in this conference.

'I did hear, Master Coliar, indeed I know from Mistress Perle herself, that she has sometimes thought of leaving the world and taking the veil. Sister Magdalen talked with her about such a vocation a few days ago, I believe. Did you know of it?'

'I knew the sister came visiting,' said Miles, his blue eyes widening. 'What they said I was not told and did not ask. That was Judith's business. She has sometimes talked of it, but less of late.'

'Did you encourage such a step?' asked Cadfael.

'I never interfered, one way or the other. It would have been her decision. I would not urge it,' said Miles forcibly, 'but neither would I stand in her way if that was what she wanted. At least,' he said with sudden bitterness, 'that would have been a good and peaceful ending. Now only God knows what her dismay and despair must be.'

'There goes a most dutiful and loving cousin,' said Hugh, as Cadfael walked beside him across the great court. Miles was striding out at the gatehouse arch with hair on end, making for the town, and the house and shop at Maerdol-head, where there might by this time be news. A frail chance, but still possible.

'He has good cause,' said Cadfael reasonably. 'But for Mistress Perle and the Vestier business he and his mother would not be in the comfortable state they are. He has everything to lose, should she give in to force and agree to marriage. He owes his cousin much, and by all accounts he's requited her very well, with gratitude and good management. Works hard and to good effect, the business is flourishing. He may well be frantic about her now. Do I hear a certain sting in your voice, lad? Have you doubts about him?'

'No, none. He has no more idea where the girl is now than you or I, that's clear. A man may dissemble very well, up to a point, but I never knew a man who could sweat at will. No, Miles is telling the truth. He's off now to turn the town upside-down hunting for her. And so must I.'

'She had but so short a way to go,' said Cadfael, fretting at the fine detail, which left so little room for doubt that she was gone, that something untoward had indeed happened to her. 'The watch at the gate spoke to her, she had only to cross the bridge and walk this short piece of the Foregate to our gatehouse. A river to cross, a short walk along open road, and in those few minutes she's gone.'

'The river,' said Hugh honestly, 'has been on my mind. I won't deny it.'

'I doubt if it need be. Unless truly by some ill chance. No man is going to make himself rich or his business more prosperous by marriage with a dead woman. Only her heir would benefit by that, and her heir – I suppose that boy must be her nearest kin? – is going out of his mind worrying over what's happened to her, as you yourself have seen. There's nothing false about the state he's in. No, *if* some wooer has determined on drastic action, he'll have spirited her away into some safe place, not done her harm. We need not mourn for the lady, not yet, she'll be guarded like a miser's gold.'

* * *

Cadfael's mind was occupied with the problem until Vespers and beyond. From the bridge to the abbey gatehouse there were but three footpaths leaving the Foregate, two that branched off to the right, one on either side the mill-pond, to serve the six small houses there, the other descending on the left to the long riverside tract of the Gaye, the main abbey gardens. Cover was sparse along the high road, any act of violence would be risky there, and the paths that served the abbey houses suffered the disadvantage, from a conspirator's point of view, of being overlooked by the windows of all six cottages, and in this high summer there would be no shutters closed. The old woman in one cot was stone deaf, and would not have heard even the loudest screams, but generally old people sleep lightly and fitfully, and also, being no longer able to get about as actively as before, they have rather more than their share of curiosity, to fill up the tedium of their days. It would be a bold or a desperate man who attempted violence under their windows.

No trees drew close about the road on that, the southern side of the Foregate, only a few low bushes fringing the pond, and the scrub-covered slope down to the river. Only on the northern side were there well-grown trees, from the end of the bridge, where the path wound down to the Gaye, to a grove some little way short of the abbey gatehouse, where the houses of the Foregate began.

Now if a woman could be drawn aside there, even into the fringe of shadow, at that early hour and with few people abroad, it would not be so difficult to seize a moment when the road was empty and drag her further into the grove, or down among the bushes, with a cloak twisted about her head and arms. But in that case the person involved, man or woman, would have to be someone known to her, someone who could detain her plausibly in talk for a matter of minutes beside the road. Which fitted in well enough with the suggestion Miles had made, for even an unwelcome suitor who was also a town neighbour would be encountered in the ordinary meetings of the day with tolerance and civility. Life in a walled and crowded borough cannot be carried on otherwise.

There might, of course, be other reasons for removing the

girl from home and family, though they would have to have something to do with the matter of the charter and the rose-bush, for surely that could not be some lunatic accident, unconnected with her disappearance. There might! But with all the cudgelling of his brains Cadfael could think of none. And a rich merchant widow in a town where everyone knew everyone was inevitably besieged by suitors out to make their fortunes. Her only safe defence was the one Judith had contemplated, withdrawal into a convent. Or, of course, marriage to whichever of the contestants best pleased or least repelled her. And that, so far, she had not contemplated. It might well be true that the one who considered himself most likely to please had risked all on his chance of softening the lady's heart in a few days of secret courtship. And keeping her hidden until after the twenty-second day of June could break the bargain with the abbey just as surely as destroying the rose-bush and all its blossoms. However many roses survived now, unless Judith was found in time not one of them could be paid into her hand on the day the rent was due. So provided her captor prevailed at last, and drove her to marry him, her affairs would then be his, and he could refuse to renew and prevent her from renewing the broken agreement. And he would have won all, not the half. Yes, whichever way Cadfael viewed the affair, this notion propounded by Miles, who had everything to lose, looked ever more convincing.

He went to his cell with Judith still on his mind. Her well-being seemed to him very much the abbey's business, something that could not be left merely to the secular arm. Tomorrow, he thought, lying awake in the dim dortoir, to the regular bass music of Brother Richard's snores, I'll walk that stretch of road, and see what's there to be found. Who knows but there may be something left behind, more to the point than a single print of a worn boot-heel.

He asked no special leave, for had not the abbot already pledged Hugh whatever men or horses or gear he needed? It was but a small mental leap to establish in his own mind that if Hugh had not specifically demanded his help, he would have done so had he known how his friend's mind was working. Such small exercises in moral agility still came easily to him, where the need seemed to justify them.

He set out after chapter, sallying forth into a Foregate swept by the long, slanting rays of the climbing sun, brilliantly lit and darkly shadowed. In the shade there was dew still on the grass, and a glisten in the leaves as a faint, steady, silent breeze ruffled them unceasingly. The Foregate on which he turned his back was bustling with life, every shop-front and house-door opened wide to the summer, and a constant traffic of housewives, urchins, dogs, carters and pedlars on the move, or gathered in gossiping groups. In this belated but lovely burst of summer, life quitted the confines of walls and roof, and moved into the sunshine. Under the west front of the church and across the gateway the knife-edged shadow of the tower fell, but along the enclave boundary it lay close and narrow, huddled under the foot of the wall.

Cadfael went slowly, exchanging greetings with such acquaintances as he met, but unwilling to be sidetracked into lingering. This first stretch of the road she could not have reached, and the steps he was retracing on her behalf were those of a pious intent which had never come to fruit. On his left, the lofty stone wall continued for the length of the great court and the infirmary and school within, then turned away at a right-angle, and alongside it went the first pathway that led past three small grace houses to the mill, on this near side of the mill-pond. Then the wide expanse of the pool, fringed with a low hedge of bushes. He would not and could not believe that Judith Perle had vanished into either this water or the waves of the river. Whoever had taken her – if someone had indeed taken her – wanted and needed her alive and unharmed and ripe for conquest. Hugh had no choice but to draw his net wide and entertain every possibility. Cadfael preferred to follow one notion at a time. Hugh would almost certainly have enlisted the help of Madog of the Dead Boat by this time, to pursue the worst possibilities of death by water, while the king's sergeants scoured the streets and alleys and houses of Shrewsbury for a live and captive lady. Madog knew every wave of the Severn, every seasonal trick it had in its power to play, every bend or shoal where things swept away by its currents would be cast up again. If the river had taken her, Madog would find her. But Cadfael would not believe it.

And if Hugh also failed to find her within the walls of Shrewsbury? Then they would have to look beyond. It's no simple matter to transport an unwilling lady very far, and by daylight. Could it even be done at all, short of using a cart? A horseman carrying such a swathed burden would need a horse powerful enough to carry the extra weight, and worse, would certainly be conspicuous. Someone would surely remember him, or even question him on the spot, human curiosity being what it is. No, she could not, surely, be far away.

Cadfael passed by the pool, and came to the second pathway, on this further side, which served the other three little houses. Beyond, after their narrow gardens, there was an open field, and at the end of that, turning sharply left, a narrow high road going south along the riverside. By that track an abductor might certainly retreat within a mile or so into the forest, but on the other hand there was no cover here along the riverside, any attack perpetrated there could be seen even from the town walls across the water.

But on the right of the Foregate, once the houses ended, the thick grove of trees began, and after that the steep path dived down sidelong to the bank of the Severn, through bushes and trees, giving access to the long, lush level of the Gaye. Beyond that, she would still have been on the open bridge, and surely inviolable. Here, if anywhere in this short walk, there was room for a predator to strike and withdraw with his prey. She had to be prevented from reaching the abbey and doing what she intended to do. There would be no second chance. And the house of the rose was indeed a property well worth reclaiming.

With every moment the thing began to look more and more credible. Improbable, perhaps, in an ordinary tradesman, as law-abiding as his neighbours and respected by all; but a man who has tried one relatively harmless expedient, and inadvertently killed a man in consequence, is no longer ordinary.

Cadfael crossed the Foregate and went into the grove of

trees, stepping warily to avoid adding any tracks to those already all too plentiful. The imps of the Foregate played here, attended by their noisy camp-following of dogs, and tearfully trailed by those lesser imps as yet too small to be taken seriously and admitted to their games, and too short in the legs to keep up with them. In the more secluded clearings lovers met in the dark, their nests neatly coiled in the flattened grasses. Small hope of finding anything of use here.

He turned back to the road, and walked on the few paces to the path that descended to the Gaye. Before him the stone bridge extended, and beyond it the high town wall and the tower of the gate. Sunlight bathed the roadway and the walls, blanching the stone to a creamy pallor. The Severn, running a little higher than its usual summer level, shimmered and stirred with a deceptive appearance of placidity and languor, but Cadfael knew how fast those smooth currents were running, and what vehement undertows coursed beneath the blue, sky-mirroring surface. Most male children here learned to swim almost as soon as they learned to walk, and there were places where the Severn could be as gentle and safe as its smiling mask, but here where it coiled about the town, leaving only one approach by land, the narrow neck straddled by the castle, it was a perilous water. Could Judith Perle swim? It was no easy matter for girl-children to strip and caper along the grassy shores and flash in and out of the stream as the boys did, and for them it must be a more rare accomplishment.

At the town end of the bridge Judith had passed, unhindered and alone; the watchman had seen her begin to cross. Hard to believe that any man had dared to molest her here on the open crossing, where she had only to utter a single cry, and the watchman would have heard her, and looked out in instant alarm. So she had arrived at this spot where Cadfael was standing. And then? As far as present reports went, no one had seen her since.

Cadfael began the descent to the Gaye. This path was trodden regularly, and bare of grass, and the landward bushes that fringed it drew gradually back from its edge, leaving the level, cultivated ground open. On the river side they grew thickly, all down the slope to the water, and under the first arch of the bridge, where once a boat-mill had been moored to make use of the force of the current. Close to the waterside a footpath led off downstream, and beside it the abbey's gardens lay neatly arrayed all along the rich plain, and three or four brothers were pricking out plants of cabbage and colewort. Further along came the orchards, apple and pear and plum, the sweet cherry, and two big walnut trees, and the low bushes of little sour gooseberries that were only just beginning to flush into colour. There was another disused mill at the end of the level, and the final abbey ground was a field of corn. Then ridges of woodland came down and overhung the water, and the curling eddies ate away the bank beneath their roots.

Across the broad river the hill of Shrewsbury rose in a great sweep of green, that wore the town wall like a coronet. Two or three small wickets gave access through the wall to gardens and grass below. They could easily be barred and blocked in case of attack, and the clear outlook such a raised fortress commanded gave ample notice of any approach. The vulnerable neck unprotected by water was filled by the castle, completing the circle of the wall. A strong place, as well as a very fair one, yet King Stephen had taken it by storm, four years ago, and held it through his sheriffs ever since.

But all this stretch of our land, Cadfael thought, brooding over its prolific green, is overlooked by hundreds of houses and households there within the wall. How many moments can there be in the day when someone is not peering out from a window, this weather, or below by the riverside, fishing, or hanging out washing, or the children playing and bathing? Not, perhaps, so many of them, so early in the morning, but surely someone. And never a word said of struggle or flight, or of something heavy and human-shaped being carried. No, not this way. Our lands here are open and innocent. The only hidden reach is here, here beside the bridge or under it, where trees and bushes give cover.

He waded the bushes towards the arch, and the last of the dew darkened his sandals and the skirt of his habit, but sparsely now, surviving only here, in the deep green shade. Below the stone arch the water had sunk only a foot or so from its earlier fullness, leaving a bleaching fringe of grass and water-plants. A man could walk through dry-shod but for dew. Even the winter level or the flush of the spring thaw never came nearer than six feet of the crown of the arch. The green growth was fat and lavish and tangled, suckled on rich, moist earth.

Someone had been before him here, the grasses were parted and bent aside by the passage of at least one person, probably more. That was nothing very unusual, boys roam everywhere in their play, and in their mischief, too. What was less usual here was the deep groove driven into the moist soil uncovered by the recent lowering of the level, and prolonged into the grass above. A boat had been drawn aground there, and no long time ago, either. At the town end of the bridge there were always boats beached or moored, handy for their owners' use. But seldom here.

Cadfael squatted close to view the ground. The grass had absorbed any marks left by feet, except for the lowest lip of the land, and there certainly at least one man had trampled the moist ground, but the mud had slithered under him and obliterated any shape he had left behind. One man or two, for the spread of slippery mud showed both sides of the groove the skiff had made.

If he had not been sitting on his heels he would never have caught the single alien thing, for there under the arch there was no glint of sunlight to betray it. But there it was, trodden into the disturbed mud, a metallic thread like a wisp of reddish-gold straw, no longer than the top joint of his thumb. He prised it out and it lay in his palm, a tiny arrow-head without a shaft, bent a little out of shape by the foot that had trodden it in. He stooped to rinse it in the edge of the river, and carried it out into the sunshine.

And now he saw it for what it was, the bronze tag which had sealed the end of a leather girdle, a delicate piece of work, incised with punch and hammer after being attached to the belt, and surely not torn from its anchorage now without considerable violence and struggle.

Cadfael turned in his tracks, strode up the steep path to the road, and set off back along the Foregate at his fastest pace.

Chapter Seven

'This is hers,' said Niall, looking up from the scrap of bronze with a fixed and formidable face. 'I know it, though I did not make it. It belongs to that girdle she took back with her, the morning Brother Eluric lay here dead. I made the new buckle to match this design, this and the rosettes round the tongue-holes. I should know it anywhere. It is hers. Where did you find it?'

'Under the first arch of the bridge, where a boat had been hauled up in hiding.'

'To carry her away! And this – trodden into the mud, you say. See, when this was set in place it was hammered home into the leather with the pattern, it would not come loose easily, even after years, and with the leather softening and thinning from use, and perhaps a little greasy with handling. Someone was rough with the girdle, to tear this away.'

'And with the lady also,' Cadfael agreed grimly. 'I could not be sure, myself, I hardly saw the girdle when she took it in her hands that day. But you could not be mistaken. Now I know. One step at least on the way. And a boat – a boat would be the simplest means of all of carrying her off. No neighbour passing close, to query such large freight, no one ashore to wonder at any passing skiff, they're common enough along the Severn. The girdle from which this came may well have been snatched to help to bind her.'

'And she to be used so foully!' Niall wiped his large, capable hands on the rag of woollen cloth on his bench, and began purposefully unfastening and laying by his leathern apron. 'What is to be done now? Tell me how best I can help – where first to look for her. I'll close my shop—'

'No,' said Cadfael, 'make no move, only keep watch still on the rose-bush, for I have this strange fancy the life of the one is bound up fast with the life of the other. What is there you could do elsewhere that Hugh Beringar cannot? He has men enough, and trust me, they're all hard at it, he'll see to that. Stay here and be patient, and whatever I discover you shall know. Your business is bronze, not boats, you've done your part.'

'And you, what will you do now?' Niall hesitated, frowning, unwilling to be left with the passive part.

'I'm off to find Hugh Beringar as fast as I can, and after him Madog, who knows all there is to know about boats, from his own coracles to the freight barges that fetch the wool clips away. Madog may be able to tell what manner of boat it was from the very dent it left behind in the mud. You bide here and be as easy as you can. With God's help we'll find her.'

He looked back once from the doorway, impressed by the charged silence at his back. The man of few words remained quite still, staring into some invisible place where Judith Perle stood embattled and alone, captive to greed and brutality. Even her good works conspired against her, even her generosity turned venomous, to poison her life. The controlled and uncommunicative face was eloquent enough at that moment. And if those big, adroit hands, so precise on his tiny crucibles and moulds, could once get a hold on the throat of whoever has rapt away Judith Perle, thought Cadfael as he hurried back towards the town, I doubt if the king's justice would have any need of a hangman, or the trial cost the shire much money.

The porter at the town gate sent a boy hotfoot up to the castle in search of Hugh as soon as Cadfael came to report, somewhat breathlessly, that there was need of the sheriff down at the waterside. It took a little time to find him, however, and Cadfael made use of the interval by going in search of Madog of the Dead Boat. He knew well enough where to find him, provided he was not already out on the water somewhere, about some curious part of his varied business. He had a hut tucked under the lee of the western bridge that opened the road into his native Wales, and there he made coracles, or timber boats if required, fished in season, ferried fares on request, carried goods for a fee, anything to do with transport by water. The time being then past noon, Madog happened to be taking a brief rest and a solitary meal when Cadfael reached the bridge. A squat, muscular, hairy elderly Welshman, without kith or kin and in no need of either, for he was sufficient to himself and had been since childhood, he yet had an open welcome for his friends. He needed no one, but if others needed him he was at their disposal. Once summoned, he rose and came.

Hugh was at the gate before them. They crossed the bridge together, and came down to the waterside and under the dim, cool shadow of the arch.

'Here in the mud,' said Cadfael, 'I found this, torn off surely in a struggle. It comes from a girdle belonging to Mistess Perle, for Niall Bronzesmith made a new buckle to match the belt fittings only a few days ago, and this was the pattern he had to copy. That puts it past doubt, he knows his work. And here someone had a boat laid up ready.'

'As like as not stolen,' said Madog judicially, eyeing the deep mark in the soil. 'For such a cantrip, why use your own? Then if it's noted, and any man smells something amiss about where it's seen and what's within it, nothing leads towards you. And this was early in the morning, yesterday? Now I wonder if any fisherman or waterman from the town has mislaid his boat from its moorings? I know a dozen could have left this scar. And all you need do, when you'd done with the skiff, would be turn it adrift to fetch up where it would.'

'That could only be downstream,' said Hugh, looking up from the little arrow-head of bronze in his palm.

'So it could! Only downstream from wherever he had done with it. And even that would surely be downstream from here, if here he set out with such a cargo. Far easier and safer than heading upstream. Early in the morning it may have been, and few people yet abroad, but by the time one rower, or even a pair, had taken a boat all round the walls of the town against the stream, as they'd have to do to get clear, there'd be folks enough about the shore and the water. Even after turning away from the town they'd have Frankwell to face – a good hour's rowing before they'd be free of notice and curiosity. Downstream, once past this stretch of the wall and out from under the castle, they could breathe easily, they'd be between fields and woodland, clear of the town.'

'That's good sense,' said Hugh. 'I don't say upstream is impossible, but we'll follow the best chance first. God knows we've dragged every alley within the walls, and ransacked most of the houses, and are still hard at it in there finishing the work. Not a soul owns to having seen or heard anything of her since last she spoke with the watchman at the gate, and started across the bridge here. And if ever she went, or was taken, back into the town, it was not by the gate. The porter passed in no cart or load that could have been hiding her, so he swears. Still, there are wickets through here and there, though most of them into burgage gardens, and it would be no easy matter to get through to the streets without the household knowing of it. I begin to believe that she cannot be within the walls, but I've set men at every wicket that gives access to a street, and made entry to every house an order under the king's justice. What's the same for all cannot well be resisted or complained of.'

'And has not?' wondered Cadfael. 'Never once?'

'They grumble, but even that under their breath. No, not one has put up any objection, nor shuffled and contrived to keep anything closed. And all yesterday until dusk I had her cousin treading on my heels, probing here and there like a worried hound on an uncertain scent. He's set two or three of his weavers to help in the hunt for her. The foreman – Bertred they call him, a strapping young fellow all brawn and brag – he's been out and about with us again all day, nose-down. He's gone with a party of my men now, out along the Castle Foregate, searching the yards and gardens in the suburb, and round to the river again. All her household is biting its nails, frantic to find her. And no wonder, for it's she who provides a living for the lot of them – a matter of twenty families or more depend on her. And never a hair of her to be found, and never a shadow of suspicion against any other creature, so far.'

'How did you do with Godfrey Fuller?' asked Cadfael, recalling what rumour said of Judith's wooers.

Hugh laughed briefly. 'I remember, too! And truth is truth, he seems as concerned about her almost as her cousin. What does he do but hand me all his keys, and bid me make free. And I did.'

'His keys for the dye-works and the fulling sheds, too?'

'All, though I needed none, for all his men were at work, and every corner open to view, and as innocent as the day. I think he would even have lent me some men to join the hunt, but that he's too fond of money to let the work slacken.'

'And William Hynde?'

'The old woolman? He's been away sleeping the night over with his shepherds and flocks, so his household said, and came home only this morning. He knew nothing about the girl going astray until then. Alan was there yesterday, and Hynde's wife made no demur, but let him look where he would, but I went back there this morning and spoke with the man himself. He's off back to the hills before night. It seems he has some hoggets up there with a rot of the feet, he and his man came back only to get a supply of the wash to treat them. And more concerned about them than about Mistress Perle, though he did say he was sorry to hear such news of her. By this time I'm certain she's not within the town. So,' said Hugh briskly, 'we may well look elsewhere. Downstream, we're agreed. Madog, come back with us to the town gate and get us a boat, and we'll take a look at what offers, downstream.'

In midstream, running with the current, and with only a twitch of Madog's oars now and then to keep them on course, they had the whole expanse of Shrewsbury's eastern side unrolling past them, a steep bank of green under the wall, here and there a cluster of low bushes at the water's edge, here and there a trailing willow tree, but chiefly one long sweep of seeding summer grass, and then the lofty grey stone of the wall. Barely a single ridge of roof showed over the crest, only the top of Saint Mary's spire and tower, and a more distant glimpse of the tip of Saint Alkmund's. There were three wickets in the wall before they reached the mouth of Saint Mary's water-lane, which gave access to the river from town and castle at need, and in places the householders within had extended their gardens to the outer side, or made use of the ground, where it was level enough, for their stores of wood or other materials for their crafts. But the slope here made cultivation difficult except in favoured spots, and the best gardens outside the wall were on the south-west, within the great serpent-coil of the river.

They passed the narrow walled chute of the water-lane, and beyond was another steep slope of grass, more cloaked in bushes here, before the town wall drew closer to the river, flanking the level, cleared strip of green where the young men were accustomed to set up the butts and practise their archery on holidays and fair-days. At the end of this ground there was one last wicket, close under the first tower of the castle, and past that the ground levelled, a sweep of open field between the water and the high road that emerged under the castle gates. Here, as on the Welsh side, the town had spilled beyond the wall for a short way, and little houses, close-set, bordered the road, huddling under the shadow of the great hulk of stone towers and curtain wall that straddled the only dry-shod approach to Shrewsbury.

The open meadows stretched away, widening, into an undulating expanse of field and woodland, peaceful and serene. The only remaining reminders of the town were here close beside the river, Godfrey Fuller's sheds and fulling-troughs and tenterground, and a short way beyond, the substantial warehouse where William Hynde's best fleeces lay corded and ready, waiting for the middleman's barge to come and collect them, and the narrow, stout jetty where it would draw alongside to load.

There were men going busily in and out here about the fulling workshop, and two lengths of bright russet cloth stretched and drying on the frames. This was the season for the reds, browns and yellows. Cadfael looked back along the castle wall to the last wicket giving access to the town, and recalled that Fuller's house lay not far from the castle precinct. So, for that matter, though a little more distant, close to the high cross, did William Hynde's. This gate was convenient for both. Fuller kept a watchman here at night, living on the workshop premises.

'Small chance of ever hiding a captive lady here,' said

Hugh resignedly. 'By day it would be impossible, with so many busy about the place, and by night the fellow who sleeps here is paid to keep a close eye on Hynde's property, too, and keeps a mastiff into the bargain. I don't recall that there's anything but meadow and woodland beyond, but we'll go a little further.'

The green banks drifted by on either side, encroaching trees overhanging both shores, but there was no thick woodland, and no building, not even a hut for half a mile or more. They were about to give up the hunt and turn back, and Cadfael was preparing to tuck up his sleeves and take an oar to help Madog back upstream, when Madog checked and pointed.

'What did I say? No need to go beyond this, here's what marks the end of the chase.'

Close under the left bank, where a curving current had hollowed the ground and exposed the roots of a small hawthorn, causing it to lean at an angle over the water, its branches had snared a fish of their own. The empty boat lay unevenly, its bow held between two thorn-boughs, its oars shipped, rocking gently in the shallows.

'This one I know,' said Madog, drawing alongside and laying a hand to the thwart to hold them together. 'It belongs to Arnald the fishmonger, under the Wyle, he moors it there at the town end of the bridge. Your man had nothing to do but row it across and hide it. Arnald will be raging round Shrewsbury clouting every lad on suspicion. I'd best do him a good turn and get it back to him, before he twists off an ear or two. He's had this borrowed once before, but at least they brought it back that time. Well, my lord, here it ends. Are you satisfied?'

'Bitterly unsatisfied,' said Hugh ruefully, 'but I take your meaning. Downstream, we agreed! Well, somewhere downstream from the bridge and upstream from here, it seems, Mistress Perle was put ashore and laid in safe-keeping. Too safe by far! For still I have no notion where.'

With the aid of a trailing mooring rope, which had been frayed to suggest that it had parted of itself, they took the stolen boat in tow, and turned to the hard pull upstream,

Cadfael taking an oar, and settling himself solidly on the thwart to try and match Madog's experienced skill. But when they drew level with the fuller's workshop they were hailed from the bank, and down to the water's edge came two of Hugh's officers, dusty and tired, with three or four volunteers from among the townsmen holding off respectfully at a little distance. Among them, Cadfael observed, was that same weaver Bertred, all brawn and brag, as Hugh had called him, bestriding the greensward with the large confidence of a man who likes himself well, and by the look of him not at all downcast at fetching up empty-handed at the end of his voluntary search. Cadfael had seen him occasionally in attendance on Miles Coliar, though he knew little of him but his appearance. Which was eminently presentable, fresh-coloured and healthy and beautifully built, with the kind of open face which may be just what it seems, or may be well adapted to conceal the fact that there is an inner chamber which is very firmly closed. Something slightly knowing about the apparently candid eyes, and a smile just a little too ready. And what was there to smile about in failing to find Judith Perle, close to the end of this second day of searching for her?

'My lord,' said the older sergeant, laying a hand to hold the boat still and inshore, 'we've been over well-nigh every tuft of grass between these two reaches of the river, both sides, and nothing to be found, nor a soul who owns to knowing anything.'

'I've done no better,' said Hugh resignedly, 'except that this must be the boat that carried her off. It was caught in thorn-branches, a little way downstream from here, but it belongs at the bridge. No need to look beyond here, unless the poor woman's been moved and moved again, and that's unlikely.'

'Every house and garden along the road we've searched. We saw you making down-river, my lord, so we took yet another look round here, but you see everything's open as the day. Master Fuller made us free of all his holding.'

Hugh looked about him in a long, sweeping, none too hopeful glance. 'No, small chance of doing anything here unperceived, at least by daylight, and it was early in the day she vanished. Someone has looked in Master Hynde's warehouse there?'

'Yesterday, my lord. His wife gave us the key readily, I was there myself, so was my lord Herbard. Nothing within but his baled fleeces, the loft all but full of them, floor to roof. He had a good clip this year, seemingly.'

'Better than I did,' said Hugh. 'But I don't keep above three hundred sheep, small coin to him. Well, you've been at it all day, as well take a rest and be off home.' He set foot lightly to the thwart and stepped ashore. The boat rocked softly to the motion. 'There's nothing more we can do here. I'd best get back to the castle, and see if by chance someone else has had better luck. I'll go in here by the eastern gate, Madog, but we can lend you two rowers, if you like, and help you back upstream with both boats. Some of these lads who've been on the hunt with us could do with a voyage back to the bridge.' He cast a glance round the group that held off respectfully, watching and listening. 'Better than walking, lads, after all the walking you've done this day. Who's first?'

Two of the men came forward eagerly to uncouple the boats and settle themselves on the thwarts. They shoved gently off into the stream ahead of Madog, and set a practised pace. And it might well be, Cadfael thought, noting how Bertred the weaver hung well back from offering his own stout arms, that his walk home from the nearby castle gate into the town was barely longer than it would have been from the bridge gate after disembarking, so that he saw small gain in volunteering. It might even be that he was no expert with an oar. But that did not quite account for the small, bland smile and the look of glossy content on his comely young face as he withdrew himself discreetly from notice behind his companions. And it certainly did not account for the last glimpse Cadfael had of him, as he glanced back over his shoulder from midstream. For Bertred had lagged behind Hugh and his henchmen as they set off briskly towards the road and the eastern gate of the town, had halted a moment to watch them as they breasted the rise, and then had turned his back and made off at a purposeful but unhurried pace in the opposite direction, towards the nearest stand of woodland, as though he had important business there.

Bertred came home for his supper only with the early dusk, to a distracted household which had lost its routine and limped through the day forgetful of work, meal-times, and every other factor that served to mark the hours in an orderly and customary fashion. Miles fretted from workshop to street a dozen times an hour, and ran out to accost any passing soldier of the garrison for news, of which there was none. In two days he had grown so tense and brittle that even his mother, for once daunted into comparative silence, tended to slip aside out of his way. The girls in the spinning room whispered and wondered far more than they worked, and foregathered with the weavers to gossip as often as his back was turned.

'Who'd have thought he cared so much for his cousin!' Branwen marvelled, awed by his strained and anxious face. 'Of course a man feels for his own kin, but – you'd have thought it was his bride he'd lost, not his cousin, he goes so grieved.'

'He'd be a sight less concerned for his Isabel,' said a cynic among the weavers. 'She'll bring him a passable dowry, and he's well enough satisfied with his bargain, but there are as good fish in the sea if she slipped off the hook. Mistress Judith is his keep and future and all. Besides, the two get on well enough, for all I could ever see. He's got every call to worry.'

And worry he did, in a nail-biting, brow-furrowing frenzy of concern and anxiety that continued unbroken through the day, and at night, when search was perforce abandoned, subsided into a mute, resigned dejection, waiting for morning to renew the hunt. But by this second twilight it seemed every corner of the town had been ransacked, and every house and garden and pasture in the suburbs at least visited, and where were they to look next?

'She can't be far,' Dame Agatha insisted strenuously. 'They'll surely find her.'

'Far or near,' said Miles wretchedly, 'she's too well hidden.

And some villain holding her, for certain. And how if she's forced to give way and take him? Then what's to become of you and me, if she lets a master into the house?'

'She never would, and she so set against marrying. No, that she won't do. Why, if a man uses her so ill, more like by far, once she's free of him – as she will be! – to do what she's thought of doing so long, and go into a nunnery. And only two days now to the day of the rent!' Agatha pointed out. 'Then what's to be done, if that passes and she still lost?'

'Then the bargain's broken, and there's time to think again and think better, but only she can do it. Until she's found there's nothing to be done, and no comfort. Tomorrow I'll go out again myself,' Miles vowed, shaking an exasperated head over the failure of the king's sheriff and all his men.

'But where? Where is there left they haven't searched already?'

A hard question indeed, and one without an answer. And into this waiting and frustrated household Bertred came sidling in the dusk, discreetly quiet and solemn about the continuing failure to find any trace of his mistress, and yet looking so sleek and bright-eyed that Miles was brutally short with him, not at all his usual good-tempered self, and followed him with a long, glowering stare when Bertred wisely made off into the kitchen. On warm summer evenings it was pleasanter to be outdoors than there in the dim, smoky room with the heat of the fire, even when it was turfed down for the night or raked out until morning, and the rest of the household had gone out on their own ploys. Only Bertred's mother Alison, who cooked for the family and its workers, was waiting there none too patiently for her truant son, with a pot still warming over the naked fire.

'Where have you been till this time?' she wanted to know, turning on him with the ladle in her hand as he tramped briskly in at the door and went to his place at the long trestle table. He gave her a casual kiss in passing, brushing her round red cheek lightly. She was a plump, comfortable figure of a woman with some worn traces still of the good looks she had handed on to her son. 'All very well,' she said, setting the wooden bowl before him with a crash, 'after keeping me waiting here so late. And much good you must have done all day, or you'd be telling me now you've brought her home, and preening yourself like a peacock over it. There were some of the men came home two hours ago and more. Where have you been loitering since then?'

In the dim kitchen his small, self-satisfied smile could barely be seen, but the tone of his voice conveyed the same carefully contained elation. He took her by the arm and drew her down to the bench beside him.

'Never mind where, and leave it to me why! There was a thing I had to wait for, and it was worth the waiting. Mother ...' He leaned close, and sank his voice to a confidential whisper. '... how would you like to be more than a servant in this house? A gentlewoman, an honoured dowager! Wait a little while, and I mean to make my fortune and yours, too. What do you say to that?'

'Great notions you always had,' she said, none too impressed, but too fond to mock him. 'And how do you mean to do that?'

'I'm telling nothing yet, not till I can say it's done. There's not one of those busy hounds out hunting all this day knows what I know. That's all I'm saying, and not a word to any but you. And ... Mother, I must go out again tonight, when it's well dark. Never you worry, I know what I'm about, only wait, and you'll be glad of it. But tonight you mustn't say a word, not to anyone.'

She held him off doubtfully to get a better look at his smiling, teasing face. 'What are you up to? I can keep as close a mouth as any where there's need. But don't you go running your head into trouble. If there's ought you know, why haven't you told?'

'And spend the credit along with my breath? No, leave all to me, Mother, I know what I'm about. Tomorrow you'll see for yourself, but not a word tonight. Promise it!'

'Your sire was just such another,' she said, relaxing into smiles, 'always full of great plans. Well, if I spend the night wakeful out of pure curiosity, so be it. Would I ever stand in your way? Not a word out of me, I promise.' And instantly she added, with a brief blaze of unease and foreboding: 'Only take care! There may be more than you out about risky business in the night.'

Bertred laughed, and hugged her impulsively in long arms, and went away whistling into the dusk of the yard.

His bed was in the weaving-shed with the looms, and there he had no companion to wake and hear him rise and do on his clothes, more than an hour after midnight. Nor was it any problem to slip out from the yard by the narrow passage to the street, without so much as risking being seen by any other member of the household. He had chosen his time with care. It must not be too soon, or there would still be people stirring. It must not be too late, or the moon would be up, and darkness suited his purpose better. And it was dark indeed in the narrow lanes between the overhanging houses and shops, as he threaded the mass of streets between Maerdol-head and the castle. The town gate there on the eastern side was a part of the castle defences, and would be closed and guarded during the night hours. For the past few years Shrewsbury had been safe enough from any threat on the eastern approach, only the occasional brief Welsh raid from the west had troubled the peace of the shire, but Hugh Beringar maintained the routine watchfulness without a break. But the most easterly wicket, giving access to the river under the very towers of the fortress, was there to be used freely. Only in times of possible danger were all the wickets closed and barred, and sentries set on the walls. Horsemen, carts, market wagons, all must wait for the gates to be opened at dawn, but a solitary man might pass through at any hour.

Bertred knew his way in the dark as well as by day, and could tread as lightly and move as silently as a cat. He stepped through the wicket into the slope of grass and bushes above the river, and drew the wooden door closed after him. Below him the flow of the Severn made fleeting ribbons and glints of moving light, just perceptible as tremors in the darkness. The sky was lightly veiled and showed no stars, and was just sufficiently less dark than the solid masses of masonry, earth and trees to show their outlines in deeper black. When the moon came up, more than an hour later than this, the heavens would probably clear. He had time to stand for a moment and think out what he had to do. There was little wind, but he had better take it into consideration, it would not do to approach the watchman's mastiff at the fulling works downwind. He wet a finger and tested. The slight, steady breeze was blowing from the south-west, from upstream. He would have to move round the bulk of the castle virtually to the fringes of the gardens along the high road, and come about from downwind in a cautious circle to reach the back of the wool warehouse.

He had taken a good look at it in the afternoon. So had they all, the sheriff and his sergeants and the townsmen helping them in the search. But they had not, like Bertred, been in and out two or three times at that warehouse, when fetching away fleeces for Mistress Perle. Nor had they been present in Mistress Perle's kitchen on the night before her disappearance, to hear Branwen declare her mistress's intent to go to the abbey early in the morning and make a new charter, rendering her gift of property unconditional. So they had not seen, as Bertred had, Hynde's man Gunnar drink up his ale and pocket his dice shortly afterwards, and take himself off in some haste, though he had seemed to be comfortably rooted for the evening. That was one more creature besides Bertred who had known of that intent, and surely had slipped so promptly away to disclose it to yet one more. Which one, the old or the young, made no matter. The strange thing was that it had taken Bertred himself so long to grasp the possibilities. The sight of the old counting-house hatch, that afternoon, securely shuttered and barred on the outer side, and probably also made fast within, had been all that was needed to enlighten him. If he had then waited patiently in the cover of the trees until dusk, to see who slipped out from the wicket in the town wall, and exactly where he headed with his rush basket, it had been only a final precaution, to render certainty even more certain.

Heavy against his side, in the great pocket stitched inside his coat, he had a long chisel and a hammer, though he would have to avoid noise if he could. The outer bar across the hatch need only be drawn back out of the socket, but he suspected the shutter was also nailed fast to its frame. A year ago a bale of fleeces had been stolen by entry through this hatch, and as the small counting-house within was already disused, old Hynde had had the window sealed against any further attempt. That was one more thing the sheriff did not know.

Bertred came down softly along the meadow beyond the warehouse, with the gentle wind in his face. By then shapes of things showed clearly, black against faded black. The bulk of the building was between him and Godfrey Fuller's workshops, the very faint shimmer of the river a little way off on his left hand. And double his own height above him was the square of the shuttered hatch, just perceptible to his night eyes.

The climb presented no problems, he had made sure of that. The building was old, and due to this rear wall backing into the slope, the base of the wall of vertical planks had suffered wet damage over the years, and rotted, and old Hynde, never one to spend lavishly, had reinforced it with split logs fastened across horizontally on top of the massive sill-beam, affording easy toe-holds high enough for him to reach up and get a grip on the rough sill under the hatch, which was just wide enough to lend him a secure resting-place with an ear to the shutters.

He drew himself up carefully, got a hand firmly on the bar that sealed the hatch, and a thigh along the sill, and drew breath and cautiously held it, wary of the first strange and unexpected thing. The shutters fitted together well, but not quite perfectly. For about a hand's-length down the centre, where the two leaves met, a hairline of light showed, too fine to give a view of anything within, a mere quill-stroke of faint gold. Perhaps not so strange, after all. Perhaps they had had the grace at least to let her have a candle or a lamp in her prison. It would pay, surely, to accommodate her in as many harmless ways as possible, while trying to break down her resistance. Force need only be tried if all else failed. But two days without gain began to look very like failure.

The chisel inside his coat was jabbing him painfully in the ribs. He worked a hand cautiously into the pocket and drew out the tools, laying them beside him on the sill, so that he could ease himself a little nearer to the sliver of light, and lay his ear to the crack.

The sudden start he made all but toppled him from his perch. For a voice spoke up, firmly and clearly, quite close on the inner side of the shutters:

'No, you will not change me. You should have known it. I am your problem. You brought me here, now get me hence as best you can.'

The voice that answered was more distant, perhaps at the far side of the room, in hopeless retreat, and the words did not come over clearly, but the tone was of desperate complaining and abject pleading, and the speaker was a man, though so unrecognisable that Bertred could not be sure whether he was old or young, master or servant.

His own plan was already awry. At best he must wait, and if he had to wait too long the moon would be up, and the risks more than doubled. The place was right, his judgement confirmed, the woman was there. But the time was ill-guessed, for her gaoler was there with her.

Chapter Eight

'You brought me here,' she said, 'now get me hence as best you can.'

In the narrow, bare room which had once been Hynde's counting-house, the small flame of the saucer lamp barely showed them to each other. He had flung away from her, and stood in the far corner, his back turned, his head bowed into the forearm he had braced against the wall, his other fist driving uselessly and painfully against the timber. His voice emerged muffled, its helpless rage degraded into a feeble wail: 'How can I? How can I? There is no way out now!'

'You could unlock the door,' she said simply, 'and let me go. Nothing could be easier.'

'For you!' he protested furiously, and swung about to glare at her with all the venom of which his nature was capable. It did not amount to much more than self-pity. He was not a venomous man, only a vain and foolish one. He wearied her, but he did not frighten her. 'All very well for you! And I should be finished, damned ... thrown into prison to rot. Once out, you'd denounce me and take your revenge.'

'You should have thought of that,' she said, 'before you snatched me away, you and your rogue servant. You brought me here to this sordid hole, locked in behind your wool bales, without comfort, without decency, subject to your man's rough handling and your insolent pestering, and do you expect gratitude? Or even mercy? Why should I not denounce you? You had best think hard and fast. You will have to release me or kill me at last, and the longer the delay, the worse will be your own plight. Mine,' she said bitterly, 'is already bad enough. What has become by now of my good name? What will my situation be when I go back to my own house and family?'

Vivian came back to her with a rush, flinging himself on his knees beside the rough bench where she had taken what rest she could, and where she sat now erect and pale, her hands gripped together in her lap, her skirts drawn close about her as though to avoid not only his touch, but the very dust and desolation of her prison. There was nothing else in the room but the broken desk where once the clerk had worked over his figures, and a stone ewer with a chipped lip, and a pile of dust and debris in the corner. The lamp stood on the end of the bench beside her, its light now full on Vivian's dishevelled hair and woeful face. He clutched at her hands imploringly, but she withdrew them so sharply that he sat back on his heels with a great gulp of despair.

'I never meant such mischief, I swear it! I thought you had a fondness for me, I thought I had only to get you to myself a while, and it would all be agreed between us ... Oh, God, I wish I'd never begun it! But indeed, indeed, I did believe you could love me ...'

'No! Never!' She had said it many times in these past two days, and always with the same irrevocable coldness. He should have recognised from the first utterance that his cause was hopeless. But he had not even been deceiving himself into the conviction that he loved her. What he coveted was the security and comfort she could bring him, the payment of his debts and the prospect of an easy life. Perhaps even the pleasure of cocking a snook at his parsimonious father – parsimonious at least in Vivian's eyes, because he had finally tired of bailing his heir out of debt and trouble. Oh, no doubt the young man had found the prospect of marriage with her pleasurable in itself, but that was not the reason he had chosen that particular morning for his bid. Why let half a fortune slip through your fingers, when with one bold stroke you might have the whole?

'How have they accounted for my vanishing?' she asked. 'Is the worst said of me already? Have they been looking for me at all? Am I thought dead?'

One faint spasm of defiance and spite passed over Vivian's face. 'Looking for you? The whole town's turned upside-down looking for you, the sheriff and all his men, your cousin and half your workmen. Not a house but they've visited, not a barn but they've searched. They were here yesterday, towards evening. Alan Herbard and three of the garrison with him. We opened the doors to them, and showed the baled fleeces, and they went away satisfied. Why did you not cry out to them then, if you wanted rescue from me?'

'They were here?' Judith stiffened, chilled by this spurt of malice. But it was the last, he had done his worst, and could not maintain it long. 'I never heard them!' she said with resigned bitterness.

'No.' He said it quite simply now, all his resistance spent. 'They were easily satisfied. The room is quite forgotten, and all those bales shut out sound. They never questioned. They were here again this afternoon, but not asking for the keys. They'd found the boat ... No, you might not hear them. Would you have cried out to them if you had?'

It was a meaningless question, and she did not answer it, but she gave it some thought. Would she have wished to be heard calling for help, and haled out of this mean prison, unprepared, dusty and stained, compromised, piteous? Might it not have been better to be silent, and make her own way out of this predicament? For the truth was that after the first confusion, indignation and alarm she had never been afraid of Vivian, nor in any danger of giving way to him, and now she would welcome as much as he would a solution which would smooth out of sight all that had happened, and leave her her dignity and integrity independent of any other soul. In the end he would have to release her. She was the stronger of the two.

He ventured a hand to clutch at a fold of her skirt. The face he lifted to her, seen clearly thus close and lit by the yellow flame of the wick, was strangely vulnerable and young, like a guilty boy pleading in extenuation of some heinous fault and not yet resigned to punishment. The brow he had braced against the wall was smeared with dust, and with the back of his hand, sweeping away tears or sweat or both, he had made a long black stain down his cheek. There was a trail of cobweb in the bright, fair, tangled hair. The wide brown eyes, dilated with stress, glinted gold from the spark of the lamp, and hung in desperate appeal upon her face.

'Judith, Judith, do me right! I could have used you worse . . . I could have taken you by force—'

She shook her head scornfully. 'No, you could not. You have not the hardihood. You are too cautious – or perhaps too decent – both, it may be! Nor would it have benefited you if you had,' she said starkly, and turned herself away to evade the desperate and desolate youth of his face, with its piercing reflections of Brother Eluric, who had agonised in silence and without hope or appeal. 'And now here we are, you and I both, and you know as well as I know that this must end. You have no choice but to let me go.'

'And you'll destroy me!' he said in a whisper, and sank his corn-gold head into his hands.

'I wish you no harm,' she said wearily. 'But it was you brought us to this, not I.'

'I know it, I own it, God knows I wish it undone! Oh, Judith, help me, help me!'

It had come to that, the bleak acknowledgement that he had lost, that he was now her prisoner, not she his, even that he was dependent upon her to save him from the trap he himself had set. He laid his head in her lap and shook as though with cold. And she was so tired and so astray that she had lifted a resigned hand to lay upon his head and quiet him, when the sudden tearing, rushing slither of sound outside the shutters at her back caused them both to start and freeze in alarm. Not a loud sound, merely like some not very heavy weight sliding down and ending in a dull fall into grass. Vivian started to his feet, quivering.

'For God's sake, what was that?'

They held their breath, straining into a silence as sudden as the sound, and as brief. Then, more distant from the direction of the riverside fulling-works, came the loud, savage alarm-baying of the chained mastiff; and after a few moments this changed abruptly into the deeper, more purposeful note of the chase, as he was loosed from his chain.

Bertred had trusted too confidently to old, worn, neglected wood, left too long uncared for on the weather side of the warehouse. The sill on which he was perched had been fixed in position with long nails, but at the more exposed end the nails had rusted in many rains, and the wood round them had rotted. When he shifted his weight further forward to ease an uncomfortable cramp, and get an ear more avidly to the crack, the wood splintered and parted, and the sill swung down before him, scraping the planks of the wall, and sent him slithering and clawing to the ground. Not a great fall nor a very loud sound, but loud enough in that depth of the night to carry to the fulling-works.

He was on his feet as he reached the ground, and leaned for a moment against the wall to get his breath back and steady his legs under him after the shock of the fall. The next moment he heard the mastiff give tongue.

Bertred's instinct was to run uphill towards the houses along the high road, and he set off in that direction, alerted to terror, only to check a moment later in the despairing knowledge that the hound was far faster than he could be, and would overhaul him long before he reached any shelter. The river was nearer. Better by far make for that, and swim across to the open spur of woodland at the end of the Gaye. In the water he could more than match the hound, and surely the watchman would call the dog off rather than let it pursue further.

He turned, and began to run in wild hare-leaps downhill across the tussocky grass, full tilt towards the river-bank. But both dog and man were out after him now, roused to a thief-hunt in the small hours, when all honest folk should be in their beds, and only malefactors could be abroad. They had traced the sound of his fall only too accurately; they knew someone had been clambering round the warehouse, and surely with no good intent. A detached part of Bertred's mind somehow had time to wonder, even as his legs and lungs strained for the speed of terror, how young Hynde managed to go back and forth by night without raising the same alarm. But of course the mastiff knew him, he was one of the guarded, an ally in the protection of property here, not an enemy and a threat.

Flight and pursuit made strangely little noise in the night, or disturbance in the darkness, and yet he felt, rather than saw, man and hound converging upon his path, and heard the rush of movement and the purposeful in-and-out of breath drawing close from his right flank. The watchman lunged at him with a long staff, and caught him a glancing blow on the head that half-stunned him, and sent him hurtling forward out of balance to the very edge of the river-bank. But he was past the man now, and could leave him behind, it was the dog, close on his heels, that terrified him, and gave him the strength for the last great leap that carried him out from the grass spur overhanging the water.

The bank was higher than he had realised, and the water somewhat lower, exposing shelving faces of rock. Instead of clearing these into deep water, he fell with a crash among the tilted stones, though his outflung arm raised a splash from the shallows between. His head, already ringing from the watchman's blow, struck hard against a sharp edge of stone. He lay stunned where he had fallen, half-concealed beneath the bushy overhang, wholly shrouded in the darkness. The mastiff, no lover of water, padded uneasily along the grassy shelf and whined, but went no further.

The watchman, left well behind and out of breath, heard the splash, caught even a brief shimmer in the fitful pallor of the river's surface, and halted well short of the bank to whistle and call off his dog. The would-be thief must be half across the river by now, no use troubling further. He was reasonably sure that the felon had not succeeded in making an entry anywhere, or the dog would have raised the alarm earlier. But he did walk round the warehouse and the dye-sheds to make sure all was in order. The dangling sill under the dark shutters hung vertically, like the planks against which it rested, and the watchman did not observe it. In the morning he would have a thorough look round, but it seemed no harm had been done. He went back contentedly to his hut, with the dog padding at his heels.

Vivian stood rigid, listening, until the dog's baying grew more distant, and finally ceased. He stirred almost painfully out of his stillness.

'Someone was prowling! Someone guesses – or knows!' He wiped sweat from his forehead with a dirty hand, prolonging the smears already there. 'Oh, God, what am I to do? I can't let you go free, and I can't keep you here any longer, not another day. If someone suspects . . .'

Judith sat silent, steadily watching him. His soiled and disillusioned beauty moved her against her will, as he could never have moved her at his most decorative and elated, the finest cock on the midden. Afraid to go on with his over-bold scheme, unable to retreat from it, frenziedly wishing he had never embarked upon it, he was like a fly in a cobweb, tangling himself ever more inextricably.

'Judith . . .' He was on his knees again at her feet, clinging to her hands, pleading, cajoling, but passionately, like a child, quite forgetful of his charm and stripped naked of his vanity. 'Judith, help me! Help me out of this! If there is a way, help me to find it. If they come and find you, I'm ruined, disgraced . . . If I let you go, you'll destroy me just the same—'

'Hush!' she said wearily. 'I don't wish you harm, I want no revenge, only to be free of you on the best terms I may.'

'How does that help me? Do you think they'll let you reappear, and ask no questions? Even if you hold your peace, how am I helped? There'll be no respite until you tell them all, and that's my undoing. Oh, if I knew which way to turn!'

'It would suit me no less than you,' said Judith, 'if we could smooth away this scandal peacably, but it needs a miracle to account for these two lost days. And I must protect myself, if that's possible. You must fend for yourself, but I'd as lief you went unharmed, too, if that may be. What now? What ails you?'

He had started and stiffened, quick to alarm, and was listening with stretched sinews. 'Someone outside,' he said in a whisper. 'Again – didn't you hear? Someone is spying . . . Listen!'

She fell silent, though she was not convinced. He was so tense and frightened by this time that he could have conjured enemies out of the air. Through a long, hushed moment she heard no sound at all, even the very slight sigh of the breeze in the shutters had ceased.

'There's no one; you imagined it. Nothing!' She gripped his hands suddenly, asserting her mastery, where hitherto she had merely suffered his touch without response. 'Listen to me! There might be a way! When Sister Magdalen visited me, she offered me a place of retreat at Godric's Ford with her, if ever I reached the end of my tether and needed a refuge and a pause for breath. As God knows I have needed both, and still do. If you will take me there by night, secretly, then I can return later and say where I have been, and why, and how this turmoil and hunt for me never came to our ears there. As I hope may be true. I will say that I fled from my life for a while, to get courage to take it up again to better purpose. And I hope to God that may also be true. I will not name you, nor betray what you have done to me.'

He was staring up at her wide-eyed, hesitant to hope but unable to resist, glowing only to doubt again the possibility of salvation. 'They'll press you hard, they'll ask why did you say no word, why go away and leave everyone to fear for you. And the boat – they know about the boat, they must know—'

'When they ask,' she said starkly, 'I'll answer, or refuse them an answer. Fret as you may, you must needs leave all that to me. I am offering you a way of escape. Take it or leave it.'

'I daren't go all the way with you,' he said, writhing. 'If I were seen it would all come out in spite of you.'

'You need not come all the way. You may leave me to go the last piece of the way alone, I am not afraid. No one need see you.'

He was flushing into hope with every word. 'My father is gone back to his flocks today, he'll stay two nights or more up there with the shepherds, and there's one good horse still in the stable, stout enough to carry two, if you'll ride pillion with me. I could bring him out of the town before the gate's closed. Best not pass through the town together, but set out this way. There's a ford a little way downstream from here, we can make our way south on the other side and get to the road to Beistan. At dusk – if we start at dusk tomorrow ... Oh, Judith, and I've done you such wrong, and can you so far forgive me? I have not deserved!'

It was something new, she thought wryly, for Vivian Hynde to suppose that his deserts were small, or that there was anything to which he was not entitled. He might yet be all the better for this one salutary fright which he had brought upon himself. He was no great villain, only a weak and self-indulgent boy. But she did not answer his question. There was one thing at least she found it hard to forgive him, and that was that he had exposed her to the rough handling of Gunnar, who had taken palpable delight in the close embrace of her body and the strength which had held her helpless. She had no fear of Vivian, but of Gunnar, if ever she encountered him without Vivian, she might be very much afraid.

'I do this for myself as much as for you,' she said. 'I've given my word and I'll keep it. Tomorrow at dusk. Agreed, it's too late to move tonight.'

He had recoiled again into doubt and fear, recalling the noises without, and the baying of the mastiff. 'But how if someone has suspicions of this place? How if they come again tomorrow demanding the keys? Judith, come back with me now, come to our house, it's not far from the wicket, no one will see us now. My mother will hide you and help us, and be grateful to you for sparing me. And my father's away in the hills, he'll never know. And there you may have rest and a bed, and water for washing, and all you need for your comfort...'

'Your mother knows of what you've done?' she demanded, aghast.

'No, no, nothing! But she'll help us now, for my sake.' He was at the narrow door which had lain hidden behind the baled fleeces, turning the key, drawing her after him, feverish in his haste to be out of here and safe in his own home. 'I'll send Gunnar to make all innocent here. If they come they must find the place bare and deserted.'

She blew out the wick of the lamp and went with him, backwards down the ladder from the loft, out through the lower door and into the night. The moon was just rising, bathing the slope in pale-green light. The air was sweet and cool on her face after the close, musty smell of dust and the smoke of the lamp in the enclosed space. It was no very long walk to the shadows of the castle towers, and the wicket in the wall.

A darker shadow made its way round the spreading plane of moonlight, by the shortest route from behind the warehouse to the cover of trees, and so roundabout to the river-bank, rapid and silent. The overhang where Bertred had made his leap to evade the mastiff was still in shadow. He lay as he had fallen, still out of his senses, though he was beginning to stir and groan, and draw the laborious breath of one quickening to the consciousness of pain. The deeper shadow that fell across his body just as the edge of the moonlight reached the river did not penetrate his dazed mind or trouble his closed eyes. A hand reached down and took him by the hair, turning his face up to view it closely. He lived, he breathed, a little patching and a few hours to recover, and he would be able to account for himself and confess everything he knew.

The shadow stooping over him straightened and stood a moment looking down at him dispassionately. Then he thrust a booted toe into Bertred's side, levered him towards the edge of the stones on which he lay, and heaved him out into deep water, where the current curled fast, bearing the body out across midstream towards the further shore.

The twentieth of June dawned in a series of sparkling showers, settling by mid-morning into a fine, warm day. There was plenty of work waiting to be done in the orchards of the Gaye, but because of the morning rain it was necessary to wait for the midday heat before tackling them. The sweet cherries were ready for picking, but needed to be gathered dry, and there were also the first strawberries to pick, and there it was equally desirable to let the sun dry off the early moisture. On the open, sunlit expanse of the vegetable plots the ground dried out earlier, and the brothers on duty were busy sowing lettuces for succession, and hoeing and weeding, before noon, but it was after dinner that the orchard party began work at the extreme end of the abbey grounds.

There was no particular need for Brother Cadfael to go out with them, but neither was there anything urgently needing his attention in the herbarium, and the mounting uneasiness of the three-day vain hunt for Judith Perle would not let him rest or settle to any routine occupation. There had been no further word from Hugh, and nothing to tell Niall when he came anxiously enquiring. The entire affair stood still, the very hours of the day held their breath, making time endless.

To fill it at least with some physical movement, Cadfael went out to the orchards with the rest. As so often in a late season, nature had set out to make good the weeks that had been lost to the spring cold, and contrived to bring on, almost at the usual time, both strawberries and the first of the little hard gooseberries on their thorny bushes. But Cadfael's mind was not on fruit-picking. The orchards lay just opposite the level where the young archers shot at the butts on fair-days, under the sweep of the town wall and in the lee of the castle towers. Only a little way beyond, through the first belt of woodland, and he would be gazing straight across the water at the fulling-works, and just downstream at William Hynde's jetty.

Cadfael worked for a while, so distractedly that he collected more than his share of scratches. But after a while he straightened his back, sucked out of his finger the latest of many thorns, and walked on along the riverside into the belt of trees. Through their leaning branches the sweeping coronal of the town wall unrolled beside him across the water, and the steep green slope beneath the wall. Then the first jutting bastion of the castle, with the narrower level of meadow under it. Cadfael walked on, through the trees and out to a broad greensward beyond, dotted with low bushes close to the bank, and here and there a bed of reeds where the shallows ran gently and the fast current sped out into midstream. Now he was opposite the tenterground, where Godfrey Fuller's men were working, and a length of brown cloth was stretched taut between the frames to dry.

He reached a spot directly opposite the overhanging bushes where they had found the stolen boat abandoned. Along the bank beyond, a small boy was pasturing goats. Sunlit and peaceful, the Severn landscape lay somnolent in the afternoon light, denying the existence of murder, malice and abduction in so lovely a world.

Cadfael had gone but a hundred or so paces further, and was about to turn back, when he reached a curve where the bank opposite was undercut and the water beneath it deep, while on his side it shallowed into a sandy shoal, and subsided into soft, innocent ripples, barely moving. One of those places Madog knew well, where whatever had gone into the river upstream might fetch up again on land.

And something had indeed fetched up here in the night just past. It lay almost submerged, at rest on the sand but barely breaking the surface, a mass of darker colour washed over by the silvery shimmer of water, and lodged in the dull gold of the sand beneath. It was the small, languid pallor, which swung lightly with the flow but was no fish, that first caught Cadfael's eye. A man's hand, at the end of a dark sleeve that buoyed it up just enough to set it swaying. A man's brown head, the back of it just dimpling the surface, all its curling locks stretching out with the ripples and stirring like drowsy living things.

Cadfael slid down the shelving bank in haste, and waded into the shallow water to get a double grip on the sodden clothing under the trailing arms, and drag the body ashore. Dead beyond doubt, probably several hours dead. He lay on his face in the sand just clear of the water, and tiny rivulets ran out of him from every fold of clothing and every tangled curl of hair. A young man, very well made and shapely. Far too late to do anything for him but carry him home and provide him a decent burial. It would need more than one man to get him up the bank and bear him back along the Gaye, and Cadfael had better be about getting help as fast as possible.

The build, the common dun-coloured coat and chausses, might have belonged to a hundred young fellows from Shrewsbury, being the common working wear, and the body was not immediately recognisable to Cadfael. He stooped to resume a careful hold under the lax arms, and turned the dead man over to lie on his back, revealing to the indifferent sunlight the smeared, pallid but still comely face of Bertred, Judith Perle's foreman weaver.

Chapter Nine

They came in haste at his call, fluttered and dismayed, though a drowned man cast up by the Severn was no such rare matter, and these young brothers knew no more of the affair than that. No doubt whispers of the outer world's crises made their way in among the elders, but by and large the novices lived in innocence. Cadfael chose the strongest and the least likely to be distressed by the contemplation of death, and sent the others back to their work. With their hoes and rope girdles and scapulars they rigged a makeshift litter, and carried it down the riverside path to where the dead man lay.

In awed silence they took up their sodden burden, and bore him back in dripping procession through the belt of woodland and all along the lush level of the Gaye, to the path that climbed to the Foregate.

'We'd best take him to the abbey,' said Cadfael, halting a moment to consider. 'That's the quickest means of getting him decently out of the public view, and we can send for his master or his kin from there.' There were other reasons for the decision, too, but he did not think fit to mention them at this point. The dead man came from Judith Perle's household, and what had befallen him surely could not be entirely disconnected from all the other disasters which seemed to be haunting the house and the heiress of the Vestier business. In which case Abbot Radulfus had a direct interest and a right to be informed, and even more surely, so had Hugh Beringar. Not only a right, but a need. Two deaths and a disappearance, all circling round the same lady and her dealings with the abbey, demanded very close attention. Even young, strong men in the most exuberant of health can drown. But Cadfael had already seen the broken bruise on the dead man's right temple, washed white and bleached of blood by the water of the river. 'Run on ahead, lad,' he said to Brother Rhun, the youngest of the novices, 'and let Father Prior know what manner of guest we're bringing.'

The boy bowed his flaxen head in the small gesture of respect with which he received any order from an elder, and was off in an instant, willing and eager. To bid Rhun run was a kindness rather than an imposition, for there was nothing in which he took greater delight than making use of the fleetness and grace he had possessed for barely a year, after coming to Saint Winifred's festival a cripple and in pain. His year's novitiate was almost over, and soon he would be admitted as a full brother. No power or persuasion could have induced him to depart from the service of the saint who had healed him. What to Cadfael was still the serious burden and stumbling-block of obedience, Rhun embraced as a privilege, as happily as he accepted the sunlight on his face.

Cadfael turned from watching the bright head and flashing feet ascend the path, and covered the dead man's face with the corner of a scapular. Water dripped through the saturated cloth as they carried Bertred up to the road, and along the Foregate to the abbey gatehouse. Inevitably there were people abroad to halt at sight of the mournful procession, and nudge and whisper and stare as they passed. It was always a mystery where the urchins of the Foregate sprang from, as soon as there was something unusual to stare at, and how they multiplied at every step, and how the dogs, their inseparable playmates, also halted and dawdled alongside them with much the same expression of alerted curiosity on their faces. Soon guess and counter-guess would be running through the streets, but none of them would yet be able to name the drowned man. The little time before it was common knowledge who he was could be useful to Hugh Beringar, and merciful to the dead man's mother. One more widow, Cadfael recalled, as they turned in at the gatehouse and left a ring of watchers gathered at a respectable distance outside.

Prior Robert came hastening to meet the procession, with Brother Jerome scurrying at his heels, and Brother Edmund from the infirmary and Brother Denis from the guest-hall converged at the same time upon the bearers and the bier. Half a dozen brothers who had been crossing the great court variously about their own proper business lingered to watch, and to draw closer by degrees to hear and see the better.

'I have sent Brother Rhun to notify the lord abbot,' said Robert, stooping his lofty silver head over the still body on the improvised litter. 'This is a very bad business. Where did you find the man? Was it on our ground you took him ashore?'

'No, some way beyond,' said Cadfael, 'cast up on the sand. Dead some hours, I judge. There was nothing to be done for him.'

'Was it necessary, then, to bring him here? If he is known, and has family in the town or the Foregate, they will take charge of his burial rites.'

'If not necessary,' said Cadfael, 'I thought it advisable he should be brought here. I believe the lord abbot will also think so. There are reasons. The sheriff may have an interest in this matter.'

'Indeed? Why should that be so, if the man died by drowning? Surely an accident not unknown here.' He reached a fastidious hand to turn back the scapular from the bleached and bluish face which in life had glowed with such self-conscious health. But these features meant nothing to him. If he had ever seen the man, it could have been only casually, passing the gates. The house at Maerdol-head lay in the town parish of Saint Chad; neither worship nor commerce would bring Bertred into frequent contact with the Foregate. 'Do you know this man?'

'By sight, yes, though little more than that. But he is one of Mistress Perle's weavers, and lives in her household.'

Even Prior Robert, who held himself aloof from those uncomfortable worldly concerns which sometimes infiltrated into the abbey's well-ordered enclave and bred disruption there, opened his eyes wide at that. He could not choose but know what untoward things had happened connected with that household, nor quite resist the conviction that any new disaster similarly connected must be a part of the whole deplorable pattern. Coincidences do occur, but they seldom cluster by the dozen round one dwelling and one name.

'Well!' he said on a long breath, cautiously noncommittal. 'Yes, the lord abbot should certainly know of this.' And with due relief he added: 'He is coming now.'

Abbot Radulfus had emerged from his garden and was approaching briskly, with Rhun attendant at his elbow. He said nothing until he had drawn back the covering from Bertred's head and shoulders and surveyed him in sombre and thoughtful silence for a long moment. Then he again covered the dead face, and turned to Cadfael.

'Brother Rhun has told me where he was found, and how, but he does not know who the man is. Do you?'

'Yes, Father. His name is Bertred, he is Mistress Perle's foreman weaver. I saw him yesterday out with the sheriff's men, helping in the hunt for the lady.'

'Who has not been found,' said Radulfus.

'No. This is the third day of searching for her, but she has not been found.'

'And her man is found dead.' There was no need to point out to him implications which were already plain. 'Are you satisfied that he drowned?'

'Father, I need to consider that. I think he did, but also he has suffered a blow to the head. I would like to examine his body further.'

'So, I suppose, would the lord sheriff,' said the abbot briskly. 'I'll send to him at once, and keep the body here for the present. Do you know if he could swim?'

'No, Father, but there are few born here who can't. His kin or his master will tell us.'

'Yes, we must also send to them. But perhaps later, after Hugh has seen him, and made what you and he between you can of the matter.' And to the bearers of the litter, who had laid it down meanwhile and stood waiting silently, a little apart, he said: 'Take him to the mortuary chapel. You had best strip him and lay him decently. Light candles for him. However and for whatever cause he died, he is our mortal brother. I'll send a groom to look for Hugh Beringar. Wait with me, Cadfael, until he comes. I want to know everything you have gathered concerning this poor girl who is lost.'

* * *

In the mortuary chapel they had laid Bertred's naked body on the stone bier, and covered him with a linen cloth. His sodden clothes lay loosely folded aside, with the boots they had drawn from his feet. The light being dim in there, they had also provided candles on tall holders, so that they could be placed wherever they gave the best light. They stood close about the slab, Abbot Radulfus, Brother Cadfael and Hugh Beringar. It was the abbot who drew down the linen and uncovered the dead, who lay with his hands duly crossed on his breast, drawn out very straight and dignified. Someone had reverently closed the eyes Cadfael remembered as half-open, like someone just waking, too late ever to complete the awakening.

A youthful body and a handsome, perhaps slightly over-muscled for perfection. Not much past twenty, surely, and blessed with features regular and shapely, again perhaps a shade over-abundant in flesh or under-provided with bone. The Welsh are accustomed to seeing in the faces of their neighbours the strong solidity and permanence of bone, and are sensitive to loss where they see it pared down and over-cushioned in others. Nevertheless, a very comely young man. Face and neck and shoulders, and from elbow to fingertips, he was tanned by outdoor sun and wind, though the brown was dulled and sad now.

'Not a mark on him,' said Hugh, looking him over from head to feet, 'barring that knock on his forehead. And that surely caused him nothing worse than a headache.'

High near the hairline the skin was certainly broken, but it seemed no more than a glancing blow. Cadfael took up the head, with its thick thatch of brown hair plastered to the broad forehead, between his hands, and felt about the skull with probing fingers. 'He has another dunt, here, on the left side, here in his hair, above the ear. Something with a long, sharp edge – through all this thickness of hair it made a scalp wound. That could have knocked the wits out of him for some time, perhaps, but not killed. No, he certainly drowned.'

'What could the man have been doing?' asked the abbot, pondering. 'At that spot on that shore, in the night? There is nothing there, no path that leads anywhere, no house to be visited. Hard to see what business a man could possibly have there in the dark.'

'The business he'd been on all yesterday,' said Hugh, 'is the hunt for his mistress. He was in Mistress Perle's service, of her household, he offered his help, and so far as I saw he gave it, unsparingly, and in good earnest. How if he was still bent on continuing the search?'

'By night? And there? There is nothing there but open meadow and a few groves of trees,' said Radulfus, 'not one cottage for some distance, once past our border, nowhere that a stolen woman could be hidden. Even if he had been found on the opposite bank it would have been more believable, at least that gives access to the town and the houses of the Castle Foregate. But even so – by night, and a dark night until late . . .'

'And even so, how did he come by two blows on the head and end in the river? A man might go too near on a shelving bank, and miss his footing in the dark,' said Hugh, shaking his head, 'but of a native Shrewsbury lad I doubt it. They know their river. We must find out if he was a swimmer, but the most of them learn early. Cadfael, we know where he was cast up. Is it possible he went into the water on the other side? If he tried to swim across, half-stunned after he got these injuries, might he fetch up about where you found him?'

'That we should ask of Madog,' said Cadfael. 'He'll know. The currents are certainly very strong and contrary in places, it would be possible.' He straightened the wet hair almost absently on the dead man's forehead, and drew up the linen over his face. 'There's nothing more he can tell us. It remains to tell his kin. At least they may be able to say when last they saw him, and whether he owned to having any plans for the night.'

'I've sent for Miles Coliar, but said nothing to him yet of the reason. Better he should break it to the mother, it will come easier for her there, in her own home – for I'm told she belongs there, in the kitchen. And Coliar will need to have the body taken back there to make ready for burial, if you see no need to keep it longer.'

'None,' said Cadfael, turning away from the bier with a sigh. 'At your discretion, both! I have done.' But at the door, last to leave the chapel, he cast one long glance back at the still white shape on the slab of stone. One more young man dead untimely, sad waste of the stuff of life. 'Poor lad!' said Cadfael, and closed the door gently after him.

Miles Coliar came from the town in haste and alone, uninformed of the occasion for the summons, but certainly aware that there must be a grave reason, and by the look of his face speculating anxiously and fearfully as to what that might be. They awaited him in the ante-room of the gatehouse. Miles made his reverence to abbot and sheriff, and raised a worried countenance to look rapidly from face to face, questioning their solemnity.

'My lord, is there news? My cousin . . .? Have you got word of her, that you sent for me here?' His pallor blanched still more, and his face stiffened into a mask of dread, misreading, it seemed, their mute and sombre looks. 'Oh, God, no! Not . . . no, she cannot be . . . You have not found her . . . ?' His voice foundered on the word 'dead', but his lips shaped it.

'No, no!' said Hugh in haste. 'Not that! No, there's nothing new, no word of her yet, no need to think the worst. This is quite another matter, though grim enough. The hunt for your cousin goes on, and will go on until we find her.'

Miles said: 'Thank God!' just audibly, and drew deep breath, the tense lines of his face relaxing. 'Pardon if I am slow to think and speak and understand, and too hasty to fear extremes. These few days I have hardly slept or rested at all.'

'I am sorry to add more to your troubles,' said Hugh, 'but needs must. It's not Mistress Perle we're concerned with here. Have you missed any man from your looms today?'

Miles stared, and scratched his bushy brown head, at once relieved and puzzled. 'None of the weavers are working today, the looms have been neglected since yesterday morning, we've all or most been out on the hunt. I've kept the women spinning, it's no work for them to go stravaging about with the sergeants and the men of the garrison. Why do you ask, my lord?'

'Then have you seen your man Bertred at all since last night? He lives in your household, I'm told.'

'He does,' agreed Miles, frowning. 'No, I've not seen him today, with the looms quiet there's no reason I should. He eats in the kitchen. I suppose he's out again on the hunt, though God knows we've knocked on every door and probed round every yard in the town, and not a housewife or goodman who hasn't been alerted to watch for any sign and listen for any word that could lead us to her. Yet what can we do but search and ask all over again? They're out on all the roads and asking at the hamlets for a mile round, now, as you best know, my lord. Bertred will be out raking the countryside with them, no question. He's been tireless for her, that I grant him.'

'And his mother – she's in no anxiety about him? Nothing has been said of things he may have had on his mind? She has not spoken of him to you?'

'No!' Miles was again looking bewilderedly from face to face. 'You'll hardly find a soul in our house who is not anxious, and they show it, but I've noticed nothing amiss with her more than with all the rest of us. Why? What is this, my lord? Do you know something of Bertred that I do not know? Not guilt! Impossible! He's run himself raw scouring the town for my cousin ... a decent man ... You cannot have taken *him* in any wickedness ... ?'

It was a reasonable supposition, when the lord sheriff began asking such close questions about any man. Hugh put him out of his defensive agitation, but without over-haste.

'I know no wrong of your man, no. He is the victim of harm, not the cause. This is bad news we have for you, Master Coliar.' Its purport was already implicit in his tone, but he put it into words bleak and blunt enough. 'An hour ago the brothers working on the Gaye plucked Bertred out of the river and brought him here, dead. Drowned.'

In the profound silence that followed Miles stood motionless, until finally he stirred and moistened his lips.

'Where is he?'

'Laid decently in the mortuary chapel here,' said the abbot. 'The lord sheriff will take you to him.'

In the dim chapel Miles stared down at the known face now so strangely unfamiliar, and shook his head repeatedly and vigorously, as though he could shake away, if not the fact of death, his own shock at its suddenness. He had recovered his down-to-earth calmness and acceptance. One of his weavers was dead, the task of getting him out of here and into his grave with proper rites fell to Miles as his master. What was due from him he would do.

'How could this be?' he said. 'Yesterday he came late in the evening for his meal, but there was nothing in that, all day he'd been out abroad with your men, my lord. He went to his bed soon after. He said good night to me, it must have been about the hour of Compline. The house was already quiet, but some of us were still up. I never saw him again.'

'So you don't know whether he went out again by night?'

Miles looked up sharply, the blue of his eyes at their widest startlingly bright. 'It seems that he must have done. But in God's name, why should he? He was tired out after a long day. I know no reason why he should have stirred again till morning. You said it was but an hour since you took him out of the Severn . . .'

'*I* took him out,' said Cadfael, unobtrusive in a dark corner of the chapel. 'But he had been there more hours than one. In my judgement, since the small hours of the morning. It is not easy to say how long.'

'And, look, his brow is broken!' The wide, low forehead was dry now, but for the damp fringe of hair. The skin had shrunk apart, leaving the moist wound bared. 'Are you sure, Brother, that he drowned?'

'Quite sure. How he came by that knock there's no knowing, but he surely had it before he went into the water. You can't tell us anything that may help us, then?'

'I wish I could,' said Miles earnestly. 'I've seen no change in him, he's said nothing to me that could shed any light. This comes out of the dark to me. I cannot account for it.' He looked doubtfully at Hugh across the body. 'May I take him home? I'll need to speak with his mother first, but she'll want him home.'

'Naturally,' agreed Hugh resignedly. 'Yes, you may fetch him away when you will. Do you need help with the means?'

'No, my lord, we'll do all ourselves. I'll bring down a handcart and decent covering. And I do thank you and this house for the care you've had of him.'

* * *

He came again about an hour later, looking strained from the ordeal of breaking bad news to a widow now childless. Two of his men from the looms followed him with a simple, high-sided handcart used for wheeling goods, and waited mute and sombre in the great court until Brother Cadfael came to lead them to the mortuary chapel. Between them they carried Bertred's body out into the early evening light, and laid him on a spread brychan in the cart, and covered him tidily from view. They were still about it when Miles turned to Cadfael, and asked simply: 'And his clothes? She should have back with him all that was his. Small comfort for a woman, but she'll want them. And she'll need what they'll fetch, too, poor soul, though I'll see she's taken care of still, and so will Judith ... when she's found. If ...' His mind seemed to be drifting back into expectations of the worst, and fiercely rejecting them.

'I had forgot,' Cadfael owned, never having handled the clothes stripped from Bertred's body. 'Wait, I'll bring them.'

The forlorn little bundle of clothes laid aside in the chapel had been folded together as tidily as haste and their sodden condition permitted, and had drained gradually where they lay. The folds of coat and shirt and homespun hose were beginning to dry. Cadfael took the pile in one arm, and picked up in the other hand the boots that stood beside it. He carried them out into the court as Miles was smoothing the blanket neatly over Bertred's feet. The young man turned to meet him and take the bundle from him, and in the exchange, as Miles leaned to stow the clothes under the blanket, the cart tilted, and the boots, just balanced at the tail, fell to the cobbled paving.

Cadfael stooped to pick them up and restore them to their place. It was the first time he had really looked at them, and the light here in the court was clear and bright. He stood arrested in mid-movement, a boot in either hand, and slowly he turned up the left one to look attentively at the sole. For so long a time that when he did look up he found Miles standing just as still in wonder, gazing at him with open mouth, his head on one side like a puzzled hound on a lost scent.

'I think,' said Cadfael with deliberation, 'I had better get leave from the lord abbot, and come up into the town with you. I need to speak once again with the lord sheriff.'

* * *

It was but a short walk from the castle to the house at Maerdol-head, and the boy sent in haste to find Hugh brought him within the quarter-hour, cursing mildly at being side-tracked on the point of further action he had intended, but reconciled by sharp curiosity, for Cadfael would not have sent for him again so soon without good reason.

In the hall Dame Agatha, attended by a tearful Branwen, volubly lamented the rockfall of disasters which had befallen the Vestier household. In the kitchen the bereaved Alison mourned with more bitter reason the loss of her son, while all the spinning-girls formed a chorus to her threnody. But in the loom-shed, where Bertred's body had been laid out decorously on a trestle table to await the visit of Martin Bellecote, the master-carpenter from the Wyle, it was quiet to the point of oppression, even though there were three of them there conversing in low voices and few words.

'There is no shadow of doubt,' said Cadfael, holding the boot sole-up to the light of a small lamp one of the girls had set at the head of the table. The light outside was still hardly less bright than in the afternoon, but half the shed was shuttered because the looms were at rest. 'This is the boot that made the print I took from the soil under Niall's vine, and the man who wore it is the man who tried to hack down the rose-bush, the same who also killed Brother Eluric. I made the mould, I know I am not mistaken. But here is the mould itself, for I brought it with me. You will find it matches exactly.'

'I take your word for it,' said Hugh. But as one who must verify for himself every morsel of evidence, he took the boot and the waxen mould, and carried them out to the doorway to match the two together. 'There *is* no doubt.' The two fitted like seal and matrix. There was the oblique tread that had worn down outer heel and inner toe, and the crack reaching half across the sole at the ball of the foot. 'It seems,' said Hugh, 'the Severn has saved us the cost of a trial, and him a worse fate than drowning.'

Miles had remained standing somewhat apart, looking from face to face with the same baffled wonder with which he had brooded over Bertred's body in the mortuary chapel.

'I don't understand,' he said dubiously at last. 'Are you saying that it was *Bertred* who got into the smith's garden to spoil Judith's rose-bush? And *killed* . . .' The same vigorous, even violent, shaking of his head, trying to toss the unwelcome belief from him, like a bull trying to throw off a dog that had him by the soft nose. And with as little success, for slowly the conviction began to penetrate his mind, to judge by the slackening of the lines of his face, and his final resigned calm and glint of rising interest. A very eloquent face, had Miles; Cadfael could follow every change. 'Why should *he* do such a thing?' he said slowly, but rather as if his own wit was already beginning to supply answers.

'The killing he never meant, as like as not,' said Hugh reasonably. 'But as for hacking down the bush – it was you yourself gave us a good reason why a man might do so.'

'But what did it benefit Bertred? All it would have done was to prevent my cousin getting her rent paid. What was that to him? *He* had no rights in it.' But there Miles halted to reflect again. 'I don't know – it seems reaching far. I know I said he fancied he had some small chance with her. He did presume, sometimes, he had a good conceit of himself. He may even have believed he might win her favour, such things have been known. Well . . . there's no denying, if he had such vaulting ideas, the Foregate house was a good half of her property, worth a man's while trying to regain.'

'As all her suitors may have reasoned,' said Hugh, 'not merely Bertred. He slept in here?'

'He did.'

'And therefore could go in and out at will, by night or day, without disturbing any other creature.'

'Well, so he could. It seems so he did, last night, for none of us within heard a sound.'

'But granted we have the proof now that links him to the death of Brother Eluric,' said Hugh, frowning, 'we are still floundering when it comes to the vanishing of Mistress Perle. There's nothing whatever to connect him with that, and we have still a second malefactor to find. Bertred has been among the most assiduous of our helpers in the search for her. I don't think he would have spent quite so much energy if he had had any knowledge of where she was, however desirable it might be to make a show of zeal.'

'My lord,' said Miles slowly, 'I never would have believed such devious work of Bertred, but now you have shown me so far into his guilt I cannot help following further. It's a strange thing, his own mother has been pouring out to us all, since we brought him home, what he said to her last night. You may ask her yourself, my lord, she will surely repeat it to you as she has to us. I would rather not be the bearer, nor risk being suspect of mangling the purport. If it means anything, let her deliver it, not I.'

The widow, bloated with tears and surrounded by her would-be comforters, was indeed still spouting words between her bouts of weeping, and had no objection to continuing her threnody for the benefit of the sheriff, when he drove her companions away for a short while, to have the bereaved woman to himself.

'A good son he was always to me, a good worker to his mistress, and deserved well of her, and well she thought of him. But great notions he had, like his father before him, and where have they got him now? How would I like, says he to me last night, how would I like to be better than a servant in this house – a gentlewoman, fit for the hall instead of the kitchen? Only wait a day or so, says he, and you'll see, I mean to make your fortune and my own. There's not one, he says, knows what I know. If there's ought you know to the purpose, I said, why haven't you told? But would he? And spend the credit along with my breath? he says. No, you leave all to me.'

'And did he say anything about what he intended in the night?' asked Hugh, slipping his question quietly and unobtrusively into the first chink in her outpourings, while she drew breath.

'He said he must go out again when it was full dark, but he wouldn't tell me where, or why, nor what he was about at all. Wait till tomorrow, he says, and not a word to any tonight. But what does it matter now? Speak or keep silent, it does him no good now. Don't you go running your head into trouble, I told him. There may be more than you out about risky business in the night.'

Her flow of words was by no means exhausted, but its matter became repetitive, for she had told everything she knew. They left her to the ministrations of the women and the diminishing bitterness of her grief as it drained away into exhaustion. The house of Vestier, Miles assured them earnestly as they left the premises, would not let any of its old servants go short of the means of a decent life. Alison was safe enough.

Chapter Ten

'Come with me,' said Hugh, setting off briskly up the hill towards the high cross, and turning his back with some relief on the troubled household at the clothiers' shop. 'Since you have honest leave to be out, you may as well join me on the errand you delayed for me a while ago. I was all but out of the town gate when your messenger came and Will came running after me to say I was wanted at the Vestiers'. I sent him on ahead with a couple of men, he's down there and at it by now, but I'd as lief see to it for myself.'

'Where are we going?' asked Cadfael, falling in willingly beside his friend up the steep street.

'To talk to Fuller's watchman. That's the one place outside the town walls where there'd be a waking witness even in the night, and a watchdog to alert him if anyone came prowling close by. If the fellow did by any chance go into the water this side the river, works and warehouse are only a little way upstream from where you found him. Fuller's man has both places in charge. He may have heard something. And as we go, tell me what you make of all that – Bertred's night affairs, and the fortune he was going to make.'

'By reason of knowing something no one else knew – hmm! For that matter, I noticed he stayed behind when your men left the jetty yesterday afternoon. He let you all go on well before, and then slipped back alone into the trees. And he came late for his supper, told his mother she should be a gentlewoman in the house instead of a cook, and went off again in the night to set about making his word good. And according to Miles he not only fancied his mistess, but had the assurance to feel there was no reason he should not bring her to fancy him.'

'And how persuade her?' asked Hugh, wryly smiling. 'By

abduction and force? Or by a gallant rescue?'

'Or both,' said Cadfael.

'Now truly you interest me! Those who hide can find! If by any chance the lady is where he put her, but doesn't know who put her there – for a Bertred can as easily find rogues to do his work for him as any wealthier man, it is but a matter of degrees of greed! – then who could better come to her rescue? Even if gratitude did not go so far as to make her marry him, he certainly would not be the loser.'

'It offers one way of accounting,' Cadfael acknowledged. 'And in its favour, the maid Branwen blabbed out what her mistress intended in the kitchen, so we are told. And Bertred ate in the kitchen, and was probably there to hear it. The kitchen knew of it, the hall knew nothing until next day, after she was lost. But there are other possibilities. That someone else took her, and Bertred had found out where she was. And said no word to you or your men, but kept the rescue for himself. It seems a simpler and a smaller villainy, for one surely not so subtle as to make tortuous plans.'

'You forget,' Hugh pointed out grimly, 'that by all the signs he had already committed murder, whether with intent beforehand or not, still murder. He might be forced into plans far beyond his ordinary scope after that, to cover his tracks and secure at least some of his desired gains.'

'I forget nothing,' said Cadfael sturdily. 'One point in favour of your story I've given you. Here is one against: If he had her hidden away somewhere, securely enough to baffle all your efforts to find her, why should it not be a safe and simple matter for him to effect that rescue of his without a single stumble? And the man is dead! Far more likely to come to grief in spite of all his planning, if he crossed the plans of some other man.'

'True again! Though for all we yet know, his death could have been pure mischance. True, it could be either way. If he is the abductor as well as the murderer, then we have no second villain to find, but alas, we still lack the lady, and the only man who could lead us to her is dead. If murderer and abductor are two different people, then we have still to find both the captor and his captive. And since it seems the most likely object of taking her is to inveigle her into marriage, we may hope and believe both that she is living, and that in the end he must release her. Though I own I'd rather forestall that by plucking her out of his hold myself.'

They were over the crest by the high cross, and striding downhill now, past the ramp that led up to the castle gatehouse, and still downhill alongside the towering walls, until town wall on their left and castle wall on their right met in a low tower, under which the highway passed. Once through that gateway, the level of the road opened before them, fringed for only a short way by small houses and gardens. Hugh turned right on the outer side of the deep, dry castle ditch, before the houses began, and started down towards the riverside, and Cadfael followed more sedately.

Godfrey Fuller's tenterground stood empty, the drying cloth just unhooked and rolled up for finishing. Most of his men had already stopped work for the day, and the last few had lingered to watch and listen at the arrival of the sheriff's men, before making for their homes in the town. A close little knot of men had gathered at the edge of the tenterground, between dye-works and wool warehouse: Godfrey Fuller himself, his finery shed in favour of stout working clothes, for he was by no means ashamed to soil his hands alongside his workmen, and prided himself on being able to do whatever he asked of them, and possibly as well or better than they could; the watchman, a thickset, burly fellow of fifty, with his mastiff on a leash; Hugh's oldest sergeant, Will Warden, bushy-bearded and massive; and two men from the garrison in watchful attendance at a few yards distance. At sight of Hugh dropping with long strides down the slope of the meadow, Warden swung away from the colloquy to meet him.

'My lord, the watchman here says there was an alarm in the night, the dog gave tongue.'

The watchman spoke up freely for himself, aware of duty properly done. 'My lord, some sneak thief was here in the night, well past midnight, climbing to the hatch behind Master Hynde's storehouse. Not that I knew then that he'd got so far, but the hound here gave warning, and out we went, and heard him running for the river. I made to cut him off, but he was past me too fast, all I got was one clout at him as he rushed by. I hit him, but did him precious little harm, surely, by the speed he made down to the bank and into the water. I heard the splash as he went in, and called off the dog, and went to look had he got into the store. But there was no sign, not to be seen in the night, and I took it he was well across and off by then, no call to make any more stir about him. I never knew till now it was a dead man came ashore on the other side. That I never meant.'

'It was not your doing,' said Hugh. 'The blow you got in did him no great damage. He drowned, trying to swim across.'

'But, my lord, there's more! When I looked round the warehouse by daylight this morning, see what I found lying in the grass under the hatch. I've just handed them over to your sergeant here.' Will Warden had them in his hands, displayed in meaning silence, a long chisel and a small clawed hammer. 'And the sill beam under the hatch broken from its nails at one end, and dangling. I reckon surely he was up there trying to break through the shutter and get in at the fleeces. A year ago when the clip was in there thieves got in and stole a couple of bales. Old William Hynde near went out of his wits with rage. Come and see, my lord.'

Cadfael followed slowly and thoughtfully as they set off round the bulk of the warehouse to the rear slope, where the shuttered hatch showed still securely fastened, though the stout beam under it hung vertically against the planks of the wall, the splintered gaps where it had broken free from its anchoring nails rotten and soft to the touch.

'Gave under his weight,' said the watchman, peering upward. 'It was his fall the dog heard. And these tools came down with him, and he had no time to pick them up, if he'd delayed a moment we should have had him. But here's good proof he was trying to break in and steal. And the best is,' said the watchman, shaking his head over the folly of the too-clever, 'if he'd got in through the hatch he couldn't have got at the fleeces.'

'No?' said Hugh sharply, turning a startled glance on him. 'Why? What would have prevented?'

'There's another locked door beyond, my lord, between him and what he came for. No, belike you wouldn't know of it, why should you? William Hynde's clerk used to work in the little back room up there, it was used as a counting-house until that time thieves broke in by this back way. By then the woolman was buying here for the foreign trade, and old Hynde thought better to bid him up to his own house and make much of him. And what with their business being all transacted there, the old counting-house was out of use. He had the door locked and barred, for an extra barrier against thieves. If this rogue had got in, it would have done him no good.'

Hugh gazed and pondered, and gnawed a dubious lip. 'This rogue, my friend, was in the wool trade himself, and knew this place very well. He fetched the fleeces for the Vestiers from here, he'd been in and out more than once. How comes it that he would not know of this closed counting-house? And my deputy had them open up here two days ago, and saw the upper floor full almost to the ladder with bales. If there's a door there, it was buried behind the wool.'

'So it would be, my lord. Why not? I doubt if a soul had gone through that door since it was first shut up. There's nothing within there.'

Nothing now, Cadfael was thinking. But was there something – someone! – there only yesterday? It would seem that Bertred thought so, though of course Bertred could be wrong. He must have known of the abandoned room, he may well have thought it worth putting to the test at a venture, without special cause. If so, it cost him dear. All those dreams of bettering his fortune by a gallant rescue, of exploiting a woman's gratitude to the limit and advancing his own cause step by step with insinuating care, all shattered, swept away down the currents of the Severn. Did he really know something no one else among the searchers knew, or was he speaking only of this hidden room as a possibility?

'Will,' said Hugh, 'send a man up to Hynde's house, and ask him, or his son, to come down here and bring the keys. All his keys! It's time I took a look within here myself. I should have done it earlier.'

* * *

But it was neither William Hynde nor his son Vivian who came striding down the field with the sergeant after a wait of some ten or fifteen minutes. It was a serving-man in homespun and leather, a tall, bold-faced, muscular fellow in his thirties, sporting a close-trimmed beard that outlined a wide mouth and a jaunty jaw with all the dandified elegance of a Norman lordling, though his build was Saxon and his colouring reddish-fair. He made a careless obeisance to Hugh, and straightened up to measure eyes with him, ice-pale eyes with only the glittering Norse-tinge of blue in them.

'My lord, my mistress sends you these, and my services.' He had the keys in his hand on a great ring, a rich bunch of them. His voice was loud, with a brazen ring to it, though his manner was civil enough. 'My master's away at his sheepfolds by Forton, has been since yesterday, and the young master's gone up there to help them today, but he'll be back tomorrow if you need him. Will it please you command me? I'm here to serve.'

'I've seen you about the town,' said Hugh, eyeing him with detached interest. 'So you're in Hynde's service, are you? What's your name?'

'Gunnar, my lord.'

'And he trusts you with his keys. Well, Gunnar, open these doors for us. I want to see what's within.' And he added, as the man turned willingly to obey: 'When is the barge expected, if Master Hynde can spare time to go in person to his flocks?'

'Before the end of the month, my lord, but the merchant sends word ahead from Worcester. They take the clip by water to Bristol, and then overland to Southampton for shipping, it cuts off the long voyage round. A rough passage they say it is, all round the south-west.' He was busy as he talked, unfastening two massive padlocks from the bar of the warehouse doors, and drawing both leaves wide open to let in the light upon a clean-swept, slightly raised floor of boards, on which the lower-grade fleeces had been stacked. This level was empty now. From the left-hand corner within the door a wooden ladder led up through a wide, open trap to the floor above.

'You're well informed concerning Master Hynde's business affairs, Gunnar,' said Hugh mildly, stepping over the threshold.

'He trusts me. I made the journey down to Bristol with the barge once, when they had a man injured and were short-handed. Will it please you go up, sir? Shall I lead the way?'

A very self-assured and articulate person, this Gunnar, Cadfael reflected, the very image of the intelligent and trusted servant of a commercial house, capable of adapting to travel, and learning from every experience. By his stature, bearing and colouring he proclaimed his northern ancestry. The Danes had reached no further south than Brigge in this shire, but they had left a few of their getting behind when they retreated. Cadfael followed without haste as they mounted the ladder and stepped on to the upper floor. Here the light was dim, reflected up from the wide doors below, but enough to show the stacked bales stretching the full length of the storehouse.

'We could do with more light,' said Hugh.

'Wait, my lord, and I'll open.' And Gunnar made no more ado, but seized one of the bales in the centre of the array and hauled it down to set aside, and after it several more, until the stout wooden planks of a narrow door were laid bare. He flourished his ring of keys with a flurry of sound, selected one, and thrust it into the lock. There were two iron bars slotted across the door in addition, and they grated rustily as he drew them from the sockets. The key creaked as it turned. 'There's been no use made of this for a while now,' said Gunnar cheerfully. 'We'll do no harm by letting in the air for once.'

The door opened inward. He thrust it wide and made straight across to the shuttered hatch, and with a lusty banging of latches and beams released the shutters and pushed them wide to let in the slanting sunlight. 'Mind the dust, my lord,' he warned helpfully, and stood back to let them examine the whole narrow room. A rising breeze blew in, fluttering trailers of cobweb from the rough wood of the hatch.

A small, barren space, an old bench against the wall, a heap of discarded fragments of vellum and cloth and wool and wood, and indistinguishable rubbish drifted into one corner, a large ewer with a broken lip, the ancient desk leaning askew, and over all the grime and dust of abandonment, of a place two years disused, and a year sealed and forgotten.

'There was a thief got in this way once,' said Gunnar airily. 'They'd have much ado to manage it a second time. But I must make all secure again before I leave it, my master'd have my head if I forgot to shoot every bolt and turn every key.'

'There was a thief tried to get in this way only last night,' said Hugh casually. 'Have they not told you?'

Gunnar had turned on him a face fallen open in sheer astonishment. 'A thief? Last night? Not one word of this have I heard, or the mistress, either. Who says it's so?'

'Ask the watchman below, he'll tell you. One Bertred, a weaver who works for Mistress Perle. Take a look at the sill outside the hatch, Gunnar, you'll see how it came down with his weight. The hound hunted him into the river,' said Hugh, offhand, gazing musingly all round the neglected room, but well aware of the look on Gunnar's face. 'He drowned.'

The silence that followed was brief but profound. Gunnar stood mute, staring, and all his light assurance had frozen into a steely gravity.

'You'd heard nothing?' marvelled Hugh, his eyes on the dusty floor, on which Gunnar's vigorous passage had printed the only pattern of footmarks perceptible between door and hatch.

'No, my lord – nothing.' The loud, confident voice had become taut, intent and quiet. 'I know the man. Why should he want to steal fleeces? He is very well settled as he is – he was . . . *Dead*?'

'Drowned, Gunnar. Yes.'

'Sweet Christ have his soul!' said Gunnar, slowly and quietly, to himself rather than to them. 'I knew him. I've diced with him. God knows neither I nor any that I know of bore Bertred any ill will, or ever wished him harm.'

There was another silence. It was as if Gunnar had left them, and was withdrawn into another place. The ice-blue eyes looked opaque, as if he had drawn a shutter down over them, or turned their gaze within rather than without. In a few moments he stirred, and asked levelly: 'Have you done here, my lord? May I close these again?'

'You may,' said Hugh as shortly. 'I have done.'

On the way back into the town through the castle gate they were both silent and thoughtful, until Hugh said suddenly: 'If ever she was there in that dusty hole, someone has done excellent work wiping out every trace.'

'Bertred thought she was,' said Cadfael. 'Though Bertred may have been wrong. Surely he was there to try and set her free, but he may have been guessing, and guessing wrongly. He knew of the room, and knew it was not common knowledge and therefore, with care, might be used for such a purpose. And he knew that young Hynde made a very possible abductor, being vain, persistent and in urgent need of money to maintain his easy life. But was it more than a guess? Did he really discover something that made it a certainty?'

'The very dust!' said Hugh. 'No mark of any foot but Gunnar's, or none that I could see. And the young fellow, the son, this Vivian – he did ride off this morning, out of the town, that I knew already, Will reported it to me. So there's no one there but the mother now. And would *she* be lying? Hardly likely he'd tell *her* if he had a woman hidden away. If he's taken the girl elsewhere after the night alarm, it would hardly be to his mother. But I'll pay the house another visit, all the same. I fancy Bertred must have been trying his luck – but that the poor wretch had no luck! No luck with the roses, no luck with the rescue. No luck in any of his schemes.'

Another long silence, while they climbed the gradual slope within the gate, and approached the ramp to the castle entrance. 'And he did not know!' said Hugh. 'He really did not know!'

'He? And know what?'

'This man Gunnar. I had my doubts about him until then. So confident and assured, light as air, until mention was made of a man's death. That I am sure came new to him. There was no pretence there. What say you, Cadfael?'

'I say there is a man who could lie and lie, whenever the occasion needed it. But who was not lying then. His very voice changed, no less than his face. No, he did not know. He was shaken to the heart. Whatever mischief he might have a part in, he had not contemplated a death. Let alone Bertred's death!' They had reached the ramp and halted. 'I must get back,' said Cadfael, looking up into a sky just veiled and softened with the approach of twilight. 'What more can we do tonight? And what will you do tomorrow?'

'Tomorrow,' said Hugh with deliberation, 'I'll have Vivian Hynde brought to me as soon as he shows his face in the town gate, and see what's to be got out of him concerning his father's old counting-house. From all I've heard of him, he should be easier to frighten than his man shows any sign of being. And even if he's a snow-white innocent, from all accounts a fright will do him no harm.'

'And will you make it public,' Cadfael asked, 'that at least Brother Eluric's murderer is known? And is dead?'

'No, not yet. Perhaps not at all, but at least let the poor woman have what peace she can find until her son's buried. What point in blazoning forth guilt where there can never be a trial?' Hugh was looking back with a frown, and somewhat regretting that Miles had been present to witness that manifestation in the loom-shed. 'If I know the sharp ears and long tongues of Shrewsbury it may yet be common talk by morning without any word from me. Perhaps not, perhaps Coliar will hold his tongue for the mother's sake. But at any rate they shall have no official declaration to grit their teeth in until we find Judith Perle. As we will, as we must. Let them gossip and speculate. Someone may take fright and make the blunder I'm waiting for.'

'The lord abbot will have to know all that I know,' said Cadfael.

'So he will, but he's another matter. He has the right and you have the duty. So you'd best be about getting back to him,' said Hugh, sighing, 'and I'd best go in and see if any of those men of mine who've been out raking the countryside has done any better than I have.'

Upon which impeccably conscientious but none too hopeful note they parted.

* * *

Cadfael arrived back at the gatehouse too late for Vespers. The brothers were in the choir, and the office almost over. A great deal had happened in one short afternoon.

'There's one here been waiting for you,' said the porter, looking out from his lodge as Cadfael stepped through the wicket. 'Master Niall the bronzesmith. Come in to him here, we've been passing the time of evening together, but he wants to be on his way as soon as may be.'

Niall had heard enough to know who came, and emerged from the gatehouse with a coarse linen bag under his arm. It needed but one glance at Cadfael's face to show that there was nothing to tell, but he asked, all the same. 'No word of her?'

'None that's new. No, sorry I am to say it. I'm just back from the sheriff himself, but without comfort.'

'I waited,' said Niall, 'in case you might bring at least some news. The least trace would be welcome. And I can do nothing! Well, I must be on my way, then.'

'Where are you bound tonight?'

'To my sister and her man at Pulley, to see my little girl. I have a set of harness ornaments to deliver for one of Mortimer's horses, though that could have waited a few days yet. But the child will be looking for me. This is the evening I usually go to her, else I wouldn't stir. But I shall not stay overnight. I'll walk back in the dark. At least to be there with the roses, if I can do nothing better for her.'

'You've done more than the rest of us,' said Cadfael ruefully, 'for you've kept the bush alive. And she'll be back yet to take the pick of its flowers from your hand, the day after tomorrow.'

'Should I read that as a promise?' asked Niall, with a wry and grudging smile.

'No, as a prayer. The best I can do. With three miles or more to walk to Pulley, and three miles back,' said Cadfael, 'you'll have time for a whole litany. And bear in mind whose festival it will be in two days' time! Saint Winifred will be listening. Who more likely? She herself stood off an unwanted suitor and kept her virtue, she'll not forsake a sister.'

'Well . . . I'd best be off. God with you, Brother.' Niall shouldered his bag of ornamental bronze rosettes and harness buckles for Mortimer's horse, and strode away along the Foregate, towards the track that led south-west from the bridge, a square, erect figure thrusting briskly into the pearly evening air cooling towards twilight. Cadfael stood looking after him until he turned the corner beyond the mill-pond and vanished from sight.

Not a man for grand gestures or many words, Niall Bronzesmith, but Cadfael was bitterly and painfully aware of the gnawing frustration that eats away at the heart from within, when there is nothing to be done about the one thing in the world of any importance.

Chapter Eleven

Niall set out from Pulley on his return walk to Shrewsbury a little before midnight. Cecily would have had him stay, urging truly enough that if he did go back it would change nothing, and stating bluntly what Cadfael had refrained from stating, that while the woman herself was still safely out of reach there was hardly likely to be any further attack on the rose-bush, for any such attack was unnecessary. No one could deliver a rose into the hand of a woman who was missing. If someone was plotting to break the bargain and recover the house in the Foregate, as by now everyone seemed to be agreed, the thing was already done, without taking any further risk.

Niall had said very little about the affair to his sister, and nothing at all about his own deep feelings, but she seemed to know by instinct. The talk of Shrewsbury found its way out here softened and distanced into a kind of folk-tale, hardly bearing at all on real life. The reality here was the demesne, its fields, its few labourers, the ditched coppice from which the children fended off the goats at pasture, the plough-oxen, and the enshrouding forest. The two little girls, listening round-eyed to the grown-ups' talk, must have thought of Judith Perle as of one of the enchanted ladies bewitched by evil magic in old nursery tales. Cecily's two shock-headed, berry-brown boys, at home in all the woodland skills, had only two or three times in their lives, thus far, set eyes on the distant towers of Shrewsbury castle. Three miles is not so far, but far enough when you have no need to cross it. John Stury came into the town perhaps twice a year to buy, and for the rest the little manor was self-supporting. Sometimes Niall was moved to feel that he must soon remove his daughter and take her back with him to the town, for fear he might lose her for ever. To a happy household, a peaceful, simple life and good company, truly, but to his own irrevocable loss and bereavement.

She was asleep long before this hour, in her nest with the other three in the loft, he had laid her there himself, already drowsy. A fair creature, with a bright sheen of gold in her cloud of hair, like her mother before her, and a skin like creamy milk, that glowed in sunny weather with the same gilded gloss. Cecily's brood were reddish-dark, after their father, with lithe, lean bodies and black eyes. She was rounded and smooth and soft. Almost from birth she had been here with her cousins, it would be hard to take her away.

'You'll have a dark walk home,' said John, peering out from the doorway. In the summer night the smell of the forest was spicy and strong, heavy in the windless dark. 'The moon won't be up for hours yet.'

'I don't mind it. I should know the way well enough by now.'

'I'll come out with you as far as the track,' said Cecily, 'and set you on your road. It's fine and warm still, and I'm wakeful.'

She walked beside him in silence as far as the gate in John's stockade, and out across the clearing of open grass to the edge of the trees, and there they halted.

'One of these days,' she said, as though she had been listening to all that he had been thinking, 'you'll be taking the little one away from us. It's only right you should, though we shall grudge her to you. As well we're not so far away that we can't borrow her back now and then. It wouldn't do to leave it too long, Niall. I've had the gift of her, and been glad of it, but yours she is, yours and Avota's, when all's said, and best she should grow up knowing it and content with it.'

'She's young yet,' said Niall defensively. 'I dread to confuse her too soon.'

'She's young, but she's knowing. She begins to ask why you always leave her, and to wonder how you do, alone, and who cooks and washes for you. I reckon you could as well take her on a visit, show her how you live and what you make. She's hungry to know, you'll find she'll drink it in. And much as she joys in playing with my brood, she never likes sharing you with them. That's a true woman you'll find there,' said Cecily with conviction. 'But for all that, it might be the best thing of all you could do for her, Niall, just now is to give her another mother. One of her own, with no rival childer by. For she's sharp enough, my dear, to know that I'm none of hers, love her as I may.'

Niall said his good night to her without comment on that, and went off with a rapid stride into the trees. She knew him well enough to expect nothing more, and turned back to the house, when he had vanished from sight, aware that he had listened and been torn. It was time he should give thought to it. The life of a respected town craftsman's daughter, with property to inherit and social skills to learn, must necessarily be different from that of a country steward's girl; her betrothal prospects must be sought among a different group of people, her upbringing be aimed at a somewhat different kind of household with a different round of duties. Sharp beyond her years, the child might begin to think that a father who leaves her too long apart from him does not really want her, but visits only out of duty. Yet she was very young, very young to be taken where there was no woman to care for her. Now if only there should be some real hope in this widow woman of whom he had nothing to say! Or, for that matter, any other decent woman with a warm heart and a cool head, and patience enough for two!

Niall walked on along the narrow path between the trees, in dark-green night, full-leaved and heady with scents, with his sister's voice still in his ears. The woods were thick and well grown here, the ground so shadowed that herbal cover was scant, but the interlacing of boughs above shut out the sky. Sometimes the path emerged for a short way into more open upland where the trees thinned and clearings of heath appeared, for all this stretch of country was the northern fringe of the Long Forest, where men had encroached with their little assarts and their legal or illegal cutting of timber and pasturing of pigs on acorns and beech-mast. But even here settlements were very few. He would not see more than a couple of small, precarious holdings before he came to the hamlet of Brace Meole, nearly half his way home.

On that thought he checked to reconsider, for it might be a little quicker to turn aside to the east on a path he knew, and hit the high road, if such a track through forest could be called a high road, well before the village, instead of staying on the forest path. Every variation on this journey was familiar to him. The path of which he was thinking crossed the one on which he was walking diagonally, striking south-west, and where the ways met there was a small open clearing, the only such space in a belt of thicker woodland. Here he halted for a moment, still undecided, and stood to savour the awesome quietness of the night, just as the hush was mysteriously broken by small, persistent sounds. In such windless silence any sound, however soft, came startlingly upon the ear. Instinctively Niall drew back from the open ground, deep into the cover of the trees, and stood with head up and ears stretched to decipher the signs.

There are always some nocturnal creatures about their business in the dark, but their small rustlings keep low to the ground and furtive, and freeze when a man is scented in the night, since every man is an enemy. These sounds proceeded steadily though softly, and were gradually drawing nearer. The dull, solid but muffled thud of hooves in deep turf, drawing near at a brisk walk from the direction of the road, and a light rustling and swish of pliable twigs brushing a passing bulk. The summer growth was at its height, the trees had reached new and tender shoots just far enough to encroach upon the path with their soft tips.

What was a horseman doing, coming this way at this hour, and by the pace and the sounds heavily laden? Niall stayed where he was, well within the trees and hidden, but looking out into the clearing, where by contrast there was light enough to distinguish shapes and degrees of grey and black. No moon, and a high, faint veil of cloud between the earth and stars, a night for dark undertakings. And though masterless men seldom ventured within ten miles of Shrewsbury, and the worst to be encountered should be only a poacher, yet there was always the possibility of worse. And when did poachers go mounted about their business?

Between the dark woodland walls of the right-hand path a

vague pallor appeared. The new foliage whispered along a horse's barrel and a rider's arm. A white horse, or a pale dapple-grey or very light roan, for his hide brought with it into the clearing its own lambent gleam. The shape of the man on his back appeared at first squat and monstrously thickset, until some unevenness of the ground set up a swaying movement that showed the mount was carrying not one person, but two. A man before, a woman riding pillion behind. One shadowy bulk, without detail, became clearly two, though still without identity, as horse and riders passed by, crossed the path and continued on their cautious way south-west. The swing of the long skirt showed, there were even points of pallor mysterious in the moving darkness, a hand holding by the horseman's belt, an oval face raised to the sky, free of the hood that had fallen back on to the woman's shoulders.

There was nothing clearer to view than that, and yet he knew her. It might have been the poise of the head with its great sheaf of hair, moving against a sky almost as dark, or the erect carriage and balance of her body, or some overstrung cord within his own being that could not but vibrate to her nearness. This woman of all women could not pass by, even in the dark and unaware of him, and he not know.

And what was Judith Perle doing here in the night, three days after vanishing from her rightful place, riding pillion behind a horseman going south-west, and she under no constraint, but going with him willingly?

He stood for so long motionless and silent that the small creatures of the night seemed to have lost all awe of him, or forgotten he was there. Somewhere across the clearing, where the path by which he had come continued, something rustled hastily from one tangle of undergrowth to another, and made off westward into safety and silence. Niall stirred out of his chilled stillness, and turned to follow the sound of the muffled hooves down the grassy ride until they died into the same profound silence.

He could neither believe in nor understand what he had seen. It was not, it could not be, what it seemed. Where she was going, who was her companion, what she intended, these were mysteries, but they were her mysteries, and in her

Niall had so strong and unquestioning a faith that no strange night venture could shake it. The one certainty was that by the grace of God he had found her, and now he must not lose her again, and that was enough. If she had no need of him, if she was in no danger or distress, so be it, and he would never trouble her. But he would, he must, follow and be near to see that no harm came to her, until all this dark interlude was over and done, and she vindicated and restored to the light. The conviction was unbearably strong within him that if he lost her now she would be lost forever.

He emerged from his cover and crossed into the path they had taken. There was no danger of losing them; through the thickening forest ahead a horse must hold to the path, especially by night, and in this darkness could not press beyond a walk. A man afoot could have outrun them, provided he knew the woods as Niall knew them. But for his purpose it was enough to recover the sounds that were his guide, and if possible approach close enough to be with her in a moment if anything untoward threatened. This ground was less familiar to him than the various ways to Pulley, having left that hamlet aside on the left, but it was similar country, and he could thread his way among the trees, aside from the path, at a faster speed than the horseman was making. Soon he recovered the small, regular beat of hooves, and the light ring of the bridle as the horse tossed its head at some sudden nocturnal stir, perhaps, in the undergrowth on the other side of the track. Twice he caught that brief, abrupt peal of bells, like a summons to service, reassuring him that he was near, and could close quickly if there should be need.

They were moving steadily south-west, deeper into the recesses of the Long Forest, and here there were fewer places where the cover became more open, and patches of heath and outcrop rock appeared. Surely more than a mile past now, and still the riders pressed on, keeping the same cautious pace. The veiled sky had grown somewhat darker with thickening cloud cover. Looking up, Niall could barely distinguish the shapes of the upper branches against the heavens. He went with hands spread to touch the trees and weave his way between, but still he kept within earshot of the horse's steady progress, and once he found he had drawn abreast of it, and was aware of movement along the path on his right, by sense rather than by sight. He hung back to let the vague blur of the pale hide draw ahead again, and then took up the patient pursuit with greater care.

He had lost all idea of how long they had been engaged in this nocturnal pilgrimage through the forest, but thought it must be almost an hour, and if the riders had come from the town they must have set out an hour earlier still. As to where they were bound, he had no notion. He knew nothing in this part of the woods, barring perhaps a solitary scratched-out assart hacked recently from the waste. They must be fairly close to the source of the Meole Brook, and riding upstream. From the higher ground on the left two or three tiny tributaries came down and trickled across the path, none of them any barrier, for any one of them could be stepped over dry-shod, at least in summer. The little serpents of water made one more tiny sound, hissing drowsily between the stones. They had gone perhaps three miles, Niall reckoned, since he first began to follow.

Somewhere not too distant on the right the woods rustled and stilled. The rhythm of the horse's gait was broken, hooves shifted, at check on a harder floor where stone came near the surface, then moved more slowly back to turf and halted. Niall crept closer, feeling his way from tree to tree and putting off the hampering branches with careful quietness. It seemed by the slight easing of the darkness that the path he was approaching had widened into a grassy ride where the sky, if clouded, could at least peer in. Then he saw through the lace of leaves the dim pallor which was the body of the horse, standing still. For the first time there was a voice, a man's, in a sibilant whisper that carried clearly through the silence.

'I should take you to the gate.'

The rider was already out of the saddle. In the forest aisle where the darkness became relative there was movement upon the ground, a blacker shape shifting across the pallor of the horse like drifts of cloud across the moon.

'No,' said Judith's voice, chill and clear. 'That was not in the bargain. I do not wish it.'

By the horse's stirring and the susurration of movement

Niall knew the moment when the man lifted her down, though still, without conviction, his voice protested: 'I cannot let you go alone.'

'It is not far,' she said. 'I am not afraid.'

And he was accepting his dismissal, for again the horse stirred and trod the turf, and a stirrup rang once. The rider was remounting. Something more he said, but it was lost as his mount turned, not to go back the way he had come, but onward to the left, uphill by another track, to cut through the rough uplands the nearest way to the road. Speed rather than secrecy was his concern now. But after a few hasty paces he did check and turn to offer again what she had refused, knowing she would still refuse it.

'I'm loth to leave you so . . .'

'I know my way now,' she said simply. 'Go, get home before light.'

At that he did turn, shake his bridle, and start along a rising ride that seemed to offer better speed and a more open and smooth surface, for in a little while the receding sound of the hooves became a cautious trot, intent on making good speed away from this mysterious errand. Judith still stood where he had set her down, quite invisible in the edge of the trees, but Niall would know when she moved. He drew nearer still, ready to follow whatever move she made. She knew her way, it was not far, and she was not afraid. But he would go at her back until she reached her chosen haven, wherever that might be.

The rider was gone, the last muted sound had died into silence, before she stirred, and then he heard her turn away to the right, out of the comparative twilight of the open ride, back into the lush, leafy blackness of thick forest, for a twig snapped under her foot. He crossed the ride and followed. There was a narrow but trodden path slanting away downhill, towards some larger tributary of the Meole, for he caught the distant small whispering of water from below.

He had gone no more than twenty paces down the path, and she was perhaps twenty before him, when there was a sudden violent threshing of bushes from the right, out of the thick undergrowth, and then Judith cried out, one wild, brief cry of alarm and dread. Niall sprang forward in a reckless run towards the cry, and felt, rather than heard or saw, the night convulsed before him with the turbulence of an almost silent struggle. His spread arms embraced two bodies, blindly and clumsily, and struggled to pluck them apart. Judith's long hair, torn from its coil, streamed across his face, and he took her about the waist to put her behind him and out of danger. He felt the upward swing of a long arm reaching past him to strike at her, and some strange trick of lambent light flashed for one instant blue along the blade of a knife.

Niall caught the descending arm and wrenched it aside, hooked a knee round the assailant's knee with a wrestler's instinct, and brought them both crashing to the ground. They rolled and strained, twigs crackling under them in the blind dark, bruised shoulders against the boles of trees, wrenched and struggled, the one to free his knife arm, the other to hold the blade away from himself or get possession of it. Their breath mingled as they strained and panted face to face, and each still invisible to the other. The attacker was strong, muscular and determined, and had a fund of vicious tricks to play, using head and teeth and knees freely, but he could not break away or get to his feet again. Niall had him by the right wrist, and with his other arm wound about the man's body, pinning the upper arm so that his opponent could only claw fiercely at neck and face, drawing blood. With a grunting effort he heaved up his body and rolled them both over to make violent impact with the bole of a tree, intent on half-stunning Niall and breaking his grip to free the knife, but he succeeded all too well, and his own knife arm, already weakened with cramps from the grip on his wrist, struck the solid timber hard, jarring from elbow to fingers. His hand started open, the knife flew wide and was lost in the grass.

Niall came dazedly to his knees, to hear his enemy gasping and moaning, groping about in the turf and leaf-mould for his weapon, and muttering curses because he could not find it. And at the first lunge Niall made to grapple with him again he dragged himself to his feet and ran, breaking through the bushes, back the way he had come. The lashing of branches and rustling of leaves marked his path through the thick woods, until the last sound faded away into distance, and he was gone.

Niall clambered to his feet, shaking his ringing head, and groped for a tree to hold by. He was no longer sure which way he was facing on the path, or where to find Judith, until a still voice said, with slow, composed wonder: 'I am here!' and the barely perceptible pallor of an extended hand beckoned him, and closed on the hand he reached out to meet it. Her touch was chill but firm. Whether she knew him or not, of him she had no fear. 'Are you hurt?' she said. They drew together very gently, rather out of a startled and mutual respect than out of any caution, and their human warmth met and mingled.

'Are *you*? He struck at you before I could reach him. Did he wound you?'

'He has slit my sleeve,' she said, feeling at her left shoulder. 'A scratch, perhaps – nothing more. I'm not hurt, I can go. But you . . .'

She laid her hands on his breast, and felt anxiously down from shoulders to forearms, and found blood. 'He has gashed you – this left arm . . .'

'It's nothing,' said Niall. 'We're lightly rid of him.'

'He meant killing,' said Judith gravely. 'I didn't know there could be outlaws prowling so close to the town. Night travellers could be butchered for the clothes they wear, let alone the money they might be carrying.' Only then did she begin to quiver with the laggard disruption of shock, and he drew her into his arms to warm the chill out of her. Then she did know him. His voice had started echoes for her, his touch was certainty. 'Master Bronzesmith? How did you come to be here? So happily for me! But how?'

'No matter for that now,' said Niall. 'First let me bring you wherever you were going. Here in the forest, if there are such scum abroad, we could still come to grief. And you may take cold from the very malice and violence of it. How far have you to go?'

'Not far,' she said. 'Down to the brook here, barely half a mile. All the stranger that footpads should be loose here. I am going to the Benedictine nuns at Godric's Ford.'

He asked her nothing more. Her plans were her own, there was nothing here for him to do but see that they were not impeded. He kept an arm about her as they set off down the path, until presently it widened into a grassy ride, where a faint light came in like mist. Invisibly beyond the trees the moon was rising at last. Somewhere before them there was the elusive gleam of water in motion, in mysterious, vibrant glimpses that shifted and vanished, and emerging from the misty air on their side of it, the sharp black edges of roofs and a fence, and a little bell-turret, the only vertical line.

'This is the place?' asked Niall. He had heard of the cell, but never before questioned where it lay, or been anywhere near it.

'Yes.'

'I'll bring you as far as the gate, and see you within.'

'No, you must come in with me. You must not go back now, alone. Tomorrow, by daylight, we shall be safe enough.'

'There's no place here for me,' he said doubtfully.

'Sister Magdalen will find a place.' And she said with sudden passionate entreaty: 'Don't leave me now!'

They came down together to the high timber fence that enclosed the cell and its gardens. Though the moon was still hidden from their sight beyond the forested uplands, its reflected light was growing with every moment; buildings, trees, bushes, the curve of the brook and cushioned strips of meadow along its banks, all emerged slowly from black obscurity into subtle modulations of grey, soon to be silvered as the moon climbed. Niall hesitated with his hand on the rope of the bell at the closed gate, such a violation it seemed to break the silence. When he did rouse himself to pull, the jangle of sound went echoing along the water, and rang back from the trees of the opposite shore. But there was only a short wait before the portress came grumbling and yawning to open the grille and peer out at them.

'Who is it? Benighted, are you?' She saw a man and a woman, both unknown to her and astray here in the forest at night, and took them for what they seemed, respectable travellers who had lost their way and found themselves in unfrequented solitudes where any shelter was more than welcome. 'You want a night's lodging?'

'My name is Judith Perle,' said Judith. 'Sister Magdalen

knows of me, and once offered me a place of refuge when I needed it. Sister, I need it now. And here with me is my good friend who has stood between me and danger and brought me safely here. I pray shelter through the night for him, too.'

'I'll call Sister Magdalen,' said the portress with wise caution, and went away to do so, leaving the grille open. In a very few minutes the two returned together, and Sister Magdalen's bright, shrewd brown eyes looked through the lattice with wide-awake interest, alert even at this hour of the night.

'You may open,' she said cheerfully. 'Here is a friend, and a friend's friend is just as welcome.'

In the tiny parlour, without fuss and without questions, Sister Magdalen did first things first, mulled strong wine to warm the last chill of shock and fright out of them, rolled back Niall's bloody sleeve, bathed and bandaged the long gash in his forearm, anointed the scratch on Judith's shoulder, and briskly repaired the long tear in her bodice and sleeve.

'It is but cobbled,' she said. 'I was never a good hand with a needle. But it will serve until you're home.' And she picked up the bowl of stained water and bore it away, leaving them for the first time alone together by candle-light, gazing earnestly and wonderingly at each other.

'And you have asked me nothing,' said Judith slowly. 'Neither where I have been all these days past, nor how I came to be riding through the night to this place, in company with a man. Neither how I vanished, nor how I got my freedom again. And I owe you so much, and I have not even thanked you. But I do, from my heart! But for you I should be lying dead in the forest. He meant killing!'

'I know well enough,' said Niall steadily, 'that you never would willingly have left us all in distress and dismay for you these three days. And I know that if you choose now to spare the man who put you to such straits, you do it of good intent, and in the kindness of your heart. What more do I need to know?'

'I want it buried for my own sake, too,' she said ruefully. 'What is there to gain by denouncing him? And much to lose.

He is no such great villain, only presumptuous and vain and foolish. He has done me no violence, no lasting wrong. Better it should all be put away. You did not recognise him?' she asked, looking at him earnestly with her penetrating grey eyes, a little bruised with tiredness.

'That was he who rode with you? No, I could not tell who he was. But if I could, I would still go with your wish. Provided it was not he,' said Niall sharply, 'who came back afoot to make sure of your silence. For yes, *he* meant killing!'

'No, no, that was not he. He was gone, you heard him go. Besides, he would not. We had agreed, he knew I would keep my word. No, that other was some wretch living wild on the pickings of the roads. And we must warn Hugh Beringar so,' she said, 'when we go back. This place is very lonely. As well he should know there are masterless men abroad here.'

She had left the great waving sheaf of her hair loose on her shoulders, ready for the sleep she sorely needed. The large, high eyelids, iris-veined and translucent, hung heavily over the grey eyes. The sheen of candle-light over her tired pallor made her look like a woman fashioned in mother-of-pearl. He looked at her, and his heart ached.

'How came it,' she asked wonderingly, 'that you were there when I so needed you? I had but to cry out, and you came. It was like the grace of God, an instant mercy.'

'I was on my way home from Pulley,' said Niall, shaken and tongue-tied for a moment by the sudden sweet intensity of her voice, 'and I saw – saw, heard, no, felt in my blood – when you passed by. I never thought to trouble you, only to see that you came safely wherever it was you wished to be.'

'You knew me?' she said, marvelling.

'Yes. Yes, I knew you.'

'But not the man?'

'No, not the man.'

'I think,' she said, with abrupt and reviving resolution, 'that you may, you of all people, that you should. I think I want to tell everything to you, you and Sister Magdalen – even what the world must not know, even what I have promised to keep hidden.'

* * *

'So you see,' she said starkly, coming to the end of her story, which had taken but a few minutes to tell, 'how shamelessly I am making use of you, Sister, in coming here. I have been lost and sought, hunted high and low, for three days, and tomorrow I must go back and face all those who have laboured and agonised for me, and tell them I have been here with you, that I fled all my troubles because they fell too heavily on me, and I took refuge without a word to any, here in this retreat, where you once offered me shelter from the world. Well, it will not be quite a lie, for I am here, if only for the half of this one night. But it shames me, so to use you. Yet I must go back tomorrow.' Though it was already today, she recalled through a haze of weariness and relief. 'I cannot leave them longer than need be in doubt and anxiety, now I'm free to return. Or God knows I would stay here, and how gladly!'

'I see no need to fret over a scruple,' said Sister Magdalen sensibly. 'If this spares both you and this idiot youth you have forgiven, and shuts the mouths of gossips, then I find it as good a way of serving as any. And the need for quietness and counsel you can declare without ever a blush, for that's no lie. For that matter, you may come back again when you will, and stay as long as you will, as once I told you. But you're right, it is but fair to set their minds at rest and call off the hunt. Later, when you're rested, you shall go back and face them all, and say that you came to me when the world and the stupidity of men – saving present company, that's understood! – bore you down to despair. But creep back afoot, no, that you shan't. Would I let a woman go so poorly provided from a retreat with me? You shall have Mother Mariana's mule – poor soul, she's bedridden now, she'll do no more riding – and I'll ride with you, to give colour and body to all. I have an errand I can do to the lord abbot at the same time.'

'How if they ask how long I have been here?' asked Judith.

'With me beside you? They won't ask. Or if they do, we shall not answer. Questions are as supple as willow wands,' said Sister Magdalen, rising authoritatively to lead them to the beds prepared, 'it's easy to brush by them and slip them aside, and no one the worse for it.'

Chapter 12

The brothers were just issuing from the church after High Mass, and the sun was climbing high into a pale blue sky, when Sister Magdalen's little cavalcade turned in at the abbey gatehouse. This was the eve of the translation of Saint Winifred, and not even for violent deaths, disappearances and disasters can the proper routine of the church be allowed to lapse into disorder. This year there would be no solemn procession from Saint Giles, at the edge of the town, to bring the relics once again to their resting-place on Winifred's altar, but there would be celebratory Masses, and day-long access to her shrine for the pilgrims who had special pleas to make for her intercession. Not so many of them this year, yet the guest-hall was well filled, and Brother Denis kept busy with provision for the arrivals, as Brother Anselm was with the new music he had prepared in the saint's honour. The novices and the children hardly realised what mortal preoccupations had convulsed town and Foregate in the recent days. The younger brothers, even those who had been closest to Brother Eluric and deeply shaken by his death, had almost forgotten him now in the cheerful prospect of a festival which brought them extra dishes at meals, and additional privileges.

Brother Cadfael was in no such case. Try as he would to keep his mind firmly on the divine office, it would stray away at every turn to worry at the problem of where Judith Perle could be hidden away now, and whether, after so many sinister happenings, the death of Bertred could really be the random and callous accident it seemed, or whether that, too, had the taint of murder about it. But if so, why murder, and by whom? There seemed no doubt that Bertred himself was the murderer of Brother Eluric, but the signs indicated that so far from being the abductor of his mistress, he had been probing that ill deed for himself, and had intended to be her deliverer, and exploit the favour to the limit afterwards. No question but the watchman was telling the truth as far as he knew it, Bertred had fallen from the hatch, roused the mastiff, and been hunted to the river-bank, with a single clout on the head to speed his flight. Yes, but only one, and the body that was drawn out of the river on the other side showed a second, worse injury, though neither in itself could have been fatal. How if someone had helped him into the water with that second blow, after the watchman had called off his dog?

If that was a possibility, who could it have been but the abductor, alarmed by Bertred's interference and intent on covering up his own crime?

And Vivian Hynde was away helping his father with the flocks at Forton, was he? Well, perhaps! Not for long! If he did not ride into the arms of the watch at the town gates before noon, Hugh would be sending an armed guard to fetch him.

Cadfael had arrived at this precise point as they emerged into the sunlight of the morning, and beheld Sister Magdalen just riding in at the gatehouse on her elderly dun-coloured mule, at its usual leisurely and determined foot-pace. She rode with the same unhurried competence with which she did everything, without fuss or pretence, and looked about her as she entered with a bright, observant eye. Close to her stirrup walked the miller from the Ford, her trusted ally in all things. Sister Magdalen would never be short of a man to do what she wanted.

But there was another mule following, a taller beast, and white, and as he cleared the arch of the gateway they saw that his rider, also, was a woman, and not in the Benedictine habit, but gowned in dark green, and with a scarf over her hair. A tall, slender woman, erect and graceful in the saddle, the carriage and balance of her head arrestingly dignified, and suddenly, startlingly, familiar.

Cadfael checked so suddenly that the brother behind collided with him, and stumbled. At the head of their company the abbot had also halted abruptly, staring in wonder.

So she had come back, of her own will, at her own time, free, composed, not greatly changed, to confound them all. Judith Perle reined her mule alongside Magdalen's, and there halted. She was paler than Cadfael remembered her. By nature her skin was clear and translucent as pearl, but now with a somewhat dulled whiteness, and her eyelids were a little swollen and heavy from want of sleep, and blanched and bluish like snow. But also there was a calm and serenity upon her, though without joy. She had the mastery of herself, she looked back into the astonished and questioning eyes that devoured her, and did not lower her own.

John Miller went to lift her down, and she laid her hands on his shoulders and set foot to the cobbles of the great court with a lightness that did not quite conceal her weariness. Abbot Radulfus had got his breath back, and started forward to meet her as she came towards him, bent the knee to him deeply, and stooped to kiss the hand he extended to her.

'Daughter,' said Radulfus, shaken and glad, 'how I rejoice to see you restored here, whole and well. We have been in great trouble for you.'

'So I have learned, Father,' she said in a low voice, 'and I take it to my blame. God knows it was never my wish that anyone should be in distress of mind for me, and I am sorry to have put you and the lord sheriff and so many good men to such a trouble and expense on my behalf. I will make amends as best I may.'

'Oh, child, pains spent in goodwill require no payment. If you are come back to your place safe and well, what else matters? But how does this come about? Where have you been all this time?'

'Father,' she said, drawing breath in a moment's hesitation, 'you see no harm has come to me. It was rather I who fled from a burden that had become too hard to bear alone. That I never said word to any you must excuse, but my need, my compulsion, was sudden and urgent. I needed a place of quietness and peace, and a time for thought, all that Sister Magdalen once promised me if ever I needed to shut out the world for a little while, until my heart could stand it. I fled to her, and she has not failed me.'

'And you are just come from Godric's Ford?' said

Radulfus, marvelling. 'All this while that you have been thought lost, you were safe and quiet there? Well, I thank God for it! And no news of this turmoil we were in here ever came to your ears there at the Ford?'

'Never a word, Father Abbot,' said Sister Magdalen promptly. She had lighted down and approached without haste, smoothing the skirt of her habit from the creases of riding with plump, shapely, ageing hands. 'We live out of the world there, and seldom feel the want of it. News is slow to reach us. Since I was last here, not a soul has come our way from Shrewsbury until late last night, when a man from the Foregate happened by. So here I have brought Judith home, to put an end to all this doubt, and set all minds at rest.'

'As hers, I hope,' said the abbot, closely studying the pale but calm face, 'is now at rest, after those stresses that drove her into hiding. Three days is not long, to bring about the healing of a heart.'

She looked up steadily into his face with her wide grey eyes, and very faintly smiled. 'I thank you, Father, and I thank God, I have regained my courage.'

'I am well sure,' said the abbot warmly, 'that you could not have placed yourself in better hands, and I, too, thank God that all our fears for you can be so happily put away.'

In the brief, profound silence the long file of brothers, halted perforce at the abbot's back, shifted and craned and peered to get a good look at this woman who had been sought as lost, and even whispered about with sly undertones of scandal, and now returned immaculate in the blameless company of the sub-prioress of a Benedictine cell, effectively silencing comment, if not speculation, and confronting the world with unassailable composure and dignity. Even Prior Robert had so far forgotten himself as to stand and stare, instead of waving the brothers authoritatively away through the cloister to their proper duties.

'Will you not have your beasts cared for here,' the abbot invited, 'and take some rest and refreshment? And I will send at once to the castle and let the lord sheriff know that you are back with us safe and sound. For you should see him as soon as possible, and explain your absence to him as you have here to me.'

'So I intend, Father,' said Judith, 'but I must go home. My aunt and cousin and all my people will still be fretting for me, I must go at once and show myself, and put an end to their anxiety. I'll send to the castle immediately to let Hugh Beringar know, and he may come to me or send for me to come to him, as soon as he pleases. But we could not pass by into the town without first coming to inform you.'

'That was considerate, and I am grateful. But, Sister, I trust you will be my guest while you are here?'

'Today, I think,' said Sister Magdalen, 'I must go with Judith and see her safely restored to her family, and be her advocate with the sheriff, should she need one. Authority may be less indulgent over time and labour wasted than you are, Father. I shall stay with her at least overnight. But tomorrow I hope to have some talk with you. I've brought with me the altar frontal Mother Mariana has been working on since she took to her bed. Her hands still have all their skill, I think you will be pleased with it. But it's packed carefully away in my saddle-roll, I would rather not delay to undo it now. If I might borrow Brother Cadfael, to walk up into the town with us, I think perhaps Hugh Beringar would be glad to have him in council when we meet, and he could bring down the altar-cloth to you afterwards.'

By this time Abbot Radulfus knew her well enough to know that there was always a reason for any request she might make. He looked round for Cadfael, who was already making his way out from the ranks of the brothers.

'Yes, go with our sister. You have leave for as long as you may be needed.'

'With your countenance, Father,' said Cadfael readily, 'and if Sister Magdalen agrees, I could go straight on to the castle and take the message to Hugh Beringar, after we have brought Mistress Perle home. He'll have men still out round the countryside, the sooner he can call them off, the better.'

'Yes, agreed! Go, then!' He led the way back to where the mules stood waiting, with John Miller solid and passive beside them. The file of brothers, released from the porch, went its dutiful way, not without several glances over shoulders to watch the two women mount and depart. While they were about it, Radulfus drew Cadfael aside and said quietly: 'If the news came so laggardly to Godric's Ford, there may still be some things that have happened here that she does not know, and not all will be pleasant hearing. This man of hers who is dead, worse, guilty . . .'

'I had thought of it,' said Cadfael as softly. 'She shall know, before she ever reaches home.'

As soon as they were on the open stretch of the bridge, going at the dogged mule-pace that would not be hurried, Cadfael moved to Judith's bridle, and said mildly: 'Three days you've been absent. Have I to give account, before you face others, of all that has happened during those three days?'

'No need,' she said simply. 'I have had some account already.'

'Perhaps not of all, for not all is generally known. There has been another death. Yesterday, in the afternoon, we found a body washed up on our side the river, beyond where the Gaye ends. A drowned man – one of your weavers, the young man Bertred. I tell you now,' he said gently, hearing the sharp and painful intake of her breath, 'because at home you will find him being coffined and readied for burial. I could not let you walk into the house and come face to face with that, and all unwarned.'

'Bertred drowned?' she said in a shocked whisper. 'But how could such a thing happen? He swims like an eel. How could he drown?'

'He had had a blow on the head, though it would not have done more than make his wits spin for a while. And somehow he came by another such knock before he went into the water. Whatever happened to him happened in the night. The watchman at Fuller's had a tale to tell,' said Cadfael with careful deliberation, and went on to repeat it as nearly word for word as he could recall. She sat on her mule in chill silence throughout the story, almost he felt her freeze as she connected the hour of the night, the place, and surely also the narrow, dusty, half-forgotten room behind the bales of wool. Her silence and her word would be hard to keep. Here was lost a second young man, withered by the touch of some fatal flaw in her, and yet a third she might scarcely be able to save, now they had drawn so near to the truth.

They had reached the gate, and entered under the archway. On the steep climb up the Wyle the mules slowed even more, and no one sought to hurry them.

'There is more,' said Cadfael. 'You will remember the morning we found Brother Eluric, and the mould I made of the boot-print in the soil. The boots we took from Bertred's body, when we carried him to the abbey dead – the left boot . . . fits that print.'

'No!' she said in sharp distress and disbelief. 'That is impossible! There is here some terrible mistake.'

'There is no mistake. No possibility of a mistake. The match is absolute.'

'But why? Why? What reason could Bertred have had to try to cut down my rose-bush? What possible reason to strike at the young brother?' And in a lost and distant voice, almost to herself, she said: 'None of this did he tell me!'

Cadfael said nothing, but she knew he had heard. After a silence she said: 'You shall hear. You shall know. We had better hurry. I must talk to Hugh Beringar.' And she shook her bridle and pressed ahead along the High Street. From open booths and shop doorways heads were beginning to be thrust in excited recognition, neighbour nudging neighbour, and presently, as she drew nearer to home, there were greetings called out to her, but she hardly noticed them. The word would soon be going round that Judith Perle was home again, and riding, and in respectable religious company, after all that talk of her being carried off by some villain with marriage by rape in mind.

Sister Magdalen kept close at her heels, so that there should be no mistaking that they were travelling together. She had said nothing throughout this ride from the abbey, though she had sharp ears and a quick intelligence, and had certainly heard most of what had been said. The miller, perhaps deliberately, had let them go well ahead of him. His sole concern was that whatever Sister Magdalen designed was good and wise, and nothing and no one should be allowed to frustrate it. Of curiosity he had very little. What he needed to know in order to be of use to her she would tell him. He had been her able supporter so long now that there were things between them that could be communicated and understood without words. They had reached Maerdol-head, and halted outside the Vestier house. Cadfael helped Judith down from the saddle, for the passage through the frontage to the yard, though wide enough, was too low for entering mounted. She had barely set foot to the ground when the saddler from the shop next door came peering out from his doorway in round-eyed astonishment, and bolted as suddenly back again to relay the news to some customer within. Cadfael took the white mule's bridle, and followed Judith in through the dim passage and into the yard. From the shed on the right the rhythmic clack of the looms met them, and from the hall the faint sound of muted voices. The women sounded subdued and dispirited at their spinning, and there was no singing in this house of mourning.

Branwen was just crossing the yard to the hall door, and turned at the crisp sound of the small hooves on the beaten earth of the passage. She gave a sharp, high-pitched cry, half started towards her mistress, her face brightening into wonder and pleasure, and then changed her mind and turned and ran for the house, shouting for Dame Agatha, for Miles, for all the household to come quickly and see who was here. And in headlong haste Miles came bursting out from the hall, to stare wildly, burn up like a lighted lamp, and rush with open arms to embrace his cousin.

'Judith . . . Judith, it *is* you! Oh, my dear heart, all this time where were you? Where *were* you? While we've all been sweating and worrying, and hunting every ditch and alley for you? God knows I began to think I might never see you again. Where have you been? What happened to you?'

Before he had finished exclaiming his mother was there, overflowing with tearful endearments and pious thanks to God at seeing her niece home again, alive and well. Judith submitted patiently to all, and was spared having to answer until they had run out of questions, by which time all the spinning-women were out in the yard, and the weavers from their looms, and a dozen voices at once made a babel in which she would not have been heard, even if she had spoken. A wind of joy blew through the house of mourning, and could not be quenched even when Bertred's mother came out to stare with the rest.

'I am sorry,' said Judith, when there was a lull in the gale, 'that you have been concerned about me, that was no intent of mine. But now you see I'm whole and unharmed, no need to trouble further. I shall not be lost again. I have been at Godric's Ford with Sister Magdalen, who has been kind enough to ride back with me. Aunt Agatha, will you prepare a bed for my guest? Sister Magdalen will stay with me overnight.'

Agatha looked from her niece to the nun, and back again, with a soft smile on her lips and a shrewdly hopeful light in her blue eyes. The girl was come home with her patroness from the cloister. Surely she had returned to that former longing for the peace of renunciation, why else should she run away to a Benedictine nunnery?

'I will, with all my heart!' said Agatha fervently. 'Sister, you're warmly welcome. Pray come into the house, and I'll bring you wine and oat-cakes, for you must be tired and hungry after your ride. Use the house and us freely, we are all in your debt.' And she led the way with the conscious grace of a chatelaine. In three days, thought Cadfael, watching apart, she has grown accustomed to thinking of herself as the lady of the house; the habit can't be shaken off in an instant.

Judith moved to follow, but Miles laid a hand earnestly on her arm to detain her for a moment. 'Judith,' he said in her ear, with anxious solicitude, 'have you made her any promises? The nun? You haven't let her persuade you to take the veil?'

'Are you so set against the cloistered life for me?' she asked, studying his face indulgently.

'Not if that's what you want, but— Why did you run to her, unless . . . ? You *haven't* promised yourself to her?'

'No,' she said, 'I've made no promises.'

'But you did go to her – well!' he said, and shrugged off his own solemnity. 'It's for you to do whatever you truly want. Come, let's go in!' And he turned from her briskly to call one of the weavers to take charge of the miller and the mules, and see both well cared for, and to shoo the spinners back to their spindles, but with good humour. 'Brother, come in with us and most welcome. Do they know, then, at the abbey? That

Judith's home again?'

'Yes,' said Cadfael, 'they know. I'm here to take back some gift Sister Magdalen has brought for our Lady Chapel. And I have an errand to the castle on Mistress Perle's behalf.'

Miles snapped his fingers, abruptly grave again. 'By God, yes! The sheriff can call off this hunt now, the quest's over. But – Judith, I'd forgotten! There must be things here you don't yet know. Martin Bellecote is here, and his boy helping him. Don't go into the small chamber, they are coffining Bertred. He drowned in the Severn, two nights ago. I wish I had not to spoil this day with such ill news!'

'I have already been told,' said Judith levelly. 'Brother Cadfael would not let me return here unprepared. An accident, I hear.' There was that in the sparsity of the words and the bleakness of her voice that caused Cadfael to check and look at her closely. She shared his own trouble. She found it almost impossible to accept that anything that had happened in connection with her person and her affairs during these June days was merely accidental.

'I am going now to find Hugh Beringar,' said Cadfael, and withdrew from them on the threshold to turn back into the street.

In Judith's own private chamber they sat down together in sombre conference, Hugh, Sister Magdalen, Judith and Cadfael, greetings over, in mildly constrained formality. Miles had hovered, unwilling to be parted from the cousin he had regained, but with a respectful eye upon Hugh, half expecting to be dismissed, but with a protective hand on Judith's shoulder, as if she might need defending. But it was Judith who sent him away. She did it with a sudden flush of family tenderness, looking up into his face with a faint, affectionate smile. 'No, leave us, Miles, we shall have time later to talk as much as you wish, and you shall know whatever you need to ask, but now I would rather be without distractions. The lord sheriff's time is of value, and I owe him all my attention, after the great trouble I have caused him.'

Even then he hesitated, frowning, but then he closed his hand warmly on hers. 'Don't vanish again!' he said, and went light-footed out of the room, closing the door firmly behind him.

'The first and most urgent thing I have to tell you,' said Judith then, looking Hugh in the face, 'I didn't want him or my aunt to hear. They have been through enough anxiety for me, no need for them to know that I've been in danger of my life. My lord, there are footpads in the forest not a full mile from Godric's Ford, preying on travellers by night. I was attacked there. One man at least, I cannot answer for more, though commonly they hunt in pairs, I believe. He had a knife. I have only a scratch on my arm to show for it, but he meant to kill. The next wayfarer may not be so lucky. This I had to tell you first.'

Hugh was studying her with an impassive face but intent eyes. In the hall Miles crossed the room, whistling, towards the shop.

'And this was on your way to Godric's Ford?' said Hugh.

'Yes.'

'You were alone? By night in the forest? It was early morning when you vanished from Shrewsbury – on your way to the abbey.' He turned to Sister Magdalen. 'You know of this?'

'I know of it from Judith,' said Magdalen serenely. 'Otherwise, no, there has been no sign of outlawry so close to us. If any of the forest men had heard of such, I should have been told. But if you mean do I believe the story, yes, I believe it. I dressed her arm, and did as much for the man who came to her aid and drove off the outlaw. I know that what she tells you is true.'

'This is the fourth day since you disappeared,' said Hugh, turning his innocent black gaze again on Judith. 'Was it wise to delay so long before giving me warning of masterless men coming so close? And the sisters themselves so exposed to danger? One of Sister Magdalen's forester neighbours would have carried a message. And we should have known, then that you were safe, and we need not fear for you. I could have sent men at once to sweep the woods clean.'

Judith hesitated only a moment, and even that rather with the effect of clearing her own mind than of considering deceit. Something of Magdalen's confident tranquillity had entered into her. She said slowly, choosing her words: 'My lord, my story for the world is that I fled from a load of troubles to take refuge with Sister Magdalen, that I have been with her all this time, and no man has anything to do with my going or my returning. But my story for you, if you will respect that, can be very different. There are true things I will not tell you, and questions I will not answer, but everything I do tell you, and every answer I give you, shall be the truth.'

'I call that a fair offer,' said Sister Magdalen approvingly, 'and if I were you, Hugh, I would accept. Justice is a very fine thing, but not when it does more harm to the victim than to the wrongdoer. The girl comes well out of it, let it rest at that.'

'And on which night,' asked Hugh, not yet committing himself, 'were you attacked in the forest?'

'Last night. Past midnight it must have been, probably an hour past.'

'A good hour,' said Magdalen helpfully. 'We had just gone back to bed after Lauds.'

'Good! I'll have a patrol go out there and quarter the woods for a mile around. But it's unheard-of for any but occasionally the lads from Powys to give trouble in those parts, and if they move we usually have good warning of it. This must be some lone hand, a misused villein gone wild. Now,' said Hugh, and suddenly smiled at Judith, 'tell me what you see fit, from the time you were dragged into a boat under the bridge by the Gaye, to last night when you reached the Ford. And for what I shall do about it you will have to trust me.'

'I do trust you,' she said, eyeing him long and steadily. 'I believe you will spare me, and not force me to break my word. Yes, I was dragged away, yes, I have been held until two nights ago, and pestered to agree to a marriage. I will not tell you where, or by whom.'

'Shall I tell you?' offered Hugh.

'No,' she said in sharp protest. 'If you know, at least let me be sure it was not from me, neither in word nor look. Within two days he was repenting what he did, bitterly, desperately, he could see no way out, to escape paying for it, and it had gained him nothing, and never would, and he knew it. Very heartily he wished himself safely rid of me, but if he let me go he feared I should denounce him, and if I was found it would equally be his ruin. In the end,' she said simply, 'I was sorry for him. He had done me no violence but the first seizing me, he had tried to win me, he was too fearful, yes, and too well conditioned, to take me by force. He was helpless, and he begged me to help him. Besides,' she reasoned strongly, 'I also wanted the thing ended without scandal, I wanted that far more than I wanted any revenge on him. By the end I didn't want revenge at all, I *was* avenged. I had the mastery of him, I could make him do whatever I ordered. It was I who made the plan. He should take me by night to Godric's Ford, or close, for he was afraid to be seen or known, and I would return home from there as if I had been there all that time. It was too late to set out that night, but the next night, last night, we rode together. He set me down barely half a mile from the Ford. And it was after that, when he was gone, that I was attacked.'

'You could not tell what manner of man? Nothing about him you could recognise or know again, by sight or by touch, scent, anything?'

'In the woods there, before the moon, it was raven-dark. And over so quickly. I have not told you yet who it was who came to my aid. Sister Magdalen knows, he came back with us this morning, we left him at his house in the Foregate. Niall Bronzesmith, who lives in the house that was mine once. How everything I am, and know, and feel, and everyone who draws near me,' she said with sudden passion, 'spins around that house and those roses. I wish I had never left it, I could have given it to the abbey and still been its tenant. It was wrong to abandon the place where love was.'

Where love is, Cadfael thought, listening to the controlled voice so abruptly vibrant and fierce, and watching the pale, tired face blaze like a lighted lantern. And it was Niall who was by her when it came to life or death!

The flame burned down a little and steadied, but was not quenched. 'Now I have told you,' she said. 'What will you do? I promised that I would not urge any charge against – him, the man who snatched me away. I bear him no malice. If you take him and charge him, I will not bear witness against him.'

'Shall I tell you,' asked Hugh gently, 'where he is now? He is in a cell in the castle. He rode in at the eastern gate not half an hour before Cadfael came for me, and we whisked him into the wards before he knew what we were about. He has not yet been questioned or charged with anything, and no one in the town knows that we have him. I can let him go, or let him rot there until the assize. Your wish to bury the affair I can understand, your intent to keep your word I respect. But there is still the matter of Bertred. Bertred was abroad that night when you made your plans . . .'

'Cadfael has told me,' she said, erect and watchful again.

'The night of his death, which may or may not be mere accident. He was prowling with intent to break in and – steal, shall we say? And it is possible that he was helped to his death in the river.'

Judith shook her head decidedly. 'Not by the man you say you are holding. I know, for I was with him.' She bit her lips, and considered a moment. There was hardly anything left unsaid but the name she would not name. 'We both were within there, we heard his fall, though we did not know then what was happening. We had heard small sounds outside, or thought we had. So we did again, or so he did, afterwards. But by then he was so fraught, every whisper jarred him from head to heel. But he did not leave me. Whatever happened to Bertred, he had no hand in it.'

'That's proof enough,' agreed Hugh, satisfied. 'Very well, you shall have your way. No one need know more than you care to tell. But, by God, *he* shall know what manner of worm he is, before I kick him out of the wards and send him home with a flea in his ear. That much you won't grudge me, he may still count himself lucky to get off so lightly.'

'He is of no great weight,' she said indifferently, 'for good or ill. Only a foolish boy. But he is no great villain, and young enough to mend. But there is still Bertred. Brother Cadfael tells me it was he who killed the young monk. I understand nothing, neither that nor why Bertred himself should die. Niall told me, last night, how things had been here in the town after I vanished. But he did not tell me about Bertred.'

'I doubt if he knew,' said Cadfael. 'It was only in the

afternoon we had found him, and though the word was going round in the town, naturally, after he was brought back here, I doubt if it had reached Niall's end of the Foregate, and certainly I did not mention it to him. How did he come to be there at hand, close by Godric's Ford, when you needed him?'

'He saw us pass,' said Judith, 'before we were into the forest. He was on his way home then, but he knew me, and he followed. Well for me! But Niall Bronzesmith has always been well for me, the few times ever we've met or touched.'

Hugh rose to depart. 'Well, I'll have Alan take a patrol down into the forest, and make a thorough drive there. If we have a nest of wild men in those parts, we'll smoke them out. Madam, there shall be nothing made public of what has been said here. That matter is finished as you would have it. And thank God it ended no worse. Now I trust you may be left in peace.'

'Only I am not easy about Bertred,' Judith said abruptly. 'Neither about his guilt nor his death. So strong a swimmer, born and raised by the river. Why should his skill fail him that night, of all nights?'

Hugh was gone, back to the castle to call off his hunters as fast as they came in to report, and either to deal faithfully with the wretched Vivian Hynde, or, more probably, leave him sweating and worrying overnight or longer in a chilly cell. Cadfael took the carefully rolled altar frontal Sister Magdalen had extracted from her saddle-roll, and set off back to the abbey. But first he looked in at the small bare room where Bertred's coffined body lay on trestles, and the master-carpenter and his son were just fitting the lid, and said a prayer for a young man lost. Sister Magdalen came out with him as far as the street, and there halted, still silent and frowning in intense thought.

'Well?' said Cadfael, finding her so taciturn.

'No, not well. Very ill!' She shook her head dubiously. 'I can make nothing of this pattern. Plain enough what happened to Judith, but the rest I cannot fathom. You heard what she said of Bertred's death? The same doubts I feel about what so nearly might have been her own, but for the smith. Is there anything in all this coil that has happened by pure chance? I doubt it!'

He was still pondering that as he started uphill towards the High Street, and as he neared the corner, for some reason he slowed and turned to look back, and she was still standing in the mouth of the passage, gazing after him, her strong hands folded at her girdle. Nothing by pure chance, no, surely not, even those happenings that seemed wanton carried a false echo. Rather a sequence of events had set off each the following one, and called in motives and interests until then untouched, so that the affair had come about in a circle, and brought up the hapless souls involved in it facing where they had never intended to go. A deal more rapidly and purposefully than he had left her, Cadfael started back towards Sister Magdalen.

'I did wonder,' she said without apparent surprise, 'what was going on in your mind. I've seldom known you sit through such a conference saying so little and scowling so much. What have you thought of now?'

'There's something I should like you to do for me, since you'll be staying in this house,' said Cadfael. 'What with the youngster's burial and Judith's return, it shouldn't be too difficult to filch a couple of things for me, and send them down to me at the abbey. By Martin's boy Edwy, if they're still here, but not a word to anyone else. Borrowing, not stealing. God knows I shan't need them for long, one way or the other.'

'You interest me,' said Magdalen. 'What are these two things?'

'Two left shoes,' said Cadfael.

Chapter Thirteen

Now that his mind was stringing together a thread of abhorrent sense out of details which hitherto had seemed to make none, he could not turn his thoughts to anything else. Throughout Vespers he struggled to concentrate on the office, but the lamentable sequence of disasters connected with the rose rent marched inexorably through his mind, gradually assembling into a logical order. First there was Judith, still deprived and unhappy after three lonely years, thinking and sometimes speaking of retreating into a nunnery, and vexed by a number of suitors both old and young, who had had an eye on her person and her wealth all this time, and wooed and pleaded without reward, and were now beginning to get desperate in case she carried out her design to become a religious. Then the attempt on the rose-bush, to retrieve at least the possibility of regaining the gift-house, and the resultant death of Brother Eluric, probably, indeed almost certainly, unplanned and committed in panic. After that, however bitterly regretted, one man at least had murder already against him, and would be far more likely afterwards to stick at nothing. But then, to confound and complicate, came the abduction of Judith, another panic measure to prevent her from making her gift unconditional, and try to persuade or threaten her into marriage. Even if he had not been named, the perpetrator of that enormity was known. And the nocturnal death of Bertred might have been logical enough, had the abductor brought it about, but plainly he had not. Judith vouched for that, and so, probably, could Vivian Hynde's mother, since it seemed clear that once the bargain was made between captive and captor, Judith had been removed to the greater comfort of a house which had already been visted in search of her, and the buried room in the warehouse hurriedly and ingeniously cleared of all traces of her presence. So far, well! But there had been listeners outside in the night, Bertred first and possibly another afterwards, unless Vivian had reached a state in which every stirring of a spider or a mouse in the roof could alarm him. The plan might well have been overheard, and the horse with the double load might have had another follower, besides Niall Bronzesmith. And that would round off the whole disastrous circle, all the more surely if he who began it was also the one who sought to end it.

For consider, thought Cadfael, while his mind should have been on more tranquil and timeless things, what an excellent scapegoat Vivian Hynde makes for whoever attacked Judith in the forest. The man who had snatched her away and tried in vain to force marriage upon her, now riding away with her into the forest by night, and perhaps not trusting to her promise not to betray him, but preferring, once he had set her down, to dismount and hurry back to put an end to her. True, as things were, Judith vindicated him, she was quite certain he had not turned back, but made all haste away home, or up to Forton, to his father's flocks. But how if the attempt had succeeded, and Judith had been left dead in the forest, and there had been no witness to do him justice?

A scapegoat provided for one murder beforehand, Cadfael pursued. How if there had been another provided for the first murder, not beforehand, since that killing was not premeditated, but afterwards? A scapegoat suddenly presented helpless and vulnerable and already trussed for execution, bringing with him in an instant the inspiration of his usefulness, and the certainty of his death? Still not chance, but the bitterly ironic consequence of what had gone before.

And all this complication of logic and guilt depended upon two left shoes, which as yet he had not seen. The older the better, he had said, when Magdalen, intelligent and immune from surprise, questioned him on detail, I want them well worn. Few but the rich own many pairs of shoes, but one of the wearers of those he had in mind had no further use for whatever he did possess, and the other must surely have more than one pair. Not the new, Cadfael had said firmly, for he surely has some that are new. His oldest he'll hardly miss.

Vespers was over, and Cadfael spared time to pay a visit to his workshop in the herb-garden before supper, in case the boy was waiting for him there. The master-carpenter's son knew his way about very well, from old acquaintance of some years past, and would certainly look for him there. But all was cool and quiet and solitary within, a single wine-jar bubbling contentedly on its bench, in a slow, drowsy rhythm, the dried bunches of herbs rustling softly overhead along the eaves without and the beams within, the brazier quenched and cold. These were the longest days of the year, the light outside was barely subdued from its afternoon brightness, but in another hour it would be mellowing into the level beams of sunset and the greenish glow of twilight.

Nothing yet. He closed the door on his small inner kingdom, and went back to supper in the refectory, and bore with Brother Jerome's unctuous reproof for being a moment late without comment or complaint. Indeed, without even noticing it, though he made appropriately placating answer by instinct. The household at Maerdol-head must be too busily awake and in motion for Sister Magdalen to manage her depredations as easily and quickly as he had hoped. No matter! Whatever she took in hand she would complete successfully.

He evaded Collations, but went dutifully to Compline, and still there was no sign. He retired again to his workshop, always a convenient excuse for not being where according to the horarium he should have been, even thus late in the evening. But it was full dark, and the brothers already in their cells in the dortoir, before Edwy Bellecote came, in haste and full of apologies.

'My father sent me on an errand out to Frankwell, and I had no leave to tell him what I was about for you, Brother Cadfael, so I thought best to hold my tongue and go. It took me longer than I thought for, and I had to pretend I'd left my tools behind as an excuse for going back to the house so late. But the sister was on the watch for me. She's quick, that one! And she had what you asked for.' He produced a bundle rolled in sacking from under his coat, and sat down comfortably, uninvited but sure of his welcome, on the bench by the wall. 'What would you be needing two odd shoes for?'

Cadfael had known him well since the boy, turned eighteen now, was a lively imp of fourteen, tall for his years and lean and venturesome, with a bush of chestnut hair, and light hazel eyes that missed very little of what went on about him. He was using them now to good effect, as Cadfael unwrapped the sacking, and tipped out the shoes on the earth floor.

'For the proper study of two odd feet,' he said, and viewed them for a moment without touching. 'Which of the two is Bertred's?'

'This. This one I purloined for her from where his few things were laid by, but she had to wait for a chance to get at the other, or I should have been here before ever I got sent out to Frankwell.'

'No matter,' said Cadfael absently, and turned the shoe sole-upward in his hands. Very well worn, the whole-cut upper rubbed thin at the toe and patched, the single-thickness sole reinforced with a triangular lift of thick leather at the heel. It was of the common sort that have no fastening, but are simply slipped on the foot. The leather thonging that seamed the instep at the outer side was almost worn through. But after all its probable years of wear, the sole was trodden straight and true from back of heel to tip of toe. No pressure to either side, no down at heel nor oblique wear at the toe.

'I should have known,' said Cadfael. 'I can't recall seeing the man walking more than half a dozen times, but I should have known. Straight as a lance! I doubt if he ever trod a sole sidelong or ground down a heel askew in his life.'

The other shoe was rather a low-cut ankle boot, made on the same one-piece pattern as to the upper, and similarly seamed at the instep, with a slightly pointed toe, a thicker lift of leather at the heel, and a thong that encircled the ankle and was fastened with a bronze buckle. The outer side of the back of the heel was trodden down in a deep segment, and the same wear showed at the inner side of the toe. The light of Cadfael's small lamp, falling close but sidelong over it, accentuated the lights and shadows. Here there was only the faint beginning of a crack under the big toe, but it showed in the same spot as on the boot that had been taken from Bertred's dead foot, and it was enough.

'What does it prove?' wondered Edwy, his bright shock-head bent curiously over the shoe.

'It proves that I am a fool,' said Cadfael ruefully, 'though I have sometimes suspected as much myself. It proves that the man who wears a certain shoe this week may not be the man who wore it last week. Hush, now, let me think!' He was in two minds whether there was any need to take further action immediately, but recalling all that had been said that afternoon, he reasoned that action could wait until morning. What could have been more reassuring than Judith's simple assumption that the attack on her had been a mere matter of the hazards of forest travel, an opportunist blow at a woman benighted, any woman, simply for the clothes she wore if she proved to have nothing else of value about her? No, no need to start an alarm and rouse Hugh again before morning, the murderer had every cause to believe himself safe.

'Son,' said Cadfael, sighing, 'I am getting old, I miss my bed. And you had better be off to yours, or your mother will be blaming me for getting you into bad ways.'

When the boy had gone, with his curiosity still unsatisfied, Cadfael sat still and silent, at last admitting into his thoughts the realisation of which even his mind had been fighting shy. For the murderer, so well persuaded now of his own skill, feeling himself invulnerable, would not give up now. Having come so far, he would not turn back. Well, his time was short. He had only this one night left, though he did not know it, and he neither would nor could attempt anything against Judith now, in her own home, with Sister Magdalen keeping her formidable company. He would prefer to bide his time, unaware that tomorrow was to see an ending.

Cadfael started erect, causing the lamp to flicker. No, not against Judith! But if he was so sure of himself, then he had still this one night to try again to conserve the house in the Foregate, for tomorrow the rose rent would be paid, and for another year the abbey's title would be unassailable. If Judith was not vulnerable, the rose-bush still was.

He told himself that he was being a superstitious fool, that no one, not even a criminal at once lulled and exhilarated by success, would dare venture anything again so soon, but by the time he had completed even the thought he found himself halfway across the garden, heading at a hasty walk out into the great court, and making for the gatehouse. Here on familiar ground darkness was no impediment, and tonight the sky was clear, and there were stars, though fine as pinpricks in the midnight blackness. Along the Foregate it was very quiet, nothing moving but the occasional prowling cat among the alleys. But somewhere ahead, near the corner of the abbey wall at the horse-fair ground, there was a small, vibrating glow in the sky, low down behind the house-roofs, and its quivering alternately lit them into black silhouette and quenched them again in the common darkness. Cadfael began to run. Then he heard, distant and muted, the flurry of many voices in half-unbelieving alarm, and suddenly the glow was swallowed up in a great burst of flame, that fountained into the sky with a crackling of wood and thorn. The babble of voices became an uproar of men shouting and women shrilling, and all the Foregate dogs baying echoes from wall to wall along the highway.

Doors were opening, men running out into the roadway, pulling on hose and coats as they came and breaking into shuffling, entangled motion towards the fire. Questions flew at random, and were not answered because no one as yet knew the answers. Cadfael arrived among the rest at the gate of Niall's yard, which already stood wide. Through the wicket into the garden the poppy-red glow glared, quivering, and above the crest of the wall the column of fire soared, breathing upward a whirlwind of burning air and spinning flakes of ash, double a tall man's height, to dissolve into the darkness. Thank God, thought Cadfael at sight of its vertical ascent, there's no wind, it won't reach either the house or the farrier's toft on the other side. And by the fury and noise of it, it may burn out quickly. But he knew already what he would see as he stepped through the wicket.

In the middle of the rear wall the rose-bush was a great globe of flames, roaring like a furnace and crackling like the breaking of bones as the thorns spat and writhed in the heat. The fire had reached the old, crabbed vine, but beyond that there was nothing but the stone wall to feed it. The fruit trees were far enough removed to survive, though their nearer branches might be scorched. But nothing, nothing but blackened, outspread arms and white wood-ash, would be left of the rose-bush. Against the blinding brightness of the flames a few helpless figures circled and flinched away, unable to approach. Water thrown from a safe distance exploded into steam and vanished in a frantic hissing, but did no good. They had given up the attempt to fight it, and stood back, dangling buckets, to watch the old, gnarled bole, so many years fruitful, twist and split and groan in its death-agony.

Niall had drawn back to the wall opposite, and stood watching with a soiled, discouraged face and drawn brows. Cadfael came to his side, and the brown head turned to acknowledge his coming, and nodded brief recognition before turning back again to resume his interrupted watch.

'How did he get this furnace going?' asked Cadfael. 'Not with simple flint and steel and tinder, that's certain, and you in the house. It would have taken him a good quarter-hour to get beyond the first smoulder.'

'He came the same way,' said Niall, without removing his bleak gaze from the tower of smoke and spinning ash surging up into the sky 'Through the paddock at the back, where the ground's higher. He never even entered the garden this time. He must have poured oil over the wall on to the bush and the vine – drenched them in oil. And then he dropped a torch over. Well alight . . . And he away in the dark. And there's nothing we can do, nothing!'

Nothing any man could do, except stand back from the heat and watch, as very gradually the first fury began to slacken, and the blackened branches to sag from the wall and collapse into the blazing heart of the fire, sending up drifts of fine grey ash that soared upwards like a flight of moths. Nothing except be thankful that the wall behind was of solid stone, and would not carry the fire towards either human habitation.

'It was dear to her,' said Niall bitterly.

'It was. But at least she has her life still,' said Cadfael, 'and has rediscovered its value. And she knows who to thank for the gift, next after God.'

Niall said nothing to that, but continued grimly to watch

as the fire, appeased, began to settle into a bed of crimson, and the flying moths of ash to drift about the garden, no longer torn headlong upward by the draught. The neighbours stood back, satisfied that the worst was over, and began gradually to drift away, back to their beds. Niall heaved a great breath, and shook himself out of his daze.

'I had been thinking,' he said slowly, 'of bringing my little girl home here today. We were talking of it only the other night, that I should do well to have her with me, now she's no longer a babe. But now I wonder! With such a madman haunting this house, she's safer where she is.'

'Yes,' said Cadfael, rousing, 'yes, do that, bring her home! You need not fear. After tomorrow, Niall, this madman will haunt you no more. I promise it!'

The day of Saint Winifred's translation dawned fine and sunny, with a fresh breeze that sprang up only with the light, and drifted the stench of burning across the roofs of the Foregate as inevitably as the first labourer to cross the bridge brought the news of the fire into the town. It reached the Vestier shop as soon as the shutters were taken down and the first customer entered. Miles came bursting into the solar with a face of consternation, like someone charged with bad news and uncertain how to convey it delicately.

'Judith, it seems we're not done yet with the ill luck that hangs around your rose-bush. There's yet one more strange thing happened, I heard it just this moment. No need for you to trouble too much, no one is dead or hurt this time, it's not so terribly grave. But I know it will distress you, all the same.'

So long and deprecating a preamble was not calculated to reassure her, in spite of its soothing tone. She rose from the window-bench where she was sitting with Sister Magdalen. 'What is it now? What was there left that could happen?'

'There's been a fire in the night – someone set fire to the rose-bush. It's burned, every leaf, burned down to the bole, so they're saying. There can't be a bud or a twig left, let alone a flower to pay your rent.'

'The house?' she demanded, aghast. 'Did that take fire? Was there damage? No harm to Niall? Only the bush?'

'No, no, nothing else touched, never fret for the smith, nor for the house, they're safe enough. They'd have said if anyone had been harmed. Now, be easy, it's over!' He took her by the shoulders, very gently and brotherly, smiling into her face. 'Over now, and no one the worse. Only that plaguey bush gone, and I say just as well, considering all the mischief it's caused. Such a queer bargain to make, you're well rid of it.'

'It need never have brought harm to anyone,' she said wretchedly, and slowly sat down again, drawing herself out of his hands quite gently. 'The house was mine to give. I had been happy in it. I wanted to give it to God, I wanted it blessed.'

'It's yours again to give or keep, now,' said Miles, 'for you'll get no rose for your rent this year, my dear. You could take your house back for the default. You could give it as your dowry if you do go so far as to join the Benedictines.' He looked sidelong at Sister Magdalen with his blue, clear eyes, smiling. 'Or you could live in it again if you're so minded – or let Isabel and me live in it when we marry. Whatever you decide, the old bargain's broken. If I were you, I would be in no hurry to make such another, after all that's happened in consequence.'

'I don't take back gifts,' she said, 'especially from God.' Miles had left the door of the solar open behind him; she could hear the murmur of the women's voices from the far end of the long room beyond, suddenly and sharply cut across by other voices at the hall door, a man's first, courteous and low, then her aunt's, with the sweet social note in it. There might be a number of neighbourly visits this day, as Bertred went to his burial. At mid-morning he would be carried to Saint Chad's churchyard. 'Let it rest,' said Judith, turning away to the window. 'Why should we be talking of this now? If the bush is burned . . .' That had an ominous biblical ring about it, the burning bush of revelation. But that one, surely, was not consumed.

'Judith, my dear,' said Agatha, appearing in the doorway, 'here is the lord sheriff to visit you again, and Brother Cadfael is come with him.'

They came in quietly, with nothing ominous about them,

but for the fact that two sergeants of the garrison followed them into the room and stood well withdrawn, one on either side the doorway. Judith had turned to meet the visitors, anticipating news already known.

'My lord, I and my affairs are causing you trouble still. My cousin has already told me what happened in the night. With all my heart I hope this may be the last ripple of this whirlpool. I'm sorry to have put you to such shifts, it shall end here.'

'That is my intent,' said Hugh, making a brief formal reverence to Magdalen, who sat magisterial and composed by the window, an admirably silent woman when the occasion demanded. 'My business here this morning is rather with Master Coliar. A very simple question, if you can help us.' He turned to Miles with the most amiable and inviting of countenances, and asked, on a silken, rapid level that gave no warning: 'The boots we found on Bertred, when he was taken out of the river – *when did you give them to him*?'

Miles was quick in the wits, but not quick enough. He had caught his breath momentarily, and before he could release it again his mother had spoken up with her usual ready loquacity, and her pride in every detail that touched her son. 'It was the day that poor young man from the abbey was found dead. You remember, Miles, you went down to bring Judith home, as soon as we heard. She'd gone to collect her girdle—'

He had himself in hand by then, but it was never an easy matter to stop Agatha, once launched. 'You're mistaken, Mother,' he said, and even laughed, with the light note of an indulgent son used to tolerating a woolly-witted parent. 'It was weeks ago, when I saw his shoes were worn through into holes. I've given him my cast-offs before,' he said turning to confront Hugh's levelled black eyes boldly. 'Shoes are costly items.'

'No, my dear,' Agatha pursued with impervious certainty, 'I recollect very well; after such a day how could I forget? It was that same evening, you remarked that Bertred was going almost barefoot, and it showed very ill for our house to let him run abroad so ill-shod on our errands . . .'

She had run on as she always ran on, hardly paying heed to anyone else, but gradually she became aware of the way her son was standing stiff as ice, and his face blanched almost to the burningly cold blue-white of his eyes, that were fixed on her without love, without warmth, with the cold, ferocious burning of death. Her amiable, silly voice faltered away into small, broken sounds, and fell silent. If she had done nothing to help him, she had delivered herself in her blind, self-centred innocence.

'Perhaps, after all,' she faltered, her lips shaking, fumbling for words better calculated to please, and to wipe away that look from his face. 'Now I'm not sure – I may be mistaken . . .'

It was far too late to undo what she had done. Tears started into her eyes, blinding her to the aquamarine glare of hatred Miles had fixed upon her. Judith stirred out of her puzzled, shocked stillness and went quickly to her aunt's side, folding an arm about her trembling shoulders.

'My lord, is this of so great importance? What does it mean? I understand nothing of all this. Please be plain!' And indeed it had happened so suddenly that she had not followed what was said, nor grasped its significance, but as soon as she had spoken understanding came, sharp as a stab-wound. She paled and stiffened, looking from Miles, frozen in his bitter, useless silence, to Brother Cadfael standing apart, from Cadfael to Sister Magdalen, from Magdalen to Hugh. Her lips moved, saying silently: 'No! No! No . . .' but she did not utter it aloud.

They were in her house, and she had her own authority here. She confronted Hugh, unsmiling but calm. 'I think, my lord, there is no need for my aunt to distress herself, this is some matter that can be discussed and settled between us quietly. Aunt, you had much better go and help poor Alison in the kitchen. She has everything on her hands, and this is a most unhappy day for her, you should not leave her to carry all alone. I will tell you, later, all that you need to know,' she promised, and if the words had a chill of foreboding about them, Agatha did not hear it. She went from the room docilely in Judith's arm, half-reassured, half-daunted, and Judith returned and closed the door at her back.

'Now we may speak freely. I know now, all too well, what this is about. I know that two people may look back on events no more than a week past, and recall them differently. And I know, for Brother Cadfael told me, that the boots Bertred was wearing when he drowned made the print left behind by Brother Eluric's murderer in the soil under the vine, when he climbed back over the wall. So it matters indeed, it matters bitterly, Miles, who was wearing those boots that night, you or Bertred.'

Miles had begun to sweat profusely, his own body betraying him. On the wax-white, icy forehead great globules of moisture formed and stood, quivering. 'I've told you, I gave them to Bertred long ago . . .'

'Not long enough,' said Brother Cadfael, 'for him to stamp his own mark on them. They bear your tread, not his. You'll remember, very well, the mould I made in wax. You saw it when you came to fetch Mistress Perle home from the bronzesmith's. You guessed then what it was and what it meant. And that same night, your mother bears witness, you passed on those boots to Bertred. Who had nothing to do with the matter, and who was never likely to be called in question, neither he nor his possessions.'

'No!' cried Miles, shaking his head violently. The heavy drops flew from his forehead. 'It was not then! No! Long before! Not that night!'

'Your mother gives you the lie,' said Hugh quite gently. 'His mother will do no less. You would do well to make full confession, it would stand to your credit when you come to trial. For come to trial you will, Miles! For the murder of Brother Eluric . . .'

Miles broke then, crumpling into himself and clutching his head between spread hands, at once to hide it and hold it together. 'No!' he protested hoarsely between rigid fingers. 'Not murder . . . no . . . He came at me like a madman, I never meant him harm, only to get away . . .'

And it was done, so simply, at so little cost in the end. After that admission he had no defence; whatever else he had to tell would be poured out freely at last, in the hope of mitigation. He had trapped himself into a situation and a character he could not sustain. And all for ambition and greed!

'. . . perhaps also for the murder of Bertred,' went on

Hugh mercilessly, but in the same dispassionate tone.

There was no outcry this time. He had caught his breath in chilling and sobering astonishment, for this he had never foreseen.

'... and thirdly, for the attempt to murder your cousin, in the forest close by Godric's Ford. Much play has been made, Miles Coliar, and reasonably enough, seeing what happened, with the many suitors who have plagued Mistress Perle, and the motive they had for desiring marriage, and marriage to her whole estate, not the half only. But when it came to murder, there was only one person who had anything to gain by that, and that was you, her nearest kin.'

Judith turned from her cousin lamely, and slowly sat down again beside Sister Magdalen, folding her arms about her body as if she felt the cold, but making no sound at all, neither of revulsion nor fear nor anger. Her face looked pinched and still, the flesh hollowed and taut under her white cheekbones, and the stare of her grey eyes turned within rather than without. And so she sat, silent and apart, while Miles stood helplessly dangling the hands he had lowered from a face now dulled and slack, and repeating over and over, with strenuous effort: 'Not murder! Not murder! He came at me like a madman – I never meant to kill. And Bertred drowned; he drowned! It was not my doing. Not murder ...' But he said no word of Judith, and kept his face turned away from her to the last, in a kind of horror, until Hugh stirred and shook himself in wondering detestation, and made a motion of his hand towards the two sergeants at the door.

'Take him away!'

Chapter Fourteen

When he was gone, and the last receding footstep had sunk into silence, she stirred and breathed deeply, and said rather to herself than to any other: 'This I never thought to see!' And to the room in general, with reviving force: 'Is it true?'

'As to Bertred,' said Cadfael honestly, 'I cannot be sure, and we never shall be quite sure unless he tells us himself, as I believe he may. As to Eluric – yes, it is true. You heard your aunt – as soon as he realised what witness he had left behind against himself, he got rid of the boots that left it. Simply to be rid of them, not then, I think, with any notion of sloughing off his guilt upon Bertred. I think he had come to believe that you really would take the veil, and leave the shop and the trade in his hands, and therefore it seemed worth his while to try and break the abbey's hold on the Foregate house, and have all.'

'He never urged me to take vows,' she said wonderingly, 'rather opposed it. But he did somehow touch on it now and then – keeping it in mind.'

'But that night made him a murderer, a thing he never intended. That I am sure is truth. But it was done, and could not be undone, and then there was no turning back. What he would have done if he had heard in time of your resolve to go to the abbot and make your gift absolute, there's no knowing, but he did not hear of it until too late, and it was someone else who took action to prevent. There was no question but his desperation then was real enough, he was frantic to recover you, fearing you might give way and commit your person and estate to your abductor, and he be left out in the cold, with a new master, and no hope of the power and wealth he had killed to gain.'

'And Bertred?' she asked. 'How did Bertred come into it?'

'He joined my men in the hunt for you,' said Hugh, 'and

by the look of things he had found you, or had a shrewd notion where you were hidden, and said never a word to me or any, but set out by night to free you himself, and have the credit for it. But he took a fall, and roused the dog – you'll have heard. The next of him was being fished out of the Severn on the other bank, next day. What happened between, and just how he came by his death, is still conjecture. But you'll recall you heard, or thought you heard, sounds as of someone else abroad in the night, after Bertred was gone. While you were making your plans to ride to Godric's Ford the next night.'

'And you think that must have been Miles?' She spoke her cousin's name with a strange, lingering regret. She had never dreamed that the man who was her right hand could strike at her with mortal intent.

'It makes sense of all,' said Cadfael sadly. 'Who else had such close opportunity to note some suspect complacency about Bertred, who else could so easily watch and follow him, when he slipped out in the night? And if your cousin then crept close, after Bertred was hunted away, and overheard what you intended, see how all things played into his hands! In the forest, well away from the town, once the other man parted from you, how simple a matter it was to leave you dead and plundered, and the blame would fall first on outlaws, and if ever that was brought in question, on the man who had held you prisoner and brought you there into remote forest, to make sure you should never betray him. I do not think,' said Cadfael with careful consideration, 'that the idea of murder had ever occurred to him until then, when chance so presented it that it must have seemed to him the perfect solution. Better than persuading you into a nunnery. For he would have been your heir. Everything would have fallen into his hands. And how if then, with this intent already filling his mind, he came upon Bertred, already half-stunned from one blow, and was visited by yet another fearful inspiration – for Bertred alive could possibly meddle with his plans, but Bertred dead could tell nothing, and Bertred dead would be found to be wearing the boots of Eluric's murderer. Thus he was provided with a scapegoat even for that.'

'But this *is* conjecture,' said Judith, wringing at disbelief. 'There is nothing, nothing to bear witness to it.'

'Yes,' said Cadfael heavily, 'I fear there is. For it so happened that when your cousin came down to the abbey with a cart, to bring home Bertred's body, he found that those who had stripped off the boy's sodden clothes had paid no heed to his boots, and neither did I pay any heed, or give a thought to them, when I brought out the bundle of clothing to the cart. Miles had to tilt the cart and spill the boots at my feet for me to pick up, before I looked at them, and knew what I was seeing. He did not intend that that infallible proof should be overlooked.'

'It was not so clever a move,' she said doubtfully, 'for Alison would have been able to tell you that her son had the boots from Miles.'

'True, if ever she was asked. But bear in mind, this was a dead murderer discovered – no trial to come, no mystery, no point in asking questions, and none in hounding a dead body, let alone a wretched, bereaved woman. Even if I had had no doubts,' said Hugh, 'and somehow a crumb of doubt there always was, I should not have kept his body from peaceable burial, or put her to any more grief than she already bore. Nevertheless, it was a risk, he might have had to brazen it out. But not even the shrewdest schemer can think of everything. And he,' said Hugh, 'was new to such roguery.'

'He must have gone in torment,' said Judith, marvelling, 'all night long since I escaped him, knowing I should return, not knowing how much I might be able to tell. And then I made it plain enough I had no notion who it was who had struck at me, and he felt himself safe ... Strange!' she said, frowning over things now beyond help or remedy. 'When he went out, he did not seem to me evil, or malicious, or aware of guilt. Only bewildered! As though he found himself where he had never thought or meant to be, in some place he could not even recognise, and not knowing how he made his way there.'

'In some sort,' said Cadfael soberly, 'I think that is truth. He was like a man who has taken the first slippery step into a marsh, and then cannot draw back, and at every step forward sinks the deeper. From the assault on the rose-bush to the attempt on your life, he went where he was driven. No wonder if the place where he arrived was utterly alien to him, and the face that waited for him in a mirror there was one he did not even know, a terrible stranger.'

They were all gone, Hugh Beringar back to the castle, to confront and question his prisoner now, while the shock of self-knowledge endured and the cold cunning of self-interest had not yet closed in to reseal a mind and conscience for a while torn open to truth; Sister Magdalen and Brother Cadfael back to the abbey, she to dine with Radulfus, having assured herself affairs in this house were in no need of her presence for a few hours, he back to his duties within the enclave, now that all was done and said that had to be done and said, and silence and time would have to be left to take their course, where clamour and haste were of no help. They were all gone, even the body of poor Bertred, gone to a grave in Saint Chad's churchyard. The house was emptier than ever, half-depeopled by death and guilt, and the burden that fell back upon Judith's shoulders was the heavier by two childless widows for whom she must make provision. Must and would. She had promised that she would tell her aunt all that she needed to know, and she had kept her promise. The first wild lamentation was over, the quiet of exhaustion came after. Even the spinning-women had deserted the house for today. The looms were still. There were no voices.

Judith shut herself up alone in the solar, and sat down to contemplate the wreckage, but it seemed rather that what she regarded was an emptiness, ground cleared to make room for something new. There was no one now on whom she could lean, where the clothiers' trade was concerned, it was again in her own hands, and she must take charge of it. She would need another head weaver, one she could trust, and a clerk to keep the accounts, able to fill the place Miles had held. She had never shirked her responsibilities, but never made a martyrdom out of them, either. She would not do so now.

She had almost forgotten what day this was. There neither would nor could be any rose rent paid, that was certain. The bush was burned to the ground, it would never again bear the little, sweet-scented white roses that brought the years of her marriage back to mind. It did not matter now. She was free and safe and mistress of what she gave and what she retained; she could go to Abbot Radulfus and have a new charter drawn up and witnessed, giving the house and grounds free of all conditions. All the greed and calculation that had surrounded her was surely spent now, but she would put an end to it once for all. What did linger on after the roses was a faint bitter-sweetness of regret for the few short years of happiness, of which the one rose every year had been a reminder and a pledge. Now there would be none, never again.

In mid-afternoon Branwen put her head in timidly at the door to say that there was a visitor waiting in the hall. Indifferently Judith bade her admit him.

Niall came in hesitantly, with a rose in one hand, and a child by the other, and stood for a moment just within the doorway to get his bearings in a room he had never before entered. From the open window a broad band of bright sunlight crossed the room between them, leaving Judith in shadow on one side, and the visitors upon the other. Judith had risen, astonished at his coming, and stood with parted lips and wide eyes, suddenly lighter of heart, as though a fresh breeze from a garden had blown through a dark and gloomy place, filling it with the summer and sanctity of a saint's festival day. Here without being summoned, without warning, was the one creature about her who had never asked or expected anything, made no demands, sought no advantages, was utterly without greed or vanity, and to him she owed more than merely her life. He had brought her a rose, the last from the old stem, a small miracle.

'Niall . . .' she said on a slow, hesitant breath, and that was the first time she had ever called him by his name.

'I've brought you your rent,' he said simply, and took a few paces towards her and held out the rose, half-open, fresh and white without a stain.

'They told me,' she said, marvelling, 'there was nothing left, that all was burned. How is this possible?' And in her turn she went to meet him, almost warily, as though if she touched the rose it might crumble into ash.

Niall detached his hand very gently from the child's grasp,

as she hung back shyly. 'I picked it yesterday, for myself, when we came home.'

The two extended hands reached out and met in the band of brightness, and the opened petals turned to the rosy sheen of mother-of-pearl. Their fingers touched and clasped on the stem, and it was smooth, stripped of thorns.

'You've taken no harm?' she said. 'Your wound will heal clean?'

'It's nothing but a scratch. I dread,' said Niall, 'that you have come by worse grief.'

'It's over now. I shall do well enough.' But she felt that to him she seemed beyond measure solitary and forsaken. They were looking steadily into each other's eyes, with an intensity that was hard to sustain and harder to break. The little girl took a shy step or two and again hesitated to venture nearer.

'Your daughter?' said Judith.

'Yes.' He turned to hold out his hand to her. 'There was no one with whom I could leave her.'

'I'm glad. Why should you leave her behind when you come to me? No one could be more welcome.'

The child came to her father in a sudden rush of confidence, seeing this strange but soft-voiced woman smile at her. Five years old and tall for her age, with a solemn oval face of creamy whiteness with the gloss of the sun on it, she stepped into the bar of brilliance, and lit up like a candle-flame, for the hair that clustered about her temples and hung on her shoulders was a true dark gold, and long gold lashes fringed her dark-blue eyes. She made a brief dip of the knee by way of reverence, without taking those eyes or their bright, consuming curiosity from Judith's face. And in a moment, having made up her mind, she smiled, and unmistakably held up her face for the acceptable kiss from an accepted elder.

She could as well have put her small hand into Judith's breast and wrung the heart that had starved so many years for just such fruit. Judith stooped to the embrace with tears starting to her eyes. The child's mouth was soft and cool and sweet. On the way through the town she had carried the rose, and the scent of it was still about her. She had nothing to say, not yet, she was too busy taking in and appraising the room and the woman. She would be voluble enough later, when both became less strange.

'It was Father Adam gave her her name,' said Niall, looking down at her with a grave smile. 'An unusual name – she's called Rosalba.'

'I envy you!' said Judith, as she had said once before.

A slight constraint had settled upon them again, it was difficult to find anything to say. So few words, and so niggardly, had been spent here throughout. He took his daughter's hand again, and drew back out of the bar of light towards the door, leaving Judith with the white rose still sunlit on her breast. The other white rose gave a skipping step back, willing to go, but looked back over her shoulder to smile by way of leave-taking.

'Well, chick, we'll be making for home. We've done our errand.'

And they would go, both of them, and there would be no more roses to bring, no more rents to pay on the day of Saint Winifred's translation. And if they went away thus, there might never again be such a moment, never these three in one room together again.

He had reached the door when she said suddenly: 'Niall ...'

He turned, abruptly glowing, to see her standing full in the sunlight, her face as white and open as the rose.

'Niall, don't go!' She had found words at last, the right words, and in time. She said to him what she had said in the dead of night, at the gate of Godric's Ford:

'Don't leave me now!'

ELLIS PETERS (a pseudonym for Edith Pargeter) was born September 28, 1913, in Horsehay, Shropshire, England. She worked as a pharmacist's assistant in Dawley, Shropshire, from 1933–40 and served in the Women's Royal Naval Service from 1940–45, becoming a petty officer and receiving the British Empire Medal for service in 1944. Pargeter published her first novel under her own name, *Hortensius, Friend of Nero*, in 1936, which she followed with dozens of historical novels and mysteries. In 1977 she decided to combine the two pursuits and launched her Brother Cadfael series, for which she is best remembered. Pargeter was also a gifted translator of Czech and published more than a dozen translations. She died October 14, 1995, near Shrewsbury.

11